1964

linguistics
epic poetry

kept

A COMPANION TO HOMER

A COMPANION
TO
HOMER

Edited by

ALAN J. B. WACE, F.B.A., Litt.D.

Sometime Laurence Professor of Classical Archaeology
in the University of Cambridge
Honorary Fellow of Pembroke College

and

FRANK H. STUBBINGS, M.A., Ph.D., F.S.A.

Fellow of Emmanuel College and Lecturer in Classics
in the University of Cambridge

LONDON
MACMILLAN & CO LTD
NEW YORK · ST MARTIN'S PRESS
1962

MACMILLAN AND COMPANY LIMITED
St Martin's Street London WC2
also Bombay Calcutta Madras Melbourne

THE MACMILLAN COMPANY OF CANADA LIMITED
Toronto

ST MARTIN'S PRESS INC
New York

PRINTED IN GREAT BRITAIN

EDITORIAL PREFACE

WHETHER this is the same *Companion to Homer* that was first conceived by Professor Wace over twenty years ago is perhaps a question for the philosophers. But some account of what has happened to it in the meantime may save the labour of anyone who is tempted to turn upon it that talent for identifying 'early' and 'late' passages so often exercised on the Homeric poems. Some of the chapters had indeed already been written before the catastrophe of 1939 which turned the energies of editors and contributors alike in other directions. Which these chapters were may not now be apparent, for ample opportunity has been given, and taken, for their revision. One exception is obvious : Professor George Miller Calhoun died in 1942, and his contribution (Ch. 14 (i)) has been left as it stood, the more easily because it is in the main a statement of unchanging evidence from the poems themselves. The supplement to it by Professor T. B. L. Webster (Ch. 14 (ii)) at once points to the explosive event which has lifted this book into a new epoch : the decipherment, in 1952, of Mycenaean writing. Work on the *Companion* was slow to get under way again after 1945 ; but delays which at the time seemed regrettable have in terms of the decipherment proved an advantage. In addition, it has been possible to use the results of excavation undertaken since 1950 at Pylos and at Mycenae, and of the full reports of Professor Blegen's excavations at Troy.

On the debit side these delays, which allowed so much to be filled in, in the picture of Mycenaean civilization, from Professor Wace's own excavations, have by his death in November 1957 deprived the book of its prime author and begetter, so that it has fallen to the Assistant Editor (himself a replacement of the original Assistant Editor) to attend to its final stages. The general arrangement of the book and the great bulk of the text had already received Professor Wace's approval. His own chapters had all been written, and have received the minimum of editorial adjustment. The final choice and arrangement of illustrations, however, are the Assistant Editor's — though wherever possible he has endeavoured to meet the wishes of contributors, in a few cases even supplying illustrations they did not ask for.

The plan of the book should be apparent from the table of contents, but it perhaps deserves a little comment here. The late Professor J. A. K. Thomson's introduction (which unfortunately he did not live to see in

v

print) places the *Iliad* and *Odyssey* squarely at the head of western literary tradition, and no further reason for reading them is required. But some help and guidance may be. This *Companion* is intended primarily for those who are reading Homer in Greek, especially those who, in school or university, are reading him for the first time. Such readers naturally cannot see features of form and style in relation to the whole, and the opening three chapters of Part One are designed to supply them in advance, as it were, with a perspective which it may need several years to make their own by a full reading of the epic. Chapter 4 is meant to do this for the actual Greek of the text ; and Chapter 5 to demonstrate Homer's place within the epic genre.

The next two chapters, on the transmission of the text and the Homeric Question, might even be deferred by the younger student until he has finished reading the *Iliad* and *Odyssey*. Their themes belong in any case to a more advanced level of scholarship and it is for that reason that those chapters are supported by a fuller array of notes and references. Of the Homeric Question the author of these two chapters has himself remarked that, if only Milman Parry's work had become known and understood, it might have died a natural death by 1932. It would still have required an obituary notice.

The general method of the first five chapters is in Part Two extensively supplemented by another : that of confronting the epic picture of the heroic world and the record of that same world as revealed by modern archaeology and scholarship. The intention here is to supply the modern reader with a background for *Iliad* and *Odyssey*. Such a background every ancient Greek reader possessed as his birthright. For him the setting of the poems was the setting of his daily life : the same seas and mountains, the same crops and crafts. Even now 'the landscape of today still fits most yesterdays in this part of the world' [a] ; but for those who cannot visit the Mediterranean some second-hand picture of that landscape is required.

But the Greek's background to Homer was not only local. The roots of his whole life were planted in Homeric soil. For him Odysseus and Agamemnon were as historical as Richard Cœur de Lion or the Black Prince to us ; nor were the *Iliad* and *Odyssey* the only memorials of early Greek history. There were heroes even before Agamemnon whose deeds and names (*pace* Horace) *were* known to their descendants. All Greek literature, not only the epic, displays how events and personalities of what we have fondly dubbed Greek *pre*-history were familiar to the classical Greeks ; nor should we forget that tangible monuments of the heroic age were far better known to the fifth century before Christ than to the nineteenth century after. Schliemann did not discover Mycenae

[a] Freya Stark, *The Lycian Shore*, p. 3.

and Troy : they had never been lost. If Cimon was mistaken in his identification of the bones of Theseus on Skyros, or Theron of Akragas over those of Minos which he returned to their Cretan home, yet their historical perspective was sound. That perspective, which the modern world would never have lost if it had been willing or able to read with faith the whole corpus of ancient Greek literature, has been restored by archaeology. We do not thereby see the Mycenaean age precisely as the classical Greek saw the heroic age ; we think more in terms of material culture than of events ; but at least we now regard it, as he did, as a historical reality. And if our record of it is found more and more to correspond to Homer's picture we should feel no surprise, for we are talking about the same age.

It may of course be argued that we can enjoy and appreciate the *Iliad* and *Odyssey* without any external knowledge of the age in which their stories are set, just as we might (perhaps) enjoy Shakespeare's *Henry V* without even the Englishman's knowledge of English history. It may be argued that we ought to examine not the age *about* which but *in* which our author wrote — whenever that was. Yet whether or not Homer lived (as most of our contributors and some who are not our contributors seem to believe) in the eighth century B.C., it is apparent that his age was singularly conscious of the heroic past, and conscious of it as a part of *Greek* history. To appreciate Homer, his modern readers need a similar consciousness. There still are those who will state that 'the Homeric world was altogether post-Mycenaean, and the so-called survivals are rare, isolated, and garbled ' [a] ; or that Mycenaean culture was 'not perhaps significant for the development of the culture which we normally mean when we speak of Greek or Hellenic'.[b] But there is another view : that without Mycenaean civilization, and the recollection of it, Hellenic culture would have been impossible. The truth of this latter view is writ large in Greek literature, and especially in Homer ; and it is confirmed by archaeology.

There has been no attempt to ensure complete consistency among the views expressed by separate contributors. Had there been, there might have been no book. Rather the intention is to present the conscientiously stated evidence of a number of special witnesses. There is no chapter of *Conclusions* ; had there been, it would have been numbered 24, and might too easily be dismissed (like *Odyssey* 24) as a 'later interpolation'. It is better that the reader should digest the evidence and do his own summing up. If, especially in Part Two, the division of matter and choice of contributors reflects a personal bias or promotes a personal view, the Editors are responsible. Happily, the personal views of scholars about the date

[a] See *Historia*, 1957, 159 ff.
[b] See *Nature*, 19 July 1958, 153.

and nature of the Homeric poems are nowadays less discordant, because less extremist, than they used to be.   A recent writer [a] was doubtless correct in stating that America is the 'home of a new and firmly based theory of Homeric unity'; but the remanent scepticism of the Old World is less than he suggests.

One editorial duty remains : to stress that this book is meant to be subordinate to the reading of Homer, not a substitute for it.   Ideally it might have been printed as an appendix to a text of the *Iliad* and *Odyssey* — but economics forbid.   It can still be used in that rôle.

FRANK H. STUBBINGS

CAMBRIDGE
September 1959

[a] Cedric Whitman, *Homer and the Homeric Tradition* (1958), *ad init.*

ACKNOWLEDGEMENTS

THE Editors' thanks are due, first and foremost, to their publishers and contributors, who have worked and waited so long and patiently for the appearance of this *Companion*. In a work by so many hands it is impossible to record specifically the contributions of the many who have helped its authors with information, advice, and criticism ; one can only confess, gratefully, that the debt is a wide and comprehensive one.

As regards illustrations, I must first express my thanks to Mrs. Wace for allowing unlimited use of the photographic archives of Professor Wace's Mycenae excavations : this has been invaluable for several chapters besides his own. Among the contributors to the text, thanks are due to Professor Blegen, for the illustrations of Troy and Pylos ; and to Professor Mylonas, for photographs of material from the second Grave Circle at Mycenae.

The names of other individuals or institutions who have kindly supplied and permitted the reproduction of photographs, as well as the nature and extent of indebtedness for permission to make use of illustrations already published elsewhere, with the sources of individual items, are indicated more particularly in the lists of plates and text-figures. Thanks are due for such permission to :

Akademie-Verlag (Fig. 52) ;
The American Philosophical Society (Pl. 36, *a*) ;
The American School of Classical Studies, Athens (Fig. 9) ;
Biblioteca Nazionale Marciana, Venice (Pl. 5) ;
The Director and Trustees of the British Museum (Pls. 1, 3, 4, 28, 36, *c*, 37, *a*) ;
The Managing Committee of the British School at Athens (Pls. 10, 11, *b*, 30, 31, *a*, 33, 39, *a* ; Figs. 27, 29, 33) ;
Messrs. Bruckmann, Munich (Fig. 14) ;
The University Library, Cambridge (Pl. 6) ;
The University Museum of Classical Archaeology, Cambridge (Pl. 12, *a*) ;
The Cambridge University Press (Figs. 66, 67) ;
The Classical Association and the Editor of *Greece and Rome* (Pl. 40 ; Fig. 68) ;
The Cyprus Museum, Nicosia (Pl. 36, *c*) ;
The French School at Athens (Pl. 27, *b*) ;
The German Archaeological Institute at Athens (Fig. 2) ;
Messrs Gleerup, Lund (Figs. 37, 38, 42, 44, 47, 65) ;
Messrs. Macmillan and Co. Ltd. (Pls. 11, *a*, 25, *b*, 26, 29, *b*, 31, *b*) ;
The National Museum, Athens (Pl. 14, *b*) ;
Max Niemeyer-Verlag (Pl. 34, *a* ; Fig. 54) ;

Messrs. Oldenbourg, Munich (Fig. 17) ;
The Oxford University Press (Figs. 3-5) ;
The Princeton University Press (Figs. 22, 50) ;
The Royal Anthropological Institute (Fig. 58) ;
Professor C. F. A. Schaeffer and the Mission Archéologique Française
   (Pl. 38) ;
The Society of Antiquaries (Pl. 32, c) ;
The Society for the Promotion of Hellenic Studies (Pl. 39, c ; Figs. 39, 40,
   43, 45, 46) ;
The Swedish Institute at Athens (Fig. 55);
Messrs. Richard Uhde, Munich (Fig. 31) ;
The Victoria and Albert Museum (Pl. 2).

I wish also to thank Mrs. Jane Rabnett (Secretary at the British School
at Athens) and Mrs. Semni Karouzou of the National Museum for their
personal help in obtaining photographs in Athens ; and Mrs. E. B.
French for taking several photographs of Mycenae specially for this work.
For the skilful preparation of prints from negatives which included some
very old and unpromising ones of my own, I am indebted to Mr. R.
Johnson of the Cambridge University Museum of Classical Archaeology,
and to Mr. L. P. Morley of the Cambridge University Museum of
Archaeology and Ethnology. Finally I must thank Mr. John Christiansen
for bringing to bear on the drawing of new text-figures and the adaptation
of old ones not only a varied technical and artistic skill but a lively interest
in the matter illustrated.

The scholarly care of Messrs. R. & R. Clark's proof-reader seems
to me to deserve a special word of thanks. So does the valued assistance
of Miss Ruth Phillips of Girton College in preparing the indexes. I am
grateful to her both for relieving me of all the real labour of them and
for her apparent enjoyment of the work.

                                                          F. H. S.

CONTENTS

PART TWO
THE PICTURE AND THE RECORD

§ A : *The Setting*

LIST OF TEXT-FIGURES

B

LIST OF PLATES

NOTES ON REFERENCES
AND ABBREVIATIONS, ETC.

¶ In references to the text of Homer the books of the *Iliad* are denoted by the Greek capital letters, those of the *Odyssey* by the Greek lower case letters. For the convenience of readers who may be using a text that only gives the Roman or Arabic numerals a concordance is printed below :

1	A	α	9	I	ι	17	P	ρ
2	B	β	10	K	κ	18	Σ	σ
3	Γ	γ	11	Λ	λ	19	T	τ
4	Δ	δ	12	M	μ	20	Υ	υ
5	E	ε	13	N	ν	21	Φ	φ
6	Z	ζ	14	Ξ	ξ	22	X	χ
7	H	η	15	O	o	23	Ψ	ψ
8	Θ	θ	16	Π	π	24	Ω	ω

¶ Notes citing sources or authorities are numbered serially for each chapter and placed at the end of the chapter, along with suggestions for further study. They are deliberately few, but should suffice to point the way to a fuller literature for those who want it. On controversial topics they also refer the reader to a statement of alternative views if these are not summarized in the text. Where such notes, etc., are enclosed in square brackets they have been supplied on editorial responsibility ; others by contributors.

¶ Cross-references within the book are indicated by lettered footnotes.

¶ Transliteration of classical and modern Greek names follows in general the conventions used in *The Journal of Hellenic Studies* and *The Annual of the British School at Athens*. Some deliberate inconsistencies have been allowed for the convenience of the reader, and it is hoped that any accidental ones that have escaped the editing process will at least prove no obstacle to understanding or reference.

¶ Abbreviations used for the titles of the principal periodicals (and some books) cited in the notes are listed below :

Act. Ant. Hung.	= *Acta antiqua Academiae scientiarum Hungaricae* (Budapest)
AE	= ᾿Αρχαιολογικὴ ᾿Εφημερίς (Athens)
AIARS	= *Skrifter utgivna av Svenska Institutet i Athen : Acta Instituti Atheniensis Regni Sueciae* (Lund)
AIRRS	= *Skrifter utgivna av Svenska Institutet i Rom : Acta Instituti Romani Regni Sueciae* (Lund)

AJA	=*American Journal of Archaeology* (Baltimore)
AJP	=*American Journal of Philology* (Baltimore)
AM	=*Mitteilungen des Deutschen archäologischen Instituts: Athenische Abteilung* (Athens)
ARV	=J. D. Beazley, *Attic Red-figure Vase-painters* (Oxford, 1942)
BSA	=*Annual of the British School at Athens*
BSR	=*Papers of the British School at Rome*
Cal. Pub. Class. Phil.	=*California University Publications: Classical Philology*
Class. et Med.	=*Classica et Mediaevalia. Revue danoise de philologie et d'histoire* (Copenhagen)
CQ	=*Classical Quarterly*
CR	=*Classical Review*
Documents	=M. G. F. Ventris and J. Chadwick, *Documents in Mycenaean Greek* (Cambridge, 1956)
FGH	=F. Jacoby, *Die Fragmente der Griechischen Historiker* (Berlin, 1923– ; Leiden, 1940–)
Gött. Gel. Anz.	=*Göttingische gelehrte Anzeigen* (Berlin)
Harv. Stud. Class. Phil.	=*Harvard Studies in Classical Philology* (Cambridge, Mass.)
JHS	=*Journal of Hellenic Studies* (Society for the Promotion of Hellenic Studies)
MMR	=M. P. Nilsson, *The Minoan-Mycenaean Religion and its Survival in Greek Religion* (2nd edition, Lund, 1950)
Mus. Helv.	=*Museum Helveticum* (Basel)
Mycenae Tablets	=E. L. Bennett, *The Mycenae Tablets*, in *Proc. Amer. Philos. Soc.* 97, no. 4 (Sept. 1953), 422–70
Mycenae Tablets II	=E. L. Bennett (ed.), *The Mycenae Tablets II*, in *Trans. Amer. Philos. Soc.*, n.s. 48, part 1 (March 1958)
PAE	=Πρακτικὰ τῆς ἐν ᾿Αθήναις ᾿Αρχαιολογικῆς ῾Εταιρείας (Athens)
P. Harris	=J. E. Powell, *The Rendel Harris Papyri of Woodbrooke College, Birmingham* (Cambridge, 1936)
P. Hibeh	=B. P. Grenfell and A. S. Hunt, *The Hibeh Papyri* (part I, 1906)
PLG	=T. Bergk, *Poetae Lyrici Graeci* (4th ed., Leipzig, 1878–82)
P. of M.	=A. Evans, *The Palace of Minos* (1921–36)
P. Rain.	=H. Gerstinger, H. Oellacher, and K. Vogel, *Mitteilungen aus d. Papyrussammlung d. Nat. Bibl. in Wien: Papyrus Erzherzog Rainer* (Baden bei Wien, 1932, 1939)
Proc. Brit. Acad.	=*Proceedings of the British Academy*
P. Ryl.	=J. de M. Johnson, V. Martin, A. S. Hunt, and C. H. Roberts, *Catalogue of Greek and Latin Papyri in the John Rylands Library* (Manchester, 1911, 1915, 1938)
RE	=G. Wissowa *et al.*, *Paulys Realencyclopädie der classischen Altertumswissenschaft* (Stuttgart, 1894–)

Rend. Linc.	= *Rendiconti dell' Accademia nazionale dei Lincei* (Rome)
Rev. Phil.	= *Revue de Philologie* (Paris)
Rh. Mus.	= *Rheinisches Museum für Philologie* (Frankfurt a.M.)
Stud. It.	= *Studi italiani di filologia classica* (Florence)
TAPA	= *Transactions and Proceedings of the American Philological Association* (Boston)
Wien. Stud.	= *Wiener Studien ; Zeitschrift für klassische Philologie* (Vienna).

¶ Reference to the Linear B tablets is as follows :

Tablets from Knossos (abbreviated KN) are cited by the numbers in A. Evans, *Scripta Minoa II*, preceded by E. L. Bennett's classification, as in *The Knossos Tablets*, by E. L. Bennett, J. Chadwick, and M. Ventris (*London Classical Institute, Suppl. Paper No. 2*, 1956), which gives the complete transliterated texts.

Tablets from Pylos (abbreviated PY) are cited by the numbers and classification prefixes as in E. L. Bennett, *The Pylos Tablets : texts of the Inscriptions found 1939-54* (Princeton, 1955).

Tablets from Mycenae (abbreviated MY) are cited by the numbers given in *Mycenae Tablets II*, ed. E. L. Bennett (*Trans. American Philos. Soc.*, n.s. 48, part 1 (March 1958)).

A classified bibliography of the tablets, their vocabulary, and subject-matter, is published annually by the London Institute of Classical Studies, under the title *Studies in Mycenaean Inscriptions and Dialect*.

¶ The phases of the Aegean Bronze Age are referred to by the usual abbreviations :

E.H.	Early Helladic
M.H.	Middle Helladic
L.H.	Late Helladic (also called Mycenaean [Myc.])
E.M.	Early Minoan
M.M.	Middle Minoan
L.M.	Late Minoan

For a *chronological table* see p. 360.

¶ Besides the *General Index*, attention is drawn to the index of *Passages of Homer cited in the text*, which should be consulted by the reader of Homer who wishes to see what the *Companion* has to say about the form, meaning, grammar, interpretation, etc., of a particular line or passage.

Greek words not appearing in transliteration in the *General Index* will be found in the separate list printed after it.

INTRODUCTION
HOMER AND HIS INFLUENCE

by J. A. K. Thomson

Hither as to thir Fountain other Starrs
Repairing, in thir gold'n Urns draw light.

AT the sources of Western civilization, themselves its main source, stand two poems on the grand scale which for sustained beauty and splendour have found no superior, perhaps no equal, in all the poetry that has followed them. This is the most remarkable fact in the history of literature. If it seems to contradict what Aristotle regards as almost a law of nature — that the arts progress by degrees — we may discover the explanation in this, that the *Iliad* and the *Odyssey* are not the beginning but the consummation of an artistic process of which the earlier stages are no longer discernible. But, while this would explain the fact, it does not explain the miracle. The miracle is the quality of the poetry, and miracles cannot be explained.

They may, however, be described and their effects observed. In his *Essays on Translating Homer* Matthew Arnold detected in the Homeric style four 'notes' or characteristic qualities : plainness of thought, resulting in directness and simplicity; plainness of style, resulting in clearness; rapidity; nobleness. It is true that Homer possesses these qualities, and what Arnold says about them is admirable. But we feel that there is in Homer something which is peculiarly his own. What shall we say it is ? It would seem that we are driven to metaphor, and the metaphor which has suggested itself to nearly every critic is taken from fire. So Pope in the Preface to his *Iliad* speaks of 'that unequal'd fire and rapture which is so forcible in Homer, that no man of a true poetical spirit is master of himself while he reads him. What he writes is of the most animated nature imaginable; everything moves, everything lives, and is put in action.' Certainly in reading Homer we have a heightened consciousness of life. But there is also the pleasure derived from his art — the enchantment of the Homeric diction and the Homeric metre — and from the story, for that must always count, perhaps count first, in a narrative poem. But the best story in the world — and the *Odyssey* has been given that

description — may be spoilt in the telling. It is the story teller who
makes the story. The world of Homer is what Homer represents it to be
in virtue of his art, of his poetry. What happens when the poetry is left
out may be seen in the *Archaeologia* of Thucydides. It is the poetry of
Homer that is the only, and sufficient, explanation of his power over the
minds of men, though this in no way detracts from the interest, the unique
interest, of his matter.

Homer, says Arnold, is the great master of 'the grand style'. We may
adopt the convenient term without committing ourselves to Arnold's
somewhat uncritical extension of it to styles so different as that of Pindar
or Aeschylus or Dante. Homer is never oracular; he can be familiar and
even humorous. Yet we never feel that he is losing control of the grand
style. It was this mastery which determined that epic poetry should be
written in the grand style. One sees this, of course, in those who might
be described as in the direct succession to Homer, in poets like Virgil and
Milton. But it is quite as striking in those who have attempted a non-
classical form of epic. Macpherson in his *Ossian*, Wordsworth in his
Prelude, have the feeling that a grand style of some kind is necessary for
them. But, if it were not for the Homeric precedent, there is no reason
why they should have this feeling at all.

An historical estimate of Homer's influence obliges us to consider not
only how far it extended but what form it took. It was not, in ancient
times, confined to literature; it affected other arts; above all it affected
education. We know that in Athens (which came more and more to
set the tone for the rest of Greece) the instruction of youth was from quite
an early period based on the reading and exposition of Homer. The fact
is perhaps better known than appreciated. For if we examine it we may
reach the conclusion that Homer is the parent of that culture which we
regard as typically classical. It is of course easy to discover 'romantic'
and even 'savage' elements in both the *Iliad* and the *Odyssey*. How could
it be otherwise in poems which draw so largely upon traditional material?
But these elements are not characteristic of Homer, they are in fact uncharacteristic. It is because they are uncharacteristic that he reduces them
to a minimum. And when we study his art we find that it has all the
qualities which are thought of as specially classical. Compare the *Iliad*
or the *Odyssey* with epics which have arisen among peoples whose culture
has been unaffected by Greek influences. Beside Homer they seem form-
less, incoherent, haunted by gloomy or grotesque fantasies sometimes
powerful but often puerile. It is frequently hard to make out their story
with any clearness; their style is apt to be stiff with conventional ornament and stereotyped phrase. Their cloudy beauties are their own, not
Homer's. He is master of his material, he is not fanciful or grotesque, he
is lucid, he is sparing (as they are not) of hyperbole. In other words he

PLATE I

Homer crowned by the World and Time. Detail from a marble relief of the second cent. B.C., found near the ancient Bovillae. Height *c.* 13 in.

PLATE 2

Pyrrhus, between Ajax and Agamemnon, receives the spurs and sword of knighthood as successor to his dead father Achilles. Detail from a Flemish tapestry of the late fifteenth century, illustrating the *Tale of Troy*, from the Château de Bayard near Grenoble

(By permission of the Victoria and Albert Museum)

is classical and they are barbaric. The classical conception of style rests on the belief that the importance of what is said very often depends on our way of saying it. In Homer, perhaps for the first time, the form is adequate to the matter, that is, suitable to it and worthy of it. *Sing, goddess, the wrath of Achilles* — only a divine utterance could do justice to so high a theme. The manner must fit the matter. That is the classical idea of style, and it comes from Homer.

It may be observed that the spirit and quality of Homeric art, though never inoperative in Greek literature, begins to affect it with peculiar force soon after the defeat of Xerxes. The preceding age had been an era of prophetism. Parmenides, Heraclitus, Empedocles, even Pindar and Aeschylus have, or often have, an oracular style, natural in men who feel that they are making a revelation of the truth, but not Homeric. Then come Sophocles and Herodotus, each ὁμηρικώτατος in the temper of his mind and the quality of his art. And that art is now purely 'classical'. But we observe the same tendency in other fields than literature. We see it in the work of Phidias, who stamped his impress on the sculpture and architecture of his age and was a main instrument in making it classical as Homer is classical. We see it in the greater and in the lesser Polygnotus. In the field of religion the Olympian gods are more distinctly conceived as Homer conceived them; the new Zeus, the new Apollo, the new Hermes, are clearly Homeric. In philosophy Socrates encounters prophetism with an ironical, Democritus with a scientific, detachment; in both we find a spirit of *sophrosyne*, that eminently classical and Homeric virtue. That this change was entirely due to Homer is altogether improbable. But it is reasonable to believe that the steady indoctrination of the Greek mind with the Homeric spirit, which was the necessary consequence of Greek education, must have been by far the most potent of all the influences at work upon it. At least Homer led the way and set the example. We have seen how this affected art; but it also influenced culture. It is the consciousness of this which inspires the polemic of Plato and other moralists against the tendency of Homeric ethics. It is the fashion to express surprise at this, but we ought to remember that Plato was arguing against people who insisted that Homer must be regarded as a moral teacher. What effect the poems may have held on private morals, we have not sufficient evidence to decide. But so far as public behaviour is concerned we do have evidence that the *Iliad* was an immense stimulus to pan-Hellenic patriotism. Thus we find Isocrates appealing to Homer in those writings which advocate that union of Greeks against Barbarians which became the policy of Philip and (at first) of Alexander. Such an appeal was effective because to the Greeks the Homeric poems were the record of their own early history. They were aware — at least the more intelligent among them — that there must be an element of fiction

C

(*pseudos*) in a poet's representation of the past.   But that Homer was
telling of things that had happened was doubted by no one.   Even to
Thucydides the Trojan War (however much he may have questioned its
extreme importance) is just as historical as the Persian or the Peloponnesian.   Such a conviction inevitably helped to mould the ideas of public
men and guide their policies.

To trace the influence of Homer in all these directions is of course out
of the question here.   The most that can be attempted is the briefest outline
of his influence on literature.

It is natural to begin with Hesiod and the 'Cyclic' poets.   We may
believe that it was the prestige of the heroic epos which led Hesiod to
adapt the metre and diction of Homer to his own matter.   That is a very
important debt, but there is not much else that the poet of the *Works and
Days* owes to Homer.   How far the Cyclics were indebted to him cannot
be determined, because their work has practically disappeared; almost
all we can say is that those parts of the Trojan matter with which they
dealt lie outside the scheme of the *Iliad* and *Odyssey*.   It is in this that their
historical importance now exists.   It is considerable, for it was from the
Cyclics rather than from Homer himself that later writers, from Aeschylus
(and earlier) to the *Posthomerica* of Quintus Smyrnaeus and the Greek
originals of Dares Phrygius and Dictys Cretensis, drew a great part of
their material.

Our chief concern must be with the direct line of succession.   From
Panyassis and earlier to Milton and later it is an almost interminable series,
and one can touch only on the more significant names.   Even so we must
remember that not only are we omitting all mention of many notable
epics but all consideration of Homer's influence on other forms of ancient
poetry and even on certain prose writers, such as Herodotus.   Of the lost
epics there is little that can be usefully said.   But the *Argonautica* of
Apollonius has survived and calls for notice.   It is in some respects what
in the jargon of contemporary criticism might be called a baroque or
even a rococo poem.   But it did reassert the Homeric tradition with
some understanding of Homeric structure and some feeling for Homeric
style.   Above all the interest is centred, apparently for the first time in
epic poetry, in a love story and a heroine.   That was to prove a momentous innovation because of what it suggested to Virgil.   It is not however
what Virgil owes to Apollonius that is our concern, but what he owes to
Homer.   That is a question of the very highest importance to the
historian of literature because of the unique position which came to be
held by the *Aeneid* in the culture of Western Europe.   All through later
antiquity, all through the Dark and the Middle Ages, up to the Renaissance and almost to the French Revolution, it was Virgil and not Homer
who was the accepted representative of epic poetry in the West.   It is

therefore essential to know how truly he represents it. The answer must be — with wonderful fidelity. Virgil's style, though even that is modelled upon Homer's, is peculiarly his own and has quite a different movement. But in the design and structure of his poem, in his management of the epic machinery, in his use of the epic conventions, in his understanding of the heroic age, Virgil stands supreme among the ancient followers of Homer. The *Aeneid* is hardly more an evidence of poetic than of critical genius. In it the art of Homer has a fresh lease of life, so far as that was possible in a different medium and an alien society. This makes it less necessary to review the post-Virgilian epic poets, for while some of them, Lucan for example, have little enough of the Homeric spirit, they all feel an obligation to revere, as Statius puts it, the footprints of Virgil. That is true even of Claudian, who comes at the end of anything that can be called 'classical' Latin literature. In him the Homeric-Virgilian tradition in antiquity may be said to blaze up once more and expire.

Contemporary with Claudian was the Christian poet Prudentius, whose *Psychomachia* was a new kind of epic. In this the actors are personified Virtues and Vices fighting Homeric duels in Homeric accoutrements. Its importance for the literary historian consists in this, that it is a main source of that flood of allegorical verse which pours in ever increasing volume through the Middle Ages down to the *Faerie Queene* and even later.

The half-literate ages which immediately followed Prudentius scarcely knew more of Homer than the name. Indeed a form so complex as the Homeric-Virgilian epic demands for its understanding an artistic education which they had not received. They had their own epics, such as *Beowulf*, which were hardly touched, if touched at all, by classical influences. There remained the memory of Aeneas and Dido and some vague notion of a Trojan War. The Trojan matter, containing much that is not in our Homer, was epitomized in the Latin Dictys and Dares, wretched little compilations from earlier compilations in Greek. They were of course forgeries, but the Dark Ages and even the Middle Ages had no suspicion of that, and their authority was preferred to Homer's. Such was the foundation on which there gradually rose a vast and glittering edifice. It may have been Geoffrey of Monmouth who began it by his invention of Brut, the Trojan-Italian *auctor* of the British nation. In the second half of the twelfth century — Geoffrey belongs to the first half — his account was greatly expanded in the Norman-French *Romans de Brut* of Robert Wace, and this in turn was greatly expanded in the English *Brut* of Layamon. If the *Brut* were not entirely innocent of plot or structure, it might pass for an epic. As it is, both it and the poem of Wace are classified as metrical romances. Such too is the *Roman de Troie* of Benoît de Sainte-Maure,[a] a French *trouvère* writing towards the close of the twelfth century. Using the Dictys-Dares matter, he is thought to have added an invention of his own, the love story of Troïlus and Cressida, whom he more correctly names Briséide. The story was embodied, with matter more authentically ancient, in the prose *Historia Romana* of Guido de Columnis, which became one of the great mediaeval sources, Chaucer for instance drawing upon it for his *Troïlus and Criseyde*. All this seems far from Homer, but it is necessary to see what happened to the substance and form of the classical epic if we are to understand the problem which confronted Boccaccio and Tasso, Camoens and even Milton.

The *Divina commedia* occupies a special position. In form it belongs to that genre of the Dream or Vision which (originating perhaps with the *Somnium Scipionis* of Cicero) holds so important a station in the literature of the Middle Ages. Yet if the *Divina commedia* is not an epic it has much of an epic character. The *Inferno*, and the *Purgatorio* up to the point where Dante reaches the Earthly Paradise, is a Christian version of the sixth Book of the *Aeneid*, which in turn was suggested by the eleventh book of the *Odyssey*. That Dante was fully conscious of his debt to Virgil is proved by his own words (*Inferno* i. 85-7). But he is also aware of Homer, whom he calls *poeta sovrano* and whose shade he meets in the underworld. One can do no more than conjecture how much he knew — from sources like the *Ilias Latina* — of the real Homer; but he evidently knew something. It has not been ascertained where he got the story of the last voyage of Ulysses as it is told in the twenty-sixth canto of the *Inferno*. It hardly looks like an invention; perhaps it was a tradition that lingered in South Italy. It is permissible to think that it would have afforded a finer ending to the *Odyssey* than the one we have.

The *Divina commedia* is a Christian, even a theological poem, and the spirit of it is accordingly unhomeric. But neither is it chivalric. By Dante's time the specially mediaeval spirit of chivalry and romantic love was passing away, though it was to be revived under a different guise by Petrarch. The combined strength of Christian feeling on the one hand and courtly love on the other was what perhaps chiefly prevented the emergence in the Middle Ages of anything very like an epic in the tradition of Homer. Thus the Knight's Tale in Chaucer, which has an almost epic scope, becomes a story of mediaeval love set against a vaguely classical background. Chaucer's original was the *Teseide* of Boccaccio, which falls to be mentioned here because it was the first attempt since the ruin of the Western Empire to produce in a vernacular tongue an epic which should have a genuinely classical character. Taking Virgil and

---

[a] Such sub-Homeric works inspired many works of visual art in the later Middle Ages, *e.g.*, the Tale of Troy tapestries woven in 1472 by Pasquier Grenier at Tournai and copied by others : see Pl. 2.

Statius as his principal models Boccaccio brings on the scene, which is pre-Homeric Greece, the chief warriors of the age of Theseus. He has learned and he uses all the traditional ornaments of the epic style. But the story remains incurably 'romantic', steeped in mediaeval sentiment and almost as far removed as *A Midsummer Night's Dream* from any conceivable *Theseid* of antiquity. Moreover it was Boccaccio who set the bad example of composing an epic in stanzas.

He was a younger contemporary of Petrarch, with whom modern literature is by many supposed to begin. It may at least be said of him that he gave a new direction to men's thoughts by turning them from mediaeval to classical models. Among ancient authors he gave the highest place, or the highest after Virgil, to Homer, whose merits, although he could never learn to read him, he divined and proclaimed. He encouraged Boccaccio to get the translation of Homer done into Latin by a Calabrian called Leo Pilatus, and in other ways used his immense contemporary fame to give an impulse to Homeric studies. His Latin epic *Africa* now hardly permits itself to be read; yet, being greatly admired at the time, it encouraged others to study the Virgilian model with equal care. In this connection it should not be forgotten that Latin epics continued to be written throughout the Middle Ages — one of the best being the *De Bello Trojano* of Joseph of Exeter — and during the Renaissance became even numerous. Some of these were not without fine poetical quality and had a definite influence on the vernacular epic. Milton, for example, had read most or all of them.

After Petrarch comes the Quattrocento and the first flowering of the Rinascimento. But although Homer was a chief object of the new enthusiasm, yet this did not to any notable extent move the Italian genius to direct imitation. Perhaps some instinct warned it that the classical *epos* belonged irrevocably to the past. At least there was this feeling about the *chansons de geste*, the metrical romances and the *poesia caballeresca* in general. Homer and Virgil however continued to be reverenced, while the *poesia caballeresca*, though vastly popular, tended to provoke, at least among the more sophisticated, that kind of sympathetic amusement which the Spanish romances were later to awaken in the mind of Cervantes. This amusement found expression in the *Orlando innamorato* of Boiardo, which appeared in 1487. A generation later there came, to complete the work of Boiardo, a still greater masterpiece, the *Orlando furioso* of Ariosto. Thus a kind of mock-heroic poetry came into existence in Italy before the serious epic, represented by the *Gerusalemme liberata* of Tasso, which did not appear until about half a century after the death of Ariosto. In the interval much had happened, and Tasso belongs to the Counter-Reformation. But, though the *Gerusalemme* is a Christian epic, which is not how we should describe the *Orlando furioso*, the later poem is in true succession to the earlier. This is perhaps more obvious to us than it was to Tasso, who made his poem as classical as he felt permissible in a Christian poet writing for more than scholars. It is as long as the *Iliad* and constructed on the classical plan, developing a heroic theme in a tone of high seriousness. The subject — the First Crusade — was an excellent choice, being glorious in itself and far enough removed in time and space to give the poet a free hand. The action is, in the Homeric manner, concentrated within the three or four months preceding the capture of Jerusalem. It is promoted by divine assistance and hindered by infernal agency. It is interrupted by digressive episodes. For the style, it has dignity and a Virgilian *mollities*. Virgil indeed is being constantly imitated or suggested, but so, though far less frequently, is Homer. Nothing so like a classical epic had yet appeared in the Italian language. And yet it is not really classical. Tasso believed it possible to compose an epic in which the continuity for the most part observed in the *Aeneid* should be relieved by incidents of a 'romantic' sort. This is done in the *Gerusalemme*. But the result has been that the romantic episodes, especially those in which the enchantress Armida plays a part, absorb most of our interest. We have in fact a romance of chivalry disguised as a classical epic. And the *ottava rima*, in which it is composed, makes it harder for us to throw off the impression that what we are reading is only another metrical romance. For all that, Tasso's poem is a milestone on the way back to Homer.

The convenience of prosecuting the Italian story must excuse a slight liberty with chronology. The *Lusiads* (*Os Lusíadas*) of Camoens (Luis de Camões) was published a few years before the *Gerusalemme liberata*. Its subject is the voyage to India of Vasco da Gama, a theme not less fit for epic treatment than the *nostos* of Odysseus. Camoens had sailed the same waters as his hero, and this gives his descriptions the vivacity (denied to Tasso) of first-hand impressions. There is perhaps no long poem since the *Odyssey* in which the sea-wind blows so free. After the long series of literary epics from Valerius Flaccus to Claudian and from Claudian to Ariosto the reader feels that here at last is the real thing again. Yet in many ways the *Lusiads* is literary enough. It is constructed rather closely on the model of the *Aeneid*, that is on the Homeric model. Thus after a proem the scene opens with a council of Olympian deities presided over by Jupiter, who directs their attention to Gama as, like Aeneas, he voyages with his little fleet over unknown waters. Counsels are divided, Bacchus expressing enmity against Gama, and Mars friendship for him. Thereafter the fortunes of the hero are alternately threatened and advanced by supernatural forces. All that is like Homer, and the parallel is continued when Gama is entertained by a native prince, to whom he gives a long retrospective narration of Portuguese history and his own adventures.

The *Lusiads* is, in the words of Hallam, 'the first successful attempt in modern Europe to construct an epic poem on the ancient model'. Yet it is open to criticism. Thus, while the tone of the *Lusiads* is ardently Christian, the machinery of it is worked by gods of Pagan mythology. The convention, perfectly natural in Homer, has already begun to appear a little absurd in Virgil; in a Catholic poet it is a mere anomaly. Again, Camoens writes in *terza rima* and in a diction which, while often attaining sublimity, is in general too diffuse and florid to suit an epic theme.

About this time there established itself in France a movement which must always engage the interest of classical scholars. It is named the Pléïade, from a group of seven writers passionately devoted to the study of ancient literature. Its leader in scholarship was Dorat, whom classical students know as Auratus, but in literature its acknowledged head was Pierre Ronsard. The group hoped to refresh and enrich the French language by naturalizing classical words, metres, and literary forms. It had a special enthusiasm for Pindar and Homer, and it is now that the modern fame of Homer begins to rival that of Virgil, who had been preferred in the generation before by critics like the elder Scaliger. Ronsard's attempt, the *Franciade*, to write a French epic after the ancient pattern was felt even by himself to be unsatisfactory; but, as we can see from his sonnets, his admiration for Homer continued undiminished and was shared by other members of the group. The importance of this fact is little affected by the circumstance that the French have never succeeded very well in their efforts to write like Homer.

The Pléïade had considerable influence upon Spenser, who translated or transplanted into English Du Bellay's *Antiquités de Rome*. It may be doubted if he went all the way with the French school in its enthusiasm for Homer, whom he would hardly be able to read, as Ronsard could, in the original without the aid of such bald Latin versions as were then available. Yet we cannot doubt that he went a good part of the way. The Trojan matter he has studied in all its ramifications from Homer to the chronicles of Brut. Nevertheless the *Faerie Queene* owes far more to Ariosto and Tasso than to any classical source; indeed in some ways he is more mediaeval than they. The fact is that the Elizabethan age did not produce an epic — unless we call the *Faerie Queene* an epic — comparable to its achievements in other fields. Chapman did his best to make his contemporaries accept Homer as their own, but his translation had no great immediate success. Even Milton's contemporaries, learned as many of them were, can hardly be said to have measured the greatness of Homer. That was left to Milton himself.

Of *Paradise Lost* it cannot be necessary to say anything here except perhaps this, that it is only in the light of earlier attempts to compose in a modern idiom an epic comparable in form and style to the Homeric

Poems that its astonishing quality is seen. Milton resolved on an experiment of extraordinary difficulty and daring. He resolved to do for English poetic style what Virgil had done for Latin. In Milton's day there was no 'standard English', so that he was free to create his own medium. He believed that he could do this by bringing his syntax and vocabulary as close to Latin as was possible without violating English idiom — which nevertheless he sometimes does violate. His metre with its over-running of line into line and its exquisitely designed verse-paragraphs is obviously modelled on Virgil's. It was Milton who settled that blank verse, and not stanzas, was the right metre for an English epic, and his choice was determined by Virgil and Homer. Both in the plan and in the conduct of his story he is careful to follow them, not slavishly but hoping to do what they had done and do it better. These things are far more important than his imitations, numerous as they are, of particular passages. Except for the subject — which Milton nevertheless claims to be 'not less but more Heroic' than any of the traditional epic themes — *Paradise Lost* is only less Homeric than the *Aeneid* itself.

The centre of interest now moves back to France. There, not long after the death of Ronsard, his influence began to wane, almost to disappear. Yet the reaction (led by Malherbe) did not attack the classical poets; it took the line of declaring that the poetry of the Pléïade was not truly classical, since it lacked the good sense, the sobriety of temper, and spareness of ornament which characterized the pure classical style. We can observe the success of this criticism in the chief writers of the age of Louis XIV. To have good sense and good taste, to be what they called 'natural', was important to them. These were qualities which, in alliance with 'sublimity', they recognized in Homer. At least one of them, perhaps the most eminent, Racine, was in a position to judge, for he had enough Greek to read Homer in the original. But the writer of that age who did most for Homer was Fénelon, whose *Télémaque* was read by old and young. The Telemachus of the *Odyssey* is already a model young man, so that it was the easier for Fénelon to make him the hero of an edifying romance, full of mildly agreeable episodes which gave readers the impression that there was nothing 'barbaric' about Homer and that his characters were *honnêtes gens*, as the age of Louis XIV understood *honnêteté*. The effect of all this was that it became a sort of literary orthodoxy, of which the high-priest was Boileau, that the best a modern writer could do was to take the ancients for his models. As Pope expressed it, 'To copy Nature is to copy them'.

But after a time doubts were felt. It was natural, though illogical, to ask if some progress had not been made since the days of Homer in the aesthetic as well as the mechanical arts. From this question arose an absurd controversy about the relative merits of ancient and modern authors in which nearly all French writers of the time became involved. The best of them, such as Racine and La Fontaine — for Molière was too sensible to have an opinion in such a dispute — tended to deprecate the efforts of their admirers to have them ranked above the ancients. But it is likely that the public in general sided with the 'moderns', because at that time it read its classics in translations which retained little or nothing of their poetry. The quarrel spread to other countries, including England, where it provoked the Phalaris controversy and suggested *The Battle of the Books*. In 1699 Madame Dacier produced a version in prose of the *Iliad*, to which she prefixed a laudatory life of Homer which was found acutely irritating by his detractors. All this tended to make at least the name of Homer very familiar, and to Alexander Pope the time seemed ripe for a translation of the *Iliad* into English verse. The influence of Pope's *Homer* on English minds and poetic diction in the eighteenth century has perhaps never been thoroughly explored; it was certainly very great. Though probably little read now, it filled a whole century with the fame of Pope and Homer.

That century was prolific in epic poetry, most of what was written in English being markedly influenced, at least in diction, by *Paradise Lost*. Since none of it rose above mediocrity, none need be mentioned. On the other hand the eighteenth century excelled in the mock-epic; we have *The Rape of The Lock*, *The Dunciad*, and *The Battle of the Books*, which is a parody of Homer rather than of Virgil. There is much in this strain to be found in Fielding, who indeed described *Joseph Andrews*, and might have described *Tom Jones*, as 'a comic epic in prose'. There is even a mock-heroic element in Cowper's *Task*. This development must not be taken to indicate any disparagement of Homer, who was translated by Pope and Cowper, and loved by Fielding and perhaps even by Swift. Outside England the most celebrated epics were probably Klopstock's *Messias* in Germany and Voltaire's *Henriade* in France. Then, in the last quarter of the century, a new conception of Homer began to gain ground. It was suggested in the main by two English books, Percy's *Reliques* and Macpherson's *Ossian*, which produced, especially *Ossian*, an extraordinary impression not only in the country of their origin but in all educated Europe, and particularly in Germany. (The hero in *Werther* is a devotee of Homer until he is swept off his feet by 'Ossian'.) The Homeric poems were now held to be, at least in origin, *Volkspoesie*, and this led to theories like that of F. A. Wolf and, later, of Lachmann. Critics were now almost unanimous in putting Homer above Virgil on the not very satisfactory ground that the *Aeneid* is, compared with the *Iliad*, an 'artificial' epic. But in the wake of this came a new and different influence, Winckelmann's Essay *Gedanken über die Nachahmung der Griechen*. In this an attempt was made to define the essence of classical art, which was said to be 'a noble simplicity and a calm greatness' (*eine edle Einfalt und eine stille Grösse*). The phrase reverberated in German minds. Lessing was stimulated to write *Laokoon*, which was widely discussed, with loud assent and dissent. Goethe — so Greek a German and so German a Greek — ardently embraced the ideal of a noble simplicity and a serene greatness, qualities which he recognized in the Attic tragedies and above all in Homer. The fruits of this enthusiasm are not all that one is entitled to expect from such a man ; but they are highly interesting. It is not possible to do more than name the *Nausikaa*, the *Achilleis*, and *Hermann und Dorothea*. The last alone could be considered a success, though few readers would think it reflects the 'heroic' temper of the *Iliad*. Yet we have it on Goethe's authority that it was inspired by Homer, that is by the more domestic scenes in the *Odyssey*.

The leaders of what is generally known as the Romantic Movement were nearly all, in greater or less degree, influenced by the ancient classics, and nearly all in England and Germany by Greek rather than Latin writers. Yet so far as Homer is concerned there is little direct imitation. Some felt and tried to recapture the Homeric largeness and simplicity, notably Mickiewicz in poetry and Chateaubriand in prose. But in spirit they are, especially Chateaubriand, incurably romantic. The truth is that the genius of the great Romantics was in the main lyrical. André Chénier — if we count him in as a precursor of the Romantic Movement — and Friedrich Hölderlin were penetrated to the very heart by the Hellenic spirit but they could not give it Homeric form. A greater genius than either, Coleridge, the true founder of the English Romantic school, failed lamentably when he tried to be epic. Wordsworth did not, but the kind of epic he invented in the *Prelude* owed to Homer almost nothing at all. Scott, who has so much of the Homeric spirit, drew his inspiration not from the *Iliad* but from the Border Ballads. It is hardly worth while speaking of Southey's epics : although they had some influence in their time they never ascend to be poetry, let alone Homeric poetry. Landor's *Gebir* may be dismissed as Miltonic. Byron in spite of his *Hints from Horace* is surprisingly unclassical. Shelley was always reading Greek but, though he translated the *Hymn to Hermes*, it is not clear that Homer was a special favourite of his. But what do these facts prove ? Only this, that the influence of Homer is not to be measured by the extent to which he has been imitated. Coleridge and Landor and Shelley read him with far better understanding and far profounder appreciation than did the eighteenth-century poetasters who wrote epics like *Leonidas* or the *Epigoniad*. How true it is that Homer's influence may penetrate deeply without showing on the surface is perhaps most strikingly illustrated in the case of Keats. In spite of its subject *Hyperion* is Miltonic, not Homeric, except in so far as Milton resembles Homer. As for *Endymion* it is not like Homer at all. Yet we know that Keats had read Pope's translation and — with a new sense of discovery — Chapman's, and we cannot doubt that this liberated and excited his genius. In fact he says as much in his famous sonnet. Homer and the Elgin Marbles — that was what Greece meant to Keats, to whom Greece meant everything. But the Homeric manner eluded him. Yet perhaps not altogether. It is perhaps not merely fanciful to think that 'the freshness of the early world', which Keats may be considered to have recaptured rather more successfully than Milton, was caught by him from Homer. With Tennyson surmise is unnecessary, for a good deal of his best work is confessedly — 'faint Homeric echoes' in his own expression — written in following or imitation of Homer. And it must be allowed that *Ulysses* and *Morte d'Arthur* reproduce the Homeric manner with admirable scholarship and a fidelity never before attained. If we cannot say this of the *Idylls of the King* that is because his model there is Theocritus rather than Homer — the Theocritus however of the *epyllia*. Nor should we disregard his fragments of translation, which combine an almost literal exactness with a diction suitably grave and beautiful. He thus opened the way for Matthew Arnold, who aimed at an even closer approximation to the Greek. He attempted this in two poems, *Sohrab and Rustum* and *Balder Dead*, of which the latter comes nearer to Homer in simplicity of syntax and particularly of detail. It is however felt by most readers to be somewhat inferior to *Sohrab* as poetry, and this suggests the reflection that too close an imitation of Homer may defeat its object. However that may be, Arnold has given us something more like Homer in English than any other poet. Yet one does not think of Arnold as a Homeric sort of person. One does not think this of William Morris, though Mackail has called *Sigurd the Volsung* 'the most Homeric poem since Homer'. It has the rush and joy of battle of the *Iliad*, but actually Sigurd is a versified saga, not an epic in the classical tradition. Although Morris composed a long quasi-epic *Life and Death of Jason*, and although half the stories in the immense *Earthly Paradise* are taken from classical sources, yet none of these rhymed romances seems classical in anything but subject. He is an excellent example of a poet strongly impressed by Homer yet remaining un-Homeric in the cast of his mind, which was mediaeval. That he was a devoted student of Homer is proved by the fact that he translated the *Odyssey*. The best Greek scholar among the Pre-Raphaelites was no doubt Swinburne. But he does not seem to care for Homer any more than Shelley cared. At any rate Homer did not influence his poetry.

The *Iliad* and *Odyssey* do not conform to the modern conception of art as a method of self-expression, for they are completely impersonal. This would explain why the romantic poets have, in spite of their admiration for Homer's art, on the whole failed to reproduce its qualities. Thus one might have expected Victor Hugo to do something Homeric. But, although he often attempts an epic strain, he is too much the victim of his temperament, he cannot be genuinely impersonal. Leconte de Lisle can; in fact to be austerely impersonal was the aim of all his writing. Moreover he had immersed himself in the study of Homer, whom he translated with a careful exclusion of all romantic colour. Yet he never attempted an epic, and only a few of his *Poèmes antiques* show any trace of Homer. Evidently the day of the classical epos was felt to be over. In a sense it had always been over — that is after Homer himself. Even *Paradise Lost* could be represented as a *tour de force* carried to success by a unique combination of scholarship and poetical genius. Yet no one who reads the poetry of the eighteenth century beside that of the nineteenth can believe that the earlier century was more deeply, was even as deeply penetrated by the Homeric spirit as the later. One evidence of that was the better understanding — the result of maturer consideration and a finer scholarship — of Homeric art. Here Matthew Arnold deserves a second mention. His lectures on translating Homer were the first adequate estimate, at least in English, of the literary qualities of the *Iliad* and *Odyssey* and did much to destroy the notion of a native genius or inspired folk-poet. Homer was now seen to be a conscious artist and took his place once for all as the chief poet of antiquity, as Dante was of the Middle Ages and Shakespeare of modern times.

In the contemporary world of letters the impact of Homer is no doubt less immediate than at some other times, notably the Renaissance. And the number of those who can read him in Greek is perhaps less now than it was a quarter of a century ago. On the other hand the number of those who have read him in translation is certainly much greater, and I should think it not less certain that he is the classical poet who means most and gives most pleasure to the general reader. Whatever the depths of his influence it never was more extensive. This may be seen from the number and popularity of translations, especially of the *Odyssey*, which in antiquity was never put quite on a level with the *Iliad*; from the interest felt in Homeric archaeology and in theories about the origin, development and authorship of these poems; from the stream of books *about* Homer. Equally significant is the way in which Homer is now accepted in circles which might have been expected to consider him out of date. It is true they put their own interpreation on his work. Thus, they like to explain the characters of the *Iliad* and *Odyssey*, especially Helen, Penelope, and Tiresias, in terms of modern psychology. This is perhaps more of a literary game than anything else, and probably more popular in France than in England or America. It is not quite so new as it looks, for allegorical and even symbolical interpretations of Homer were very common in the ancient world and began at a surprisingly early date.

Perhaps the *Ulysses* of James Joyce calls for special mention as having some Homeric significance. And other names will suggest themselves of writers who have been under a greater or less obligation to Homer. But it is not names that are important so much as the persistence of the tradition they maintain. It is the classical tradition, and of that Homer is not only the founder but the still unchallenged master. As such he has been the centre of attraction and repulsion for European literature through all its history

NOTE

The bibliography of so wide a subject must be highly selective and even a little arbitrary. In the short list which follows deficiencies may be supplied from sources like the catalogues of the Warburg Institute (London University), which specializes in tracing the classical tradition through the ages. Several of the books listed have good bibliographies of their own. Much may be gathered from standard editions and commentaries, not only on Homer but on his successors, such as Virgil. Besides this the scholar must take account (so far as is humanly possible) of the vast periodical literature touching on a subject so important in the history of Western culture.

Arnold, Matthew, (1) *On translating Homer.* Three lectures given at Oxford (1861).
     (2) *On translating Homer : last words.* (Reply to F. W. Newman (1862).)
Bowra, Sir C. M., *From Virgil to Milton* (1945).
Butler, E. M., *The tyranny of Greece over Germany* (1935).
Chamard, H., *Histoire de la Pléïade* (1939–40).
Conway, R. S., *Vergil as a student of Homer* (1929).
Dixon, W. Macneile, *English epic and heroic poetry* (1912).
Finsler, G., *Homer in der Neuzeit von Dante bis Goethe* (1912).
Hallam, H., *Introduction to the literature of Europe in the 15th, 16th, and 17th centuries*
     (1937–9).
Highet, G. A., *The classical tradition* (1949).
Mazon, P., *Madame Dacier et les traductions d'Homère en France* (1949).
Murray, G., *The classical tradition in poetry* (1929).
Rigault, A. H., *Histoire de la querelle des anciens at des modernes.* (*Œuvres complètes*,
     vol. i (1859).)
Routh, H. V., *God, man, and epic poetry* (1927).
Schadenwaldt, W., *Winckelmann und Homer* (1941).
Scott, J. A., *Homer and his influence* (1925).
Toffanin, G., *Omero e il rinascimento italiano* (1949).
Trevelyan, H., *Goethe and the Greeks* (1941).

PART I

THE HOMERIC POEMS AND THEIR AUTHORSHIP

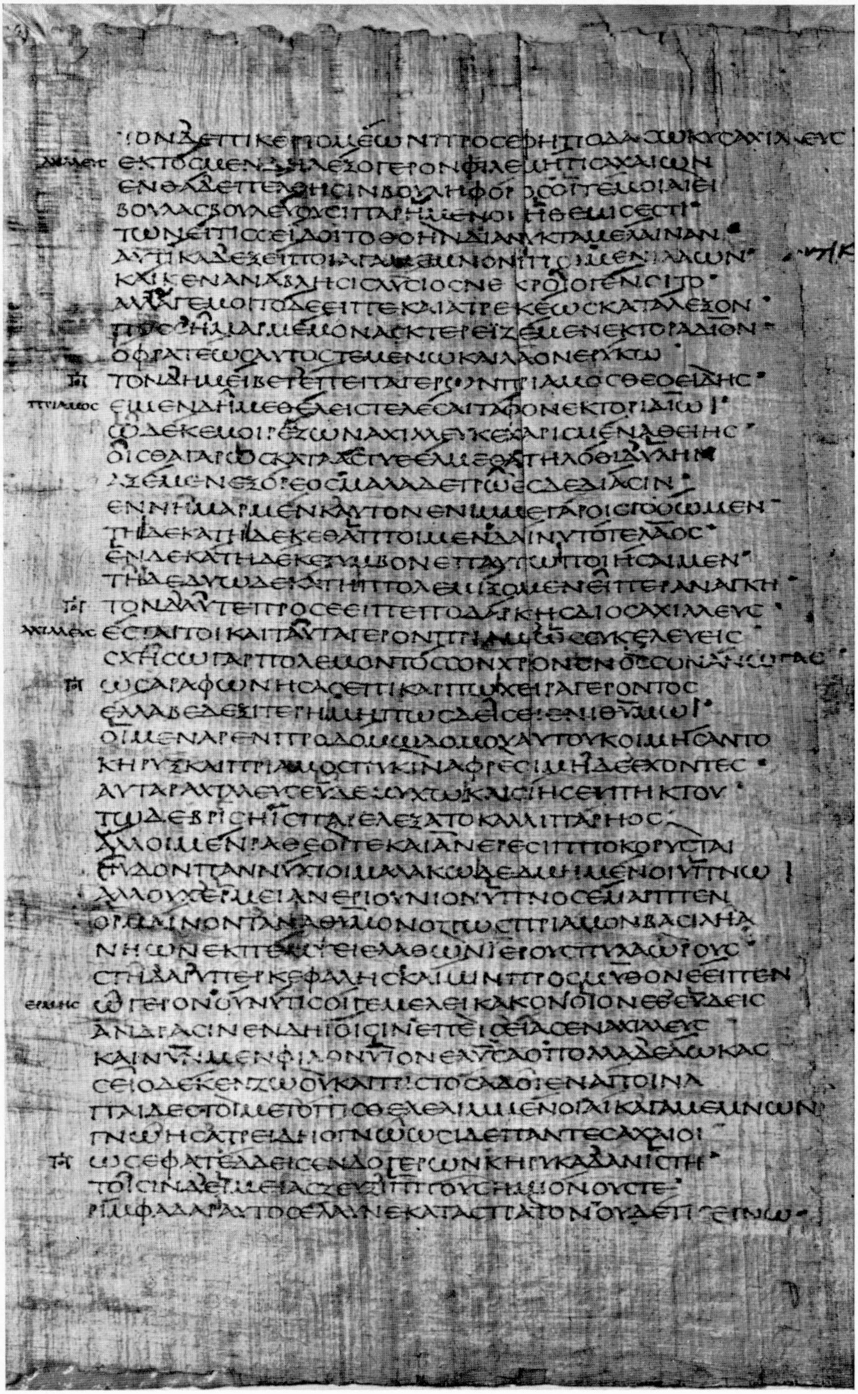

PLATE 3

The Bankes Homer Papyrus of the second century A.D. (Brit. Mus. Papyrus cxiv.) The column illustrated shows Ω 649-91. Height $9\frac{1}{2}$ in.

PLATE 4

A fifth-century rhapsode. From an Attic red-figured amphora found near Vulci. Height of figure 7¾ in.

§A: THE POEMS

CHAPTER I

METRE

by Sir Maurice Bowra

THE Homeric poems, like the works of Hesiod, the Homeric Hymns, and a few lines scratched or painted on vases from the latter part of the eighth century, are composed in dactylic hexameters or what Herodotus calls ἐν ἑξαμέτρῳ τόνῳ (i. 47) or ἐν ἔπεσι ἑξαμέτροισι (vii. 220). Like all ancient Greek metres, the dactylic hexameter is quantitative in the sense that the metrical value of a syllable is decided not by its accent, or loudness, but by its quantity, that is by the time taken to pronounce it. All such metres depend on the relation of long and short syllables, and the simpler among them have a regularly repeated unit or 'foot'. The hexameter has six feet, and each foot is ideally a dactyl. Thus, like trochaic verse, it has what is called a 'falling rhythm', since the emphasis comes at the beginning of each foot, not, as in anapaestic or iambic verse, at the end. But it is not absolutely dactylic or perfectly a hexameter. First, a spondee can always be substituted for a dactyl, though hardly any line consists entirely of spondees, since the dactylic rhythm must always be present in some degree. Secondly, the last or sixth foot is never a dactyl but a trochee or a spondee. The reason for this is that the end of a line must be marked to show that it is the end and to allow the reciter a slight pause for breath. This means that the fifth foot is normally a dactyl — for otherwise the dactylic lilt might be impaired — though sometimes, notably with proper names, a line may end with two spondees after a dactyl. The hexameter may then be schematically displayed as follows:

$$-\,\cup\,\cup\;|\;-\,\cup\,\cup\;|\;-\,\cup\,\cup\;|\;-\,\cup\,\cup\;|\;-\,\cup\,\cup\;|\;-\,\underline{\cup}$$

The form is absolute. There are no hypermetric or incomplete lines. Each line stands by itself as a metrical unit, and there is no hint that lines were ever arranged in regular groups to create anything like stanzas. Since each line is complete, it always ends with the end of a word, and there is no objection to 'hiatus' between lines, that is, to one line ending with a vowel and the next line beginning with another.

The hexameter is constructed on the principle that at any point a spondee may take the place of a dactyl, provided that this does not happen at every place. This is a special application of the assumption that in

D   19 quantitative verse a long syllable is the equivalent of two shorts. This seems to be very rare in any language, and even in Greek it is almost limited to dactyls and anapaests. It is probably based on the simple notion that the dactyl and the anapaest belong to the γένος ἴσον in rhythm, which consists of four unit-times. The special character of each is secured by making the first two unit-times of the dactyl and the last two of the anapaest a single long syllable, but so long as this is done, the other syllables can either be kept as two shorts or replaced by a single long.

The hexameter is conventionally divided into two halves at the τομή or caesura, which may come (1) after the first syllable of the third foot:

$$\text{μῆνιν ἄειδε, θεά, | Πηληϊάδεω Ἀχιλῆος} \qquad \text{(A 1)}$$

or (2) after the second syllable of the third foot if that foot is a dactyl:

$$\text{ἄνδρα μοι ἔννεπε, Μοῦσα, | πολύτροπον, ὃς μάλα πολλά} \qquad \text{(a 1)}$$

or (3) after the first syllable of the fourth foot:

$$\text{Διογενὲς Λαερτιάδη, | πολυμήχαν' Ὀδυσσεῦ.} \qquad \text{(ε 203)}$$

Of these forms the first two are much the most common. In the first 100 lines of the *Iliad* the first occurs 48 times, the second 51, and the third only once. Indeed the comparative rarity of the third can be seen from its general use in the *Iliad*, where it varies from 1 in 50 to 1 in 100, and in the *Odyssey*, where it varies from 1 in 100 to 1 in 200. The caesura is certainly indispensable to the hexameter, but the question is rather what it means in the structure of the verse.

It seems unlikely that it was a real break.[1] Such a break was provided at the end of the line, and to have an earlier break is not only unnecessary but detrimental to the rhythm of what is essentially a unit. Nor is it always clear where the break would actually come. For instance a line may contain all three kinds of caesura, like

$$\text{Ἀτρεΐδη, ποῖόν σε ἔπος φύγεν ἕρκος ὀδόντων} \qquad \text{(Δ 350)}$$

or formally contain the first but in practice the third, as in

$$\text{Ἀτρεΐδης τε ἄναξ ἀνδρῶν καὶ δῖος Ἀχιλλεύς.} \qquad \text{(A 7)}$$

The real reason for the existence of the caesura seems rather to be that the hexameter is a unit whose character is maintained by the balance of its parts and that it secured its effect, as most rhythms do, by making its words run against its strictly metrical divisions. Even if a poet could make each foot end with the end of a word, it would soon become insufferably monotonous and lose the variety which comes from making the rhythm dominate the whole line instead of each foot separately. The caesura helps the line to remain a unity by interlocking its different parts at different points according to the metrical nature of the words used.

That the hexameter was conceived as a whole and treated as such can be seen from its avoidance of any rhythm which might seem to indicate that it falls into parts or ends earlier than it does.[2] The first explains why it very seldom has a break at the end of the third foot, since this would divide it into two equal halves. Sometimes it does this, as in

$$\mathring{\eta} \ o\mathring{v} \ \mu\acute{\epsilon}\mu\nu\eta \ \mathring{o}\tau\epsilon \ \tau' \ \mathring{\epsilon}\kappa\rho\acute{\epsilon}\mu\omega \ \mathring{v}\psi\acute{o}\theta\epsilon\nu, \ \mathring{\epsilon}\kappa \ \delta\grave{\epsilon} \ \pi o\delta o\mathring{v}\nu \qquad (O \ 18)$$

but it is very rare, and we can see why the poets avoided it. So too a break after a trochee in the fourth foot might give the impression that the line ends there as a dactylic tetrameter, and though this is found in

$$\Pi\eta\lambda\epsilon\acute{v}s \ \theta\acute{\eta}\nu \ \mu oi \ \mathring{\epsilon}\pi\epsilon\iota\tau a \ \gamma\upsilon\nu a\mathring{\iota}\kappa a \ \gamma a\mu\acute{\epsilon}\sigma\sigma\epsilon\tau a\iota \ a\mathring{v}\tau\acute{o}s \qquad (I \ 394)$$

Aristarchus felt that it was wrong and emended to $\gamma\epsilon \ \mu\acute{a}\sigma\sigma\epsilon\tau a\iota$. It does indeed occur on a few other occasions (Z 2; Ψ 760), but it is very unusual, and sometimes it is more apparent than real as in

$$\kappa a\acute{\iota} \ \kappa\epsilon\nu \ \tau o\mathring{v}\tau' \ \mathring{\epsilon}\theta\acute{\epsilon}\lambda o\iota\mu\iota \ \Delta\iota\acute{o}s \ \gamma\epsilon \ \delta\iota\delta\acute{o}\nu\tau os \ \mathring{a}\rho\acute{\epsilon}\sigma\theta a\iota \qquad (a \ 390)$$

where $\Delta\iota\acute{o}s \ \gamma\epsilon \ \delta\iota\delta\acute{o}\nu\tau os$ forms a single, formulaic phrase and can hardly be broken into constituent elements. So too the fourth foot usually avoids ending with the end of a spondaic word, as in

$$\mathring{o}\phi\rho a \ \phi\acute{\epsilon}\rho oi \ \nu\mathring{\eta}\acute{a}s \ \tau\epsilon \ \kappa a\grave{\iota} \ a\mathring{v}\tau o\acute{v}s\cdot \ o\mathring{v}\delta' \ \mathring{a}\rho' \ \mathring{\epsilon}\mu\epsilon\lambda\lambda\epsilon\nu, \qquad (\kappa \ 26)$$

and may even resort to unusual creations to avoid it like

$$\mu\epsilon\iota\delta\iota\acute{o}\omega\nu \ \beta\lambda o\sigma\upsilon\rho o\mathring{\iota}\sigma\iota \ \pi\rho o\sigma\acute{\omega}\pi a\sigma\iota\cdot \ \nu\acute{\epsilon}\rho\theta\epsilon \ \delta\grave{\epsilon} \ \pi o\sigma\sigma\acute{\iota}\nu \qquad (H \ 212)$$

where $\pi\rho o\sigma\acute{\omega}\pi a\sigma\iota$ looks like an invention made for the occasion, to prevent any impression that the line ends at this point. The hexameter is welded firmly together, and most effects which would interfere with the impression of unity are avoided.

Though the complete absence of any Greek verse earlier than the hexameter makes it impossible to dogmatize about its origins, these have been sought in its actual structure, and it has been claimed that it is built from a combination of more primitive *metra*, which exist in lyrical verse and may well be very ancient.[3] This might happen in more than one way :

1. A *hemiepes* $- \cup\cup - \cup\cup -$ is combined with an *enoplion*, $- - \cup\cup - \cup\cup - \cup$

$$\mu\mathring{\eta}\nu\iota\nu \ \mathring{a}\epsilon\iota\delta\epsilon, \ \theta\epsilon\acute{a},$$
$$\Pi\eta\lambda\eta\ddot{\iota}\acute{a}\delta\epsilon\omega \ '\mathrm{A}\chi\iota\lambda\mathring{\eta}os \qquad (A \ 1)$$

with the variation of combining $- \cup\cup - \cup\cup - \cup$ with $\cup - \cup\cup - \cup\cup - \cup$

$$\mathring{\eta}\rho\acute{a}\mu\epsilon\theta a \ \mu\acute{\epsilon}\gamma a \ \kappa\mathring{v}\delta os\cdot$$
$$\mathring{\epsilon}\pi\acute{\epsilon}\phi\nu o\mu\epsilon\nu \ "\mathrm{E}\kappa\tau o\rho a \ \delta\mathring{\iota}o\nu \qquad (X \ 393)$$

2. *Two dactylic dipodies* are followed by an *adonius* or *two spondees*:

οἴδ᾽ ἐπὶ δεξιά,
οἴδ᾽ ἐπ᾽ ἀριστερὰ
νωμῆσαι βῶν.   (H 238)

3. A *dactylic tetrameter* is followed by an *adonius*:

αὖτις ἔπειτα πέδονδε κυλίνδετο
λᾶας ἀναιδής.   (λ 598)

In principle it is not impossible that the hexameter was developed from some more simple metre or combination of metres. But we have no evidence that it was, and the attempts to derive it from the metres of extant lyric poetry are open to considerable objections. First, the hexameter is so plainly a unity that attempts to break it up into original parts fail to convince, since it can be broken up equally convincingly in more than one way, and there is no reason to think that one is more likely to be right than the others. Secondly, we may in principle doubt whether the hexameter would be likely to owe anything to the metres of lyrical verse. Heroic narrative of the Homeric kind is a distinct and separate art from song. While song uses the stanza for its unit of composition, heroic poetry uses the single line; while song is sung to a recognizable tune, heroic poetry is at the most intoned to a very simple chant; while song may be sung by a choir and even accompanied by a dance, heroic poetry is sung by a single bard and has no dance. In the absence of any independent evidence it seems unwise to claim that the hexameter is derived from the measures of lyric verse. There is no reason why it should not have been developed simply as a measure of narrative poetry, and if it has any connection with lyric verse, it may be no more than through some distant common source which has been shaped into two quite different directions.

That the hexameter was originally not spoken but sung is clear enough. First, when Homer tells of Achilles or Demodocus or Phemius, he makes them sing to the accompaniment of the φόρμιγξ or lyre (I 185 ff.; θ 261; χ 332). Secondly, he himself summons the Muse to sing, ἄειδε, of the wrath of the Achilles (A 1). There is no doubt that he himself was acquainted with the practice of singing heroic lays, but it is possible that even in his time the practice changed or was matched by another practice of speaking. Nothing much can be deduced from his use of the word ἔννεπε to the Muse (α 1; B 761), since it simply means 'tell' and is applicable equally to song and to speech. On the other hand it is noteworthy that when Hesiod tells how the Muses summoned him to be a poet, he does not mention a lyre, but says that they have given him a staff (*Theog.* 30), and this anticipates the practice of the rhapsodes in the fifth century, as we know them from vases (Pl. 4) and from Pindar's words on Homer, κατὰ ῥάβδον ἔφρασεν (*Isth.* iv. 42). If we press the meaning of ἔφρασεν, it is that the rhapsodes of Pindar's time recited instead of singing. This may well have been the later practice. But in Homer's own time we can hardly doubt that singing was normal. It is most unlikely that this implies any real tune or indeed anything more than some primitive chant, and if we wish to establish the essential difference between the hexameter and the metres of lyric verse, it is that it was sung to some musical accompaniment which probably allowed full play to its metrical character.

The hexameter is not ideally fitted for an easy use of the Greek language. It excludes, because of their scansion, many words, especially those which contain a cretic (– ◡ –) or have more than two short syllables in succession. That is why Homer excludes certain words which must have been known to him but could not be fitted into his metre. Thus he has κτήματα and κτήμασι but not κτημάτων, παύομαι but not παυόμην, δυσμενέες but not δυσμενής. The traditional language provided him with useful alternatives such as ἤματα for ἡμέρας, μῆχος for μηχανή, κραδίη for καρδίη. When two alternatives suit the metre, he uses whichever meets his immediate need; we find on the one hand πευθόμεθα, πευθοίαθ', πευθέσθω, and on the other πυνθάνομαι and πυνθανόμην. The Greek language, as we know it, does not fall so easily into the hexameter as into the iambic trimeter, of which Aristotle says, 'it is the most speakable of metres, as is shown by the way in which we very often fall into it in conversation' (*Poet.* 1449 a 25).

This difficulty has prompted the suggestion that the Greeks took over the hexameter from some other language, such as Minoan or Hittite, for which it was more naturally adapted.[4] This is not inconceivable, though the present state of our knowledge affords no evidence for it. Yet it is none the less possible that the hexameter is a Greek invention. Not all metres are ideally suited to the languages which use them, and the hexameter is so fine a measure that it may well have become popular, despite its limitations, because of its irresistible rhythm. It certainly gives prominence to some essential qualities of the Greek language, notably its high proportion of short to long syllables and its ability to differentiate between them on the principle that one long is the equivalent of two shorts. This view receives some support from the Mycenaean tablets in Linear Script B. These are not in verse and have very little to do with its usual subjects and vocabulary, but they tell enough about early Greek to show that it could fall without undue strain into hexameters. It must of course be an accident that some phrases on the tablets such as τοιχοδόμοι δεμέοντες, ἕνεκα χρυσοῖο ἱεροῖο and ἐρέται Πλευρωνάδε ἰόντες look as if they were parts of hexameters, but the likeness conceals an important fact. Because this archaic Greek had a large number of short syllables, it was possible to evolve a metrical system based on the proportion of longs and shorts. A simple test can be taken with proper names. Of fifty-eight names given by the first decipherers of the script fifty-two can be fitted at once without change into hexameters,[5] as can twenty-one place-names of Greek origin in the Pylos tablets.[6] Nor is this difficult to explain. At this stage Greek still preserved a large number of uncontracted vowels, and in such words as κτοινοόχος, ὀπισκαφεῆϜες and κλαϜιφόρος, these betray the metrical capacities of the language. Its words fall more easily into a dactylic rhythm than do the contracted words of a later age, and though the iambic may then have been closer to ordinary speech, this is not necessarily true of Mycenaean times. Since for other reasons it is likely that the epic tradition goes back to these times, it is likely that the hexameter itself is a Mycenaean measure, if not a Mycenaean invention.[7]

Even so the hexameter was an exacting metre, and the difficulties which attended its composition were by no means solved by the use of alternative forms. Homer shows abundantly how, almost in defiance of prosody, intractable words could be introduced into it, especially by the artificial lengthening of short syllables.[8] To some extent our texts conceal what has happened when they write ου for ο, ει for ε, and λλ, μμ, νν for λ, μ, ν; in fact when we read ἔλλαβε, ἔμμεναι, ἔννεπε, Οὔλυμπος, εἰλήλουθα, these are not real forms but the scribe's way of indicating a special metrical treatment of ἔλαβε, ἔνεπε, Ὄλυμπος, ἐλήλυθα. Artificial lengthening is extremely common in the Homeric poems and shows how the tradition has evolved its own means of adapting to the hexameter words which would otherwise not fall into it. It observes not indeed exact rules for this but at least recognizable tendencies. Lengthening occurs most commonly in (1) the first syllable of three shorts as in Πρῑαμίδης, κῡάνεος, ᾱθάνατος, ᾱκάματος, ᾱγοράασθε; (2) the first syllable of an antispast, ∪−−∪, as in Ᾱπόλλωνα, εἰλήλουθα; (3) a short syllable between two long syllables when it is followed by a digamma, as in ἐμπνείησι (ἐμπνέϜησι); (4) a short syllable between two long syllables when it is followed by a vowel, as in ὑπεροπλίῃσι, ἀκομιστίη, κακοεργίης. Such lengthenings usually take place at certain places in the line, notably (1) the first syllable of the first foot, producing the στίχος ἀκέφαλος as in

$$\delta\iota\grave{\alpha}\ \mu\grave{\epsilon}\nu\ \dot{\alpha}\sigma\pi\acute{\iota}\delta o\varsigma\ \mathring{\eta}\lambda\theta\epsilon\ \phi\alpha\epsilon\iota\nu\mathring{\eta}\varsigma\ \ddot{o}\beta\rho\iota\mu o\nu\ \ddot{\epsilon}\gamma\chi o\varsigma\ ;\qquad (\Gamma\ 357)$$

(2) the second syllable of the first foot when it consists of a single trochaic word as in πολλὰ λισσόμενος, and (3) the first syllable of the sixth foot, which may be disguised as συφείου or νέμεσσι or produce a στίχος μείουρος as in

$$T\rho\hat{\omega}\epsilon\varsigma\ \delta'\ \dot{\epsilon}\rho\rho\acute{\iota}\gamma\eta\sigma\alpha\nu\ \ddot{o}\pi\omega\varsigma\ \ddot{\iota}\delta o\nu\ \alpha\dot{\iota}\acute{o}\lambda o\nu\ \ddot{o}\phi\iota\nu.\qquad (M\ 208)$$

Short vowels are more commonly lengthened before the liquids λ, μ, ν, than before other consonants, but, in general, lengthening seems to be decided by the needs of the verse at certain places where the dactylic rhythm is most obvious, and that is why it occurs at them.

The usual technique of the hexameter shows what efforts were made to extend its capacities and how carefully its practitioners adapted their language to it. In this process two factors call for notice. First, the influence of musical accompaniment, no matter how simple, must have counted for something. The bard who chanted a verse would be able to make his words conform more closely to the requirements of metre than if he had merely spoken them with the usual attention that speech gives to the quantity of a syllable. Secondly, since the distinction between long and short syllables is in the last resort settled by rules, and since the assumption that a long is the equivalent of two shorts is a matter of convention, the poets could treat their words with some freedom and make them conform to the metre without imposing too great a strain on the natural limitations of the language. What counts with the hexameter is its dominating dactylic rhythm. Once this was established, much could be done to extend its scope and to make intractable words fit into it. The hexameter remains not only a powerful instrument of narrative poetry, such as is to be found hardly anywhere else in the world, but in its own way a precise and careful means for keeping language at an impressive level of music and movement. It has its skilfully devised rules, and these illustrate what mastery Homer had of it and what versatility he displayed in combining an elaborate technique with a straightforward manner of telling a story.

NOTES TO CHAPTER 1

1. S. Bassett, *The Poetry of Homer*, 145-9.

2. W. R. Hardie, *Res metrica*, 21.

3. T. Bergk, *Über das älteste Versmass der Griechen* (1854); H. Usener, *Altgriechischer Versbau* (1887); U. von Wilamowitz-Moellendorf, *Die Ilias und Homer*, 352; K. Witte in *RE*, *s.v.* 'Homeros'.

4. A. Meillet, *Les Origines indo-européennes des mètres grecs*, 57-71.

5. M. Ventris and J. Chadwick, 'Evidence for Greek dialect in the Mycenaean archives' in *JHS*, lxxiii. 94.

6. E. G. Turner, *Bulletin of the Institute of Classical Studies*, London, i. 17-20.

7. *Cf.* M. Ventris and J. Chadwick, *Documents*, 107 f.

8. W. Schulze, *Quaestiones epicae* (1892); *cf.* W. Leaf, *Iliad*, i. 590-8. *Cf.* Arist. *Poetic* 1458 b for ancient comment on the practice.

[On Mycenaean survivals in Homer's language see also Ch. 4.]

CHAPTER 2

STYLE

by Sir Maurice Bowra

HOMER'S language can never have been spoken by men. It contains too many alternative forms, too many synonyms, too many artificial forms for it to be in any sense a vernacular. It is a language created for poetry by the needs of composition. To its remarkably expressive and wide-ranging effects various layers of Greek have contributed. If the most predominant element is the Ionic of the eighth century, this is inextricably combined with other elements which might be thought to come from various districts outside Ionia. There are words and forms which survived in historical times in Thessaly and Aeolis, in Arcadia and Cyprus; there are others so unusual that we cannot give them a historical place. Conversely, there are Greek peoples who made no distinctive contribution to Homeric language, notably the speakers of Western Greek, including the Dorians of the Peloponnese and Crete. The explanation of this is that the Ionian poets adapted a traditional language to Ionic in order to make it more intelligible to their own people and easier to compose in it themselves. But they retained, because they were useful as well as ornamental, words and forms which are not Ionic but seem to come from an older Greek language which was spoken in the Mycenaean age but later broke into separate dialects. The existence of this language has long been suspected. We can now begin to see what it was and to identify some features of Homeric usage which have not hitherto been satisfactorily explained.

The language of the tablets in Linear Script B, which may be called Mycenaean, contains elements which survive in Homer,[a] but are rare, if not absent, elsewhere, notably the genitive singular in -οιο (elsewhere found only in some Thessalian inscriptions) and in -αο; the genitive plural in -αων; the form Ποσειδάων; frequent nouns of agent in -ηρ, which are regular in Cyprus but unusual outside it; the suffixes -δε denoting direction towards and -θεν denoting direction from; the termination -φι denoting locative, comitative, or instrumental force, reminiscent of the way in which Homer uses the clearly archaic ἶφι and sometimes keeps ὄρεσφι when he might use ὄρεσσι (Λ 474; Χ 139, 189). The Homeric πότνι' 'Αθήνη is an easy transposition of the Mycenaean 'Αθάνα πότνια. Some forms, which have not survived into

[a] Cf. Ch. 4.

Homeric Greek, seem to lie behind their Homeric equivalents and perhaps to explain them, as when Mycenaean provides infinitives in -εεν
instead of -ειν or -ην, and may account for the mysterious Homeric
infinitives in -εειν, while the artificial Homeric ἔασι may have been
fashioned as a substitute for the Mycenaean ἔενσι. Mycenaean keeps
both initial and internal digamma, and shows that the uncertainty of
Homeric practice in this respect is due to the competing claims of traditional language and contemporary Ionic. Though the evidence is not
plentiful, it proves that certain forms of ancient origin were deeply
embedded in Homeric Greek, while others were transformed into
artificial substitutes with the same metrical value. The Mycenaean forms
in Homer survived because they were preserved by a living, oral tradition
of poetical composition and were thought worthy of preservation both
for their antiquity and for their usefulness.

Though we may be fairly confident that the beginnings of the Homeric
language are to be found in the Mycenaean age, we cannot point to this
or that passage and say that it is Mycenaean, or even with any confidence
draw up a list of Mycenaean words. What is clear is that some words,
which in historical times were found only in Cyprus or Arcadia, are
almost certainly Mycenaean in the sense that they come from the language
which was spoken in the Peloponnese before the Dorian invasion or the
colonization of Ionia. A recent confirmation of this can be seen in the
use of τέμενος in Arcadian to mean a piece of land marked off as a
special domain. This is the sense which it has not only in Homer (Z 194;
I 578; ζ 293) but in Mycenaean tablets from Pylos, but not elsewhere
in Greek. It is more than likely that many of the Homeric epithets,
especially for the gods, come from the Mycenaean age: πότνι' Ἀθήνη
certainly does; ἐριούνιος used of Hermes is best explained from Arcadian
as meaning 'fast runner'; Cypriot explains why Apollo is called
Σμινθεύς (A 39); as the sender of plague he is addressed as the mouse-
god, since mice carry it. We may hope that future discoveries will
throw more light on the Mycenaean origins of Homeric words, but for
the moment it must suffice to know that such origins undoubtedly exist.

The language, which began on the Greek mainland, seems to have
passed through two main stages afterwards. First, after the collapse of
the Mycenaean civilization in the twelfth century B.C., the tradition of
epic song survived most probably in Athens and for a time in Pylos, and
possibly elsewhere; second, after the Ionian migration of c. 1000 B.C.,
it passed to Ionia, and there reached the form which we know from the
Homeric poems. Such a history explains both its predominantly Ionic
exterior and its many archaic elements. Less easy to explain are the so-
called Aeolic elements, words and forms which lie outside Ionia and find
their historical parallels in Thessaly or in Aeolis. Some of these are so

deeply embedded in the text that they cannot be moved, but others are certainly preserved because they belong to the tradition, and for this reason survive when an Ionic substitute could easily take their place. That some of these Aeolic forms come from Mycenaean is reasonably certain, since patronymics in -ιος are found in the Pylos tablets. On the other hand we cannot yet rule out the possibility that Ionian poets sometimes introduced an Aeolic form or word because the two dialects, notably in Chios, were not entirely distinct.

Homeric language is then the fruit of a long tradition which preserved relics of Mycenaean times. It was able to do this because it was formulaic. Its copious formulae were devised to assist the bard in the task of oral composition. Since he composed for hearers and much of his work was necessarily improvised, he needed a large number of formulaic phrases to help him. Even if writing existed, and it seems unlikely that it did between c. 1200 and c. 750,[a] the bard would not rely upon it, but form his poems in his head and deliver them by word of mouth. All oral poetry needs and uses formulae, and indeed cannot exist without them. If the poet has them in full control, he can produce a poem on almost any subject at short notice. This must be the way in which Homer's imaginary bards, Phemius and Demodocus, perform (χ 347-8; θ 44-5), and we cannot doubt that when Homer learned his craft what he mastered was a rich store of formulae connected with heroic legends and ready to meet almost any emergency. Once a phrase met a need and was found to have an appeal to the poets' audiences, it might come to stay, while others less worthy were abandoned and replaced by new phrases. This is how an oral tradition works, and we may assume that this is what happened before Homer found the art in existence and made his own magnificent use of it. The formula makes the Homeric style what it is and is fundamental to any understanding of it.

The study of the Homeric formulae was undertaken by Milman Parry[1] with remarkable results. He showed not only that it is far more pervasive than had hitherto been thought but that its use is governed by unexpectedly consistent rules. For convenience formulae may be divided into three classes: (1) short phrases, notably noun-adjective combinations containing the famous Homeric epithets; (2) single phrases used for the machinery of the story and repeated when a similar occasion occurs; (3) blocks of lines, or themes, which describe conventional actions. Each of these shows its own special usage and its own rules, and each is undeniably formulaic in the sense that a given set of words is normally used for a like occasion whenever it occurs. It is not always easy to say what is formulaic or what is not. Some occasions are so unusual that they occur only once, but they may none the less belong to the poet's repertory or

[a] Cf. Ch. 23, esp. pp. 551 ff.

contain phrases which do and which are now put together in a new combination. Homer operates far less with single words than with phrases,
and these phrases may often be of some length.

First, the shorter formulae may best be examined in the noun-adjective combinations, which are used not merely for god sand men but for
all sorts of inanimate objects such as spears, swords, the sea, and the sky.
In using these Homer follows marked rules with few variations from
them, and the rules are determined by the demands of the hexameter
and the inflected nature of Greek syntax. Just because Greek nouns are
declined and have different metrical values according to their cases, so
the formulae have been worked out with consummate care and skill to
be ready for all cases in the declension and for every space or place to be
occupied in the hexameter. For instance, there are 56 different noun-
adjective combinations for Achilles, but each is determined by the case
of the noun and the position to be occupied in the verse. With certain
exceptions, which we shall consider, this is Homer's normal practice, and
it indicates an ancient and powerful tradition which has invented such
combinations for almost every need. At times it looks a little mechanical,
as when certain epithets are not so much otiose as out of place. Thus we
hardly expect the Cyclops Polyphemus to be called 'god-like' (α 70) or
great-hearted (κ 200), or the mother of the beggar Irus to be 'lady
mother' (σ 5) or the herdsman Philoetius to be 'leader of men' (υ 185).
Such cases suggest that even for Homer some epithets had little meaning
and were useful chiefly for filling a place in the verse. At other times
epithets, which in most places are suitable and even charming, do not fit
their contexts, as when the sky by day is called 'starry' (Θ 46; Ο 371;
ι 527) or beached ships 'swift' (Κ 306; Λ 666; Π 168) or dirty linen
'shining' (ζ 26). Here the familiar epithet is retained in its usual place in
the verse, even though it conflicts slightly with the sense.

The second kind of formula, the repeated line, presents no such
difficulties. It is complete in itself either as a main sentence, such as that
which tells of a warrior falling in battle :

$$\delta o \acute{u} \pi \eta \sigma \epsilon \nu \; \delta \grave{\epsilon} \; \pi \epsilon \sigma \acute{\omega} \nu, \; \mathring{a} \rho \acute{a} \beta \eta \sigma \epsilon \; \delta \grave{\epsilon} \; \tau \epsilon \acute{u} \chi \epsilon' \; \mathring{\epsilon} \pi' \; a \mathring{u} \tau \widehat{\omega}$$

or it forms a temporal clause, such as that which tells of a new day coming :

$$\mathring{\eta} \mu o s \; \delta' \; \mathring{\eta} \rho \iota \gamma \acute{\epsilon} \nu \epsilon \iota a \; \phi \acute{a} \nu \eta \; \rho o \delta o \delta \acute{a} \kappa \tau \upsilon \lambda o s \; \text{'} H \acute{\omega} s.$$

In either case it needs no such variations and adjustments as the noun-
adjective combination does. The result is that for much of his machinery
of action Homer uses such lines abundantly without change. They are
useful for almost any action which is necessary for the development of a
story but does not call for too much attention to be drawn to it, whether
for the coming of dawn or night, the minor details of fighting, the be-

ginning or the end of a meal. There are however, times when Homer
abandons the stock form for something more elaborate, as when the fall
of Sarpedon or Asios is told not in the usual single line for a man falling
in battle, but with a simile :

ἤριπε δ’ ὡς ὅτε τις δρῦς ἤριπεν ἢ ἀχερωΐς,
ἠὲ πίτυς βλωθρή, τήν τ’ οὔρεσι τέκτονες ἄνδρες
ἐξέταμον πελέκεσσι νεήκεσι νήϊον εἶναι.

(N 389-91 ; Π 482-4)

No doubt he does this because he wishes to make something special of
the occasion and to give it its own appropriate poetry. None the less
the three lines used are themselves as formulaic as the single line ; they
differ only in being reserved for special occasions. So too he sometimes
forsakes the usual line for the coming of dawn and substitutes a variation
which is not a dependent temporal clause but stands paratactically to what
follows. Of this he has four variations, which bear some resemblance to
one another but are none the less different (1 : H 421-2 ; τ 433-4. 2 : Θ 1.
3 : T 1. 4 : ε 1.). Since each of these precedes a marked change in the
action, that may be why they are used. It is quite possible that these variations are themselves based on a common formula, and that their slight
differences indicate the poet's desire to improve upon the traditional form.
The third kind of formula, the repeated theme, is considerably more
elastic. Though certain actions, such as the putting of a ship to sea or
bringing it to land or the entertainment of guests, receive little variation,
yet others do, and there seems to be some system in them. For instance,
the arming of a warrior is a common theme and Homer may well have felt
that it could not always be treated in exactly the same way.[2] So the line

κνημῖδας μὲν πρῶτα περὶ κνήμῃσιν ἔθηκε

occurs in four places and in each is developed differently. (1) In Γ 328 ff.
it is confined to a normal description of arming. (2) In Λ 16 ff. it is
expanded by an account of Agamemnon's breast-plate and shield. (3) In
Π 130 ff. it is combined with the harnessing of horses. (4) In T 369 ff.
it goes further in the prodigy of the horse Xanthus speaking to its master.
Moreover, each of these occasions marks an important new movement
in the action. The first begins the fighting in the *Iliad*; the second the
general engagement which brings the Achaeans, without Achilles, near
to disaster; the third the counter-attack led by Patroclus; the fourth the
final onslaught when Achilles takes at last to the field. A somewhat
similar variation occurs in the treatment of sacrifices. This may, if it is
not very important, be reduced to four lines (A 315-18), but it is usually
expanded, whether by a prayer (A 447 ff. ; B 402 ff.), or by the presentation of the chine of the sacrificed beast to Ajax (H 314 ff.) or the gilding
of the heifer's horns (γ 430 ff.). Each of these variations has its own rele-

vance or significance in the context, and we can understand why Homer
has introduced it.   Behind it lies the standard, formulaic theme, and
though he builds his scene on this, he is not tied to it.

Homer's occasional elasticity in his treatment of such themes may be
matched by certain variations in his noun-adjective combinations.   There
are occasions when he might use a standard form and does not do so,
and we can usually see why.³   When Circe realizes who Odysseus is, the
conventional epithet διίφιλος is replaced by πολύτροπος (κ 330).   When
the size and strength of some great warriors call for a moment's attention, the usual epithets are abandoned and their place is taken by πελώριος
for Achilles (Φ 527; X 92), Hector (Λ 820) and above all Ajax (Γ 229;
Η 211; P 360).   Though after a masculine caesura Odysseus in the
nominative is usually called δουρίκλυτος, he is twice called by the metrically interchangeable Ἰθακήσιος (β 246; χ 45), which refers to his
position as the true king of Ithaca and the only man who can restore
order there.   On one occasion the familiar ἐϋκνήμιδας Ἀχαιούς is replaced by ὑπερκύδαντας Ἀχαιούς (Δ 66, 71), when Athene and Hera
plot for the victory of the Achaeans, and the word strengthens their case.
When Achilles prepares the funeral of Patroclus, he is not πόδας ὠκύς
but μεγάθυμος (Ψ 168), as if on this solemn occasion it were inappropriate
to stress his speed of foot and right to stress his greatness of heart, when
he pays the last rites to his friend.   When Penelope prays that Apollo
will strike Antinous, she calls the god not Διὸς υἱός but κλυτότοξος
(ρ 494), which is certainly more suitable for one who sends arrows of
vengeance.   Such substitutions would cause no trouble to the poet and
would enable him to make rather a finer point than if he had kept the
traditional formula.

Though some of the Homeric formulae must be very ancient and go
back to the Mycenaean age, it is clear that in the long tradition of oral
poetry between that time and Homer's own many new formulae were
invented, and there is no good reason to think that, when the *Iliad* and the
Odyssey were composed, they had to rely entirely on existing, traditional
phrases.   Indeed the evidence of other formulaic epic suggests that poets
were able to fashion new phrases for new needs.   But in general we can
see some of the ways in which new formulae were made.   It was indispensable that they should not only meet the metrical needs of composition
but fit into the general poetical atmosphere.   Thus we often find echoes
between one formula and another, and the similarities suggest different
ways of invention.   First, we may perhaps assume that two different
phrases have a common origin.   The Hours are entrusted with watching
the entrances and exits of Olympus :

ἠμὲν ἀνακλῖναι πυκινὸν νέφος ἠδ᾽ ἀναθεῖναι.   (Θ 395)

So Odysseus protects the entrances and exits of the Wooden Horse:

$$\mathring{\eta}\mu\grave{\epsilon}\nu\ \mathring{a}\nu\alpha\kappa\lambda\hat{\iota}\nu\alpha\iota\ \pi\nu\kappa\iota\nu\grave{o}\nu\ \lambda\acute{o}\chi o\nu\ \mathring{\eta}\delta'\ \mathring{\epsilon}\pi\iota\theta\hat{\epsilon}\iota\nu\alpha\iota.\qquad (\lambda\ 525)$$

We may surmise that νέφος and λόχον are both variations on some word for 'door' and have been substituted for it to provide a more precise picture. Secondly, one idea may suggest another. If two men killed in battle are called εἰδότε χάρμης (E 608), it is but a small step to call two dogs εἰδότε θήρης (K 360). If men in battle ἐπ' ἀλλήλοισιν ὄρουσαν (Ξ 401), there is no real reason against saying of thistledown πρὸς ἀλλήλησιν ἔχονται (ε 329). Thirdly, a familiar phrase can be altered to secure an ironical effect. When Dionysus and Hephaestus find a safe haven in the sea, we hear that Θέτις δ' ὑπεδέξατο κόλπῳ (Z 136; Σ 398), and some such form may have prompted the phrase στυγερὸς δ' ὑπεδέξατο κοῖτος (χ 470) for the hanging of the maidservants of Odysseus, who have found a hateful κοῖτος in death. Somewhat differently, a phrase may provoke another which is almost humorous. When Hector complains that much of the wealth of Troy has perished ἐπεὶ μέγας ὠδύσατο Ζεύς (Σ 292), his formula must lie behind another, which certainly contains a pun, when Athene asks her father about Odysseus τί νύ οἱ τόσον ὠδύσαο, Ζεῦ; (α 62). Fourthly, the echo may be almost entirely of sound. The structure of some familiar phrase suggests, perhaps unconsciously, another which sounds like it but has a different meaning. So ἠεροειδέα πέτρην (μ 233) may have been suggested by the familiar ἠεροειδέα πόντον (Ψ 744; β 263, etc.); the description of Ithaca as πίονα δῆμον (ξ 329) by πίονα δημῷ, the epithet for an ox (Ψ 750); the sound of Odysseus's bow-string χελιδόνι εἰκέλη αὐδήν (φ 411) by the simile used of Athene χελιδόνι εἰκέλη ἄντην (χ 240). These, and other cases like them, indicate that the oral style fostered the formation of new phrases on the analogy of others already existing. When a bard composes without the aid of writing, he has a keen sense of sound as well as of sense, and it is inevitable that, just as one situation suggests another and provokes a similar form of words, so a sound-sequence may suggest another similar in rhythm or in tonal value or in balance of words. The new formulae fit easily into the old pattern and strike no discordant note in it.

Homer's dependence on formulae and copious use of them need not have prevented him from breaking at times into what we may call free composition. In principle it is not improbable that he described scenes for which his formulae were not fully adequate and invented new phrases for them. Even if he composed without writing, he may well have been able to think out certain passages in his head and to remember them without requiring formulae to help him with them. We cannot say which such passages are, since a phrase which occurs only once in Homer may in fact be a formula used by other poets and its rarity in his work

simply an accident.   But we can at least notice some passages in which
his own formulae are rare and which have the air of being new creations.
Even so he does not choose his words individually as literary poets do.
He still relies on certain mannerisms and phrases of the formulaic style,
even if he assigns minor functions to them.   For instance, the vision of
Theoclymenus is certainly an unusual event, and we expect it to contain
unusual words :

> ἆ δειλοί, τί κακὸν τόδε πάσχετε; νυκτὶ μὲν ὑμέων
> εἰλύαται κεφαλαί τε πρόσωπά τε νέρθε τε γοῦνα,
> οἰμωγὴ δὲ δέδηε, δεδάκρυνται δὲ παρειαί,
> αἵματι δ' ἐρράδαται τοῖχοι καλαί τε μεσόδμαι·
> εἰδώλων δὲ πλέον πρόθυρον, πλείη δὲ καὶ αὐλή,
> ἱεμένων Ἐρεβόσδε ὑπὸ ζόφον· ἠέλιος δὲ
> οὐρανοῦ ἐξαπόλωλε, κακὴ δ' ἐπιδέδρομεν ἀχλύς.   (υ 351-7)

In this are some undeniable formulae, notably ἆ δειλοί (Λ 816; κ 431),
νέρθε τε γοῦνα (Χ 452), δεδάκρυνται δὲ παρειαί (Χ 491), and καλαί τε
μεσόδμαι (τ 37).   But these do no more than provide a structure for the
really significant phrases which look like inventions made for the unusual
occasion.   For one indeed we may trace an origin : κακὴ δ' ἐπιδέδρομεν
ἀχλύς may well be derived from words used to describe the brilliant
light on Olympus, λευκὴ δ' ἐπιδέδρομεν αἴγλη (ζ 45), to which it provides
a counterpart and an antithesis.   So too, when Achilles plans shameless
deeds against the dead body of Hector, they must be revealed in their
horror and pathos.   So indeed they are :

> τοῦ δ' ἦν ἑλκομένοιο κονίσαλος· ἀμφὶ δὲ χαῖται
> κυάνεαι πίτναντο, κάρη δ' ἅπαν ἐν κονίῃσι
> κεῖτο πάρος χαρίεν· τότε δὲ Ζεὺς δυσμενέεσσι
> δῶκεν ἀεικίσσασθαι ἑῇ ἐν πατρίδι γαίῃ.   (Χ 401-4)

The only certain formula here is ἐν πατρίδι γαίῃ, which occurs seven
times elsewhere, while the placing of both ἐν κονίῃσι and δυσμενέεσσι at
the end of the line is common form and hardly less formulaic.   Homer
often works in this way when he has something special to say and wishes
to give full weight to it.   Even in his battle-scenes he uses phrases which
do not occur elsewhere and may therefore not be true formulae, and when
he deals with something more unusual, he may well allow himself a
certain freedom in combining traditional forms with others of his own
invention.

Though Homer is able to vary his formulae and to achieve an almost
individual style in his combinations of them, he remains an oral poet, who
expects his words not to be read but heard.   His way of using them is
one to which the Western world is no longer accustomed, and it raises
questions of literary and aesthetic interest which are relevant to any true

understanding and criticism of it. The oral poet does not work like the literary poet, whose success lies in the unusual and striking combination of single words and who aims at making his style as personal as possible, and thinks it below his dignity to follow his predecessors too closely. The oral poet both belongs to a tradition which circumstances force him to follow and is proud to do so, because it connects him with an honoured past and gives him a special authority as an expert on it. He is interested not in the *mot juste* as such but in a more extended effect which depends on different methods. Much of his work has already been done for him. His formulae have survived because of their intrinsic usefulness and brilliance and may be regarded as the best of all available means for their purpose. Since he starts with them and uses them abundantly, his originality is to be judged by what he does with them. To understand such an art we must try to see it at work in its own conditions, and put ourselves in the position of people who do not read but hear, who assume that a poet will use a traditional style, who respond to salient effects rather than to small points, and may well not notice matters which would trouble a watchful and critical reader.

Since the formulaic style was devised in the first place for the help of the bard rather than for the benefit of his audience, it does not always have the precision which we expect from poetry. This is particularly clear in noun-adjective combinations. We may at its first appearance feel that there is some special point in πολύμητις 'Οδυσσεύς or ἄναξ ἀνδρῶν 'Αγαμέμνων, but we soon cease to feel this and begin to treat the phrase as a functional element which adds little or nothing to the meaning of a passage. Even if such inventions are delightful when taken in isolation, their appeal is dulled by repetition, and the original audiences, who were more accustomed to them than we are, must have been no less unresponsive. Yet in the general pattern of poetry they have their function. Because they are so familiar, and do not trouble us, they emphasize the words to which they are attached, and help the clear flow of the narrative which would be slower and less easy to absorb if the poet adorned his nouns with too many different epithets or thought that, whenever they appear, they must be made to add something new to the poetry. The noun-adjective combinations may be negative in their effect, but so far from being an obstacle to story-telling, they are a help, because they allow the action to proceed on broad, simple lines.

With some necessary adjustments something of the same kind may be said of the formulaic, repeated lines. They too are essentially functional, but that does not mean that they lack poetical virtues. Indeed many of them, taken by themselves, are rich in a noble, simple poetry, and that no doubt is why they were taken into common use instead of other less deserving lines. With them too we must identify ourselves with a listening audience. They work in a way which is not commonly to be found in written poetry. Though they perform an essential task, they must be considered in their individual contexts, since it is from these that they often take their meaning and their worth. A simple example is the little formula μίνυνθά περ οὔ τι μάλα δήν. It is used by Thetis to Achilles about the shortness of his life and has almost a tragic grandeur in its concentrated brevity (A 416). When Adamas is struck by Meriones, it is applied to his dying agonies and catches his last brief struggles (N 573). When Odysseus hangs the maidservants who have slept with the suitors, he punishes them with a terrible death, but its horror is tempered by its brief duration (χ 473). More striking are lines which do not look very distinguished in themselves but, when they occur, are so well knit into their context that they develop a different character on occasion and make us see more clearly what the action means. Such is

$$\text{ὣς ἔφατ᾽, ἔδεισεν δ᾽ ὁ γέρων καὶ ἐπείθετο μύθῳ.}$$

Used of Agamemnon's dismissal of Chryses, it stresses the power of the king and the helplessness of the priest (A 33), but when it is applied to Priam, after Achilles's warning that he must not provoke him by complaints, it assumes a grave and almost tragic pathos (Ω 571). Even a quite unobtrusive line may gain greatly from its context. Take for instance

$$\text{αὐτὰρ ὁ ἔγνω ᾗσιν ἐνὶ φρεσὶ φώνησέν τε.}$$

With slight variations, this is used when the heralds come to take Briseis from Achilles, and are too ashamed to speak, but he understands the situation at once (A 333); when Zeus finds Athene and Hera sitting apart in silence and bursts into anger against them (Θ 446); when Glaucus, after praying to Apollo, is healed of his wounds and knows that the god has done what he asked (Π 530); when Hector, tricked by Athene into thinking that Deiphobus is near and ready to help him, calls on him and finds that he has vanished (X 296). In turn the line presents quick understanding, angry discovery, grateful recognition, and horrified realization. The repeated line of this kind is not a self-sufficient unit; it derives its character and its strength from its context, and through this becomes an important and effective instrument in the poetical result.

It follows that when a repeated line has a different colour in different settings we must take it on its merits as it comes and not think of its other appearances. This is certainly what a listening audience would do, and such awkwardness as we may feel is due to our dependence on books and our slow study of them. It is no matter for distress that ἐννέα πάντες ἀνέσταν should describe both nine champions getting ready for battle (H 161) and nine judges getting ready to judge sports (θ 258); that ἄνδρεσσι μελήσει should follow not only πόλεμος δ᾽ (Z 492) but

E

μῦθος δ᾽ (α 358) and τόξον δ᾽ (φ 352); that μαίνεται (μαίνεαι) οὐκέτ᾽ ἀνεκτῶς should refer both to the furious career of Hector in battle (Θ 355) and to the disgusting habits of the Cyclops (ι 350); that σμερδαλέον κονάβησε should describe not only the noise of an army, whether in its shouts (Β 334; Π 277) or its tread (Β 466) or the din of its armour (Ν 498; Ο 648; Φ 255, 593), but the noise of Telemachus's sneeze (ρ 542). In such applications of formulae to very different situations, we may feel that one or the other is original and authentic and the rest are imitations. But this is not how Homer's audience would take it. What matters is the immediate effect in the moment of recitation, and if we look at this without comparisons or prepossessions, we cannot deny that the repeated phrase is perfectly apt and adequate.

The Homeric style is formulaic because it belongs to a tradition in which poems were normally improvised. This does not mean that a bard performed without taking thought for his subject or was not able often to prepare his poem in advance. But it does mean that he did not necessarily always recite the same story in exactly the same words and that he could make additions or corrections during recitation if a happy thought came to him. There are many degrees and kinds of improvisation, and many oral bards, who know nothing of writing, are able to carry large tracts of poetry in their memories and to work on them and improve them with time. Homer was certainly brought up in an art of improvisation and learned his language from it, but it is unlikely that he improvised the *Iliad* and the *Odyssey* in any ordinary sense of the word. They imply long and hard thought, and it would not be surprising if the two poems together were the main work of a lifetime. They are certainly meant to be recited, and their art presupposes this at every point. Poets in other countries have produced oral poems of even greater length, and there is nothing impossible in the idea of Homer being unable to read or write and composing his poems in his head.

At the same time we cannot but ask if he depended in any way on writing. The new alphabet came to Greece in the eighth century, and it is likely that Homer knew of it. What is clear is that even if he knew of it, his style remained oral and formulaic and shows few signs of that precise choice and variation of words to which poets take when they know how to write. Yet the Homeric poems were written down, and it is likely that this happened in the poet's own lifetime. The question is whether he wrote them himself or dictated them to someone else who did it for him. This is perhaps insoluble, but either alternative would account for certain features in the poems. In both methods composition would be relatively slow and make it easy for the poet to say what he wished without undue hurry, to choose his formulae with care and occasionally to alter them, to avoid any obvious awkwardness or in-

equality, to exploit his devices with skill, and to give an artistic shape
both to individual episodes and to whole poems.   Each would allow a
certain degree of free composition in the sense of dispensing with formulae
and paying more attention to the choice of individual words.   Of the
alternatives it is perhaps more likely that Homer dictated than that he
wrote.   But the important thing is that though he used a formulaic language which was devised for improvisation, he used it so skilfully that
his style is richer and fuller and more expressive than almost any other
oral poetry known to us. For this he was certainly indebted beyond
calculation to the long Greek tradition which evolved formulae with so
astonishing a capacity and foresight, but he showed his own genius in his
management of them.   It is quite as difficult to work with them as with
individual words, and equal judgement and insight are needed by the poet
who is to make an original and effective use of them.   It is Homer's
extraordinary achievement that he not only made very few slips in an
art in which they are all too easy but kept his whole performance at an
unfailing level of high, heroic poetry.

NOTES TO CHAPTER 2

1. Milman Parry, *L'Épithète traditionnelle dans Homère*, and *Les Formules et la métrique
d'Homère* (both 1926); 'Studies in the epic technique of oral verse-making' in *Harv. Stud.
Class. Phil.* xli. 73-147 and xliii. 1-50.

2. G. M. Calhoun, 'Homeric repetitions' in *Cal. Pub. Class. Phil.* xii. 11-12.

3. M. Parry, *L'Épithète traditionnelle*, 197-203.

4. G. M. Calhoun, *op. cit.* 7-8.

[On oral and formulaic epic generally see Ch. 5.]

CHAPTER 3

COMPOSITION

by Sir Maurice Bowra

THE *Iliad* and the *Odyssey* are epic poems in the sense that they are long narratives in verse, but we shall not understand their peculiar nature if we compare them with the *Aeneid* or *Paradise Lost*. They are more profitably classified as heroic poems composed for oral performance. As such they belong to a class of poetry which once held pride of place in a large part of the world and is still practised in many parts of Asia and in some parts of Europe. They have the main characteristics of their kind — the choice of stories from a time when a superior race of men lives for action and for the honour and renown which it brings, the realistic presentation of minor details to form a solid background, the use of the single line instead of the stanza as the metrical unit, the taste for speeches, often of some length, spoken by the different characters, literary devices to vary or assist the narrative, such as similes, repeated passages, and incidental stories, the reluctance of the poet to assert his own personality, the dependence on a tradition which is passed from generation to generation and from poet to poet and supplies stories, themes, and language. Oral heroic poetry shows many of the same characteristics wherever it occurs, because they rise immediately from the demands of composition and performance. Its examples vary enormously both in manner and in quality, but the form maintains certain constant elements. In this body of poetry the *Iliad* and the *Odyssey* are exceptional in their length and almost unique in their poetical accomplishment. In considering their composition, we must bear in mind both the class of poetry to which they belong and the somewhat unusual place which they have in it.

In an art of this kind the poet is not necessarily concerned with being original. His first task is to tell traditional and familiar tales in a traditional and familiar way. It is his ability to do this which establishes his claim to be a bard, and Odysseus follows convention when he praises Demodocus for telling of the troubles of the Achaeans κατὰ κόσμον (θ 489). The oral poet's normal staple consists of stories, whose outlines are established and known, and of many passages, which were once indeed the creation of individual talent but have passed into common currency because they are both useful and delightful. There is no question of plagiarism or copyright, and any bard is free to make full use of the inventions of others. Indeed he does not think of them in this way, but regards them as the legitimate and indispensable instruments of his craft, without which he would not be able to tell his tales as he should. His skill lies in knowing a large number of such stories and passages and in using them to the best of his ability. This means that in criticizing the Homeric poems we must not look for originality in the way that we do with most poetry which depends on writing. The use of writing means that a poet tries above all to say something new in his own original way; the oral tradition makes no such assumption and no such demands. When we read Homer, we may indeed enjoy it very much as we enjoy other poetry, but we can hardly ever say that it is because of the poet's originality; for in the last analysis we may never be certain what is his own invention and what he has taken from tradition. Indeed, however original an oral poet may be, he must always conform to the traditional manner and his inventions must be adapted to it and made to look at home in it. This means that, when we speak of the poet or poets of the Homeric poems, we must always remember that any passage or phrase may well be inherited from other poets before them.

At the same time, though oral poetry has its strict conventions, within them it allows a certain freedom to its practitioners. They are expected to keep the main outline of a story, but they are free to include what details they choose and even to change the whole temper of its events. They may also invent new stories, especially if these fit into the body of traditional material and fill gaps in it or pursue themes already adumbrated. When there are competing versions of a story, the poet is free to make his choice between them or to combine elements from different versions into a new whole. If he has more time than usual at his disposal for recitation, he may well expand a familiar story with details and episodes not hitherto associated with it. Above all he may show his individual touch in the treatment of small devices which are part of his craft but can be used with very different degrees of skill. It is in such matters, rather than in any given line or lines, that we can sometimes discern the poet at work in his own way, and even though the Homeric poems are indeed difficult to analyse in any attempt to distinguish between what comes from the poet and what from his tradition, there are certain moments when we feel the poet's own touch. None the less, just because the *Iliad* and the *Odyssey* are the fruit of a long tradition and contain elements which have been matured over some six centuries, any discussion of their composition must admit that whatever part we ascribe to its final author or authors, this must always be seen in relation to the tradition from which it grew.[a]

<hr/>

[a] For a full discussion of oral epic see Ch. 5, pp. 179-211.

From the time of Aristotle onwards the Greeks, almost without exception, believed that the *Iliad* and the *Odyssey* were both composed by a man called Homer. In Alexandrian times there were indeed scholars, known as οἱ χωρίζοντες, who claimed that the two poems were the work of different poets, but they were not treated very seriously. It was generally believed that Homer was an Ionian, and in the sixth and fifth centuries he was associated with Smyrna or Chios or Kolophon. But here agreement ends, and we are lost in legends and speculations. The ancient Lives of Homer are built partly from the poems themselves, partly from folklore, but can hardly be treated as historical. Though Homer is a real name, nothing at all is known about the man who held it. Even if we dismiss those Greek antiquarians who made him a contemporary of the Trojan War, his date remains without external authority, since Herodotus (ii. 53. 2) puts him in the ninth century, and Theopompus in the seventh (fr. 203 Jacoby). The tradition that he composed the *Iliad* and the *Odyssey* becomes less impressive when he is credited by different authorities with the *Thebais, Epigonoi, Cypria,* and *Nostoi.* Though his name was known to Xenophanes (fr. 9-10) and Heraclitus (frs. 42 and 56), yet it is not associated with either the *Iliad* or the *Odyssey,* while Simonides (fr. 32) and Pindar (*Pyth.* iv. 277, *Nem.* vii. 21, fr. 280) regard him as the author of other poems not known to us. Before Aristotle reduced the works attributed to him to the *Iliad,* the *Odyssey,* and the *Margites,* he seems to have been treated uncritically as the author of almost any ancient epic. Even what look like quotations from or references to the Homeric poems in early times may be no more than references to traditional themes or echoes of traditional phrases. The mention of Nestor's cup on a vase of the eighth century from Ischia [1] and verbal similarities or echoes in Hesiod, Archilochus, Alcman, Tyrtaeus, and Stesichorus may be due either to a common poetical tradition, which employed these themes or phrases, or to other poems which were known to whoever composed the *Iliad* and the *Odyssey.*

Two possible references show how difficult the question is. In the Homeric Hymn to Apollo the poet speaks to his audience and tells them that, if they are asked in whose songs they take most delight, they should say :

τυφλὸς ἀνήρ, οἰκεῖ δὲ Χίῳ ἔνι παιπαλοέσσῃ,
τοῦ πᾶσαι μετόπισθεν ἀριστεύουσιν ἀοιδαί.   (172-3)

Thucydides (iii. 104. 4) thought that this was the actual work of Homer, in which he speaks of his own poems. But for stylistic reasons it is hard to believe that the Hymn comes from the same hand as the *Iliad* or the *Odyssey,* and the lines are undeniably mysterious. Of many possibilities two, perhaps, are the most likely. Either the bard, who is otherwise unknown to us, speaks of his own poems and commends them, or he somehow identifies himself with Homer, who is so well known that he can be referred to as the blind man who lives in rocky Chios. If the latter is right, it does indeed suggest that the poems and their poet were familiar in the seventh century, when this part of the Hymn seems to have been composed. But this is at the best a speculation, and we cannot base conclusions on it. A like uncertainty attaches to another poem of early date, of which the surviving lines begin:

$$\text{ἐν δὲ τὸ κάλλιστον Χῖος ἔειπεν ἀνήρ·}$$
$$\text{‘οἵη περ φύλλων γενεή, τοίη δὲ καὶ ἀνδρῶν.’}$$

Stobaeus, who quotes them, ascribes them to Simonides (iv. 34), but this has reasonably been questioned, and they have been credited to Semonides of Amorgos,[2] who is said to have lived in the seventh century. If this is right the 'man of Chios' was famous for at least one line, familiar to us from Z 146. But though the lines do not look like the work of Simonides, there is no sure reason to think them the work of Semonides. It is quite possible that they were written by some other poet of the sixth or fifth century and were ascribed to Simonides, as other pieces were, because they were in elegiacs. These passages cannot be taken to prove anything very conclusive. The second certainly suggests that in classical times the *Iliad*, or part of it, was regarded as the work of a Chian poet; the first may imply no more than that in the seventh century there was a school of poetry in Chios.

Yet, despite these confused and confusing testimonies, a few facts emerge. First, the poet or poets of the *Iliad* and the *Odyssey* were connected with Ionia. This is a reasonably certain deduction from the large part played by Ionic in the Homeric language and receives some support from the knowledge displayed by the poems of the western seaboard of Asia Minor. Secondly, the main body of the poems may have reached something like its present state about 700 B.C., since they refer to certain matters, such as a seated statue (Z 303), the wealth of Apollo's shrine at Delphi (I 404-5), and the brooch of Odysseus (τ 226-31), which are not likely to be earlier,[a] and at the same time they contain no elements which are demonstrably later. The Homeric world of heroic kings is quite different from the new world of aristocracies which dominated the seventh century and of which there is no hint at all in the poems. Thirdly, it is significant that the poems were after all ascribed by name to Homer. It is not customary to ascribe an oral poem to anyone, and some oral bards claim that their work is not their own but inspired by a god or learned from unnamed masters. Such poets as are remembered owe it either to inserting their names somewhere in the text or through some local tradition which preserves them, usually not for long. The preserva-

[a] See, however p. 500.

tion of Homer's name suggests that some special means existed to preserve it, and this may be the existence of something like a guild of poets in Chios, who called themselves the Sons of Homer and made a business of reciting the poems. However flimsy their claims to actual descent from anyone called Homer may have been, they would hardly have made them if his name had not been sufficiently famous to be thought worthy of preservation with the works attributed to him. The existence of the Sons of Homer may account for the connection of Homer with Chios, as it was known to 'Simonides' and to Pindar (fr. 279). At the same time the renown of Homer's name may account for the ascription to him of other poems, whose authors had in fact been forgotten but which could conveniently be credited to a poet whose name survived with honour from the past.

The authorship of the Homeric poems provokes two main questions : first, is either poem the work of one poet, and second, if both are, is the same poet the author of both ? These are separate questions and must be considered separately. At times both poems have been regarded as more or less haphazard collections strung together by not very skilful editors from separate short lays. This seems to be unlikely. If the poems are in some sense compounded from other poems, the work has been done with considerable skill, since both the *Iliad* and the *Odyssey* have their own distinctive structure, and though this may contain the work of more than one poet, it is not haphazard or incompetent. Though the structure of the *Iliad* differs from that of the *Odyssey*, both are praised by Aristotle for their marvellous superiority to other epic poems in their unity of action (*Poet.* 1459 a 30). Each combines a main theme with a subsidiary or complementary theme, which extends the whole field of narrative and gives a striking background to the central plot. In the *Iliad* the theme of the wrath of Achilles is set against the wider theme of the Trojan War ; in the *Odyssey* the return of Odysseus to Ithaca is set against what happens there in his absence. Both poems contain incidental stories which are not indispensable to the plot but enrich it by showing how wide the heroic world is and what a wealth of stories the poet has at his disposal for reference or relaxation. Both have a well balanced scheme of characters. In the *Iliad* the almost exclusively male life of the Achaeans in their camp is countered by the full society of Troy with its old and young men, its women and children ; in the *Odyssey* Odysseus, his son, and the faithful Eumaeus form an antithesis to the suitors and their supporters, while Penelope remains a distressed and indecisive victim between their competing claims. In both poems a generous scale of narrative allows for many actions to be treated at full length and for the characters to speak with a copious eloquence, and in both, though the poet hardly ever ventures his own explicit opinions, there is a subtle discrimination between the characters who live up to heroic standards and those who do not.

The *Iliad* has a capacious and majestic plan. It falls roughly into three main parts, of which the first is preceded by a prologue and the last followed by an epilogue. The prologue in Book I tells how the wrath of Achilles begins. Then the first section, Books II to VIII, tells how the Achaeans try to carry on the battle without him, and, despite splendid efforts by individual heroes, fail. Book IX marks the transition to the second section. The Achaean leaders try to persuade Achilles to return to battle, and Agamemnon offers handsome amends, but Achilles refuses and again the Achaeans try to carry on without him. This time they meet with greater reverses than before, and their ships are in danger of destruction by Hector. The third section, which begins with Book XVI, tells how Achilles begins to relent, sends out Patroclus to fight, and, when he is killed, goes out himself and kills Hector in Book XXII. Though the death of Hector seals the doom of Troy, the poem does not tell of it, but closes instead with an epilogue in Books XXIII and XXIV. After the Games, in which Achilles is still half-stunned with grief at the death of Patroclus, he receives Priam who offers ransom for Hector's body. Achilles is moved by compassion for the old man, and with it his wrath is healed. In this scheme Book XXIV balances Book I. In the first the wrath begins, in the last it ends. In both Thetis intervenes with her son, and strengthens his will, in Book I by praying to Zeus that the Achaeans may be humiliated by defeat, in XXIV by softening Achilles's heart towards Priam. Despite the many individual episodes which may have little to do directly with the wrath of Achilles, the *Iliad* is held together by it. It recurs as a dominating theme at the main stages of the story and enables it to end on the same issue with which it begins, after showing what this has meant for Achilles himself, his friends, and his enemies.

The *Odyssey* too has a controlling design, though it is more closely knit and in some ways more elaborate than that of the *Iliad*. Books I-IV are introductory. Odysseus does not appear in them, though he is never far from our minds and we see what his long absence means to his family, his kingdom, and his friends like Nestor and Menelaus. The poet builds up his picture of the suitors and shows how base they are, until they reach the point of plotting the murder of Telemachus. The introduction also gives a picture of the Greek world in the years after the Trojan War, tells what has happened to the chief personalities, and what place Odysseus holds in their esteem and their memories. It prepares the stage for his return and his vengeance on the suitors. The second section presents a remarkable contrast with it. From the moment when Odysseus prepares to leave Calypso to his arrival in Ithaca the story moves in another world, or indeed in two other worlds, of which that which contains Odysseus's account of his wanderings is even more remote and more wonderful than Phaeacia where he tells of them. The third section, from his arrival in Ithaca to his recognition by Penelope, is more violent and more complex than the introduction but in effect reverts to its setting and its characters. It is a heroic tale of vengeance and moves at the appropriate level for such a theme. Each main part of the *Odyssey* has its own preponderant temper, but all three parts are held together by the personality of Odysseus and the impression which he makes, even when absent, on all who know him. The *Odyssey* is much more immediately concerned with him than the *Iliad* is with Achilles, and for this reason presents an air of greater unity. It is less obviously episodic than the *Iliad*, if only because it has a smaller cast of characters and gives a bigger part to its protagonist, but both the *Odyssey* and the *Iliad* rise to a crisis through a series of individual episodes and relate their incidental events to a central theme.

The main design of the *Iliad* and the *Odyssey* suggests that each is the work of a poet who knows how to build separate episodes into an artistic whole and does so consciously and carefully. But when we examine the poems in detail we find many small points which we, who are used to reading books, may find unfamiliar and troubling. There are, for a precise taste, too many contradictions, too many places where the poet says something which is not easily harmonized with what he says elsewhere. It is only natural that attention should be focused on these and that they should form the basis of far-reaching analytical theories which distribute the poems among several authors, even if they allow a considerable part to some final poet who marshals the disparate elements together. Nor is it a final refutation of analytical methods to say that the analysts do not agree with one another and that each has his own private theory about the composition of the poems. In a matter of such complexity it is hard, if not impossible, to reach any final agreement, and what matters is the validity of the doubts and questions raised. If they are really unanswerable, we must accept in principle the multiple authorship of the poems in the sense that they are not sufficiently coherent to be the work of single poets.

How composite works of this kind could come into being is a matter for ingenious debate. But one point seems to be clear. So long as poems are recited without help from writing, the bard performs at each recitation what is in effect a new poem. He may well keep his main outlines, but he is always liable to vary the details, since he is not tied to any text and probably has no notion of what a completed, unalterable poem is. At such a stage it is meaningless to speak of interpolation from other poems. The bard indeed uses a mass of traditional material, which may sometimes be of some length, but he uses it in his own way, and the poem at each recitation is to this degree his own. But as soon as the poem is written down, and each performance of it is not determined by the poet's own creation but by the reciter's fidelity to a text which he has learned by heart, additions and alterations can be made to it, especially from other poems which have also been written down and are available for loans at various points. In such conditions it is not inconceivable that some reciter, who is himself something of a poet, should fashion a large new poem from pieces of other poems which he may have incorporated into his repertory for recitation. For the *Iliad* and the *Odyssey* this means that if they contain the work of more than one poet and are in any sense compilations or expansions or largely interpolated texts, this must have happened after the first versions were written down. The additions need not necessarily have been new. It is, for instance, quite conceivable that an old poem could be taken from a written text and incorporated with some suitable adjustments. On the other hand it is most unlikely that before the poems were committed to writing they were learned by heart and passed from bard to bard by memory.[3] For such a process there is no evidence and no parallel. Though genealogies and the like may be learned by heart and transmitted orally over a long period, this seems never to happen to narrative verse. Indeed it is difficult to imagine how it could happen or how long poems could be learned without texts to learn them from. It follows that if composite authorship is to be considered seriously, it must come after the poems have taken some sort of shape and been written down. What this first shape was is a matter for speculation from critic to critic. What concerns us is whether after being written down *c.* 700 B.C., as the poems seem to have been,[4] they were subjected to serious alterations and accretions.

That something of the kind could happen and has happened could be argued from λ 568-626, which tells of scenes in Hades, and looks inconsistent with the previous account of ghosts appearing at a trench.[5] The discord is not easily explained away and seems to violate the Homeric practice of making the given scene or moment entirely clear. Nor is it difficult to surmise why the passage has been interpolated. Life beyond the grave is a subject of too general an interest for Homer's special account of it to be left unspoiled. In so far as he did not satisfy later, or other, notions of it, someone else felt that he must correct his version. So too in the same book 225-332 also look like an interpolation. Though the appearance of the heroines creates less of a contradiction in the story, it is none the less out of place in a scene where Odysseus speaks only to Tiresias, his mother and a few friends, and its whole manner, brief, summary, and like a catalogue, suggests that it is an addition. For somewhat different reasons we may suspect two other, longer passages. Both were questioned by Alexandrian scholars, who had more information about the sources and transmission of the Homeric texts than we have and did not lightly make suggestions of this kind. The first is the continuation of the *Odyssey* from ψ 297 to the end of ω. Though it has its own charming poetry, it is an anti-climax after the recognition of Odysseus by Penelope, and some of its linguistic usage is different, but not very different, from that of the rest of the *Odyssey*.[6] It looks as if it may have been added, partly to tidy up some loose ends, as in the second Νέκυια, which brings the chief heroes of the *Iliad* back for a final appearance, and the scene between Odysseus and Laertes, which gives the old man at least a place in the poem, partly to prepare the way for some other poem which picked up the story soon after the slaughter of the suitors and needed a point to start at. Similar doubts were also felt about K, which also shows linguistic oddities and is more realistic and more brutal than we expect from the rest of the *Iliad*.[7] It may well be an independent poem, which, if not itself ancient, certainly draws upon ancient material, and perhaps was added because some bard felt a need for a variation in the action between the failure of the embassy to Achilles in I and the resumption of fighting in Λ.

With these exceptions, it is not easy to point to any substantial part of the *Iliad* or *Odyssey* as an interpolation. It is more than likely that with a formulaic style single lines and short passages have been displaced or added, but they need not disturb the story. It is also possible that new details have been incorporated to bring a stock passage up to date or make it more intelligible. But we must in principle beware of accusing lines of being interpolations just because they do not suit our theories. We must instead try to understand the methods of oral composition and ask if the inconsistencies can be explained by them. Evidence from such methods in the modern world shows that the oral performance of poetry presupposes conditions quite different from those presupposed by writing and that a listening audience must be treated by means uniquely appropriate to it. An examination of such poems suggests that many of the alleged Homeric inconsistencies are inherent in the oral manner and more suitably explained by it than by theories of additions and alterations. If the text has been changed, we must find a reason for it, and this is too often not forthcoming, and analysts have to rely on denunciations of incompetence or vague assumptions that a later poet must necessarily be worse than an earlier. Oral conditions indicate three main directions in which composition is affected. First, the actual conditions of performance impose on the poet certain obligations which we do not expect to find in books. Secondly, the poet has behind him a large mass of stories, among which there may be several variations of a single story, and from these he has to make his choice. Thirdly, the time available for the recitation of a story or an episode inevitably affects the manner of telling it.

The conditions of oral performance mean that the poet cannot turn back pages to recall what he has already said and may easily fall into mistakes which a poet who is helped by writing can avoid. Nor are such mistakes likely to be noticed by an audience, unless they are remarkably flagrant. The poet's duty is to make his chief movements and his chief situations as clear and firm as he can, to present them as directly as possible, and to concentrate entirely on what is most significant in them. This means that he can do only one thing at a time, that he cannot interfere with his action by presenting it from more than one angle or allow minor details to blur its character. When he moves from one episode to another, the change must be clean and sharp, and the new episode must from the start have its own marked development and temper. The Homeric clarity rises directly from the needs of oral performance. Without it the audience would soon be confused, lose the thread of the story, and not understand what is happening. From this certain results follow which an analyst might think to be evidence of incompetence or multiple authorship, but, if we look at them in their right setting, we see that they are appropriate and indeed inevitable.

Though minor details are important because they give reality to heroic actions, they must not become too prominent and interfere with the central subject in hand at the moment. If there is any danger of this, they must be neglected or omitted, and this happens in more than one way. The simplest is to neglect some actions which have had their use in their place but later mean nothing to the story. When Poseidon comes to the battlefield, the poet lingers affectionately on his golden chariot and his horses with golden manes, whom he tethers with golden shackles (N 23 ff.), but when he leaves the field, nothing is said about the horses or untethering them (O 218-19). When Athene and Hera come to help the Achaeans, they turn their horses out to graze (E 775), but when their work is done, we hear no more than that they go back to Olympus (*ibid.* 907). Achilles lays down his spear by a tamarisk that he may use his sword (Φ 17), but soon afterwards has his spear in his hand, though we do not hear that he has taken it up (*ibid.* 67). When Hector meditates on his forthcoming encounter with Achilles, he rests his shield against the wall of Troy (X 97), but he has it again when the fight begins (*ibid.* 111 ff.). When Athene comes to Ithaca in the form of Mentes, she leaves her spear in a spear-stand by a pillar (α 127), but later, when she disappears in the form of a sea-bird (*ibid.* 320), nothing is said about the spear, which is conveniently forgotten that no embarrassing questions may be asked about it. If in any of these places the poet had worried about such details, the story would have suffered. It is enough for them to be mentioned when they are needed and later to be neglected. To do more would interfere with the straight course of the story.

The same need to say one thing at a time affects more important matters than these. Though first-class heroes, like Agamemnon, Diomede, and Odysseus are wounded so seriously that they are forced to leave the battlefield, they are all back on it before long, and though nothing is said of their recovery, we must take it for granted. The centre of interest has shifted from their wounds to a new phase of the fight, and all our attention must be given to this. More complex is the case of Diomede, who says to Glaucus:

$$\text{εἰ δέ τις ἀθανάτων γε κατ' οὐρανοῦ εἰλήλουθας,}$$
$$\text{οὐκ ἂν ἔγωγε θεοῖσιν ἐπουρανίοισι μαχοίμην.} \qquad \text{(Z 128-9)}$$

We are certainly surprised that Diomede should be so wary of fighting against a god, since in the previous book he has wounded both Aphrodite (E 335 ff.) and Ares (*ibid*. 855 ff.). We can understand that for the moment he has had enough of attacking gods, but less easily that he finds it hard to recognize them. The answer is that in the earlier fight Athene gives him the power to recognize a god (*ibid*. 127), but now, though we are not told so, this power has ceased. Other matters are afoot, and there is no need to mention it. Something of the same kind happens when Odysseus has his shape and appearance changed by Athene into that of a broken old beggar (ν 429 ff.). This seems to be forgotten when he prepares to box with Irus and the poet dwells on his strength and size (σ 67) and when Eurycleia, in washing his feet, notices at once his resemblance to the Odysseus whom she knew of old (τ 380 ff.). He has evidently regained his original shape without our hearing about it, and the reason is that the poet has not mentioned it because he has already quite enough on his hands and must keep his eye on his new developments. The audience, intent on what happens at the moment, would not notice, and indeed embarrassment only begins when we read and study the text in books and are able to look back and compare what has happened before with what happens afterwards.

This concentration on the dramatic present impels the poet to place certain high occasions where they can stand out in their splendour and not be interfered with by other episodes. This may mean that such passages occur sometimes where we do not expect them and may even think them inappropriate. For instance the scene between Hector and Andromache (Z 370 ff.) is not only complete and satisfying in itself but has something which suggests that it is their last meeting, that it it is almost a farewell. No doubt it is placed comparatively early in the poem to avoid any need for repeating it later when our attention must be given to other matters. We are not in fact told that they meet again, and so this scene has an air of pathetic finality. Yet if we press the details of the text, husband and wife do in fact meet again ; for at H 310 the Trojans go back to Troy and spend the night there, and we must assume that Hector spends it with Andromache. The poet tactfully says nothing of it, and we are probably wrong to think of it. A somewhat similar technique is used for the parting between Odysseus and Calypso. When Calypso knows that he must leave her, she addresses a moving speech to him, and he replies with graceful and grateful courtesy (ε 203 ff.). But in fact he does not leave her till the fourth day after this, and in the interval they see each other and sleep together as before (225-7). Here, as with Hector and Andromache, one thing is done at a time. The farewell is got out of the way before the poet gets on to the business of Odysseus building his raft. This has a different purpose and a different temper, and must be kept separate and undisturbed.

This concentration on the moment becomes more important when an action is spread over more than one book or begun at one point and taken up after an interval. Here the need for concentration is even greater, and the poet must be careful not to allow his new developments to be disturbed by harking back to what has happened before. When Achilles has refused the overtures of Agamemnon in I, it is surprising to find him saying a little later, when the battle is going badly for the Achaeans :

> νῦν ὀΐω περὶ γούνατ' ἐμὰ στήσεσθαι 'Αχαιοὺς
> λισσομένους· χρειὼ γὰρ ἱκάνεται οὐκέτ' ἀνεκτός.   (Λ 609-10)

It looks as if he had forgotten all that has just happened and the conclusion has been drawn that I is a later addition.[8] So too a little later, when he yields to Patroclus's entreaties to be allowed to join the battle, Achilles seems to be no less oblivious of what has happened, when he says that all would be well

> εἰ μοι κρείων 'Αγαμέμνων
> ἤπια εἰδείη.   (Π 72-3)

Yet in an oral art these apparent contradictions are natural and explicable. The first passage shows how Achilles still refuses to relent and enjoys his vengeance on Agamemnon by seeing the humiliation of the Achaeans. In the second he realizes, as he should, the need for the Achaeans to be united against their enemies. We may, if we wish, go further and say that in the first he is still so occupied with his own injured pride that he has dismissed Agamemnon's apologies from his mind and in the second he may well feel that Agamemnon is not likely to be well disposed towards him after his obdurate refusal to be appeased. But this is not necessary. What counts is that the poet concentrates on the moment and gives everything to it.

A somewhat similar case is the wall of the Achaean camp, which has caused some trouble.[9] The alleged difficulties are: (1) at H 435 the

wall is built, but at Ξ 31 it seems to have been built at the beginning of
of the war; (2) at M 10-33 it remains ἔμπεδον till the end of the war, but
at Ξ 361 ff. it is destroyed by Apollo, as a child destroys a sand-castle;
(3) in M and N it is sometimes present and sometimes absent. The answer
to these troubles is to be found in the Homeric way of telling a story.
Each point is made emphatically in its own place because it is relevant
to the context, and though we may complain that insufficient notice is
taken of what is said elsewhere, there is in fact no real contradiction. (1)
H 435 refers to no more than the strengthening of a wall which already
exists; a rampart is reinforced by the addition of towers and battlements.
(2) At Ξ 361 Apollo does not destroy the whole wall — why indeed
should he? — but only that part where he himself is fighting. For the
moment this is the only part that matters, and its destruction receives full
attention. (3) The alleged presence of the wall at some places and its absence at others are due simply to the technique of mentioning only what is
relevant to the plot. So it is mentioned at M 62 when Polydamas summons Hector to cross it, and not mentioned later, because in the general
excitement of the battle which then rages it has ceased to be of interest.

A similar technique appears in the loan of Achilles's armour to Patroclus. It has been claimed that there is no real dramatic motive for this
and that it takes place simply to provide an excuse for introducing the
new armour which Hephaestus makes for Achilles.[10] Now it would
have been easy for the poet to describe the new armour without inventing
so complex a scheme for its introduction. But in fact the loan to
Patroclus has its own dramatic motivation. Achilles assumes that the
Trojans will think that he himself has returned to the battle and will be
frightened of Patroclus. It is a fair and natural assumption, and at first
it is justified by events. Patroclus thinks that the trick will work (Π 40-3),
and for a time it does. The Trojans at first believe that Achilles has
joined the fight and are frightened (*ibid.* 280-2). Then gradually they
begin to realize the truth, and Sarpedon, feeling that something is wrong
with the man whom they believe to be Achilles, calls the bluff:

ἀντήσω γὰρ ἐγὼ τοῦδ' ἀνέρος, ὄφρα δαείω
ὅς τις ὅδε κρατέει· καὶ δὴ κακὰ πολλὰ ἔοργε
Τρῶας, ἐπεὶ πολλῶν τε καὶ ἐσθλῶν γούνατ' ἔλυσεν. (423-5)

Once Patroclus has been recognized, there is no need to speak any more of
the attempted deception which has done its poetical task, and the interest
shifts to his impending doom and concentrates on it.

Something of the same kind may be seen in the much discussed removal of arms from the hall of Odysseus. Before going to the palace
Odysseus gives careful instructions to Telemachus that at a sign from
himself he must remove the arms from the hall, but keep two sets for

themselves, and if the suitors ask questions, he is to give a suitable answer
(π 281 ff.). We need not be surprised that these instructions are not
carried out. That is common enough in Homeric narrative and is part
of the technique of surprise. Events develop differently and more quickly
than Odysseus has anticipated, and the arms are removed hurriedly at
night with the help of Athene (τ 1 ff.). There is no need for Odysseus
to make a sign to Telemachus, since there is nobody present to hear their
conversation; nor in fact do the suitors ask about the removal of the
arms until much later, when the killing begins, and Telemachus's planned
answer is not needed. The important fact is that, when the arms are
removed, none are kept for Odysseus and Telemachus, with the result
that later, when the fight is becoming dangerous, they need weapons and
have to seek them from outside. The poet's omission to say anything
about this failure in Odysseus's plan is surely deliberate. He concentrates
for the moment on the single point of clearing the hall, and allows us to
forget about the need for two suits of arms. Then later, with a characteristic surprise, he makes much of the failure because then it is really indispensable to his story. If he had dwelt on it at the time of the removal
he would have spoiled the mysterious atmosphere of the scene.

The conditions of oral recitation create a special difficulty in the
treatment of time. The writer of a book can without trouble form a
scheme for its events, which allows for concurrent or simultaneous actions
and moves to some sort of timetable. But the oral poet, who has to
concentrate on the immediate subject in hand, is almost unable to do this
and under no obligation to trouble about it. Since he usually composes
for people who have no clocks or calendars, he is not very interested in
chronology. Just as the Homeric poems give no hint of a date for the
Trojan War, so the poet is not much worried by problems raised by time
in his story. It is indeed possible to find a scheme of days for the action
of each poem, and this may be of interest, but it tells us little about the
poet's constructive intentions. What is more illuminating is his disregard for some elements which we might think important and his
difficulty in placing events in his own scheme. This is common enough
in oral poetry, but its consequences are important for any discussion of
the Homeric poems.

The action of the *Iliad* takes part in the tenth and last year of the siege
of Troy. The point is not made very emphatically, but Agamemnon
says that nine years have passed (B 134) and Odysseus implicitly confirms
it soon afterwards (*ibid.* 329). But this does not prevent the poet from
producing certain episodes which would be more appropriate to the
first year of the war than to the tenth. The division of troops proposed
by Agamemnon (B 126 ff.), the duel between Paris and Menelaus in Γ,
and the identification of Achaean heroes by Helen to Priam would all

F

be more suitable before the outbreak of hostilities.[11]   The first seems an ordinary military mobilization; the second is entirely appropriate as an alternative to general slaughter and should be tried before full warfare begins; the third surely comes a little late in the day.   The explanation of these anomalies is that the poet combines two rather different subjects, the wrath of Achilles and the whole theme of the Trojan War.   The wrath must come towards the end of the war because it precedes his death. This is an important element in its tragic character.   Achilles, who has so little time to live, wastes it in sorrow and disaster.   That is why his impending doom is foretold by Thetis (A 417), the horse Xanthus (T 411-23), Achilles himself to Lycaon (Φ 108-13) and the dying Hector to Achilles (X 356-60).   Since the death of Achilles comes soon before the capture of Troy, the wrath comes late during the war.

On the other hand the poem is not an *Achilleid* but an *Iliad*. Round the theme of the wrath is built the story of the siege of Troy.   The death of Hector is indeed the beginning of the end of Achilles's wrath, but it is also the beginning of the end for Troy (X 410-11).   To give a proper notion of the siege the poet introduces episodes which belong to its start but are none the less necessary to get his full-scale story going.   Without them we should not have the impression that the war is a prodigious affair, nor should we see the Achaean leaders so clearly as we do through Helen's description of them.   The poet produces these scenes to give the right start and the right background for his tale, and is able to do so because chronology means very little either to him or to his audience. More striking than these is the way in which he introduces the Catalogues of the Achaean ships and the Trojan allies.   These indeed belong not so much to the beginning of the war as to the period just before it.   The Achaean ships are described as they gathered at Aulis before starting for Troy (B 303), and the Catalogue, which looks as if it were based on ancient material, is introduced to show the extent of the Achaean forces. It does not matter that it mentions many characters who do not appear again and that some characters, like Odysseus, who are important elsewhere, are of little importance for it.   It sets the stage for a poem about the war and gives us not so much a list of *dramatis personae* as a general picture of the Achaean world and of its constituent states, their relative size, and their rulers.

We may now turn to the second chief characteristic of oral tradition — the variant versions of a story of which the poet chooses the one which he thinks most appropriate.   In choosing one he may not completely rid himself of traces of another, especially since his formulae may be to some extent concerned with the one which he rejects.   The older the story, the more likely that there was more than one version of it, especially if it was based on folktale or fairy-story.   A simple case of this can be seen in the blinding of Polyphemus.[12] Homer's version of this ancient and wide-spread tale differs from most other versions in that the Giant's eye is put out by a wooden stake and not by the iron spit on which he intends to roast his victims before eating them. We do not know why our poet chose this version or indeed invented it, as he may well have, but we can see that the other is not far from his mind. He keeps skilfully to his own version, except at one point. When the stake of olive wood has been heated in the fire, he says:

$$\text{ἀλλ' ὅτε δὴ τάχ' ὁ μοχλὸς ἐλάϊνος ἐν πυρὶ μέλλεν}$$
$$\text{ἅψεσθαι, χλωρός περ ἐών, διεφαίνετο δ' αἰνῶς . . .} \quad (\iota \; 378-9)$$

The first part of this is quite correct. A stake of unseasoned wood would catch fire if left too long in the flames, but the last three words apply not to a wooden stake but to an iron spit and are a formula left over from an alternative version.

Often enough the poet uses more than one variant on a familiar theme or story and makes them so different that we hardly suspect their common origin. In the *Odyssey*, which deals with the universal and immemorial theme of the Wanderer's Return, the Wanderer is twice delayed by more or less divine women on remote islands, first by Circe and then by Calypso. Behind them lies the common theme of the Witch who falls in love with the Wanderer and keeps him until somehow he escapes from her. That both of them were witches of some sort may be deduced from their names which mean 'the Hawk' and 'the Concealer'. But the poet has created two entirely separate episodes from them. Circe is a true witch who turns men into beasts and lives in a palace; Calypso is a nymph who lives in a cave. If Circe has her sinister side, Calypso is entirely considerate and affectionate. In the plot they perform different functions. Circe has, among her other tasks, that of instructing Odysseus how to sail to the edge of the world and call up the ghost of Tiresias; Calypso is useful because she hides Odysseus long enough for his fate to be a mystery and his death to be thought probable. They may have been differentiated before the poet of the *Odyssey* heard of them, or perhaps, as has been thought, Calypso is his own invention to explain the hero's long absence.[13] In either case they show how a single theme would be turned into two different and yet complementary or contrasted themes.

A simpler example of this kind are the two duels in the *Iliad* between Menelaus and Paris and between Ajax and Hector. Such duels must have been extremely common in heroic poetry, especially between the leading figures in opposing armies. That between Menelaus and Paris is closely connected with the plot of the *Iliad* in that they are mainly responsible for the war. But we may ask why, having told of it, the poet proceeds to tell of another duel for which the motives are much less clear. The answer is surely that the theme was so popular that it deserved to be treated more than once, and of course simple audiences have no objection to repetitions of this kind. The two duels have indeed certain points of resemblance. In both the Achaeans are technically victorious. Paris is spirited off by Aphrodite; Hector is wounded by Ajax, but further fighting stops on an appeal to the approach of night. And both duels are inconclusive in the sense that after them the fighting continues as before. Yet the poet has made them different. The first is between the two men most responsible for the war, the second between the two best soldiers still in the field. The first shows how the war is fought for Helen's sake, the second how it has passed beyond its first issue and become a fight to the death for Troy. The details too are different. There is a contrast between the slap-dash methods of Paris and the true heroism of Hector, between the careful confidence of Menelaus and the unimaginative courage of Ajax. The two duels are separate and distinct, and there is no need to think that one is a later version or adaptation of the other.[14] Both come from a single source, the stock subjects of oral tradition.

The problem of treating different versions by combining them into a single whole is well illustrated by the later part of the *Odyssey*. The theme of the Wanderer's Return fostered a number of stories about him making himself known by some sign on his arrival in his home. Our poet makes use of at least three such signs, and though originally each may have been sufficient in itself, oral poetry likes things to come in threes, and the poet uses them with a fine sense of development and climax. First is the sign of the scar, which Odysseus got when he was wounded by a boar twenty or more years earlier. This has a dramatic but limited task. The old woman Eurycleia sees it when she is washing Odysseus's feet in the presence of Penelope, recognizes her master from it, and is saved only by his presence of mind from giving it away (τ 386 ff.). Later, it enables Odysseus to reveal himself to Eumaeus (φ 217 ff.). Its function, in fact, is to reveal him to his faithful servants. The second sign is that of the bow, and turns on the ability of Odysseus, alone among men, to string the great bow which has been kept carefully in his home ever since he went to Troy. Though the stringing is soon followed by the slaughter of the suitors, the sign need not necessarily have been connected with so dramatic a finale. But, when Odysseus strings the bow, it is indeed a dramatic occasion, since it tells the suitors who he is (φ 392 ff.), and creates terror among them. Just as Penelope did not see the sign of the scar, so she is out of the way for the sign of the bow. It is for her that the third sign, of the bed, is kept. Odysseus has built the bed for her and himself, and almost alone they know its secret. When he tells her of it, she knows that he is really her husband, and the story of the Return really ends where Aristarchus thought the Odyssey ended, with the words:

$$οἱ μὲν ἔπειτα$$
$$ἀσπάσιοι λέκτροιο παλαιοῦ θεσμὸν ἵκοντο.$$ (ψ 295-6)

By taking the three signs as separate stages in a single process the poet makes a different use of each until at last the returned Wanderer is known to everyone.

The existence of variant versions of a theme or story made it possible for the poet to exploit a special kind of surprise by leading his audience to expect one result and then to provide them with another. It is more than likely that in some songs Achilles, after killing Hector, mutilated his body. It would be in full accord with the raging thirst for vengeance which possesses him, and such a story would have been known to audiences, who would reasonably expect something of the same kind in the *Iliad*. Homer takes full advantage of this. When Achilles prepares to go out and fight Hector, he tells the dead Patroclus that he will bring back Hector's armour and head, and this certainly means that he will cut off his head (Σ 334-5). When he drags the body behind his chariot, he plans ἀεικέα ἔργα against it (Χ 395) and a little later declares his intention of throwing it to the dogs (Ψ 20-1). We are led to expect that he will do this, and may even assume that it is characteristic of him. From this it has been deduced that the present end of the *Iliad* has replaced a lost version in which Achilles carried out his threats and no doubt satisfied his desire for revenge.[15] But, as we read the story, we see that the poet works on a subtle plan. After suggesting that Achilles is going to behave in this way, he makes him relent and yield to Priam's entreaties. We have, in fact, misjudged him, and he is a nobler hero than we have thought. Mere vengeance is not enough to close the *Iliad*, and the existing end not only restores Achilles in our estimation but heals the wrath with which the poem began.

The same technique can be seen in the more complex tales which are used in the *Odyssey*. In the versions of the Wanderer's Return there was a tale that he was saved from the sea by the king's daughter, whom he afterwards married. The theme was too fruitful to be abandoned, and yet Odysseus, who must return to Penelope, cannot marry a princess on the way home. Homer introduces this theme in Nausicaa. From her first appearance onward her approaching marriage is more than once forecast. Athene speaks of it when she appears to her in a dream (ζ 33 ff.), and Nausicaa herself has it in mind when she asks her father for a waggon and mules for the laundry (*ibid.* 66-7). When Odysseus has been washed and anointed, Nausicaa says with charming candour to her maidens:

$$αἲ γὰρ ἐμοὶ τοιόσδε πόσις κεκλημένος εἴη$$
$$ἐνθάδε ναιετάων, καί οἱ ἅδοι αὐτόθι μίμνειν,$$ (*ibid.* 244-5)

and her instructions to him on how to come to her home have the conscious propriety of a young woman in love. So far the poet uses the old theme skilfully and carefully. But it cannot go on. There is more for Odysseus to do in Phaeacia than dally with Nausicaa, and though his prowess in the games may belong to the story of the Wanderer's wooing of the king's daughter, Nausicaa fades from the scene. We have been led to expect that something will happen between her and Odysseus, not indeed marriage because we know of Penelope, but still something, and it comes in the short and touching scene when Odysseus meets her on his way from the bath, and she says to him :

χαῖρε, ξεῖν', ἵνα καί ποτ' ἐὼν ἐν πατρίδι γαίῃ
μνήσῃ ἐμεῖ', ὅτι μοι πρώτῃ ζωάγρι' ὀφέλλεις.   (θ 461-2)

Odysseus thanks her for what she has done for him, and we hear no more of her. The technique of the 'false clue' is used differently from Achilles's treatment of Hector, but not less successfully.

Surprise and suspense are indeed essential to the art of oral poetry, and the Homeric poems exploit both to a high degree in more than one way. Since the audience was more or less familiar with the outline of the tale, the poet keeps it guessing about his own treatment of it. It is therefore no matter for complaint that the opening lines of the *Iliad* and the *Odyssey* give but a vague notion of what actually follows. The first correctly stresses the wrath of Achilles as the main theme and then goes on to speak in very general terms of the deaths which it will cause. What the poet does not say is that the deaths include those of Patroclus and Hector. This is his special concern, and he is not going to reveal it at the start. So too the *Odyssey* begins with five lines about Odysseus, who is not named but described and whose doings are forecast in terms no less vague and general than those which forecast the action of the *Iliad*. Then, rather to our surprise, the poet gives four lines to the comrades of Odysseus and tells how they failed to come home because they ate the oxen of the Sun. We might think that this pays too much attention to what is after all only one episode among many. But it has its point. The poet is concerned mainly with Odysseus, and for an important part of his poem with Odysseus alone. He returns to Ithaca single and unaided and has to rely on his own exertions to regain his home. The lines on his companions emphasize this isolation, which is indeed a marked characteristic of the *Odyssey*. The poet gives a hint, but not much more, of what he is going to say, and so leaves the way clear to develop his own version of a tale which he knows to be familiar :

τῶν ἁμόθεν γε, θεά, θύγατερ Διός, εἰπὲ καὶ ἡμῖν.   (α 10)

The audience must now wait to see how the poet is going to treat the old story.

This art of surprise is also applied to the speeches of the characters themselves, who give instructions or forecast a course of action which we expect to be carried out but which in fact is not. A striking case is the relation in the *Odyssey* between Telemachus and Theoclymenus. The poet prepares the way for it with an account of Theoclymenus's previous career, which is indeed dramatic and explains his peculiar behaviour. He is a homicide in flight from his avengers (o 223 ff.) and he approaches Telemachus with none of the formality which heroic manners demanded of strangers. Instead of waiting to be asked his own name, he asks Telemachus what his is, and without more ado begs for asylum in his ship. So far the episode might seem to have little point except as the kind of thing that may happen to a man on his travels. Later, on arriving at Ithaca Theoclymenus asks where he should go, and to our surprise, Telemachus recommends his own enemy, the suitor Eurymachus (*ibid.* 508 ff.). The simplest interpretation of this is that Telemachus speaks in bitter irony, as one who feels that he has no home of his own worthy of the name and that the real lords of Ithaca are his enemies like Eurymachus.[16] The words show his despondent spirit on coming back to his own island. Then the whole situation changes. A hawk flies overhead carrying a dove, and Theoclymenus interprets this as a sign of the power of the family of Odysseus in Ithaca. This transforms Telemachus's mood, and makes him feel quite differently towards Theoclymenus:

$$
\begin{aligned}
&\text{αἲ γὰρ τοῦτο, ξεῖνε, ἔπος τετελεσμένον εἴη·}\\
&\text{τῷ κε τάχα γνοίης φιλότητά τε πολλά τε δῶρα}\\
&\text{ἐξ ἐμεῦ, ὡς ἄν τίς σε συναντόμενος μακαρίζοι.}\quad\text{(o 536-8)}
\end{aligned}
$$

We now see why Theoclymenus has been introduced. He is necessary in order to make Telemachus start on his new adventures in a confident spirit, and the poet shows dramatically how this happens.

A more complex case of this kind happens early in the *Odyssey*, when Athene, disguised as Mentes, tells Telemachus what to do (a 269 ff.). First, he must summon an assembly of the Ithacans and at it tell the suitors to disperse to their homes; secondly, if his mother is eager for marriage, she must go to her father's house, where her family will arrange for it and her dowry; thirdly, Telemachus himself must go abroad in search of his father; and fourthly, on his return he must give his mother a husband and then kill all the suitors at the palace. The instructions are by no means clear. The marriage of Penelope is assigned first to her family, then to Telemachus; the suitors must first be sent to their homes and then, it seems, be killed in the palace of Odysseus. In fact Athene really offers alternative lines of action, and leaves us guessing which will take place. Telemachus summons the assembly and tells the suitors to go home, but they refuse to do so; he considers sending Penelope to her father but decides that it is impossible (β 130 ff.). On the other hand he goes in search of news of Odysseus and in the end takes a part in the slaughter of the suitors in the palace. Part of Athene's complex instructions are carried out, part not, and this is in accordance with the poet's technique of not showing his full hand at the start.

A third characteristic of oral recitation is that the bard has to shape his poem to suit the time at his disposal. If this is more or less unlimited, he can, of course, continue so long as his audience is prepared to listen, and in modern times Tatar bards have produced oral poems longer than the *Iliad* and the *Odyssey*. But on the whole long heroic poems are rare, and their existence is usually to be explained by special reasons, such as national festivals or patrons who call for something out of the usual run. The normal heroic poem is quite short, and that this art was familiar to the Homeric poems is clear alike from the songs of Phemius and Demodocus, which tell of single episodes, and the κλέα ἀνδρῶν which Achilles sings in his tent and for whose conclusion Patroclus waits (I 189 ff.). Moreover, such an art certainly lies behind the technique of the *Iliad* and the *Odyssey*. Many parts of the *Iliad* have the air of being complete poems in themselves and can be enjoyed without reference to the larger whole which contains them. It is true that they often have references to other parts of the poem, but the doings of Diomede in E or of Agamemnon in Λ, the deception of Zeus in Ξ, the Funeral Games in Ψ, and the ransoming of Hector's body in Ω can certainly be read in isolation and have their own balance and completeness. Even quite short episodes have a similar completeness. For instance, the story of Glaucus and Diomede begins with a theme to be found wherever heroic poetry exists, of two warriors meeting on a battlefield, and follows a common pattern by advancing at once to the point:

$$\text{Γλαῦκος δ' Ἱππολόχοιο πάϊς καὶ Τυδέος υἱὸς}$$
$$\text{ἐς μέσον ἀμφοτέρων συνίτην μεμαῶτε μάχεσθαι,}\quad\text{(Z 119-20)}$$

while it ends suddenly and brilliantly with an exchange of armour:

$$\text{ἔνθ' αὖτε Γλαύκῳ Κρονίδης φρένας ἐξέλετο Ζεύς,}$$
$$\text{ὃς πρὸς Τυδείδην Διομήδεα τεύχε' ἄμειβε}$$
$$\text{χρύσεα χαλκείων, ἑκατόμβοι' ἐννεαβοίων.}\quad\text{(ibid. 234-6)}$$

The poet clearly knows this kind of short lay and makes his own new and happy use of it.

In the *Odyssey* the method is a little different. The whole plot is more closely interwoven than in the *Iliad*, and the poet seems to have moved further away from the short lay. Yet traces of it survive. The stories told by Menelaus and Helen imply its existence; Telemachus's voyage can be treated as a complete episode; the adventures of Odysseus are indeed skilfully combined to show how he gradually loses his ships and his companions, but each is satisfying in itself; the stringing of the bow and the fight in the hall have their own unity. In both poems the structure is largely piecemeal, and though this is partly dictated by the necessity of dealing with only one theme at a time, it certainly owes much to the existence of short lays on whose technique the poet may have been trained and with which he was clearly familiar. But the individual episodes are so well fitted into the main design that they suggest a controlling mind at work in them. Their technique indicates that in Ionia, as in other lands, the long heroic poem grew from the short heroic lay and inevitably kept some traces of it.

We do not know how this happened, or why the poet should compose on a large scale. It has been suggested that the *Iliad* and the *Odyssey* were composed for performance at some great festival like the Panionia at Mycale,[17] where the bard would have far more time at his disposal than he would normally have at a feast in the household of such kings as Odysseus and Alcinous. After the middle of the sixth century the poems were recited at the Panathenaea at Athens, but it is improbable that they had not by then found their main shape and size. It is more than likely that before this they were recited at festivals, and if the Homeric Hymns are indeed, as Thucydides calls them, προοίμια (iii. 104. 4) and were sung as preludes to the actual poems, this kind of recitation may go back to Ionian festivals of the seventh century in Delos and other places. Our evidence is too scanty to show how the Homeric poems were performed, but there is no difficulty in assuming that they could be performed, if occasion allowed, in their entirety or that the poet took advantage of favourable circumstances to abandon the small scale of the lay for the full scale of the epic.

At the same time the poet cannot always have been able to recite his poems completely. There must have been occasions when he was asked to recite only this or that episode. Then his technique of episodic construction would help him, since he would be able to produce a section reasonably complete and satisfactory in itself. This would cause little difficulty in the *Iliad*, of which almost any section can be detached for separate performance, but it causes rather more difficulty in the *Odyssey* and may perhaps account for a very unusual feature in it. At the opening of α the gods meet on Olympus, and Athene raises the question of Odysseus. Zeus decides that Hermes shall be sent to Ogygia to tell Calypso to release him, and that Athene shall go to Ithaca to encourage Telemachus. At the opening of ε the gods again meet, and after a much shorter debate, decide to send Hermes to Ogygia. In the complete poem this is undeniably difficult. If we assume that the two councils are different, we must ask why a second council has to be held to take again a decision which has already been taken; if we assume that they are the same, we must ask why the second is introduced with words that indicate that it is new. A possible solution is that the second council was performed as an alternative to the first for occasions when the poet had to begin his tale not with the situation in Ithaca but with the wanderings of Odysseus. That audiences should ask for this is perfectly understandable, and without some such beginning the story would start too informally and too abruptly. We know too little about the way in which the poems were first written down to be able to suggest how or why both councils were included in the text. But perhaps it was felt that, since the departure from Ogygia begins a totally new section, it needed an introduction and the second council met this need.

If some of the contradictions and inconsistencies in the Homeric poems can be explained by the circumstances of oral recitation, we may well ask whether they form after all a solid basis for theories of multiple authorship. If we accept this explanation of them, we follow a sound rule of criticism in judging a work of art by the rules and technique proper to its time and conditions. If, on the other hand, we apply our own modern standards to this different and unfamiliar form, we must apply the same standards when we try to explain why such contradictions have arisen. The difficulty then is to show how additions and changes were made which are presumably inadequate and may even spoil something that already existed. This, of course, may have happened, but it seems more likely that what are thought to be contradictions are really an inevitable feature of oral composition. It would indeed be too much to hope that our Homeric texts are almost the same as the first originals, and we must surely assume that passages have been displaced or remodelled or interpolated. But, apart from the obvious cases which we have considered, this is more likely to be true of smaller and less important passages than of greater and more impressive. The absence of final and conclusive arguments for the multiple authorship of either poem must be considered with the two powerful arguments for their unity, the main, dominating design of each poem and the remarkably consistent use of formulae in them. The first indicates a poet in each case who has his material in full control and is unlikely to be an editor or a compiler; the second surely indicates an individual touch, since, however many formulae were provided by tradition, there were certainly alternatives among them, and their rigorous discipline in the poems suggests a poet who had made his own choice and kept to it.

It does not necessarily follow that the two poems are the work of one poet, and even advocates of unity sometimes deny this. The Greek attribution of both to Homer is not after all very impressive when we remember that his name was a useful label for any ancient heroic poem.

Nor is common authorship proved by the way in which the *Odyssey* pre-supposes the *Iliad* and takes a knowledge of it for granted. It certainly looks as if it were composed after the *Iliad*, but that does not mean that it must have been the work of the same man. Even if the *Little Iliad*, the *Iliou Persis*, and the *Nostoi* were composed to fill the gap between the *Iliad* and the *Odyssey*, it proves no more than that the *Odyssey* was famous at an early date and regarded as in some sense a continuation of the *Iliad*.

We cannot deny that there are obvious differences between the *Iliad* and the *Odyssey*. The *Iliad* tells of war in a more or less realistic spirit; the *Odyssey* combines romantic and marvellous adventures on the edge of the world with brutal slaughter in a king's palace. The difference of subject is matched by a difference of temper. The mood in which Achilles kills Hector is more passionate and more truly heroic than the cold determination with which Odysseus kills the suitors. The *Iliad* has no transformations of shape such as we find in the *Odyssey* and re-stricts its marvels to a few outstanding occasions, as when the horse of Achilles speaks, but the *Odyssey* makes them the staple of some of its most brilliant episodes. The *Iliad* has not indeed a tragic end, but it is conceived in a tragic spirit, in which the brevity of human life makes the wrath of Achilles more painful because it brings the death of Patroclus, and the doom of Hector means the doom of Troy, but the *Odyssey* despite its bloodshed has a happy end, while much of its story is indeed, as 'Longinus' says, οἱονεὶ κωμῳδία τις ἠθολογουμένη, a comedy of man-ners (*de Sublimitate* ix. 15). Yet these differences can be explained by the difference between the two subjects, both equally traditional and both expected to display a certain temper and character. Tradition sets its mark on stories and insists that they belong to certain categories, and might well demand that the story of the *Iliad* should be told in one way and that of the *Odyssey* in another. There is indeed a certain overlap between the two, and there are certain scenes of domestic life in the *Iliad* which recall the *Odyssey* and of fighting in the *Odyssey* which recall the *Iliad*. But the temper of the two poems is certainly different, and this can be equally explained whether we postulate two poets or two manners of telling traditional stories.

Nor is it easy to avoid the impression that the poetical intensity of the *Odyssey* is less sustained than that of the *Iliad*. The *Odyssey* indeed deals with many subjects which do not call for such intensity, but when it approaches a truly dramatic subject like the killing of the suitors, we may feel that it lacks the concentration which the *Iliad* would have given to it. This is partly due to the more leisurely scale of the narrative and to the care with which a situation is developed. Yet this would surely be explicable if the *Odyssey* were composed by the poet of the *Iliad* later in life. As he moved further away from the technique of the short lay and from the unquestionably heroic themes of war, he would naturally try new effects, make his actions more detailed, and pay more attention to smaller matters. There is still something to be said for the view of 'Longinus' that Homer wrote the *Iliad* at the height of his inspiration and the *Odyssey* in his old age ὅθεν ἐν τῇ ᾿Οδυσσείᾳ παρεικάσαι τις ἂν καταδυομένῳ τὸν Ὅμηρον ἡλίῳ, οὗ δίχα τῆς σφοδρότητος παραμένει τὸ μέγεθος (ix. 13). That in certain directions there is a contraction of power we cannot deny, but in other directions new fields of poetry are exploited, and that is after all to be expected in a poet who turns from a subject which is essentially dramatic and thrilling to another which calls for a quieter and less fiery art. Yet, even if the *Odyssey* is the work of old age (and after all that is no more than a guess), γῆρας δ᾿ ὅμως Ὁμήρου.

We might hope that a more conclusive answer could be found in a comparison of the language of the two poems, but here we are faced by a puzzling phenomenon. On the one hand, a large mass of formulae is common to both poems and displays a regular uniformity throughout, whether in noun-adjective combinations or 'stock' lines or repeated themes. More strikingly, some of the rare abnormalities are also common to both poems. Thus instead of the normal πολυφλοίσβοιο θαλάσσης, νεφεληγερέτα Ζεύς, κλυτὸς ᾿Εννοσίγαιος, we find also the rare θαλάσσης εὐρυπόροιο, Ζεὺς τερπικέραυνος, κρείων ᾿Ενοσίχθων.[18] This looks as if it indicated a personal taste or idiosyncrasy of a single poet operating alike in both poems. On the other hand there are no less remarkable differences. Though the different subjects of the two poems mean that many words are used in one which are not used in the other, there are undeniably both words and formulae which we might well expect to appear in both, since they are certainly serviceable, but do not. With individual words this is perhaps not very disturbing, and it may not matter very much that the *Odyssey* alone uses such words as βασίλεια, δέσποινα, δημιοεργός, ἐλπωρή, δύη, χρήματα, πρῆξις, φήμη, ὕμνος, ἑξῆς, ὄνομα, ἐλπίς,[19] but it is more significant that it has a number of formulae which would be at home in the *Iliad* but are not found in it, such as φρεσὶ (κακὰ) βυσσοδομεύων, τετληότι θυμῷ, ἤρχετο μύθων, πολυκλύστῳ ἐνὶ πόντῳ, γόον δ᾿ ὠίετο θυμός, Κακοΐλιον οὐκ ὀνομαστήν, μοῖρ᾿ ὀλοὴ καθέλῃσι, τερψιμβρότου ἠελίοιο.[20] However much we may be impressed by the similar use of formulae in the two poems, we must admit that there are also differences which call for explanation.

Our solution for this problem must depend on what we mean by a poetical tradition and on the degree of liberty which it allows to those who are trained in it. If the poet had been brought up on books and composed his poems on paper, the linguistic difference between the two poems would not trouble us, since a literary poet usually alters his vocabulary and style with years and incorporates new words and new phrases from what he reads or hears. The difference between the *Iliad* and the *Odyssey* is not so great as that between *Titus Andronicus* and *The Tempest* or between *Comus* and *Samson Agonistes*. But because the Homeric poems are derived from an oral tradition, we cannot apply to them analogies from written texts. They must be judged in their own setting of a traditional, formulaic art, where unfortunately parallels do not give much help. If Yugoslav and Russian poems belong to a very narrow school which allows or encourages few linguistic innovations, this is not true of the Asiatic Tatars whose work in this century differs in many respects from that in the last. In principle we must expect the Greek tradition to be severe just because the hexameter demands a large number of carefully devised phrases, and innovations are less likely, because less easy, than in a freer and easier metre. If we insist that this tradition allowed few innovations, the right conclusion is that the *Odyssey* comes from a different branch of it from the *Iliad* and that the differences of language mean two poets working in different schools, each of which had its own mannerisms and preferences. Such a difference may have been determined by time or place or simply training. That both poems are derived ultimately from the same tradition is clear from their many similarities, but this tradition may have produced more than one branch, and the two poems may reflect such a division in it.

This view is based on two assumptions; first, that once an oral bard has formed a style he does not alter it, and second, that a poetical tradition like the Greek was so firmly fixed that even small differences of language must indicate a real difference of origin. Neither of these assumptions is capable of proof, and indeed neither is in principle very likely. An oral tradition like the Greek must for centuries have created new formulae and adopted new words to keep itself up to date. The poet of the *Odyssey* may well reflect the views of his own generation when he makes Telemachus say to Penelope:

> τὴν γὰρ ἀοιδὴν μᾶλλον ἐπικλείουσ᾽ ἄνθρωποι,
> ἥτις ἀκουόντεσσι νεωτάτη ἀμφιπέληται.   (α 351–2)

He certainly does not look as if he worked in a tradition so fossilized that nothing new could be done with it. New subjects call for new formulae, and it is at least possible that our poet learned or adapted or formed new phrases as he matured his art and moved to fresh subjects. Nor does the Greek tradition, as we know it in the Homeric poems, seem to be so fixed that it excludes variety. Indeed, as we have seen, it does in fact admit certain alternatives both in recurring lines and in noun-adjective combinations, and if it does this, the difference of language between the *Iliad* and the *Odyssey* need not necessarily represent a difference of origin or of authorship. It may imply no more than that even so highly disciplined a style as this was still capable of absorbing new elements, as it must have been in the earlier centuries when it was being fashioned for its multifarious duties.

Another, but no less serious, difficulty may be found in the way in which the two poems treat the gods. It may be of no great importance that the *Odyssey* confines its scenes on Olympus to two councils and to the story sung by Demodocus, while the *Iliad* abounds in them, or that Athene's relations with Odysseus, intimate, humorous, and unfailingly loyal, have no clear parallel in the *Iliad*, where Aphrodite treats Helen with tyrannical wilfulness and Apollo deserts Hector in his hour of need. More striking is the apparent difference of attitude adopted by the gods towards the doings of men. When Agamemnon speaks of his treatment of Achilles, he blames not himself but superior powers:

> ἐγὼ δ᾽ οὐκ αἴτιός εἰμι,
> ἀλλὰ Ζεὺς καὶ Μοῖρα καὶ ἠεροφοῖτις Ἐρινύς,
> οἵ τέ μοι εἰν ἀγορῇ φρεσὶν ἔμβαλον ἄγριον ἄτην. (T 86-8)

When the gods discuss the murder of Agamemnon by Aegisthus, Zeus says:

> ὢ πόποι, οἷον δή νυ θεοὺς βροτοὶ αἰτιόωνται.
> ἐξ ἡμέων γάρ φασι κάκ᾽ ἔμμεναι· οἱ δὲ καὶ αὐτοὶ
> σφῇσιν ἀτασθαλίῃσιν ὑπὲρ μόρον ἄλγε᾽ ἔχουσιν. (α 32-4)

The second passage contradicts the assumptions of the first, and shows a different view of the responsibilities of men for what happens to them. We can of course argue that religious and ethical notions must not be expected to be very consistent and that, while Agamemnon is simply making excuses for himself, Zeus may be taken to represent the poet's own view. This would be acceptable if this difference did not seem to go deeper and to affect the essential structure of both poems.

While the *Odyssey* is built on the notion that the suitors are punished for their wickedness and, as Penelope says, δι᾽ ἀτασθαλίας ἔπαθον κακόν (ψ 67), the *Iliad* has no such obvious message. Though the poet makes the wrath of Achilles a truly tragic force as the cause of his anguish at the death of Patroclus, and though he calls his intended treatment of Hector's body ἀεικέα ἔργα, he does not condemn him or point any moral about him. He is concerned not with the goodness or badness of his actions but with the agonizing misery of the short time at his disposal. If Achilles himself has any views on the matter, it is that the gods treat men as they please, giving both good and evil to some men, to others only evil (Ω 525 ff.). The *Iliad* certainly gives the impression that the gods are less concerned with the worth of human actions than they are in the *Odyssey*. Yet this difference is perhaps not so great as it appears. The gaiety of the

Olympian scenes in the *Iliad* does not necessarily exclude a divine interest in right and wrong ; [they belong to tradition and are needed in a poem of bloodshed to make a contrast between the gods in their ease and men in their sufferings, between divine immortality with all its security and human mortality with its obligation to fill life with great doings.] Nor are the gods without their interest in the actions of men. The poet has at least his own explanation for the doom of Troy and all the sufferings which it brings, and towards the end of the poem he reveals it. It is the Judgement of Paris, which has won the undying hatred of Athene and Hera for Troy :

> Ἀλεξάνδρου ἕνεκ' ἄτης
> ὃς νείκεσσε θεάς, ὅτε οἱ μέσσαυλον ἵκοντο,
> τὴν δ' ᾔνησ' ἥ οἱ πόρε μαχλοσύνην ἀλεγεινήν.   (Ω 28-30)

This explains why Aphrodite fights for Troy, while Athene and Hera are implacably bent on its destruction. But it does more than this. It implies a moral judgement. The word μαχλοσύνη is a harsh one, and the poet gives as his own opinion that it was this which was ultimately responsible for the fall of Troy.[21]

There is, then, perhaps less ultimate discrepancy between the theological and ethical outlooks of the two poems than we might think. None the less there is a difference, if not of fundamental assumptions, at least of emphasis. The *Odyssey* is certainly built on a more obviously ethical plan than the *Iliad*. This may, of course, be due to difference of authorship, especially as the notion that the gods are concerned with the doings of men grew in force in the seventh century.[22] On the other hand, if such ideas were already in the air, it is possible that a poet, who already held them to some extent, clarified and strengthened them as he grew older. On this point, as on others, the difference between the *Iliad* and the *Odyssey* can be explained either by the development of a single poet's outlook over a period of years or by the existence of two poets, of whom the second was well acquainted with the work of the first, belonged to the same tradition, and learned much from him, but made his own alterations in technique and outlook to suit his own tastes. There perhaps the question might be left. For those who feel that the two poems come from the same poet, it is at least a tenable view ; for those who feel that the differences are too great for this to be possible, there remains the consolation that both poems come from the same tradition and reflect the same world of the heroic imagination. Whatever decision we reach must in the end be partly subjective and determined by our sense of poetical quality. But some of us may think that from the poems emerges a personality, remote indeed and not easily defined, but none the less individual and too distinctive to belong to two separate poets or to be the result of a composite tradition.

The first and most remarkable resemblance between the two poems lies in the vivid reality of their characters. They may indeed be conceived on broad and simple lines, but they are lifelike in the sense that they make a personal appeal to us and that we think of them as living people. They reveal themselves partly in their words, partly in their behaviour, seldom in any comment, however allusive, from the poet. The *Odyssey* presents a smaller gallery of characters than the *Iliad* but they are no less vivid. In both poems the standard is set by the chief heroes, who maintain a high style and courtesy even in the most testing conditions, whether it is Achilles who receives the envoys of Agamemnon or Odysseus who approaches Nausicaa in his nakedness. They are extremely sensitive to any slur on their honour, whether it is Achilles who is insulted by Agamemnon or Odysseus who is derided by Euryalus. Nor does the simplicity of presentation exclude considerable insight and even subtlety. Helen makes few appearances in the *Iliad* but on each she reveals something new in her character, her charming relation with old Priam, her resigned helplessness in the presence of Aphrodite, her grief for Hector. Penelope is far more present in the *Odyssey*, but she too has her surprises for us, when through her long acquaintance with suffering she turns away from any possibility or sight of violence or refuses to recognize her husband until the evidence is too strong to resist. If the character in the *Iliad* who shows the greatest development is Achilles, as he moves from one crisis to another and in each reveals a different facet of his heroic personality, in the *Odyssey* it is Telemachus, who begins as an inexperienced boy, unable to deal with the situation in which he finds himself, but ends as the true son of his father, at whose side he fights with cool determination. Whatever information or aid tradition gave to the poet in his characters, there is surely a personal hand at work in their creation, and this hand seems to be the same both in the *Iliad* and in the *Odyssey*.

This view is supported by the portrayal of characters who appear in both poems. Odysseus in the *Odyssey* is ten years older than in the *Iliad*, but he is unchanged in his courage, resourcefulness, courtesy, vigorous appetites, and capacity to deal with other men. In the *Odyssey* Helen has returned to her first husband and left Troy behind her, but she has the same elusive detachment from her surroundings, the same quick instinct for the feelings of those about her, the same sense that she has brought untold sufferings into the world and the same patient acceptance of it. In both poems Nestor is equally garrulous, kindly, reminiscent, full of himself, and yet able always to recall the right precedents and to give the right advice. In Book λ of the *Odyssey* the ghosts of Agamemnon and Achilles are still their old selves, Agamemnon in his fierce pride, which now takes the form of a desire for vengeance for his murder, and

Achilles in his longing for the life of action, which is his no longer, and his delight in hearing of the prowess of his son. Such a degree of life and personality is not necessary to the figures of heroic poetry and is indeed rare among them. That both poems maintain it consistently argues for a close connection between them.

The same interest in human beings can be seen in quite unimportant characters, who are introduced to serve a momentary need and yet are illuminated by some brief, vivid touch of description, like Axylus, who lives in Arisbe and welcomes all who pass on the road (Z 13-15); Dresus, whom a nymph bore among the flocks on a mountain (*ibid.* 22); Meges, who wears a breast-plate from Ephyra (O 529 ff.); Iphition, who was born in a rich land under snowy Tmolus (*ibid.* 382 ff.); Theano, the priestess, who nurses her husband's bastard son (E 70); Aegyptius, who is bent with age, and whose son has been eaten by the Cyclops (β 15 ff.), and Ikmalios, who made Penelope's chair of ivory and silver (τ 56-7). In the same way small realistic touches enliven actions which the poet might well omit, but which evidently appeal to him. The supper in the quarters of Achilles (I 205-21) is very like that in the hut of Eumaeus (ξ 443); when Eurymachus as a child sits on the lap of Odysseus (π 443 ff.), he recalls the child Achilles on the lap of Phoenix (I 488-91); the blow which Odysseus gives to Thersites (B 265-9) and the kick which he himself receives from Melanthius (ρ 233) are equally sudden and violent. No doubt the formulae gave much help in such matters, but it was the poet's task to make a good use of them, and in such cases we can see how he does so.

The poet was, of course, obliged to tell of a distant past when men were stronger and braver than in his own day. The *Iliad* and the *Odyssey* accept this obligation not only by making their chief characters live up to a heroic ideal but by pouring contempt on those, like Thersites or Melanthius, who are below it. But this does not mean that the poet was not interested in common men and women or forced to exclude them from his tales. If faithful servants like Eurycleia and Eumaeus are common enough in heroic poetry, our poet was allowed another way of showing his care for humanity and took full advantage of it. This was the simile. The Homeric similes show how deeply he felt the claims of ordinary people, and we cannot doubt that he drew much of his material from what he saw around him, such as the mother who wards off flies from her child (Δ 130 ff.), the reapers in the barley (Λ 67 ff.), the boys who beat an ass which has broken into a cornfield (Λ 557 ff.), the woman working at her wool to save her children from poverty (M 433 ff.), the child who treads down his sand-castle (Ξ 362 ff.), the traveller uncertain of his way (O 80 ff.), the inexperienced cowherd who cannot keep off a lion (O 631 ff.), the fisherman with his line and hook (O 433 ff.), the

G

craftsman who puts gold on silver (ζ 332 ff.), the woman whose husband is killed in war and who is herself dragged into slavery (θ 522 ff.), the shipwright who bores a ship's timber (ι 384 ff.), the smith who tempers an axe by dipping it in water (ι 391 ff.), the man who watches a bard as he sings (ρ 518-19). The Homeric similes reveal a personal interest in human beings who lie outside the scope of the heroic tale, and in them the poet surely displays his own wide sympathy and understanding.

A poet who deals with human beings inevitably chooses some subjects which appeal to him and rejects others which do not. However wide his sympathies, there will be some themes from which he shrinks, because they shock or horrify him. Many of the Greek legends contained brutal or revolting elements which we know from later poetry and art and which must have had their birth in the poetical tradition as legitimate parts of its repertory. The sacrifice of Iphigeneia, the incest of Oedipus, the cannibal banquet of Thyestes, and many other such stories were told in later times, but do not appear in the Homeric poems. In the account of the gathering at Aulis nothing is said about Iphigenia, and if, as is not certain, she is the same as Iphianassa, whom Agamemnon offers to Achilles in marriage (I 415), the story of her sacrifice is quietly contradicted; the fate of Oedipus is reduced to a single, non-committal mention of his death at Thebes (Ψ 679); in the various accounts in the *Odyssey* of the vengeance of Orestes no word is said that he killed his mother; the love of Achilles and Patroclus is implicitly denied (I 633-8); no more is said of Ganymede than that Zeus made him his cup-bearer because of his beauty (Υ 234). Sometimes indeed tradition forced a brutal or unsavoury theme on the poet, and then he despatched it as quickly as possible, as when Phoenix sleeps with his stepmother and plots to murder his father but does not (I 451 ff.). When authority said that Alcinous was married to his sister Arete the poet recorded it but explained that they were really cousins (η 54 ff.). At one point we are indeed surprised to hear of human sacrifice, when Achilles kills twelve Trojans at the pyre of Patroclus. This may indeed be a very ancient memory, since it has an archaeological parallel in the king's tomb at Dendra, where human and animal bones are found in a pit by the actual grave, but in the *Iliad* it is told to show the state of vengeful anger which still obsesses Achilles, and the poet does not conceal his own distress but comments κακὰ δὲ φρεσὶ μήδετο ἔργα (Ψ 176). It has been thought that this delicacy is due to a later expurgation of the poems which once contained such material,[23] but it seems more likely that it represents a personal distaste for horrors, to be expected in a poet who does not allow Achilles to mutilate the body of Hector. We cannot ascribe it to tradition, since it is clear that some poets at least did not share it.

A similar personal touch may be observed also in some relatively minor points of technique, which are indeed derived from tradition but show a careful, selective discrimination in their use. First, since the poet composes on what is probably an unusually large scale and has to deal with a long stretch of events, the poem marks certain main features by forecasting them. This may be simply to keep us more or less aware of what is going to happen, as when Athene tells Achilles that he will receive threefold recompense for Agamemnon's arrogance to him (A 213 ff.) or the poet himself tells that the time has come for Odysseus to return home (α 15 ff.). Or it may not forecast events so distant as these, but refer to something in the immediate future, as when we hear that Hector will set fire to the Achaean ships (O 596 ff.) or Penelope prays that her son may be saved, and the poet adds θεὰ δέ οἱ ἔκλυεν ἀρῆς (δ 767). Conversely, sometimes the hopes of men are shown at the start to be futile. Both when Agamemnon hopes to capture Troy during the next day (B 413 ff.) and when both Achaeans and Trojans hope that the duel of Menelaus and Paris will end the war (Γ 302), the failure of such hopes is curtly expressed by the words οὐδ' ἄρα πώ οἱ ἐπεκραίαινε Κρονίων. More impressively, the central actions of both poems, the death of Patroclus and the slaughter of the suitors, are both forecast more than once, and each occasion adds something to the tragic or sinister nature of what is to come. The doom of the suitors is first hinted at when Athene says that Odysseus will certainly return (α 203); it is explicitly foretold at the Ithacan assembly when the seer Halitherses sees it foreshadowed in the actions of birds (β 167 ff.); Menelaus says that it will come to pass (δ 333); Theoclymenus sees an omen of it in an eagle holding a dove (ο 351) and prophesies it in dark and mysterious words when the suitors are struck to temporary madness in their cups (υ 351 ff.). The death of Patroclus is first forecast when, in answer to the summons of Achilles, he comes out of his tent, κακοῦ δ' ἄρα οἱ πέλεν ἀρχή (Λ 604). Later, when he begs Achilles to let him go to battle, the poet is even more explicit:

> ὣς φάτο λισσόμενος μέγα νήπιος· ἦ γὰρ ἔμελλεν
> οἷ αὐτῷ θάνατόν τε κακὸν καὶ κῆρα λιτέσθαι,   (Π 46-7)

and finally when Achilles prays to Zeus that the Trojans may be driven from the ships and Patroclus come home safe, we hear that Zeus grants the first part of the prayer but not the second (ibid. 248-52). This art of forecasting not only helps to hold a long story together but, by approaching an event from different angles, makes it more dramatic and more exciting when it comes.

A second device which looks like a personal touch is the way in which the poet makes his characters know certain things which they cannot strictly be expected to know. This is useful to him since it enables him to keep his narrative simple and unobstructed by tiresome or distracting explanations. The audience, without knowing it, automatically fills the gap, and supplies the information which we might expect to be supplied by the poet. Thus, though he has no means of doing so, Achilles knows that Chryses has prayed to Apollo (A 380), because the poet has said so (*ibid.* 35); Sarpedon has made the first successful attack on the Achaean wall (M 387), but Patroclus, who has not heard of it, speaks of it (Π 558); Ajax fears that Patroclus's body will be thrown to the dogs (P 241), but it is we, and not he, who know that this is Hector's intention (*ibid.* 126 ff.); Penelope knows that Antinous has thrown a stool at Odysseus (ρ 500 ff.), though she did not see it happen and nobody has told her about it. More simply, the poet may omit something just because it would be boring to tell it too often. So Zeus instructs Hermes that Odysseus is to build a raft (ε 33), but Hermes says nothing of it to Calypso, although she passes it on to Odysseus as part of the message which Hermes has given her (*ibid.* 112). In a rather similar way the poet sometimes creates in his narrative what is strictly an inconsistency in order to keep his story clear. Eumaeus tells Penelope that the Beggar has spent three days and three nights with him in his hut (ρ 515), but if we look into it carefully, the figure should be not three but four. We remember the three nights because each has its own events and character; we do not remember the fourth. The poet shows consideration for us and keeps to the essential point of the narrative. The ghost of Anticleia speaks of Telemachus as if he were already fully grown (λ 185-7). So indeed he is as we have seen him in Ithaca, but when she speaks, he cannot be more than a boy. To treat him otherwise would be to disturb us for a moment on a matter in which clarity is more important than precision. Oral recitation imposes its own obligations, and chief among these is the need to maintain a straightforward narrative. Our poet does this by many means, of which this consideration for his audience is one of the more subtle.

Thirdly, a personal touch may surely be seen in the placing of similes. Though the *Iliad* has four times as many as the *Odyssey*, that is because it deals with battle-scenes, where they are needed to relieve the monotony, and that is why in it 164 are in battle-scenes and 38 outside them. More illuminating for our purpose is the way in which they are used to mark pauses in the action or changes in it. When Diomede starts his adventures, his head is like the bright star of autumn (E 5); when Hector and Paris go to join the Trojans, they come like a breeze to tired mariners (H 4-6); the embassy to Achilles begins by comparing the divided minds of the Achaeans with a sea driven by winds (I 4-7); the fatal adventure of Patroclus starts with his tears falling like a stream from a rock (O 3-4); the last fight of Achilles and Hector is heralded by the Trojans flying like frightened fawns (X 1); the release of Odysseus from Ogygia begins with Hermes flying like a sea-bird (ε 51-3); Odysseus's first sight of

Phaeacia cheers him as the sons of a sick father are cheered when he begins to recover (ε 394-7); the beginning of Eumaeus's exploits with Telemachus is like the meeting of a father with a son who has been long away (π 17-19); when Odysseus starts his final action against the suitors, he turns his thoughts this way and that, like a man turning a blood-pudding over a fire (υ 25-7); when the climax at last comes, he strings the great bow as a harper strings his harp (φ 406-8).

In the same way similes are used to end scenes both large and small. The exploits of Diomede close with his blood drying like congealing milk (E 902-3). The first part of Achilles's warfare in pursuit of Hector ends with a comparison of him to a devouring fire and to oxen treading corn (Υ 490-7). Hector's first attack on the Achaeans ends with the Trojan watch-fires burning like stars around the moon (Θ 555-9). Odysseus's ride on the raft ends with its pieces being scattered like chaff (ε 368-9). When he sleeps in a bush after his long swimming, it is like a man who hides a torch in the hot ashes (ε 488-90). His long stay on Phaeacia closes with a parallel between his desire to depart and a man's relief at sundown after a day's ploughing (ν 31-4), and the killing of the suitors and their collaborators is marked by the simile in which the faithless serving-women are strung up like thrushes or doves (χ 468-70). This is not the only way of using similes, but it is sufficiently noticeable to suggest that they are so placed because the poet feels a need to mark his beginnings and his finishes, and has an apt means of doing so.

Fourthly, the poet seems sometimes to invent a detail which looks as if it referred to some story outside his immediate subject but is in fact an invention brought in to serve a passing need. By this he suggests that there is much more in a situation than meets the eye and gives to it an enhanced interest. Naturally, the critics have assumed that this is due to multiple authorship or editorial muddle, but the simpler explanation is more likely, that it is simply a means to give importance to otherwise not very important actions. So before his duel with Paris, Menelaus insists on an oath being taken because Priam's sons are not to be trusted (Γ 106). The theme occurs nowhere else, and there is no need to assume that there is a lost saga behind it. Its task is simply to make the oath more impressive and to provide a good reason for what would otherwise be a mere 'stock' theme. Again, on Olympus Hera speaks of the trouble she had in collecting a host to fight against Priam (Δ 25 ff.). Of course, this may refer to Hera's connection with Argos and come from another cycle, but in its place it is adequately explained by the need to strengthen her appeal for help against the Trojans. Similar circumstantial inventions can be seen when Andromache tells Hector that the Achaeans have assaulted Troy three times at a certain place (Z 435 ff.), or Aeneas lags behind because he is always angry with Priam (N 459 ff.), or Achilles says that his mother foretold the death of Patroclus (Σ 9), or the Phaeacian ship finds the harbour of Phorcys because the sailors have been there before (ν 113), or Antinous says that the Beggar cannot be Odysseus because he remembers him from his childhood (φ 95). Of course, narrative poets invent many details to give verisimilitude to their stories, but in the Homeric poems touches such as these seem to be intended to create an impression of a whole, crowded world of events behind the actual story.

Lastly, it is worthy of notice that both in the *Iliad* and in the *Odyssey* the poet puts forward, quietly indeed and not very emphatically, his own theory of the connection between human suffering and song. When Helen uncovers her grief and her guilt to Hector, and speaks of the doom which belongs to her and to Paris, she not only ascribes it to Zeus but explains his reason for it :

οἷσιν ἐπὶ Ζεὺς θῆκε κακὸν μόρον, ὡς καὶ ὀπίσσω
ἀνθρώποισι πελώμεθ' ἀοίδιμοι ἐσσομένοισι.   (Z 357-8)

When Alcinous refers to the way in which Odysseus weeps when he hears the song of Demodocus on the sufferings of the Achaeans, he says :

τὸν δὲ θεοὶ μὲν τεῦξαν, ἐπεκλώσαντο δ' ὄλεθρον
ἀνθρώποις, ἵνα ᾖσι καὶ ἐσσομένοισι ἀοιδή.   (θ 579-80)

This is the nearest approach in the Homeric poems to a theory of poetry. In expressing his belief that suffering is sent by the gods that men may have subjects for song, the poet reveals his high conception of his art, which is that the only survival, other than as shadows among other shadows, which men can expect after death is on the lips and in the ears of men. This atones for their sufferings and provides an explanation of them. Such a belief seems both too tentative and too unusual to be common form, and in it we may surely see a poet's personal defence of his art and of its concern with the sorrows and sufferings of men.

These details may not be very important in themselves, but they have some relevance to the discussion of Homeric authorship because it is in such small matters that a poet reveals himself and his own tastes, especially if he is working inside a traditional, conventional frame. This does not allow him to produce such startling novelties as a literate poet can to display his originality, and we must look elsewhere for his individual touch. Points of this kind are indeed born of a tradition, but it does not instruct the poet where or how they can best be used, and most of them are so unobtrusive that it is unlikely that more than one poet would use them in so strikingly consistent a way. They indicate a poet who was such a master of his craft that he could turn the most humble devices to unexpected purposes. He is in full control of them and uses them to keep his story radiantly clear and to hold his audience's attention for each episode as he tells it. If the conditions of oral performance imposed certain obligations on him, and his tradition, fashioned through many centuries, meant that he was sometimes inconsequent in the handling of material details, he was still free to make the most of his technique and to apply it as he thought most suitable to the different elements in his tale. He knew its difficulties, and once at least speaks of them:

$$\mathring{\alpha}\rho\gamma\alpha\lambda\acute{\epsilon}o\nu\ \delta\acute{\epsilon}\ \mu\epsilon\ \tau\alpha\hat{\upsilon}\tau\alpha\ \theta\epsilon\grave{o}\nu\ \mathring{\omega}s\ \pi\acute{\alpha}\nu\tau'\ \mathring{\alpha}\gamma o\rho\epsilon\hat{\upsilon}\sigma\alpha\iota,\qquad\text{(M 176)}$$

but he had behind him the vast resources which he had learned in his apprenticeship and in what he gained from the Muse's inspiration in actual performance. When he made his Phemius say

$$\alpha\mathring{\upsilon}\tau o\delta\acute{\iota}\delta\alpha\kappa\tau os\ \delta'\ \epsilon\mathring{\iota}\mu\acute{\iota},\ \theta\epsilon\grave{o}s\ \delta\acute{\epsilon}\ \mu o\iota\ \mathring{\epsilon}\nu\ \phi\rho\epsilon\sigma\grave{\iota}\nu\ o\mathring{\iota}\mu\alpha s$$
$$\pi\alpha\nu\tauo\acute{\iota}\alpha s\ \mathring{\epsilon}\nu\acute{\epsilon}\phi\upsilon\sigma\epsilon\nu,\qquad\qquad\qquad\qquad\text{(χ 347-8)}$$

he could hardly expect anyone to believe that he himself was self-taught, but he could rightly claim that a god had given him all the ways of song and that he followed these alike in his stories, his language, and his many poetical devices.

Much indeed of our delight in the poems comes from the tradition behind them. The rich, varied, resourceful language, the many ways in which a story can be made more dramatic or more human, the ability to combine convention and surprise, the sense of a heroic world and of the grandeur of brave exploits, the vision of the gods and the unique distinction which human life gains from being set against the darkness of death, all these we owe in large degree to the tradition, and it is conceivable that, if we had not the *Iliad* and the *Odyssey* but only the work of some uncreative bard who relied entirely on traditional material, we might well be impressed and delighted by it. Yet when we have made every allowance for this, we must still feel that there is something else, not easily defined and in the last resort beyond precise analysis, which reveals a great poet at work. It lies largely in his vision of humanity, seen almost always with affection, sometimes with compassion, sometimes with admiration, sometimes with humour. These men and women live for us because they are portrayed from the inside. Human nature gave the poet his chief inspiration and made him extend his stories beyond their immediate subjects to contain a whole world of real characters. But these characters are set in surroundings as real as themselves. They are seen from without as well as from within, and play their parts in scenes which the poet loves hardly less than them and describes with affectionate care, from the constellations and the sea to birds and flowers and insects. If this is needed as a setting for his crowded events, it too lives in its own right and has its own enchanting reality. It is certainly possible for more than one poet to combine these gifts and use them effectively, but it seems less likely that they should be combined with so sure a touch and so unflagging an inspiration. Despite all the arguments to the contrary, it is not unreasonable to believe that a single poet composed both the *Iliad* and the *Odyssey* and, since the Greeks said that his name was Homer, and there is no other name by which we may call him, we may perhaps be content with it.

NOTES TO CHAPTER 3

1. G. Buchner and C. F. Russo, 'La coppa di Nestore', *Rend. Linc.* x (1955), 215-34.
2. U. von Wilamowitz-Moellendorff, *Sappho und Simonides*, 273-4.
3. For a different view *cf.* E. R. Dodds in *Fifty Years of Classical Scholarship*, 15 ff.
4. C. M. Bowra, *Homer and his Forerunners*, 9-13.
5. U. von Wilamowitz-Moellendorff, *Homerische Untersuchungen*, 140 ff.
6. D. L. Page, *The Homeric Odyssey*, 102-11, makes the most of such arguments.
7. For a different view *cf.* A. Shewan, *The Lay of Dolon.*
8. W. Leaf, *The Iliad* (2nd edn.), i. 370.
9. *Idem* i. 297
10. E. Bethe, *Homer*, i. 206 ff.
11. Leaf, *op. cit.* i. 117-18.
12. Page, *op. cit.* 9-12.
13. W. J. Woodhouse, *The Composition of Homer's Odyssey*, 216-17.
14. Leaf, *op. cit.* i. 296-7.
15. U. von Wilamowitz-Moellendorff, *Die Ilias und Homer*, 92-115.
16. For a different view *cf.* Page, *op. cit.* 83-8.
17. H. T. Wade-Gery, *The Poet of the Iliad*, 2-6.
18. M. Parry, *L'Épithète traditionnelle dans Homère*, 238-40.
19. D. B. Monro, *Homer's Odyssey*, ii. 334-5.
20. Page, *op. cit.* 151-2.
21. K. Reinhardt, *Von Werken und Formen*, 11-36.
22. E. R. Dodds, *The Greeks and the Irrational*, 28 ff.
23. G. Murray, *The Rise of the Greek Epic*, 125-40.

CHAPTER 4

THE LANGUAGE OF HOMER

by L. R. Palmer

FOREWORD

WITHIN the limits of the present chapter it is not possible to offer an exhaustive grammar of the Homeric language. The following contribution represents, therefore, a Homeric supplement to an Attic grammar, wherein the divergences from Attic usage have been explained as far as possible by a comparative and historical treatment. The student will find that his understanding of the morphology in particular is facilitated by a knowledge of certain philological facts and principles. These are set out at the beginning as 'Preliminary notions' distinguished by Roman numerals. It is to these that indications in the text such as '(IV)' refer.

The grammatical works most consulted by me have been D. B. Monro, *A Grammar of the Homeric Dialect* (1891), Kühner-Gerth, *Grammatik der griechischen Sprache*, ii : *Satzlehre* (1898–1904), and J. v. Leeuwen, *Encheiridion dictionis epicae* (1894). From C. Mohrmann's *Homerische Spraakleer* (Nijmegen, 1933) I have derived some valuable hints on the selection and arrangement of the facts. But I have thought it advisable to devote considerably more space to syntax than the Dutch scholar's sixteen pages.

The chapter was completed in its first form before the appearance either of the syntax volume of E. Schwyzer's great *Griechische Grammatik* (1950) or of P. Chantraine's *Grammaire homérique* (i, 1942, ii, 1953). It was, however, possible to profit by the delay in publication to undertake a thorough revision in the light of these fundamental studies. It was also necessary to make some reassessment of the genesis of the epic dialect in the light of the newly deciphered Linear B tablets. However, as is argued in detail below, the impact of the new evidence on Homeric studies has been much exaggerated.

Reference to individual topics will be facilitated by the subjoined synopsis.

SYNOPSIS OF CONTENTS, CHAPTER 4

i. PRELIMINARY NOTIONS

PHONOLOGY

I. Original $\bar{a}$ becomes η in Attic-Ionic : thus to μάτηρ, δᾶμος, etc. in Doric, etc., there correspond Attic μήτηρ, δῆμος, etc. This change, complete in Ionic, was inhibited in Attic by a preceding ρ, ι, or ε : thus forms like χώρη, οἰκίη, etc., distinguish Ionic from Attic, which has χώρᾱ, οἰκίᾱ, etc.

II. Attic is distinguished from other dialects by the extensive *contraction of vowels* which were elsewhere left uncontracted. Thus εα, εο, and εω remain open in Ionic, so that Attic γένη, γένους, πυλῶν are opposed to Ionic γένεα, γένεος, πυλέων.[a]

III. Attic-Ionic are further distinguished from other dialects by the phenomenon known as *quantitative metathesis* : that is to say a trochaic succession of vowels in hiatus becomes iambic, *e.g.*, ηο 〉 εω. Thus a

---

[a] See below.

common Greek form ναός became (according to I) first νηός and then, by quantitative metathesis, νεώς. Other examples of the same kind are λᾱός 〉 ληός 〉 λεώς, ἴλᾱος 〉 ἴληος 〉 ἴλεως. This change is important for the understanding of the genitive singular of masculine nouns of the first declension. Thus the early genitive of a word like πολίτας was πολίτᾱ-ο, a form of the genitive preserved in the Aeolic dialects; πολίτᾱο in Ionic 〉 πολίτηο 〉 πολίτεω.[a] The genitives Πηληϊάδεω, etc., in Homer are consequently Ionic forms. Quantitative metathesis affects also early Greek -ηο-, -ηα- in Attic-Ionic, so that βασιλῆος, θήομεν,[b] etc. become βασιλέως and θέωμεν, etc., and βασιλῆα becomes βασιλέᾱ.

IV. IE γ at the beginning of a word appears variously either as ζ or as the rough breathing. Thus Lat. iugum = ζυγόν; but Lat. iēci corresponds to ἧκα.

Between vowels γ is dropped and the vowels contracted: thus Sanskrit trayas = Gk. *τρέι̯ες 〉 τρεῖς. In combination with consonants γ brings about sundry changes. Note: (1) κ, χ+ι̯ 〉 σσ: e.g., *φυλάκ-ι̯ω 〉 φυλάσσω, *ταράχ-ι̯ω 〉 ταράσσω. (2) δ, γ+ι̯ 〉 ζ: *ἐλπίδ-ι̯ω 〉 ἐλπίζω, μέγ-ι̯ων 〉 μέζων. (3) ρ+ι̯ 〉 ρρ in Aeolic, but other dialects lengthen the preceding vowel: hence *φθέρ-ι̯ω produces Aeolic φθέρρω but Attic φθείρω.[c]

V. A. w (written F, the digamma) disappeared at an early period in Attic-Ionic. In other dialects it is better preserved, particularly at the beginning of a word before a vowel. Thus the congener of Eng. work is in Doric Fέργον; other examples are: Foῖδα (cf. vidi), Foῖνον (cf. vinum), Foῖκος (cf. vicus), etc. We shall discuss below the question of digamma in the text of Homer.

B. The treatment of the combinations νF, ρF, and λF provides us with a valuable criterion for the distinction of Ionic from the other dialects, for, whereas in most dialects the F disappears without trace, in Ionic it produces a compensatory lengthening of the preceding vowel: thus κόρFᾱ, 'a maiden', appears in Attic as κόρη, but in Ionic as κούρη.[d] Thus the contrast between Ionic μοῦνος, οὖρος, οὖλος, ξεῖνος, κᾱλός, etc. on the one hand, and Attic μόνος, ὄρος, ὅλος, ξένος, κᾱλός, etc. on the other, is due to the digamma in the original forms μόνFος, ὄρFος, ὅλFος, ξένFος, καλFός, etc.

VI. m, n. These sounds, when syllabic as in the English seven (sevṇ), rhythm (riđṃ), are usually represented by Indo-Europeanists as ṃ, ṇ. These so-called sonant nasals of Indo-European appear in Greek as α: e.g., *dekṃ (Latin decem) 〉 δέκα; so, too, the ending of the accusative

---

[a] Attic substitutes -ου borrowed from the masculine second declension.
[b] On these subjunctives see p. 81.
[c] Note that ει is the graphic representation of a lengthened ε̄.
[d] Note that ου is the graphic representation of a lengthened o as ει is of ε̄.

singular of consonant stems: *φύλακ-ṃ (cf. iudic-em) 〉 φύλακ-α. The corresponding representation of ṇ is seen in the past participle of *ten 'to stretch' (the present tense *τέν-ι̯ω 〉 τείνω): *tṇtos [a] 〉 τατός.

VII. The sonant liquids ṛ and ḷ appear as ρα, αρ and λα, αλ: e.g., ἔδρακον (〈 *dṛk the weak grade [b] of *derk); καρδία and κραδίη (〈 *kṛd); ἔσταλται (〈 *stḷ, the weak grade of *stel); cf. πί-πλα-μεν = Sanskrit pi-pṛ-mas.

VIII. *Labio-Velars.*—Perhaps the most remarkable sound changes which obscure the etymological relationships of Greek words with their congeners in other languages are those affecting the IE labio-velars. These were guttural plosive sounds (k, g, gh) pronounced with a protrusion of the lips, and they are represented as q^u, g^u, and g^uh. In Attic they become dentals (τ, δ, θ) before front vowels (ι, ε, η) and labials (π, β, φ) before back vowels (α, ο, ω) and consonants, with the proviso that in the neighbourhood of a *u*-sound they appear as pure gutturals (κ, γ, χ). This development may be exemplified in the forms of the interrogative-indefinite pronoun *$q^u$is (Latin *quis, quod*, etc.). Thus we have in Attic before a front vowel τις, before a back vowel ποῦ, πόθεν, etc., and in the neighbourhood of a *u*-sound οὐκί.

Further examples follow:

		Front Vowel	Back Vowel	Consonant
q^u	*q^uel 'to turn'	τέλομαι	πόλος	περι-πλόμενος
g^u	*g^uel 'to strike'	δέλλω (Arcadian)	βάλλω, βόλος	ἐβλήθην
g^uh	*g^uhen 'to strike'	θείνω (θέν-ι̯ω)	φόνος	ἔ-πε-φν-ον

Aeolic, however, is distinguished from Attic, in that it does not differentiate between the treatment before front and back vowels but has labials even before ι and ε. Thus Aeolic πέλομαι, for instance, contrasts with Attic τέλομαι. This, as we shall see, is one of the most important criteria for the Aeolic dialect.

IX. *s.*—A. This sound at the beginning of a word before a vowel appears in Greek as a rough breathing (which is lost in the Asiatic dialects and sporadically elsewhere): thus *sex* = ἕξ, *septem* = ἕπτα (〈 *sept-ṃ, see VI). Intervocalically this *h* disappears and in Attic the resulting hiatus is removed by contraction (II): thus γένος, *γένεσος, *γένεσα, etc., become in non-Attic dialects γένεος, γένεα, etc. Similarly the forms of the second person singular middle of the verb, which were originally *λύεσαι (cf. λύεται), *ἐλύεσο (cf. ἐλύετο), *ἐλύσασο (cf. ἐλύσατο), etc., became λύεαι, ἐλύεο, ἐλύσαο respectively, which were contracted in Attic to λύῃ, ἐλύου, ἐλύσω, etc. The open forms, as we shall see, are found in Homer.

---

[a] On this reduction of the root *ten to *tṇ see below on *Ablaut*.
[b] See below on *Ablaut*.

B. In combination with sonants and nasals (*r, l, m, n*) *s* underwent a variety of transformations. In *-ns-* and *-ms-* the *s* disappeared and compensatory lengthening took place, which in Aeolic took the form of *a doubling of the consonant* as against *a lengthening of the vowel in other dialects.* Hence we get the following distinctive dialect forms:

$$*\ddot{\acute{e}}\text{-}\mu\epsilon\nu\text{-}\sigma a \rangle \text{ Aeol. } \ddot{e}\mu\epsilon\nu\nu a \quad \text{Attic-Ionic } \ddot{e}\mu\epsilon\iota\nu a \ ^a$$
$$*\ddot{\acute{e}}\text{-}\nu\epsilon\mu\text{-}\sigma a \rangle \quad \text{,, } \ddot{e}\nu\epsilon\mu\mu a \quad \text{,,} \quad \text{,, } \ddot{e}\nu\epsilon\iota\mu a$$

A similar change took place in the groups *-sm-, -sn-, -sl-, -sr-*: hence Aeolic φαεννός (*φαεσ-νός, *cf.* φάος), ἐρεβεννός (*ἐρεβεσ-νός), ἀργεννός (*ἀργεσ-νός), ἐμμί (*ἐσ-μί), etc.; contrast with Attic-Ionic φαεινός, ἐρεβεινός, ἀργεινός, εἰμί, etc. This change took place also in the first and second person plural personal pronouns, which it will be convenient to discuss here.

C. The accusative forms meaning 'us' and 'you' are to be traced to *ἀσμε (*n̥s-me) and *γυσ-με (Sanskrit *yuṣmān*) respectively. According to the rules discussed above these should yield Aeolic ἄμμε, ὔμμε and Attic-Ionic *ἧμε (⟨ *ᾱμε) and *ῦμε. Actually the Attic-Ionic forms have received new endings ἡμᾶς and ὑμᾶς (Ionic ἡμέας, ὑμέας), but the characteristic treatment of *-σμ-* in the different dialect groups yields us the following criteria for the distinction of the dialects.

	Aeolic	Attic-Ionic
N.	ἄμμες, ὔμμες	ἡμεῖς, ὑμεῖς
A.	ἄμμε, ὔμμε	ἡμᾶς (-έας), ὑμᾶς (-έας)
G.	ἀμμέων, ὑμμέων	ἡμῶν (-έων), ὑμῶν (-έων)
D.	ἄμμι(ν), ὔμμι(ν).	ἡμῖν, ὑμῖν.

D. *sm-, sn-*, etc. at the beginning of a word simply drop the *s*, so that νίφα (*sn-*) contrasts with ἀγά-ννιφος A 420, which exhibits the Aeolic doubling. Similarly (σ)νέω 'to spin' forms the past tense ἔννεον Φ 11 and the compound εὔννητος Σ 596. But this 'internal' treatment of *-sm-*, etc. is not confined to the interior of single words: we find traces of it in closely-knit word groups such as prepositional phrases. Hence we find κατὰ μοῖραν Π 367; *cf.* further ὥς τε νιφάδες, περὶ δὲ ῥόος,[b] etc., but we should add that purely metrical lengthening also takes place before words in which initial *m, n*, etc. were never preceded by an *s-*.

E. On the simplification in Attic-Ionic of *-σσ-* (from σ-σ, -τσ-, τ̣ι, etc.) see below.

---

[a] ει=lengthened ε (see above): note φέρουσι, too, for φέρον-σι from φέροντι, where ου=δ.

[b] These should perhaps be written κατὰ μμοῖραν, etc.

MORPHOLOGY

X. *Root, suffix, stem, inflection.*—The structure of a Greek (or Indo-European) word may be analysed into the following parts. A *root* is the constant element found in a given group of etymologically related words such as δί-δω-μι, ἔ-δω-κα, δῶ-ρον, δω-τήρ, δώ-τωρ, δω-τίνη, etc. In a noun or verb, further, we find endings which indicate the relationship which the word bears to the rest of the sentence. Thus in δωτήρ-ος δωτήρ-α, etc., the elements -ος, -α, etc. are case *inflections*, which if struck off leave us with the bare *stem*. Thus from the *root* δω we can form a *nominal stem* (agent noun) by the addition of a *suffix* -τηρ. In verbs, too, such as δίδωμι we say that the *present stem* δι-δω- is formed by reduplication, that the aorist ἔ-δο-μεν has a *root stem* (δο without the addition of any suffix). δείκ-νυ-μι, on the other hand, forms its present stem from the root by the addition of a formant -νυ, while its aorist ἔ-δεικ-σ-α exhibits a formant -σ : this is the so-called sigmatic aorist. λα-ν-θ-άν-ω, μα-ν-θ-άν-ω, etc., further, form their present stems from the root by *infixing a nasal* (λα-ν-θ) [a] and adding -αν-, such verbs having root aorists ἔ-λαθ-ον, ἔ-μαθ-ον, etc.

XI. *Thematic and athematic.*—If we examine a verb like λύω, λύ-ο-μεν, λύ-ε-τε, we notice that a vowel ο/ε intervenes between the inflections -μεν, -τε, etc., and the stem, whereas in δείκνυ-μεν, δείκνυ-τε, etc., no such vowel is found. This linking vowel is called the thematic vowel, and nouns and verbs which exhibit it are called *thematic*, whereas those without the vowel are called *athematic*. The distinction is important because athematic tenses of verbs form their subjunctive, optative, and infinitive moods differently from thematic tenses. Moreover, athematic verbs exhibit *Ablaut* of the stem (see next section).

A. The *Subjunctive* of an athematic verbal tense was originally formed by inserting the thematic vowel : thus ἴμεν 'we go' had as its subjunctive ἴομεν 'let us go, we will go'. This *short-vowelled subjunctive*, as it is called, was once characteristic of all athematic verbs, but Attic has generalized the long-vowelled type, which was originally proper only to thematic tenses : ἴωμεν, etc., like λύωμεν.

B. *Optative.*—The mood sign of the thematic tenses is an invariable -ι- which, combined with the thematic vowel ο, produces the -οι- which is characteristic, for instance, of the optative of λύω : λύ-οι-μι, λύ-οι-ς, λύ-οι. The optative sign of the athematic tenses, however, appears with an alternation *iē/i* : thus from the verb *es* 'to be' we get *es-iē-m,*[b] plural *es-ī-men* ⟩ εἴην, εἶμεν.

---

[a] An infixed nasal is also found in the Latin *iungo*, ⟨ root *iug*.

[b] Note that the full form of the root *es* is restored in Greek, whereas Latin *siem* and Sanskrit *syām* have the original zero grade *s*- (for *Ablaut* see below).

C. *Infinitive.*—The ending of the infinitive of athematic tenses is in Attic-Ionic -ναι, in other dialects variously -μεν and -μεναι. Thus the verb **es* forms its Attic infinitive **ἔσ-ναι*, which according to IX B becomes εἶναι with loss of the -s- and compensatory lengthening. In Lesbian, on the other hand, we find ἔμ-μεναι from **ἔσ-μεναι* with the Aeolic doubling of the consonants discussed above.

Most other dialects (including the Aeolic dialects Thessalian and Boeotian) have the -μεν form : ἔμμεν, ἦμεν, etc.

XII. *Primary and secondary inflections in the verbal conjugation.*—The so called primary forms of the verb (present, future, subjunctive) have in some persons different inflections from the secondary forms (imperfect, aorist, optative). The most important differences are :

Active 1st pers. sing. *Primary -ω* (thematic), *-μι* (athematic) ; *secondary -m* (developing
                          to *-ν* after a vowel and to *-α* (⟨ṃ, see VI) after a consonant).
        2nd pers. sing. *Primary -si* (possibly *-s*, see p. 118) ; *secondary -s.*
        3rd pers. sing. *Primary -ti* (developing to *-σι* in East Greek) ; *secondary -t*
                          (which is dropped in Greek).
        3rd pers. plur. *Primary -(e/o) nti, -ṇti* (after consonant) ; *secondary -(e/o) nt,*
                          -ṇt (after consonant).

Middle 1st pers. sing. *Primary -mai* ; *secondary -mān.*
        2nd pers. sing. *Primary -sai* ; *secondary -so.*
        3rd pers. sing. *Primary -tai* ; *secondary -to.*
        3rd pers. plur. *Primary -ntai, -ṇtai* ; *secondary -nto, -ṇto.*

XIII. *Ablaut* or *vowel gradation.*—An important morphological device of IE was the alternation of vowels such as we observe, for instance, in the English *drive, drove, driven*, an alternation to which we find a counterpart in the Greek πείθω, πέποιθα, ἔπιθον. This *Ablaut*, as it is called, is found both in the nominal and in the verbal systems, *e.g.*, *a drove, a drift* ; πειθώ, πίστις (= πιθ-τις).[a] If we examine these alternations we find that one grade contains the vowel *e*, another the vowel *o*, and that in another the vowel disappears : *e.g.*, ἔχω, ὄχος, ἔ-σχ-ον (these being respectively the *e-grade*, the *o-grade*, and the *zero grade* of the root **segh*.[b] If the root contains a diphthong, then in the zero grade the second element of the diphthong becomes syllabic : *e.g.*, λείπω, λιπεῖν, κλέϝομαι, κλυτός. Where the second element of the diphthong is a sonant (*m, n, r, l*), in the zero grade the changes outlined in VI and VII take place. Thus we find the following examples of *Ablaut* :

[a] The development of two adjacent dental consonants from θτ, δθ, etc., to στ, σθ, etc., is an important sound change in Greek : note **οἶδ-θα, *ἴδ-τε, *ἴδ-θι* > οἶσθα, ἴστε, ἴσθι.

[b] The expected present tense would be **ἔχω*, but Greek does not tolerate a succession of syllables beginning with an aspirate but removes one of the breathings, usually the first. This rule is known as Grassmann's Law : thus we find θρίξ, but gen. τριχός for **θριχός*, and τρέφω for **θρέφω*, cf. θρέψω.

E-grade	O-grade	Zero-grade
ἀγείρω (*ἀγέρ-ι̯ω)	ἀγορά	ἀγρ-όμενος
(F)είκω	(F)έ(F)οικα	(F)ε(F)ίκ-την
Fείδομαι	Fοῖδα	Fίδμεν
λείπω	λέλοιπα	ἔλιπον
δέρκομαι	δέδορκα	ἔδρακ-ον (*dr̥k)
μείρομαι (*smer-ι̯omai)	μοῖρα	εἵμαρτο (‹ *se-smr̥-to [a])
πένθος	πέπονθα	ἔπαθον (*pn̥θ)
μένος	μέμονα	μεμαFώς, μέ-μα-μεν
πέρθω	πτολί-πορθος	ἔπραθον
θείνω [b]	φόνος [b]	ἔ-πε-φν-ον,[b]
		πέ-φα-νται.

Such *Ablaut* of the root is also observed within the conjugation of a verbal tense or the declension of a noun, where the vowel alternations were presumably evoked by changes in the position of the accent: εἶμι, ἴμεν for instance, is paralleled in Sanskrit by *émi, imás*, where the original accentual shift in the plural from the root to the ending can still be observed. Such a change we see, further, in Homeric perfects such as μέμονα, μέ-μα-μεν (representing the zero grade *mn̥*), πέπονθα, πέπασθε (where *πn̥θ-θε ‹ πασθε in accordance with the law enunciated above, p. 82). In the noun, too, IE exhibited similar alternations: in Sanskrit, for instance, *rājā* 'king' has its accusative singular *rājān-am* with the strong form of the stem, whereas the genitive singular and other oblique cases have *rajñ-as*, etc. with the weak form. Such an alternation we see in the Greek ἀνήρ, ἀνέρα, *ἀνρός,[c] etc. But this primitive irregularity of conjugation and declension is acted upon by a powerful solvent — analogy, a phenomenon we must now discuss.

XIV. *Analogy.*—There is a general tendency in language for words of related function to become similar in form. *Height*, for instance, becomes *heighth* because of its functional relationship with *depth*, etc. This unifying force, which is known by the somewhat vague term *analogy*, is particularly strong in producing unity within a given conjugation or declension: e.g., οἶδα, οἶσθα, ἴσμεν, ἴστε, etc. became in Hellenistic times οἶδα, οἶδας, οἴδαμεν, οἴδατε, etc. Such a unification of a conjugation or declension, which is a special instance of analogy, I shall call *integration* ('making whole'). It is well exemplified in the Homeric declension of *r*-stems such as ἀνήρ. We saw above that there are two forms of the stems ἀνερ- and ἀνρ- (ἀνδρ-), the first of which is proper to the strong cases (accusative singular and nominative plural; note that the nominative singular has the extended form), and the second to the

[a] *se-* ‹ *ἑ-* (IX), and *-sm-* produces compensating lengthening of ἑ- to εἱ- (IX B).
[b] See VIII.

[c] The -δ- in ἀνδρός is merely a glide consonant which has developed in the group -νρ-, just as English *cinder*, French *cendre*, have developed from *cin(e)rem*.

H

other oblique cases of the singular and plural (the dual we ignore for the moment). Thus the original declension was as set out in the centre columns of the following table. 'Integration' subsequently worked on this primitive declension in two ways: either the form ἀνερ- or the form ἀνρ- was generalized. Thus we find the following forms of such nouns in Homer:

	Sing.			Plur.		
N.		ἀνήρ		ἄνδρες	ἀνέρες	
V.		ἄνερ				
A.	ἄνδρα	ἀνέρα			ἄνδρας	ἀνέρας
G.		ἀνδρός	ἀνέρος		ἀνδρῶν	
D.		ἀνδρί	ἀνέρι		ἀνδράσι(ν)	

Similarly we find θυγατέρα, θυγατρός, etc., but also θύγατρα, θυγατέρος, θυγατέρι, θυγατέρες and θύγατρες, θυγατέρας and θύγατρας; πατέρος and πατρός, πατέρι and πατρί, πατέρων and πατρῶν; μητέρος and μητρός, μητέρι and μητρί. The dative plurals such as πατράσι, etc. are legitimate descendants of IE *patr̥si; for the new Aeolic dative plurals in -εσσι (θυγατέρ-εσσι) see below (p. 85 f.).

ii. THE GREEK DIALECTS

In post-Mycenaean Greece the political disunity was matched by a linguistic fragmentation, for each state used in its public documents a language which reflects more or less faithfully the local dialect. Yet this multiplicity of dialects falls clearly into three or four major groups. (See the map, fig. 1.)

(1) Attic-Ionic, as the name implies, comprises the dialects spoken in Attica (and the adjoining Euboea) together with those of the Ionic colonies situated on the southern half of the western seaboard of Asia Minor and certain of the intervening islands.

(2) Aeolic, which includes the dialects spoken in Boeotia and Thessaly (both of which are strongly coloured by intrusive West Greek elements) and in a purer form the dialect of Lesbos with an adjacent strip of the Asiatic mainland.

(3) Arcado-Cypriot, this being the name given to the presumed ancestral form which it is necessary to postulate to account for the virtual identity of the dialects of Arcadia and Cyprus in post-Mycenaean times.

(4) West Greek, which embraces the so-called North-west Greek dialects of Aetolia, Phocis, and Locris, with Elean as a bridge dialect leading to the Doric dialects used in the Peloponnese (with the exception of Arcadia) and in a southerly band of islands including Crete and Rhodes. We should add the western colonies in Sicily and Magna Graecia.

This last group played no part in the formation of the Epic dialect, and it will not be further described. We shall therefore confine ourselves to an examination of the so-called East Greek dialect group, which comprises the first three of the above groups, and note merely one important division between East and West: τι is preserved in all the West Greek dialects but it becomes σι in East Greek so that a Doric δίδωτι contrasts with an East Greek δίδωσι. The importance of this dialect boundary ('isogloss') has been recently impugned (but see below, p. 88 ff.).

THE CHARACTERISTICS OF ATTIC–IONIC

1. ᾱ ⟩ η : δῆμος (see I).
2. No other dialects have the movable euphonic -ν-: ἔλυσε(ν), etc.
3. Prepositions are not apocopized (see p. 140) : thus always κατά, never κάτ.
4. The athematic infinitive ends in -ναι (see XI).
5. The secondary ending of the 3rd plur. such as in ἔθε-ν appears as ἔθε-σαν (see p. 119).
6. The 'potential' particle is ἄν, whereas Aeolic has κε and West Greek κᾱ.

Ionic is distinguished from Attic by :
1. The complete change of ᾱ ⟩ η : χώρη (see I).
2. The absence of contraction in -εα, -εο, and -εω (see II).
3. The treatment of -νϝ-: ξεῖνος as opposed to ξένος (see V).
4. -εω in the gen. sing. of masculine A-nouns (see III).
5. -εων in the gen. plur. of A-nouns : πυλέων.[a]
6. The analogical genitives βασίλεος for βασιλέως (by quantitative metathesis from βασιλῆος : see III).
7. ἤν = Attic ἐάν, ἄν.

THE CHARACTERISTICS OF AEOLIC

1. The labio-velars appear as labials even before front vowels (see VIII) : thus πέμπε = Attic πέντε (⟨ *penqʷe).
2. The doubling of consonants as opposed to Attic-Ionic lengthening of vowels in ἐμμί, ἀργεννός, etc. (see IX B).
3. The patronymic adjective is used instead of the genitive of the father's name : Τελαμώνιος for (Αἴας) Τελαμῶνος.
4. ἴα for μία.
5. The dative plural of the third declension ends in -εσσι, a form of the inflection which originated in neuter s-stems such as ἔπεσ-σι :

---

[a] This represents a shortening of -ηων (⟨ -ᾱων).

and was thence transferred to other stems such as ἄνδρεσσι, πολίεσσι, etc.

6. -σσ-, both original (as in ἐτέλεσ-σα, etc.) and the product of *τi̯, *θi̯, -δσ-, etc. (ὅσσος, μέσσος, ἐκόμισσα), is retained whereas Attic simplified to -σ-. Thus the following forms in Homer may be considered Aeolic: ἐτέλεσσα, ζέσσε, ἔσσεται, ὅσσος, δάσσασθαι, etc.

7. The athematic infinitive ends in -μεναι, -μεν: ἔμμεναι, δόμεν, etc. (see XI C).

8. The perfect participle active has the endings of the present participle: ἐληλύθων, -οντος.

9. The potential particle is κε.

10. The -μι inflection of contracted verbs: φίλημι.

THE CHARACTERISTICS OF ARCADO-CYPRIOT

1. The final o has a tendency to be raised to υ so that, for instance, the genitive singular in -αο appears as -αυ, and verbal forms in -το as -τυ.

2. The preposition-adverb corresponding to πρός is πός (a different word !).

3. κάς instead of καί.

4. σίς for τίς (from *qʷis).

5. The dative case after prepositions meaning 'from' such as ἀπό, ἐξ, etc.

THE INTERRELATIONSHIPS OF THE GREEK DIALECTS

The map (fig. 1) reveals a peculiar fact of linguistic distribution. The dialect spoken in Arcadia, the mountainous centre of the Peloponnese, although it is practically identical with that of Cyprus, the most easterly outpost of Greek speech until the Hellenistic expansion, is completely surrounded by regions of Dorian dialects. From this fact philologists long ago drew the conclusion that dialects of Arcadian type had once extended to the coast of the Peloponnese, whence colonists had sailed to Cyprus before the coming of the Dorians. These were later intruders who conquered most of the Peloponnese, isolating the pre-Dorian Greeks in their mountain fastness. In other words it was maintained that beneath the Dorian of the Peloponnese there underlay a substratum of Arcado-Cypriot.

This conclusion has been confirmed by the discovery and decipherment of tablets in the Linear B script at Pylos and Mycenae, to say nothing of those from Cretan Knossos which are believed to date from the fifteenth

century. The dialect revealed by the great work of the late Dr. Michael
Ventris shows most of the main characteristics of the postulated Arcado-
Cypriot. Most remarkable are the primary middle endings in *-to* such
as *e-u-ke-to* (= εὔχετοι), which is co-ordinated with *e-ke* (= ἔχει), and
the datival construction after 'from' prepositions such as *pa-ro* (= παρό).

As we should expect in texts of such early date, there are archaisms
which no longer appear in the Arcadian and Cypriot texts, which are

FIG. 1. Language-map of the Aegean in classical times

some eight hundred years later. We may single out the genitive singular
in *-o-jo* (later found in Lesbian and the Homeric dialect) and the instru-
mental-locative (and ablative ?) case forms in *-pi* (= -φι, see pp. 106, 107).

Before proceeding to evaluate the new evidence it will be well to
clarify a point of principle. Arcado-Cypriot is merely the name given
to a group of linguistic features common to the dialects of post-Mycenaean
Arcadia and Cyprus : these are so peculiar that the resemblances are most
plausibly accounted for by ascription to some ancestral linguistic community from which they are both descended. But this does not imply
a completely uniform language in the Mycenaean Peloponnese. In other
words a common physiognomy does not exclude individual differences

of features. In fact the documents of Arcadia and Cyprus show local differentiations. There is evidence both for ἄν (ἀνά) and ὄν (ὔν). In Tegea and Mantinea the labio-velars are represented by (ṣ), elsewhere by τ. The infinitives at Tegea end in -εν, at Lycosoura in -ην (*-εεν). Thus we may expect to find in the Mycenaean inscriptions forms which are different from Arcado-Cypriot not because they are more archaic, but because they represent a variety of Mycenaean in some respects different from the dialect(s) of which Arcadian and Cypriot are the later descendants. Thus both these dialects show nominatives of the type ἱερής and this resemblance is too peculiar to be attributed to independent development after their separation. Yet the Linear B tablets show consistently many examples of the type ἱερεύς. Other examples of considerable importance for assessing the affinities of Mycenaean (cf. the treatment of the labio-velars, the name Ποσειδάων, the verb βούλομαι) will be discussed below.

Scholars have long pointed out that Arcado-Cypriot has certain striking similarities to Aeolic. These are the prepositions ἀπύ and ὄν, the tendency for the vowel o instead of a to appear in the reflections of the sonant liquids and nasals (so that for instance ṛ appears as oρ instead of the Attic-Ionic αρ/ρα), and the conjugation of contracted verbs as athematic (type example φίλημι).

Now the new Mycenaean evidence has confirmed the preposition ἀπύ and shown conclusively that this is not to be explained as a mere phonetic development of ἀπό, but, as many scholars had asserted, that it is a separate word compounded of ἀπ+υ (the latter adverbial prefix being attested as it happens for Cypriot and Mycenaean) whereas the second element of ἀπό is the adverb ὀ (found in ὀ-κέλλω, ὀ-τρύνω, etc.).

Linear B words of the type to-pe-za (τόρπεζα) again show that the distinctive differentiation from Attic-Ionic τράπεζα had already taken place by Mycenaean times.

From these 'notable points of agreement between Arcado-Cyprian and Aeolic . . . which cannot be accidental' Buck concluded, 'it is probable that the connections with Aeolic reflect a remote period of geographical contiguity with Aeolic peoples in northern Greece or even before the migration into Greece'.

Recently, however, this analysis and conclusion have been impugned and attempts have been made to bring Mycenaean and Arcado-Cypriot into close relationship with Attic-Ionic: these dialects, it is suggested, formed a South-Greek unity separate from proto-Aeolic, this unity representing the parent language from which the later Attic-Ionic has evolved. This new hypothesis, however, runs foul of certain facts.

In the first place we have in Arcado-Cypriot a very remarkable syntactical innovation: 'from' prepositions like ἀπύ, quite contrary to inherited case usage, take the dative instead of the genitive. Because both Arcadian and Cypriot show this feature it was safe to conclude that it characterized the dialect of the Peloponnese at the time when the Cyprian colonists left its shores. The Linear B tablets give evidence of the same construction. Thus this dialect had already diverged from the more conservative Attic-Ionic by the thirteenth century.

Nor can we derive an Attic-Ionic preposition ἀπό from the 'South Greek' ἀπύ. We may add the evidence of another preposition. Arcado-Cypriot shows πός against the Attic-Ionic πρός. Mycenaean offers po-si. Some confusion of thought has arisen in the assessment of this phenomenon. It must be emphasized that πός contains a different word stem from πρός. Each is extended by the endings -ς or -τι so that the Greek dialect map offers us four different words for 'towards': πός, ποτί: πρός, προτί (see C. D. Buck, Greek Dialects ³, p. 107 f.).ᵃ The primary division is one of vocabulary, that is into regions which use the word πο- and those which use προ-. In this respect, too, Arcado-Cypriot and Attic-Ionic belong to different linguistic worlds; it is not correct to classify them together on the basis of the final -ς of πός and πρός and to ignore altogether the Mycenaean form ποσί.

There is one morphological characteristic which separates Arcado-Cypriot from the rest of the Greek dialects: this is the primary middle endings -τοι, -ντοι (type example λύετοι). We have seen that this again is a mark of the Mycenaean dialect. Thus the new hypothesis can be saved only by the assumption that Arcado-Cypriot, so far from innovating, is the only linguistic community in the whole Indo-European world to have preserved the original endings of the parent language. Yet if we send our dialect field workers into every nook and cranny of the Hellenic world, from Aetolia to Lesbos and from Tarentum to Rhodes, we shall find that all communities except the Arcado-Cypriot say λύεται and not λύετοι. If the latter is the archaism, then the remarkable common innovation observed in all the other Greek dialects, if we are to be true to our principles, must be taken as evidence for a one-time linguistic unity from which only the speakers of Arcado-Cypriot were excluded. In other words we are driven to the conclusion of a unity embracing West Greeks, Aeolians, and Ionians. The proponents of the new theory have shrunk from this conclusion and attempt to save the hypothesis by the assumption that the innovation -ται first arose among the West Greeks before the Dorian migration, and was imposed by them on the Aeolians

---

ᵃ Homer shows πρός, προτί, and ποτί. The last occurs in Thessalian and Boeotian but it is shared with all the West Greek dialects (except Cretan πορτί). Homeric ποτί with unassibilated -τι (a characteristic of West Greek) is puzzling: perhaps it conceals ποσί, which was changed to the more familiar ποτί when it had disappeared from the spoken dialects.

and Ionians before their respective migrations eastwards across the Aegean, but after the proto-Ionians had become separated from their South-Greek linguistic kinsmen. Thus the proto-Ionians of Attica, who repulsed the Dorians, succumbed to West Greek influence in this point alone. The new hypothesis is thus driven to the conclusion that the only Greeks who resisted the all-powerful West Greeks in this respect were the Arcadians, who were completely surrounded by them. This may rank as a classic example of an *ad hoc* saving hypothesis. It would be wise in such delicate matters of interpretation to be guided by the scientific principle of economy of hypotheses. We should not disregard the overwhelming weight of testimony for the primacy of the endings -ται, -νται. The Arcado-Cypriot -τοι is most simply regarded as an Arcado-Cypriot innovation of structural origin : it was formed simply by adding -ι, the mark of the primary endings, to the secondary -το just as in the active primary -ει contrasts with secondary -ε. This, the old explanation, is linguistically plausible and does not involve any further saving hypotheses so historically improbable as that just criticized. But as we have seen, Mycenaean exhibits this important morphological innovation. In this respect, too, the linguistic gulf between Arcado-Cypriot and the rest of the Greek world was already in existence by the thirteenth century.

With this in mind we may reconsider another important dialect boundary or 'isogloss'. It will be recalled that in Hellenic times the West Greek, Aeolic, and Ionic (Attic) areas are clearly differentiated by κα, κε, and ἄν respectively. Arcado-Cypriot again presents a problem. The island colony, isolated and likely to preserve archaisms, has κε, but Arcadian uses ἄν. But as Buck writes (134.2a) 'Arcadian once had κε like Cyprian and a relic of this is to be seen in the κ' which appears where there would be otherwise hiatus between εἰ and a following ἄν, which had regularly replaced κε as a significant element'. Buck is referring to such examples as εἰκ ἄν διελαυνόμενα τύχη (Tegea), where it is arbitrary to divide thus rather than εἰ καν. Thus the Arcado-Cypriot evidence for these particles is best listed as Cypriot κε, Arcadian (κ)αν.

The discussion of the interrelationships of these different particles has been obscured by the intrusion of etymological fantasies. ἄν has been identified with the *an* of Latin and Gothic, neither of which is used as a potential particle. This identification implies that an Indo-European *an* of unknown function persisted through the common proto-Greek period and was preserved solely by the speakers of Attic-Ionic and Arcadian (not Cypriot !), who employed it to differentiate the prospective subjunctive and the potential optative, whereas the other groups of Greeks, though making essentially the same syntactical differentiation (this is the essential common feature of all the Greek dialects), used another word. Such procedure violates the first law of etymology, which has been phrased 'Look for Latin etymologies first on the Tiber'. It will therefore be wise not to approach the question of origin until the facts have been accurately observed.

The geographical distribution is as follows:

West Greek		Aeolic	
κᾱ		κε	
		Attic-Ionic	
		ἄν	
Arcadian			Cypriot
(κ)αν			κε

We must now add the evidence of the Homeric poems. Here we find two particles of identical function κεν and ἄν, the former being three to four times more frequent than the latter. Important is the observation that 'in negative clauses there is a marked preference for ἄν'. This last is a fact of great importance: any explanation must account for this peculiar distribution.

In pursuance of the above principle I propose to attempt an explanation[a] which eschews appeal to facts outside Greek and accounts for all the known Greek facts including the distribution of ἄν in our earliest literary text. I find the origin of the potential particle in the well-known demonstrative stem κε-. The full form κεν has an adverbial formant -ν of vocative function: κεν means accordingly 'in this case'. The example of the Latin si, which goes back to the Old Latin sei, the locative case of the demonstrative stem so-, immediately occurs as a parallel. This particle could occur in both parts of correlated sentences, one containing the full form κεν and the other the reduced form κη̥ (cf. the Thessalian μέν : μά, the latter from μη̥). Now the reduced form would appear in Greek as κα before consonants and καν before vowels. This gives us the forms κεν : κα, καν. From these possibilities the various Greek dialects generalized one or the other. There is evidence, as we have seen, in Arcadian for καν.[b] As for the Aeolic κε, there are two possibilities. It is either the pure demonstrative stem without the adverbial -ν or (this I prefer) the opposition κεν : κα was levelled analogically to κεν : κε. There remains the Attic-Ionic ἄν. Here we neglect at our peril the distributional facts relating to its occurrence after the negative. I propose to account for these facts by the hypothesis that an original οὐ κάν τις (with the ante-vocalic form) was falsely divided as οὐκ ἄν τις. An immediate parallel for this is available in the emergence of the Latin ubi from *cubi (as in alicubi) through the false division of si cubi. The accentuation of

[a] An almost identical explanation has now been published by Miss K. Forbes in Glotta, 37 (1958), 179 ff.

[b] West Greek κᾱ is an adverbial form of the type ταυτᾶ (also found in West Greek). The meaning is basically 'in this case'.

the Attic-Ionic ἄν is secondary and due to the frequent occurrence of the phrases οὐ κάν τις, οὐ κάν τι, etc.

This explanation may claim preference over the current one because (1) it appeals solely to Greek facts; (2) it brings the facts of Arcadian and Cyprian into harmony without the *ad hoc* hypothesis that κε in Cypriot is an Aeolic 'borrowing'; (3) it releases the Attic-Ionic group from its strange isolation from the other Greek dialects and its attachment to Latin and Gothic, and also explains the affinity of ἄν for the negative; (4) it accounts for the function diagnosed as 'in this case'.

Certain important consequences flow from this. Cypriot (and presumably Arcadian) is brought once again into significant relationship with Aeolic. ἄν is revealed as an extraordinary innovation of Attic-Ionic, and there is nothing which implies that this is in any way 'recent'. It sets another severe obstacle in the way of those who urge that Attic-Ionic has evolved from a South Greek close to the language revealed in the Linear B tablets and the later Arcado-Cypriot.

Now that the bonds connecting the dialect of the Mycenaean Peloponnese with Aeolic have been reaffirmed, we may add a few more details the effect of which will be accumulative. The Pylian documents show a verb *te-re-ja* 3rd pers. sing. present corresponding to an infinitive *te-re-ja-e*. The meaning of the root is uncertain but the morphology is explicable only by postulating an unthematic vowel-stem verb. This is, in fact, the proposal also of Ventris and Chadwick. Accepting this as a fact of the dialect of Mycenaean Pylos, we search for parallels. The only Greek dialect of post-Mycenaean times which thus conjugates unthematic vowel stems is Lesbian. Buck writes (155.3): 'In Lesbian the present infinitive of unthematic vowel stems . . . ends in -ν not -μεναι, e.g., δίδων, κέρναν . . .'. Evidently this important point of morphology must be added to the Arcado-Cypriot and Aeolic links.

In Aeolic, as we have seen, the labio-velars are represented by labials even before front vowels. The position of Arcado-Cypriot is again confused. In certain words a sibilant appears (Arcadian σίς and Cypriot σίς). But Cypriot also has the form πείσει which has been explained away as an analogical formation. The Linear B script has a special series for the labio-velars, but their phonetic value is unknown. All we can say is that they were still phonemically distinct from the labial and dental series. There are, however, a few spelling alternations which suggest that the changes of the labio-velars are in the direction of the labials: *qe-re-qo-ta* / *pe-re-qo-ta*, *o-pe-pa₂* / *o-qe-pa₂*, *i-po-po-qo-i* / *i-qo*. This again would lend support to the view that the Mycenaean dialect revealed in the Linear B texts had somewhat closer affinities to Aeolic than either Arcadian or Cypriot.

Further evidence points in the same direction. Thus a phrase *e-re-*[·]

qe-ro-me-no is most plausibly interpreted as ἐρέεν gʷέλομενοι 'willing to row'. βέλλομαι is the form of this verb attested for Thessalian whereas Arcadian, Cypriot and Lesbian all show the vowel -*o*- in this verb, as does Attic-Ionic. Again the feminine nouns of the ā-declension have a dual in -*o* : *to-pe-za* 'table(s)', *to-pe-zo* 'two tables'. The only parallel for this in later texts is the Hesiodic καλυψαμένω, and Hesiod is a Boeotian poet. So this fact may be allowed to add its little weight to the thesis we are propounding.

The word transcribed conventionally *su-za* is now generally agreed to stand for συκίαι 'fig trees', the zeta series of the Linear B script standing in reality for palatalized plosives. Ionic, the alleged close kinsman of this dialect, shows συκέη and more frequently the contracted form συκῆ. Once again we find an echo in Aeolic : συκία is quoted from an inscription of Mytilene. Finally *to-so-ne* appears to be a demonstrative the only exact counterpart of which is to be found in the Thessalian ὄνε although Arcadian offers ὀνί and Cypriot ὄνυ.[a]

Thus the evidence taken point by point is overwhelmingly in favour of the old established view that Aeolic and Arcado-Cypriot (add now the new Mycenaean evidence) are members of a larger unity to which the name 'Achaean' has been given. These linguistic affinities should not be ignored in attempts to reconstruct Greek settlement history. But if the interrelationships of the Greek dialects continue to be used for this purpose, one may insist on a fact which will affect the time-scale involved. The differences between the Greek dialects are comparatively trivial and no great length of time need be allowed for their differentiation. As Professor E. Risch has reminded us, in medieval times there was no Swiss German patois which was clearly differentiated from Swabian and Alsatian. Thus it would be ample to allow a few centuries for the Greek dialects to reach the state of differentiation observed. The linguistic evidence does not justify the old hypothesis of three distinct waves of Greeks. Nor is there any need to go so far back as the Middle Helladic invasion of *c.* 1900 B.C. to account for the dialectal distinctness of proto-Ionic. If then we may take this as a minimum hypothesis to account for the essential 'Greekness' of all the Greek dialects, it is worth while, within this framework of a single invasion of Greek-speaking tribes, making the attempt to translate these shifting patterns of dialect resemblances into the realities of settlement history and migration. In the first place one must beware of attributing a monolith 'unity' to proto-Achaean or proto-Aeolic. Once again we insist that these terms are simply the names which philologists bestow on a given group of linguistic features whose distribution in the observed dialects is best explained by attribution to an ancestral linguistic community. But this postulated community doubtless

[a] τόν(νε) is now quotable from Cypriot (see T. B. Mitford in *Minos*, vi (1958), 40).

showed dialect differentiation which may be mirrored in the descendant dialects.   Thus the 'proto-Achaean' which some philologists have postulated to account for the striking resemblances between Arcado-Cypriot and Aeolic may have comprised a number of sub-groups settled, shall we say, in Thessaly and Boeotia.   The settlement of the Peloponnese may have originated in the south part of this region and the settlers in question would then have been close neighbours of the Mycenaeans of Attica.   But the pattern of dialect resemblances analysed above implies that they were more closely linked with the speakers of proto-Aeolic. The exclusive dialect peculiarities of Arcado-Cypriot were developed after the settlement of the Peloponnese.   As we can now see, the Linear B inscriptions give us a terminus *ante quem*.

iii. TRADITION AND CORRUPTION

Before venturing on an analysis of the Homeric dialect in the light of the above criteria we must first consider the state of the text which is the source of our knowledge of this dialect.   This is discussed more fully in Chapter 6, and we need do no more than recall that the text contained in our best manuscript, Venetus A, goes back in the last instance to editions compiled by Alexandrian scholars.   Metrical study, however, combined with linguistic analysis has made it evident that this Alexandrian text contains many forms which must be regarded as modernizations or corruptions of the original.

In A 344, for instance, an optative plural μαχέοιντο is read.   But an ending -οιντο is attested only for Attic, and even in this dialect it is a comparatively late innovation which competes with the original -οιατο throughout the fifth century.   Consequently, unless we are prepared to say that the passage in which this form stands was inserted by a hand which, even if not Attic, was at least exposed to Attic influence, we must deny this form of the optative a place in Homeric grammar and adopt the emendation μαχεοίατ' or μαχεόνται.   Late, too, is ἧντο for original ἥατο.[a]   Another questionable optative form is σταίησαν, which is read in P 732 (ὅτε . . . σταίησαν).   This is the only Homeric example of an optative 3rd pers. plur. in -ιησαν, a type which, further, is rare even in post-Homeric Greek.   Moreover, in this passage there is no suggestion of repeated action, so that the optative is also suspect on syntactical grounds. There can be little doubt, therefore, that the correct reading is ἔστησαν or some equivalent form.   We may further view with suspicion the optatives φοροίη (ι 320) and φιλοίη (δ 692), for this type of optative formation in contracted verbs is peculiar to Attic, even the closely related

[a] On this inflexion see p. 120.

Ionic having the normal φορέοι, etc. In Aeolic, however, as we saw, contracted verbs are conjugated according to the athematic type (φίλημι), and Homer actually exhibits the athematic infinitive φορήμεναι. This being so, it is probable that the authentic forms were *φορείη, *φιλείη, which were Atticized in the tradition to φοροίη, φιλοίη.

Our text, further, contains two forms of the genitive of o-nouns: -οιο and -ου. The authenticity of the latter is guaranteed *inter alia* by readings such as παρὰ μηροῦ at the end of the verse. It is possible, however, to produce evidence for the attribution of yet a third form of the inflexion to the Homeric language. Some verses will scan only if we resolve -ου into the -οο from which it must have been contracted: *e.g.*, in βῆν εἰς Αἰόλου κλυτὰ δώματα, κ 60, the impossible cretic Αἰόλου is removed if we read Αἰόλοο. Sometimes this false intrusion of the contraction -ου into the text brings about consequential alterations. Well-known examples of this are ἐπιδημίου ὀκρυόεντος, I 64, and κακομηχάνου ὀκρυοέσσης, Z 344, where a false division of words, due to misunderstanding of ΕΠΙΔΕΜΙΟΟ, etc., resulted in the distortion of κρυόεντος to ὀκρυόεντος. The correct readings are, therefore, κακομηχάνοο and ἐπιδημίοο. ἀδελφειοῦ κταμένοιο, again, may be due to false interpretation of a reading ΑΔΕΛΦΕΟ ΚΤΑΜΕΝΟΙΟ, the correct rendering of which is ἀδελφεόο κταμένοιο. In the same way ὄου κλέος in B 325 (*cf.* α 70) should be altered to ὄο; but it is noteworthy that on the analogy of οὗ : ὄου an entirely artificial ἔης was extracted from ἧς. We have thus no fewer than three forms of the genitive singular of o-nouns, -οιο, -οο, and -ου, which represent a chronological series [a] and constitute a valuable indication of the different linguistic strata which may be detected in the Homeric language.

A further distortion which the tradition brought about in the Homeric language is the so-called epic diectasis ('distension'). In -αω verbs forms such as ὁράεις, ὁράει, ὁράοντες, ὁράεσθαι were in Attic contracted to ὁρᾷς, ὁρᾷ, ὁρῶντες, ὁρᾶσθαι. As long as the verse was merely recited and not committed to writing, the rhapsodists could make a concession to contemporary pronunciation without disturbance to the metre merely by distributing the contracted vowels -ᾳ- and -ω- over two syllables. When, however, the poems came to be written down, metrical integrity was formally established by writing ὁράᾳς, ὁράᾳ, ὁράασθαι, ὁρόωντες.[b] Precisely similar is the case of φόως, which represents a re-expansion of φῶς, the contraction of φάϜος. There can be little doubt that the open

---

[a] Improbable is the view that -οο is different in origin from -οιο, deriving from an inflexion *-οσο. Arcado-Cypriot has -ō (with some examples of -ōν in Cypriot), but Mycenaean shows -οιο.

[b] There is less probability in the theory that -ααι and -οω represent an assimilation of the two vowels as a preliminary to the later contraction.

forms were proper to the language in which the epics were composed, but whether these open forms represent Aeolic elements in the dialect or whether they were also features of an earlier Attic-Ionic it is impossible to say in view of the comparatively late date of the inscriptional evidence available to us.

The traditional text underwent a further distortion during the so-called μεταγραμματισμός. Greek had inherited from Indo-European two e sounds: the short ε of ἐστί and the long η of ἔθηκα, the latter being a more open sound roughly equivalent to the vowel of the English *dare*. Both these sounds appeared as the first components of diphthongs: ει and ηι. The same is true of the o sounds. Greek distinguished the short o from the more open ω. In the early alphabets, however, no distinction was made between the short and long vowels, E or O serving respectively for both varieties. The Ionic alphabet, however, which was later adopted in Athens and elsewhere, contained distinct signs for the long vowels: H and Ω. A further refinement was the use of the diagraph EI to represent the long ε. This was a new sound in Greek and had arisen from the contraction of εε in hiatus (as in ἐλύει for ἐλύεε) or from the compensatory lengthening of an ε (as in εἰμί for *ἐσ-μί). This long ē had a more closed pronunciation than the original inherited long ē: it was much like the first element of the diphthong in English *day*. The use of the digraph ει arose in the following way. EI was first used to indicate the diphthong ε+ι, but in Ionic pronunciation this developed to a long vowel with a quality much as in the Scottish pronunciation of *day* as [de :]. An exactly parallel development brought about the use of the digraph ου for the long closed vowel ō (as in English *bone*) which was eventually raised to [u:] (as in *boon*).

We now attempt to envisage the difficulties faced by scribes who had the task of transcribing texts written in the older alphabet where ε and o each represented three distinct sounds. Their problem was essentially where to substitute H or EI and Ω or OΥ.

The scribes experienced no difficulty as long as they could get guidance from their contemporary spoken language. When, however, they were faced with words and forms not contained in their spoken dialect, they often experienced embarrassment in deciding whether Ē should be EI or H and whether Ō should be transcribed as OΥ or Ω. In η 107, for instance, our texts read καιροσέων δ' ὀθονέων. But the adjective 'closely-woven' is a derivative of καῖρος 'row of thrums on the loom', so that the correct spelling is καιρουσσέων (with synizesis of -εων). Faced with an unfamiliar form ΚΑΙΡΟΣΕΟΝ (we have a parallel to the archaic spelling in the Miletan ΤΕΙΧΙΟΣΗΣ) the scribe was misled by the metre into construing the first foot as a dactyl and marking ΟΣ as a short syllable, so that he wrote καιροσέων. Another misunderstood form was

ΘΕΟΔΕΣ, which must be scanned ‿ – –, where the length of the second syllable is due to the original digamma (see below) in θεοδϜεής. In ignorance of this fact the scribes expressed the length of the syllable by writing ου for ο, so that we find θεουδής. On the other hand in ἔδ(Ϝ)εισεν the length of the first syllable found expression in a doubling of the consonant — ἔδδεισεν, with which contrast δείδιμεν for δέδ(Ϝ)ιμεν. Still more remarkable is the apparent present form δείδω which conceals δέδϜω, this being the contracted form of δέδϜοα which goes back to δέ-δϜοι-α, the regular perfect of the root *dwei* on the pattern of λέ-λοιπ-α as the perfect of the root λειπ-. The morphological transparency has been obscured first by the loss of intervocalic -ι̯- and then, much later, by loss of digamma and vowel contraction in Ionic.

Similar misinterpretations occur where quantitative metathesis (III) made the later forms unmetrical. Thus ἦος (from ἆος) may stand at the beginning of a verse, whereas the later ἕως is impossible. Consequently where the metre demanded length of the first syllable in ΕΟΣ, this was represented as εἵως before a consonant, where positional length of the second syllable permitted a transcription of Ο as ω, and εἷος before a vowel: e.g., εἵως Πηνελόπειαν, δ 800, εἷος ἐγώ, δ 90. Precisely similar misrepresentations affected subjunctives such as θήομεν, στήομεν, which in later times were transformed by quantitative metathesis to θέωμεν, στέωμεν, etc. Here, too, scribes interpreted ΕΟ as -ειο-, so that forms like θείομεν and στείομεν for long disfigured Homeric grammars.[a] By such spellings ει and ου the later editors also expressed purely metrical lengthenings such as εἰν and οὔνομα, where there was no historical reason for the long syllable. The substitution of ει for ε and ου for ο was facilitated by the fact that an Ionic ξεῖνος (from ξένϜος) and μοῦνος (from μόνϜος) corresponded to Attic ξένος and μόνος (see V).

iv. THE CONSTITUTION OF THE HOMERIC DIALECT

After this preliminary sifting of the linguistic facts presented in our text of Homer, we shall now proceed to ascertain the dialect constituents of the Homeric language in the light of the criteria enumerated above. At first sight the treatment of the ᾱ reveals that the dialect is basically Ionic, an impression which is confirmed by the presence of all the characteristic features of this dialect noted above. But we may establish, further, the presence of certain unmistakably Aeolic features:

1. πίσυρες, πελώριον, πέλομαι, etc. (with π from qᵘ, see p. 79 above).

[a] Note that this false diphthong in θείομεν, etc., is only found before α, ο, and ω. This may well be a reflection of the widespread tendency throughout the history of Greek to raise a front vowel in hiatus before a back vowel.

2. ἄμμε, ὔμμε, ἄργεννος, etc. (see IX B, C).
3. Datives in -εσσι.
4. A perfect participle κεκλήγοντες (there are further certain artificial forms in -ῶτας, etc., which may conceal earlier -όντας, etc.).
5. Infinitives in -μεναι, -μεν.
6. Patronymics such as Τελαμώνιος Αἴας.
7. Apocope of prepositions (see p. 140).
8. Third person plurals such as ἤγερθεν for ἠγέρθη-σαν.
9. Athematic conjugation of contracted verbs (φορήμεναι).

The ancient authors, too, had already characterized Homer's language as mixed: οὐ μόνον ἐξὸν αὐτῷ τὰς ἄλλας γλώττας μιγνύειν τὰς τῶν Ἑλλήνων καὶ ποτὲ μὲν αἰολίζειν ποτὲ δὲ δωρίζειν, ποτὲ δὲ ἰάζειν ἀλλὰ καὶ διαστὶ διαλέγεσθαι (Dio Chrys. Or. xi. 13). With the *caveat* that there is no trace of Doric, to say nothing of the 'language of Zeus', we may now pose the problem how this dialect mixture in Homer's language came about.

We can at once rule out the suggestion that such a mixed dialect represents the spoken language of any historical Greek community. It is true that we have evidence of a northward advance of the Ionians and their occupation of originally Aeolic towns such as Smyrna. It is true, further, that the dialect inscriptions of Chios exhibit Lesbian features such as πρήξοισι for πρήξουσι. The dialects of Boeotia and Thessaly, too, are a remarkable compound of West Greek and Aeolic elements. But for the type of mixture we observe in the Homeric poems we can produce no parallel in a spoken language. Indeed it is difficult to believe that a living dialect possessed at one time so many genitive singulars for a single noun type as -οιο, -οο, and -ου, so many different forms of the personal pronouns as ὔμμε, ὑμέας, ὑμᾶς, etc.; or that it could use a form ἐλέλιχθεν in one sentence and ἐλελίχθησαν in the next. The very first line of the *Iliad* contains the name Πηληϊάδεω, where we have a form with the specifically quantitative metathesis,[a] followed by 'Αχιλῆος, where this change has not taken place. A similar collocation of different forms is to be observed in πολυφλοίσβοιο (Aeolic) θαλάσσης (Ionic); so, too, we find κύνεσσιν in l. 4 but πᾶσι in l. 5; ἀγορήνδε (Ionic) καλέσσατο λαόν (Aeolic) in l. 54. In the speech of Achilles (ll. 59 ff.) there occur the Aeolicisms ἄμμε, κε, ἱερῆα, τόσσον, but he ends with the Ionic infinitive ἀμῦναι. The speech of Calchas (ll. 74 ff.) contains the Aeolicisms ἑκατη-βελέταο, ὄμοσσον, χολωσέμεν, τελέσσῃ, but also the Ionic forms ἔπεσι and χερσίν. στήθεσσιν (l. 83) deserves a special note. The form of the dative is, of course, Aeolic, but the ν-ephelkustikon 'is a marked characteristic of Attic-Ionic, where it appears from the earliest inscriptions

[a] In the genitive ending: -āο⟩ -ηο⟩ -εω.

on with increasing frequency and before both vowels and consonants.
. . . Only in the dative plural does it appear in other dialects and even
here only in Thessalian (χρέμασι) and Heraclean' (Buck, *Greek Dialects*²,
78). Moveable -ν, then, is a specifically Attic-Ionic characteristic, so
that within the single word στήθεσσιν we may establish different dialect
elements. The artificiality of the language of the poems could hardly
be exemplified in a more striking way.

Certain scholars have questioned the validity of the evidence of such
forms as Ἀχιλλῆος, ἱκέταο, λαόν, πολέμοιο, etc. They hold that the
Ionic of the Homeric poems goes back to a much earlier date than that of
our earliest attested inscriptions, so that -οιο, for instance, the ancestor of
the later -οο and -ου, may have existed in primitive Ionic and not necessarily be a specifically Aeolic feature. Similarly ἱκέταο may, according
to this view, be Ionic of a date before the change of ᾱ ⟩ η and the quantitative metathesis of ηο ⟩ εω.[a] Monro even questioned whether -εσσι was
a mark only of Aeolic. He pointed out that such datives are found not
only in Aeolic but also in certain West Greek dialects and concluded that
there was a general tendency towards these forms, so that the dialect of
Homer may have shared in this tendency without being thereby proved
to be non-Ionic. The occurrence of -εσσι in the Peloponnese and elsewhere is, however, in itself no evidence of a general tendency: for there
is general agreement to-day that an 'Achaean' substratum underlies the
Doric dialects of that region (see above). We may conclude, therefore,
that even when we make the fullest concessions to the archaists, there
still remains a stubborn core of forms which find their parallel only in
the Aeolic dialects of historical times. Such are the specifically Aeolic
innovations like the datives in -εσσι, the perfect participle in -ων and the
-μι conjugation of contracted verbs (φορήμεναι). There is no evidence
for their occurrence in the Ionic dialects.

August Fick, in an attempt to explain the indubitable dialect mixture
in Homer, put forward the theory that the poems were originally composed in Aeolic and subsequently translated into Ionic; whereby the
Aeolic forms were left standing if they were not metrically equivalent
to the corresponding Ionic forms. Apart from the linguistic evidence,
he pointed out that the story of the *Iliad* revolves round an Aeolic hero,
Achilles from Phthia in Thessaly, and that the very Ionic regions with
which tradition connected Homer were adjacent to Aeolic territory,
while Smyrna had actually at one time been an Aeolic city before its
capture by the Ionians. The theory, however, fails to fit the facts in two
ways: there are Aeolicisms such as πέλομαι, ἄμμιν, which could easily

---

[a] 'Ionic' is the name given to a dialect with certain enumerated characteristics. If we
go back far enough and strip off these identification marks, then the term 'Ionic' ceases
to have linguistic significance.

I

be turned into the corresponding Ionic forms (ἧμιν before a vowel, ἡμῖν before a consonant), while many Ionicisms occur which are not metrically equivalent to the Aeolic forms : thus in Z 106 we find ἐλελίχθησαν with the Aeolic form ἐλέλιχθεν three lines later. Even the comparatively simple matter of the particle ἄν is an obstacle to the reconstruction of the postulated Aeolic text, for, as Monro pointed out, it is impossible to make any change, for instance, in such combinations as οὐδέ γὰρ ἄν (Ω 566), since οὐδὲ γάρ κε would produce a cretic and οὐδέ κε γάρ is an impossible word order. There remains no other choice than to accept dialect mixture as *a characteristic of the language in which the Homeric poems were actually composed.* How such an artificial language developed is a matter for surmise. It is likely that it was the product of a long tradition of oral poetry, which passed over from an Achaean to an Ionic milieu, whereby certain Achaean elements, preserved particularly in stereotyped formulae, were transmitted from one generation to another of professional bards as picturesque, traditional elements in 'poetic diction'. That the Aeolic personal pronouns, for instance, and adjectives such as ἀργιόεις, φαιδιμόεις, etc., were used in such a sophisticated and self-conscious way has been made probable. We may see, too, similar archaistic-poetical devices in the use of the dual and the digamma.

The dual was progressively eliminated from all the Greek dialects, among which Attic showed in this respect the greatest conservatism, whereas in Ionic the dual has completely disappeared. In Homer, too, its decay is made evident by the fact that even χεῖρε, an expression where a dual might be expected to survive longest, is less frequent than the plural χεῖρες. Even where the archaism χεῖρε is used it is often combined with a plural adjective. e.g., χεῖρε πετάσσας ἀμφοτέρας, Φ 115. But it is passages such as those quoted on p. 128 f. that reveal to us the purely conventional-traditional use of the dual by the Homeric poets and constitute unmistakable indications of the essential artificiality of the Homeric language.

We now turn our attention once more to the digamma. This sound, which, as we saw, was equivalent to the English *w*, disappeared at an early date in Attic-Ionic. Our texts of Homer contain no indication of this sound, but its presence in the Homeric language is attested by unmistakable metrical effects. Hiatus of a short final vowel, for instance, is extremely rare before a word beginning with a vowel or with a rough breathing which has emerged from an initial simple *s-*. On the other hand, before words which began with a Ϝ- or sϜ- over 2000 examples have been counted, thus we can remove the hiatus in these cases by inserting the Ϝ: *e.g.*, Ἀτρεΐδης τε̆ Ϝάναξ (Α 7), θαρσήσας μάλα Ϝειπέ (Α 85), οἴσετε Ϝάρν᾽ ἕτερον (Γ 103), αἷμά τε̆ Ϝαρνῶν (Δ 158). In other verses an apparently short syllable acquires by position the length demanded by the metre if F is supplied: ἐς δίφρον Fάρνας (Γ 310). Most remarkable are examples like φίλε ἑκυρέ and πατερὶ ὧι, where the lengthening of the short vowel in hiatus is due to the double digamma FF- which resulted from the original initial sw- in *swekuros and *swos. But such treatment is by no means constant, for there are numerous cases where a digamma is ignored, so that a vowel is elided and a short syllable suffers no lengthening by position. A case of elision is ἠδ᾽ ἄρ᾽ ἐκέλευον, Γ 119 although, as we saw above, Fάρνα, etc., is often demanded by the metre. We have, further, neglect of the digamma as a position-making factor in μένος καὶ θυμὸν ἑκάστου.[a] A certain number of these adverse cases can be removed by trifling alterations of the verse: for instance, in ἐν χερσὶν ἑκηβόλου Ἀπόλλωνος the ν-ephelkustikon may be dropped and the digamma inserted. For χειρὸς ἑλοῦσ᾽ ἐπέεσσι προσηύδα E 30 we may read ἑλοῦσα Fέπεσσι; in fact it is probable that ἐπέεσσι is a purely rhapsodic form evoked by the apparent irregularity of the metre. Similarly the apparent cretic in μειλιχίοισ᾽ ἔπεσσι was avoided by alteration μειλιχίοισ᾽ ἐπέεσσι, whereas the true reading is μειλιχίοισι Fέπεσσι. But when all ingenuity has been expended, there remains a not inconsiderable number of cases where the digamma is treated as non-existent. Actually it has been calculated that against 3354 places where the influence of the digamma is metrically evident there are 617 places where it is neglected. We have, then, yet another example of chronologically or dialectically different elements in the language of Homer. The explanation of such inconsistency lies in the poetical traditions of which Homer was the heir. In the earliest period digamma formed an element in the spoken language and phrases and formulae were coined wherein F played its part as a full consonant. In the course of time F was dropped in Ionic, so that while the previous poetical tradition was continued, the spoken language began to make its influence felt in the neglect of the digamma. We may conclude that F, like the archaisms we have already discussed, was merely a traditional 'poetical' colour on the palette of the Homeric artist.

It remains to ask how far this picture of the genesis of the epic dialect needs modification in the light of the newly deciphered Mycenaean texts. Ventris and Chadwick wrote 'If this was the language of Nestor and of Agamemnon, then it was presumably also that of Demodokos and the poets of that time. Should we not conclude that the Aeolic stratum which so obviously underlies the text of Homer is not the Aeolic of Lesbos but a much older Achaean form which had already set the conventions of epic verse within the second millennium B.C.?

'Attention has been drawn to similarities especially in vocabulary between Cyprian and Homer. But to suppose two transpositions, first

[a] Note also the contracted genitive.

from Achaean to Aeolic and then from Aeolic to Ionian, is stretching credulity too far. If the original stratum was of this archaic Mycenaean type, many of the difficulties disappear.'[a]

Why have scholars maintained that there are *Aeolic* features present in the epic language ? Simply because certain features are found only in the Aeolic of Lesbos together with supporting evidence from the closely related dialects of Thessaly and Boeotia. We take some test samples to see if we can now dispense with the 'Aeolic' phase. The new inscriptions do not contain infinitives of the type -μεναι.[b] If we consider the characteristic dative plurals in -εσσι we again draw blank. Here the new evidence is definitely against, for the dative plurals of the athematic class end in the inherited -σι and there is no trace of the Aeolic innovation. The same is true of the perfect participles in -ων, for at Pylos and Knossos we find the very archaic endings –wōs, plural –wŏ-e, –wŏ-a. More might be added, but this will suffice to show that the new evidence, so far from enabling us to eliminate Aeolic as a factor in the genesis of the Homeric language, actually disposes of the theoretical possibility that such features may be inherited directly from a Mycenaean Old Achaean and makes plain that the key features just discussed are an innovation of Aeolic, or 'North Achaean'.

What then has the new evidence contributed ? As we have seen, it has confirmed what had in any case been a near certainty — that the ancestral form of Arcado-Cypriot was spoken in the Mycenaean Peloponnese. It has increased the number of Arcado-Cypriot words in the Epic vocabulary ; φάσγανον, for instance, occurs in inventories of swords and so may be added to the words listed previously from this dialect : κέλευθος, λεύσσω, ἀπύω, ἀνώγω, ἕλος, κασίγνητος, etc.

This does not prove, however, that such words found their way into the epic vocabulary directly from Arcado-Cypriot sources. All this need imply is that words in common use in Mycenaean Greece *as a whole* happened to survive in ordinary use only in the Arcadian and Cypriot dialects. The fact that the 'poetic' word *delve* is in ordinary use, shall we say, among Cheshire gardeners has no significance for the origin of poems which prefer to use this word instead of the common English *dig*. The point may be illustrated by the verb ἆσαι 'drink one's fill'. The verb has been found in the introductory formula of a Pylian inventory of σιαλοί. Doubts have been expressed about the identification, but the great antiquity of the verb in this technical sense has been confirmed by recent discoveries in the Anatolian group of languages which were in use in Asia Minor throughout the second millennium B.C. Here ḫas- occurs in precisely the same meaning as the Homeric and the Mycenaean verb, and a derived noun, *hasas* 'surfeit, abundance' also occurs to match

[a] *JHS*, lxxiii. 103.   [b] There is one possible athematic infinitive in -me(n).

the Greek noun ἄση. Thus although our earliest inscriptional evidence for the verb happens to come from a Peloponnesian source, it may safely be ascribed also to the vocabulary of 'North Achaean' at the same time.

The new evidence has done, therefore, little to modify the current hypotheses relating to the genesis of the epic dialect. Basically Ionic, it nevertheless shows well established Aeolicisms of frequent use. As P. Chantraine has recently written: 'Les traits éoliens de la langue homérique apparaissent donc moins importants qu'on ne l'avait cru du temps de Fick, mais ils restent, quand même, bien établis sur certains points'. On the other hand there is no pervasive feature of the epic dialect which compels us to add the hypothesis of a one-time 'South Achaean' participation in the formation of Homer's language. Here too the scientific principle of economy of hypotheses must guide our judgements.

In conclusion the philologist may be asked what bearing his analysis has on the question of the 'unity' of the Homeric epic. There is a consensus of opinion among linguists that 'centuries of poetic practice were required before the language of the Greek epic assumed the form which it presents to us'. Few would question the statement that an unbroken tradition of formulaic diction reaches back into the Mycenaean age. But the most determined philological analysts have been forced to admit Ionic influence even in the earliest strata of the *Iliad*. Until recent years philologists in general shared in the general tendency towards 'unitarianism' which has been evident in the 'Homeric question' since the turn of the century. Mazon begins his analysis with a virtual denial of the relevance of the linguistic evidence. My own views as recorded in 1939 [a] were: 'While it is possible to stigmatize individual lines or passages as late on the grounds of forms such as the indubitably Attic ἦντο in Γ 153, on the artistic unity or multiplicity of the poems as a whole in the form in which they have come down to us the philologist *qua* philologist can pass no judgement'.

Some recent work, however, has made it difficult to maintain this attitude of neutrality and non-intervention. Professor G. P. Shipp has made a systematic study of the distribution in the *Iliad* of forms classified as late in P. Chantraine's *Homeric Grammar*. He has found that they occur predominantly in similes, digressions, and 'comments'. Now if we accept the above view that the epic 'linguistic palette' was virtually complete by the eighth century and that 'Homer' was at liberty to choose any 'colour', early or late, according to his pleasure and convenience, then if we plot the 'early' and 'late' forms in different colours on the pages of our Homeric texts, we should expect to find a fairly even distribution. If we accept Professor Shipp's results, the unevenness of

[a] In the original version of this chapter.

the distribution is a fact which cannot be ignored. It might be explained by reference to the conventions of Greek literature in varying its language according to the genre. The Homeric flavour of messenger speeches in tragedy is a well-known example. Thus it might be argued that a more modern linguistic tone might have been regarded as appropriate in similes drawn from contemporary life. But late linguistic forms are also found, for instance, in the visit of the old women of Troy to the temple of Athena in Z 264 ff. Nor would the genre theory explain the lateness of the Nestor passages which will be discussed below.

Professor M. Leumann has approached the question of 'stratification' from a different angle. As we have seen, the traditional formulae preserved words and grammatical forms which were no longer in use in the spoken language, some of them going back to the Mycenaean age. Such words are liable to be misunderstood. A notorious example from Hellenistic poetry is the Pseudo-Theocritean στῆτα (Syr. 14) 'woman', which is due to a wrong analysis of διαστήτην ἐρίσαντε in A 6 as διὰ στήτην 'because of a woman'. Leumann has detected such misunderstandings within the Homeric poems. If these examples are confirmed, it would be reasonable to suppose that no poet would thus misinterpret his own work. We should in that case have incontrovertible evidence that the passages of the στῆτα type were composed by a different author from those of the 'correct' διαστήτην type.

By way of illustration we may begin with the technical word παρήορος. In Π 470 f. it would appear to be used in its proper sense of 'what is attached alongside' (of an extra horse in the chariot team). This extra horse is struck and confusion results: the two horses separated, the yoked creaked and the harness was tangled ἐπεὶ δὴ κεῖτο παρήορος ἐν κονίῃσι 'since the παρήορος lay in the dust'. Here we have an authentic technical detail from an incident of presumably Mycenaean chariot fighting. If we now turn to H 154 f. we read 'I fought with him and Athena granted me my prayer. He was the tallest and strongest man I ever slew. For there he lay a great bulk sprawling this way and that.' The last sentence translates the words: πολλὸς γάρ τις ἔκειτο παρήορος ἔνθα καὶ ἔνθα. It will be apparent that the phrase κεῖτο παρήορος of the first passage has been wholly misunderstood. The speaker is Nestor. We may add another linguistic observation: 'The combination πολλός τις is common in Herodotus, but it is not elsewhere found in Homer' (Leaf ad loc.).

The search may now be carried to the Games in Ψ 602 f. Menelaus says 'I will yield to you, angry though I am. For you were not previously παρήορος or ἀεσίφρων.' Here again the word παρήορος is used in a wholly different sense from that above. The man addressed by Menelaus is Antilochus, the son of Nestor.

Another technical word shows similar distortions. The following passages contain the word κύμβαχος :

$$κύμβαχον ἀκρότατον νύξ' ἔγχεϊ ὀξυόεντι. \qquad (Ο\ 536)$$

$$ἔκπεσε δίφρου \ .\ .\ .\ κύμβαχος ἐν κονίῃσι. \qquad (Ε\ 585\text{-}6)$$

It will be seen that in both passages a man is struck on the head and both tumble in the dust. But in the first κύμβαχος is evidently the technical word for a part of the helmet, whereas in the second it is an adjective meaning something like 'head first'. The misunderstanding is like that of παρήορος : in both a technical word of military equipment has been interpreted as an adjective. It remains to add that the hero of the second exploit is Antilochus, the son of Nestor.

We may now turn to the study of a false quantity. The adjective φοινῑκόεις from the noun φοινῑκ- occurs in the following passages :

$$ἀπὸ δὲ χλαῖναν βάλε φοινικόεσσαν, \qquad (ξ\ 500)$$

where Odysseus relates how he secured the cloak of Thoas one cold night before Troy.

$$ἦ καὶ ἀπ' ὤμοιιν χλαῖναν βάλε φοινικόεσσαν. \qquad (φ\ 118)$$

This is said of Telemachus in the notorious 'axes' passage.

$$ἀμφὶ δ' ἄρα χλαῖναν περονήσατο φοινικόεσσαν. \qquad (Κ\ 133)$$

The person concerned is Nestor.

$$Νέστωρ δ' ἐν χείρεσσι λάβ' ἡνία φοινικόεντα. \qquad (Θ\ 116)$$

Here φοινικόεντα is a variant for σιγαλόεντα. The person concerned is again Nestor.

$$σμώδιγγες \ .\ .\ .\ αἵματι φοινικόεσσαι ἀνέδραμον. \qquad (Ψ\ 716\text{-}17)$$

The passage in question is taken from the wrestling match in the Games.

The form φοινῑκόεσσα with its false quantity is a rhapsodic reformation of the Mycenaean φοινίκϝεσσα forming a double spondee which can occupy the last place in the line. Later such derivatives in -ϝεντ- from athematic stems received the thematic vowel o and this necessitated the false scansion of the preceding syllable. However, it is notable that the word occurs in the final position in all instances except the last, and its formulaic connection with the cloak is apparent. What is notable is that in two of the three Iliad passages the person concerned is Nestor. The Games example is the only one where the adjective has been set free from its formulaic position and this may be considered a mark of its lateness.

We now turn to a peculiarity of spelling. The verb ὀφείλω occurs in two guises. In the *Odyssey* the Aeolic form ὀφέλλω with the doubled consonant occurs whereas the *Iliad* shows three examples of the Ionic form ὀφείλω, all from Book Λ. This distribution has puzzled philologists. Chantraine finds it 'enigmatic', while Wackernagel acknowledges himself baffled, particularly because the Ionic (*i.e.*, 'later') spelling occurs in the *Iliad*. But as Shipp points out, all the Iliadic examples come from Nestor's Elean War. But they must have been inserted after the alleged metagrammatism. Before that there would have been no difference of spelling, for both dialect forms would have been spelt ΟΦΕΛΟ. The peculiarity of the distribution of the different orthographies is explicable only if we conclude that this Nestorian episode, characterized by the aberrant spelling, was a later insertion into the text of the *Iliad*. In Attica the inscriptions of the fifth century still maintain the distinction between the inherited diphthong written EI and the lengthened ε̄ written E. Spelling of the modern type became regular from about the beginning of the fourth century, although sporadic examples occur much earlier: ὀφείλοντες is quotable from 428 B.C.

The chronology suggested by the spelling applies only to the insertion of the episode in the canonical text and not to the date of its composition. However, if the convergence of so many different lines of inquiry strongly suggests that some Nestorian passages are late, it is legitimate to ask the question *cui bono*? The fact that Peisistratus claimed descent from the Neleids of Pylos may be now regarded as adding weight to the arguments for a Peisistratean recension.[a]

v. THE MORPHOLOGY OF THE HOMERIC DIALECT

A. THE NOUN

THE CASE ENDINGS

In Greek the original eight IE cases have been reduced to five, the genitive taking over the functions of the original genitive and ablative while the dative, which is formally partly dative and partly locative, functions as dative, locative, and instrumental (see Syntax).

Genitive singular.—In the 2nd declension we find the endings -οιο, -οο, and -ου (πολέμοιο, ἀνεψίοο, μηροῦ), which form a chronological series. -οιο goes back to IE -asyo (*cf.* Skt. *aśvasya* ' of a horse '). -οο is best regarded as a later chronological stage (see above); but some scholars postulate a separate genitive ending -o-so, comparing τέο with OBulg. *česo* (IE *qʷeso*).

---

[a] Discussed in Ch. 6 (p. 219 f.) and Ch. 7 (p. 238 f.).

Genitive plural.—The influence of the demonstrative made itself felt also in the ending of the 1st declension. The oldest forms -άων (Aeolic), which are preserved mainly at the end of the verse, have been taken over from the pronominal τᾱ(σ)ων (*cf.* Lat. *is-tarum*, Skt. *tāsām*). Since ᾱ > η in Ionic (I), with shortening of the long vowel we get genitives in -έων (θυρέων, ὁπλέων, βουλέων).

Dative plural.—An old locative ending -σι, -συ is preserved in the forms in -οισι, which we found also in other dialects, including Ionic and early Attic, the -οι being derived ultimately from the pronominal τοῖσι (-*oisu* in other languages [a]). The by-forms in -οις may have arisen either from elided forms -οισ' or they may be descendants of instrumentals in -οις (*e.g.*, Skt. *devāis*). But it should be noted that forms in -οις are more frequent in the *Odyssey* than in the *Iliad* and that the majority of the *Iliad* examples occur in 'late' passages. In the dual the dissyllabic -οιιν for Attic -οιν would appear to be due to the analogical influence of the singular -οιο. On quantitative metathesis in such words as νᾱός, etc. see p. 77 f. In the 1st declension the original form of the ending is seen in the Old Attic 'Ἀθήνη-σι; but -ῃσι became -ῃισι under the influence of -οισι, and was transformed further to -αισι according to the analogy -οι : -οισι :: -αι : -αισι. -ῃσι is by far the most frequent Homeric ending. The few certain examples of -ης before a consonant or at the end of the line may have arisen from elided forms. -αις is found in Aeolic, but the Homeric examples of this ending may well be due to Atticization of the text. The Aeolic ending -εσσι is usually considered to have originated in neuter s-stems, but it may likewise be explained as the attachment of -σι to the nominative plural -ες. It is found in Aeolic both with vowel and with consonant stems of the 3rd declension: πολίεσσι, ἄνδρεσσι.

-φι, -θεν, -δε, -θι.—These case endings illustrate the process whereby a post-posited adverb becomes an inflection—possibly all case endings originated in this way. -φι occurs in a variety of functions: as singular and plural (ναῦφι, ὀστεόφι, ὄρεσφι); as instrumental (ἶφι, βίηφι, etc.), ablative (παρὰ ναῦφι), locative (ὄρεσφι) and, more rarely, genitive ('Ἰλιόφι κλυτὰ τείχεα), and dative (φρήτρηφι B 363). In combination with the stem vowel of the 2nd declension it appears as -οφι occasionally also in nouns of other declensions: κοτυληδονόφιν, δακρυόφι.

The particle -δε denoted motion towards and bore an independent accent like a post-posited preposition: οἶκον δέ, ἀγορὴν δέ, etc. It is usually accented οἴκόνδε, etc. We find this adverb further in the forms οἴκαδε, 'Ἀθήναζε (= 'Ἀθήνας-δε), where the language had lost the feeling for the underlying accusative forms οἶκα (stem οἰκ-) and 'Ἀθήνας. In 'Ἀϊδόσδε we find -δε added to a genitive of the same type as the Attic εἰς "Ἀιδου.

[a] The correspondence of Greek -ι to -*u* in other languages presents difficulties.

-θεν denotes motion from, and as such forms ablatival cases : Τροίηθεν, οἴκοθεν, ἐμέθεν, σέθεν, ἔθεν, etc. But in view of the fusion of the ablative and genitive in Greek it came also to be used in genitival functions, particularly with the pronouns.

Position in or at may be expressed by the addition of a particle -θι : Κορινθόθι οἰκία ναίων, Ἰλιόθι πρό, οὐρανόθι πρό, ἠῶθι πρό.

A-STEMS

(1) On the preservation of the long ā in Aeolic forms see p. 78. For forms in -άων, -ησι, -ηισι, and -αις see above.

(2) The masculines were in IE declined exactly like feminines (cf. Lat. nauta, etc.). In Greek, however, analogical influences from the 2nd declension produced changes : (a) in the nominative singular, which became -ā-s, -η-s ; (b) in the genitive singular, which became -ā-o (on subsequent changes ⟩ -ηο ⟩ -εω see III).

(3) Homer contains some archaic nominatives (more rarely vocatives) in -ᾰ : ἱππότα Νέστωρ, νεφεληγερέτα Ζεύς, ἱππηλάτα Πηλεύς, μητίετα, εὐρύοπα, etc. They are probably petrified vocatives, embedded in traditional formulae belonging to the oldest strata of the epic tradition. Later epic writers even used them as indeclinables : πατρί τε κυανοχαῖτα.

4. In the vocative note νύμφᾰ, which, like the masculines τοξότα, etc., represents the IE ending -ə. On the other hand Ἀτρείδη, Ἑρμεία are analogical innovations.

O-STEMS

The only forms which call for comment are the genitive singulars in -οιο, -οο, and -ου. On their origin see p. 106. Though it is often possible to substitute o-jo (with consonantal -i) for -οο and -οι' for -ου (a genitive singular in -οι appears in Thessalian), there is little doubt that the three Homeric endings form a chronological series, -οιο being the earliest and -οο representing the transition to the contracted (Attic) -ου (see p. 106). On the dative plurals in -οισι, -οις see p. 107.

A dual ending -οιϊν is attested : e.g., ἵπποιϊν, ὤμοιϊν, ὀφθαλμοῖϊν, βλεφάροιϊν, etc. This ending may be reflected in certain Mycenaean forms in -o-i.

THE THIRD DECLENSION

1. R- and N-Stems.—On Ablaut in these nouns see p. 83.

2. S-Stems.—The declension of nouns such as γένος, γένεσ-ος, γέρας, γέρασ-ος has been complicated by the disappearance of -σ- and in Attic by the subsequent vocalic contraction (see p. 79). Types such as γένεος, γέραος, etc., preserve the non-Attic open forms. The late

Ionic genitive in -ευς, which occurs in a few words (θέρευς, θάμβευς, etc.) should be written -εος and scanned with synizesis. Precisely similar phenomena are accusatives such as ἀκλέα, δυσκλέα which the MSS occasionally offer, but always before a vowel. The declension of compounds in -κλεϜος is -κλε(ϝ)ης, -κλε(ϝ)εα, -κλε(ϝ)εος, etc. Consequently the above forms should be corrected to ἀκλεέ᾽, δυσκλεέ᾽, etc. On the other hand in εὐκλέος, εὐκλέϊ, etc., we have hyphaeresis, whereby one of three adjacent vowels such as -εεο-, -εεα-, etc. was dropped. The derived adjectives in -ης exhibit the expected accusative plural in -ας, the Attic ending exemplified in εὐγενεῖς being an innovation. On the Aeolic datives γένεσσι and the rhapsodic distortions γενέεσσι see pp. 99, 101.

		Sing.		Plur.	
Sing.	N.A.	γένος	Plur.	γένεα	
	Gen.	γένεος		γενέων	
	Dat.	γένεϊ		γένεσσι, γενέεσσι	

The neuters in -ας exhibit the non-contracted forms: γήραος, γήραϊ, etc. (⟨*γήρασος, *γήρασι, etc.). The word κρέας is also treated as a member of this class although in fact it is of different origin. The genitive plural κρειῶν is presumably due to μεταγραμματισμός of ΚΡΕΟΝ which conceals an archaic κρεάων. The plural sometimes has a short vowel κρέᾰ, which may well represent an original *κρεϜα, a root noun without a suffix.

The nouns γέλως and ἔρως have thematic doublets γέλος and ἔρος which are Aeolic forms.

3. *Dental Stems.*—On dative plurals in -σσι (⟨τ-σι) see p. 107. Note the non-Attic accusative singulars of barytones in -ις and -υς: ἔριδα, κόρυθα.

4. *ι- and υ-Stems.*—The original *Ablaut* (see XIII) of these stems *i : ei* and *u : eu* is preserved in the alternation of ι : ε and υ : εϜ which characterizes the Greek declension of these nouns (πόλις, πόλεις (⟨*πόλε(ι)-ες), πῆχυς, πήχεος (⟨*πήχε(ϝ)ος). This alternation is, however, best preserved in the *u*-stems, for in the *i*-stems the ι of the weak cases has been carried through the whole declension except in Attic: e.g., πόλις, πόλιν, πόλιος, πόλῑ (⟨-ι+ι), πόλιες, πόλῑς (⟨*πόλι-νς), but also πόλιας, πολίων, πολί-εσσι (Aeolic). The form of the stem seen in the Attic πόλεως (earlier πόληος, see III) originated in the locative πόληϊ. In Homer we find it in πόληες, πόληας. In Ionic the genitive πόλεως has been substituted by an analogical form πόλεος. The following, then, is the Homeric declension of such nouns:

Sing.			Plur.	
Sing.	N.	πόλις	Plur.	πόλιες, πόληες
	V.	πόλι		πόλιες
	A.	πόλιν		πόλῑς, πόλιας, πόληας
	G.	πόλεος, πόλιος, πόληος		πολίων
	D.	πόλεϊ, πόλει, πόλῑ, πόληι		πολίεσσι

In Indo-European there existed another type of ι and υ stems not distinguished by *Ablaut* of the stem. It may be exemplified by the word for 'sheep': *owi-s, *owi-m, *owi̯-os, etc., the Greek representative of which is ὄϝις, ὄϝιν, ὀιός (⟨*ὀϝιός⟩), etc. Note the dative plural ὄ-εσσι, where a new stem ὄ- has apparently been extracted from the accusative plural ὄ-ις.

The υ-stems are less varied. The accusative plural was originally -ῡς (from -υνς), but on the analogy of the nominative plural in -ε(ϝ)ες a new ending -εας was coined: εὐρέας, etc., and this in its turn gave rise to a new accusative singular εὐρέα for εὐρύν. Note further the Aeolic datives εὐρέεσσι, etc.

	Sing.				Plur.		
Masc.	N.	εὐρύς	Neut.	εὐρύ	Masc. εὐρέες	Neut.	εὐρέα
	A.	εὐρύν, εὐρέα		εὐρύ	εὐρέας		εὐρέα
	G.	εὐρέος			εὐρέων		
	D.	εὐρέϊ			εὐρέεσσι		

Disguised υ-stems are γόνυ and δόρυ. In the oblique cases we have lengthening of the root vowel according to V: γουνός, γουνί, etc. ⟨ *γονϝός, *γονϝί, etc. A parallel declension γούνατος, etc., is modelled on neuter stems such as ὄνομα.

	Sing.	Plur.
N.A.	γόνυ	γοῦνα, γούνατα
G.	γουνός, γούνατος	γούνων
D.	(γουνί, γούνατι)	γούνεσσι

5. *Stems in -ῑ and -ῡ.*—The archaic accusative singular of ϝῖς ϝῖν, corresponding exactly to the Latin *vim*, occurs three times and always before a vowel, where the MSS read ἶν'. Similar is λῖν Λ 480. Of ῡ-stems, besides the older form of the accusative plural ἰχθύας, νεκύας, etc., we find the later analogical forms σῦς, ὀφρῦς, νεκῦς, etc., which are based on the singular forms σῦν, etc. Note the dative plurals νέκυσσι, γέννυσσι, which may be graphic forms (*vide* p. 96) for *ΝΕΚῩΣΙ, etc. On the Aeolic datives νεκύεσσι, etc. see above.

6. *Heteroclite υ-Stems*: υἱός.—The complicated Homeric declension of this word is to be explained as follows. The IE word for 'son' appears with a suffix -i̯, *sui̯-us ⟩ υἱύς, which, with the disappearance of intervocalic -i̯-, is declined:

Sing.	N.	*sui̯u-s	⟩	υύς	Plur.	*sui̯eu-es	⟩	υέϝες, υέες
	V.	*sui̯u		⟩	υύ			
	A.	*sui̯u-m	⟩	υύν		*sui̯u-n̥s	⟩	υἷϝας, υἷας
	G.	*sui̯u-os	⟩	υἱϝός, υἱός, etc.	*sui̯u-ō̆m	⟩	υἱϝῶν, υἱῶν

The irregularities of this primitive declension were subjected to analogical levelling in a number of ways: (1) the stem υἱ- is generalized as in υἱύς, υἱέες, etc.; (2) the stem form ὑε- is generalized as in ὑέ-ος, etc.; (3) we get a contamination of the two stems in υἱέος; (4) on the genitive plural υἱῶν a new nominative υἱός is constructed, which is declined regularly as an o-stem; (5) a new dative υἱάσι is substituted for *ὑ(ι)ύσι on the analogy of other 'relationship' words such as πατράσι. Thus the declension of the noun in Homer is a medley of old and new.[a]

Sing.		Dual.	Plur.	
N.	υἱός	υἷε	υἱέες, υἱεῖς, υἷες	
V.	υἱέ			
A.	υἱόν, υἷα, υἱέα (?)		υἱέας, υἷας	
G.	υἱοῦ (?), υἱέος, υἷος [b]		υἱῶν	
D.	υἱέϊ, υἱεῖ, υἷι (?)		υἱοῖσιν, υἱάσι	

The declension of πολύς exhibits a variety of forms. πολύν, πολέος, πολέες, πολέας, πολέων, πολέσι, follow the declension of a u-stem like εὐρύς; others are based on a thematic stem πολλός, πολλή. The complete paradigm is as follows:

	M	N	F
Sing. N.	πολύς, πολλός	πολύ, πολλόν	πολλή
A.	πολύν, πολλόν	πολύ, πολλόν	πολλήν
G.	πολέος	πολέος	πολλῆς
D.	πολλῷ	πολλῷ	πολλῇ

	M	N	F
Plur. N.	πολέες, πολλοί	πολλά	πολλαί
A.	πολέας, πολλούς	πολλά	πολλάς
G.	πολέων, πολλῶν	πολλῶν	πολλάων, πολλέων
D.	πολέσι, πολέσσι	πολλοῖσι	πολλῇσι
	πολέεσσι, πολλοῖσι		

7. *Diphthong Stems*: (i) βασιλεύς.—The regular declension of this type was βασιλεύς, βασιλεῦ, βασιλῆϜα, etc., βασιλήϜεσσι or βασιλεῦσι. In Attic with quantitative metathesis (III) the accusative and genitive singular became βασιλέᾱ and βασιλέως. In Ionic and West Greek the genitives in -εος were due to the shortening of η in hiatus. This form of the stem is seen in the Homeric Ἀτρέος, etc.

It should be noted, however, that all these genitives with a short o belong to nouns with a long first syllable. They are therefore probably metrically conditioned since - ⌣ - is impossible in a hexameter.

Sing.		Plur.	
N.	βασιλεύς	βασιλῆ(Ϝ)ες	
V.	βασιλεῦ	βασιλῆ(Ϝ)ες	
A.	βασιλῆ(Ϝ)α, Τυδέα,	βασιλῆ(Ϝ)ας	
G.	βασιλῆ(Ϝ)ος, Τυδέος	βασιλή(Ϝ)ων	
D.	βασιλῆ(Ϝ)ϊ, Τυδέϊ	βασιλεῦσι, (ἀριστή(Ϝ)εσσι)	

[a] Metrical considerations governed the choice of form used in different parts of the line. [b] The accentuation of υἷος and υἷι is Aeolic.

(ii) *Stems in -ωι.*—The uncontracted forms are more usual : $\Lambda\eta\tau\hat{\omega}(\iota)$, $\Lambda\eta\tau o\hat{\iota}$, $\Lambda\eta\tau o(\iota)$-α, $\Lambda\eta\tau o(\iota)$-$o\varsigma$, $\Lambda\eta\tau o(\iota)$-$\ddot{\iota}$. The contracted form of the genitive ($\Lambda\eta\tau o\hat{\upsilon}\varsigma$) is demanded by the metre in A 9, Ξ 327, that of the dative ($\Pi\upsilon\theta o\hat{\iota}$) in I 405, θ 80.

(iii) $Z\epsilon\hat{\upsilon}\varsigma$.—The IE declension $*d\underline{\imath}\bar{e}us$, $*d\underline{\imath}\bar{e}m$, $*di\underline{\upsilon}os$, etc., is preserved in the Greek $Z\epsilon\hat{\upsilon}\varsigma$, $Z\hat{\eta}\nu$, $\Delta\iota(F)\acute{o}\varsigma$, etc. Analogical levelling took place in two ways : (1) the accusative $Z\hat{\eta}\nu$ (occurring at the end of the verse and then only if the next verse begins with a vowel) was normalized to $Z\hat{\eta}\nu\alpha$ and the stem $Z\eta\nu$- was then carried throughout the declension : $Z\eta\nu\acute{o}\varsigma$, etc. ; (2) the stem $\Delta\iota F$- was carried into the accusative, $\Delta\acute{\iota}(F)\alpha$, a form found eleven times in Homer.

(iv) $\beta o\hat{\upsilon}\varsigma$.—The accusative singular $\beta\hat{\omega}\nu$ [a] (H 238) is derived regularly from IE $*g^u_o\bar{o}m$ and is a parallel form to $Z\hat{\eta}\nu$. The Attic $\beta o\hat{\upsilon}\nu$ is a transformation of this archaic accusative with the vocalism of the nominative singular. The rest of the Homeric declension is as in Attic with the exception of the accusative plural $\beta\acute{o}\alpha\varsigma$ (Attic $\beta o\hat{\upsilon}\varsigma$ is modelled on the accusative singular) and the Aeolic dative $\beta\acute{o}$-$\epsilon\sigma\sigma\iota$.

(v) $\nu\alpha\hat{\upsilon}\varsigma$.—The IE $*n\bar{a}us$, $*n\bar{a}\underline{\upsilon}$-$m$, $*n\bar{a}\underline{\upsilon}$-$os$, etc., should appear in Attic-Ionic [b] as $\nu\alpha\hat{\upsilon}\varsigma$, $\nu\hat{\eta}\alpha$, $\nu\eta\acute{o}\varsigma$, etc. The Homeric nominative singular $\nu\eta\hat{\upsilon}\varsigma$ has its stem form from the other cases. So, too, we find dative plural $\nu\eta\upsilon\sigma\acute{\iota}$ for the regular $\nu\alpha\upsilon\sigma\acute{\iota}$ (cf. $\nu\alpha\upsilon\sigma\acute{\iota}\kappa\lambda\upsilon\tau o\varsigma$). The Ionic forms with a shortened stem vowel, e.g., $\nu\epsilon\acute{o}\varsigma$, $\nu\acute{\epsilon}\epsilon\varsigma$, $\nu\acute{\epsilon}\alpha\varsigma$ (and, with the Aeolic ending, $\nu\acute{\epsilon}$-$\epsilon\sigma\sigma\iota$) are rarer in Homer.

Sing.		Plur.	
N.	$\nu\eta\hat{\upsilon}\varsigma$	$\nu\hat{\eta}\epsilon\varsigma$, $\nu\acute{\epsilon}\epsilon\varsigma$	
A.	$\nu\hat{\eta}\alpha$, $\nu\acute{\epsilon}\alpha$	$\nu\hat{\eta}\alpha\varsigma$, $\nu\acute{\epsilon}\alpha\varsigma$	
G.	$\nu\eta\acute{o}\varsigma$, $\nu\epsilon\acute{o}\varsigma$	$\nu\eta\hat{\omega}\nu$	
D.	$\nu\eta\ddot{\iota}$	$\nu\eta\upsilon\sigma\acute{\iota}$, $\nu\acute{\eta}\epsilon\sigma\sigma\iota$, $\nu\acute{\epsilon}\epsilon\sigma\sigma\iota$	

8. *Heteroclite Neuters.*—A very ancient type of noun is seen in the neuters whose nominative and accusative singular ends in a sonant (i, u, r, l) which is replaced by an $-n$ in the oblique cases : e.g., Lat. *femur, feminis*. These suffixes are often extended by consonantal elements t/d, k/g, such as appears, for instance, in the Sanskrit word corresponding to *iecur*: $yak\underline{r}$-t, genitive singular $yakn$-as. It is this consonantal element that appears in Greek nouns such as $\hat{\eta}\pi\alpha\rho$ ($\langle$ -$\underline{r}$), $\H{\eta}\pi\alpha\tau o\varsigma$ ($*$-$\underline{n}$-t-os). Of such nouns we find in Homer :

(i) with $-i$: $\H{\alpha}\lambda\phi\iota$, $\H{\alpha}\lambda\phi\iota$-$\tau$-$\alpha$, $\mu\acute{\epsilon}\lambda\iota$, $\mu\acute{\epsilon}\lambda\iota$-$\tau$-$os$.

(ii) with $-u$: $\gamma\acute{o}\nu\upsilon$, $\gamma o\acute{\upsilon}\nu\alpha\tau os$ (but see above, 110).

(iii) with $-\underline{r}$: $\hat{\eta}\mu\alpha\rho$, $\H{\eta}\mu\alpha\tau os$, $o\H{\upsilon}\theta\alpha\rho$, $o\H{\upsilon}\theta\alpha\tau os$, etc. $\phi\rho\epsilon\acute{\iota}\alpha\tau\alpha$ Φ 197 is a graphic expression (p. 96) for $\phi\rho\acute{\eta}F\alpha\tau\alpha$ from $\phi\rho\hat{\eta}F\alpha\rho$, which in Attic by quantitative metathesis (III) gives $\phi\rho\acute{\epsilon}\bar{\alpha}\rho$, $\phi\rho\acute{\epsilon}\bar{\alpha}\tau os$.

---

[a] In the meaning 'shield'.
[b] Before quantitative metathesis took place.

The word for 'head' appears in a variety of forms. We may start from the root *ker, *kr̥, which appears in Greek as κάρ. This root is extended by various suffixes: thus κρᾱατος derives from *kr̥-s-n̥tos and appears also in a contracted form κρᾱτός; κάρηνα, according to a recent analysis, contains the extended base *ker-əs (whence κέρας) in the zero grade *kr̥-es combined with an n-suffix, *kr̥əs-no- producing quite regularly κάρηνο-; on the other hand κάρᾱ is to be traced to *kr̥-əs-n̥ ⟩ *κάρασα; then with loss of intervocalic -s- and contraction αα ⟩ ᾱ. Transformed to κάρη under the influence of κάρηνα, it was made the basis of yet another series of forms — καρήατα, etc. A Mycenaean ᾱ-declension is required to account for the instrumental plural ka-ra-a-pi, dual ka-ra-o-i. This would be the s-stem karas- extended by -ᾱ with loss of intervocalic s: καρα(h)ᾱ.

ADJECTIVES

Comparison.—The suffix -tero- is used of contrasted pairs in many IE languages: e.g., magister, minister, dexter, sinister, cf. δεξιτερός, ἀριστερός. This suffix could be added to nouns: note, for instance, ἀγρότερος as opposed to ὀρέστερος; θεώτερος 'belonging to gods' (and not to mortals), κουρότερος 'young' (as opposed to old), κύντερος, βασιλεύτερος. It was from this usage that the comparative developed. The 'contrast' function is still clearly seen in ἐλαφρότεροι πόδας εἶναι ἢ ἀφνειότεροι α 164, 'to be swift of foot rather than wealthy'.

-ιων. The stem of the comparative formed with this suffix was originally strong whereas the weak grade (XIII) was characteristic of the superlative. Hence we have κρατύς, κρέσσων, κράτιστος. Analogical levelling has, however, mostly removed this ancient distinction, which was partially restored by a secondary lengthening of the vowels in ἐλάσσων, θάσσων, μᾶλλον, and the Attic μείζων, κρείττων[a] (μέζων and κρέσσων in other dialects).

Comparatives of this type are often obscured by the combination of -i̯- with the final consonant of the stem (IV): e.g., ταχύς, θάσσων (⟨ *θαχ-ι̯ων), μακρός, μάσσων (⟨ *μακ-ι̯ων). Non-Attic comparatives of this type are βράσσων (βραχύς), πάσσων (παχύς).

The comparative λωΐων is in reality a neuter noun λώϊον, which stands in the same relationship to the verb λῆν 'to want, wish' as ζώϊος to ζῆν. ἀμείνων, too, is based on a neuter noun ἄμεινον, and the Homeric χέρειον may well be a neuter of χέρειος. Other forms of this comparative in Homer are χείρων and χειρότερος. ἀρείων is a derivative from a neuter ἄρος 'use, profit, help' (originally 'acquisition, possession'). The oblique forms of -ιων comparatives are usually -ονα, ονος, etc.,

[a] These forms in Homer are presumably due to Atticization of the text.

the archaic (Attic) forms -ω, -ους, etc. (contracted from -ο(-σ)α, -ο(σ)ος, etc.) being extremely rare and usually in the last foot — a notorious storehouse of archaisms.

NUMERALS

Cardinals.—On the Aeolic forms ἴα = μία, πίσυρες = τέσσαρες, πέμπε (in πεμπώβολα) see p. 85.

Both δύο and δύω occur, and are indeclinable in Homer, as is ἄμφω. The former is, perhaps, the older, the second being due to the influence of the dual of o-stems. Apart from these we have the collective forms δοιώ, δοιοί (*cf.* ἐν δοιῇ = *in dubio* I 230). These are adjectival derivatives: *δϜο-ιος.

Of τέσσαρες note the reduced grade in τρυ-φάλεια.[a]

ἐννέα. There are two distinct IE forms of this numeral: (1) *neun 〉 novem (analogical for *noven), etc.; (2) *enun 〉 Gk. ἐνϜα, which = Ionic εἰνα- (V) as in εἰνάνυχες. In the Homeric compounds ἐννέάβοιος, ἐννεόργυιος, ἐννέωρος, ἐννῆμαρ, etc., we see the same form of the numeral as in the Attic ἐν-νέ(Ϝ)α, where we have a prefix ἐν- denoting 'full number' (*cf.* ἐν-ενήκοντα).

ἐείκοσι(ν). The original base is seen in Dor. Ϝῑ-κατι 〈*wī-knti̯. Attic εἴκοσι stands for ἐ-Ϝίκοσι, which may well be the form which the Homeric ἐ(Ϝ)είκοσι attempts to represent. Another possibility is that it may be a variant of εἴκοσι on the lines of εἶπον, ἔειπον (for which see p. 117).

Ordinals.—Greek πρῶτος, like German *erst*, Latin *primus*, etc., is a superlative. In Homer we find an additional superlative suffix attached: πρώτιστος. The non-Attic by-forms of other ordinals such as τρίτατος, ἑβδόματος, ὀγδόατος owe their extension -ατος to the influence of τέτρατος (with -ρα- from r̥) and ἔνϜα-τος (with α from n̥).

THE PRONOUNS

Personal Pronouns

	1. Pers.	2. Pers.	Reflexive
Sing.			
N.	ἐγώ(ν)	σύ, τύνη	
A.	ἐμέ, με	σε	ἑ(Ϝ)ε, (Ϝ)ε
G.	ἐμέο (ἐμεῖο), μεῦ, μευ, ἐμέθεν	σέο (σεῖο), σεῦ, σευ, σέθεν, τεοῖο	ἕο (εἷο), εὗ, ἕθεν
D.	ἐμοί, μοι	σοί, τοι, τεῖν	ἑοῖ, οἷ

[a] That the first part of the compound means 'four' has received support from the fact that Linear B armour texts regularly list 'four o–pa–wo–ta [? 'plates'] of the helmet'.

Dual

N. νῶϊ	σφῶϊ, σφώ	
A. νώ, νῶϊ	σφῶϊ, σφώ	σφωέ
G. νῶϊν	σφῶϊν, σφῷν	σφωΐν
D. νῶϊν	σφῶϊν, σφῷν	

Plur.

N. ἄμμες, ἡμεῖς	ὔμμες, ὑμεῖς	
A. ἄμμε, ἡμέας, ἤμεας	ὔμμε, ὑμέας	σφέ, σφας, σφέας
G. ἀμμέων, ἡμέων (ἡμείων)	ὑμμέων, ὑμέων (ὑμείων)	σφέων, σφείων, σφῶν
D. ἄμμιν, ἡμῖν, ἤμιν, ἧμιν	ὔμμι(ν), ὑμῖν, ὔμιν, ὗμιν	σφίσι(ν), σφί(ν)

Notes. The following forms are inherited from IE:

1. ἐγώ(ν), (ἐ)με, μοι (*cf.* ego, me), νώ (acc.)
2. τύ, τεϜε, τϜε,[a] τοι (*cf.* tu, te, tovos), σφώ.
3. ἐϜε, Ϝε, ἐϜοι, οἱ (*cf.* se, sovos).

On the Aeolic forms ἄμμες, ἄμμε, ὔμμες, ὔμμε, see p. 80. The strengthened form τύνη is found also in Doric dialects. The genitives ἐμε, τεϜε, ἐϜε, with the corresponding enclitic forms με, τϜε, hϜε, were originally uninflected, but received genitive endings: (1) ἐμέ-ο, σέ-ο, whence ἐμεῖο, etc. by metrical lengthening, ἐμεῦ, etc. (Ionic), and ἐμοῦ (Attic) by contraction; (2) -θεν (on this see above): ἐμέ-θεν, etc.; (3) τεοῖο is the genitive of the possessive adjective τεϜός, which is used as the genitive of the pronoun (*cf.* Latin mei, tui, etc.). The MSS contain the parallel forms ἐμοῖο, σοῖο, while ἑοῖο occurs in Apollonius Rhodius. The datives ἄμμι(ν), etc. have the original short vowel, -ῑν in Attic being a secondary lengthening. The datives τε(Ϝ)ίν, νῶϊν, σφωΐν are modelled on ἄμμιν, etc. The nominative νῶ(Ϝ)ι is a combination of the old nominative *Ϝι (= 'we') and the accusative stem νώ. The plural forms in σφ- are not found in the related languages. It is possible that they originated in the case forms σ-φει, σ-φι(ν) to which an accusative σφέ was coined on the analogy of ὔμμι(ν) : ὔμμε.

μιν is an accusative which is used for all genders, both anaphorically and as a reflexive. It originated in a reduplicated form of the accusative of is: *imim (*cf.* O. Latin emem), which was reduced by dissimilation to *mim, whence Greek μιν.[b]

The Possessive Adjectives.—τεός, ἑός (from *tevos, *sevos) are exact correspondents of the Latin tovos, sovos. The by-forms σός, ὅς contain a reduced form of the root τϜ-, σϜ- (on the sound development see p. 100 f.). The Doric forms ἁμός and ὑμός, which occur occasionally in the MSS,

---

[a] τϜ 〉 σ- in Greek.

[b] Final -m becomes -ν in Greek; *cf.* iugom : ζυγόν. Enclitic mi(n) is attested in the Linear B texts.

K

should be replaced by the Aeolic ἄμμος, ὕμμος. On the analogy of these forms σφός was created. In the plural we find another suffix -tero (cf. noster, etc.), which was discussed above : ἡμέτερος, ὑμέτερος, νωΐτερος, σφέτερος, σφωΐτερος.

The Demonstratives.—Note the following points :

(1) ὁ, ἡ, and τό are used as demonstratives, e.g., ὁ γὰρ νοῦσον . . . ὦρσεν A 9 (see Syntax). The nominative in -s, ὅς, has a wider application than in Attic, where it is confined to set phrases (ἦ δ᾽ ὅς).

(2) The nominative plurals τοί, ταί are the IE forms which survived also in West Greek dialects. οἱ and αἱ are analogical forms with the rough breathing of the nominative singular.

(3) On the genitives τοῖο, τάων, and the datives τοῖσι, ταῖσι see above (p. 106 f.).

(4) In the dative plural of ὅδε, which is a compound of ὁ + the enclitic particle -δε, we occasionally find both parts inflected : τοῖσδεσσι, τοῖσδεσι (cf. Thessalian τό-νε, τοῖ-νεος, τοῦν-νεουν).

The Relative.—The genitive form ὅ-ο was in Attic contracted to οὗ, which was then re-expanded (*vide* p. 95) to ὅου to suit the metre. On the analogy οὗ : ὅου we find also ἕης for ἧς.

In the forms compounded with ὅς- and ὁ- the first element is often not declined : ὅτινα, ὅττεο, ὅτεῳ, ὅτεων, ὁτέοισι. In the accusative, however, both parts may be declined.

The Interrogative-Indefinite.—The form of the stem in dative τέῳ, genitive plural τέων, dative plural ὁτέοισι has been abstracted from the genitive singular τέο (on which *vide* p. 106). τῷ and τοῖσι are contracted forms. The neuter plural σσα (τ 218) is the legitimate phonetic descendant of IE *$q^u i \mathfrak{d}$, which appears also in Latin *quia* : εἰπέ μοι ὁπποῖ᾽ ἄσσα περὶ χροῒ εἵματα ἕστο. ὁπποῖα σσα was later wrongly divided into ὁπποῖ᾽ ἄσσα.

B. THE VERB

REDUPLICATION

Reduplication in the IE verb is a mark of intensified or repeated action. It is found in the present, aorist, and perfect stems and takes the following forms : (*a*) the whole root is repeated, e.g., *present* : βαμβαίνω (= βαν-βαν-ίω), καρκαίρω, μορμύρω, μαρμαίρω, etc.; *aorist* : ἀγ-αγ-εῖν; *perfect* : ἐλ-ήλ-ατο, ὀδ-ωδ-α, ὀρ-ωρ-ε, etc.

(*b*) The first consonant is reduplicated with the vowel ι, a procedure confined to the present stem : βί-βας, λι-λαίομαι, δί-δωμι, τι-ταίνω, τι-τύσκομαι, etc.

(*c*) In the perfect and thematic aorist the reduplicating vowel is ε. The frequency of such reduplicated aorists is a distinctive mark of the

Homeric verb system. Note that the root in such formations has the reduced or weak grade (see XIII): πείθω, ἐ-πέ-πιθ-ον, κήδω, κε-καδ-ών, πάλλω, πε-παλ-ών, τέρπω, τε-τάρπ-ετο. The present tense of ἔ-τε-τμ-ον 'I reached', τέμει, is read in N 707 and is almost certainly authentic despite the harshness of the syntax. The sense of the passage is: 'just as two oxen come to a halt when they *reach* the headland (τέλσον), so did those two stand'.

In roots beginning with F or an s the reduplication is often obscured by phonetic developments (p. 100 f.).

Ϝελ 'turn':   Ϝε-Ϝελ-μένος ⟩ ἐελμένος
Ϝεργ 'work, force': ϜέϜοργα   ⟩ ἔοργα
Ϝεπ 'say':   ἔ-Ϝε-Ϝπ-ον   ⟩ ἔειπον (where the second Ϝ becomes ι
                                            by dissimilation)
ser 'join together' σε-σερ-μένος ⟩ ἐερμένος (for ἐ-)
slagᵘ 'take'   σέ-σλᾱφα   ⟩ εἴληφα (for εἴ-).

AUGMENT

The augment was originally a detachable adverb which was not a necessary and integral part of the verb as it later became. This more primitive condition is preserved in Homer, where the augment is optional: e.g., πλάγχθη but ἔπερσεν a 2, ἴδεν but ἔγνω a 3, πάθεν a 4, φύγον a 11, ἔσαν a 12, etc., etc. ἧκα on the other hand may be a contraction of ἔηκα (so A 48) or it may be unaugmented.

Note that the augment appears in a lengthened form η- before some roots beginning with F: e.g., ἀπήυρα ⟨ *ἀπ-ή-Ϝρα, ἠ-Ϝείδη. Attic forms like ἑώρων show the action of quantitative metathesis: ⟨ *ἠ-Ϝόρα-ον; but the Homeric ἐῳνοχόει, ἐῴκει, and ἐώργει are probably Atticistic substitutions for ἐϜοινοχόει, ϜεϜοίκει, and (ἐ)ϜεϜόργει.

THE PERSONAL ENDINGS (see XII)

We distinguish (1) primary endings, *i.e.*, those of the primary tenses and the subjunctive; (2) secondary endings, *i.e.*, those of the imperfect, aorist, and optative; (3) the endings of the perfect.

A. ACTIVE

First Person Singular.—(*a*) Primary: the athematic ending -μι intrudes not only into the optative (as in Attic φέρο-ι-μι) but also into the subjunctive: ἐθέλωμι, ἀγάγωμι, εἴπωμι, etc.

(*b*) Secondary: the IE ending -*m* after a vowel proceeds regularly to -ν (ἔλυο-ν, etc.); but after a consonant when -*m* becomes sonant, to

-α [a] (*ἔλυσ-ῃι 〉 ἔλυσα). This we can see in ἦα 'I was' (*ἔ-εσ-ῃι), whence ἔᾱ by quantitative metathesis (III), and in ἤϊα from *ἔ-ει-ῃι.

(c) Perfect: -α as in οἶδα, etc. There are grounds for postulating IE -ḷα.

Second Person Singular.—In Greek, with the exception of ἐσσί, the primary ending is everywhere -ς: τίθη-ς, φέρει-ς, φέρῃ-ς, etc. A curious form for 'thou art', εἰς, occurs some twenty times in Homer, of which nineteen are before a vowel. The current explanation is that to εἶ (from *ἐσ-ι) an -ς of the 2nd pers. sing. has been added. The facts suggest, however, that this form is an archaic survival rather than a short-lived analogical innovation, and it is more probable that εἰς is merely a graphic rendering (see above) of a long syllable ΕΣ = ἐσ-ς (*cf.* Plautine *ess*), so that the verb 'to be' is conjugated exactly like any other -μι verb: *ἐσ-μί, ἐσ-ς, ἐσ-τί like τίθη-μι, τίθη-ς, τίθη-τι. If this is true, then ἐσσί should be explained as a transformation of *ἐσς under the influence of ἐστί. A precisely similar, but misunderstood, form is the Hesiodic εἶ-ς 'thou goest'.

Another peculiarity of the Homeric verb is the frequency of -θα in the 2nd pers. sing. This ending was originally confined to the perfect: οἶσ-θα 〈 *οἶδ-θα. [b] In the imperfect of the verb 'to be', however, confusion arose owing to the phonetic convergence of *ἦσ-ς and *ἦσ-τ, both of which became ἦς. Hence -θα was introduced into the 2nd pers. to recreate an essential distinction: ἦσ-θα. From this beginning it became possible to attach -θα as an optional extension to the 2nd pers. sing., in Attic to past tenses such as ἔφησθα, and in Aeolic to indicatives, subjunctives, and optatives of all kinds. In Homer, too, such forms are frequent: τίθησθα, διδοῖσθα, ἐθέλῃσθα, βάλοισθα, etc. It is, however, hardly correct to speak of an ending -σθα: the existing ending -ς is extended by means of -θα. διδοῖσθα is illuminating in this respect, for here the -θα is added to the Ionic contracted form διδοῖς.

In Ionic and the κοινή -θα was replaced even in the perfect by -ας. The earliest example of this process is the Homeric οἶδας (α 337).

Third Person Singular.—The athematic ending -σι (-τι), like -μι, also appears in the subjunctive: φέρῃ-σι, ἴῃ-σι, ἀνέχῃ-σι, etc.

Second Person Plural.—The ending is everywhere -τε. The only apparent exception is πέπασθε (so Aristarchus in Γ 99), which is, however, merely the regular phonetic development of *πέ-παθ-τε (see p. 82 n.).

Third Person Plural.—(a) Primary.—The original ending ε/ο-ντι (West Greek δίδοντι) has become obscured in East Greek owing to the passage of -τι 〉 -σι and the phonetic complications resulting from the combination -νσ- (see IX). Thus φέροντι 〉 Attic φέρουσι and Lesbian

---

[a] See VI.
[b] See p. 82 n. for the phonetic change of -δθ- 〉 -σθ-.

φέροισι. The Homeric forms διδοῦσι, τιθεῖσι, ἱστᾶσι are thus (apart from the accent, for which see below, p. 121) legitimate phonetic descendants of δίδοντι, τίθεντι, ἵσταντι. On the other hand, after a consonant -n̥ti ⟩ -ατι ⟩ -ᾱσι,[a] e.g., λελόγχᾱσι λ 304. In some dialects -ατι was transformed to -αντι, -ντ- being regarded as the proper mark of the 3rd pers. plur. It is from -αντι (⟩ -ανσι) that the Attic -ᾱσι has developed: hence we get ἴσ-ᾱσι (for *ἴδασι with ἰσ- from ἴστε ⟨ *ἴδ-τε), and then, by analogical extension on the model of ἴσμεν : ἴσασιν, ἴ-μεν : ἴ-ᾱσι, δείκνυ-μεν : δεικνύ-ᾱσι, and, further, the Homeric ἔσμεν : ἔᾱσι, βέβα-μεν : βεβά-ᾱσι, μέμα-μεν : με-μά-ᾱσι.

(b) Secondary.—The IE ending -nt loses its final plosive in Greek: *ἔφεροντ ⟩ ἔφερον. By a further change a long vowel followed by a sonant + a consonant (i̯, u̯, r, l, m, n + consonant) is shortened, so that *ἔβᾱντ, *ἔστᾱντ, *ἔφθᾱντ, *ἔθηντ, etc. ⟩ ἔβᾰν, ἔστᾰν, ἔφθᾰν, ἔθεν, etc. In Attic these forms were replaced by new forms with -σαν from the s-aorist: ἔβη-σαν, etc. Both types are found in Homer; ἔβαν, ἔσταν, ἔκταν, ἔτλαν, φθάν, ἐλέλιχθεν, etc., which are presumably Aeolic constituents of the dialect; ἔβησαν, ἔστησαν, ἐλέλιχθησαν, etc.

ἴσαν 'they knew' (Σ 405, δ 772) is remarkable both for the form of the stem ἰσ- (elsewhere ᾐδ- in the pluperfect) and for the ending. It is most probably due to an analogical process whereby on the model of φᾱσί : φάν ἴσασι has given rise to ἴσαν.

Dual.—Note -τον (metrical for Attic -την) in the imperfects διώκετον Κ 364, ἐτεύχετον Ν 346, λαφύσσετον Σ 583. The penultimate vowels in συναντήτην π 333, ἀπειλήτην λ 313, συλήτην Ν 202 are not Attic but Aeolic, and it has been suggested that these are Aeolic elements which came to the Ionians in the form -ητᾱν and were then Ionicized to -ητην, the penultimate vowel being left unchanged because they possessed no native forms in -είτην, -άτην, which would be the expected Ionic contractions of ε-ετην and α-ετην.

B. MIDDLE

Second Person Singular.—(a) Primary.—The original ending -σαι was obscured by the loss of the intervocalic -σ- and further, in Attic, by the subsequent contraction of vowels (*vide* p. 79): *λύεσαι ⟩ λύεαι ⟩ Attic λύῃ. So Homeric βούλεαι, ὄψεαι, ἵκηαι, etc. -σ- was lost also in the athematic verbs, e.g., δίζηαι, but here the -σ- was restored on the analogy of stems ending in a consonant. Thus on the model of ἧσται : ἧσαι κεῖσαι was recoined from κεῖται. So in Homer we find also δύνασαι, δαίνυσαι, δάμνασαι, παρίστασαι, etc. In the perfect, too, the lead

[a] We recall that τι ⟨ σι is a mark of East Greek (see p. 85). Note that both the Homeric examples for -ᾱσι (the above and πεφύκασι, η 114) occur in passages regarded as 'late'.

of λέλειπται : λέλειψαι, etc. is followed by δέδοται : δέδοσαι, μέμνημαι : μέμνησαι, etc.

(b) *Secondary.*—The -σ- of the original ending -σο was similarly lost: *ἐλύσεσο ⟩ ἐλύσεο ⟩ ἐλύσου; *ἐλύσασο ⟩ ἐλύσαο ⟩ ἐλύσω. This -ς- is rarely restored in the secondary tenses, where -εο, -αο, etc. are the regular Homeric endings. Note, however, κεῖσο (Σ 178, etc.) and παρίστασο (Κ 291), both injunctives (*i.e.* unaugmented preterites serving as imperatives).

First Person Plural.—The forms in -μεσθα for -μεθα, with -σθα on the analogy of -σθε of the second person, was possibly a metrical device to avoid a succession of three shorts -ομεθᾰ. In view of the new Hittite evidence, however, it may well be an authentic IE inflection.

Third Person Plural.—(a) *Primary.*— -ntai after a consonant became -αται (⟨ -ṇtai). This form of the ending is found regularly in Ionic in the perfect even after a vowel where one would expect -νται: so Homeric βεβλήαται, κεκλίαται, εἰρύαται, ἥαται (⟨ ἡσ-ṇται), πεποτήαται, etc. On Attic ἧνται see p. 94. A curious composite ending -δαται is seen in ἐρράδαται υ 354 (*cf.* ἐληλάδατο, η 86). Its origin is obscure.

(b) *Secondary.*— -ṇto ⟩ -ατο after a consonant, but here, too, we observe analogical spread: ἐτετράφατο, ὀρωρέχατο, ἥατο, βεβλήατο, πευθοίατο, ἐλασαίατο, etc. On the optative μαχέοιντο see p. 94.

First Person Dual.—περιδώμεθον Ψ 485 is a Greek innovation, the analogical process being represented by the formula λύεσθε : λύεσθον :: λυόμεθα : λυόμεθον.

FORMATION OF THE TENSE STEMS

1. *The Present Stems*

In the athematic verbs (XI) note the *Ablaut* alternations with strong forms in the singular, and weak forms in the dual and plural active, and in the middle. We distinguish:

(a) *Root presents*: εἶμι, ἴμεν; φημί, φᾰμέν, etc. Some of the peculiarities of εἰμί have already been discussed: εἶς, ἐσσί (p. 118), ἔ-ᾱσι (p. 119), ἧα, ἔᾱ (p. 118). The 3rd pers. sing. of the imperfect ἧεν is formally a plural which took the place of the ambiguous *ἧσ-τ (p. 118). The unaugmented form is ἔεν [a] and the contracted form ἧν, while ἔην [b] is an artificial contamination of these two forms. A few forms are conjugated like thematic verbs: pres. participle ἐών, 1st pers. sing. imperf. ἔον (Λ 762, etc.), and the optative ἔοις (Ι 284), ἔοι (Ι 142, etc.).

εἶμι: On ἴᾱσι see p. 119; on ἴσαν *ibid.*

---

[a] This form is not actually attested, but it may be substituted for ἔην before a consonant.
[b] ἤην Λ 808, etc., appears to be founded on ἔην, which was regarded as unaugmented. Such forms are purely artificial rhapsodic inventions.

κεῖμαι: Note the 3rd pers. plur. κέαται (Λ 659), κείαται (Ω 527) ⟨ *kei̯-ntai. κέονται (X 510, etc.) is thematic. On the subjunctive κεῖται see below.

ἧμαι: On the purely graphic forms of the 3rd pers. plur. εἵαται, εἵατο for ἧαται, ἧατο cf. p. 96.

Some verbs waver between the athematic and the thematic conjugation: so δέχαται [a] (-ηται) M 147, δέγ-μενος B 794, etc., δέξο T 10, δέχθαι A 23; φέρ-τε (I 171), cf. Latin fers, fert.

(b) Reduplicated presents: ἵστημι, ἵσταμεν, πίμπλημι, πίμπλαμεν, τίθημι, τίθεμεν, etc. In Ionic these verbs tend to pass to the class of verba contracta. Such forms are also found in our texts of Homer, especially in the third person plural: τιθεῖσι, διδοῦσι, etc. It is doubtful, however, whether this accentuation is authentic since the normal conjugation of these verbs — *τίθεντι, *δίδοντι — by regular phonetic development would produce *τίθενσι, *δίδονσι ⟩ τίθεισι, διδοῦσι (δίδοισι in Aeolic). Similarly ἀνιεῖς, μεθιεῖς, διδοῖς, ἐδίδους, ἐδίδου, etc. may be later substitutions for ἀνίης, δίδως, etc. δίδημι (imperative διδέντων μ 54) is a new analogical formation coined from the aorist ἔδησα. βιβάς is the sole attested form of an athematic verb on which is based the Attic βιβάζω.

(c) Stems in -νῡ, -νῠ: This alternation has replaced the original IE -neu, -nu. Homer has many such verbs which are not found elsewhere: ὄρνυμι, δαίνυμι, ἄγνυμι, στόρνυμι, ἐέργνυμι, τάνυμι, γάνυμαι, etc. The third person plural of these verbs was originally of the type δεικνύουσι (⟨ -οντι), etc., which in Attic was replaced by δεικνύᾱσι (⟨ -αντι), and in Ionic by δεικνῦσι. Thus Homeric forms such as ῥηγνῦσι are more recent than the type τανύουσι, which, being identical in ending with the thematic class, gave rise to further thematic forms such as ὤμννε and ὀμννέτω.

Note ἤνυτο (ε 243) from *ἄνυμι, but with thematic forms ἦνον γ 496, ἄνεται K 251 (on the supposed optative ἄνοιτο see below).

(d) Stems in -νᾱ, -νᾰ: δάμνησι, δάμνᾰται, πίλναται, μάρναται, etc.

In later Ionic and the κοινή the -μι verbs pass over into the thematic class. In Homer we find apparent anticipations of this process, but forms such as ἀνιεῖς, μεθιεῖς, διδοῖς, ἵειν, ἵεις, etc., ἐτίθει, ἐδίδους may possibly stand for ἀνίης, δίδως, ἵην, ἐτίθη, etc., while for the 3rd pers. sing. ἱεῖ, τιθεῖ, διδοῖ, etc., we may read the Aeolic forms ἵη, τίθη, δίδω, etc.

2. Iteratives and Imperfects in -σκω

IE possessed a category of verbs distinguished by the suffix -σκ (preserved in English 'wash, wish'). Such verbs had iterative-durative force, and it is from them that an iterative-continuative past tense developed in Ionic, characterized by -σκ. Such forms may be built on imperfect

---

[a] The root originally contained an unaspirated κ—*dek (cf. δωροδόκος); the χ probably originated in forms like δέχθαι.

and aorist stems of any type, and on all present stems except, of course, those in -σκω.

Present stems : ἔσκεν, παρεκέσκετο, φεύγεσκε, ἔδεσκε, ἔχεσκες, πωλέσκεο, etc., etc. Note γοάασκεν (θ 92), περαάσκε (ε 480), etc. for γοάεσκεν, etc.

Aorist stems : δόσκον, εἴπεσκε, ἴδεσκε, στάσκεν, προβάλεσκε, εἴξασκε, γενέσκετο, etc.

3. The Aorist

We distinguish the athematic -s aorist (ἔλυσα), the thematic strong aorist (ἔλιπον, ἀραρών), the athematic asigmatic aorist (γέντο), and the aorist passives in -ην, -θην.

(a) The sigmatic aorist has -σα in the first person from -sṃ (VI), and this -α spread by analogy throughout the conjugation. Epic Greek, however, has a number of archaic middle forms which do not exhibit this analogical -α, so that the -s of the stem, coming between two consonants, disappeared : thus we have ἆλ-σο, ἆλ-το, ἄλ-μενος (< *ἁλίομαι, cf. salio). So further δέκ-το, ἐλέλικτο, λέκτο, ἐλέγμην, μίκτο, ὦρτο (< ὄρνυμι), πέρθαι (< *πέρθ-σ-θαι). It is, however, also possible to regard these forms as athematic root aorists (see below).

In stems ending in an -s or a dental plosive this final consonant combines with the sigma of the aorist to form -σσ- : ἐτέλεσ-σα, *ἐδατ-σάμην > ἐδασσάμην. This -σσ- was simplified in Attic but was retained in Aeolic and spread by analogy to vowel stems : so ὀμόσσαι, ἐλάσσαι, δαμάσσαι, etc. (see p. 86). In stems ending in a liquid or nasal the groups ρσ, λσ, μσ, and νσ underwent the phonetic changes outlined IX B (so ἔφθερρα, ἔφθειρα, etc.). In some verbs -λσ- and -ρσ- are preserved for reasons which are obscure : ἐνέκυρσε, κέρσαι, πέρσαι, etc.

(b) The thematic aorist :

(i) without reduplication. The root has the weak grade : ἤγρετο (ἀγείρω), ἔλιπον, ἔδρακον (δερκ-), ἤρυγε (ἐρευγ-), (εὔαδον (< ἔ-σϝαδ-ον), ἄμπνυε (πνεϝ-), περι-πλ-όμενος (qʷel-), ἐπ-έ-σπ-ον (*sep-, ἐφέπω), σπέσθαι (*seqʷ), ἔ-σχ-ον (< *segh), etc.

(ii) with reduplication (see above, p. 116 f.) : δέ-δα-ε, ἔειπον (< ἔ-ϝε-ϝπ-ον), τεταγών, ἔ-πε-φν-ον (*gʷhen-, θείνω), ἔ-τε-τμ-ον, κεκαδών, κέκλετο, λέλαθον, πεπιθεῖν, τετάρπετο, πεφιδέσθαι.

(c) The athematic asigmatic aorists. We distinguish :

(i) Roots with a short vowel (e.g., χεϝ-), which exhibit weak grade : ἔ-χυτ-ο, ἔ-φθι-το, ἔσσυ-το, ἔ-κτα-μεν [a] (ktṇ, weak grade of κτεν-), ἀπ-έ-κτα-το.

---

[a] The ἄ was introduced by analogy into other persons of the active : ἔκταν 'I killed', ἔκτα 'he killed', ἔκταν 'they killed'. Note further the thematic form ἔκτανον and the sigmatic aorist ἔκτεινα.

(ii) Of roots with a long vowel some aorists exhibit *Ablaut* alternation, others not.

(*a*) With *Ablaut*: ἔθη-κα, ἔ-θε-μεν,[a] etc.; ἔφην, ἔφαμεν; ἔβην, βάτην; ἔφθην, φθάς.

(*β*) Without *Ablaut*: ἔστην, ἔστημεν; ἔβην, ἔβημεν; ἔτλην, τλῆ-το. Nearly all such formations are intransitive in meaning, e.g., ἔσβη 'went out, was extinguished' but transitive ἔσβεσα; συμβλήτην 'they met'.

(iii) After a consonant the ṃ of the 1st pers. sing. appears as -α, which was carried throughout the conjugation. Here belong the Homeric-Ionic ἔνεικα (which is from a root *seik and quite distinct from ἤν-εγκον), εἶπα (also ἔειπον, see above), ἔκηα (‹ *ἔκηϝṃ), χεῦα,[b] ἔσσευα, ἠλεύατο (with Aeolic -ευ-).

(*d*) To this class we can possibly assign the aorists ἆλσο, γέντο (‹ *gem 'to grasp'), δέκτο, λέκτο, etc., which some scholars regard as sigmatic aorists with phonetic loss of the characteristic sigma.

(*e*) There are a number of so-called *mixed aorists* which exhibit the sigma together with the thematic inflection: ἄξετε, λέξεο, οἶσε, οἴσετε, ὄρσεο, πελάσσετον. But they are, perhaps, best regarded as futures (see below).

(*f*) Aorist passive in -η-, -θη-: IE had no separate forms for the passive, and in Homer the middle aorist may still function as a passive (see Syntax). The distinctive mark of the new Greek passive, -η-, was originally a formant of intransitives: e.g., ῥύη 'it flowed', ἐχάρη 'he rejoiced', (κατα) ἐκάη 'burnt itself out', etc. It is interesting to observe that nearly all -η- 'passives' in Homer are used intransitively, whereas about a quarter of the -θη- aorists are purely passive. -θη- arose from a combination of the suffix -θ-, which expresses a state (e.g., τελέθω), with the suffix -η-.

4. The Future

On the old athematic subjunctives functioning as futures such as ἔδομαι 'I shall eat' see p. 126. The normal Greek future is formed with the old desiderative suffix -s-, which was preserved or restored between vowels, as in λύσω, owing to the influence of consonant stems such as δείξω, etc. Note the reduplicated futures (which were originally independent of the reduplicated aorists and perfects). In Homer we find the following *future perfects*: δεδέξομαι, κεχολώσεται, πεφήσεται (which in P 155 means 'will appear' and is consequently based on the perfect πέφη· ἐφάνη, which Hesychius preserves), εἰρήσεται, κεκλήσηι.

Aorist futures: κεκαδησόμεθα (also active κεκαδήσει), πεφιδήσεται,

---

[a] The introduction of the long vowel and the κ-formant into the plural is a feature of Ionic; the examples found in Homer, e.g., ἔθηκαν, ἧκαν, ἔδωκαν, are to be regarded as later developments of the Epic dialect.

[b] Original *ἔχεϝα, *ἔχευ-s, *ἔχευτ- was levelled to ἔχευα, ἔχευας, etc.

πεπιθήσω. τετεύξεται, however, is built neither on the aorist nor on the perfect, but has the same stem form as the future τεύξεται.

To disyllabic roots in -ε and -α (καλε-, δαμα-) we find future formations in -εσω and -ασω, which after the disappearance of -σ- became identical with the present: καλέω. This type of future was extended to stems ending in a liquid or nasal consonant; so we find θενῶ, κτενέω,[a] στελέω, κερέω, μενέω, etc. In Attic-Ionic, further, this contracted future is a feature of verbs in -ιζω. Homer has, however, not only this type[b] (κομιῶ, κτεριῶ, ἀγλαϊεῖσθαι, etc.), but also the Aeolic type in -ισσω (ἐρίσσεται, ἐφοπλίσσουσι, ξεινίσσουσι) and, further, examples of the predominantly West Greek type in -ξω (with analogical guttural on the model of στηρίζω: στήριξα, etc.): πολεμίξω, ἐναρίξω, κτερεΐξω, δνοπαλίξω.

Where such disyllabic verbs have a sigmatic aorist in -σσα, there we find not only futures in -εω, -αω but also types in -εσ(σ)ω, -ασ(σ)ω: ὀλεῖται and ὀλέσσει, δαμᾷ and δαμάσσεται. But owing to uncertainty of reading in many cases and the identity of some forms of the future and the short-vowelled subjunctive (p. 126) it is difficult to decide what -σ(σ)ω futures are attested in Homer (see Monro² 57 f.). ἔσομαι is regarded as a short-vowelled subjunctive whereas ἔσσομαι is formed with the desiderative suffix -σο-.

Another type of future in -σε- (possibly a contamination of -σω and -ε(σ)ω) is particularly characteristic of Doric dialects. In Homer we find only ἐσσεῖται, but this has been explained as a contamination of ἔσσεται and *εῖται ⟨ *ἔσεται.

The examples of the so-called 'mixed aorist' (see above) such as οἶσε, οἰσέτω, δύσεο, λέξεο, etc., are in origin futures. The future οἴσετε occurs as a polite imperative Γ 103, etc., and οἶσε is merely a back-formation extracted from it on the analogy of ἐλθέ, ἔλθετε. On the other hand δύσετο δ' ἠέλιος is a past future and = occasurus erat,[c] and the same was perhaps true of βήσετο. But the aorist ἷξε is more probably a secondary transformation of ἷκε.

The future passive in -θησομαι does not occur in Homer, and the only two examples of -ησομαι (δαήσεαι γ 187 and μιγήσεσθαι Κ 365) are both intransitives (see above).

5. Perfect and Pluperfect

The perfect tense originally exhibited in many verbs the o-grade of the Ablaut in the singular and the zero grade in the dual and plural:

---

[a] κτανέω also occurs. Cf. aorist ἔκτανον above.

[b] This accentuation, however, probably represents a later, Attic-Ionic pronunciation. The Homeric futures in -ιω to -ιζω verbs were coined on the analogy of the type -ασα : -άω and should be written -ίω, since κτεριέουσι would produce *κτεριεῦσι in Ionic.

[c] In view of the meaning it is hardly probable that δύσετο and βήσετο are imperfects of desideratives δύσομαι and βήσομαι.

πέποιθα, ἐ-πέ-πιθ-μεν; μέμονα, μέ-μα-μεν (μα ⟨ mn̥), με-μα-(ϝ)ώς. Further examples of the weak grade which have been obscured by phonetic development are εἵμαρτο[a] (⟨ *se-smn̥-to), πέφα-νται (⟨ πέ-φn̥-νται, root θεν-, φον-, φν-), ἔϊκτον (ϝέ-ϝοικ-α, ϝέ-ϝικ-τον), ἐκγεγάτην[b] (γέγονα, *γε-γn̥-την), πέπασθε (πέπονθα, *πέ-πn̥θ-θε).

δείδω is a rhapsodic form representing *δέ-δϝοι-α, which after the loss of intervocalic -ι- and the resulting contraction became δέδϝω. The weak form was δέ-δϝι-μεν, which is represented as δείδι-μεν, and from this form a new stem δειδι- was extracted, which is seen in δείδιε. There is, further, a by-form of the perfect characterized by -κ-: δέ-δϝοι-κ-α (see below).

Note that the extension of the -α of the 1st pers. sing. to forms like πεποίθ-α-μεν is post-Homeric. In the middle, however, we find a thematic vowel sometimes intercalated to relieve difficulties of pronunciation: ὀρώρεται for *ὄρωρ-ται, μέμβλεται for *μέ-μλ-ται, etc. The κ- perfect is a Greek innovation which in Homer is found only where a long vowel or diphthong precedes the -κ, and further, apart from a few exceptions, only in the singular of the indicative and the subjunctive: ἕστηκα, δείδοικα, πέφυκε, βέβηκα, βέβληκα, κέκμηκας, etc., but ἑστᾶσιν, βεβάασιν, πεφύασιν, etc.

The perfect was originally intransitive in meaning (e.g., ἕστηκα), but the growing transitive use led to the coinage of new intransitive (middle) forms. Hence we find κεκορηότε and κεκορημένος, τετιηώς and τετιημένος, πεφευγώς and πεφυγμένος, etc.

Of the *Pluperfect* three types may be distinguished:

(1) With (optional) augment and secondary endings: μέ-μα-σαν, ἐ-δείδιμεν, βέβα-σαν, etc.; middle ἐπέπυστο, ἐτέτυκτο, ἠλήλατο.

(2) With the thematic vowel (found in Homer and the 'Achaean' dialects: ἄνωγον, ἐμέμηκον (3rd plur.), ἐπέπληγον, γέγωνε.

(3) The Attic-Ionic forms in -εα (-η), -εας (-ης), -εε (-ει), -εμεν, -ετε, -εσαν: πεποίθεα, ἠνώγεα, ἐπεποίθει, ἐοίκεσαν. ᾔδεα Θ 366, etc., stands for *ἠϝίδεα, the weak form of the stem having been taken over from the plural. On the other hand ἠείδης Χ 280 contains an extended form of the stem, ϝ(ε)ιδ-η-, which is seen in the future εἰδήσω and in the Latin *vid-ē-re*; it is consequently not a pluperfect in origin. The 3rd sing. -ει, frequent in Homer, may conceal an original pluperfect in -η.

THE MOODS

1. *Imperative*

The bare stem functions as the imperative in IE. To this stem various

---

[a] But note ἔμμορε ⟨ *se-smor-e with Aeolic treatment of -sm- and loss of the aspiration (psilosis). [b] On γεγά-ᾱσι, etc., see p. 119.

particles and personal endings were attached. Note thematic φέρε, but athematic φέρ-τε.

τῇ Ξ 219 is an adverb used as an imperative 'here !' A plural form τῆ-τε is found in Sophron; cf. further δεῦρο, δεῦ-τε and the Latin cedo, cette.

The extension by means of the ending -σο is a Greek innovation : ἔσ-σο, φάο, μάρναο, δέξο, λέξο, etc. On the forms -(σ)εο see above.

The ending -θι, which is proper to the athematic 2nd pers. sing. (e.g., ἴθι, ἴσθι, γνῶθι, etc.), appears as an optional element in ὄμνυθι (but δαίνῡ), δίδωθι, ἐμπίμπληθι. Note further the perfects ἄνωχθι, τέτλαθι, δείδιθι, τέθναθι, and the 'intransitive' aorist φάνηθι. κέκλυθι (and κέκλυτε), however, are not perfects, but are prefixed with the particle κε- seen in the Latin cedo, etc. But analysis as reduplicated aorists with zero grade -κλυ- is also possible.

The 3rd pers. of the imperative is characterized by -τω (originally the ablative case of the demonstrative *tod used to form future imperatives as in Latin with the meaning 'do so and so from that point'). Such forms were both singular and plural, but Greek evolved a number of plural forms such as -ντω, -των, -ντων. The last type is frequent in Homer : ἀγειρόντων, καιόντων, φιλεόντων, ἀγγελλόντων, etc. Apart from these we find only one other type : -των in ἔσ-των (α 273).

In the same way various pluralizations of the middle -σθω were coined : e.g., -σθων, -νσθω, -νσθων, etc. Homer has only forms in -σθων : λεξάσθων, ἐπέσθων, πιθέσθων.

2. Subjunctive

The Epic dialect, in common with many Greek dialects, exhibits a subjunctive which Attic no longer possessed : that is the short-vowelled type in ε/ο, which was proper to athematic indicatives, particularly the asigmatic aorist (see XI A).

E.g., ς- aorists : ἐρύσσομεν, τείσομεν, ἱλασόμεθα, ἀμείψεται, etc., etc.

Other types : ἴομεν (indic. ἴ-μεν), εἴδομεν (indic. ἴδ-μεν), χεύομεν (indic. ἔχευα), φθίεται (indic. φθί-το), πεποίθομεν (indic. πέποιθα).

Some of these subjunctives function as futures (see Syntax) : ἔδομαι, πίομαι.

This type was gradually replaced by the long-vowelled thematic type in η/ω. Thus we find in Homer on the one hand κεῖται (= κεῖ-εται) Ω 554, κέεται Τ 32, κατακείομεν, etc., and on the other κέηται (contracted κῆται). So also θή-ομεν, βή-ομεν, στή-ομεν (written θείομεν, etc.[a]) together with θήῃς, θήῃ, στήῃς, στήωσι, δαμήω, etc. In the latter type there took place further either a shortening of the first vowel (so

---

[a] See above, p. 97.

στέωμεν, ἔωμεν, θέωμεν, ἀφέῃ) or contraction (γνῶμεν, θῆσι, βῇ, δῶσι, etc.).
On the personal endings -μι, -(σ)θα, -σι in the subjunctive see above.

3. *Optative*

Two types must be distinguished: (1) the athematic optative where
the mood sign exhibits *Ablaut*: -*ie*, *ī* (so Latin *siem*, *simus*, Greek *ἐ̄(σ)-
ίη-ν*, *ἐ̄((σ)-ί-μεν)*; (2) the thematic optative where the non-alternating
mood sign -ι- combines with the thematic vowel to produce -οι.

In (1) the strong form -ιη- appears in the sing. active, -ῑ- being proper
to the dual and plur. active and to the middle. In Ionic, however, -ιη- is
often extended to the plural (εἴημεν, etc.); but in Homer the only
example is σταίησαν P 733 (on which see p. 94).

In some forms phonetic development has obliterated the mood-sign:
thus δαινῦτο Ω 665 stands for *δαινύιτο; so also the 3rd plur. δαινύατο
σ 248, and αἰνῦτο, δύη, ἐκδῦμεν, λελῦτο, φθῖτο. Note, further, the
intrusion of the thematic type in ἔοις, ἔοι, and ἴοι. Apart from the last
form εἶμι has a number of different forms. The IE *i-i̯ē-t would in
Greek become *ἴη; this appears as εἴη Ω 139 with a restoration of the
full grade ει (cf. ἐ(σ)ίην, where Sanskrit *syām* and Latin *s-iem* still preserve
the zero grade *s*-). εἴη, however, was homonymous with εἴη from εἰμί,
to obviate which ἰ-είη Τ 209 was formed.

The contracted verbs have the expected thematic forms: καλέοι,
φιλέοι, etc. In Attic these were replaced by φιλοίην, etc., forms which
were coined on the analogy διδοῖμεν : διδοίην :: μισθοῖμεν : μισθοίην.
In Homer only two such forms are attested: φιλοίη δ 692 and φοροίη ι 320,
which may be regarded as Atticisms (see above, p. 94).

THE VERBAL NOUNS

1. *The Infinitive*

On the dialectal distribution of the athematic types in -μεν, -μεναι,
and -ναι see p. 82. It should be noted that all these types occur in all
tenses of athematic verbs with the exception of the perfect, where -μεν,
-μεναι are alone attested.

The ending -μεν is attached also to thematic types in the Aeolic
dialects Boeotian and Thessalian; this happens occasionally in Homer
both with -μεν (ἀγέμεν, φερέμεν, σχέμεν, εἰπέμεν, etc.) and with -μεναι
(ἀγινέμεναι, ἀγορευέμεναι). The thematic vowel appears even in the aorist
infinitive κελευσέμεναι.

Note that ἔμμεναι and ἔμμεν sometimes appear without the lengthened
consonant which is the expected product in Aeolic of -σμ-: ἔμεναι and
ἔμεν.

On the other hand, though the athematic conjugation of contracted verbs (φίλημι, etc.) is a characteristic of Aeolic, Lesbian[a] perversely has the thematic infinitive of such verbs (κάλην). In Homer, however, we find the expected athematic infinitives of contracted verbs: γοήμεναι, καλήμεναι, φορήμεναι, etc.

The thematic type in -ειν is contracted from -ε(σ)εν. ἰδέειν Γ 236, etc., βαλέειν Β 414 are perhaps rhapsodic forms, blends of ἰδεῖν, etc., and the uncontracted ἴδε-εν, etc., which may, however, often be substituted in the verse for ἰδέειν, etc.

2. The Participles

On the Aeolic perfect participles in -ων -οντος and the rhapsodic forms in -ωτος see above.

vi. THE SYNTAX OF THE HOMERIC DIALECT

A. THE NOUN

NUMBER

The usage whereby a noun in the neuter plural takes a singular verb is often transgressed in Homer: e.g., λύντο δὲ γυῖα Η 16, ἄρματα ('a chariot' !) . . . ἐπέτρεχον Ψ 503 f., τόσσ᾽ ἄρα τοῦ ἑκάτερθεν ἔσαν πτερά Ω 319, etc.

The use of the plural for nouns of mass such as ἅλες, πυροί, ζεαί, ξύλα, ψάμαθοι, is well known, as is that in nouns denoting objects of complex structure such as πύλαι, θύραι, ὄχεα, ἄρματα. Noteworthy is the compact group of plurals in abstract nouns denoting human qualities and defects: πολυκερδείῃσι, ἀεσιφροσύνῃσι, ἀϊδρείῃσι, μεθημοσύνῃσι, νηπιέῃσι, ποδω-κείῃσι, προθυμίῃσι.

Metrical convenience often determines the choice of singular or plural, e.g., ἄλφιτα but ἄλφιτον. Yet where the poet has a choice of singular or plural the use of the latter gives the expression greater concreteness and palpability. In a word, the 'poetic plural' is more vivid; as Aristotle observed, it gives greater ὄγκος to the style.

In the use of the dual, too, which was progressively eliminated during the history of Greek, Attic shows itself more archaic than Homer and still more so than the close cousin Ionic, which has completely eliminated the dual. The artificiality of Homeric usage (see p. 100) is illustrated by ὣς τώ γ᾽ ἀντιβίοισι μαχεσσαμένω ἐπέεσσιν ἀνστήτην, λῦσαν δ᾽ ἀγορὴν παρὰ

[a] One such infinitive is attested for Linear B: te–re–ja–e corresponding to indicative te–re–ja.

νηυσὶν Ἀχαιῶν Α 304 f.; τὼ μὲν ταρβήσαντε καὶ αἰδομένω βασιλῆα στήτην, οὐδέ τί μιν προσεφώνεον οὐδ' ἐρέοντο Α 331 f.; cf. Γ 340 ff., Χ 145 ff., etc., etc.

The dual is in full vigour in the Mycenaean documents: *to-pe-zo*, 'two tables', *ko-to-no*, 'two *ktoinai*', *i-qi-jo*, 'two *hippiai*', *a-mo-te*, 'two *harmata*'.

THE CASES

Greek preserved (apart from a few remnants such as the ablative οἴκω) only five of the original eight IE cases, whose functions were distributed thus:

Function	IE	Greek
	Nominative	Nominative
	Vocative	Vocative
→∣ [a]	Accusative	Accusative
⊙	Genitive⎱	
⊢→	Ablative⎰	Genitive
⇢	Dative ⎫	
↓	Locative ⎬	Dative
→←—	Instrumental ⎭	

1. *The Nominative* is frequently used for the vocative: (1) for the second of two persons addressed: Ζεῦ πάτερ . . . Ἠέλιός θ' Γ 276 f.; (2) in the attribute of a noun in the vocative: φίλος ὦ Μενέλαε Δ 189 (but note the MSS readings οὐλε ὄνειρε Β 8, πάτερ ὦ ξεῖνε θ 408, Θέτι τανύπεπλε Σ 385, where the metre demands a restoration of the nominative); (3) where two people are addressed γαμβρὸς ἐμὸς θυγάτηρ τε τ 406.

Close to this vocative use is the exclamatory noun phrase as in δημοβόρος βασιλεύς, ἐπεὶ οὐτιδανοῖσιν ἀνάσσεις Α 231.

The use of the introductory particle ὦ differs from that of Attic: in Homer it lends a tone of abruptness, impatience, familiarity, etc. Thus Gods and superiors (*e.g.*, husbands) are addressed without ὦ.

On the *Nominative Pendens* cf. p. 156, on anacoluthon.

2. *The Accusative.*—The function of this case may be defined as the end, aim, or result, towards which the action proceeds or is directed. It may be represented thus: →∣ [b] The nature of the movement or direction ('down to', 'up to', 'towards', etc.) could be indicated more precisely

---

[a] For an explanation of the signs see below.

[b] The view is widely held that the accusative of the historical Indo-European languages combines two originally separate functions: (1) the case of the direct object and (2) a 'lative' function expressing the limit or goal towards which the action expressed by the verb proceeds.

by the insertion of independent adverbs (εἰς, ἐπί, κατά, etc.). These adverbs through constant use in the course of time came to be regarded as necessary adjuncts and thus developed into prepositions 'governing' the cases which follow them (see p. 139 f.). In Homer, however, we still observe the base case functioning with much of its original independence : ὃς δέ κ' ἀνὴρ ἀπὸ ὧν ὀχέων ἕτερ' ἅρμαθ' ἵκηται, '. . . comes to another chariot' Δ 306; ἡ δὲ ξυνάγουσα γεραιὰς νηὸν 'Αθηναίης, 'gathering the old wives to the temple of Athena' Z 87-8; νῦν δὲ σὺ μὲν 'Αΐδαο δόμους . . . ἔρχεαι, 'now shalt thou come to the abode of Hades' X 482, etc.

This type of accusative in πεύθετο γὰρ Κύπρονδε μέγα κλέος Λ 21 is to be explained as a contamination of 'the rumour reached Cyprus' and 'he heard the rumour in Cyprus'.

Noteworthy is the function (of Indo-European origin) which the verbal prefix has of making a verb transitive : ἀνεδύσετο κῦμα, 'she emerged from the sea' A 496. Still stranger to our feeling is κατέβαιν' ὑπερώϊα, 'she descended from the upper chamber' σ 206, as contrasted with θάλαμον κατεβήσετο, 'went down into the store room'.

The aims, objects, or results of the verbal action may be classified variously according to the meaning of the verb : thus in 'to dig the ground', where ground is exposed to the action of digging, we have a so-called external accusative ; but in 'to dig a trench' 'trench' expresses the result towards which the action is directed. Such accusatives are known as *internal accusatives*. Homer has some curious examples : γεφύρωσεν δὲ κέλευθον, 'he built a causeway' O 357; ἀγγελίην ἐλθόντα [a] Λ 140, 'going on an embassy' with an accusative as in our 'running an errand'. This type of accusative is combined in a strange fashion with an external accusative in ἤγαγε Σιδονίηθεν . . . τὴν ὁδὸν ἣν 'Ελένην περ ἀνήγαγεν Z 291-2, where ὁδὸν ἀνάγειν is merely an extension of the usage seen in ἀγγελίην ἐλθεῖν and ἦλθον . . . ὁδόν [b] ζ 164, ὁδὸν οἴχεσθαι. Cf. τὸν . . . ἀνώγεα αὐτὴν ὁδὸν ἡγήσασθαι κ 263 as in our 'lead the way'.

The adverbial accusative is a special development of the internal accusative. As in Latin, it is particularly frequent with the neuter singular and plural of pronouns and adjectives. Such accusatives are particularly a feature of Homer's language, which does not exhibit many examples of the adverbs in -ως : τάδε μαίνεται Ε 185, τόδ' ἱκάνεις Ξ 298, αἶν' ὀλοφυρόμεναι χ 447, ἄλληκτον πολεμίζειν Β 452, ὀξέα κεκληγώς Β 222, εὐρὺ ῥέοντος Β 849, μεγάλα κλάζοντε Π 429 (cf. οὖλον κεκλήγοντες, 'shrieking doom'), ἅ . . . πείσεσθαι, 'to obey which orders' A 289, etc.

The so-called *cognate accusative*, too, is merely a special instance of the internal accusative in which the object noun is etymologically related to the verb : μάχην μάχεσθαι.

---

[a] But note ἤλυθε . . . ἀγγελίης Γ 205 (see below).   [b] Cf. longam viam ire.

Often we find a double limitation or direction of the verbal action: τόν ῥ' Ὀδυσεὺς ἑτάροιο χολωσάμενος βάλε δουρὶ κόρσην ... τὸν δὲ σκότος ὄσσε κάλυψε Δ 501 ff., 'O. struck him (and more precisely) his temple'. This second accusative may be 'retained' when the verb is in the passive: χερμαδίῳ γὰρ βλῆτο ... κνήμην δεξιτερήν Δ 518-19. From this usage such *accusatives of respect* as we observe in χεῖρα καμεῖται Β 389 developed. On the other hand, true accusatives of respect such as ὄνομα, μῆκος, etc., are examples of an IE usage which particularly flourished in Greek. A noteworthy example is οἱ περὶ μὲν βουλὴν Δαναῶν Α 258, 'ye who are superior to (the best of) the Greeks in counsel'. In Γ 158 the accusative is strengthened by means of the preposition εἰς, which shows clearly that the Greeks felt such an accusative as a directional case 'with regard to ...', just as the later use of ἀπό with the genitive of comparison brings out its essentially ablatival force: αἰνῶς ἀθανάτῃσι θεῇς εἰς ὦπα ἔοικεν Γ 158, 'she is wondrously like the immortal goddesses in countenance'.

3. The Greek *Genitive*, as emerges from the above schema, fulfils the functions of both the genitive and the ablative in IE. We discuss its functions, therefore, under these two headings. Hittite has an ablative case in -*ts*. This would have become -*s* in Greek. So the syncretism of ablative and genitive may have been due to phonetic causes.

1. *The Pure Genitive*.—A. In Indo-European the genitive is considered by some to have been primarily an adverbal case, the adnominal use being a secondary and narrowly restricted development. But if we confine our analysis to the Greek facts, we may say that the basic function of the genitive when constructed with another noun (the *adnominal genitive*) is to denote the sphere or frame in which the governing noun is placed. It may be represented: ⊙. Thus a πόλεμος Ἀχαιῶν is war limited or circumscribed by the idea 'Achaeans': *i.e.* a war in which the Achaeans are concerned, an 'Achaeans-war'. Whether it is a war by, against, or on behalf of the Achaeans can only be deduced from the context. Similarly in ἦ νύ τοι οὔ τι μέλει Τρώων πόνος the genitival phrase must be translated 'toils, efforts with regard to, or directed against the Trojans'. It is, in fact, what is known as an objective genitive. Further, ἕρκος πολέμοιο is a 'war-bulwark', *i.e.* a barrier against war, with which one may compare σκέπας ... ἀνέμοιο, 'a wind ... shield' ε 443; ἕρκος ὀδόντων, on the other hand, a 'teeth-barrier', is a barrier consisting of teeth, that is a qualitative genitive, a usage we may compare with the appositional genitive τέκμωρ Ἰλίου, 'the goal that is Ilion'. But such special terms as subjective, objective, qualitative, partitive, possessive, etc., with which grammarians label the special instances of the genitive, should not conceal the essential unity of the genitive in denoting the sphere, milieu, or

L

environment in which a noun is placed or a verbal action takes place. Thus there is no particular syntactical difficulty about B 356 τείσασθαι δ' Ἑλένης ὁρμήματά τε στοναχάς τε = 'avenge the efforts and the griefs connected with Helen'. The authenticity of the line is disputed; but it was written by a Greek who knew his language and so demands syntactical exegesis.

The particular specialization of the genitive of quality which we observe in the Latin genitive of price and value was not highly developed in ancient Greek (for occasional adverbal usages of this genitive see below).

B. *Adverbal Functions.* Here too the central core of usage may be designated as the sphere of the verbal action. It may be the sphere *within which* the verbal action takes place: διέπρησσον πεδίοιο Γ 14, 'they sped over or through the plain'; cf. πόλεος πεδίοιο θέουσαι Δ 244; νέφος δ' οὐ φαίνετο πάσης γαίης οὐδ' ὀρέων Ρ 372, 'no cloud was seen over all the earth and mountains'; λοεσσάμενος ποταμοῖο Φ 560, etc. A purely local use in the sense 'in the region of, close to' is seen in ἀντίον ἷζεν . . . τοίχου τοῦ ἑτέροιο I 218-19, cf. Ω 598, ψ 90. Similar are the *genitives of time* [a] such as τοῦδ' αὐτοῦ λυκάβαντος τ 306, 'this same month', ὀπώρης Χ 27, 'in autumn', οὐδὲ . . . χείματος οὐδὲ θέρευς η 118, νηνεμίης Ε 523, 'in still weather', τῶν προτέρων ἐτέων, 'in previous years', etc.

The action may be directed towards, or referred to, a sphere. Such usages were already present in Indo-European and explanations of their origin can consequently only take the form of unverifiable hypotheses. It is conceivable to find a starting point in partitives such as ὕδατος πίνειν, whence by a natural association the construction spread to such expressions as 'to want to drink water', 'to be thirsty for water' (διψῆν and πεινῆν may both take a genitive), 'long for water' (οὐδεὶς ποτοῦ ἐπιθυμεῖ), etc. In this field of expansion we find the verbs of desiring, aiming at, reaching for, reaching, achieving, touching, and the like. Homeric examples are: ὄστευσον Μενελάου Δ 100, 'aim your shafts at Menelaus'; οὗ παιδὸς ὀρέξατο φαίδιμος Ἕκτωρ Ζ 466, 'glorious Hector reached out for his son'; σέθεν ἀντιάσαιμεν Η 231, 'we should go to meet you' (so also ἀντιάαν πολέμοιο, ἀντιόων ἑκατόμβης, etc.). Less obvious examples of the same kind are ἀλλήλων ἀφίκοντο and τύχε γάρ ῥ' ἀμάθοιο βαθείης, 'he fell in the deep sand', which Monro classifies as 'quasi partitive'. The genitives found after verbs of emotion such as οἰκτίρειν, χολοῦσθαι, etc., might be regarded as embodying genitives expressing the sphere *from which* the verbal action proceeds. But it is difficult to distinguish this usage from the genitives of the sphere referred to usual after *verba iudicalia*. A pure example of such a 'referential' genitive of the sphere is τί μοι ἔριδος καὶ ἀρωγῆς Φ 360, 'what concern have I with strife and succour'. The genitives with verbs of perceiving,

---

[a] Such genitives are also attested in the Linear B tablets.

learning, too, may be variously interpreted as denoting the *sphere from which*, or they may be grouped among the partitive genitives usual after verbs of filling, sharing, tasting, etc. They follow on quite naturally from the series discussed above: reaching, touching, grasping, comprehending, perceiving. But there is little point in splitting logical hairs over the assignment to this or that compartment of usage: the adverbal genitive refers a verbal action vaguely to a sphere, and, as with the adnominal genitive, the precise relationship is to be deduced from the context. The categories to which grammarians affix their various labels are nothing more than the associational groups or 'fairy rings' [a] into which words naturally fall in virtue of their meaning. The following examples are noteworthy: διδασκόμενος πολέμοιο Π 811, 'to learn warfare', and πολέμοιο δαήμεναι Φ 487, have the construction of verbs of perceiving, remembering, etc. (Note, however, the unexpected accusative in Τυδέα δ᾽ οὐ μέμνημαι Ζ 222). ἤλυθε . . . ἀγγελίης Γ 206 and Ν 252, ἀγγελίης οἴχνεσκε Ο 640 are referential genitives which contrast with the internal accusative construction ἀγγελίην ἐλθεῖν discussed above. *Cf.* further examples of 'referential' genitives of the sphere: εἴτ᾽ ἄρ ὅ γ᾽ εὐχωλῆς ἐπιμέμφεται ἠδ᾽ ἑκατόμβης Α 65 and, still more remarkable, εἰπὲ δέ μοι πατρός τε καὶ υἱέος ὃν κατέλειπον λ 174. But the last may be an extension of the partitive use as in τῶν ἁμόθεν γε . . . εἰπὲ καὶ ἡμῖν α 10.

One of the most developed functions of the genitive of the sphere is to denote the whole from which a part is taken, used, tasted, etc. A less familiar example is μὴ τάχα ἄστυ πυρὸς δηΐοιο θέρηται Ζ 331, 'lest the city be burnt with consuming fire', where the genitive has contact on the one hand with partitives such as χείλεα φύρσω αἵματος σ 21 f., and on the other with local genitives such as ποταμοῖο λοεσσάμενος. The locatival dative construction is also found with λοῦσθαι. Interpretation of the genitives as partitives seems the most attractive solution of ἀλλ᾽ οὔ πῃ χροὸς εἴσατο Ν 191, 'but no flesh was anywhere visible', cf. φαίνετο . . . λαυκανίης [b] Χ 324-5, 'the throat was partially visible'.

The *genitive of price* had its origin [c] in the genitive of quality: *e.g.*, λόγου ἐλαχίστου ἐστί, *res est mille denarium*, etc. We note some peculiar analogical extensions of this usage: ὥ ποτ᾽ Ἀχιλλεὺς . . . ἔλυσεν ἀποίνων Λ 104 f., 'whom Achilles released for a ransom'; ἢ τρίποδος περιδώμεθον ἠὲ λέβητος Ψ 485, 'let us wager a tripod or a cauldron'. Of a similar type are the genitives with verbs of exchanging: ἢ χρύσον φίλου ἀνδρὸς ἐδέξατο λ 327, 'who took gold for her own husband'; τεύχε᾽ ἄμειβε χρύσεα χαλκείων Ζ 235 f., 'he exchanged golden armour for bronze'.

---

[a] On this technical term see L. R. Palmer, *The Latin Language*, 284-5.

[b] λαυκανίην is also read.

[c] Wackernagel traces the usage to an old adverbial -ī case exemplified in the Latin *lucri facere*.

11. *The Ablatival Genitive.*—The IE ablative designated the point of departure, the origin of the action. We represent it: ↦. This case, too, in the primitive usage required no supporting preposition, so that we find in Homer constructions such as the following: ἀλλὰ τὰ μὲν πολίων ἐξεπράθομεν A 125, 'the things we plundered from the cities'; ὡς ὅτε μήτηρ παιδὸς ἐέργῃ μυῖαν Δ 130 f., 'as when a mother wards off a fly from her child'; after verbs denoting separation, deprivation, distance from (λείπομαι), falling short of (δεύομαι): διώκετο οἷο δόμοιο σ 8, 'was chased from his home'; πυλάων χάσσασθαι Μ 171-2, 'to withdraw from the gates'; ἀτεμβόμενος ἴσης Λ 705, cf. Ψ 445, 'debarred from, cheated of, his proper portion'. The genitive after verbs of beginning may be interpreted as ablatival as in σεῦ δ' ἄρξομαι I 97, but they are intimately connected by association with verbs of opposite meaning 'to cease': λῆξαν δὲ φόνοιο Ζ 107. This *genitive of separation* is found also with ἀμύνω: ἀμυνέμεν οὐκ ἐθέλουσι νηῶν ὠκυπόρων Ν 109 f., 'they do not wish to ward off from the swift-faring ships', *i.e.* defend the ships); cf. ὁ δ' οὐδ' οὗ παιδὸς ἀμύνει Π 522.

The frequent use of the genitive to express the cause or source of an emotion may also be at least partly ablatival in origin: ἑτάροιο χολωσάμενος Δ 501, ἱρῶν μηνίσας Ε 178 (but it is more probably a pure referential genitive, see above on εὐχωλῆς ἐπιμέμφεται). The *genitive of comparison*, too, is ablatival in origin, representing the point of view or standard from which a quality is judged to be excessive or inferior. We find it after the adverb περί 'exceedingly' in οἳ περὶ μὲν βουλὴν Δαναῶν, 'who excel the Greeks' A 258; cf. γυναικῶν περίειμι τ 325-6.

4. *The Dative* : ⇢

In accordance with the above schema we must distinguish between pure datival, locatival, and instrumental usages.

A. *The Pure Dative.* The original function of the pure dative was to indicate the person concerned or implicated in the verbal event or state of affairs. The extension to non-personal nouns was secondary. The reference is a vague one implying that the person is indirectly affected by the event in question, whether favourably, unfavourably, or merely as an interested observer. It may be represented: ⇢. As such it is often equivalent to a possessive genitive (cf. Latin *mihi est*): κυκήθησαν δέ οἱ ἵπποι as in the German *Die Pferde liefen* ihm *davon*. This practical equivalence of genitive and dative explains sense constructions such as τοῦ δέ τ' ἐρητύεται κραδίη καὶ θυμὸς ἀγήνωρ ποινὴν δεξαμένῳ I 635 f., 'his heart and proud spirit are restrained when he has received the blood-money'.

Note, further, the *dativus iudicantis* in πᾶσι δέ κε Τρώεσσι χάριν καὶ κῦδος ἄροιο Δ 95, 'you would win favour and glory in the eyes of all the

Trojans'. The *datives of direction* exemplified in such expressions as ψυχὰς
Ἄϊδι προΐαψεν Α 3, τρήρωνες, ταί τ' ἀμβροσίην Διὶ πατρὶ φέρουσι μ 63,
Αἰθίκεσσι πέλασσεν Β 744, etc., are merely developments of the personal
dative of advantage found with verbs of giving. A less obvious example,
which has been misunderstood by some editors,[a] is αὐτὸς δ' ἐννοσίγαιος
ἔχων χείρεσσι τρίαιναν ἡγεῖτ', ἐκ δ' ἄρα πάντα θεμείλια κύμασι πέμπε
Μ 27 f., 'the Earthshaker, holding the trident in his hands, was leading
them and sweeping all the foundations out to sea'.

B. *The Instrumental* is not aptly named, since it was also used to express
the association, conjunction, or co-operation of persons or things. We
represent it: →←.

The following usages call for comment:

The case may stand without a supporting preposition: ἦ νῦν δὴ
Τροίηθεν ἀλώμενος ἐνθάδ' ἱκάνεις νηΐ τε καὶ ἑτάροισι λ 160-1, etc.

Frequent, too, is the instrumental of accompanying circumstances:
σε κακῇ αἴσῃ τέκον Α 418, 'I bore thee under an evil star'; νῶϊ δέ τ' ἄψορροι
κίομεν κεκοτηότι θυμῷ Φ 456, 'we came back with angry hearts', etc.
But such instrumentals often shade off into causal usages: οἱ δ' ἄλλοι
φιλότητι νεώτεροι ἄνδρες ἕπονται γ 363, 'the others, the younger men,
accompany him out of friendship', cf. Γ 453; θηλύτεραι δὲ θεαὶ μένον
αἰδοῖ οἴκοι ἑκάστη θ 324, 'the goddesses remained at home out of mo-
desty'.

On the other hand we have as in Latin, Sanskrit, etc., an *instrumental
of the price* whereby something is acquired: τήν ποτε Λαέρτης πρίατο
κτεάτεσσιν ἑοῖσιν α 430. Less obvious examples of the normal instrumental usage are: γαῖα φάνεσκε ψάμμῳ κυανέη μ 242 f., 'the earth came
to view with its dark sand'; but the reading may be κυανέη, in which
case the expression 'dark with sand' is parallel with τεύχεσι παμφαίνων
Ζ 513.

I am inclined to classify here the dative expressing the time taken to
accomplish something (*i.e.* basically = 'by means of'): e.g., ω 118 μηνὶ
δ' ἄρ' οὔλῳ πάντα περήσαμεν εὐρέα πόντον. This interpretation derives
support from Aristarchus's ἐν οὔλῳ.

C. *The Locative* is often used without a preposition: τόξ' ὤμοισιν
ἔχων Α 45; cf. ἀγρῷ Ε 137, Ἄργεϊ μέσσῳ Ζ 224, στὰς μέσῳ ἕρκεϊ Ω 306,
etc., etc. Here, too, we should classify such usages as ὅο κράτος ἔσκε
μέγιστον πᾶσι Κυκλώπεσσι, *i.e.* 'among the Cyclops' α 70 f.; ἐπεὶ οὐτιδανοῖσιν ἀνάσσεις Α 231. Semantically we may classify here the verbs
meaning 'to be pre-eminent (among)', 'rule', 'command', and the like
although they belong simultaneously to several associational 'fairy rings'.
The explicit preposition used in ἐν ὀφθαλμοῖσι ὁρᾶσθαι Γ 306 makes it

---

[a] Monro regards it as a 'sociative' dative. But the syntactical development is no greater
than between 'give the dog a bone' and 'throw the dog a bone'.

probable that the Greeks felt datives such as θυμῷ, φρεσί, ὀφθαλμοῖς, etc., as locatives rather than instrumental. We find, however, an instrumental use of ἐν in later Greek : e.g., γράφε ἐν ἥλῳ κυπρίνῳ, 'write with a copper nail', in a magical papyrus. We also find locatives of time as ὥρῃ, νυκτὸς ἀμολγῷ, τῇδε . . . νυκτί, etc.

THE ARTICLE

The article of classical times was in origin nothing more than a weakened form of the demonstrative ὁ, ἡ, τό (cf. the development of the Romance definite article from the Latin illum, illam). In Homer ὁ, ἡ, τό, still preserve much of their original demonstrative force and independence : they may be used substantivally, adjectivally, and as relative pronouns.

1. *Substantival Use*: ὁ γάρ . . . ὦρσε A 9 ; ὁ γὰρ ἦλθε l. 12 ; τὴν δ' ἐγὼ οὐ λύσω l. 29 ; τοῦ δ' ἔκλυε Φοῖβος Ἀπόλλων l. 43 ; ὁ δ' ἤϊε l. 47 ; τῷ γὰρ ἐπὶ φρεσὶ θῆκε θεὰ λευκώλενος Ἥρη l. 55 ; τοῖσι δ' ἀνιστάμενος l. 58, etc.

Such demonstratives are used to denote a contrast either where there is a change of subject or where the same subject engages in contrasted activities : Θέτις δ' οὐ λήθετ' ἐφετμέων παιδὸς ἑοῦ, ἀλλ' ἥ γ' ἀνεδύσετο κῦμα θαλάσσης A 495 f., 'Thetis did not forget her son's behest, but she rose up from the swell of the sea' ; τοῦ μὲν ἅμαρθ', ὁ δὲ Λεῦκον . . . βεβλήκει Δ 491, where there is no contrast between τοῦ and ὁ, but between the actions of missing and hitting by the same subject ὁ ("Αντιφος) ; cf. στήθεσσιν λασίοισι διάνδιχα μερμήριξεν, ἦ ὅ γε φάσγανον ὀξὺ ἐρυσσάμενος παρὰ μηροῦ τοὺς μὲν ἀναστήσειεν, ὁ δ' Ἀτρείδην ἐναρίζοι . . . A 189 ff., where note the double contrast of the actions ἀναστήσειν and ἐναρίζοι (subjects ὅ γε . . . ὁ δέ) and the objects τοὺς μέν . . . Ἀτρείδην. The use of the demonstrative with a particle (ἀλλ' ὁ, ὁ δέ, etc.) to denote a change of subject hardly requires illustration : . . . οὐδ' ἀπίθησε μύθῳ Ἀθηναίης. ἡ δ' Οὔλυμπόνδε βεβήκει A 220, etc., etc. Contrast within the sentence is often effectively expressed by a collocation of two demonstratives : ἧος ὁ τὸν πεδίοιο διώκετο πυροφόροιο Φ 602, 'and while he pursued him over the wheat-bearing plain' ; πρὸ ὁ τοῦ ἐνόησεν K 224, 'one perceives before the other'.

As a step towards the purely adjectival use we find the demonstrative in apposition with a noun which follows and explains it (this is possibly the origin of the adjectival use, which, however, is also Indo-European, so that any attempt at a history of its development is pure speculation) : αὐτὰρ ὁ βοῦν ἱέρευσεν ἄναξ ἀνδρῶν Ἀγαμέμνων πίονα πενταέτηρον ὑπερμενέϊ Κρονίωνι B 402 f., where the schema of the sentence is first sketched in the three words ὁ βοῦν ἱέρευσεν, which is then filled out and explained — 'he sacrificed a bull, namely Agamemnon, a fat, five-year-old one, to mighty Cronion'. *Cf.* Δ 502 ἡ δ' ἑτέροιο διὰ κροτάφοιο πέρησεν αἰχμὴ χαλκείη, 'it passed through the other temple, the spearpoint of bronze'. Where the demonstrative is followed immediately by the noun in apposition, it is difficult to distinguish from the later article. But note in παῖδα δ' ἐμοὶ λύσαιτε φίλην, τὰ δ' ἄποινα δέχεσθαι Α 20, 'may you release my dear child and receive this ransome I bring', as contrasted with ἔνθ' ἄλλοι μὲν πάντες ἐπευφήμησαν 'Αχαιοὶ αἰδεῖσθαί θ' ἱερῆα καὶ ἀγλαὰ δέχθαι ἄποινα ll. 22 f., where Attic would have required the article with ἄποινα as being already known to the speaker (so also l. 95).

This appositional use is no different in principle from the anticipatory, where it is followed by an explanatory clause:

(1) *Relative*: τὰ γὰρ φρονέεις, ἅ τ' ἐγώ περ Δ 361; *cf.* κείνοισι δ' ἂν οὔ τις τῶν οἳ νῦν βροτοί εἰσιν, ἐπιχθόνιοι μαχέοιτο Α 271 f., 'not one of those who . . .'; τὴν γὰρ ἀοιδήν . . . ἥ τις ἀκουόντεσσι νεωτάτη ἀμφιπέληται α 351 f.

In such constructions the demonstrative is often brought nearer to the relative by placing it after the noun; ὁππότε κεν καὶ ἐγὼ μεμαὼς πόλιν ἐξαλαπάξαι τὴν ἐθέλω ὅθι τοι φίλοι ἀνέρες ἐγγεγάασι Δ 40 f., 'whenever I in eagerness wish to lay waste a city, such a one wherein men dear to you have been born'; οὐδ' υἱὸς Καπανῆος ἐλήθετο συνθεσιάων τάων ἃς ἐπέτελλε βοὴν ἀγαθὸς Διομήδης Ε 319 f.; ἦ τ' ἐφάμην σὲ περὶ φρένας ἔμμεναι ἄλλων τῶν ὅσσοι Λυκίην ἐριβώλακα ναιετάουσι Ρ 171 f.

(2) *Substantival* clause introduced by ὅ, ὅτε, ὅτι, etc.: λεύσσετε γὰρ τό γε πάντες, ὅ μοι γέρας ἔρχεται ἄλλῃ Α 120, 'for you all see this, that my prize is going elsewhere'; ἦ ἄρ τι τόδ' ἀμφοτέροισιν ἄρειον ἔπλετο . . . ὅτε νῶϊ . . . μενεήναμεν Τ 56 ff., 'was this then better for us two when we raged . . .?'

(3) Introducing *Epexegetic Infinitive*: τὸ δὲ ῥίγιον αὖθι μένοντα βουσὶν ἐπ' ἀλλοτρίῃσι καθήμενον ἄλγεα πάσχειν υ 220 f., 'this is worse . . . to suffer pain'; so also ἀνίη καὶ τὸ φυλάσσειν πάννυχον ἐγρήσσοντα υ 52, 'it is a grievous thing to keep watch all night', which is the nearest approach we find in Homer to an articular infinitive (see below, pp. 153 ff.).

(4) The demonstrative may be followed by a clause without explicit mark of dependence: ἀλλὰ τὸ θαυμάζω· ἴδον ἐνθάδε Μέντορα δῖον . . . δ 655, 'but this I marvel at: I saw here noble Mentor'.

2. *Adjectival Use.* Certain Attic usages already appear in Homer:

(1) Denoting parts and divisions: τοὺς μὲν τέσσαρας αὐτὸς ἔχων ἀτίταλλ' ἐπὶ φάτνῃ, τὼ δὲ δύ' Αἰνείᾳ δῶκεν Ε 271.

(2) Substantivizing adjectives, adverbs, etc.: τὸν ἄριστον 'Αχαιῶν Ε 414, τὸν ὁμοῖον Π 53, τῶν τότε Ι 559, τά γ' ὄπισθε Λ 613.

(3) With the attributive adjective, adverb, etc. : τὰ μακρότατα ἔγχεα, οἱ ἔνερθε θεοί, Αἴας ὁ μέγας, etc.

(4) Occasionally in a possessive sense : ὡς ἄν μοι τὸν παῖδα . . . ἐξαγάγοις Τ 331 f. (but contrast λυσόμενός τε θύγατρα Α 13 ; cf. ll. 20, 95, etc.) ; οὐδ' ἄν μοι τὴν γαστέρ' ὀνειδίζων ἀγορεύοις σ 380.

In view, however, of the distinct demonstrative force which the article still retained, it is not surprising to find it omitted where in Attic it would have been essential : e.g. βουλή Α 5, Διὸς υἱός l. 9, λαοί l. 10, νῆας l. 12, θύγατρα l. 13, Πριάμοιο πόλιν l. 19, ἱερῆα l. 23, Δαναῶν l. 56, etc., etc. Briefly one may say the 'article' has a more insistent force in Homer even when it is no longer strictly demonstrative. It draws attention to contrast, or some peculiarity, often with a note of contempt.

There remain, however, not a few examples where the original demonstrative force has been so whittled away that we have no alternative but to classify them under the heading of 'article'. These examples are more frequent in the *Odyssey* than in the *Iliad* where they have been detected chiefly in Books Κ, Ψ, and Ω (P. Chantraine, *Grammaire homérique*, ii. 164).

3. *Relative.*—The use of the 'article' as a relative pronoun has developed from the demonstrative use. In a sentence, for instance, such as 'Απόλλωνι ἄνακτι, τὸν ἠΰκομος τέκε Λήτω, the parenthetic or paratactic demonstrative clause 'him Leto bore' becomes by a shift of tempo and emphasis 'whom Leto bore' (cf. the development of the relative *that* in English). Examples are to be found *passim* : μαντοσύνην τήν οἱ πόρε Φοῖβος 'Απόλλων Α 72 ; τὰ μὲν πολίων ἐξεπράθομεν, τὰ δέδασται l. 125 ; ναὶ μὰ τόδε σκῆπτρον, τὸ μὲν οὔ ποτε φύλλα καὶ ὄζους φύσει l. 234 ; Νέστωρ . . . τοῦ καὶ ἀπὸ γλώσσης μέλιτος γλυκίων ῥέεν αὐδή l. 247, etc.

THE PRONOUNS

1. ὅς.

Note the use of demonstrative ὅς, which survives in the Attic ἦ δ' ὅς : μηδ' ὅς φύγοι Ζ 59, 'may not he escape' ; ἀλλὰ καὶ ὅς δείδοικε Φ 198, 'even he fears' ; ὅς κέν τοι εἴπῃσιν ὁδόν δ 389, 'he will tell you the way' ; ὡς ὁ τὸν οὐ δύνατο μάρψαι ποσίν, οὐδ' ὅς ἀλύξαι Χ 201, 'so the one cannot catch up the other, nor the other escape' ; ἀλλ' ὅς μέν θ' . . . ἐλίσσεται Ψ 319, 'but he wheels round'.

2. ὅδε, οὗτος, ἐκεῖνος.

The original distinctions between these pronouns (ὅδε = 'this here, mine', οὗτος = 'this (yours)' (*iste*), ἐκεῖνος = 'that' (not present to the speaker in time or space)) appear clearly in the Homeric language :

Φόρκυνος μὲν ὅδ' ἐστὶ λιμήν . . . τοῦτο δέ τοι σπέος εὐρύ . . . ν 345 ff.,
'this harbour (near) . . . this cave (further away)'; εἵματα ταῦτ'
ἀποδὺς σχεδίην ἀνέμοισι φέρεσθαι κάλλιπ' . . . τῇ δέ, τόδε κρήδεμνον ὑπὸ
στέρνοιο τάνυσσαι . . . ε 343 ff., 'take off your clothes . . . stretch my
head-cloth'; cf. τοῦδ' ἕνεκα Α 110, 'because of my action'; but τήνδε
θεῷ πρόες l. 127, 'give up this (your) girl'.

κεῖνός: δεῦρ' ἴθ'· Ἀλέξανδρός σε καλεῖ οἰκόνδε νέεσθαι. κεῖνος ὅ γ' ἐν
θαλάμῳ Γ 390 f., 'he is absent yonder in his chamber'; κεῖνος ὅ γε . . .
ἧσται ὀδυρόμενος ἕταρον Τ 344, 'yonder sits he bewailing his comrade'.

Among the grammatical-metaphorical usages which have grown out
of the purely deictic function we may note:

(1) ὅδε may refer to what follows while οὗτος refers to what precedes: ταῦτα μὲν οὕτω δὴ τελέω, γέρον, ὡς σὺ κελεύεις· ἀλλ' ἄγε μοι τόδε
εἰπέ δ 485; but cf. εἰ δ' ἄγε δή μοι τοῦτο, θεά, νημερτὲς ἐνίσπες μ 112,
where there is no contrast with ὅδε.

(2) As a correlative to the demonstrative to the relative pronoun we
find οὗτος, whose demonstrative force is less strongly marked than ὅδε
and ἐκεῖνος. οὗτος, however, is most frequently employed anaphorically,
that is with reference to a noun already mentioned or assumed to be
known. (a) Anticipating the relative: τοῦτο δέ τοι ἐρέω ὅ μ' ἀνείρεαι
Γ 177, 'I will tell you what you ask'; οὐκ ἐσθ' οὗτος ἀνήρ . . . ὅς κεν
. . . ἵκηται ζ 201 f.; (b) anaphoric: ἡμῖν μὲν τόδ' ἔφηνε τέρας μέγα
μητίετα Ζεύς, . . . ὡς οὗτος κατὰ τέκν' ἔφαγε ὥς . . . πτολεμίξομεν . . .
Β 324 ff., 'Zeus revealed this great portent to us. Even as it (οὗτος) ate
up its children . . . so shall we make war'; cf. οὗτος δ' αὖ Λαερτιάδης
πολύμητις Ὀδυσσεύς Γ 200, 'the man you mention [contrasts with
purely deictic ὅδε in l. 192] is Odysseus'; so also Γ 229; κλήρῳ νῦν
πεπάλασθε διαμπερές, ὅς κε λάχῃσιν· οὗτος γὰρ δὴ ὀνήσει . . . Ἀχαιούς
Η 171 f., 'shake up the lots now (to see) who shall be chosen; for he
(the one chosen) shall profit the Achaeans'. Note that the Attic use of
οὗτος to mark famous or notorious persons or things (τούτους τοὺς
συκοφάντας) is not found in Homer, who uses the article (see above).

THE PREPOSITIONS

1. *The Prepositions as Adverbs.*—This title, though convenient, reverses
the chronological order of events, for, as we saw above, the prepositions
have developed from independent adverbs which merely served to under-
line and give precision to the case ending. Homer still uses these adverbs
with some of their original independence and freedom of position in the
sentence.

ἀμφί.   ἀμφὶ δὲ Ἀθηναῖοι Δ 328, 'about him were the Athenians'.
ἐν.   πολέες γὰρ ἅμ' αὐτῷ λαοὶ ἕποντ', ἐν δ' αὐτὸς ἀριστεύεσκε

μάχεσθαι Π 550 f., 'and he was pre-eminent among them in the fray'.

μετά.   τεῖχος μέν ῥ᾽ ἄλοχοί τε φίλαι καὶ νήπια τέκνα ῥύατ᾽ ἐφεσταότες, μετὰ δ᾽ ἀνέρες οὓς ἔχε γῆρας Σ 514 f., 'and with them were the men whom old age possessed'.

παρά.   παρὰ δὲ χρυσόθρονος Ἥρη Α 611, 'and beside him (slept) Hera of the golden chair'.

περί.   πολλοὶ περὶ κτείνοντο Δ 538, 'many were killed about (them)'.
πέρι μὲν πολέμῳ ἔνι καρτερός ἐσσι Ι 53, 'you are surpassing valiant in battle'.
οἳ περὶ μὲν βουλὴν Δαναῶν Α 258, 'who are superior in counsel'.

πρό, ἐπί.   ὣς Τρῶες πρὸ μὲν ἄλλοι ἀρηρότες, αὐτὰρ ἐπ᾽ ἄλλοι Ν 800, 'so the Trojans in close array, some in front and others close behind', etc., etc.

When such adverbs qualify verbs their freedom of position is maintained, whereas in classical Greek they are prefixed to their verb. Viewed from the classical angle the Homeric usage appears as the separation of the preposition from its verb. Hence later grammarians spoke of τμῆσις (cutting), a term which is as historically misleading as 'preposition'. Examples are to be found on every page of Homer: Σμινθεῦ, εἴ ποτέ τοι χαρίεντ᾽ ἐπὶ νηὸν ἔρεψα, ἢ εἰ δή ποτέ τοι κατὰ πίονα μηρί᾽ ἔκηα Α 39 f., where the classical verbs would be ἐπερέφω, κατακαίω. The comparative looseness, however, of the attachment even in classical times is revealed by the fact that the augment comes between the preposition and the verb.

2. *Apocope.*—In other dialects than Attic the prepositions have shortened forms such as κάτ, πάρ, ἄπ, ἄν, etc. This phenomenon is particularly characteristic of Thessalian — an Aeolic dialect. In Homer, too, we have numerous examples, whereby we note that the final consonant of the shortened preposition is assimilated to the initial consonant of the following word: e.g., κάββαλε (for κάτ-βαλε), κὰρ ῥοόν, καμ-μονίη, κὰγ γόνυ, κάλ-λιπε, καπ-πεδίον, etc. The following apocopized forms are attested: ἄν, ἀπ-, ὑπ-, κατ-, πάρ.

3. *Dialect Forms.*—πρός, προτί, and ποτί are all found in Homer. These are the representatives of two distinct groups: (1) with ρ, πρός and προτί, and (2), without ρ, ποτί and πός (the last not found in Homer). πρός is the Attic-Ionic form, while προτί apart from Homer is found in Cretan, which is, roughly speaking, a Doric dialect with an Achaean substratum; ποτί, on the other hand is Thessalian and Boeotian (*i.e.* possibly Aeolic) and West Greek.[a]

It is curious that πεδά, which is the Aeolic preposition κατ᾽ ἐξοχήν, is

─────────
[a] It should be noted that προ- and πο- are different words. Linear B has po-si.

nowhere found in Homer.[a] Possibly Fick's thesis holds good here so that πεδά has everywhere been replaced by the metrically equivalent μετά. The forms ὑπείρ and εἰν are merely graphic representations of metrical lengthening (see p. 97).

4. *Usages.*—The following prepositional usages call for comment:

(1) ἀμφί, originally 'on both sides', then 'around', often enforces a locative dative: Ἀχαιοὶ ἕστασαν ἀμφὶ Μενοιτιάδῃ P 266-7; αὐτὰρ ὅ γ' ἀμφ' ὤμοισιν ἐδύσετο τεύχεα καλά Γ 328, etc., etc. Then like the English 'to fight *over*' it developed a causal meaning: ἀμφ' Ἑλένῃ καὶ κτήμασι πᾶσι μάχεσθαι Γ 70, 'to fight over (for) Helen and all her possessions'; then, with still vaguer meaning (like our colloquial 'about the matter we spoke of, I've already seen to it'): ἀμφὶ δὲ νεκροῖσιν κατακαιέμεν οὔ τι μεγαίρω, 'with regard to the bodies, I do not grudge their burning' H 408. We find, further, instances of ἀμφί with the genitive, where later prose would use περί: μάχεσθον πίδακος ἀμφ' ὀλίγης Π 824-5, 'they fight for a scanty spring' (cf. θ 267). The genitive here is one of respect: 'in the matter of', 'as regards', etc. (see above).

(2) ἀνά accompanies the genitive case νηός in three Odyssean examples: ἂν δ' ἄρα Τηλέμαχος νηὸς βαῖν' β 416 (cf. ι 177, ο 284), where the genitive must be local with the force 'within the ship'. The interdependence of these three examples, all dealing with the business of embarking and untying the πρυμνήσια, is evident.

ἀνά, too, is used with a locative dative: στέμματ' ἔχων . . . χρυσέῳ ἀνὰ σκήπτρῳ, 'having the fillets on the top of a golden sceptre' Α 14-15; ἄρματα δ' ἂμ βωμοῖσι τίθει Θ 441, 'he set the chariot on its stand', cf. Ξ 352, Σ 177, etc.

(3) ἀπό is used not only in its classical sense of motion away from but also in the meaning 'far from': ἀπολέσθαι ἀπ' Ἄργεος N 227, 'to perish far from Argos'; μένων ἀπὸ ἧς ἀλόχοιο B 292. As such, ἀπό reinforces adverbs as in the combinations τῆλε ἀπό, νόσφιν ἀπό, ἐκτὸς ἀπό. The instrumental use in two passages dealing with death by arrows from a bow has obviously developed from the ablatival use of the cause or source: τόξου ἄπο κρατεροῦ Τρώων ὀλέκοντα φάλαγγας Θ 279; τοὺς μὲν Ἀπόλλων πέφνεν ἀπ' ἀργυρέοιο βιοῖο Ω 605.

(4) διά, which originally meant 'in two', was used in the complementary semantic fields of 'through' and 'separate'. With the genitive it is always local in meaning; that is to say, it merely serves to reinforce such local genitives as πεδίοιο, etc. (see above).

With the accusative, too, it is mostly local: διὰ δώματα Α 600, διὰ στόμα Κ 375, δι' ἄκριας κ 281, etc. Even in the set phrase διὰ νύκτα the

---

[a] pe-da wa-tu occurs on a Linear B tablet from Knossos and the phrase is readily interpreted as πεδὰ Ϝάστυ 'to the town'.

predominant notion is spatial: 'through the darkness'.*a* Occasionally, however, it is used of the agent and the instrument: διὰ μαντοσύνην A 72, διὰ . . . Ἀθήνην θ 520. It may, further, express the motive or occasion for an act: Χλῶριν . . . τήν ποτε Νηλεὺς γῆμεν ἐὸν διὰ κάλλος λ 281 f., 'whom Neleus married for her beauty'; Ἴτυλον φίλον, ὅν ποτε χαλκῷ κτεῖνε δι' ἀφραδίας τ 522 f., 'whom he killed because of his folly'.

(5) ἐπί as we say above, besides 'on, upon' also means 'close to, next to, after, succeeding, in addition'. This is its force in the compound adverbs ἔπ-ειτα, ἐπ-ύπερθεν.

ἐπί is constructed with:

(a) The locatival dative (e.g., ἐπὶ χθονί) with metaphorical usages such as ἐπὶ Πατρόκλῳ, 'in honour of P.', ἐπ' ὄεσσι, '(watching) over the sheep', ἐπ' αὐτῷ ἡδὺ γέλασσαν, 'they laughed over [i.e. 'at'] him'. The sense of proximity is evident in ἐπὶ νηυσί, with which we may classify ἐπὶ ἵστορι πεῖραρ ἑλέσθαι, 'get the verdict in the presence of [we should say 'before'] the judge'. The close association of the meanings 'upon' and 'after' is clearly apparent in ὄγχνη ἐπ' ὄγχνη γηράσκει, μῆλον δ' ἐπὶ μήλῳ η 120, 'pear after [or 'upon'] pear grows old, apple after apple'. From this usage ἐπί came to be used after a comparative: οὐ γάρ τι στυγερῇ ἐπὶ γαστέρι κύντερον ἄλλο ἔπλετο η 216-17, 'there is nothing more shameless than the hateful belly'. In this connection it is worth recalling that our word 'than' is nothing more than a specialization of 'then'.

The temporal usage as in ἐπὶ νυκτί Θ 529, ἐπ' ἤματι Τ 229 is found in poetry and late prose.

(b) The local genitive (ἐπὶ χθονός, ἐπ' ἀγροῦ, ἐφ' ἵππων 'in the chariot'). With verbs of motion, ἐπὶ νηὸς ἔβαινεν, etc., the genitive originally conveyed the motion 'in the direction of, towards' but even in Homer the distinction between this and the more precise accusatival construction, implying that the destination is reached, has been blurred. On the other hand, ἐπί with the genitive coincides with the datival construction in indicating the end-point of the action (κατέθηκεν ἐπὶ χθονός Γ 293, κατέθηκεν ἐπὶ χθονί Ζ 473).

The combination with the genitive of persons in the sense 'in the presence of' is found only in the phrase ἐφ' ὑμείων Η 195, '(pray in silence) by yourselves'.

The temporal genitive use is rare: ἐπ' εἰρήνης Β 797, Ι 403, Χ 156, ἐπὶ προτέρων ἀνθρώπων Ψ 332.

(c) The use with the accusative of the goal requires no exemplification. ἐπί also reinforces the accusative of extent: ἐπὶ οἴνοπα πόντον, 'over the . . . sea' Η 88, ἐπ' ἐννέα κεῖτο πέλεθρα λ 577, ὅσσον τ' ἐπὶ οὖρα πέλονται ἡμιόνων Κ 351-2, 'how far apart the boundary marks of

---

a This phrase, the only temporal use in Homer, occurs in the *Odyssey* and Books Κ and Ω of the *Iliad* (Chantraine, *op. cit.* ii. 96).

mules are wont to be'. With persons in the sense 'among, throughout' we find πάντας ἐπ' ἀνθρώπους K 213, Ω 535, and a 299 (cf. Ω 202, ψ 125, ω 201), a significantly 'late' distribution.

(6) μετά still preserves much of its original meaning. With the dative it is predominantly an epic construction reinforcing a locative-dative with the meanings 'among', 'in the midst of': μετὰ δὲ τριτάτοισιν ἄνασσεν A 252, 'he was lord among the third generation'; ζώει . . . Πηλεὺς μετὰ Μυρμιδόνεσσιν Π 15, etc., etc.

With the accusative μετά means (1) 'into the midst of': νεκροὺς ἔρυσαν μετὰ λαὸν 'Αχαιῶν E 573, 'they dragged the bodies among the host of the Achaeans'; the accusative is one of extent rather than goal in such examples as καὶ βουλῇ μετὰ πάντας ὁμήλικας ἔπλεν ἄριστος I 54. (2) 'to go *after*', 'to make *for*' (in a hostile sense): ἐπαΐξαι μεθ' ἑὸν βέλος N 513, 'to dart after his spear'; πλεῖν μετὰ χαλκόν a 183-4, 'to sail in search of bronze'; ἵνα θᾶσσον ἵκηαι ἐς Πύλον ἠγαθέην μετ' ἀγαυοῦ πατρὸς ἀκουήν β 307 f., 'that you may come more speedily to holy Pylos in search of news about your noble sire'; βῆ δὲ μετὰ Ξάνθον E 152, 'he made for Xanthos'. (3) 'between': ἔφερον . . . ἅρμα μετὰ Τρῶας καὶ 'Αχαιούς Λ 533.

The preposition never has the temporal meaning 'after'.

There are two straightforward examples of the usage with the genitive, both in the *Odyssey*: μετὰ δμώων τ' ἐνὶ οἴκῳ πῖνε καὶ ἦσθε π 140-1; μετ' ἄλλων λέξο ἑταίρων κ 320.

Of the examples in the *Iliad*, N 700 (μετὰ Βοιωτῶν ἐμάχοντο) is likely to have been a late insertion; Φ 458 (μεθ' ἡμέων) occurs in the appeal of Poseidon to Apollo, who then compares men 'who like leaves are full of fire and eat the fruit of the field'; Ω 400 τῶν μέτα παλλόμενος κλήρῳ λάχον ἐνθάδ' ἔπεσθαι, 'from among them casting lots I was chosen . . .', may be compared with παλλομένων δὲ λαγχάνει ἐκ πάντων Βαγαῖος ὁ 'Αρτόντεω Herodotus iii. 128.

(7) περί may be a case of an old noun *per* meaning 'boundary', 'limit'. It is constructed with three cases. The *accusative* construction is used in speaking of motion or activity 'round about', 'in the neighbourhood of', an object: περὶ τέρμαθ' ἑλισσέμεν Ψ 309, 'to whirl round the turning-post'; οἳ πολλοὶ περὶ βόθρον ἐφοίτων λ 42, 'who swarmed about the trench', etc., etc. The construction with the locative *dative* on the other hand (which is rare in Attic prose), originally suggested a more or less static activity around a given point. The distinction is clear in μαρνάμενοι περὶ ἄστυ Z 256, as against μάρναντο περὶ Σκαιῇσι πύλῃσι Σ 453. As we observed with ἀμφί, a metaphorical usage, with the meaning 'about', 'concerning' developed: ἀνὴρ περὶ οἷσι μαχειόμενος κτεάτεσσιν ρ 471; περὶ γὰρ δίε νηυσίν I 433, 'for he feared for the ships'; ἔδεισεν δὲ περὶ ξανθῷ Μενελάῳ K 240; ὄφρα φίλῳ περὶ παιδὶ μάχης ὀλοὸς πόνος εἴη

Π 568, 'that there might be grievous toil of battle over his dear son' (note ἀμφὶ νέκυι κατατεθνηῶτι μάχεσθαι l. 565).

With the *genitive* περὶ is found only twice in a local sense: ἡ δ' αὐτοῦ τετάνυστο περὶ σπείους γλαφυροῖο ἡμερὶς ἡβώωσα ε 68-9, 'around the hollow cave was stretched a luxuriant vine', and in the same book τὸν μὲν ἐγὼν ἐσάωσα περὶ τρόπιος βεβαῶτα οἷον ll. 130-1, 'him I saved alone sitting astride the keel'. The figurative usage 'about', 'concerning' is, of course, frequent and a common prose idiom. Note, however, the analogical extension of the construction in ἠμὲν ἐμαρνάσθην ἔριδος πέρι θυμοβόροιο Η 301. In a sentence such as περὶ νηὸς μάχοντο, 'they fought about a ship', 'they fought over a ship', περὶ νηὸς may be regarded as the cause of the strife. So we may translate the sentence just quoted as 'the two fought over or because of a soul-devouring quarrel'. In view of the progressive approximation of ὑπέρ and περί in this figurative sense it is interesting to compare this example with one from Euripides's *Andromache* 490: κτείνει δὲ τὴν τάλαιναν . . . δύσφρονος ἔριδος ὑπέρ.

On περί with a comparative genitive in the meaning 'exceeding', 'superior to' see above.

(8) πρό.—The local sense 'in front of' develops to the notion of 'in defence of': μάχεσθαι . . . πρό τε παίδων Θ 56-7. In Ρ 667 πρό reinforces an ablatival genitive of the source or cause: πρὸ φόβοιο ἕλωρ . . . λίποιεν. The temporal use is confined to the *Odyssey* and the late book Κ of the *Iliad*: πρὸ ὁ τοῦ ἐνόησε Κ 224, 'one perceives before the other'.

(9) πρός reinforces the locative dative ('close to', 'towards'), ποτὶ γαίῃ (cf. ποτὶ πέτρῃ, πρὸς οὔδει) being a set phrase. The use with the accusative of the goal needs no comment.

The genitival usages are best explained as ablatives of origin 'proceeding to us from', a type of phrase which becomes specialized in indications of orientation: αὐτὸς δὲ ποτὶ πτόλιος πέτετ' αἰεί Χ 198, 'he sped ever on the city side'; cf. πρὸς βορέαο . . . πρὸς νότου ν 110 f. The phrases naming the source or authority are likewise ablatival: οἵ τε θέμιστας πρὸς Διὸς εἰρύαται Α 238-9. Closely related are the genitives indicating the authority appealed to in oaths: οὐδ' ἐπιορκήσω πρὸς δαίμονος Τ 188.

(10) ὑπέρ is constructed as in Attic with both genitive and accusative. Note the accusatival usage in the sense 'beyond', 'in transgression of': πειρᾶν δ' ὥς κε Τρῶες ὑπερκύδαντας Ἀχαιοὺς ἄρξωσι πρότεροι ὑπὲρ ὅρκια δηλήσασθαι Δ 66 f., 'essay that the Trojans may begin first, in transgression of their oaths, to do hurt to the Achaeans'; Αἰνεία, πῶς ἂν καὶ ὑπὲρ θεὸν εἰρύσσαισθε Ἴλιον αἰπεινήν; Ρ 327-8, 'Aeneas, how could you save steep Ilion even in defiance of a god?' So also ὑπὲρ αἶσαν, ὑπὲρ μοῖραν, etc.

(11) ὑπό reinforces the locative dative. Noteworthy are the instances which indicate the agent, presumably a development of the originally

local usage 'under (a king, commander, etc.)' : ὡς δ' ὑπὸ λαίλαπι πᾶσα κελαινὴ βέβριθε χθών Π 384; τὸν ὑπ' Ἀδμήτῳ τέκε δῖα γυναικῶν Β 714.

Combinations with a local genitive such as ἧχι βάθιστον ὑπὸ χθονός ἐστι βέρεθρον Θ 14 are clearly distinct from ablatival usages such as ὑπὸ θρόνου ὦρτο χ 364, ὑπ' ἀπήνης ἡμιόνους ἔλυον η 5-6, etc.

Such ablatives of origin lie behind the well-known usage to indicate cause, agent, etc.

B. THE VERB

GENERA

The main opposition of 'voice' in the Indo-European verb was between active and middle, the latter indicating the especial interest of the subject in the event referred to by the verb, or that the action takes place in the person of the subject.

The distinctive passive voice in the IE languages has developed from the use of the intransitive middle.[a] Even in classical Greek there were still no separate passive forms for the present tense. Homeric Greek has advanced still less in its creation of distinct passive forms. There are, as yet, no future passives in -(θ)ησομαι, but the same form serves for both passive and middle: πόλις . . . πέρσεται ω 728-9; τρώσεσθαι μ 66, etc., etc. On the other hand middle aorists in a passive function are rare and all examples are of the older type of aorist: ἐβλήμην, ἐκτάμην, and ἐσχόμην. E.g., πρὶν βλῆσθαι Μενέλαον Δ 115, ἀπέκτατο πιστὸς ἑταῖρος Ο 437, πᾶν δ' ἐξηράνθη πεδίον σχέτο δ' ἀγλαὸν ὕδωρ Φ 345 (but note intransitive δὴν δέ μιν ἀμφασίη ἐπέων λάβε· τὼ δέ οἱ ὄσσε δακρυόφι πλῆσθεν, θαλερὴ δέ οἱ ἔσχετο φωνή δ 704 f.). It is noteworthy that no middle of an s-aorist is used in a passive function, which suggests that the above usages are fossilized survivals. A parallel phenomenon is the formation of aorist tenses to deponent verbs; for even here we find a gradual expansion of the passive type at the expense of the middle. Thus we find not only ἠδέσθην, the Attic aorist of αἰδέομαι, but also ἠδε(σ)σάμην, while for ἥδομαι, ἐράμαι, ἄγαμαι Homer has only ἠσάμην, ἠρασσάμην, ἠγασσάμην as against Attic ἥσθην, ἠράσθην, ἠγάσθην.

There remains to be mentioned one peculiarity of the Homeric language — the tendency of verbs expressing perception to take on the middle form, e.g., ὁρῶμαι, ἀκούομαι. Such a usage underlines the interest of the subject in the action, and it may be related with a still more widespread phenomenon of the Greek verbal system — the tendency for future tenses to appear in the middle voice. This is doubtless due to the

---

[a] We find an extension of this intransitive type particularly with verbs which express some mental activity or perception. Thus Homer has ἀκούετο λαὸς αὐτῆς Δ 331, ὁρᾶτο Α 56, etc., ἴδωμαι Α 587, etc.

fact that future formations have developed from expressions of will and wish (see p. 123), where it was natural for the interest of the subject to be stressed.

THE TENSES

Indo-European by means of its tense stems distinguished three types of verbal aspect.　(1) The present stems describes the action as a process in being : φεύγει, 'he is in flight'.　We shall call it 'the durative aspect'. (2) The aorist refers to the action as a total event, a unit of history : ἀπέθανε, 'his death took place', 'he breathed his last'.　We shall call it 'the momentary or punctiliar aspect'.　(3) The perfect expresses the state which is the result of an action : τέθνηκε, 'he is dead', 'he is in his grave' ; ἀμφιβέβηκας, 'thou hast taken thy stand about', 'dost protect' ; προβέβουλα, 'I have made my choice', 'I prefer' ; κέκευθε 'he has hid', 'has in store'.　These distinctions made in prevalent philological doctrine do not do full justice to the observed facts of Homeric and later Greek usage. A concrete example from Plato will serve to illustrate this.

The friends of Socrates, hearing that the Salaminian galley has arrived in port, assemble outside the prison.　The warder comes out and invites them to enter.　The scene is set by verbs in the aorist (συνελέγημεν . . . ἐξήλθομεν . . . ἐπυθόμεθα . . . παρηγγείλαμεν . . . εἶπεν . . . μὴ . . . παριέναι . . .).　Then Phaedo continues 'We went in and found Socrates just released and Xanthippe sitting beside him'.　The verb 'find' is in fact καταλαμβάνω, where the prefix κατα- gives the verb a clear completive or confective force so that it has the meaning 'seize', 'overtake', 'surprise', and the like.　As such it can refer only to events of a momentary duration.　Yet in this passage of the Phaedo (60 A) Plato uses the imperfect κατελαμβάνομεν, the so called 'infective' of modern theorists, despite the fact that there is a successful completion of the action and there is no sustained process about 'clapping one's eyes on' a person.　The distinction between the aorist and the present stem would appear to be rather that whereas the former refers to the event globally and colourlessly as an item of history regardless of the objective duration, the 'present' brings us face to face with the scene.　It is the presentative, the eyewitness aspect, the news-reel aspect.　I propose to call it the 'autoptic'.　Thus one and the same event may be described by the use of aorist or 'presentative-autoptic' according to the stylistic purpose of the author.　In Homer we may add metrical convenience.

1. The Imperfect

The above considerations may explain puzzling alternations in Homer of aorist and imperfect which appear to be indistinguishable in function :

e.g., ἵππους δὲ Τρῳοὺς ὕπαγε ζυγόν Ψ 291, but ὑπὸ δὲ ζυγὸν ἤγαγεν ὠκέας ἵππους three lines later. *Cf.* Ἀτρεὺς δὲ θνῇσκων ἔλιπεν πολύαρνι Θυέστῃ, αὐτὰρ ὁ αὖτε Θυέστ' Ἀγαμέμνονι λεῖπε φορῆναι Β 106 f.; ἵππους δ' οἷς ἑτάροισι δίδου μετὰ νῆας ἐλαύνειν Ε 165, where δίδου does not mean 'he offered'; ἐν δ' ἐτίθει δύο κῆρε τανηλεγέος θανάτοιο Χ 210; and the bewildering alternation of tenses in the description of Hera's toilet Ξ 178 ff.: ἀμφὶ δ' ἄρ' ἀμβρόσιον ἑανὸν ἔσαθ', ὅν οἱ Ἀθήνη ἔξυσ' ἀσκήσασα, τίθει δ' ἐνὶ δαίδαλα πολλά. χρυσείης δ' ἐνετῇσι κατὰ στῆθος περονᾶτο. ζώσατο δὲ ζώνῃ ἑκατὸν θυσάνοις ἀραρυίῃ, etc. In the description, too, of Agamemnon arraying himself Β 42 ff., we find successively ἔνδυνε, βάλλετο, ἐδήσατο, βάλετο.

2. *The Aorist*

This tense, too, is often used in a way which, at first sight, seems to be contrary to its basic function: *e.g.*, κάτθαν' ὁμῶς ὅ τ' ἀεργὸς ἀνὴρ ὅ τε πολλὰ ἐοργώς Ι 320, 'death comes alike upon the indolent and upon him that has done much'; ξυνὸς Ἐννάλιος καί τε κτανέοντα κατέκτα Σ 309, 'impartial Enyalios slays even him that would slay'; *cf.* Hesiod's παθὼν δέ τε νήπιος ἔγνω, 'even a fool learns by suffering'. These are instances of the so-called *gnomic aorist*, where this tense, so far from referring to single momentary acts, is used to express general truths. It has been suggested that such a usage is an extension of the aorist which would be used in negative adages of the type 'faint heart never won fair lady'. It should be noted, however, that the aorist in such expressions as the above always refers to the moment of inception or completion of an action: 'death comes upon . . .', 'Enyalios puts to death . . .', 'suffering opens the eyes . . .', etc., so that such usages may be regarded as survivals of a state where the aorist indicative was as timeless as the other moods still are in classical Greek and was used merely to express type of action. Closely allied with such usages are the aorists which appear in similes: *e.g.*, ὡς δ' ὅτε τίς τε δράκοντα ἰδὼν παλίνορσος ἀπέστη οὔρεος ἐν βήσσῃς, ὑπό τε τρόμος ἔλλαβε γυῖα, ἄψ τ' ἀνεχώρησεν, ὦχρός τέ μιν εἷλε παρειάς Γ 33 ff., 'as when a man espying a snake in the dells of a mountain starts back and trembling seizes his limbs and pallor comes upon his cheeks'; ὡς δὲ θεὸς ναύτῃσιν ἐελδομένοισιν ἔδωκεν οὖρον, ἐπεί κε κάμωσιν ἐϋξέστῃς ἐλάτῃσι . . . ἐλαύνοντες Η 4 f., 'and as a god grants a fair breeze to sailors in their longing when they grow weary pulling at the well-polished oars'. Such instances may be explained in two ways. We may suppose the speaker to have in mind a particular concrete event, 'a god sent a breeze . . .', or here, too, we may understand the aorist as expressing a momentary action: 'trembling gets hold of his limbs', 'he starts back', etc., where the aorist indicative is timeless, the decisive

M

element in the choice of tense being the momentary nature of the event or the conception of the event.

This essential timelessness of the IE aorist is illustrated in another series of examples, where English must translate variously with past, present, and even the future: ἦ μάλα δή τινα Κύπρις Ἀχαιϊάδων ἀνιεῖσα Τρωσὶν ἅμα σπέσθαι, τοὺς νῦν ἔκπαγλα φίλησε E 422-3, 'surely now Cypris has been urging one of the Achaean women to go off with [aorist!] the Trojans, whom she now loves wondrously' (or 'has fallen deeply in love with'); cf. μή μ' ἔρεθε, σχετλίη, μὴ χωσαμένη σε μεθείω, τὼς δέ σ' ἀπεχθήρω ὡς νῦν ἔκπαγλα φίλησα Γ 414 f. These examples are only slightly different from those instances where the aorist refers to an event which has just happened and whose effect is still felt, aorists which, in fact, are almost indistinguishable from the perfect: οὔτε σὺ τούτῳ ἔσσεαι, Ἕκτορ, ὄνειαρ, ἐπεὶ θάνες X 485 f., 'nor will you be a help to him, Hector, since you are dead'; νῦν μὲν γὰρ Μενέλαος ἐνίκησεν Γ 439. We find, further, aorists referring to the future in sentences such as εἴπερ γάρ τε καὶ αὐτίκ' Ὀλύμπιος οὐκ ἐτέλεσσεν, ἔκ τε καὶ ὀψὲ τελεῖ, σύν τε μεγάλῳ ἀπέτεισαν Δ 160 f., 'for even if the Olympian does not fulfil immediately, he will bring it to pass and they will pay dearly for it'; εἰ μέν γ' αὖθι μένων Τρώων πόλιν ἀμφιμάχωμαι, ὤλετο μέν μοι νόστος, ἀτὰρ κλέος ἄφθιτον ἔσται I 412 ff., 'if I stay here and do battle about the city of the Trojans, then lost is my return, but deathless shall be my fame'. Such usages of the aorist occur, however, only in conditional clauses, where the future reference is unmistakable, so that the aorist tense stem may be chosen to emphasize the nature of the aspect — 'that wipes out my chance of return', 'they get their deserts', etc.

In all these instances the aorist indicative is as timeless as in the infinitive σπέσθαι, 'run off with' or the participle νοστήσαντα in ὄφρ' ἔμπεδον αὖθι μένοιεν νοστήσαντα ἄνακτα N 37 f., 'that they might steadfastly await the moment of return of their lord'. The only common factor is that the action is viewed as a bald fact,[a] a sudden or complete occurrence.

3. *The Perfect*, as we saw, expresses the state which is the result of the action. In many Homeric perfects we can still sense yet another function — the intensive-iterative force which it is in the nature of the reduplication to express (see above, p. 116). This is clear, for instance, in the perfects denoting:

    1. *noises*: τέτριγα, 'I squeak', βέβρυχα, 'I roar', μέμηκα, 'I bleat', μέμυκα, 'I bellow', etc., etc.
    2. *emotions*: κέκηδα, 'I am anxious', γέγηθα, 'I am joyful', τετιηώς, 'grieved', κεκοτηώς, 'angered'.

    [a] Such a downright statement in a context referring to the future conveys the impression of certainty and inevitability. We could therefore translate ἀπέτεισαν in Δ 160 as 'they are sure to get their deserts'.

3. *perceptions*: δέδορκε, ὄπωπα, 'I see'.
4. *physical states and gestures*: τέθηλα, 'I flourish', τέθηπα, 'I waste', βέβριθα, 'I am loaded', ἔρριγα, 'I shudder', κέκμηκα, 'I am weary', κέχηνα, 'I gape', βέβηκε, 'he strides'.

The Homeric perfect is, however, subject to an important limitation not observed in Attic usage: it cannot be used of an action the results of which persevere in *the object*. In other words it is essentially intransitive. Thus while the type σπάρτα λέλυνται, 'the cords are loosened', is frequent enough, we never find the type λέλυκε σπάρτα, which is a later active rendering of the passive construction. For here it is in the state of the object that the result of the action persists and is to be observed. On the other hand, given the basic meaning of the perfect, it is easy to see how the *active* perfect, for instance, of a perception-verb δέρκομαι may be used, because it is in the subject of δέδορκε that the experience and knowledge which result from the action of seeing persist. Thus it is that the perfect of the IE root *weid*, 'to see', is used to express the notion 'I know': Ϝοῖδα.

THE MOODS

Subjunctive and Optative

In Greek we can observe a rough parallelism of usage between these two moods, each of which may be used in two distinct ways: (1) the voluntative subjunctive expresses the will of the speaker towards the event in question: ἴδωμ' ἅτιν' ἔργα τέτυκται, 'I want to see . . .'. The corresponding function of the optative is to express a wish. (2) The prospective subjunctive indicates the speaker's *expectation* of an event. It is roughly equivalent to the Latin periphrasis with the future participle with its various shades of possibility, expectation, and intention. To this the optative corresponds with the well-known potential use to indicate the *possibility* of the event. In other words the subjunctive both looks forward to an event and at times expresses the speaker's desire for the event, so that γένηται, for instance, may mean 'it will happen' and 'I will that it happens'. In the same way the optative envisages a possibility and/or a desirable possibility, so that γένοιτο may mean either 'it would happen' or 'I would that it happens'. This distinction is often a subtle one and it is not surprising that in strict classical usage we find the potential optative distinguished from the wish optative by the addition of the particle ἄν, the Aeolic correspondent of which is κε. Attic abandoned the use of the prospective subjunctive, so that the question of differentiation did not arise. In Homer, however, we find κε and ἄν used to differentiate the prospective subjunctive from the voluntative. It must, however, immediately be pointed out that the distinction is not everywhere clear cut. Particularly in the first person, where the willer-wisher is also the bearer of the action, there tends to occur a confusion, familiar in our own language, between the modes of expression 'I shall, I should' and 'I will, I would'. In this uncertainty and looseness Homer links on to later colloquial usage. With these words of explanation and warning we propose to discuss some peculiarities of Homeric use of the moods under these main headings.

1. *Subjunctive.* (Negative μή)

A. *Voluntative.*—This usage, as in Attic, is practically confined to the 1st person. In the singular it is invariably introduced by some exhortatory particle such as εἰ δ' ἄγε, etc. : δεῦτε, δύω, μοι ἔπεσθον, ἴδωμ' ὅτιν' ἔργα τέτυκται Χ 450, 'come hither, two of you, accompany me, I will see what deeds have been wrought'; ἀλλ' ἄγεθ', ὑμῖν τεύχε' ἐνείκω θωρηχθῆναι χ 139, 'I will bring you harness to arm yourselves'; ἀλλ' ἄγε οἱ καὶ ἐγὼ δῶ ξείνιον υ 296, 'come now, I too will give him a guest-present'. It is easy to see how the usage in final clauses could develop from this : 'two of you follow that I may see' (see below, p. 159).

It is, however, a constantly recurring phenomenon that expressions of 'willing' tend to weaken and to become mere expressions of futurity. One recalls the development of Latin futures such as *faxso* from aorist subjunctives and further the use of θέλω ἵνα (θά) in Greek as the expression of the future. In Homer, too, we find a corresponding use of the subjunctive which is practically indistinguishable from the future (*cf.* ἔλθω, 'I shall come', in late vulgar Greek): οὐ γάρ τίς με βίη γε ἑκὼν ἀέκοντα δίηται Η 197, 'for no man shall put me to flight by force pitting his will against mine'; οὐκ ἔσθ' οὗτος ἀνὴρ οὐδ' ἔσσεται οὐδὲ γένηται π 437, 'for the man does not exist, nor will he live or be born . . .'; καί νύ τις ὧδ' εἴπησι κακώτερος ἀντιβολήσας ζ 275, 'and some malicious person meeting us will say'. This usage is known as the *prospective subjunctive*. The difficulty of distinguishing between voluntative and prospective is felt most in the first person,[a] where an 'I rather think I shall' readily passes to 'I want to' and vice versa. Thus οὐδὲ ἴδωμαι Α 262, 'nor do I expect to see' is obviously different from ἴδωμαι Χ 450, 'I want to see'. The latter is, in fact, an exact parallel to ἐγὼ δέ κ' ἄγω Βρισηΐδα Α 184, 'I intend to take Briseis', which, however, is classified by Delbrück as prospective. The truth is that out of the original unity of the subjunctive these two typical functions of will and expectation were gradually developed, that the second usage came to be distinguished by the

---

[a] Such border-line cases are the 'voluntatives' with κε, ἄν: note κεν ἕλωμαι Α 137 which is followed by the future ὁ δέ κεν κεχολώσεται l. 139; so πέμψω and ἐγὼ δέ κ' ἄγω l. 184, κεν ἕλωμαι and ἔσται l. 324; κε ἰδέω and δώσω Ξ 235 ff., κε τελέσσω and δώσω Ψ 559 f., and finally the often recurring line οὐκ ἄν ἐγὼ μυθήσομαι οὐδ' ὀνομήνω δ 240, etc.

'potential' particles κε (ἄν) but that, as always in language, there are border-line cases and petrified archaisms which disturb the grammarian's ideal symmetry. With this proviso we can lay down some general rules of reasonably wide validity.

B. The *prospective subjunctive* (negative οὐ) is distinguished by κε (ἄν). Exceptions: καί ποτέ τις εἴπῃσιν ἰδὼν κατὰ δάκρυ χέουσαν Z 459, 'someone will say, I expect . . .', with which we may compare ὥς ποτέ τις ἐρέει at the end of the same speech l. 462; οὐ γάρ πω τοίους ἴδον ἀνέρας οὐδὲ ἴδωμαι A 262, 'I have never seen such men nor do I expect to see'.

With κε (ἄν): ἧς ὑπεροπλίῃσι τάχ' ἄν ποτε θυμὸν ὀλέσσῃ A 205, 'through his headstrongness he will presently, I think, lose his life'; τὴν (sc. νῆα) δέ κέ τοι πνοίη Βορέαο φέρῃσιν κ 507, 'the breath of Boreas will bear the ship'; ἄλλον κ' ἐχθαίρῃσιν βροτῶν, ἄλλον κε φιλοίη δ 692, ('a king) will hate one man, another he may love', an example which brings out the close relationship between the prospective subjunctive and the potential optative (see below p. 161).

2. *Optative*

A. *Wishes* (negative μή).—Contrary to Attic usage (with the exception of the phrase ὡς ὄλοιτο) the optative may express unfulfilled wishes: (1) referring to the present: αἴθ' ὅσον ἥσσων εἰμί, τόσον σέο φέρτερος εἴην Π 722, 'O ! that I were so much stronger than you as I am weaker'; εἴθ' ὡς ἡβώοιμι βίη δέ μοι ἔμπεδος εἴη Λ 670, 'O that I were young and my strength as firm'; cf. H 132 f., Ψ 629, ξ 468, where the similarity of the formula is evidence that the usage is a petrified archaism. There are very few examples in Homer where a wish optative refers to the past: νῦν μὲν μήτ' εἴης, βουγάϊε, μήτε γένοιο σ 79, 'O that you were not living nor had ever been born, braggart',[a] an imprecation of the same type as the Attic ὡς ὄλοιτο. The extreme tenacity of such phrases is illustrated by the fact that μὴ γένοιτο has survived down to the present day although the optative disappeared from colloquial use in the Graeco-Roman period.

The use of the wish optative as a polite command, injunction, or concession is, of course, not unknown to Attic: ἀλλά τις ὀτρηρῶς Δολίον καλέσειε γέροντα δ 735, 'but let someone speedily call the aged Dolios'; ἀλλ' εἴ μιν ἀεικισσαίμεθ' ἑλόντες τεύχεά τ' ὤμοιιν ἀφελοίμεθα Π 559 f., 'come let us capture him and work shame on him and strip the armour from his shoulders'; κτήματα δ' αὐτὸς ἔχοις καὶ δώμασι σοῖσιν ἀνάσσοις α 402, 'the property you may have yourself and be master in your own house'; λῆγ' ἔριδος, Τρῶας δὲ καὶ αὐτίκα δῖος Ἀχιλλεὺς ἄστεος ἐξελάσειε· τί μοι ἔριδος καὶ ἀρωγῆς Φ 359 f., 'cease from strife and as for the Trojans

[a] Cf. αἰ γὰρ ἐγὼν οὕτω γε Διὸς πάϊς αἰγιόχοιο εἴην . . . τέκοι δέ με πότνια Ἥρη N 825.

let god-like Achilles drive them straightway from the city; what concern of mine is strife and succour?'

B. *The potential optative* (negative οὐ).—As with the prospective subjunctive the particle κε (ἄν) has not yet become obligatory: χερμά-διον . . . μέγα ἔργον, ὃ οὐ δύο γ' ἄνδρε φέροιεν, οἷοι νῦν βροτοί εἰσί E 303-5, 'a stone — a mighty deed — which not even two men such as there are now could carry'; ῥεῖα θεός γ' ἐθέλων καὶ τηλόθεν ἄνδρα σαώσαι γ 231, 'a god, if he wish, could easily save a man even from afar'; τούτου γ' ἑσπομένοιο καὶ ἐκ πυρὸς αἰθομένοιο ἄμφω νοστήσαιμεν, ἐπεὶ περίοιδε νοῆσαι K 246 f., 'if he come with me we two would return safe even out of blazing fire, for he is surpassing in wisdom'; ὦ γέρον, οὔ τις κεῖνον ἀνὴρ ἀλαλημένος ἐλθὼν ἀγγέλλων πείσειε γυναῖκά τε καὶ φίλον υἱόν ξ 122 f., 'no wanderer bringing that message would persuade his wife and dear son'; ἐγγὺς ἀνήρ . . . ὅς μοι ἑταῖρον ἔπεφνε τετιμένον· οὐδ' ἄρ' ἔτι δὴν ἀλλήλους πτώσσοιμεν ἀνὰ πτολέμοιο γεφύρας Υ 425 f., 'nigh is the man who slew the comrade I honoured; not long shall we yet shrink from each other along the paths of war', where the optative is almost equivalent to a prospective subjunctive or future indicative; but note the variant οὐδ' ἄν . . .; for οὐδ' ἄρ' . . .; οὐ μὲν γάρ τι κακώτερον ἄλλο πάθοιμι Τ 321, 'I could not suffer a worse blow'.

A further point of interest is that the potential optative, like the wish optative, is timeless, so that it may refer also to imagined (1) present and (2) past situations where Attic would use ἄν with the indicative of the imperfect and aorist respectively: (1) εἰ μὲν γὰρ μὴ δῶρα φέροι, τὰ δ' ὄπισθ' ὀνομάζοι Ἀτρείδης, ἀλλ' αἰὲν ἐπιζαφελῶς χαλεπαίνοι, οὐκ ἂν ἐγώ γέ σε μῆνιν ἀπορρίψαντα κελοίμην Ἀργείοισιν ἀμυνέμεναι I 515 f., 'for if Atreides were not bringing gifts and naming others hereafter, but were persisting in furious anger, I should not bid you cast aside your anger and defend the Argives'; ἦ μὲν καὶ νέος ἐσσί, ἐμὸς δέ κε καὶ πάϊς εἴης I 57, 'verily you are young indeed and could be even my son'. (2) καί νύ κεν ἔνθ' ἀπόλοιτο ἄναξ ἀνδρῶν Αἰνείας, εἰ μὴ ἄρ' ὀξὺ νόησε Διὸς θυγάτηρ Ἀφροδίτη E 311-12, 'and now would Aeneas lord of men have perished had not Zeus's daughter Aphrodite been quick to notice'; ὡς οἱ μὲν πονέοντο κατὰ κρατερὴν ὑσμίνην· Τυδείδην δ' οὐκ ἂν γνοίης ποτέροισι μετείη E 84 f., 'thus they toiled in mighty combat; but you could not have known to which side Tydeides belonged'; ἔνθ' οὐκ ἂν βρίζοντα ἴδοις Ἀγαμέμνονα Δ 223, 'you would not have seen Agamemnon slumbering', etc. (see Conditional Sentences).

We noticed above that the distinction between voluntative and prospective subjunctive tends to become blurred especially in the first person. It is precisely in the first person, too, that the majority of border-line cases between the wish and the potential optative occur. In X 252, for instance, νῦν αὖτέ με θυμὸς ἀνῆκε στήμεναι ἀντία σεῖο· ἔλοιμί κεν ἤ κεν ἁλοίην we may interpret the last phrase either as a concessive use of the wish-optative or as a potential (see Leaf's note); cf. αὐτίκ᾽, ἐπεί κε κεῖνος ἰὼν ἑὰ δώμαθ᾽ ἵκηται, ἔσσαι με χλαῖνάν τε χιτῶνά τε, εἵματα καλά· πρὶν δέ κε, καὶ μάλα περ κεχρημένος, οὔτι δεχοίμην ξ 153 f., 'when first he comes to his house, then clothe me in a cloak and tunic, fine raiment; but before that, though I be in sore need, may I not receive aught'; εἰ μέν κεν πατρὸς βίοτον καὶ νόστον ἀκούσω, ἦ τ᾽ ἄν, τρυχόμενός περ, ἔτι τλαίην ἐνιαυτόν β 218 f., 'if I should hear that my father is alive and safe, verily though sore pressed I should be willing to endure the year round'; καὶ δέ κεν αὐτὸς ἐγὼ τοῦ τόξου πειρησαίμην φ 113, 'I myself would like to try the bow'; cf. μ 387, ο 313, σ 166, τ 579, υ 326, etc., where the first person of the optative with ἄν (κε) occurs in the meaning 'I should like to . . .', or perhaps as a tentative question 'could I perhaps . . .?'.

3. *The Future* tense, originating as we saw in voluntative-desiderative expressions, is more conveniently treated as a mood than as a tense, the more so in that in Homer it has the closest relationship with the subjunctive. In the first place, parallel with the *prospective subjunctive* (with ἄν, κε) we find a corresponding use of κε (ἄν) with the future: ὁ δέ κεν κεχολώσεται ὅν κεν ἵκωμαι Α 139, 'the one to whom I came will be wroth'; καί κέ τις ὧδ᾽ ἐρέει Τρώων ὑπερηνορεόντων Δ 176, 'and one of the overweening Trojans will say thus, I expect'; ἔπειτα δέ κ᾽ αὐτὸς ὀνήσεαι, αἴ κε πίῃσθα Ζ 260, 'you shall have profit of it yourself if you will drink', etc. This usage is particularly frequent in relative clauses (see p. 167).

The original *voluntative* sense is still preserved in Attic usage (Tragedy) such as τί λέξεις; 'what do you want to say?', 'what do you mean?'. In Homer, too, we find this voluntative element still evident in expressions of intention, necessity and the like. In I 60 f., ἀλλ᾽ ἄγ᾽ ἐγών, ὃς σεῖο γεραίτερος εὔχομαι εἶναι, ἐξείπω καὶ πάντα διΐξομαι, for instance, we find a future indicative co-ordinated with a voluntative subjunctive. Cf. further οὐδὲ γυνὴ ποδὸς ἅψεται ἡμετέροιο τ 344, 'nor shall any woman touch my feet'; ἀτὰρ ἠῶθέν γε τὰ σὰ ῥάκεα δνοπαλίξεις ξ 512, 'but at dawn you must wrap your rags about you'; ἀλλ᾽ ἄγε δὴ καὶ δουρὸς ἀκωκῆς ἡμετέροιο γεύσεται Φ 60 f., 'but come now, he shall taste of my spear's point', etc.

4. *The Infinitive*

The infinitives of Greek are in origin cases of verbal nouns (see p. 127). We may discern cognate accusatives in such turns of phrase as βάν δ᾽ ἴμεν, 'they went their way' which proliferates in the innumerable infinitival phrases of the type ἔβαν . . . νέεσθαι. An accusative of respect is clearly evident from the parallelism in περὶ μὲν βουλὴν Δαναῶν, περὶ δ᾽ ἐστὲ μάχεσθαι Α 258, 'superior in counsel and in battle'. Datival function may be detected in the large group of final and consecutive uses.

A. *Final use*: ὡς ὅτε τίς τ' ἐλέφαντα γυνὴ φοίνικι μιήνῃ . . . παρήϊον ἔμμεναι ἵππων Α 141 f., 'as when a woman stains ivory with crimson . . . to be a cheek-piece for horses'; νηὶ μελαίνῃ, ἥ ῥ' ἐν μεσσάτῳ ἔσκε γεγωνέμεν ἀμφοτέρωσε Λ 6, 'by a black ship, which was in the middle for shouting to both sides'; πίτυς . . . τήν τ' οὔρεσι τέκτονες ἄνδρες ἐξέταμον πελέκεσσι νεήκεσι νήϊον εἶναι Ν 390 f., 'a pine which craftsmen fell in the mountains with newly-whetted axes, to be a ship's timber'. Such an infinitive is found after ἐπέσσυτο: ἔνθα δέ μοι μάλα πολλὸν ἐπέσσυτο θυμὸς ἀγήνωρ . . . κτήμασι τέρπεσθαι Ι 398 f., 'there my proud spirit did eagerly desire to have joy of the possessions'. *Cf.* the same construction introduced by ὥς τε: εἰ δέ τοι αὐτῷ θυμὸς ἐπέσσυται ὥς τε νέεσθαι Ι 42, while in Ζ 361 f. ἐπέσσυται is constructed with a purpose clause introduced by ὄφρα: ἤδη γάρ μοι θυμὸς ἐπέσσυται ὄφρ' ἐπαμύνω Τρώεσσι.

B. *Consecutive use*: ἐπεὶ οὔ σφι λίθος χρὼς οὐδὲ σίδηρος χαλκὸν ἀνασχέσθαι Δ 510 f., 'since their flesh is not stone or iron so that it can resist the bronze'; *cf.* καὶ τό γε . . . ὦσεν ὑπὲκ δίφροιο ἐτώσιον ἀϋχθῆναι Ε 853 f., where the infinitive is ambiguous: 'she thrust it to speed in vain' or . . . 'so that it sped in vain'. There is a particularly bold usage of this construction in Β 291: ἦ μὴν καὶ πόνος ἐστὶν ἀνιηθέντα νέεσθαι, 'verily there is toil enough that a man should become disheartened and return'.

C. In *commands* the use of the infinitive is widespread in IE languages. The infinitive in such cases is usually equivalent to a second person of the imperative,[a] although it is occasionally also found for the third person: τεύχεα συλήσας φερέτω κοίλας ἐπὶ νῆας, σῶμα δὲ οἴκαδ' ἐμὸν δόμεναι πάλιν Η 78 f., 'having stripped me of my armour let him take it to the hollow ships, but my body let him give back'; εἰ μέν κεν Μενέλαον Ἀλέξανδρος καταπέφνῃ, αὐτὸς ἔπειθ' Ἑλένην ἐχέτω . . . εἰ δέ κ' Ἀλέξανδρον κτείνῃ . . . Μενέλαος, Τρῶας ἔπειθ' Ἑλένην . . . ἀποδοῦναι Γ 281 ff., 'if Alexander slays Menelaus let him keep Helen; but if Menelaus slays Alexander, then shall the Trojans give back Helen'. Two points should be noted about these examples: in each case the infinitive is preceded by a third person imperative (φερέτω, ἐχέτω) and the subject of the infinitive is in the accusative.[b] When, however, the infinitive

---

[a] An imperatival use lies behind infinitives such as ἥδε . . . ἀρίστη φαίνετο βουλή, Νέστορ' ἔπι . . . ἐλθέμεν Κ 17 f., 'this seemed the best advice: go to Nestor . . .' where the purely logical grammatical analysis yields 'an explanatory opposition' (Chantraine, *op. cit.*, ii. 303).

[b] The only example in Homer of a third person imperatival infinitive with the subject in the nominative, Ζ 87 ff., is perhaps to be classed as anacoluthon due to the separation of subject from the infinitive by ll. 88-91: ἡ δὲ συνάγουσα γεραιάς . . . πέπλον . . . θεῖναι Ἀθηναίης ἐπὶ γούνασιν.

represents a second person imperative, the subject is in the nominative: ἀλλὰ σὺ τόν γ' ἐπέεσσι καθάπτεσθαι μαλακοῖσι A 582, 'but do you accost him with soft words'; τῷ νῦν μή ποτε καὶ σὺ γυναικί περ ἤπιος εἶναι λ 441, 'now therefore be thou never gentle to thy wife'.

D. The use of the infinitive in two passages of the *Odyssey* to express a *wish* possibly arose from contamination with the construction with αἴθ' ὤφελον. At the same time we should bear in mind that the distinction between wish and command is often vague. The examples are: αἲ γάρ . . . . παῖδά τ' ἐμὴν ἐχέμεν καὶ ἐμὸς γαμβρὸς καλέεσθαι η 311 f., 'O! that you would have my daughter to wife and would be called my son-in-law' — a wish referring to the future; αἲ γάρ . . . . τεύχε' ἔχων ὤμοισιν ἐφεστάμεναι καὶ ἀμύνειν ἄνδρας μνηστῆρας ω 376 ff., 'O that I with armour on my shoulders had stood at your side and warded off the suitors', this being a wish refering to the past. Rather different are the wish constructions where we must understand a verb such as δός or εὔχομαι[a]: Ζεῦ ἄνα, Τηλέμαχόν μοι ἐν ἀνδράσιν ὄλβιον εἶναι καί οἱ πάντα γένοιθ' ὅσσα φρεσὶν ᾗσι μενοινᾷ ρ 354, where εἶναι is co-ordinated with the optative γένοιτο; Ζεῦ . . . . μὴ πρὶν ἐπ' ἠέλιον δῦναι καὶ ἐπὶ κνέφας ἐλθεῖν B 412 f., 'may not the sun set nor darkness come upon us', etc.

C. THE COMPLEX SENTENCE

PARATAXIS

It is an axiom of historical syntax that sentences of the complexity such as we find in the highly developed prose of a Cicero or a Demosthenes have developed from simpler types where the constituent parts existed side by side without explicit relationship or subordination one to the other. Such simplicity of structure is a feature both of archaic and of colloquial styles. The letters of Cicero, for instance, and the plays of Plautus abound in such turns as *faxso adferat* where an old aorist subjunctive used as a future is simply followed without any conjunction by a jussive subjunctive: 'I shall see to it: let him bring'. Such parataxis, as it is called, is a feature of the liveliness and directness of Homeric style. In μή μιν ἐγὼ μὲν ἵκωμαι ἰών· ὁ δέ μ' οὐκ ἐλεήσει X 123, for instance, we have a simple co-ordination of 'let me not approach him' and 'he will not pity me', the logical connection of the parts (the second clause is distinctly causal) being left to the hearer or indicated by pause and intonation. *Cf.* further νῆσος δενδρήεσσα, θεὰ δ' ἐνὶ δώματα ναίει α 51, 'a wooded island, a goddess has her home on it', where a more developed

---

[a] *E.g.*, ὑμῖν μὲν θεοὶ δοῖεν . . . ἐκπέρσαι Πριάμοιο πόλιν A 18 f., where strictly ἐκπέρσαι is the direct object: 'grant destruction'.

style would use a relative clause. *Cf.* further δυσμενέες δ' ἄνδρες σχεδὸν ἥαται· οὐδέ τι ἴδμεν· μή πως καὶ διὰ νύκτα μενοινήσωσι μάχεσθαι Κ 100 f., 'the enemy are encamped hard by; we know naught; perhaps even (save the mark !) the urge may come upon them to do battle even through the night', where the punctuation of the passage has caused difficulties to the editors (see Leaf *ad loc.*). The passage is, however, best left as a series of phrases whose very disconnectedness effectively conveys Agamemnon's agitation. A similar passage is θάπτε με ὅττι τάχιστα· πύλας 'Αΐδαο περήσω Ψ 71, 'bury me with all speed. I want to pass within the gates of Hades', where in the loose attachment of a voluntative subjunctive we find the germ of the subordinate purpose clause introduced by an explicit conjunction such as ὡς, ὅπως, etc. Another transparent example of parataxis as the precursor of a complex syntactical type is seen in ἀλλ' εἴ μοί τι πίθοιο· τό κεν πολὺ κέρδιον εἴη Η 28, 'may you obey me : that would be far better', where a wish construction is juxtaposed with a potential optative — a combination from which developed conditional sentences of the pattern 'if you were to believe me, it would be far better'.

It is not merely in paratactical constructions of this type that the primitive and colloquial nature of Homeric syntax is revealed. We miss, too, the logic and consistency of careful prose. Thus when there are alternative means of expression, the sentence may begin one way and end in another. Such is the nature of anacoluthon — a phenomenon so common and self-explanatory that it needs little in the way of illustration. Note a remarkable example in ἀλλ' εἴ τίς μοι ἀνὴρ ἅμ' ἕποιτο καὶ ἄλλος· μᾶλλον θαλπωρὴ καὶ θαρσαλεώτερον ἔσται. σύν τε δύ' ἐρχομένω, καί τε πρὸ ὁ τοῦ ἐνόησεν ὅππως κέρδος ἔῃ Κ 222 ff., 'if only some other man would go with me ! There will be greater comfort and confidence. Two going together . . . one discerns before the other how it is best'; and in Αἰνείας δ' υἱὸς μὲν ἀμύμονος 'Αγχίσαο εὔχεται ἐκγεγάμεν, μήτηρ δέ οἵ ἐστ' 'Αφροδίτη Ε 247 f., where the clumsiness of a long *oratio obliqua* is avoided by recourse in the second clause to direct narrative : 'Aeneas boasts that he is the son of blameless Anchises, and his mother is Aphrodite'.

SUBORDINATE CLAUSES

1. *The Moods*

It follows from the above that the functions of the moods in subordinate clauses must have developed from their use in principal clauses. Consequently, although analogical developments have obscured and complicated the original distinctions, in the following we shall attempt to classify modal usages under the headings introduced above : the voluntative and prospective uses of the subjunctive and the wish and potential uses of the optative.

2. Indirect Statements

The Attic form of indirect speech with its modal sequence and retention of the tense of the direct words is foreign to Homer, where messengers merely deliver their messages as personal experiences. Compare, for instance, the words of Agamemnon in I 127 ff. with the report by Odysseus *ibid.* 269 ff.

. . . ὅσσα μοι ἠνείκαντο	. . . ὅσσ' Ἀγαμέμνονος ἵπποι
ἀέθλια μώνυχες ἵπποι.	ἀέθλια ποσσὶν ἄροντο.
δώσω δ' ἑπτὰ γυναῖκας	δώσει δ' ἑπτὰ γυναῖκας
ἀμύμονα ἔργα ἰδυίας	ἀμύμονα ἔργα ἰδυίας
Λεσβίδας, ἃς ὅτε Λέσβον	Λεσβίδας, ἃς ὅτε Λέσβον
ἐϋκτιμένην ἕλεν αὐτὸς	ἐϋκτιμένην ἕλες αὐτὸς
ἐξελόμην, αἳ κάλλει	ἐξέλεθ', αἳ τότε κάλλει
ἐνίκων φῦλα γυναικῶν.	ἐνίκων φῦλα γυναικῶν.
τὰς μέν οἱ δώσω, μετὰ δ'	τὰς μέν τοι δώσει, μετὰ δ'
ἔσσεται ἢν τότ' ἀπηύρων,	ἔσσεται ἢν τότ' ἀπηύρα,
κούρη Βρισῆος· ἐπὶ δὲ	κούρη Βρισῆος· ἐπὶ δὲ
μέγαν ὅρκον ὀμοῦμαι . . .	μέγαν ὅρκον ὀμεῖται . . .

It will be seen that the speech is an 'egocentric' narrative of Odysseus, where the words of the original are preserved as nearly as possible, only minor adaptations being made according to the exigencies of the metre. Note that the imperative infinitives νηήσασθαι 1. 279 and ἑλέσθαι 1. 281 are chosen as being metrically equivalent to νηησάσθω 1. 137 and ἑλέσθω 1. 139.

Indirect statements are introduced by the particles ὅ, ὅ τε, ὅτι, ὡς, and οὕνεκα.[a] It is pointed out, however, that such clauses are far more common after verbs of 'knowing, hearing, remembering', etc., than after verbs of 'saying'.

3. Indirect Questions

These are introduced (apart from the somewhat rare use of interrogative pronouns, adverbs, etc.) by the particles εἰ (ἄν) and ἦ. The mood is the same as the direct question. We find:

A. The *prospective subjunctive* (with and without κε, ἄν): γνώσῃ ἔπειθ' ὅς θ' ἡγεμόνων κακός, ὅς τέ νυ λαῶν ἠδ' ὅς κ' ἐσθλὸς ἔῃσι B 365 f., 'you will find out then who of the captains will be a craven and who among the host and who will be brave'; ὄφρα καὶ Ἕκτωρ εἴσεται ἦ ῥα καὶ οἶος ἐπίστηται πολεμίζειν ἡμέτερος θεράπων Π 242 f., 'that Hector

[a] See below.

may know whether even alone my squire shall have understanding of battle'.

B. *Deliberative subjunctive*[a] : μητρὶ δ' ἐμῇ δίχα θυμὸς ἐνὶ φρεσὶ μερμηρίζει, ἢ αὐτοῦ παρ' ἐμοί τε μένη καὶ δῶμα κομίζῃ, . . . ἦ ἤδη ἄμ' ἕπηται . . . π 73 ff., 'my mother's mind is divided this way and that, shall she remain with me and watch over the house or now shall follow . . .'; μερμήριζε κατὰ φρένα ὡς Ἀχιλῆα τιμήσῃ[b] B 3 f., 'he was pondering in his heart how he should honour Achilles'.

One subjunctive which Monro classes as final undoubtedly belongs here: μάρνασθ' ὁπποτέροισι πατὴρ Ζεὺς κῦδος ὀρέξῃ E 33, 'fight (to decide) to which of the two father Zeus shall grant glory'.

C. The *oblique optative* is fully developed in indirect questions, although, as we saw, this construction has not yet spread to indirect statements. ἀλλήλους τ' εἴροντο τίς εἴη καὶ πόθεν ἔλθοι ρ 368, 'they asked one another who he was and whence he came'; μερμήριξε . . . ἠδὲ ἕκαστα εἰπεῖν ὡς ἔλθοι καὶ ἵκοιτ' ἐς πατρίδα γαῖαν ω 235 ff., 'he pondered . . . or should he tell all how he returned and came to his native land'; οἴχετο πευσόμενος μετὰ σὸν κλέος εἴ που ἔτ' εἴης ν 415, 'he went away to inquire after news of you, whether you are still living'; δίζε γὰρ ἠὲ μάχοιτο . . . ἦ λαοὺς ἐς τεῖχος ὁμοκλήσειεν ἀλῆναι Π 713 f., 'he debated whether he should do battle . . . or should call the people to gather within the wall'; κλήρους . . . πάλλον . . . ὁππότερος . . . ἀφείη Γ 316, 'they were casting lots . . . which of the two should let fly'. So also λ 331, Ξ 507, Z 177, etc.

In one example this optative is accompanied by κε: ὁρμαίνων ἤ κεν θάνατον φύγοι ἦ κεν ἁλώῃ ο 300, 'pondering whether he would escape death or be slain'. The corresponding direct form to this is seen in νῦν αὖτέ με θυμὸς ἀνῆκε στήμεναι ἀντία σεῖο· ἕλοιμί κεν ἤ κεν ἁλοίην X 252 f., a passage which has been discussed above (p. 152 f.).

4. *Causal Clauses* are introduced by ὅ, ὅτι, ὅ τε, οὕνεκα (see below). The oblique optative in such clauses is unknown to Homer. After a question a causal clause often expresses the reason for asking the question: τί νύ σε Πρίαμος Πριάμοιό τε παῖδες τόσσα κακὰ ῥέζουσιν ὅτ' ἀσπερχὲς μενεαίνεις Ἰλίου ἐξαλαπάξαι ἐϋκτίμενον πτολίεθρον Δ 31 ff., 'in what do Priam and the sons of Priam work such evil on you that you rage unceasingly to sack the well-built city of Ilios'. This idiom, which has doubtless arisen from a double question ('why do you desire to sack? What harm do we do?'), is particularly characteristic of Homeric style: οὔ νυ καὶ ὑμῖν οἴκοι ἔνεστι γόος, ὅτι μ' ἤλθετε κηδήσοντες Ω 239 f., 'Have you, too, no wailing at home? Why have you come to vex me?'

---

[a] On the voluntative nature of this subjunctive see p. 161.
[b] Allen reads τιμήσει' with the scholiasts but against the majority of the MSS.

5. *Consecutive Clauses.*—ὥς τε and the infinitive occurs only twice in Homer. θυμὸς ἐπέσσυται ὥς τε νέεσθαι I 42, has been discussed above (p. 154). The other example is οὐ γὰρ ἐπὶ σταθμοῖσι μένειν ἔτι τηλίκος εἰμί, ὥς τ' ἐπιτειλαμένῳ σημάντορι πάντα πιθέσθαι ρ 20 f., 'for I am no longer of an age to abide at the sheep-folds and obey in all what a master commands'. Apart from this, possible or intended result is expressed by the simple infinitive. The Attic use of ὥστε and the indicative to indicate actual result is unknown. Instead of this we find a loosely attached main clause, the logical connection of which remains unexpressed: ὁ γὰρ βασιλῆϊ χολωθεὶς νοῦσον ἀνὰ στρατὸν ὦρσε κακήν, ὀλέκοντο δὲ λαοί A 9 f., 'for he sent an evil pestilence throughout the host, so that the people were perishing'; ἐκ γάρ τοι τούτων φάτις ἀνθρώπους ἀναβαίνει ἐσθλή, χαίρουσιν δὲ πατὴρ καὶ πότνια μήτηρ ζ 29 f., 'from these things a man's good fame arises, so that his father and lady mother have joy'.

6. *Final Clauses* are introduced by ὄφρα, etc., while relative and temporal clauses, too, are often final in force [a] (*cf.* the Latin use of *qui, dum, donec, priusquam,* etc.). In a final clause the speaker or narrator refers to an event which is the willed, expected, or desired result of the event or action described in the main clause. Will, expectation, and desire, as we have seen, could be expressed in Greek variously by the subjunctive (voluntative and prospective), the optative (wish and potential), and the future indicative. In Homer we find examples of all these modes of expression in final clauses.

A. The *subjunctive* used in such clauses may be regarded variously as voluntative (without κε, ἄν) or prospective (with κε, ἄν) in origin; but, the distinction, always a fine one, has become blurred by analogical extension. There is, however, a noteworthy difference of usage with the different conjunctions: ἵνα never takes the potential particle κε, ἄν [b]; ὡς is rarely without it; while ὄφρα has κε only in a few instances. The origin of the subjunctive in such constructions may be seen in paratactic forms such as ἀλλ' ἄγε νῦν ἐπίμεινον, ἀρήϊα τεύχεα δύω Z 340, 'but come now wait a while, I want to put on my armour', which gradually merges into 'wait until I put on', 'wait for me to put on', etc. *Cf.* further ἀλλ' ἄγε νῦν ἰθὺς κίε Νέστορος ἱπποδάμοιο· εἴδομεν ἥν τινα μῆτιν ἐνὶ στήθεσσι κέκευθεν γ 17 f., 'but come now go straight to horse-taming Nestor; we want to know what counsel he has stored in his breast'. Thence: αὐτὰρ ἐγὼν Ἰθάκην ἐσελεύσομαι ὄφρα οἱ υἱὸν μᾶλλον ἐποτρύνω α 88 f., 'but I shall go to Ithaca that I may spur on his son'. βουλὴν δ' Ἀργείοις ὑποθησόμεθ' ἥ τις ὀνήσει ὡς μὴ πάντες ὄλωνται Θ 36 f., where the negative μή clearly marks the voluntative nature of the subjunctive.

---

[a] In Attic such final relative and temporal clauses take the future indicative, which is used in the voluntative function.   [b] The sole possible exception is discussed below.

In other examples the prospective (distinguished by κε, ἄν) makes itself apparent. The opposition is particularly clear in ἀλλ' ἄγε μοι δότε νῆα θοὴν καὶ εἴκοσ' ἑταίρους ὄφρα μιν αὖτις ἰόντα λοχήσομαι . . . ὡς ἄν ἐπισμυγερῶς ναυτίλεται εἴνεκα πατρός δ 669 ff., 'give me a ship that I may ambush him [voluntative] . . . so in that case he will ruefully go voyaging' (prospective).[a] This may be the reason for the preference of ὡς for the potential particle; for as we have seen, ὡς means 'so', 'thus' while κεν, ἄν originated in the demonstrative stem κε- and meant 'in this case', 'thus'. However, an envisaged result shades imperceptibly into a willed result, so that 'final' clauses are traceable to these two sources. They still leave their traces, however, in the varying preferences of the different conjunctions for the potential particles.

Many usages classified by some grammarians as final voluntative are better regarded as *prospective*: ἔσσεται ἦμαρ ὅτ' ἄν ποτ' ὀλώλῃ Ἴλιος ἱρή Z 448, 'there will come a day when sacred Ilios shall perish'; ἔσται μὰν ὅτ' ἄν αὖτε φίλην γλαυκώπιδα εἴπῃ Θ 373, 'truly there will be a time when he shall again call me his bright-eyed maid'; ἀλλ' ἴθι, μή μ' ἐρέθιζε· σαώτερος ὥς κε νέηαι A 32, which may be regarded as paratactic: 'but go, stop provoking me; so you will go the safer'.

Such prospective subjunctives are often introduced by εἰ (αἰ)+ἄν (κε): ἔρχεο πευσόμενος πατρὸς δὴν οἰχομένοιο ἤν τίς τοι εἴπῃσι α 281 f., 'go and inquire after your father, who has been long absent, if haply someone may tell'; cf. πατρὸς ἐμοῦ κλέος εὐρὺ μετέρχομαι, ἤν που ἀκούσω γ 83; αὐτάρ τοι πυκινῶς ὑποθήσομεθ', αἴ κε πίθηαι Φ 293, 'but we will make you a wise proposal that you may obey it'; βάλλ' οὕτως, αἴ κέν τι φόως Δαναοῖσι γένηαι Θ 282, 'strike on thus that you may be a light of deliverance to the Danaans'; καί οἱ ὑποσχέσθαι δυοκαίδεκα βοῦς . . . ἱερευσέμεν, αἴ κ' ἐλεήσῃ ἄστυ τε καὶ Τρώων ἀλόχους καὶ νήπια τέκνα, ὥς κεν Τυδέος υἱὸν ἀπόσχῃ Ἰλίου ἱρῆς Z 93 ff., 'and promise to sacrifice to her twelve kine, if haply she may take pity on the city and the wives and infant children of the Trojans; in that case she will hold back the son of Tydeus from sacred Ilios'. This construction is parallel with that of the Latin *si forte*, and the subjunctive conveys *hope, eager expectation*, a mode of thought which, as we saw above, closely verges on *wish*. The sense of the first example, for instance, expressed paratactically, is 'go and inquire after your father: so perhaps someone will tell you', which shades off into 'I hope someone will tell you'. A loosely attached clause of this kind is found in A 66 f., αἴ κέν πως ἀρνῶν κνίσης αἰγῶν τε τελείων βούλεται ἀντιάσας ἡμῖν ἀπὸ λοιγὸν ἀμῦναι, 'in the hope that receiving the savour of lambs and unblemished goats he may be minded to ward off the pesti-

---

[a] A corresponding potential optative is found in T 331 f. ὡς ἄν μοι τὸν παῖδα . . . ἐξαγάγοις καί οἱ δείξειας ἕκαστα '(I thought that I should die and you would return to Phthia): so in that case you would bring him from Scyrus and show him everything . . .'.

lence from us', where βούλεται is a short-vowelled subjunctive.

The same construction is found also without ἄν, κε : e.g., τιμὴν δ' Ἀργείοις ἀποτινέμεν ἥν τιν' ἔοικεν, ἥ τε καὶ ἐσσομένοισι μετ' ἀνθρώποισι πέληται Γ 286 f., 'to pay such recompense to the Argives as is fitting and such as shall live among generations to come'. But in μάρνασθ' ὁπποτέροισι πατὴρ Ζεὺς κῦδος ὀρέξῃ E 33, 'to fight (to decide) on which of the two Zeus shall bestow glory', it is hardly necessary to interpret the omission of κεν (ἄν) as indicating 'the vagueness of the future event contemplated, i.e., the wish to exclude reference to a particular occasion' (Monro ² 258). The subjunctive is best regarded as deliberative (see above), with which ἄν is not required.

B. After historic tenses, as in Attic, both the optative and the subjunctive are used, the former being about four times the more frequent. Note the following final temporal clauses with such optatives : δέγμενος . . . ὁπότε λήξειεν ἀείδων I 191, 'waiting for him to cease'; μοχλὸν ὑπὸ σποδοῦ ἤλασα πολλῆς, ἧος θερμαίνοιτο ι 375 f., 'I thrust the bar beneath a pile of embers until it should be heated' (see below on 'until' clauses).

Optatives are occasionally found even *after a primary tense*. But these are not properly 'oblique' optatives; they have arisen from a paratactic wish construction, which, as we mentioned above, is in close psychological relationship with the voluntative subjunctive. Examples are : ἐν δ' αὐτοῖσι πύλας ποιήσομεν εὖ ἀραρυίας, ὄφρα δι' αὐτάων ἱππηλασίη ὁδὸς εἴη H 339 f., 'let us build gates in them, well-fitted that through them there may be a road for the chariots'; τόν ποτ' ἐγὼν ἐπὶ νηὸς ἐϋσσέλμοιο μελαίνης ἄξω τῆλ' Ἰθάκης, ἵνα μοι βίοτον πολὺν ἄλφοι ρ 249 f., 'him shall I carry sometime in a black well-benched ship far from Ithaca that he may bring me a goodly sum'.

On the other hand we find optatives with ἄν after a primary tense. Such constructions may be traced to paratactic potential optatives. Examples are : ἡγείσθω φιλοπαίγμονος ὀρχηθμοῖο, ὥς κέν τις φαίη γάμον ἔμμεναι ἐκτὸς ἀκούων ψ 134 f., 'let him lead the sportive dance; thus one would say, hearing it from without, that it is a wedding'; ἀλλ' ἐρέω μὲν ἐγών, ἵνα εἰδότες ἤ κε θάνωμεν ἤ κεν ἀλευάμενοι θάνατον καὶ κῆρα φύγοιμεν μ 156 f., an example in which the prospective subjunctive alternates with its opposite number (see p. 151) the potential optative. This is the only example in Homer where a final clause introduced by ἵνα has the potential particle. It should be noted, however, that the sense is not 'I will tell you all, that we may die or escape death' but 'that we may all *know* . . .'. Thus the subjunctive with κε is prospective; the optative with κεν is the remoter potential. Such an optative is also found after a historic tense : ῦε δ' ἄρα Ζεὺς συνεχές, ὄφρα κε θᾶσσον ἁλίπλοα τείχεα θείη M 25 f., 'Zeus rained constantly that he might more quickly turn the walls to jetsam'.

C. We have discussed above the interrelationship of the various modes of referring to the future — the subjunctive, the optative, and the future indicative. In a final construction, too, we find a *future indicative*: θέλγει ὅπως ᾽Ιθάκης ἐπιλήσεται α 57, 'she beguiles him that he may forget'. This is the only instance [a] in Homer of the Attic construction of ὅπως with the future indicative after verbs of 'planning, striving', etc. Apart from this we find always the subjunctive or optative.

7. *The Conditional Sentences*, as we discussed above, have emerged from the parataxis of two independent clauses the first of which poses a situation or event and the second sets forth the consequence of such a premise. Such a correlation we see at its baldest in 'no rain: no crops', where the situation posed is timeless. It may, however, contain a reference to future, present, and past time and it will be convenient to discuss the Homeric conditional sentences from the angle of their temporal reference.

A. *Future.*—We have already discussed the interrelationship and the interaction of the various modes of referring to the future — fact, will, wish, expectation, and imagination, expressed by the future indicative, the voluntative subjunctive, the wish-optative, the prospective subjunctive, and the potential optative respectively. The instability of these distinctions is exemplified most drastically in the Homeric future conditions. We find no more or less rigid division into *future vivid*, or *eventual* (ἐάν+subjunctive followed by the future indicative) and *future vague*, or *potential* (εἰ+the optative followed by the potential optative +ἄν). Instead of this all the modes of referring to the future may be interchanged in both the protasis and the apodosis, and κε (ἄν) [b] may or may not be used. Thus all the following combinations are theoretically possible: εἰ (κε) κελεύσει, κελεύῃ (κελεύσῃ), κελεύοι (κελεύσειε)+(κε) ποιήσει, ποιήσῃ, ποιήσειε; and there is no effort at consistency within one and the same sentence: e.g., ἦ γάρ κεν δειλός τε καὶ οὐτιδανὸς καλεοίμην, εἰ δὴ σοὶ πᾶν ἔργον ὑπείξομαι . . . Α 293 f., 'indeed I should be called a coward and a good-for-nothing if I yield to you in every matter'; εἰ δέ κεν εὐπλοίην δώῃ κλυτὸς ἐννοσίγαιος, ἤματί κε τριτάτῳ Φθίην ἐρίβωλον ἱκοίμην Ι 362 f., 'if the renowned Earth-Shaker shall grant us fair voyage, on the third day I should come to deep-soiled Phthia'. There follow some typical examples of these various combinations.

Future indicative+future indicative: εἰ γὰρ ᾽Αχιλλεὺς οἶος ἐπὶ Τρώεσσι μαχεῖται, οὐδὲ μίνυνθ᾽ ἕξουσι ποδώκεα Πηλεΐωνα Υ 26 f., 'for if Achilles shall fight even alone against the Trojans, not even for a short while will

---

[a] A 136 ὅπως ἀντάξιον ἔσται has more the force of 'how' than 'in order that'.

[b] Homer presents numerous examples of the contracted form ἤν which is under suspicion of being a late intrusion into the text. In the following account the text is taken as it stands and ἤν is classified with the uncontracted εἰ+ἄν.

they keep back the swift-footed son of Peleus'.

Future+(*prospective*) *subjunctive*: εἰ δέ μοι οὐ τίσουσι βοῶν ἐπιεικέ' ἀμοιβήν, δύσομαι εἰς 'Αΐδαο καὶ ἐν νεκύεσσι φαείνω μ 382 f., 'but if they do not pay me a meet recompense for my oxen, I shall go down to Hades and shine among the dead'.

Future+*optative* (κεν): εἴη κεν καὶ τοῦτο τεὸν ἔπος, ἀργυρότοξε, εἰ δὴ ὁμὴν 'Αχιλῆϊ καὶ "Εκτορι θήσετε τιμήν Ω 56 f., 'even what you say might come to pass, Archer of the Silver Bow, if indeed you shall hold Achilles and Hector in equal honour'. *Optative without* κεν: μηκέτ' ἔπειτ' 'Οδυσῆϊ κάρη ὤμοισιν ἐπείη . . . εἰ μὴ ἐγώ σε λαβὼν ἀπὸ μὲν φίλα εἵματα δύσω . . . Β 259 ff., 'may Odysseus's head no longer rest on his shoulders . . . if I do not take you and strip you of your fine clothes . . .'.

Future (κε)+*future*: σοὶ μὲν δή, Μενέλαε κατηφείη καὶ ὄνειδος ἔσσεται, εἴ κ' 'Αχιλῆος ἀγαυοῦ πιστὸν ἑταῖρον τείχει ὕπο Τρώων ταχέες κύνες ἑλκήσουσιν Ρ 556 ff., 'disgrace and rebuke will be yours, Menelaus, if the swift dogs shall rend the trusty comrade of lordly Achilles beneath the wall of the Trojans'.

Future (κε)+*the subjunctive* is apparently not found. For the *future* (κε)+*potential optative* no example is attested, but note *future* (κε)+*wish optative*: εἰ δέ κε νοστήσω καὶ ἐσόψομαι ὀφθαλμοῖσι πατρίδ' ἐμήν . . . αὐτίκ' ἔπειτ' ἀπ' ἐμεῖο κάρη τάμοι ἀλλότριος φώς, εἰ μὴ ἐγὼ τάδε τόξα φαεινῷ ἐν πυρὶ θείην (note the double protasis) Ε 212 ff., 'if I shall return and look with my eyes upon my native land . . ., then may some stranger cut off my head if I do not place this bow in the blazing fire'.

Subjunctive+*future*: εἴ περ γάρ σε κατακτάνῃ, οὔ σ' ἔτ' ἐγώ γε κλαύσομαι ἐν λεχέεσσι Χ 86 f., 'if he shall kill you, no longer shall I bewail you . . .'. This subjunctive is also followed by an *imperative* (Α 341) and by βούλομαι (μ 348) but apparently never by the subjunctive or the optative. On the other hand we find many combinations with the *subjunctive*+κε.

Subjunctive (κε)+*future*.—This is, of course, (with ἄν) the regular Attic construction: αὐτὰρ 'Αχαιοὶ τριπλῇ τετραπλῇ τ' ἀποτείσομεν, αἴ κέ ποθί Ζεὺς δῷσι πόλιν Τροίην εὐτείχεον ἐξαλαπάξαι Α 127 ff., 'but we Achaeans shall pay you back threefold and fourfold if ever Zeus grants us to sack the strong-walled city of Troy'.

Subjunctive (κε)+*subjunctive* (κε): εἰ δέ κε μὴ δώωσιν, ἐγὼ δέ κεν αὐτὸς ἕλωμαι ἢ τεὸν ἢ Αἴαντος ἰὼν γέρας Α 137 f., 'if they do not give it, I shall come and take either your prize or Aias's'.

Subjunctive (κε)+*subjunctive*: εἰ δέ κε τεθνηῶτος ἀκούσω μηδ' ἔτ' ἐόντος, νοστήσας δὴ ἔπειτα φίλην ἐς πατρίδα γαῖαν σῆμά τέ οἱ χεύω . . . β 220 ff., 'if I hear that he is dead and no longer alive then on my return to my native land I shall raise a barrow to him . . .'.

N

Subjunctive (κε)+*optative* (ἄν): εἰ μέν κεν πατρὸς βίοτον καὶ νόστον ἀκούσω, ἦ τ' ἄν, τρυχόμενός περ, ἔτι τλαίην ἐνιαυτόν β 218 f., 'if I hear of my father's survival and safety, then indeed, though it go hard with me, I should gladly endure a year round'. In the next example we have:

Subjunctive (κε)+*constative aorist*+*future*+*potential optative*: εἰ δέ κεν οἴκαδ' ἴκωμι φίλην ἐς πατρίδα γαῖαν, ὤλετό μοι κλέος ἐσθλόν, ἐπὶ δηρὸν δέ μοι αἰὼν ἔσσεται, οὐδέ κέ μ' ὦκα τέλος θανάτοιο κιχείη I 414 ff., 'but if I come home to my native land, lost is my good fame, but long shall be my life nor would the end of death come swiftly upon me'.

Optative+*future*: ἀλλ' εἴ τίς μοι ἀνὴρ ἅμ' ἔποιτο καὶ ἄλλος, μᾶλλον θαλπωρὴ καὶ θαρσαλεώτερον ἔσται K 222 f., 'but if some other would accompany me, there will be greater comfort and confidence'.

Optative+*future* (κεν): εἰ δ' Ὀδυσεὺς ἔλθοι, καὶ ἵκοιτ' ἐς πατρίδα γαῖαν, αἶψά κε σὺν ᾧ παιδὶ βίας ἀποτίσεται[a] ἀνδρῶν ρ 539 f., 'if Odysseus should come back to his native land, with his son he shall give requital for the outrages of the men'.

Optative+*subjunctive* (κεν): εἰ μὲν δὴ ἀντίβιον σὺν τεύχεσι πειρηθείης, οὐκ ἄν τοι χραίσμῃσι βιὸς καὶ ταρφέες ἰοί Λ 386 f., 'if you would but vie with me in armour, your bow and swift arrows would not avail you'.

Optative+*future*+*subjunctive* (ἄν): πληθὺν δ' οὐκ ἂν ἐγὼ μυθήσομαι οὐδ' ὀνομήνω, οὐδ' εἴ μοι δέκα μὲν γλῶσσαι, δέκα δὲ στόματ' εἶεν . . . B 488 f., 'their number I should not tell nor name, not even though I had ten tongues and ten mouths'.

Optative+*optative* (κεν): εἰ δέ σύ γ' . . . ὠμὸν βεβρώθοις Πρίαμον . . . τότε κεν χόλον ἐξακέσαιο Δ 34 ff., 'if you were to devour Priam raw . . . then you would heal your anger'.

Optative+*optative*: εἰ δ' αὖ πως τόδε πᾶσι φίλον καὶ ἡδὺ γένοιτο, ἦ τοι μὲν οἰκέοιτο πόλις Πριάμοιο ἄνακτος Δ 17 f., 'if this would somehow be welcome and pleasing to all, then verily would the city of lord Priam still be dwelt in'.

Optative (κεν)+*optative* (κεν): εἰ τούτω κε λάβοιμεν, ἀροίμεθά κε κλέος ἐσθλόν E 273, 'if we should take these two, we should win good fame'; cf. I 141, Θ 196, τ 589, etc. Note εἴ χ' ὑμεῖς γε φάγοιτε, τάχ' ἄν ποτε καὶ τίσις εἴη β 76, 'if you were to consume them, there might some day be recompense too' (with κε . . . . ἄν).

Optative (κεν)+*future* (κεν): εἰ δέ κεν εἰς Ἰθάκην ἀφικοίμεθα, πατρίδα γαῖαν, αἶψά κεν Ἡελίῳ Ὑπερίονι πίονα νηὸν τεύξομεν μ 345 ff., 'if we should come to Ithaca, our native land, swiftly shall we rear a goodly temple to Helios Hyperion'.

The manifold variety of the 'mixed' conditionals illustrated above does not mean that these modes of expression are equivalent in force and

[a] This may be, of course, a short-vowelled subjunctive.

meaning. The shades of meaning which distinguish the subjunctive of will and expectation on the one hand from the optative of wish and imagination on the other lose little of their validity. But such change of colour and variety of expression are characteristic of the nervous and energetic Homeric style. On the other hand only a sturdy subjectivism will detect shades of insistence and non-insistence in the insertion or omission of the potential particles κε(ν) and ἄν.

B. *Unreal Conditions* (contrary to fact).—The *aorist indicative* with κε (ἄν) is used as in Attic to express a past unreal (unfulfilled condition): καί νύ κεν ἔνθ' ὁ γέρων ἀπὸ θυμὸν ὄλεσσεν εἰ μὴ ἄρ' ὀξὺ νόησε βοὴν ἀγαθὸς Διομήδης Θ 90 f., 'and now would the old man have lost his life had not Diomede, good at the war-cry, been quick to notice him'. The corresponding use, however, of the *imperfect indicative* to represent present unreal conditions (*diceret si adesset*) seems not to be Homeric. There are three doubtful examples: . . . εἰ νῶϊν ὑπεὶρ ἅλα νόστον ἔδωκε νηυσὶ θοῇσι γενέσθαι 'Ολύμπιος εὐρύοπα Ζεύς, καί κέ οἱ "Αργεϊ νάσσα πόλιν καὶ δώματ' ἔτευξα . . . καί κε θάμ' ἐνθάδ' ἐόντες ἐμισγόμεθ'· οὐδέ κεν ἡμέας ἄλλο διέκρινεν φιλέοντέ τε τερπομένω τε δ 172 ff., '. . . if Zeus had granted him a safe return . . . I should have built him a house . . . and we should have had many meetings . . . and nothing else would have separated us' (until death), where it is just possible that ἐμισγόμεθα = 'we should be having many meetings'. In Ω 220, too, εἰ μὲν γάρ τίς μ' ἄλλος ἐκέλευεν might be translated 'if another were ordering me'; but 'if another had been ordering' is equally possible. Apart from this the imperfect in such constructions has its normal meaning of past continuous action: καί νύ κε δὴ ξιφέεσσ' αὐτοσχεδὸν οὐτάζοντο, εἰ μὴ κήρυκες . . . ἦλθον Η 273 ff., 'and now they had been wounding one another with swords at close quarters, had not the heralds come'; οὐ δ' ἄν πω χάζοντο κελεύθου δῖοι 'Αχαιοί, εἰ μὴ 'Αλέξανδρος . . . παῦσεν ἀριστεύοντα Μαχάονα Λ 504 ff., 'nor would the divine Achaeans have given ground from their way, had not Alexander stayed Machaon in his exploits'.

Another Homeric peculiarity is the use of the *potential optative* with reference to present and past events (see above, p. 152): εἰ μὲν νῦν ἐπὶ ἄλλῳ ἀεθλεύοιμεν 'Αχαιοί, ἦ τ' ἄν ἐγὼ τὰ πρῶτα λαβὼν κλισίηνδε φεροίμην Ψ 274 f., 'if we Achaeans were holding games in another's honour, surely I should win and take to my hut the first prize' (this the sole example containing an optative in both protasis and apodosis). Note the double apodosis in οὐκ ἄν τόσσα θεοπροπέων ἀγόρευες, οὐδέ κε Τηλέμαχον κεχολωμένον ὧδ' ἀνιείης β 184 f., '(if you had died) you would not have uttered[a] such incredible prophecies nor would you thus be spurring on Telemachus in his anger'; καί νύ κεν ἔνθ' ἀπόλοιτο ἄναξ

---

[a] Or possibly 'you would not be uttering', in which case add this example to the doubtful cases of the imperfect + ἄν.

ἀνδρῶν Αἰνείας, εἰ μὴ ἄρ' ὀξὺ νόησε Διὸς θυγάτηρ Ἀφροδίτη Ε 311 f.,
'and now would Aeneas, lord of men, have perished had not Aphrodite,
daughter of Zeus, been quick to notice', cf. ἔνθα κε ῥεῖα φέροι κλυτὰ
τεύχεα Πανθοΐδαο Ἀτρεΐδης, εἰ μή οἱ ἀγάσσατο Φοῖβος Ἀπόλλων Ρ 70 f.

C. *Iterative and General Conditionals* in *present time* are characterized
as in Attic by the use of the subjunctive+ἄν (κε), although the particle is
more often replaced by the generalizing τε (see below, p. 176); εἴπερ
γάρ τε χόλον γε καὶ αὐτῆμαρ καταπέψῃ, ἀλλά τε καὶ μετόπισθεν ἔχει
κότον . . . Α 81 f., 'for even if he swallows down his wrath for the
moment, yet he nurses his grudge thereafter'. This generalizing τε is
found in such conditionals in Ε 262, Κ 226, Λ 116, Μ 239, Π 263, Χ 191,
etc., but apparently never in the *Odyssey*.

We find the *plain subjunctive* in four passages: εἴπερ γὰρ φθάμενός
μιν ἢ οὐτάσῃ ἠὲ βάλῃσιν, ἀλλά τε καὶ περὶ δουρὶ πεπαρμένη οὐκ ἀπολήγει
ἀλκῆς Φ 576 ff., 'even if a man be first to wound and strike her, yet
even though transfixed by the spear she does not cease from her fury';
cf. η 204 f., ξ 372 ff., π 97 ff. Two passages classified here by Goodwin
are not of the same kind: νῦν δ' ὁ μὲν ὣς ἀπόλωλε κακὸν μόρον, οὐδέ τις
ἡμῖν θαλπωρή, εἴ πέρ τις ἐπιχθονίων ἀνθρώπων φῇσιν ἐλεύσεσθαι α 166 ff.,
which may well be a future conditional of the type discussed above:
'nor will it be any solace if one of earthly men shall tell us that he will
come back'. In the other passage αὐτοῦ δ' ἰχθυάᾳ, σκόπελον περιμαιμώωσα,
δελφῖνάς τε κύνας τε καὶ εἴ ποθι μεῖζον ἕλῃσι μ 95 f., the subjunctive is
prospective, of the type we discussed above (p. 160): 'there she fishes,
questing round the rock (in the hope that) somewhere she may catch
dolphins', etc. Apart from these examples we find two examples of the
subjunctive with ἤν: ἤν ποτε δασμὸς ἵκηται, σοὶ τὸ γέρας πολὺ μεῖζον
Α 166 f., 'if ever a division comes, your share is much bigger', cf. λ 159;
two examples of εἴ κε, both in the *Iliad*: ἦτ' ἄλλως ὑπ' ἐμεῖο, καὶ εἴ κ'
ὀλίγον περ ἐπαύρῃ, ὀξὺ βέλος πέλεται Λ 391 f., 'truly in another way is
my spear wont to be sharp when sped by me, even though it but graze a
little', cf. Μ 302; and finally one example of εἴ περ ἄν: μάλα γάρ τε
κατεσθίει (note the generalizing τε), εἴπερ ἂν αὐτὸν σεύωνται ταχέες
τε κύνες θαλεροί τ' αἰζηοί Γ 25 f., 'eagerly does he devour it even if the
swift hounds and vigorous youths assail him'. Thus εἴ κε (ἄν) is found
five times in such constructions, εἰ and the pure subjunctive in four
passages, while εἴ τε occurs in seven.

In *past iterative conditionals* the use of the *optative* is post-Homeric with
the exception of one passage at the end of the *Iliad*: ἀλλ' εἴ τίς με καὶ
ἄλλος ἐνὶ μεγάροισιν ἐνίπτοι . . . ἀλλὰ σὺ τόν γ' ἐπέεσσι παραιφάμενος
κατέρυκες Ω 768 ff., 'but if someone else in the house did chide me, you
would restrain him prevailing upon him with words'. The optative was
not in itself 'iterative': the meaning was 'suppose some one chid me [on

this 'timeless' use of the optative see above], then you would restrain him'.

8. *Relative Clauses*

A. *Final use.*—Whereas in Attic these clauses exhibit the future indicative, Homer uses the subjunctive (usually with κε, ἄν) in primary sequence and the optative (without κε, ἄν) in secondary sequence. The nature of the moods in such constructions has already been discussed above, pp. 159 ff.

Subjunctive: ἕλκος δ' ἰητὴρ ἐπιμάσσεται ἠδ' ἐπιθήσει φάρμαχ', ἅ κεν παύσῃσι μελαινάων ὀδυνάων Δ 190 f., 'the leech probes the wound and lays on simples which shall stay the black pangs'; cf. I 165, etc. One passage is quoted for the omission of ἄν: τιμὴν ἀποτινέμεν ἥντιν' ἔοικεν, ἥ τε καὶ ἐσσομένοισιν μετ' ἀνθρώποισι πέληται Γ 459 f., 'pay such recompense as is meet and which shall live in the memory of generations to come'. But this is a prospective subjunctive.[a] μή τίς τοι τάχα "Ιρου ἀμείνων ἄλλος ἀναστῇ, ὅς τίς σ' ἀμφὶ κάρη κεκοπὼς χερσὶ στιβαρῇσι δώματος ἐκπέμψῃσι . . . σ 334 ff., '(take care) lest some other, a better man than Irus arise who shall send you forth from the house . . .', is likewise clearly prospective. Monro quotes further μάρνασθ' ὁπποτέροισι πατὴρ Ζεὺς κῦδος ὀρέξῃ Ε 33 as a final usage, but, as we saw above (p. 161), this is deliberative. Prospective, too, are the 'generic' subjunctive introduced by a negative antecedents clause: οὐκ ἔσθ' οὗτος ἀνὴρ διερὸς βροτὸς οὐδὲ γένηται, ὅς κεν Φαιήκων ἀνδρῶν ἐς γαῖαν ἵκηται ζ 201 f., 'no mortal man exists nor will there be born who shall come to the land of the Phaeacians'; and, without κε, νῦν δ' οὐκ ἔσθ' ὅς τις θάνατον φύγῃ Φ 103, 'now there is not one who shall escape death'.

In such constructions as the above Attic used the future indicative, while in poetry we find occasionally the optative. The germs of both these constructions are found in Homer, for, as we have repeatedly discussed (above, pp. 162 ff.), the modes of future reference are to some extent interchangeable even though they are not exactly equivalent. Thus we find the future indicative with κε: πάρ' ἔμοιγε καὶ ἄλλοι οἵ κέ με τιμήσουσι A 174 f., 'there are others in my service who will honour me, I dare say'; κηδεμόνες δέ οἱ ἐνθάδ' ἀολλέες αὖθι μενόντων, οἵ κέ μιν ἐξοίσουσι Ψ 674 f., 'let his kinsmen remain here all together that they may bear him away', etc.

It is the use of the *optative* after negative antecedents which has given rise to a great deal of discussion as to the origin and nature of the mood in such clauses. The Homeric examples are (1) οὐκ ἔσθ' ὃς σῆς γε κύνας κεφαλῆς ἀπαλάλκοι, οὐδ' εἴ κεν δεκάκις τε καὶ εἰκοσινήριτ' ἄποινα στήσωσ' ἐνθάδ' ἄγοντες, ὑπόσχωνται δὲ καὶ ἄλλα, οὐδ' εἴ κέν σ' αὐτὸν χρυσῷ

---

[a] See above, p. 161.

ἐρύσασθαι ἄνωγοι Δαρδανίδης Πρίαμος Χ 348 ff., 'there is not one who would keep off the dogs from your head, not though they should bring here and weigh out ten-fold and twenty-fold ransom, and should promise still more, not even if Priam Dardanides should bid weigh your body with gold'. In this sentence we have a clear example of the alternation of the modes of future reference such as we saw in the conditionals, and there can be little doubt that those scholars are right who regard this optative as a potential without ἄν. (2) The only other Homeric example has κεν: οὐδέ οἱ ἄλλοι εἴσ᾽ οἳ κεν κατὰ δῆμον ἀλάλκοιεν κακότητα δ 166 f., 'he has no others who would protect him from ill among the people' (or 'in the land'). But this potential with κε (ἄν) is not infrequent after positive antecedents: ἀλλ᾽ ἄγε δή τινα μάντιν ἐρείομεν ἢ ἱερῆα . . . ὅς κ᾽ εἴποι Α 62 ff., 'but come now let us ask a seer or a priest . . . who would tell us'; ὀρύξομεν ἐγγύθι τάφρον, ἥ χ᾽ ἵππους καὶ λαὸν ἐρυκάκοι ἀμφὶς ἐοῦσα Η 341 f., 'let us dig a trench hard by, which shall encircle us and keep back horse and host'. Finally we find such an optative also after an historic tense representing the prospective subjunctive after a primary tense: οὐ γὰρ ἔην ὅς τίς σφιν ἐπὶ στίχας ἡγήσαιτο Β 687, 'for they had no man who would lead them into the ranks'. This optative, too, must be regarded as potential (without the particle) for, as we saw above (p. 152), this mood was originally timeless and could express an imagined situation or event in past, present, or future.

The purely *final use of the optative* in relative clauses is rare, the future indicative being the usual mode of expression. An example is καὶ τότ᾽ ἄρ᾽ ἄγγελον ἧκαν, ὃς ἀγγείλειε γυναικί ο 458, 'and then they sent a messenger to bring the news to his wife'. But most of the Homeric examples quoted by Monro are still strongly tinged with the potential force: (Athene saw to it) ὡς Ὀδυσεὺς ἔγροιτο, ἴδοι τ᾽ εὐώπιδα κούρην, ἥ οἱ Φαιήκων ἀνδρῶν πόλιν ἡγήσαιτο ζ 113 f., 'that O. should wake up and see the fair-faced girl who would lead him to the city of the Phaeacians', which is almost identical in form with that in Β 687 quoted above. *Cf.* further Ξ 107, ε 240. On the other hand both the subjunctive in Ε 33 and the optatives in ι 332, Γ 316, Ξ 507, etc., classified by Monro as final, are indirect dubitatives (see above, p. 158).

B. *Indefinite relative clauses* (under which are included those which refer to the future) in Attic have the subjunctive+ἄν after a primary tense and the optative without ἄν after a secondary tense. Homeric usage, as we have learned to expect, is not so canonized: we frequently find the subjunctive without κε (ἄν), while the optative sometimes appears with the particle.

Pure subjunctive: ἀλλὰ μάλ᾽ εὔκηλος τὰ φράζεαι ἅσσ᾽ ἐθέλησθα Α 554, 'but at your ease devise whatever you will'; οὐ δηναιὸς ὃς ἀθανάτοισι μάχηται Ε 407, 'not long-lived is he who battles with the immortals';

ῥεῖα δ' ἀρίγνωτος Διὸς ἀνδράσι γίγνεται ἀλκή, ἠμὲν ὁτέοισιν κῦδος ὑπέρτερον ἐγγυαλίζῃ, ἠδ' ὅτινας μινύθῃ Ο 490 ff., 'the aid which comes to men
from Zeus is easy to discern, both to whom he grants greater glory
and those whom he brings low'; cf. α 351, 415, λ 428, μ 40, etc., etc.

Instead of ἄν, too, we find, as in the conditionals (see above), the
generalizing particle τε: ἀντί νυ πολλῶν λαῶν ἐστιν ἀνὴρ ὅν τε Ζεὺς
κῆρι φιλήσῃ Ι 116 f., 'worth many folk is the man who becomes the
favourite of Zeus'; ἀντὶ κασιγνήτου ξεῖνός θ' ἱκέτης τε τέτυκται ἀνέρι,
ὅς τ' ὀλίγον περ ἐπιψαύῃ πραπίδεσσι θ 546 f., 'equal to a brother is a
guest and suppliant in the eyes of a man who has the least breath of
understanding', etc.

The frequent use of this subjunctive (and of τε) in similes is merely
a special instance of the indefinite: ἀστέρ' ὀπωρινῷ ἐναλίγκιον, ὅς τε
μάλιστα λαμπρὸν παμφαίνῃσι Ε 5 f., 'like unto a star at harvest time which
shines most brightly'; ὁ δ' αὖτ' ἔπεσεν μελίη ὥς, ἥ τ' ὄρεος κορυφῇ . . .
χαλκῷ ταμνομένη τέρενα χθονὶ φύλλα πελάσσῃ Ν 178 ff., 'he fell like an ash,
which on the mountain-top cut by the bronze brings its tender leaves to
the ground'; cf. Ρ 110, etc., etc. Note that such subjunctives in similes
are only used of exceptional situations and events; where comparison
is made to banal and everyday phenomena, to natural characteristics of
man or beast, the indicative is used: e.g., ἠΰτε μυιάων ἀδινάων ἔθνεα
πολλὰ αἵ τε κατὰ σταθμὸν ποιμνήϊον ἠλάσκουσιν Β 469 f., 'even as the
numerous swarms of flies which flit about the herdsman's steading'.

On relative clauses introduced by negatives such as οὐδείς ἔστι . . .
see Relative Clauses: A. Final use.

The optative without ἄν in indefinite relative clauses is also found in
Homer: ὅν τινα Τυδεΐδης ἄορι πλήξειε παραστάς, τὸν δ' Ὀδυσεὺς
μετόπισθε λαβὼν ποδὸς ἐξερύσασκεν Κ 489 f., 'whomsoever Tydeides
stood by and struck with his sword, him would Odysseus seize from
behind by the foot and drag away'; ὅς τις δὲ Τρώων κοίλης ἐπὶ νηυσὶ
φέροιτο σὺν πυρὶ κηλείῳ . . . τὸν δ' Αἴας οὔτασκε Ο 743 ff., 'whoever of
the Trojans rushed upon the ships with blazing fire, . . . him would Ajax
wound'; οὔ τινα γὰρ τίεσκον ἐπιχθονίων ἀνθρώπων, οὐ κακὸν οὐδὲ μὲν
ἐσθλόν, ὅτις σφέας εἰσαφίκοιτο χ 414 f., 'for they honoured not one of
earthly men, neither evil nor good, whosoever would come to them'.

Apart from this use after frequentative forms in -σκ- (see p. 121 f.) we
find the optative (clearly potential in force and in origin) after an optative
in the antecedent clause (both potential and wish, or, as a substitute for
this, the imperative).

Without ἄν: ὡς ἀπόλοιτο καὶ ἄλλος ὅτις τοιαῦτά γε ῥέζοι α 47, 'may
another perish, too, whoever should do such things'; cf. λ 490, etc.;
ὃς τὸ καταβρόξειεν, ἐπεὶ κρητῆρι μιγείη, οὔ κεν ἐφημέριός γε βάλοι κατὰ
δάκρυ παρειῶν δ 222 f., 'the man who should swallow it when it has

been mixed in a bowl, not short-lived would he shed tears down his cheeks' (here the optative is clearly potential in force).

With ἄν (κε): ἐς οἶκον ἀπερρίγασι νέεσθαι Ἰκαρίου, ὥς κ' αὐτὸς ἐεδνώσαιτο θύγατρα, δοίη δ' ᾧ κ' ἐθέλοι β 52 f., 'they shrink from going to the house of Icarius that he may give his daughter in marriage to whom it pleases him'; ἡ δέ κ' ἔπειτα γήμαιθ' ὅς κε πλεῖστα πόροι καὶ μόρσιμος ἔλθοι φ 161 f., 'she afterwards would marry the man who should bring most gifts and should come as the choice of destiny'. Note, further, after an imperative in the antecedent clause: δῶρον δ' ὅττι κέ μοι δοίης, κειμήλιον ἔστω δ 600, 'whatsoever gift you give me, let it be a jewel'.

9. The *Temporal Clauses* are almost entirely parallel in their constructions to the relative clauses, from which, of course, they have developed. Thus we find:

A. *Final uses*, which are discussed below together with 'until' clauses.

B. *Indefinite temporal clauses*:

Subjunctive without ἄν: οὐ μὲν σοί ποτε ἶσον ἔχω γέρας, ὁππότ' Ἀχαιοὶ Τρώων ἐκπέρσωσ' εὖ ναιόμενον πτολίεθρον Α 163 f., 'never have I a prize equal to yours whenever the Achaeans lay waste a well-peopled stronghold of the Trojans'; ἀλλ' ὅτε δὴ καὶ λυγρὰ θεοὶ μάκαρες τελέσωσι, καὶ τὰ φέρει ἀεκαζόμενος τετληότι θυμῷ σ 134 f., 'but when the blessed gods bring evils to pass, these too he bears them all unwilling yet with enduring heart'; αἰεὶ γὰρ τὸ πάρος γε θεοὶ φαίνονται ἐναργεῖς ἡμῖν, εὖτ' ἔρδωμεν ἀγακλειτὰς ἑκατόμβας η 201 f., 'for always hitherto have the gods appeared manifest to our gaze whenever we offer splendid hecatombs'; ἦμος δ' ἠέλιος μέσον οὐρανὸν ἀμφιβεβήκῃ, τῆμος ἄρ' ἐξ ἁλὸς εἶσι γέρων ἅλιος νημερτής δ 400 f., 'when the sun stands at the zenith, then the infallible old man of the sea comes forth from the water'.

There are numerous examples of great similarity to the above where κε(ν) or ἄν accompanies the verb. With Α 163 compare ἐγὼ δ' ὀλίγον τε φίλον τε ἔρχομ' ἔχων ἐπὶ νῆας ἐπεί κε κάμω πολεμίζων Α 167 f., 'I go to my ships with a small portion but my own when I have grown weary in the fight'; and further ἀλλὰ τὸ μὲν καὶ ἄνεκτον ἔχει κακὸν ὁππότε κέν τις ἤματα μὲν κλαίῃ . . . νύκτας δ' ὕπνον ἔχῃσι υ 83 ff., 'that sorrow is endurable, when a man weeps by day but has sleep of nights'. These examples show that little is involved in the inclusion or exclusion of κε(ν) or ἄν, although some scholars hold that κε(ν) insists on a particular happening or moment. That κεν means etymologically 'in this case' has been argued above.

Here, too, generalizing τε may take the place of ἄν: Διὶ ὥς τερπικεραύνῳ χωομένῳ, ὅτε τ' ἀμφὶ Τυφωέι γαῖαν ἱμάσσῃ Β 781 f., 'like Zeus, that hurls the thunderbolt in his wrath when he scourges the land about Typhoeus'; cf. Δ 259.

Optative without ἄν: ἀλλ' ὅτε δὴ πολύμητις ἀναΐξειεν Ὀδυσσεύς, στάσκεν Γ 216 f., 'but whenever Odysseus of many wiles sprang up, he would stand'; cf. ibid. 233. Cf. a similar construction with κε: οὕτω καὶ τῶν πρόσθεν ἐπευθόμεθα κλέα ἀνδρῶν ἡρώων, ὅτε κέν τιν' ἐπιζάφελος χόλος ἵκοι I 524 f., 'even so have we heard report of heroes of former times whenever furious wrath came upon one of them'. The optative is used even with reference to the future, the usage being assignable to the potential optative. σὸν δὲ πλεῖον δέπας αἰεὶ ἕστηχ' ὥς περ ἐμοὶ πιέειν ὅτε θυμὸς ἄνωγοι Δ 262, '. . . for you to drink whenever the spirit should move you'. In the following example where ἐπὴν . . . refers to an indefinite future the optative is due to attraction from the optative in the antecedent: αὐτίκα γάρ με κατακτείνειεν 'Αχιλλεὺς ἀγκὰς ἑλόντ' ἐμὸν υἱόν, ἐπὴν γόου ἐξ ἔρον εἵην Ω 226 f., 'straightway may Achilles slay me when I have clasped my son in my arms and have had my fill of lamentation' (for this attraction of mood see the corresponding section of *Relative Clauses*); cf. further τοιούτῳ δὲ ἔοικας, ἐπεὶ λούσαιτο φάγοι τε, εὑδέμεναι μαλακῶς ω 254 f.,[a] where the optative, in any case, is potential in force. Another example is νῦν γάρ χ' "Εκτορ' ἕλοις, ἐπεὶ ἂν μάλα τοι σχεδὸν ἔλθοι I 304, 'for now you could slay Hector, when he should come nigh'.

C. '*Until*' *clauses*, which may combine temporal and final sense (*cf.* donec, dum, priusquam, etc., in Latin), deserve a special examination. In a purely temporal sense Attic uses the prospective subjunctive+ἄν with reference to the future and the aorist indicative with reference to the past: *e.g.*, ἀλλ' ἀναχασσάμενος νῆχον πάλιν ἧος ἐπῆλθον ἐς ποταμόν η 280 f., '. . . I swam back till I came to the river'; μίμνετε πάντες, ἐϋκνήμιδες 'Αχαιοί, αὐτοῦ, εἰς ὅ κεν ἄστυ μέγα Πριάμοιο ἕλωμεν Β 331 f., . . . 'remain . . . until we take'; αὐτὰρ ἐγὼ . . . μαχήσομαι . . . ἧός κε . . . κιχείω Γ 290 ff., 'I shall fight . . . until I reach', etc.

The *subjunctive without* ἄν, however, also occurs: ἔχει κότον ὄφρα τελέσσῃ Α 82, 'he nurses his grudge until he pays it back' (*cf.* above, p. 170); κοιμήσας δ' ἀνέμους χέει ἔμπεδον, ὄφρα καλύψῃ ὑψηλῶν ὀρέων κορυφὰς καὶ πρώονας ἄκρους Μ 281 f., 'and lulling the winds he pours down (snow) continually until he has covered the peaks of the lofty mountains and the high headlands'; ὁ δ' ἀσφαλέως θέει ἔμπεδον ἧος ἵκηται ἰσόπεδον Ν 141 f., 'and it runs . . . until it reaches the level ground'; but ἕως and εἰς ὅ are always followed by the subjunctive with κε (ἄν).

In these clauses, too, the *optative*+κε (ἄν) is found where the governing clause contains an optative: τόφρα γὰρ ἂν κατὰ ἄστυ ποτιπτυσσοίμεθα

---

[a] This should mean 'you resemble such a one in sleeping comfortably when he has bathed and eaten' (*cf.* ἐοικότα μυθήσασθαι 'in speech resembling [your father]'); but the sense required is 'for such a one it is meet that he should sleep comfortably . . . for such is the right of old men'. Consequently it is difficult to resist emending ἔοικας to ἔοικεν as v. Leeuwen does.

μύθῳ χρήματ' ἀπαιτίζοντες, ἔως κ' ἀπὸ πάντα δοθείη β 77 f., 'so long should we importune you with speech throughout the city demanding our money until it was all paid back'; ἐκ τοῦ δ' ἄν τοι ἔπειτα παλίωξιν παρὰ νηῶν αἰὲν ἐγὼ τεύχοιμι διαμπερές, εἰς ὅ κ' Ἀχαιοὶ Ἴλιον αἰπὺ ἔλοιεν Ο 69 ff., 'then after that should I bring about a retreat from the ships until the Achaeans take steep Ilion'. Apart from these the following is the only example where an optative+ἄν occurs in an 'until' clause without an optative in the main clause: δὴ τότε κεῖτ' . . . ἐν πολλῇ κόπρῳ, ἥ οἱ προπάροιθε θυράων ἡμιόνων τε βοῶν τε ἅλις κέχυτ', ὄφρ' ἂν ἄγοιεν δμῶες Ὀδυσσῆος τέμενος μέγα κοπρήσοντες ρ 296 ff., where, however, the meaning is not certainly final but oscillates between 'the dung was piled there until the serfs should cart it away' and '. . . for the serfs to cart away'. The use of the optative with ἄν in purely final clauses has been discussed above (p. 161).

The use of ἔως deserves a special note: in the *Odyssey* it is used in five separate passages in a purely final sense with little or no temporal connotation: ὦρσε δ' ἐπὶ κραιπνὸν Βορέην, πρὸ δὲ κύματ' ἔαξεν, ἧος ὁ Φαιήκεσσι φιληρέτμοισι μιγείη διογενὴς Ὀδυσσεύς ε 385 ff., 'she aroused blustering Boreas and broke the waves before him that god-born Odysseus might reach the land of the seafaring Phaeacians'; cf. ζ 79, δ 799, ι 375, τ 367.

D. πρίν. In Homer the construction with the infinitive predominates. We find no example of the Attic usage, according to which the indicative is used where the πρίν clause denotes the limit up to which the action of the main clause is continued: e.g., οὐδέ τι θυμῷ τέρπετο, πρὶν πολέμου στόμα δύμεναι αἱματόεντος Τ 312 f., 'nor did he rejoice in his heart until he entered the mouth of bloody war'; οὐ δ' ἀπολήγει πρὶν χροὸς ἀνδρομέοιο διελθέμεν Υ 99 f., 'nor does it cease until it pierces the flesh of a man'. The nearest approach to an indicative construction is seen in those sentences where πρίν γ' governs a clause introduced by ὅτε δή: ὡς μὲν τῶν ἐπὶ ἶσα μάχη τέτατο πτόλεμός τε, πρίν γ' ὅτε δὴ Ζεὺς κῦδος ὑπέρτερον Ἕκτορι δῶκε Μ 436 f., 'thus were their battle and strife stretched evenly until Zeus granted greater glory to Hector'; ἥμεθ' ἀτυζόμεναι . . . πρίν γ' ὅτε δή με σὸς υἱὸς ἀπὸ μεγάροιο κάλεσσεν ψ 42 f., 'we sat distraught until your son called me from the hall'. In these turns of phrase the paratactic origin is clearly apparent: 'it was level pegging at least prior to (πρίν γε) the moment when Zeus . . .'. The prospective subjunctive occurs in β 374 (πρίν γ' ὅτ' ἄν . . . γένηται) and the corresponding optative with reference to the past in I 488 f. (πρίν γ' ὅτε δή . . . ἄσαιμι).

When πρίν refers to the future, the construction with the subjunctive is frequent, but whereas in Attic the potential particle ἄν regularly accompanies the mood, it is nowhere found in Homer. This suggests that the subjunctive in such constructions has arisen from the voluntative, which is exemplified in ἀλλὰ σὺ μὲν μήπω καταδύσεο μῶλον Ἀρῆος, πρίν γ᾽ ἐμὲ δεῦρ᾽ ἐλθοῦσαν ἐν ὀφθαλμοῖσιν ἴδηαι Σ 134 ff., which may be translated paratactically 'do not enter the battle . . . I want you to see me coming first'. So also οὐ γάρ πω καταδυσόμεθα . . . εἰς Ἀΐδαο δόμους, πρὶν μόρσιμον ἦμαρ ἐπέλθῃ κ 174 f., 'we shall not go down to the home of Hades — let the destined day come first'. On the other hand the parataxis quoted by Goodwin as illustrating the origin of the construction is hardly satisfactory: οὐδέ μιν ἀνστήσεις· πρὶν καὶ κακὸν ἄλλο πάθῃσθα Ω 551, 'you will not raise him up again; before that you will suffer some other misfortune' is wholly different in meaning from 'you will not raise him up until you suffer some other affliction'. In the former case the subjunctive is prospective, whereas to get the second meaning a voluntative is necessary — you must suffer some other misfortune first.

The *optative* is used after πρίν in only one passage: οὐκ ἔθελεν φεύγειν, πρὶν πειρήσαιτ᾽ Ἀχιλῆος Φ 580, 'he was unwilling to flee — might he make trial of Achilles first'. This example throws light on the origin of the 'oblique' optative in such constructions: the optative here obviously represents a wish, and we have seen above (p. 149) how the wish optative suggests in a more 'remote' form a desire for which the voluntative subjunctive is a more direct expression. It thus came to be used after historic tenses to correspond to the subjunctive after primary tenses.

THE PARTICLES

1. ἀτάρ, αὐτάρ.—These are identical in force. Their functions may be divided into (1) *adversative*: e.g., τὼ μέν . . . στήτην, οὐδέ τί μιν προσεφώνεον οὐδ᾽ ἐρέοντο· αὐτὰρ ὁ ἔγνω ᾗσιν ἐνὶ φρεσὶ φώνησέν τε Α 331 ff., 'but the two stood and spoke not to him nor questioned him; but he knew in his heart and spoke'; εἰ δὲ θανόντων περ καταλήθοντ᾽ εἰν Ἀΐδαο, αὐτὰρ ἐγὼ καὶ κεῖθι φίλου μεμνήσομ᾽ ἑταίρου Χ 389 f., 'if they forget the dead in Hades, yet will I even then remember my dear comrade'.

(2) *progressive*: Ἥφαιστος μὲν δῶκε Διὶ Κρονίωνι ἄνακτι, αὐτὰρ ἄρα Ζεὺς δῶκε διακτόρῳ ἀργεϊφόντῃ, etc. Β 102 f., 'Hephaestus gave it to Zeus Kronion and Zeus gave it to the messenger Argeiphontes'.

2. ἄρα, ἄρ (before consonants), ῥα.—This is one of the most frequent of Homeric particles. It signifies 'interest' and 'excitement' of every kind, whether in the novel, the unexpected, the disappointing, etc. E.g., δράκων . . . τόν ῥ αὐτὸς Ὀλύμπιος ἧκε φόωσδε, βωμοῦ ὑπαΐξας πρός

ῥα πλατάνιστον ὄρουσεν Β 308 ff., 'a serpent . . . which the Olympian himself sent forth to the light, flashed from beneath the altar and darted to the plane tree'; ὁ δὲ κλισίηθεν ἀκούσας ἔκμολεν ἶσος Ἄρηϊ, κακοῦ δ' ἄρα οἱ πέλεν ἀρχή Λ 603 f., 'and he heard and came forth from the hut like unto Ares; and that was for him the beginning of woe'; οὐδ' ἄρ' ἔμελλε . . . ἂψ ἀπονοστήσειν Μ 113 ff., 'nor was he destined . . . to return safely'.

ἄρα is often combined with other particles calculated to quicken the hearers' interest: e.g., ἤ ἄρα, ἤ ῥά νύ τοι, etc.

3. δέ.—The continuative and adversative uses are common as in prose and require no illustration. At times, however, and particularly after a wish, Homer links on with δέ a causal clause which prose would express more explicitly by γάρ: πίθεσθ'· ἄμφω δὲ νεωτέρω ἔστον ἐμεῖο Α 259, 'trust me; you are both younger than I'; ἐμέθεν ξύνες ὦκα· Διὸς δέ τοι ἄγγελός εἰμι Β 26, 'listen quickly to me: I am, you know, the messenger of Zeus', etc.

A use peculiar to Homer and Herodotus is the so-called 'apodotic', where it marks the entrance of the main clause after a preceding subordinate clause: οἵη περ φύλλων γενεή, τοίη δὲ καὶ ἀνδρῶν Ζ 146; ὅσσον Φαίηκες περὶ πάντων ἴδριες ἀνδρῶν νῆα θοὴν ἐνὶ πόντῳ ἐλαυνέμεν, ὣς δὲ γυναῖκες ἱστῶν τεχνῆσσαι η 108 ff., 'as much as the Phaeacians surpass all men in skill in sailing a swift ship on the sea, even so are their women skilful workwomen at the looms', etc.

4. ἦ.—This particle is used by Homer only in speeches, where it has a strong asseverative force — 'verily', 'in sooth'. ἦ μέγα πένθος Ἀχαιΐδα γαῖαν ἱκάνει Α 254, 'verily a great grief has come to the land of Achaea'; and passim.

This particle, too, is often combined with particles of similar force: note ἦ μέν, ἦ μήν, ἦ τοι, ἦ ἄρα, ἦ ῥά νύ τοι, ἦ γάρ, etc. It may further be used as an adjunct in ἐπεὶ ἦ, τί ἦ (also written τιή), and further in combinations ἠμέν . . . ἠδέ ('verily on the one hand . . . verily on the other'), e.g., νῦν δ' εἶμι Φθίηνδ', ἐπεὶ ἦ πολὺ φέρτερόν ἐστιν οἴκαδ' ἴμεν Α 169 f., 'but now I shall go to Phthia since it is indeed far better to return home'. τί ἦ τοι ταῦτα ἰδυίη πάντ' ἀγορεύω; Α 365, 'why indeed should I tell this to you who know everything?'; ἠμὲν δή ποτ' ἐμεῦ πάρος ἔκλυες εὐξαμένοιο . . . ἠδ' ἔτι καὶ νῦν μοι τόδ' ἐπικρήηνον ἐέλδωρ Α 453 ff., 'verily in the past you were wont to hearken to my prayer . . . and even so now fulfil this wish of mine'. In most examples, however, ἠμέν . . . ἠδέ has little more force than 'both . . . and'.

5. θην.—This particle is rather weaker in force than δή: οὔ θην οὐδ' αὐτὸς δηρὸν βέῃ Π 852 f., 'indeed not long shall you yourself live'; ὥς

θην καὶ σὸν ἐγὼ λύσω μένος P 29, 'even so shall I loose your might';
οὔ θήν μιν πάλιν αὖτις ἀνήσει θυμὸς ἀγήνωρ νεικείειν βασιλῆας ὀνειδείοις
ἐπέεσσιν B 276 f., 'never again, I am sure, will his proud heart urge him
to revile the kings with abusive words'; ἦ θήν σ' ἐξανύω γε καὶ ὕστερον
ἀντιβολήσας Λ 365, 'verily I will make an end of you . . .'.

6. μέν.[a]—It has been suggested that μέν (like δέ) is an old demonstrative stem, which would satisfactorily account for the opposition μέν
. . . δέ. μέν by itself clearly has this deictic-demonstrative force in
thrusting some aspect of a situation on the attention of the hearer.

The Homeric use differs from Attic in that it may be used to produce
emphasis without a following contrast denoted by δέ: χρὴ μὲν σφωΐτερόν
γε, θεά, ἔπος εἰρύσσασθαι A 216, 'a man certainly must obey the words of
you two, O goddess !'; οὐ μὲν σοί ποτε ἶσον ἔχω γέρας A 163, 'never do
I have a prize equal to yours'; αὐτίκα δ' ἀσπίδα μὲν πρόσθ' ἔσχετο
M 294, 'his shield straightway he held before him' (but here there is an
implied contrast with δύο δοῦρε τινάσσων which follows in l. 298);
νημερτὲς μὲν δή μοι ὑπόσχεο A 514, 'promise me quite without fail'.

Note the combination γε μέν, which in Homer is either (1) adversative: οὐδὲ μὲν οὐδ' οἳ ἄναρχοι ἔσαν, πόθεόν γε μὲν ἀρχόν B 703, 'nor
were his men leaderless, yet they longed for their leader'; αἷμα μέλαν
κελάρυζε, νόος γε μὲν ἔμπεδος ἦεν Λ 813, 'the black blood was gushing;
yet was his spirit steadfast'; (2) concessive: τὸν ξεῖνον ἐρώμεθα εἴ τιν'
ἄεθλον οἶδέ τε καὶ δεδάηκε· φυήν γε μὲν οὐ κακός ἐστι θ 133 f., 'let us
ask the stranger if he knows and is skilful at some sport; in build at least
he is not bad'. ἦ μέν like ἦ μήν is strongly asseverative: ἦ μέν σ'
ἐνδυκέως ἀπεπέμπομεν, ὄφρ' ἂν ἵκοιο πατρίδα σήν κ 65 f., 'truly in kindness
we sped you on your way that you might come to your native land'.
Similar combinations are ἦ μὲν δή and ἦ τοι μέν.

7. μήν (μάν) uncombined with another particle seems to be used only
to emphasize negative statements: οὐ μήν οἱ τό γε κάλλιον οὐδέ τ' ἄμεινον
Ω 52, 'verily that will neither be fairer nor better for him' (= 'he shall
have neither profit nor honour from it'); ἀλλ' οὐ μάν σ' ἔτι δηρὸν
ἀνέξομαι E 895, 'but no longer shall I endure you'. Note the com-

---

[a] Wackernagel reminds us (Untersuchungen, 18 f.) that μάν is the form of this particle
in all dialects except Attic-Ionic. In Ionic we find μέν while μήν is exclusively Attic. In
Homer μάν is confined to ante-vocalic positions where a long syllable is metrically required,
while μέν is found mostly before a consonant. Thus ἦ μάν appears before a vowel in B 370,
N 354, etc., and ἦ μέν before a consonant A 77, E 197, etc. It is difficult in the face of these
facts to resist the conclusion stated by Monro: 'an original μάν was changed into μέν
whenever it came before a consonant, and preserved when the metre made this corruption
impossible'. The presence of μήν in our Homeric texts must, therefore, be ascribed to
Attic or Atticistic influence.

binations (1) εἰ δ' ἄγε μὴν πείρησαι A 302, 'come now try (if you dare)' ; (2) καὶ μήν: ὧδε γὰρ ἐξερέω, καὶ μὴν τετελεσμένον ἔσται Ψ 410, 'for thus shall I speak out and it shall indeed be accomplished' ; (3) ἦ μήν: ἦ μὴν καὶ πόνος ἐστὶν ἀνιηθέντα νέεσθαι B 291, 'in good sooth there is toil enough to make a man become disheartened and depart'.

8. οὖν.—This particle has a limited function in Homer, where it appears almost solely in temporal clauses in the combinations ἐπεὶ οὖν, ὡς οὖν and seems to mean no more than 'when in fact' (it is possible that οὖν/ὦν is the present participle of the verb 'to be', in which case it is identical with the English 'sooth'): οἱ δ' ἐπεὶ οὖν ἤγερθεν A 57, 'when they were actually gathered together' (οὖν refers to ἀγορήνδε καλέσσατο λαὸν Ἀχιλλεύς l. 54).

9. περ concentrates attention on the word it follows, such emphasis often implying exclusion or contrast: ἐπεί μ' ἔτεκές γε μινυνθάδιόν περ ἐόντα, τιμήν πέρ μοι ὄφελλεν Ὀλύμπιος ἐγγυαλίξαι A 352 f., 'since bear me you did (γε) short-lived though I am, honour at least ought the Olympian to have vouchsafed me'; οἴκαδέ περ σὺν νηυσὶ νεώμεθα B 236, 'home let us go with our ships'; ἐπεὶ οὔ κε θανόντι περ ὧδ' ἀκαχοίμην, εἰ μετὰ οἷς ἑτάροισι δάμη Τρώων ἐνὶ δήμῳ a 236 f., 'since not even if he had died should I grieve thus if he had been brought low with his comrades in the land of the Trojans'.

10. τε.—Besides its common prose function as a connective, in Homer τε exhibits a specifically epic function: it denotes habitual (natural, expected) action. We have already discussed its attachment to the subjunctive in frequentative clauses, and we have, further, observed its presence in similes where the subjunctive occurs. It can, however, also appear in similes where the indicative is usual (see p. 169): Βορέης καὶ Ζέφυρος, τώ τε Θρήκηθεν ἄητον I 5, 'Boreas and Zephyrus, which blow from Thrace'; Παλλάδ' Ἀθηναίην . . ., ἥ τέ τοι αἰεί . . . παρίσταμαι ν 300 f., 'Pallas Athene, I who ever stand by your side'; ὥρῃ ἐν εἰαρινῇ, ὅτε τε γλάγος ἄγγεα δεύει B 471, 'in the season of spring when the milk drenches the pails'. τε is used, further, in general aphorisms such as ῥεχθὲν δέ τε νήπιος ἔγνω P 32, 'even a fool recognizes a fact'; καὶ γάρ τ' ὄναρ ἐκ Διός ἐστιν A 63, 'for a dream, too, as you know, comes from Zeus'.

There seems every possibility that this τε is etymologically different from connective τε (= Latin -que, *qᵘe). In the first place we note the resemblance of function to τοι in general aphorisms: πλεόνων δέ τοι ἔργον ἄμεινον M 412, 'many hands make light work'. Moreover, ἥ τε, 'which presents considerable difficulties on any theory of τε' (Denniston), is almost indistinguishable from ἦτοι (for which see below): ἐξ αὖ νῦν ἔφυγες θάνατον, κύον· ἦ τέ τοι ἄγχι ἦλθε κακόν Λ 362 f., 'once again have you escaped death, dog that you are; in truth did bane come near to you'. Denniston notes, further, the 'contact' between στρεπταὶ μέν τε φρένες ἐσθλῶν Ο 203, 'placable are the hearts of the good, you know' and ἀκεσταί τοι φρένες ἐσθλῶν Ν 115. In view, then, of this parallelism and partial identity of usage between τε and τοι it is possible to suggest an explanation of τε which accounts for the hitherto inexplicable 'generalizing' function of τε: τε involves an apostrophe of the hearer, and it bears the same morphological relationship to σε [a] as τοι to σοι. Its function is roughly 'as you know, of course', whereas τοι = 'as you have perhaps forgotten'; e.g., τὸν δ' ἐξήρπαξ' Ἀφροδίτη ῥεῖα μάλ' ὥς τε θεός Γ 380 f., 'but Aphrodite snatched him up full easily, just as you would expect a goddess to'. So, too, in the above quoted similes 'the winds which, as you know, blow from Thrace'; 'the season when, as you know, the milk drenches the pails', etc.

We may list here certain elliptical comparisons indicating measurement characterized by τε: τὴν δὲ γυναῖκα εὗρον ὅσην τ' ὄρεος κορυφήν κ 112 f. (cf. ὅσσον θ' ἱστὸν νηός ι 322; τὸν δὲ χιτῶν' ἐνόησα . . . οἷόν τε κρομύοιο λοπόν τ 233; πεῖσμα δ' ὅσον τ' ὄργυιαν κ 167; βόθρον . . . ὅσον τε πυγούσιον κ 517). All the examples are from the *Odyssey*. Here belongs too, the post-Homeric use of οἷός τε 'capable of'.

11. τοι, in origin a 'datival' form of τύ (σοι comes from τϜοι), calls the attention of the reader to a fact which he has forgotten: it may be roughly translated 'mark you'. It remains true to its origin in that it always implies the presence of a hearer, and in Homer the vast majority of instances occur in speeches, particularly in dialogue. The usage hardly requires illustration. Note the combinations (1) ἀλλά τοι, (2) ἤτοι, (3) ἤτοι μέν, (4) τοιγάρ.

(1): ἀλλά τοι οὐκ ἐθέλησα Ποσειδάωνι μάχεσθαι πατροκασιγνήτῳ, ὅς τοι κότον ἔνθετο θυμῷ ν 341 f., 'but, mark you, I was not willing to fight with Poseidon, my father's brother, who planted rancour in his heart'.

(2): ἀλλ' ἤτοι ἔπεσιν μὲν ὀνείδισον Α 211, 'but by all means revile him with words'.

(3): ἀλλ' ἤτοι μὲν ταῦτα μεταφρασόμεσθα καὶ αὖτις Α 140, 'but, mark my words, we shall take thought of this another time' (*i.e.* 'you haven't heard the last of this').

(4): τοιγὰρ ἐγὼν ἐρέω Α 76, 'therefore will I speak' (note, however, that τοι- may be here a part of the demonstrative root *to-*).

12. κε(ν), ἄν.—It will be convenient to summarize here the usages of these 'potential' particles. κε, as we saw, is Aeolic, while ἄν is the

---

[a] τε was, of course, not originally an accusative but an old invariable form.

corresponding Attic particle.[a] Their function, as we have seen, derives from their demonstrative origin 'in this case', etc. As such it serves to mark the prospective subjunctive from the voluntative and the potential optative from the optative of wish (see, however, pp. 149 ff.). But this usage has not yet become canonized and the prospective subjunctive appears without κε, ἄν, as does the potential optative, while conversely the particle may occasionally accompany the voluntative subjunctive and the wish optative (p. 153). The same uncertainty applies to the use of the particle in subordinate clauses (q.v.). We must see in the stricter Attic usage an example of the process whereby every developed and disciplined prose style orders and sifts out from the vagueness and multiplicity of colloquial usage those carefully differentiated forms of expression which writing, lacking as it does gesture and intonation, the commentators and interpreters of speech, finds necessary for achieving precision and clarity.

[a] κε(ν), however, is between three and four times more frequent than ἄν, which is most common after the negative οὐ(κ). As P. Chantraine observes, ii. 345: 'on a observé que la vulgate homérique écrit presque toujours οὐκ ἄν, mais que οὔ κεν et οὔ κε sont exceptionnels'. I cannot agree with the finding that ἄν is more emphatic than κε(ν). The dialectical distribution of the particles must be the primary fact on which to base interpretations. That ἄν and κε(ν) are different forms of the same word has been argued above (pp. 90 ff.).

CHAPTER 5

HOMER AND OTHER EPIC POETRY

by A. B. Lord

THE field of epic poetry is vast. Our texts cover a period of some four thousand years, from the ancient Babylonian epic of Gilgamesh, of about 2000 B.C., to the present day. They come from many parts of the world, including such widely separated places as the northern tip of Sumatra and the barren lava fields of Iceland.[1] The poems themselves vary greatly in length from less than a hundred lines to many thousands, and naturally their quality is as varied as their length. We know the names of some of the poets who gave us these texts and in some instances we know the circumstances of composition. In other cases we are ignorant of both the name of the poet and the time and place and manner of composition.

A study of other epic poems and traditions has afforded us a greater insight into Homeric poetry and the Greek tradition than we have had hitherto, but much still remains to be done. The Chadwicks, especially in *The Growth of Literature*, and C. M. Bowra in *Heroic Poetry* have brought enlarged vistas of epic to our view of Homer and in doing so have taken the camera from the hands of the separatists; for we now realize that to compare Homer with other epic songs does not necessarily entail the theory of multiple authorship. Yet the most significant advance came in the early thirties of this century when Milman Parry proved that the Homeric poems were oral traditional songs, and collected material among the Yugoslavs that would enable us to discover exactly what the implications of his proof were for Homeric studies. The present chapter will attempt to synthesize the most important of these implications in so far as they are now understood.

THE OCCURRENCE AND NATURE OF ORAL EPIC

Epic poetry is still practised, or was until recently at least, in Russia and central Asia, Afghanistan and Persia, and in Yugoslavia, Bulgaria, and Albania. The Western Hemisphere and the Pacific Islands have yielded us no texts from the past, nor is there any indication that there ever was singing of epic in those parts, although argument from absence of evidence is far from conclusive. An Ainu epic has recently been published,[2] and from the last century we have information about an epic

among the Moslem Achehnese in northern Sumatra.[3] There is indication
that among the Touaregs, also Moslems, in northern Africa there is epic
poetry.[4] It is possible, of course, that epic poetry was practised in many
parts of the world in the past and then disappeared entirely without having
been written down. In fact, no matter how rich our texts from earlier
periods are, they represent only an infinitesimal part of what must have
been.

If epic poetry exists now only in out-of-the-way regions of the world,
we know that it was still alive in the Middle Ages in most parts of Europe.
We have not only descriptions but texts themselves from France, Spain,
England, Iceland, Germany, and Greece. From ancient times we have,
in addition to the Homeric poems, Sumerian, Akkadian, and Hittite
epic texts from as early as 2000 B.C. Even at this time epic is fully
developed, so that its practice must go very far back in the history of
mankind.

Epic is narrative song; it is a tale which is sung. In Russia, Afghanistan, Turkestan, Arabia, Albania, Yugoslavia, and Bulgaria, indeed,
wherever epic poetry is still practised today, it is sung, and the melodies
of its chant have been recorded on discs. There are abundant indications
from the Middle Ages, both in outside sources and in the mediaeval
poems themselves, in France, Germany, England, and Spain, that the
jongleurs and minstrels, *scops*, and *Spielmänner* sang epic poetry.[5] Tacitus
noted that the Germanic tribes sang of their famous men.[6] Homer's
bard (ἀοιδός) sang the tale of Troy.[7] Although the evidence is very
scanty, there is every reason to believe that the oldest of our epics from
Babylonia and Sumeria were also stories in song.[8]

When Homer refers to epic it is in the term ἀείδειν, and the man who
practises epic song is an ἀοιδός. Homer uses ἔπος, sometimes in
combination with μῦθος, to emphasize the content, 'what is or has been
uttered', thus underlining the narrative element in ἀείδειν.[9] Homer
himself teaches us that the basic idea of epic is narrative song. The
formula at the beginning of the *Iliad* stresses the song: Μῆνιν ἄειδε,
θεά; that at the beginning of the *Odyssey*, the story: Ἄνδρα μοι ἔννεπε,
Μοῦσα.

Other epic traditions than that of the ancient Greek use similar words.
Romance tradition has its *chansons* to which Roland refers when he
addresses his men before the battle at Roncevals: 'Now let each have a
care that he strikes good blows and great, that no man may mis-say us in
his songs'.[10] The famous Spanish epic is entitled *El Cantar de Mio Cid*.
In the Anglo-Saxon *Beowulf* a number of words are used to indicate epic
song. *Gid* (verb *giddian*), *leoth*, and the verb *singen* all emphasize the
importance of the song. When the minstrel in Heorot concludes the
tale of Finn, the poet uses all three of these words: 'The song was sung,

the glee-man's measure'.[11]　In modern times South Slav epics are always referred to as songs, *pjesme*, (the bard is a *pjevač* ('singer'), as in the lines, 'And then let us sing a song which is true and for the assembled company'.[12]　In a variant of these lines the singer also uses the verb *pričati*, to 'tell' : 'And then I shall tell you a song, a short one, one sung before, one which is true and shall be for the assembled company'.[13]

Singing of tales which we call epics is almost everywhere accompanied by instrumental music.　Homer pictures it thus : 'A herald brought a beautiful lyre and handed it to Phemius the minstrel, whom they had pressed into their service.　He had just struck the first notes for some delightful song, when Telemachus leaned across to the bright-eyed Athene and whispered to her.'[14]　Typical of the lines referring to singing in the *chansons de geste* is one which combines singing and playing the *vielle* : 'After eating the minstrels played and sang'.[15]

Even in those parts of the world where no musical accompaniment is used, as for instance in Russia and in central and western Yugoslav Macedonia, epics are still sung, and we know, furthermore, that in the past an instrumental accompaniment was present but was abandoned for known reasons.[16]　Ordinarily it is the singer who plays the instrument for his own accompaniment.　There is evidence, however, for example in France and Germany in the late Middle Ages, that the accompaniment was sometimes played by another person.[17]　Where it is used the musical instrument is a great aid to the singer in setting the rhythm of his lines and the tempo of his performance.　Under his control it can assist him in smoothing over lines which in the speed of composition are faulty.

In its pre-literary form epic poetry was a necessary part of the social life of a family or of a community.　Whatever its functions may have been in its earliest pre-history and in its origins, we find it in historical times serving as tribal, family, or national history, panegyric, political propaganda, as a model for education, and finally as entertainment.　It is sung at religious festivals, both pagan and Christian, at the courts of princes, at community gatherings, at solemn family feast days, and in the peasant hut.　The audience for epic song seems never to have been exclusive.　Although sung in the courts of princes, it was also sung for the farmers, and was not restricted to any single group.

While epic may not have been intended for the ears of any special class, it is frequently performed and practised by a special group.　The very fact of being a singer sets the individual apart even in the simplest society.　The ancient Greeks looked upon the *aoidos* as divinely inspired, and in some of the central Asiatic tribes the singer is actually a shaman or seer and priest.[18]　He is the intermediary between the world of spirits and of the spirit and the ordinary every-day world of man.　Frequently the singer is professional or semi-professional, and this professionalism may be of great moment in maintaining a tradition. But professionalism is not a *sine qua non* for oral epic. Achilles singing in his tent was not a paid bard any more than is the patriarch of a Serbian family when he sings at the family's solemn feast day.

It is not uncommon to find that epic poetry is sung by two men to-gether. Such seems to have been the practice in Finland,[19] and one can still hear this kind of performance in Albania and Yugoslav Macedonia to-day.[20] In these cases, however, only one man is the composer of the song. He sings the lines and his companion repeats them. Even when a singer accustomed to such a tradition sings alone he repeats each line. The musical pattern in these instances is constructed of two lines with a final cadence at the end of the second. Whether this form arises from antiphonal singing is not known, but it is a boon to the poet, because it allows time for him to think of the following line. It has drawbacks, however. It is not suited for really long epic poems. The tempo of performance is so slow that the dramatic force of a narrative is weakened. The audience finds its attention wandering during the repetitions. Hence the songs which come from regions where this practice holds tend to be short.

Of the actual practice of epic poetry among the ancient Babylonians and their neighbours we know little, and the poems themselves give us no description of minstrelsy that can definitely be labelled 'epic' as we understand the term. The Sumerian poem, *The Death of Gilgamesh*, gives a list of the hero's family and retinue, and in it is mentioned 'his musician, (his beloved) entertainer'.[21] Perhaps this was an epic singer, a Sumerian *jongleur*.

The most vivid description of minstrelsy in ancient times is in the *Odyssey*, which abounds in references to the singing of tales as enter-tainment at a feast. The courts at Ithaca and in Phaeacia maintain bards, and it is natural to suppose that Homer is describing something very similar to what must have been his own experience. Quite early in the *Odyssey* we find the suitors listening to Phemius singing (to Penelope's distress) about the Achaeans' return from Troy (α 325-59). In this passage it is clear that the bard has his own choice of songs, a right which Telemachus is ready to defend. This is decidedly the singer's point of view. We find it again more fully when Odysseus is being entertained at the court of Alcinous (in the eighth book). Demodocus the bard is much in demand throughout, whether to sing epic lays within the palace (θ 72-84) or, after his tale of the quarrel of Odysseus and Achilles has reduced Alcinous's guest to tears, to accompany on his lyre out of doors the dancing which is part of the alternative entertainment provided by the considerate host (θ 254-65). Afterwards he sings of the love of Ares and Aphrodite (θ 266-366), and again, after dinner, at the specific request of Odysseus, the tale of the Wooden Horse (θ 487-520). Finally, on the following day, he performs at the farewell banquet to Odysseus (ν 27-8). In all these scenes Homer's eye is on Demodocus, and no chance is missed of giving the bard the praise and respect due to his art. He is beloved of the Muse above all others, though bereft of his sight (θ 63-4), and meets with the kindly consideration that such a one deserves. There is always someone at hand to give him a chair, to place his lyre within easy reach, and to set beside him a table with food and drink to refresh him between songs (θ 65-70, 471-3), or to lead him by the hand when the party go outside (θ 106-7). Nor does Homer omit to note the delight of the audience at his singing (θ 367-9), and Odysseus is especially complimentary: he sends a serving-man across the hall with a special portion of meat for the bard, and richly praises his singing and narrative powers (θ 474-91).

The details which Homer gives are applicable to-day. They are integral and even necessary accompaniments to the oral art. As Homer has noted, the singer must stop from time to time in his long song to rest.[22] At these times he takes refreshment, and when Demodocus was first brought in a table with wine on it was set near him. In the Balkans to-day when the epic singer stops to rest, his audience buys him coffee or some more spirituous beverage.

It may be wrong to conceive of Demodocus as being a member of the court of Alcinous. Demodocus is sent for and while he is being fetched other activity takes place, activity which indicates that it was some little time before the bard arrived. It is quite possible that he was not brought from another part of the palace but rather from another section of the town. Were he a regular adjunct of the court his lyre might be expected to be already on a peg in the hall, and he would not need to be instructed as to where the instrument was. He seems to be a famous *jongleur* of the district rather than a minstrel permanently and officially attached to the court.

The status of the bard among the Yugoslavs is not unlike that of Demodocus. During the last century and up to the Balkan Wars, when the southern districts of Yugoslavia were provinces of the Turkish Empire, there was an aristocracy of beys and pashas which still found entertainment in its courtly circles from the singing of epics. There are Moslem Slav singers alive to-day in these districts who recall those days and who themselves sang at such gatherings or learned from other singers who had been called in by the local aristocracy.[23] The Turkish nobles did not actually, it would seem, maintain a permanent court bard. We have heard of local beys who had a great interest in epic singing, who practised the art themselves, and thought nothing of finding a kindred spirit in a bard who was not of the nobility, keeping him at their court for indefinite periods of time.[24]   Such a patron and his friends provide the ideal audience for the epic singer, and King Alcinous and his court seem also to have been that kind of patron and audience.   That Homer appreciated such circumstances for singing one can be sure; the care given to the description of the feast in Phaeacia bears witness to just that.

While indeed the audience and the occasion and the musical accompaniment are of great significance in the practice of oral epic poetry, needless to say, it is the singer who is the centre of attention and the chief actor.   He is the carrier of the tradition; he composes the songs.   He must be sensible of both occasion and audience, but it is ultimately his skill or lack of it which will please, instruct, move to tears or laughter, or incite to action.   The fate of the songs is in his hands.   He may corrupt a good story, or he may enhance and set right a story which he received from the tradition in a corrupt state.   He is no mere mouthpiece who repeats slavishly what he has learned.   He is a creative artist.

THE ORAL TECHNIQUE: (A) FORM

The greatest service which the study of living epic traditions has performed for the Homerist has been to explain the way in which the epic singer composes and transmits his songs.[25]   The craft of a singer is a most demanding one.   Consider what he has to do and the nature of the material available to him.   He must sit before a critical or unruly audience and at a rapid speed tell a story in a restricted, perhaps even highly complex, verse form, for a period of anywhere from twenty minutes to six or seven hours.   Had he memorized exactly a fixed text, his task would have been comparatively easy, requiring little skill. What the oral poet does is much more difficult, because he must compose as he sings at sometimes breakneck speed.

One of the most common misconceptions which has arisen from the use of the word 'oral' is that the singer has memorized a song and is presenting it as he learned it word for word as exactly as possible.   This is oral presentation of a fixed text.   It implies that the singer sat at the feet of another singer and heard the song over and over again until he had memorized it, or that he had a manuscript from which he memorized the song.   In neither of these cases would the term 'oral composition' be applicable.   Those who memorized the Homeric songs from a manuscript and then sang them were not bards, but mere reciters.   It would be perfectly possible for a person aspiring to be a reciter to sit at the feet of such a one and by dint of memory finally learn the song.   The reciter could learn from a manuscript or from another reciter orally.   But it is quite impossible for the singer in an oral tradition, in the technical sense of the word, to memorize a song by sitting at the side of another singer.

One can memorize only a fixed text, and in oral tradition a song is never sung twice word for word exactly the same. The differences between performances, however, are not mere lapses of memory. This again would be possible only if there were a fixed text to begin with. The key to understanding oral style lies in the fact that the singer and the generations of singers who preceded him are unlettered. They have no concept of a fixed text for epic song. Each performance represents a new composition of the song, and it is this method of composition among unlettered bards which we call 'oral composition'. It is a special technique which came into being long before the art of writing was invented by man. It is a technique of remembering rather than of memorization.

In order to understand this distinction, we must discover what the young singer 'remembers'. As a boy he hears the old men sing, and he absorbs the stories and becomes acquainted with the phraseology and language of the poetry and with its rhythms. They become a part of him and his young mind begins to remember the tales and to form his thoughts in the patterns of the song. The process in the early stage is as unconscious as that of the child learning to speak, when he first listens to the sounds which his elders are making. It becomes conscious when the boy decides to try to sing himself. He is still in his early 'teens when he begins to learn the art of oral composition. He does not learn this art from a set of rules, but he learns it by composing, by trial and error, by experience. He listens, and then in private he sings; and this is repeated many times.

The learning, or remembering, starts when the boy picks up the instrument that accompanies the singing and begins to play awkwardly and to sing a few lines. He watches the fingers of an older singer and he imitates; he hears the melody and he imitates it; he remembers a few phrases; he tries to fit fingering, melody, and phrase together. The fingering and the melody are repeated over and over again, and they are soon mastered to the extent that the singer is at ease with them and needs to give them no thought. In this respect the playing of the instrument and the singing of the melody are learned first, but they are not learned apart from the words or phrases. Learning of all three begins at the same time, but the first two are less complicated and are hence learned faster because they are more often repeated. Learning the phrases goes on for a much longer period of time; there are more phrases and they are not repeated so often.

If memorization takes place at any point, it is in the period of apprenticeship when the young singer is learning the phrases and lines of the poetry. The song has no fixed text, but the phrases and lines of the poetry are more or less stable. They exist to make oral composition possible; they have been worked out by countless generations of singers.

The boy must learn them. These are the 'formulae' of oral poetry, the distinguishing feature of its style. They express the ideas of the poetry; they are useful and necessary; hence they persist from age to age. The boy learns enough of them to sing the song of his choice. He sings it over and over again; at first only part way through, then all the way through. Meanwhile he continues to listen to this and to other songs. But the ability to sing one song from beginning to end is a landmark in his learning.

The next song is easier, because many of the ideas are the same and the formulae can be used again. In fact, not only are the same formulae useful, but also some of the ideas, some of the action, are the same in both stories. In one tale a letter was written and dispatched, a journey was made. The same happens in the other tale. The singer already knows how to do this. He already has the ability to express the repeated situations in the poetry. These are the 'themes' of oral poetry, another distinguishing feature of its style. Their usefulness is apparent when the singer learns his second song.

And thus the singer continues until he is master of the formulae and themes of the poetry, the necessary and characteristic elements of oral composition. The art has then been learned; the singer is fully fledged.

To the singer a song is a story and he is concerned, after he has learned this art of story telling, with what happened and with the actors in the tale. As he proceeds in the telling he remembers the themes and the formulae necessary to the rapid expression of the ideas of the song within the limits of the metre. But the song is not in a fixed form in his mind; he remakes its form each time he tells it; each time the configuration of the themes may be somewhat different and their expression in formulae will fit the requirements of the moment, metrical, melodic, psychological. The singer translates the elements of the story as he remembers them into the themes of the tradition, and these he expresses in formulae. This is the process which he goes through at every performance. This is oral composition.

Let us illustrate the formulaic and thematic structure which comparative study has revealed to us. Each linguistic tradition has its own set of patterns on which its formulae rest. In Serbocroatian an epic line is decasyllabic with an inviolable diaeresis after the fourth syllable: *Vino pije | Kraljeviću Marko* ('Kraljević Marko is drinking wine'). Its formula structure is based, therefore, on units which are either four, six, or ten syllables in length. The general metrical movement of the line is trochaic. The line in the *Song of Roland* is sometimes hendecasyllabic with a diaeresis after the fourth syllable, and its metrical movement is iambic: *Carles li reis, | nostre emperere magnes* [26] ('King Charles, our great emperor'). Its formula structure is based on units which are either four, seven, or eleven syllables in length. Most of the Old French lines are decasyllabic with iambic movement : *Si recevrez | la lei de chrestiens* [27] ('You will receive the law of the Christians') ; hence they are very similar to the Serbocroatian line. The Old Germanic metre of the Anglo-Saxon *Beowulf* is not founded on syllabic principles, but rather on the number of stresses in the line, there being two in each half line, with a caesura in the middle of the line. There is a certain amount of freedom in the number of syllables between stresses, but the metrical patterns fall into a given number of definite types. The two hemistichs are joined by alliteration : *monegum maegþum | meodosetla ofteah* [28] ('Wrested the mead-benches from troops of foes'). Here the basic formula structure is somewhat more varied than in the previous instances ; half lines of two stresses with given types of syllabic distribution, and whole lines of four stresses with alliteration, double in the first hemistich, single in the second. The Homeric hexameter is a longer line than any of these, and the number of places in it where a diaeresis or caesura may occur multiplies the possible lengths for formula units. Its basic formula structure is more varied even than that of the Old Germanic line.[a] Yet it is still fundamentally a system of parts of lines and of whole lines. In the ninth line of the *Iliad*, for example, the first formula in the line ends after the second syllable of the third measure : Λητοῦς καὶ Διὸς υἱός· | ὁ γὰρ βασιλῆϊ χολωθείς, but in the following line the break comes after the first syllable of the fourth measure : νοῦσον ἀνὰ στρατὸν ὦρσε κακήν, | ὀλέκοντο δὲ λαοί.

As generations of bards have poured their ideas into the metrical patterns outlined briefly above, the grammatical sequence of their thoughts has come to form syntactic patterns, and the syntactic patterns are part of the characteristic make-up of the formulae. They represent the rhythm of the singer's thought, even as the metrical patterns represent the rhythm of the stresses. Thus in Serbocroatian epic one of the most common syntactic patterns for the four-syllable formula which begins a line is conjunction+verb : *pa otide* ('then he departed') or *pa pokupi* ('then he gathered') ; and in the second half of the line one frequently has an adjective+direct object combination : *careve ordije* ('the imperial hosts'). In *Roland* a frequent initial formula has the syntactic pattern noun-subject+verb : *Charles respunt* ('Charles answered') or its reverse : *Dient Franceis* ('the French said'). In the second half of the Old French line a relative clause is a common syntactic pattern, as in : *Guenes i vint | ki la traisun fist* [29] ('Guenes arrived, who did the treachery').

While the formulae built on these metrical and syntactic patterns have arisen to meet all the needs of the singer, they should not be con-

---

[a] *Cf.* Ch. 1.

sidered as simply set phrases which are fitted together mechanically. They range in flexibility in proportion to the frequency of their use in a single singer's practice. Those which are used most frequently, such as the formulae for speech, are stable, because they satisfy the simple need of saying 'he or she said'. Yet the number of formulae which come into being in any tradition to express the various manners of speaking, the various speakers with names of differing metrical length, is large. Such a system must include the needed expression of tense, aspect, number, gender. Not all of these formulae will be the same, since some will be used frequently, some very seldom. Those which are used frequently come to the singer's mind automatically, without his thinking about them; but the less frequent ones he may even recompose each time, and in this recomposition he uses analogy with other formulae which are in his mind. The core of the formulaic technique and of its resulting structure is formed by the metrical and syntactic patterns; these patterns have been established by the most common of the formulae over the years, and the most common formulae at any given time reflect and set the tone of these patterns. The formulaic technique of oral composition enables the singer to compose secondary formulae for the less common ideas within the rhythms of these patterns and by analogy with the more common formulae. This is an entirely different matter from learning formulae to express all the ideas of the poetry, which would, of course, imply that the formulae were fixed and so regarded by the singer. If the oral poet is never at a loss for a word or group of words to express his idea,[30] it is because the formulaic technique has provided him, not with the formula for every idea, but with a means of constantly recomposing the formulae for the less common ideas, with a sufficient variety of patterns so that the idea can take almost instantaneous form in the rhythm of his song.

THE ORAL TECHNIQUE: (B) SUBJECT

The formulaic technique accounts for the singer's ability to build his lines in the rapidity of performance, but it does not account for his ability to tell his tale, to build his story, and to learn new ones. For that, generations have developed what we may call the thematic technique of oral story making in verse. This technique can be best seen where we have a number of songs by the same singer and several versions of the same song by the same singer. The examples are from the first published volume of the Parry Collection.

The *Song of Bagdad* (No. 1) tells of the capture of Bagdad by a Bosnian hero after the failure of the sultan's campaigns of twenty years. It begins with an assembly of the pashas and viziers in which the sultan informs them of his failure and asks for their advice. Such assemblies are common in the poetry and constitute one of the most easily recognized themes. There are two more assemblies of the sultan's councillors in this same story; one when the Bosnian hero arrives at Stambul with his army on the way to Bagdad and is summoned to appear before the sultan; a second when the Bosnian army returns from Bagdad and the hero appears again before the sultan to receive his reward. When the same singer tells the story of a Greek War in which he himself participated, his song (No. 10) begins with an assembly of all the seven kings in the French city of Paris. Still another song in his repertory, the capture of Candia by the Turks in the seventeenth century (No. 15), also includes an assembly of pashas and viziers in which the sultan asks for advice. Here the situation is the same as in the assembly at the beginning of the *Song of Bagdad*.

In the Bagdad story, our Bosnian hero gathers an army to capture the city. He begins by writing seven letters to Bosnian chieftains (each letter is given in full) and dispatching them by messengers. He then sends retainers to gather provisions for the army and prepares tents and kitchens on the plain. In due time the army begins to arrive, and the appearance of each chieftain is described as well as his reception by our hero and the disposition of his men. Thus we have a catalogue of the Bosnian forces.

We have two other versions of this same song from the same singer (Nos. 2 and 3). In Numbers 2 and 3 the hero first writes letters to the Bosnian chieftains and sends forth seven messengers, but he does not list the chieftains by name, nor are the letters given in full. Then he assembles the provisions, and finally the chieftains arrive and the catalogue of forces is given. In none, however, of these three versions is the catalogue exactly the same. It can thus be seen that within a theme considerable variety occurs — even when the theme is a catalogue !

This theme is used again by the same singer in another song, *The Wedding of Ćejvanović Meho* (No. 12). The letters of invitation in this case are sent to chieftains who are listed, but in some cases the letter is quoted in full and in other cases its contents are summarized. The list is substantially like that given in the Bagdad song, but again not exactly so. The gathering of provisions is essentially the same as in Bagdad. A catalogue is thus useful to the singer in more than one song.

The assembly and the catalogue are two of the commonest and most useful themes in all epic poetry. The reader is immediately reminded of Homeric parallels. The *Song of Roland* presents the same themes. It opens with King Marsila holding council with his dukes and counts in a garden at Saragossa and asking their advice about what he should do, since Charles is ready to attack him. This scene of assembly is followed shortly by an assembly of Charles and his chevaliers who receive Marsila's envoy, Blancandrin, and discuss his message. Even as Homer catalogues both Greeks and Trojans, so the singer of the *Roland* gives a catalogue of the forces of Charlemagne as they assemble against the emir, which is followed in turn by a catalogue of the chieftains in the emir's army and the number of men whom they command.[31]

As another example of the theme of the assembly in epic song, we shall cite the beginning of the Sumerian poem *Gilgamesh and Agga*, written on tablets dating from the first half of the second millennium B.C.[32] The envoys of Agga make proposals to Gilgamesh in Erech. Gilgamesh puts their ultimatum of submission or war to the assembly of the elders of Erech, and they advise submission, but Gilgamesh is not pleased with their answer and persuades them in speeches to make war. In the Kara Kirghiz *Song of Bokmurun* there is not only a catalogue of the heroes who are invited to the funeral feast, but also a list of horses which are to be entered in the horse race at the feast.[33]

We have seen that a theme is not always constant in regard to its content, even in the same song by the same singer. It can be contracted or expanded as the singer wishes; it can be presented in its barest essence or ornamented with details. The better the singer, the greater the amount of ornamentation.[34] Of many possible examples of a short and a long treatment of the same theme, the following from the *Iliad* will suffice: in Γ 330-8 the arming of Paris is described:

330 κνημῖδας μὲν πρῶτα περὶ κνήμῃσιν ἔθηκε
καλάς, ἀργυρέοισιν ἐπισφυρίοις ἀραρυίας·
δεύτερον αὖ θώρηκα περὶ στήθεσσιν ἔδυνεν
οἷο κασιγνήτοιο Λυκάονος· ἥρμοσε δ' αὐτῷ.
ἀμφὶ δ' ἄρ' ὤμοισιν βάλετο ξίφος ἀργυρόηλον
335 χάλκεον, αὐτὰρ ἔπειτα σάκος μέγα τε στιβαρόν τε·
κρατὶ δ' ἐπ' ἰφθίμῳ κυνέην εὔτυκτον ἔθηκεν
ἵππουριν· δεινὸν δὲ λόφος καθύπερθεν ἔνευεν·
εἵλετο δ' ἄλκιμον ἔγχος, ὅ οἱ παλάμηφιν ἀρήρει.

The following line (339) shows the theme in its shortest compass:

ὣς δ' αὔτως Μενέλαος ἀρήϊος ἔντε' ἔδυνεν.

It is instructive to compare with these themes of arming that of Agamemnon in Λ 17-44, that of Patroclus in Π 131-44, and, of course, that of Achilles in Τ 369-91. All three begin with the same three lines given above. Patroclus's arming is exactly the same as that of Paris except that the line: 'starry and elaborate of swift-footed Aeacides' takes the place of line 333. In both cases it is a borrowed corslet and the ownership is stated. Lines 140-4 of the Patroclus passage are perhaps not part of the arming because they tell us what Patroclus did *not* take, namely, 'the spear of blameless Aeacides'. The theme of the arming of

Achilles has its own very special features, but it is not long; it does not need to be, because the armour has already been described at length. The arming of Agamemnon is the longest and most ornate of the passages cited. It can be seen that Homer had a basic theme for arming, which is given in its normal form in the arming of Paris and of Patroclus. The theme is adjusted in the case of the other two heroes to fit the particular circumstances.

We may say that any song is a grouping of themes which are essential to the telling of the tale plus such descriptive or ornamental themes as the singer chooses either habitually or at the moment of performance to use as decoration for the story. We can, therefore, expect that a song as sung by a given singer may vary in respect of minor or ornamental themes, themes of details, but that it will not vary in respect of the essential themes of the story. In fact, singers boast that they sing a song word for word as they heard it [35]; they mean, essential theme for essential theme. They say that they always sing it in the same way and never change anything either by addition or subtraction; they are really talking about essential themes, because to them the story consists of those themes.

Experiment with oral singers shows that their statements are true within certain limits and with certain qualifications. Two versions of the story of the rescue of Mustajbey's children by Bojičić Alija were given to Parry by the same singer in 1934; the versions are separated by a period of four months. They vary much in details, and this can be seen dramatically from the fact that when one version is at line 1078 in the story the other is at line 621. Yet essentially the tales are the same through to the very end, although the divergences are greater toward the end of the story than at the beginning; a secondary heroine bargains for a husband as a price for assisting in the rescue of the children, additional heroes appear in the final rescue in one version but not in the other, but the methods of rescue are the same. One tale has 698 lines and the other 1369 (Nos. 24 and 25).[36]

In 1951 the singer sang the song again for the recording apparatus. He had actually boasted in 1934 that, were he to sing the song twenty years later, it would be word for word the same. The latest version is somewhat longer than the longer of the two earlier ones, 1429 lines, and the singer has kept his word about variations, because the story is essentially the same and the divergences of details are no greater, in fact less so, over the seventeen year period than over the four month period.

We are fortunate in having a version of this song from the singer from whom our first singer learned it, and thus we can test whether Zogić, the first singer, was right when he said that he sang it exactly as he heard it. Again there is considerable divergence in detail (more than between the versions by the same singer), and no large theme of the story varies. Yet there is one major theme in Zogić's tale which is not found in that of his teacher. Our young hero, Bojičić Alija, having accepted the challenge to rescue the children, goes home and laments to his mother that he has no arms or horse or disguise for his journey. His mother goes to Sarajevo and borrows them from her brother. When Alija arrives in the enemy city he goes to an inn, and Mary the innkeeper recognizes him from the way in which he drinks. Identity is proved because he is wearing the breastplate of a Christian hero whom he had killed in battle and which he always wore ! This is Zogić's version, and the inconsistency of recognition by the habitual armour, when as a matter of fact the hero was on his first raid and had only borrowed clothes and weapons, is a glaring one which Zogić had not noticed or changed over seventeen years. The episode is not in his teacher's version at all. After accepting the challenge, Alija goes home and prepares himself and departs. There is no borrowing of armour. There is consequently, however, no proving of identity by armour. The singer merely says that Alija declared his identity and he and Mary embraced.

Essential themes, then, seem to remain constant. But the essential themes in a story are large enough and can be couched in general enough terms to allow for great variety. The essential theme is that Alija goes home and prepares himself for the journey ; in one case, however, it is elaborated with a whole episode of borrowed armour. Again, the essential theme is that Alija and Mary recognize one another ; in one case the means of proof of identity is complex, in another the simple statement of revelation suffices. Thematic content is fluid in oral epic tales.

We can see from the preceding example one of the ways in which narrative inconsistencies can arise in oral composition. On one hand there is flexibility of content of a song ; on the other, there is a varying stability of any given theme. In the forming of a song a mixture of themes which are not compatible in the context of the song is thoroughly possible. Here the talent of the individual singer is most evident.

The deeper our study of oral composition penetrates, the more we come to a realization that this traditional method of composition allows the individual singer some latitude and play for his original talents. The method aids the singer to tell his story ; but even when the tradition furnishes the main outlines of the story, the resulting performance is the singer's own. He is not the mouthpiece of tradition ; he *is* the tradition.

The formulaic technique allows for innovation and for the entry of new words into the scheme of the formulae. While the tradition may be conservative in that the singer is not consciously striving to coin a new phrase, knowingly seeking to be original, yet he is not stifled by the tradition if he wishes to express something new. He does not need writing to find the felicitous phrase.

The thematic technique too is flexible enough, so that it is possible to say that the treatment given any story in a particular text is that of the individual singer, even though the story be as old as time itself, and in spite of forces which tend to make a tradition conservative.

But the individuality and originality of the oral epic poet must be sought in the terms of his traditional art with an understanding of oral epic composition. When we analyse and interpret Homer's poems from that basis, we shall be able to judge whether *Iliad* and *Odyssey* are by the same man. Only then shall we be able to see wherein and how Homer was original and individual.[37]

ORAL AND WRITTEN: HOMER'S PLACE

It is to the period of writing that we owe the texts of traditional epic which we possess. What the collector does in effect is to petrify a particular performance of a given song by a given singer. Except for those texts which have in recent times been recorded by phonograph apparatus, our epic texts have come to us through a middleman, and are the results of circumstances which are abnormal for the singers. The very presence of the collector may be a disturbing element in the performance.

The importance of this disturbance should not, however, be overestimated. The presence of the collector may have little influence on the singer. Much depends on the personality and methods of the collector and of the singer. If the collector waits for normal performance, he may, in theory at least, capture the performer in the milieu to which the singer is accustomed. Interestingly enough, this method scarcely ever works in practice. The collector finds too often that the interest of the singer's audience has moved from the singer to the collector.

Moreover, normal performance is not usually ideal, even without the collector. Only rarely does a singer find himself before an ideal audience which will listen enraptured to his every word. Ordinarily his audience is unlike the paying public at a theatre; it is not necessarily a quiet audience. The effect of this situation on traditional songs is apparent in the fact that the last half of songs tends to vary more than the first half. The singer does not always have an opportunity to finish his song; hence he knows the latter part less well than the first part, and when he hears other singers, he is apt to hear only the first part of a song and not the whole. The collector wants a circumstance of performance which will give him the whole song. Normal performance, then, is not by any means the best time for collecting.

There is, besides, another practical consideration: normal performance is rapid, and the collector cannot possibly write down the words fast enough to get a whole song down, except in those few traditions in which each line is sung twice, as in some places in Yugoslav Macedonia and Albania, for example. Attempts to have a singer sing the same song several times so that the collector may fill in the gaps and correct 'mistakes' fail. The singer does not sing the same song twice exactly the same. This method of collecting cannot possibly yield anything close to a true text.

The collector, then, finds himself forced to take the singer aside and to have him dictate his song line for line, while the collector or his scribe writes. This method is beneficial even when collecting with a recording apparatus, because it removes the singer from the vagaries of a doubtful audience. If the collector has previously convinced the singer that he forms an appreciative, well instructed, critical audience, the resulting text will probably be better than the text of normal performance. The singer knows that he has an audience on which he can count for the duration of the song. The collector has thus reproduced the circumstances of 'ideal' performance. The singer has time and has been stimulated to do his best.

Even in 'ideal' performance before a microphone, the singer makes his normal mistakes in forming lines, mistakes which arise from the very nature of rapid singing performance. Collecting by dictation, oddly enough, may result in the finest texts, in the texts which one might say the singer carries as an ideal in his own mind. That is because the singer may edit his text himself as he dictates. This does not mean that he goes back over the text and changes anything, but rather that he has time between lines to form the next line in his mind at his leisure. Yet the method of collecting by dictation is the most difficult to apply.

There are two chief difficulties for the singer. He is not accustomed to slow composition, and his mind frequently runs ahead of the hand of the scribe. He may thus inadvertently omit parts of his song. Secondly, he is not accustomed to forming lines without the aid of musical accompaniment to set the rhythm, and he may have great difficulty in forming metrically perfect lines, which in normal performance he would find easy. If the collector or scribe can overcome these difficulties of slow composition without instrumental accompaniment, he has only one other matter with which to concern himself, namely, boredom or fatigue on the part of both singer and scribe. He must be constantly alert to what the singer is doing, and he must keep the singer interested. In the method of collecting by dictation the collector or the scribe has great responsibility. He has been the forgotten man in the study of those poems which have come down to us from the past, which must have been taken down from dictation, since there is no other way in which they could be recorded.[38]

Boredom and fatigue are the main enemies. They may make the singer shorten his song, leave out the poetic ornamentation which is typical of epic breadth of style, confuse themes, and so on. If the singer can overcome boredom and fatigue in the dictating process, he can produce a poem of great length, provided that he is a singer of talent and experience and his tradition is rich in formulas and themes. The scribe must be wary. There is a tendency for scribes, when they are in a hurry, to neglect to write down actually as dictated passages which they recognize as repetitions of passages previously dictated. They assume that the repetition will be word for word, and hence they note down simply that at a given point certain lines are to be repeated. It is worth consideration that some of the repeated passages in the Homeric poems may have been set down in this way.

We must stress the fact that dictated texts are not exactly as sung at any time by any singer. Dictating offers the singer a rare opportunity to produce a long song. The question of length long troubled Homerists, but we know from the Yugoslav material that the oral singer can compose unified songs as long as the *Iliad* or *Odyssey* without any difficulty, and our research in the method of composition shows how this is possible. Our knowledge of Moslem tradition in Yugoslavia indicates that songs ranging from 3000 to 8000 lines are not rare. Long songs and how they are made are no longer mysteries.[39]

The problem that remains for us is to posit the occasion when long songs are sung. There is a possibility that at festivals lasting for several days a song might be continued from one day to the next. The ancient Greek festivals would give such an opportunity [40]; the Moslem feast of Ramadan with its thirty nights also provides an occasion. In both instances a fairly stable audience can be counted on to be present. There is no doubt that such festivals fostered long songs, and that because of them the tradition became enriched to the extent of making long songs possible. Evidence, however, that a song was ever actually carried over from one day to another is not very convincing. The probability is that this was not the practice. At such festivals the epic is not the only form of entertainment, as we have seen earlier in this chapter. Probably the longest songs which would be sung would range between 5000 and 8000 lines, depending on the speed of performance, the stamina of the singer, the length of the line in the given tradition, and the ability of the singer to hold his audience.

While it is pleasant to think of the *Iliad* being performed from beginning to end as we have it at one of the festivals of ancient Greece, the evidence is against it. It is highly probable that Homer sang the *Iliad* at a festival and that all the essential themes of the tale were there; it is highly probable that his song was a long one, but not so long as our text.

P

Our text must be a performance for a 'collector', regardless of how long or short it is, regardless, indeed, of whether it was ever sung over a period of days at a festival and attained this or even greater length in performance.

Our text is not a normal performance, and from what we know of dictated texts taken down by a skilful collector, it is very probably superior to Homer's ordinary performance of the song.

Homer is not a shadowy figure. He is the poet of the *Iliad* and perhaps of the *Odyssey*; perhaps also of some of those poems which disappeared but which were ascribed to him. It is the collector who has eluded us. The real riddle is who wrote down the poems and why. Did Homer write them down himself? The possibility of a literate oral poet writing down his own song is very attractive to Homerists, more attractive than the idea that someone else wrote down the *Iliad* and the *Odyssey* from Homer's dictation. It appears to be a welcome compromise; Homer could thus be both an oral poet, as his style indicates, and also a literary poet, as some scholars feel he must be in order to have composed such long and artistically well unified poems.[41] What are the facts about literate oral poets? First, they are not rare; they can be found in Yugoslavia to-day. Second, most of them do not write very well, but have only an elementary knowledge of writing, which is for them only a means of recording, not a means of composition. Third, they are still basically oral singers, because they still follow the process of oral composition outlined above. They are in a dangerous position, because as soon as they come to the conclusion that the written text must be reproduced exactly, as soon as they have the concept of a fixed text, their singing days of oral songs are over. Their ability to compose orally is lost when this happens, and they become mere reciters. It is a demonstrable fact that when this point is reached, the singer cannot sing a song unless he has memorized it; and when he forgets a word or a line, he is no longer able to fill it in with the formulae.

There are singers who change from oral composition to written composition as well as to recitation. They know writing well enough and have read enough so that they can begin to compose in writing, not merely to record what they compose orally, but to 'write' a song. What is significant, however, is that this is detectable in the style. One can tell when a song has been 'written'. The writer no longer has the necessity to abide by the formulaic style of oral composition; he has leisure which the singer lacks. Homer's style is too consistently formulaic to allow us to place him in this category. We have, moreover, no evidence that singers who have gone through this 'sea-change' in their lifetime have ever attained any excellence in literary technique.

In the last analysis, however, the crucial question is: why would an oral singer write down his song? To preserve it? It has never occurred

to him that it would disappear.   To preserve it in the exact form in which
he has just sung it ?   He knows nothing of fixed texts.   As an aid to memory ?   He has a style of composition which was evolved for that purpose.   No, the fact is that it would never come to his mind to write it down.
Only an outside force from the world of writing would suggest it to him.[42]
It is only to the writing mind that this process would occur.   If Homer,
then, wrote down his own songs, he had not done enough writing to corrupt his oral method of composition, and it must have been suggested by
someone else ; for that Homer's style is formulaic there is no doubt.[a]

The deciphering of the Linear B Script does not change the facts of
Homer's oral style one whit.   There must, of course, have been writing
in Homer's day, as we have said above.   How far back into the past this
skill extended is not actually relevant to the problem of the writing down
of the Homeric poems.   Indeed, even were one to prove that Homer
lived in an age of a developed written literature, one would not by any
means prove that the Homeric poems belonged in that category.   Were
one to discover epics written in Linear B having all the characteristics of
oral narrative poetry, one would have uncovered another period of
collecting.   We know now that the answer to whether the Homeric
poems are oral or not lies in the analysis of their style and not in the
presence or absence of writing, or even in the presence or absence of a
literary tradition.[43]

It seems to me that it is precisely the oral character of the Homeric
poems and all that this implies which scholars are eager to avoid.   They
are still trying to refute Wolf's thesis that there was no writing in Homer's
day.   They are tormented by the apparent contradiction between
Homeric excellence and a conception of the poetry of illiterate peoples
as something crude.   Could it be that we have failed to recognize the
intricacy of oral poetry ; that we have not looked deeply enough into
it to appreciate its artistic qualities ?   Perhaps we have been misled by the
romantic idea of the 'simple peasant'.   Surely the songs of Avdo
Međedović [44] and, to a lesser extent, those of his confrères in the Balkans,
place before us a potential of great artistry, even at times greatness itself.
If it is not the sustained art of Homer, we should not be surprised ; for
the Balkans of the twentieth century do not present as felicitous a background for the practice of oral epic as most certainly the eighth century
B.C. afforded in Greece and the Aegean.

RITUAL AND MAGICAL ORIGINS OF EPIC

As we learn more about the practice of epic song in many parts of the
world and reach a clearer understanding of the texts we seem to discover

---

[a] On the 'Peisistratean recension' see Ch. 6, p. 220.

some evidence to indicate that the deep seriousness of epic poetry, its fundamental concern with life and death and rebirth, with mortality and immortality, spring from its prehistoric past.[45]   These are concerns which have brought forth not mere poetic musing or intellectual search for understanding, but rather, perhaps, an effective means (or so it was forever hoped) of overcoming death, of finding life. The myths of a people, be they cosmic myths or myths of lesser pretensions, are dynamic. By the telling of the myth or by its enactment symbolically one takes part in its meaning. It could be hypothesized that when myth became ceremonial, told in chant and verse, epic was born. Many ages later when epics were recorded in writing, they still carried marks of their origin.

In the earliest epics we find man seeking for knowledge of and power over the unknown and especially the mysteries of death. The heroes of the Gilgamesh epic, like their counterparts in the Homeric poems, are men of this world striving with the superhuman forces of a divine world. The lines with which the Akkadian text of Gilgamesh begins might apply to Odysseus :

> He who saw everything (to the end)s of the land,
> (Who all thing)s experienced, (conside)red all ! . . .
> The (hi)dden he saw, (laid bare) the undisclosed.
> He brought report of before the Flood,
> Achieved a long journey, weary and (w)orn.[46]

There are indications from sources going back to the second millennium B.C. that connect epic with incantation and with festival ceremony in which the epic is recited by a priest. The Akkadian *Creation Epic* was 'recited with due solemnity on the fourth day of the New Year's festival'.[47] 'The Temple Programme for the New Year's Festivals at Babylon' gives the following entry in part for the events and rituals of the fourth day : 'After the second meal of the late afternoon, the *urigallu*-priest of the temple of Ekua shall recite (while lifting his hand ?) to the god Bel the (composition entitled) *Enuma eliš*. While he recites *Enuma eliš* to the god Bel, the front of the tiara of the god Anu and the resting place of the god Enlil shall be covered.'[48] Part of the *Atrahasis Epic* from Akkadia was used in later times as an incantation for childbirth.[49]

There are echoes of the ritual function of epic poetry in the poems themselves. The hero of the *Kalevala* is a magician and singer, and by his singing he accomplishes his great works. His song gives him power over the forces of nature and over men. Väinämöinen and the youthful Joukahainen contend in magic song. Their contest consists in telling what each knows about nature.

> Sang the aged Väinämöinen ;
> Lakes swelled up, and earth was shaken,
> And the coppery mountains trembled,
> And the mighty rocks resounded.
> And the mountains clove asunder ;
> On the shore the stones were shivered.
> Then he sang of Joukahainen,
> Changed his runners into saplings,
> And to willows changed the collar,
> And the reins he turned to alder, etc.[50]

In the Russian *bylina* of *Sadko* the power of the song of the great minstrel and merchant is extolled.[51]   The ancient Greek *aoidos* is pictured as divinely inspired by the Muse and perhaps we can see in this not merely a convention designed to give the illusion of veracity and history, as Bassett believed,[52] but also acknowledgement of the source of the bard's power.   It is well to remember that the Homeric Hymns were very likely used as preambles to epic.   In much the same way the Yugoslav singer of our own day calls upon Allah or upon God to aid him in his song of the deeds of the great men of long ago whom he wishes now to remember. His invocation to the musical instrument, the *gusle*, abounds in magical significance.   We learn from the Finnish epic [53] and from the spells of all peoples, that power over something is gained by knowledge and description of it.   Thus the Yugoslav singer describes the *gusle*, not primarily for the purpose of enhancing his song, but rather that he may have power over the instrument which is symbolic of the song itself.

> *Gusle* mine, gift of God,
> Last night I told you
> That you were cursed
> From the time when you were covered with skin ;
> The skin on you is of a goat
> And over it runs a string of foal's hair.[54]

We are reminded of the Hittite text of *The Festival of the Warrior-God*, in which musical instruments called the 'Ishtar instruments' play an important role in the ritual [55] ; and the elaborate ritual preserved in an Akkadian text, to be followed by the *Kalu*-priest when covering the temple kettle-drum, illustrates the sacred character of some musical instruments.[56]

That the narration of epic tales had a practical purpose can be seen from the following passages from epic poetry and saga found at two widely separated poles of Indo-European tradition, India and Ireland. At the end of the story of Nala and Damayanti in the *Mahabharata* we read :

And those who will recite this great adventure of Nala, and those who will

hear it attentively, misfortune shall not visit them. His affairs shall prosper
and he shall attain wealth. Having heard this ancient story whose excellence
endures eternal, he shall have sons and grandsons, wealth in cattle and pre-
eminence among men. He shall be free from sickness and rich in love most
certainly.[57]

And in the satirical *Vision of MacConglinne* one reads:

There are thirty virtues attending this tale, and a few of them are enough
for an example. The married couple to whom it is related on their first night
shall not separate without an heir; they shall not be in dearth of food or
raiment. The new house in which it is the first tale told, no corpse shall be
taken out of it; it shall not want food or raiment; fire does not burn it. The
king to whom it is recited before battle or conflict shall be victorious. On the
occasion of bringing out ale, or of feasting a prince, or of taking inheritance or
patrimony this tale should be told.[58]

It is worthy of note that the emphasis is on fertility, new life, and
prosperity.

The very fact that the stories of epic poetry are told in verse, sung or
chanted to an instrumental accompaniment, probably indicates an origin
or at least a connection with ritual ceremony. It would seem that prose
would be the easiest and most natural way to tell a story. Singing a tale
in verse requires special skills not possessed by everyone. There must be
some important reason why men would begin to tell stories in song, why
they should choose a difficult method of narration rather than a simple
one, why they should maintain and elaborate that method until it became
a highly complex art. We can see the magic qualities of this intricate
art in the patterns of alliteration and assonance; Germanic, Slav, Irish,
and Finnish epic most notably are characterized by these devices.[59] They
are frequently onomatopoetic and set the mood of a line or passage. A
Russian spell intended to stop the flow of blood in a wound abounds in
kr alliterations, which suggest throughout the incantation the word for
blood, *krov*, over which the singer wishes to obtain power.[60]

Alliteration and assonance are very common in the Homeric poems
and, as in other oral epics, these features are clustered about the key
words of a passage. The first sixteen lines of *Iliad* xxi illustrate this
phenomenon:

> ᾿Αλλ᾿ ὅτε δὴ πόρον ἷξον ἐϋρρεῖος ποταμοῖο,
> Ξάνθου δινήεντος, ὃν ἀθάνατος τέκετο Ζεύς,
> ἔνθα διατμήξας τοὺς μὲν πεδίονδε δίωκε
> πρὸς πόλιν, ᾗ περ ᾿Αχαιοὶ ἀτυζόμενοι φοβέοντο
> ἤματι τῷ προτέρῳ, ὅτε μαίνετο φαίδιμος ῞Εκτωρ·   5
> τῇ ῥ᾿ οἵ γε προχέοντο πεφυζότες, ἠέρα δ᾿ ῞Ηρη
> πίτνα πρόσθε βαθεῖαν ἐρυκέμεν· ἡμίσεες δὲ

ἐς ποταμὸν εἰλεῦντο βαθύρροον ἀργυροδίνην,
ἐν δ᾽ ἔπεσον μεγάλῳ πατάγῳ, βράχε δ᾽ αἰπὰ ῥέεθρα,
ὄχθαι δ᾽ ἀμφὶ περὶ μεγάλ᾽ ἴαχον· οἱ δ᾽ ἀλαλητῷ   10
ἔννεον ἔνθα καὶ ἔνθα, ἑλισσόμενοι περὶ δίνας.
ὡς δ᾽ ὅθ᾽ ὑπὸ ῥιπῆς πυρὸς ἀκρίδες ἠερέθονται
φευγέμεναι ποταμόνδε· τὸ δὲ φλέγει ἀκάματον πῦρ
ὅρμενον ἐξαίφνης, ταὶ δὲ πτώσσουσι καθ᾽ ὕδωρ·
ὡς ὑπ᾽ Ἀχιλλῆος Ξάνθου βαθυδινήεντος   15
πλῆτο ῥόος κελάδων ἐπιμὶξ ἵππων τε καὶ ἀνδρῶν.

πόταμός and Ξάνθος set the most pervasive alliterative patterns of this passage, which abounds with p, b, ph, t, d, th, m, n. The clusters of sounds play upon the various syllables of ποταμός and Ξάνθος; po-, tam-, and anth- are especially productive of echoes. Anth- is helped by the verb forms in -nto and by ἔνθα, βαθεῖαν, and βαθύρροον in lines 7 and 8, accompanying ποταμόν in line 8 and looking backward in sound to Ξάνθου, and again by βαθυδινήεντος in line 15 following Ξάνθου in the same line and ποταμόνδε in line 13. Thus the river Xanthus is placed explicitly at the beginning, middle, and end of this passage and is reflected acoustically throughout. The k, t alliterations begin in line 2 with τέκετο, are picked up at the end of line 3 in δίωκε, and reach their climax in Ἕκτωρ in line 5. The mist which Hera spreads is another key idea in the passage, and we can watch its development in the -er- clusters from -rei- in line 1 to περ in line 4, followed in exactly the same position in the next line by the -ter- of προτέρῳ, in which it is linked with ποταμός alliteration and assonance (a linking, indeed, which also began in line 1 with πόρον and continued with πρός in line 4, προχέοντο in line 6 and πρόσθε in line 7), until it is realized in line 6, beginning with τῇ ῥ᾽ and culminating in the almost tangible ἤερα δ᾽ Ἥρη. The cluster -er- is repeated after the key word as well as before it and we find it in ἐρυκέμεν in line 7, where already the clusters of a new key word are forming, namely the -ur- of πυρός in line 12. This new cluster is given real life in line 8 with βαθύρροον and ἀργυροδίνην. These examples give but a hint of the complexity of sound structure of this passage around the key words and ideas as they come to the singer's mind. Image, sound, formula, and idea merge. To us the effect is poetic magic, the magic of Homer's hexameters.

But it is more than that. It is also a technique of oral epic that aids the singer in moving from one line to another; the association of sounds has a compositional purpose. Yet the effect which results was surely calculated by the originators of this device, not for poetic, but for practical magic. This is a dynamic method of emphasis used by incantation and inherited by oral epic, if I am not mistaken, from far distant times. Magic spells throughout the world use alliteration and assonance to make the charm effective. Note, for example, the alliteration and assonance in the following Latin and Greek charms:

> Stulta femina super fontem sedebat
> et stultum infantem in sinu tenebat,
> siccant montes, siccant valles,
> siccant venae, vel quae de sanguine sunt plenae.[61]

> Θειοτάτη βοτάνη βοτρυηφόρε, ἄμπελος λευκή, μήτηρ τῶν βοτανῶν, εὔδιε
> κυμβαληφόρε, γῆς ἐν φυτοῖς ἡ πρώτη, ἐνὶ εὐγρίνων φρενῶν μου, τήρησόν μου
> νοὸς φρένας, εὔθυμος οὖσα εἰς θειοτάτην ὑγίειαν· ἠωω ἀεκ ιαω ἐαωε.[62]

There is one kind of ritual song, the lament, which has a special place in epic poetry. It is set into the epics. Perhaps this peculiar treatment of lament indicates the closeness of the epic's connection with cults of the dead; for the lament is given as part of the full account of funeral rites. Hector's funeral begins with:

> And the others, when they had brought him to the famous house, laid him on a fretted bed, and set beside him minstrels, leaders of the dirge, who wailed a mournful lay, while the women made moan with them.
>
> (Ω 719-22, trans. Lang, Leaf, and Myers.)

And this passage is followed by the laments of Andromache, Hecuba, and Helen. The laments over Patroclus also, of course, are justly famous in the *Iliad*. The epic of *Beowulf* ends with references to two kinds of lament. The funeral pyre has been lighted for Beowulf and the warriors stand about it.

> Sad in heart, they lamented the sorrow of their souls, the slaying of their lord; likewise the women with bound tresses sang a dirge . . . the sky swallowed up the smoke.

After the burial mound has been built, the poem continues:

> Then men bold in battle, sons of chieftains, twelve in all, rode about the mound; they were minded to utter their grief, to lament the king, to make a chant and to speak of the man; they exalted his heroic life and praised his valorous deed with all their strength.
>
> Thus it is fitting that a man should extol his friendly lord in words, should heartily love him, when he must needs depart from his body and pass away. Thus did the men of the Geats, his hearth-companions, bewail the fall of their lord; they said that among the kings of the world he was the mildest of men and most kindly, most gentle to his people and most eager for praise.[63]

One of the most moving laments in all epic literature is that of Gilgamesh over Enkidu:

> Hear me, O elders (and give ear) unto me!
> It is for Enkidu, my (friend), that I weep,

Moaning bitterly like a wailing woman.
The axe at my side, the (bow) in my hand,
The dirk in my belt, (the shield) in front of me,
My festal robe, my (greatest) joy —
An evil (demon) rose up and (robbed) me!
(O my younger friend), thou chasedst
    The wild ass of the hills, the panther of the steppe,
Enkidu, my younger friend, thou who chasedst
    The wild ass of the hills, the panther of the steppe!
We who (have conquered) all things, scaled (the moun-
    tains,)
Who seized the Bull (and slew him),
Brought affliction on Hubaba, who (dwelled in the Cedar
    Forest)!
What, now, is this sleep that has laid hold (on thee)?
Thou art benighted and canst not hear (me)! [64]

In Slav epic the most famous lament is that of Yaroslavna in the Igor'
tale, which begins thus:

But what I hear is Yaroslavna's voice like a cuckoo singing without
    tidings at morn.
'I will fly', quoth she, 'like a cuckoo down the Don.
I will dip my sleeve of beaver-fur in the Kayali river.
I will wipe off the Prince's bloody wounds on his lusty body!'
Yaroslavna weeps at morn at Putivl' on the city wall, wailing:
'Wind, O Wind! Wherefore, Lord, blowest thou so fiercely?
Wherefore carriest thou the Huns' arrow upon thy carefree wings
    against the warriors of my beloved?
Is it not enough for thee to blow on high, beneath the clouds, rocking
    ships upon the blue sea?
Wherefore, Lord, hast thou scattered my joy over the grass of the
    plains?' [65]

When we realize that the Homeric poems share with other oral epics
throughout the world not merely a generic process of composition and
transmission, but also probably the traces of a ceremonial past that we
have just noted, we should not be surprised that there are similarities
with other oral epics in the stories which they tell. It could be, of course,
that these similarities, like the laments we have just been considering,
are simply descriptions of the heroic world, real or imaginary, with which
epic deals. Yet it is possible that, hidden in the history of these tales,
there is a deeper meaning than glorification of 'the heroic'. To ignore
this possibility would be short-sighted.

Our study of the form of oral epic and of techniques of composition
and transmission tends to emphasize variation and multiformity; we
sometimes forget the highly conservative character of this style in respect
to essential narrative elements. Names, places, ornamental details change,

but essentials remain in the story and they remain for very long periods of time.   The basic narrative themes of epic even as we have them to-day are preserved by the oral form from very remote times.   The stories of epic, especially those most characteristic of the genre, such as the return of a man who has been absent in another world, or the search for something or someone in the world beyond, may very well go back to the origins of epic.   The oral technique shows us the way in which the central core and essential details are preserved.   The surface of a traditional story or myth may be constantly changing, but the kernel of myth and its significance remain intact.

Ritual is most generally centred on moments of transition either in the life of an individual or of groups: birth, puberty, marriage, death, the renewing of the kingship.   The ritual assures the success of the transition and looks ever from death to life, from the old man to the new. Death is necessary to life, and must be experienced, symbolically or by substitution, before life is possible.   Sacrifice and purification ensure the continuance of life.[66]

Once one is aware of this, certain parts of Homer's narrative begin perhaps to take on another dimension.   Achilles, it might be said, undergoes the ritual experience of death three times and in three different ways. First, he departs from the company of his fellows with the curses of the leader of the hosts on his head and returns in glory with new and divine armour, having lost his own.   Second, he experiences death in the person of Patroclus, the substitute, who, when he puts on Achilles's armour, becomes Achilles and is slain in his stead.   Third, he fights with death in the form of the river, from which he is saved only by the miracle of god-sent fire.   Achilles is the kind of hero who attracts these symbolic deaths.   He has an unusual birth and an unusual upbringing; significantly, information about both is not lacking in the *Iliad* (I 434 ff.).

Parallels in other traditional epics or sagas would seem to support this interpretation, or, at the very least, to emphasize the persistence of these essential clusters of themes in traditional lore.   Examples from non-traditional material must be excluded, of course.   Gilgamesh, it would seem, was fashioned by several gods who made him two-thirds god and one-third human.   His youth was stormy, and he 'dies' in the person of his animal companion, Enkidu, who is his Patroclus.   Digenis Akritas's unusual origin is emphasized in the first word of his name; his father was Moslem and his mother Christian.   His boyhood deeds depict him as a precocious hunter (like Gilgamesh) and he slays a serpent-dragon which emerges from a spring.[67]   An even more striking parallel to the fight with the river can be found in Genesis xxxii. 24-32, where it is told of Jacob that he wrestled with an angel at the ford of the Jabbok.   Here Jacob receives the name Israel, symbolic of a new life for him.   He has 'striven with God and men and prevailed'. Jacob, it will be recalled, had an unusual birth in his parents' old age, and a twin brother, perhaps significantly enough, a hairy man, Esau. Beowulf is a supreme example of a specialist in struggling with water demons. Of his youth we are informed that he was despised. There seems to be nothing extraordinary about his lineage as given in the poem, but there may be some confusion here with the other Beowulf who belongs to the Scaefing line and goes back to divine origin. It is worthy of note also that Beowulf's fight with Grendel is preceded by the monster's devouring of one of his companions, which might seem to be unnecessary carnage, unless one could see in it a possible element of sacrifice.

Other parallels could be cited, but these will be sufficient to illustrate the essential narrative pattern of a struggle with death, in the form of water spirits, and escape from it, by a hero of unusual birth and upbringing who often has a special companion associated with him.[68]

Odysseus's journey to the realm of Hades may be said to symbolize a search for life. It has parallels in the ancient Gilgamesh epic, the *Kalevala*, and elsewhere. In the *Kalevala* the aged hero Väinämöinen sets out to build a boat, but he is lacking three magic words with which to finish it. He betakes himself to the dread abode of Tuoni, the world of death, to find them. He is rowed across the river by Tuoni's daughter. His trip is in vain, however, and he escapes with difficulty from the lower world. He then seeks the words in the belly of the giant Vipunen, where he is at last successful and returns to complete his boat.[69] Gilgamesh too travels to the other world to consult with Utnapishtim, the hero of the Deluge, on how to obtain immortality. Utnapishtim tells him the story of the Flood and dwells with considerable detail on the building of the boat which we know in Biblical legend as the Ark. Odysseus's wanderings also are comparable to those of Gilgamesh, who visits the scorpion-man, travels to a garden of jewels, visits the ale-wife Siduri, 'who dwells by the deep sea', and is finally provided with a boat by Urshanabi, Utnapishtim's boatman, to cross the waters of death.[70] Journeys to the other world can be found in almost all epic traditions. The Kara Kirghiz song of *Er Toshtuk* tells of the hero's sinking into the ground and of his many adventures underground before his return to his bride.[71] Throughout its history from Gilgamesh and Homer to Virgil, Dante, and Milton, the epic is preoccupied with the journeys of heroes into the world beyond, the world of the spirit.

THE PURPOSES OF EPIC: HISTORY, TEACHING, ENTERTAINMENT

Yet to say that epic may have had its origin in ritual, and that it may have kept something of this function well on into the Christian era, and even to our own day, does not in any way imply that the Homeric poems had that purpose or that Homer was aware of the magic properties of the tales and of the style which he had inherited. He sang them, I believe, as heroic tales of the past for the entertainment and edification of his own generation. Traditional lore, however, is fraught with the meanings and symbolism of the past. Because of his history the hero retains certain characteristics, and elements of the story persist. The present always carries some degree of awareness of the past. What Achilles is and what he does is in part conditioned by his epic genealogy; Homer is not a completely free agent in forming his character, though he may have considerable latitude in the way in which he presents it.

Perhaps the first great change to come over epic tradition in many of the cultures in which it is known was its secularization. This has happened nearly everywhere but at different times in the various traditions. Seldom has it led to complete emancipation from myth and ritual. One might hypothesize that when the god of the ritual was replaced by the demigod, the divine king, and then by the symbolic human substitute, man became the central figure of the narrative. Whatever the process may have been, the result is clear. The ritual story of the god became the adventures of a hero, and thus it was possible to include actual historical events and historical persons in epic. The field of epic widened. Battles with monsters, strife with symbols of death, could become war on human enemy armies. Epic in this way took on the shape of history and of glorification of the man of mighty deeds; it became the epic as we commonly use the term.

There were two forces which tended to preserve the mythic elements even when they were submerged in history. The first was the conservatism of religious belief itself, the aura of mystery, of the unknown and the fantastic. All the great epics of mankind have a quality which stems from this element. The second is to be found in the necessities of the oral traditional style. Themes which already form a tradition admit new thematic material only very slowly. It is easier for the singer to modify an already existing theme than it is to invent a new one. Both of these strong forces have preserved much from epic's primitive sophistication. We are possibly not wrong in seeing far in the distant past a mythic model for the most obviously historical epic.

In its guise as history epic fulfilled also another serious purpose. It became morally didactic. An example of this can be found in the Balkans to-day. Among the Serbian Orthodox Yugoslavs the greatest festival of the year is the *Slava*.[72] It is a family festival and a very solemn one. From the time of the introduction of Christianity among the South Slavs, this festival is said to commemorate the day when the family was converted to Christianity, and it is celebrated on the feast day of the family's patron saint. The customs associated with this festival, however, indicate an origin from pagan times. The ceremonial cakes are undoubtedly reminiscent of and perhaps even identical with the sacrificial foods connected with pagan funeral practices. Among the Yugoslavs the singing of epic poetry has long been an important and integral part of the celebration of the *Slava*. This is still true in rural communities in Yugoslavia. After the feast of which the elders of the family and their distinguished guests partake, these same men pass the *gusle* from one to another, each contributing a song as he can. One is here reminded of Caedmon [73] and his feeling of shame at not being able to sing when the harp was passed to him in a somewhat similar situation. In his dream, it will be remembered, he was told to sing of the Creation. This story could be taken as symbolic of the change in Anglo-Saxon epic tradition from pagan to Christian.

When the Yugoslav elders sing of the glorious deeds of the past, the young men of the family and of the community assemble outside the circle and listen. They are being instructed by the chiefs of their family. Such is the situation described by Lönrot also in the opening of the *Kalevala*:

> Let us sing a cheerful measure,
> Let us use our best endeavours,
> While our dear ones hearken to us,
> And our loved ones are instructed,
> While the young are standing round us,
> Of the rising generation,
> Let them learn the words of magic,
> And recall our songs and legends.[74]

Thus the singer is a teacher. From him the youth learn the history of the past and also the moral wisdom of their nation. The gnomic passages which are to be found in all epic poetry are not, then, mere insertions, mere sententious interpolations. The oral epic of the ancient Greeks taught the wisdom of the Achaeans long before Homer became the educator of Hellas. The epic stories themselves embody moral lessons. Whatever the standards may be in each tradition, they are inculcated by epic poetry.

History was didactic centuries before Thucydides wrote his famous words to that effect. Both he and Herodotus looked upon the Homeric poems as history, even though they criticized them as being unscientific.[75] In mediaeval times the earliest chroniclers, consciously writing annals for history, drew from the traditional epics their accounts of man's activities before the memory of contemporary eye-witnesses. Thus, for example, in Spain we know of epic themes and epic stories from the Chronicle of the Pseudo-Isidore and from the First General Chronicle

(*Primera Crónica General*).[76]   Epics of contemporary events were also entered in the chronicles.   The Anglo-Saxon Chronicle has preserved the *Battle of Brunanburh*.   Indeed, the belief in the historicity of epic poetry is still alive among those who practise it to-day.   The Yugoslav singer insists that the stories he tells are true, no matter how fantastic their content.   He has ever before him the ideal of singing a song exactly as he heard it;   he even says that to change it would be to falsify history.

This does not mean, of course, that the events described in epic poems bear any exact relationship with actual happenings, but the audience and the singer believed them to be faithful to history.   The historian of events will rightly be sceptical, but the writer of intellectual history cannot ignore them, because the fact that they were considered as history meant that they were influential in the thinking and in the behaviour of their times.

The history contained in epic poems has indeed a force which a Thucydides or a Toynbee might well envy.   Wise leaders of men have recognized this force and have used it.   We are told that at the battle of Hastings the Normans sang the *Song of Roland*.[77]   Centuries later the Yugoslav soldiers fighting against the Turks used to sing in their camps the deeds of their national hero, Marko Kraljević.   And from Turkish times in Yugoslavia, the Moslem singers sang of the importance of their home province, Bosnia, in the great empire of Sulejman the Magnificent. For example, from Milman Parry's collection of South Slav epic texts comes a passage in the preamble to the song of the *Wedding of Meho, son of Smail*:

Now to you, sirs, who are gathered here I wish to sing the measures of a song, that you may be merry.   It is the song of the olden time, of the deeds of the great men of old and the heroes over the earth in the time when Sulejman the glorious held empire.   Then was the empire of the Turks at its highest. Three hundred and sixty provinces it had, and Bosnia was its lock, its lock it was and its golden keys, and place of all good trust against the foe.[78]

This is history not as a dry record of the past, but as a vital memory of the past as exhortation to present action.   It was national pride which to no small extent led men in the nineteenth century to record and collect the oral epics.   Each nation vied with its neighbour in discovering what it called its 'national treasure'.

So far we have seen the serious or ceremonial uses of epic poetry. Yet the oral epics which we have and the practice of epic poetry as we know it best fall rather into the category of entertainment.   Even while epic is didactic, it is entertaining.   It teaches by stories and it praises by telling a tale.   Indeed, the moral is the more forceful, the praise the more vivid, by being cast in narrative form.

We have already described the minstrel as entertainer in Yugoslavia and as he is depicted in the *Odyssey*. Of especial interest in the Phaeacian scene cited is the presence of the bard Demodocus at games and dancing out of doors. At first blush it may seem surprising to find the epic muse in such surroundings. Yet a glance at reports of epic poetry from other ages and from other climes provides abundant evidence that in this respect also Homer's picture is realistic. In France in the Middle Ages we are told that the *jongleurs* were divided into many groups, but those who sang epic poetry were of a more dignified and solemn aspect. A much quoted passage from the *Romance of Flamenca* gives a description of the entertainment provided by a group of *jongleurs* after a feast. They played upon many instruments, they danced and performed acrobatic feats, they had marionettes. Some of them sang of the histories of kings, marquises, and counts. Their repertory extended from the classical stories of Priam and Helen and Odysseus to more recent history including stories of Charlemagne, Clovis, and Pepin.[79] The scene depicted seems confused and excessively luxuriant compared with the well-ordered feasting and games in Phaeacia. Yet the elements of the outdoor entertainment given by King Alcinous are found in the mediaeval setting. Demodocus's amusing tale of Ares and Aphrodite is accompanied by dancers and followed by acrobats. The singer is the same who shortly before had sung of Troy and who later was to sing another serious tale. Like the *jongleurs* Demodocus was not limited in subject matter to the deeds of men. One is reminded of the comments on actors (*histriones*) in a thirteenth-century *Summa de poenitentia*, which divides its third category of actors, those who play musical instruments for the entertainment of men, into two classes: the first sing lascivious songs, but the second, called *joculatores*, sing of the deeds of nobles and the lives of saints.[80]

In the *Iliad* as well as in the *Odyssey* Homer refers to the minstrel performing in the company of dancers. With one exception (that of Achilles singing in his tent, where the song is obviously epic, since none but epic would celebrate κλέα ἀνδρῶν), the songs mentioned in the *Iliad* are laments; but on the shield of Achilles there is worked a dancing-place:

There young men and maidens of price danced holding one another by the wrist. . . . Now they circled on practised feet, light and smooth as a potter's wheel when he sits and tries with a touch of his hands whether it will run; now they would scamper to meet in opposite lines. A crowd stood round enjoying the lovely dance; a heavenly minstrel twangled his harp, and two tumblers twirled about among them leading the merry sport.

(Σ 593–606, trans. Rouse.)

In a mountain village in Yugoslav Macedonia not far from the Bulgarian border, an epic singer performed several epics for recording in 1950 to the accompaniment of a three-stringed instrument called the *ćemane*. This instrument is none other than the mediaeval lyre. The singer also performed humorous songs and love songs for dancing to the accompaniment of this same instrument. It was surprising because the musical instrument most commonly used in Yugoslavia to-day to accompany epic, the one-stringed *gusle*, is never used for any other purpose. On the northern Dalmatian coast, in a district in which epic poetry has now disappeared, although we know that it was practised there several generations ago, the same three-stringed bowed instrument is used to accompany a dance which is not at all unlike the one described on the shield of Achilles. In Dalmatia this instrument is called *lirica*. Thus in the Balkans to-day epic poets can still be found who also perform lighter songs to the accompaniment of dancing.

Whether this association of the epic singer and of narrative songs with dancing and games has any significance for the origin of epic poetry in the funeral games and rituals associated with them may be a moot point. Yet the fact remains, whatever its explanation or significance may be, that from Homeric times to the present the epic singer's repertory has its lighter moments and the singer himself descends from the lofty isolated throne of the great muse to be joined by other entertainers of a different sort.

Oral epic continues its life as long as it has a purpose in the tradition and as long as the way of thinking of its singers remains oral. Its disappearance is usually slow, but foreign conquest or government decree may shorten the process of disintegration.

In modern times the epics even as entertainment have died out because another form or forms of entertainment have taken their place and subsumed their function. For the growing reading public the novel and short story satisfy the taste for the heroic or romantic. The cinema and the radio, when introduced into a society in which the practice still survives, eventually take the place of epic. And when the epic continues in some sense as entertainment of a reading public, it is a different kind of epic, namely the literary derivative of oral epic, which is read, and the public is a select and restricted one.

Literary epic then fulfils the same purposes as oral epic from which it derives. These purposes, as we have seen, arise from the circumstances of the practice of oral epic. As the audience becomes literate and therefore cognisant of ideas beyond the scope of oral tradition, there may be greater emphasis on the religious, philosophical, and didactic. There may be less attention paid to the lighter side of oral epic. Yet the earlier functions of the genre are retained. It still relates the connection of man with the unseen forces of the world beyond, whether it be Jason and his Argonauts in their journey to Colchis, rich in magic, or Virgil guiding Dante through Hell and Purgatory, or Vasco da Gama and his Lusiads on their crusade to India. It still relates the history of a nation as Ennius does in his *Annales* or as Camoens in his *Lusiads*. Epic keeps throughout the ages its moral, didactic purpose. Virgil and Milton are great moralists and teachers. And even when the moral itself is not so clearly stated, when the epic seems to be merely a fine story well told, it holds its heroes and heroines up as models for imitation, as men and women who accomplished great things in the past. There is thus a continuity of exalted purpose and serious meaning, a solemnity of greatness in the tradition of epic poetry, whether oral or literary. In a larger sense Homer is the epitome of all epic; a singer of tales of the traditional school, he set the tone which a literary age was later to imitate and finally to make its own.

NOTES TO CHAPTER 5

1. For a survey of world epic poetry consult: C. M. Bowra, *Heroic Poetry* (1952); H. M. and N. K. Chadwick, *The Growth of Literature* (3 vols., 1932–40); W. J. Entwistle, *European Balladry* (1939).

2. *Botteghe oscure*, vii.

3. C. Snouck-Hurgronje, *The Achehnese* (Leyden, 1906). Translated by A. W. S. O'Sullivan.

4. H. M. and N. K. Chadwick, *op. cit.* iii. 650 ff.

5. *Cf.*, *e.g.*, E. Faral, *Les Jongleurs en France au moyen-âge* (1910).

6. Tacitus, *Ger.* 2–3.

7. α 325 ff. and θ 471 ff. are the principal relevant passages.

8. See below, note 21.

9. *Cf.* δ 597; λ 561.

10. *The Song of Roland*, trans. Isabel Butler (1932), lines 1013–14.

11. *Anglo-Saxon Poetry*, selected and translated R. K. Gordon (1926), lines 1159–60.

12. N. Šaulić, *Srpske Narodne Pjesme* (Belgrade, 1929), p. xxxv.

13. *Ibid.* p. xxxix.

14. α 153–7. For the *phorminx* see, *e.g.*, ρ 260–3.

15. 'Les Enfances Godefroi', line 1738, Faral, *op. cit.* 284: *Apres mengier vielent et content cil jogler*.

16. For ecclesiastical hostility as a reason see Y. M. Sokolov, *Russian Folklore* (1950), 299. For the situation in Macedonia see B. Rusić and A. Schmaus, 'Guslar Vandjel iz Ohrida', *Prilozi proučavanju narodne poezije* (Belgrade, 1936), sv. 1–2. Also B. Rusić, 'Prilepski guslar Apostol', *Prilozi* (Belgrade, 1940), *poseb. izd. br.* 2.

17. G. Reese, *Music in the Middle Ages* (1940), 203. This seems to have been true also in Finland.

18. Chadwick, *op. cit.* iii. 3 ff.; see especially the chapters on 'Heroic Poetry and Saga' (II) and 'The Shaman' (X).

19. D. Comparetti, *The Traditional Poetry of the Finns* (1898), 69 ff.

20. This remark is based on my own experience in northern Albania in 1937 and in Yugoslav Macedonia in 1950. My Albanian collection is in the Houghton Library at Harvard University, and the Macedonian is with the Milman Parry Collection in Widener Library.

Q

21. J. B. Pritchard, *Ancient Near Eastern Texts* (1950), 51.

22. A. B. Lord, 'Homer and Huso. I: The Singer's Rests in Greek and Southslavic Heroic Song' in *TAPA*, lxvii. 106-13.

23. See, *e.g.*, the conversation with the singer Salih Ugljanin in *Serbocroatian Heroic Songs*, collected by Milman Parry, edited and translated by A. B. Lord, vol. i (1953).

24. Of especial interest are conversations with Ćamil Kulenović in Kulen Vakuf, Texts Nos. 524 and 1957 in the Milman Parry Collection at Harvard.

25. This section is based on my own experiences in Yugoslavia and Albania and on research on the Milman Parry Collection of Southslavic Texts. The subject is treated more fully in my book, *The Singer of Tales*, in the series *Harvard Studies in Comparative Literature*, 24 (Cambridge, 1960).

26. *Roland*, line 1.

27. *Roland*, line 38.

28. *Beowulf*, line 5.

29. *Roland*, line 178.

30. See Parry, 'Studies in the Epic Technique of Oral Verse-Making. I. Homer and Homeric Style', *Harv. Stud. Class. Phil.* xli. 73 ff., esp. 146. H. T. Wade-Gery in *The Poet of the Iliad*, 38-41, in criticizing Parry merely indicates his lack of information concerning the technique of the formulae. This failure is in part due to the fact that Parry had not time to elaborate his ideas, as Wade-Gery himself points out. See my 'Homer's Originality: Oral Dictated Texts', *TAPA*, lxxxiv. 124-34.

31. *Roland*, lines 3023 ff.

32. Pritchard, *op. cit.* 44 ff.

33. Chadwick, *op. cit.* iii. 32 ff.

34. See A. B. Lord, 'Composition by Theme in Homer and Southslavic Epos', *TAPA*, lxxxii. 71 ff.; and A. Schmaus, 'Episierung im Bereich der slavischen Volksdichtung', in *Münchener Beiträge zur Slavenkunde*, Festgabe für Paul Diels, München, 1953.

35. See the conversations with singers in vol. i of *Serbocroatian Heroic Songs*. *Cf.* Comparetti, *op. cit.* 2.

36. An analysis of these versions, with a translation of one of them, can be found in the Notes to vol. i of the Parry Collection.

37. See F. M. Combellack, 'Contemporary Unitarians and Homeric Originality', in *AJP*, lxxi. 337-64.

38. Although the illuminating statements of such an eminent and trustworthy collector as Radlov are frequently quoted, their full implications are not understood. *Cf.* Chadwick, *op. cit.* iii. 179-83, where statements are quoted from Radlov, *Proben der Volkslitteratur der türkischen Stämme* (St. Petersburg, 1866–1904), v, pp. xv and xvi. *Cf.* also Snouck-Hurgronje, *op. cit.* ii. 101.

39. For information on the phenomenal Yugoslav singer, Avdo Međedović, who gave Parry two long songs of over 12,000 lines, see my 'Homer, Parry, and Huso', *AJA*, lii and 'Avdo Međedović: Guslar', *Journal of American Folkore*, lxix. 320-30. For my synopsis of one of these, the poem of Osman Delibegović and Pavičević Luka, see Bowra, *Heroic Poetry*, 352-3, with Bowra's comments on pp. 359-60. See also the excellent article by J. A. Notopoulos, 'Continuity and Interconnexion in Homeric Oral Composition', *TAPA*, lxxxii. 81 ff. Notopoulos is one of the few Homerists besides Parry who have gone into the field to collect and study oral poetry.

40. Wade-Gery's comments on the Panionia, *op. cit.* 2 ff., are worthy of note.

41. The most recent is Wade-Gery (*op. cit.*), who goes so far as to say that Homer may even have invented the Greek alphabet in order to write the *Iliad* !

42. On the 'Peisistratean recension' see J. A. Davison, 'Peisistratus and Homer', *TAPA*, lxxxvi. 1-21.

43. See Sterling Dow, 'Minoan Writing', *AJA*, lviii. 77-129, and C. M. Bowra's Andrew Lang Lecture, *Homer and His Forerunners* (1955).

44. For more on this singer see my 'Avdo Međedović', *Journ. Amer. Folklore*, lxix. 320-30.

45. In this section I am especially indebted to the stimulating, if controversial, book of G. R. Levy, *The Sword from the Rock* (1953).

46. Pritchard, *op. cit.* 73.

47. *Ibid.* 60. For Homer and festivals see H. T. Wade-Gery, *The Poet of the Iliad*.

48. *Ibid.* 332.

49. *Ibid.* 104.

50. *Kalevala*, translated from the Finnish by W. F. Kirby (1907), Rune iii. 295-304.

51. For a German translation of this *bylina* see Reinhold Trautmann, *Die Volksdichtung der Grossrussen* (1935), 222 ff. Russian examples of wizardry can be found also in the Igor' tale (see Grégoire, Jakobson, and others, *La Geste du prince Igor'* (1948)) and in the *bylina* of Volk' Vseslavevich (Trautmann, pp. 215 ff.). See R. Jakobson and M. Szeftel, 'The Vseslav Epos', *Russian Epic Studies*, 1949, 13 ff.

52. S. E. Bassett, *The Poetry of Homer* (1938), 22 ff.

53. *Kalevala*, xlvii. 67-364 ; xlvi. 355-458 ; ix. 29-258 ; xxvi. 295-758. See Comparetti, *op. cit.* 27 ff.

54. Šaulić, *op. cit.* p. xxxviii.

55. Pritchard, *op. cit.* 358 ff.

56. *Ibid.* 334 ff.

57. *Mahabharata* (Poona ed.), 3. 78. 12-13. Quoted from Myles Dillon, 'The Archaism of Irish Tradition', The Sir John Rhys Memorial Lecture, British Academy, 1947 (*Proceedings of the British Academy*, xxxiii. 4).

58. Meyer, *Vision of MacConglinne*, 110-12. Quoted *ibid.* 5.

59. As is well known, Germanic and Finnish epic use alliteration and assonance as a formal principle. For these devices in Slav epic see D. Čiževsky, 'On Alliteration in Ancient Russian Epic Literature' in *Russian Epic Studies* (*Memoirs of The American Folklore Society*, xlii. 125-30), and my 'The Role of Sound Patterns in Serbocroatian Epic' in *For Roman Jakobson*, 509-13. I am indebted to Professor John V. Kelleher of Harvard for examples of Irish 'rhetorics' ; *cf. The Táin Bó Cúailnge*, ed. by J. Strachan and J. G. O'Keefe (1912), 36-7.

60. L. Majkov, *Velikorusskija zaklinanija* (1869), 60 ff. ; E. E. Pantzer, 'Serbocroatian and Russian Epic Preambles' (Doctoral dissertation, Harvard, 1953), 62 ff.

61. R. Heim, *Incantamenta magica graeca latina* (1892), 498.

62. Heim, *op. cit.* 539.

63. Lines 3148-55 ; lines 3169-82.

64. J. B. Pritchard, *op. cit.* 87. *Cf.* David's lament over Jonathan in 2 Samuel i. 19-27.

65. Translated by S. H. Cross in 'La Geste du prince Igor'', *Annuaire de l'institut de philologie et d'histoire orientales et slaves*, viii. 175.

66. For further details see G. R. Levy, *The Sword from the Rock*. See also C. Lévi-Strauss, 'The Structural Study of Myth', *Journ. Amer. Folklore Soc.* lxviii. 428-44.

67. An English translation is now available, John Mavrogordato, *Digenes Akrites* (1956).

68. The Irish parallels to Beowulf given in James Carney's *Studies in Irish Literature and History* (1955) are illuminating, although I have some reservations about his general thesis.

69. *Kalevala*, Runes xvi and xvii.

70. Pritchard, *op. cit.* 72 ff.

71. Chadwick, *op. cit.* iii. 84 ff.

72. I am especially indebted to Dr. Milenko Filipović, of the Ethnographic Institute

of the Serbian Academy of Sciences, now Professor at Sarajevo University, for his kindness in describing and interpreting the *Slava*.

73. An English translation of The Venerable Bede's account of the poet Caedmon from his *Historia Ecclesiastica Gentis Anglorum* can be found in Faust and Thompson, *Old English Poems* (1918). For the whole subject of the oral character of Anglo-Saxon poetry see F. P. Magoun, Jr., 'The Oral-Formulaic Character of Anglo-Saxon Narrative Poetry' in *Speculum*, xxviii. 446-67.

74. *Kalevala*, i. 23-30.

75. Thucydides, i. 21. Herodotus, of course, is less critical than Thucydides, but *cf.* such passages as ii. 23 and 120.

76. See R. Menéndez Pidal, *Poesía juglaresca y juglares* (Madrid, 1924), 2nd edn. (Buenos Aires, 1945), 189 ff.

77. The story is told by William of Malmesbury (*c.* 1080–1143) in his *Gesta Regum* (1125), and by Robert Wace (1100–75), *Roman de Rou* (after 1160). Wace's passage about the singer Taillefer is famous. Guy of Amiens also mentions Taillefer in his Latin poem on the battle of Hastings, written before 1076.

78. Text No. 6840, lines 25-36. The translation is by Milman Parry. This poem has 12,312 lines and will be published in vols. iii and iv of the Parry Collection.

79. See Faral, *op. cit.* 100-2.

80. Hermann Reich, *Der Mimus* (1903), ii. 814 n.

CHAPTER 6

THE TRANSMISSION OF THE TEXT

by J. A. Davison

La prudenza è qui figliuola della dottrina — PASQUALI

Εἰ καὶ ὡς ἄνθρωπος ἔσφαλα, σύγγνωτέ μοι—BYZANTINE SCRIBE

THE purpose of this chapter is to describe, so far as possible, the processes by which the text of the Homeric poems (limited for this purpose to the *Iliad* and *Odyssey*) has been transmitted to us from the time at which it was first committed to writing.[1] A really authoritative history of these processes cannot be given here: in those cases where the sources are immediately accessible, lack of space prevents full discussion of the ambiguities and obscurities which many of them contain, and in other cases the material which might be used as evidence if it were accessible has not been adequately studied.[2] This chapter is therefore offered only as a preliminary and provisional account of the matters with which it deals.

The sources from which a history of the transmission of the Homeric text might ultimately be written are of two main kinds. I. The *direct sources* include (*a*) a large number of mediaeval (and even some post-mediaeval) manuscripts on parchment or paper[3]; (*b*) many fragments of texts of the Graeco-Roman period, mostly on papyrus[a] but some on parchment or other materials[4]; (*c*) verbatim quotations of Homer in other authors and on archaeological objects.[5] II. The *indirect sources* include indirect allusions in other authors, especially the earlier writers from Archilochus to Pindar, and the learned commentaries of great scholars of the Ptolemaic and Roman periods, which can be to some extent reconstructed from papyrus fragments (*e.g.* the commentary on Φ 1-363 by one Ammonius, which is preserved in Oxyrhynchus Papyrus 221), from quotations and allusions in the works of later writers (mainly grammarians, but including Plutarch, Lucian, and Athenaeus), and above all from the Byzantine lexica (especially that formerly ascribed to Suidas but now more accurately called *the Suda*[6]) and commentaries, whether written between the lines or in the margins of the text to which they refer (*scholia*) or (more rarely) existing as separate works (the classical

[a] See Pl. 3.

example is the great commentary on both poems compiled by Eustathius, archbishop of Salonica, in the last years of the twelfth century).[7]

As was emphasized by Robert Wood in his *Essay on the Original Genius and Writings of Homer*,[8] the Homeric poems describe a form of society in which reading and writing are almost entirely unknown, and which depends for all matters, whether of business or literature, on word of mouth.[9] Wood therefore argued, mainly on *a priori* and analogical grounds, that Homer had been as illiterate as his own heroes ; he backed up his conclusion by reference to Josephus, who in arguing for the superiority of Hebrew society over Greek, alike in antiquity and in cultural development, quotes certain unnamed (and unidentifiable) authorities for the statement that 'not even Homer left his poetry behind him in writing, but it was preserved by memorization and put together out of the songs'.[10] Wood's suggestion that Homer was illiterate was taken up by F. A. Wolf in his *Prolegomena ad Homerum*,[11] and has been accepted by many scholars since ; but it should be noted that the evidential value of Josephus's statement is very slight (he was writing polemic, not history), and that the belief in Homer's illiteracy really rests upon inferences from the content and style of the poems.

Of these, the argument from the content of the poems is merely an argument from silence, and proves nothing by itself; the argument from style is more important. It has been conclusively shown, by the work of Milman Parry and others, that the diction and narrative technique of the Homeric poems very closely resemble the practice of Yugoslav (and especially Serbo-Croat) bards (*guslyare*) who at the present day travel round the country, singing their ballads and songs to the people. Like Demodocus or Phemius in the *Odyssey*, these *guslyare* improvise their songs afresh for each performance, though the diction which they employ is always, and the subjects on which they sing are usually, traditional.[a] It is therefore argued that the Homeric poems were composed in conditions similar to those now prevailing in Yugoslavia (and elsewhere in the Slavonic world, to go no farther afield) ; and some scholars (notably Professor E. R. Dodds and Professor D. L. Page) have gone so far as to assert that Parry's work proves decisively that the *Iliad* and *Odyssey* are oral compositions.[12] The situation is not, however, as simple as these scholars would have us believe. In the first place the oral style exists almost as much to help the audience to follow a long narrative as to assist the poet with his improvisations ; and the fact that 'Homer' employs the oral style may prove only (what no one doubts) that the poems were composed for oral delivery. In the second place Dodds himself admits that there are some signs in the *Iliad*, and still more in the *Odyssey*, that the author or authors who gave these poems their final

[a] See Ch. 5 for fuller discussion of oral epic.

form did not always make appropriate use of the traditional formulae which are characteristic of the oral style; he argues that this 'suggests that parts of the *Odyssey* date from a period of declining oral technique', and it is at least arguable (though Dodds dismisses the possibility very summarily) that one of the causes of this decline may have been the introduction of writing.[13] In the third place there is no evidence that any *guslyar* ever produced an impromptu narrative poem of anything like the complexity of the *Iliad* or *Odyssey* (poems of comparable length are on record, but their design seems to be much cruder than that of the Homeric poems), and it might reasonably be argued that poems so elaborately designed as the *Iliad* and *Odyssey* could not have been produced at all without recourse to writing. Thus we are still at liberty to believe, if we wish to do so, that the *Iliad* and *Odyssey* were either composed in writing or (as Lord has shown to be more probable) [a] dictated at the time of composition to an amanuensis; and hence that the history of the poems as physical objects begins at the moment when they were first composed. But though we may believe this, we cannot prove it; all that we can do is to try to establish the earliest and latest dates for the first writing down of the Homeric poems.

For our present purpose the fact that the documents written in the so-called Minoan Linear B script, both those from Crete and those from the Greek mainland, have now been proved to be written in Greek [14] seems to be of comparatively little importance. There is no evidence yet that the script was used to record anything deserving the name of literature; and even if there were, there is no evidence available that knowledge of the script survived the 'dark age' which followed the end of the Mycenaean period. Thus the introduction of the alphabetic script in the eighth century (most probably about the middle of the century) [15] may be regarded as representing a new birth of literacy in Greece; and we have therefore to consider the relation of the literary profession to this new development.[b]

The Homeric poems recognize literature as a craft, which is already distinct from the related activities of the priest, the seer, and the herald; but within the literary craft there seems to be little or no specialization — any professional ἀοιδός will produce any type of composition which may be needed. The compositions mentioned by Homer include two types of narrative poetry: a more formal type, in which the singer stands up and is accompanied by dancers, and a less formal type, for which the singer remains seated and there is no accompanying 'chorus'. So in the *Iliad* (I 189) Achilles sits singing κλέα ἀνδρῶν. In both cases the singer accompanies himself upon a stringed instrument (κίθαρις, φόρμιγξ).

[a] *Cf.* Ch. 5, pp. 193-7.
[b] For a full discussion of the early use of writing in Greece see Ch. 23.

Hesiod uses the name ἀοιδός too, but he seems to limit the singer's functions to the recital of κλέα προτέρων ἀνθρώπων and of hymns to the gods.[16] By the end of the seventh century specialization had gone farther; the recognition of the αὐλός had necessarily produced a distinction between those who sang to an accompaniment played by another, and those who continued to accompany themselves; and we can also trace a third class who recited verses without any musical accompaniment at all.[17] Of these three classes only the third directly concerns us here; but the fact that the earliest surviving remnants of Greek lyric poetry belong to the last years of the eighth, and the early years of the seventh, centuries, suggests that literary men in general were quick to employ the new technique for the recording of their works.[18]

The professional reciters (ῥαψῳδοί, rhapsodes) (Pl. 4) differed from the Homeric ἀοιδός in that the rhapsodes were primarily executants, performing works composed by others, rather than original composers.[19] Their connection with 'Homeric' poems (not necessarily, or even probably, the Iliad and Odyssey) is attested by Herodotus (v. 67. 2) as having existed before the tyranny of Cleisthenes at Sicyon (c. 600–c. 570), and Plato (Ion 531 A) gives us reason to think that some rhapsodes included Hesiod and even Archilochus in their repertoires. A rhapsode might specialize in the works of a single author (as Ion himself specialized in Homer), but even so his professional equipment must have included great powers of memorization and the ability to explain the texts which he recited. Thus the very nature of the epic style made it easy for the skilled rhapsode deliberately or insensibly to revise the texts which he recited, and even to insert 'cadenzas' of his own composition. This tendency was enhanced by the existence of regular competitions for rhapsodes, such as those which Cleisthenes suppressed at Sicyon or those which Plato mentions as taking place at Epidaurus and Athens (Ion 530 A-B), the natural result of which was the appearance of the virtuoso, more concerned with the effectiveness of his 'interpretation' than with strict fidelity to his author's intentions.

Thus as long as books were rare, and in any case not easily accessible to the members of the rhapsode's public, a written text was not indispensable to a professional rhapsode, and might even be a hindrance to him; but it is certain that the result of the rhapsodes' activities was to put into circulation many divergent versions of the poems ascribed to Homer. One of the worst offenders, we are told, was a Chian named Cynaethus, who is said to have composed many lines and inserted them into Homer's poetry.[20] Another source of divergent texts was the school; two anecdotes about Alcibiades preserved by Plutarch (Alcib. vii. 1), and presumably ben trovati at the worst, mention the schoolmaster who took his pupils through Homer 'without book', and the even more dangerous type of pedagogue who had a text of Homer revised by himself. On the other hand there were certain influences resisting the 'pollution' of the text by the rhapsodes (though they were less effective against the schoolmasters). In the first place there was the corporation of the Homeridae, who claimed to be descended from Homer, and whose existence in Chios in the sixth century is attested by the contemporary chronicler, Acusilaus of Argos (2 F 2 Jacoby). For our purpose it matters little whether the relationship of the members to Homer was nominal (like that of the Coan Asclepiadae to Asclepius) or real; in Plato's time the corporation had a great care for Homer's reputation, and Pindar's scholiast shows that they claimed to recite Homer's poems ἐκ διαδοχῆς ('by right of succession'). This does not compel us to assume that they had texts in writing in the sixth century; but their claim would obviously be easier to maintain against sceptics if manuscripts could be produced in support of it. The possibility must therefore be borne in mind that already in the sixth century the Homeridae possessed manuscripts of the poems which, they claimed, contained the authentic texts bequeathed to them by Homer himself.[21] In the second place the competition mechanism could itself be used to resist the encroachments of the rhapsodes. The fourth-century dialogue *Hipparchus*, which is included in the Platonic *corpus*,[22] tells us (228 B) that Hipparchus 'first brought the poems of Homer to this land [*i.e.* Attica], and compelled the rhapsodes at the Panathenaea to perform them according to the cues [ἐξ ὑπολήψεως], in due order, as they still do to this day'. The existence of the Panathenaic rule in 332 B.C. is attested by the orator Lycurgus (*c. Leocr.* 102), and both he and 'Plato' show that the motive for the rule was admiration for the quality of the poems; but for our present purpose it is more important to note that the creation of the rule implies the existence of an official text, to which both judges and competitors could refer. It also seems necessary to suppose that this text was so authoritative that the competitors, even in the sixth century when the Panathenaea was a festival of very little importance, were willing to submit to the rule in order to compete. This is the first point at which we have any direct justification for assuming the existence of a written text of the Homeric poems; and the question of the source from which it was obtained is still unsolved.[23]

An obscure and scarcely datable historian of Megara, named Dieuchidas, who is quoted by Diogenes Laertius (i. 57) in his life of Solon, seems to have accused Peisistratus of some mishandling of the passage referring to the Athenians in the *Iliad* (B 546 ff.); and a third-century Megarian writer, named Hereas, is said (by Plutarch, *Theseus* xx. 1-2) to have reported that Peisistratus added a line in praise of Theseus to the *Odyssey* (λ 631). There were also doubts in antiquity about the authenticity of B 558, which either Peisistratus or Solon was said to have foisted into the Catalogue of Ships.[24] Minor interpolations of this sort in the name of local patriotism were common form down to the middle of the second century B.C.,[25] and these stories would have no significance at all for the history of the text, were it not for a report, first attested in Cicero (*de Oratore* iii. 137) and after him with various embellishments in several writers, that the Homeric poems *confusos antea* were first arranged as we now have them by Peisistratus. Hence comes the belief that Peisistratus was responsible for a 'recension' of the Homeric poems, or even for the creation of the *Iliad* and *Odyssey* (or at least for their first reduction to writing, which comes to very much the same thing). These stories cannot be disproved, but it can be shown that the sources from which they come are late and almost certainly prejudiced; and the alternative view, that Hipparchus brought what was to be the Panathenaic text of Homer to Athens from elsewhere (probably from Ionia, as we shall see, and perhaps from the Homeridae themselves), is at least equally plausible, and has the additional merit of explaining why the Panathenaic text was accepted as authoritative for its purpose from its first promulgation.[26 a]

In any case, the Panathenaic text of Homer is the oldest whose existence is attested by external evidence, and with it we enter what may be called the 'proto-historic' period, *i.e.* that in which written texts are known to have existed, although we still have no direct evidence of their nature or content. Verbatim quotations from poetry are extremely rare in the sixth and fifth centuries; and there are almost none from the *Iliad* or *Odyssey* before Herodotus, who is the first author to mention either poem by name (*Iliad* and *Odyssey*, the second perhaps an interpolation: ii. 116; *Odyssey*: iv. 29), but there is a considerable increase in the number of indirect references from about 530 B.C. onwards, and the references to something like scholarly activity begin with Theagenes of Rhegium, who is said to have been a contemporary of Cambyses (king of Persia 529–522). Theagenes was the first person to write about Homer, and he is also the first person named in connection with a variant reading[27]; his successors included Stesimbrotus of Thasos, Metrodorus of Lampsacus, one Glaucus (perhaps also of Rhegium), Thrasymachus of Chalcedon, and Democritus of Abdera. All these were concerned primarily with questions of interpretation, especially the meanings of uncommon words ($\gamma\lambda\hat{\omega}\sigma\sigma\alpha\iota$), and there is no reason to suppose that any of them concerned himself with anything which we should recognize as textual criticism in the modern sense. A further difficulty is that we have only the haziest information about the conditions of book-production in the fifth century. The earliest surviving mention of reading as a pastime is in a fragment of Euripides's *Erechtheus* (370 Nauck), produced between 424 and 421,[28] and it seems that the book in question is a privately made scrap-book or commonplace book; the first datable mention of a book-trade at Athens is in the *Birds* of Aristophanes (line 1288), produced in 414. But there is no reason to suppose that the reading public in the late fifth century (or for two centuries after that) had any feeling that such a thing as a 'correct' text of the poems was desirable, much less attainable, or that it was the booksellers' business to provide it. So long as the versions on sale were readable and sufficiently alike to be acceptable as versions of the same poem, both readers and booksellers seem to have been satisfied; even Plato, though his quotations show that his text resembled ours very closely at many points,[29] cannot be supposed to have had a text identical with that on which ours is based. The truth seems to be that the versions of the Homeric poems which were current, even in Athens, in the fourth century were produced in an extremely haphazard way; and any attempt to speak of a single 'pre-Alexandrian vulgate', and still more to create out of it a version of the Panathenaic text by arguing back to sixth- or fifth-century Athens from the conditions which existed in Egypt after the establishment of the Alexandrian library, is doomed to failure from the beginning.[30]

Texts revised by individuals (διορθώσεις; ἐκδόσεις κατ᾽ ἄνδρα) [31] are said to have been prepared by the poet Antimachus of Colophon about the end of the fifth century (Schol. on A 298 and *passim*), and also by the younger Euripides, nephew of the tragedian (Eustathius on B 865), but the first mention of a text which might perhaps deserve to be called 'critical' is that which Alexander the Great is said to have taken with him when he invaded Persia; the preparation of this is ascribed to Aristotle, and it was known as ἡ ἐκ τοῦ νάρθηκος (sc. ἔκδοσις) because Alexander was said to have kept it in a richly decorated cylinder (νάρθηξ) which he had taken from the Persian treasury (Plut. *Alex.* viii, Strab. xiii. 594). Aristotle's own quotations from Homer [32] need further study, but it seems clear that his text diverged more than that used by Plato from the ancestor of our texts; and it is unlikely that the *Narthex* edition, even if it was produced by Aristotle, is of any great significance for the later history of the Homeric text.

With the third century we enter alike the full historical period, with the appearance of actual texts on papyrus, and also the first period in which scholars practised something worthy of the name of textual criticism.[33] Demetrius of Phalerum, it is said, convinced Ptolemy I of Egypt that a rich and powerful kingdom ought to have a centre for advanced studies on the model of that which had been developed by Aristotle in the Lyceum; and an essential part of this foundation was a great library. The growth of the new library, established in the Brucheum at Alexandria, was spectacular, and when in the reign of Ptolemy II it became possible to study the collections properly, it soon came to light that the many texts of Homer which had been collected (not always perhaps by the fairest means) from all over the Greek world [34] showed remarkable divergences, not only in the wording of individual lines but in the number of lines devoted to the various episodes. The early papyri, some of which are of very considerable extent (the third-century papyrus Pack 536 contains parts of *Iliad* iii–v, and Pack 762, of the same century, has much of *Iliad* xxi–xxiii), show very clearly the difficulties with which the first Alexandrian scholars had to contend; and the fragmentary records of their activities which are preserved in the mediaeval commentaries show that it was some time before they were able to evolve satisfactory methods of grappling with those difficulties.

It is not possible to deal in detail here with all those who contributed to the criticism of Homer in the great period of scholarship which begins early in the third century B.C. and ends in the second century A.D.; but there are some who cannot be passed over in silence. The first of these is Zenodotus of Ephesus who, like Theocritus, had been a pupil of Philetas of Cos, and who became head of the Alexandrian library before the middle of the third century B.C. The peculiarities of his revision of Homer are known to us only at second or third hand, and very incompletely; it seems that he did not write a commentary ($\dot{\upsilon}\pi\acute{o}\mu\nu\eta\mu a$) to accompany his text, and his reasons for preferring one reading to another can only be inferred. His text seems to have been considerably shorter than ours (in several cases the scholia remark of a line or passage $Z\eta\nu\acute{o}\delta o\tau o s$ $o\dot{\upsilon}\delta\dot{\epsilon}$ $\ddot{\epsilon}\gamma\rho a\phi\epsilon\nu$), and even among the lines which he did retain he seems to have regarded many as un-Homeric [35]; these he marked with a horizontal stroke ($\ddot{o}\beta\epsilon\lambda o s$, —) in the left-hand margin, and this sign was used in the same sense by his successors. Thus there are two grades of rejection: complete omission, and *athetesis* which denotes the sort of suspicion which would lead a modern editor to consider the use of square brackets. It will be disputed until the end of time whether Zenodotus's employment of one or other of these grades of rejection rests upon any more substantial basis than his own feelings; we do not know in the least what manuscripts were available to him or what their texts were like, but it is difficult to suppose that he let himself be guided solely by manuscript authority in making his excisions or in retaining the lines which he obelized. If he had manuscripts of this kind, it can only be said that their authority was not such as to commend itself to his great successors, Aristophanes and Aristarchus, neither of whom was so drastic as Zenodotus in his recourse to excision.

Zenodotus's drastic measures were natural in the circumstances; he was the first major scholar to contend against the corruptions of the current texts of Homer, and if he used the scalpel more freely than was strictly justifiable, the fault was clearly on the right side. Thanks to his pioneer work, his successor Aristophanes of Byzantium, who was head of the library from 195 to 180, could afford to make more moderate use of excision than Zenodotus, but he made up for this by more frequent recourse to athetesis; his edition is quite often quoted in the scholia, but though he is said to have made a special study of Homeric lexicography, it does not seem that he left a systematic commentary behind him. He used the *obelus* as Zenodotus had done, and he added other signs, especially the κεραύνιον (T) to mark groups of athetized lines, the ἀντίσιγμα (Ͻ) to draw attention to the use of tautology, and the ἀστερίσκος (✱) to denote passages in which the sense seemed incomplete. On the whole we know less of Aristophanes's contributions to Homeric criticism than of Zenodotus's, largely it seems because Aristarchus disagreed more frequently with Zenodotus than with Aristophanes. But so far as we can see Aristophanes, like Zenodotus, was still struggling to make critical sense of the many divergent texts in the library, and had failed to find an Ariadne's clue to guide him through the labyrinth.

It seems that the finding of this clue was left to Aristarchus of Samothrace (*c.* 215–*c.* 145 B.C.),[36] to whose outstanding work as a Homeric critic it is reasonable to ascribe the great change which came over the text of Homer in the latter part of the second century B.C. Henceforward 'wild' papyri (*i.e.*, those which differ in length, or materially in wording, from the text on which our editions are based) are the exception rather than the rule; and though variations in wording persist, as is inevitable in a text with such a mixed ancestry as Homer's, we can at last speak with some confidence of a 'standard' text of the *Iliad* and *Odyssey*. The difficulty in ascribing this text to Aristarchus is that, according to the information which we can collect from the scholia and other sources, it is by no means what Aristarchus would have regarded as the most satisfactory text possible. Of the readings which, we are told, Aristarchus preferred, only comparatively few have been preserved in the text of the post-Aristarchean papyri and in the generality of the Byzantine manuscripts. It is customary to explain this state of affairs as resulting from a victory of the vulgate text over the scholarly recension of Aristarchus; but it has been argued above that there never was (nor could have been) a single vulgate, and even if there had been it could hardly have stood a chance in the Graeco-Roman book-market against a standard text prepared by the head of the Alexandrian library or under his direction.

The text which, from Aristarchus's time down to that of Wolf, held the field against all comers, must, as its orthography shows, have come to Alexandria by way of Athens [37]; and there is reason to think that at

some time in its career it had been transliterated from an alphabet similar
to that of the seventh- (or early-sixth-) century inscription on the statue
dedicated by the Naxian Nicandre at Delos [38] into the late Ionic alphabet
of twenty-four letters which became the official alphabet at Athens in
the archonship of Eucleides (403/2). Thus there is a certain degree of
possibility that Aristarchus, who, we are told, believed Homer to have
been an Athenian and to have lived about 140 years after the Trojan war
(*Vit. Hom.* ed. Allen, ii. 13, v. 7-8 ; Proclus 58-62 Severyns), based his
second and final revision of the text of Homer upon the Panathenaic text,
which had either not been available to or not been so highly valued by
his predecessors. There is no reason to think that he made serious changes
in the wording or content of his basic text, whatever it was ; his διόρθωσις,
even in its final form, clearly contained much with which he was not
personally in sympathy ; and his own conjectures, together with the
variant readings from other texts which he either preferred or thought
worth recording, were set down in the commentary which he prepared
to accompany his text, or in one or other of the great series of mono-
graphs (συγγράμματα) which he devoted to specific problems. In his
text he made use of most of the critical signs used by his predecessors,
though he gave a new meaning to the asterisk (which henceforth denoted
a line wrongly repeated elsewhere) and to the *antisigma* (which now
marked a line which he thought to be out of place), and he added some
new signs : the διπλῆ (>) to indicate that a note on some point in the
line would be found in the commentary, the διπλῆ περιεστιγμένη (⩒)
to indicate a line in which his text differed from Zenodotus's, and the
στιγμή (·) to indicate a line which he suspected of being un-Homeric
but was not prepared to obelize outright ; the στιγμή combined with the
antisigma (Ɔ) indicates a line after which a re-arrangement should be made,
the line or lines to be moved to the new place being marked with a
σίγμα ἐστιγμένον (Ϲ).[39] All this apparatus of reference was, of course,
intended for professional scholars ; the enormously greater frequency
of Homer, compared with other writers, among the surviving literary
papyri makes it clear that there *was* a general reading public for Homer ;
but they took little interest in anything but the text. In these circumstances it is easy to understand how the text which Aristarchus's respect
for evidence imposed upon him, against his own personal feelings about
what was truly Homeric, might become the standard text for general
circulation without carrying with it more than a very small percentage
of the readings from other sources which Aristarchus himself regarded
as superior to those of the standard text.

But whether or not it is true that (as has been shown to be possible)
the text which became current in the late second century B.C. was based
upon the Panathenaic text, and behind it upon an Ionic (and perhaps

Homerid) text, there is no doubt at all that the second-century text is the ancestor of almost all our surviving witnesses to the text of Homer since that time. Lists can be made of all the scholars since Aristarchus who are credited by the scholiasts with the defence of variant readings (see, for example, Allen's *Homeri Ilias*, i. 203-4), but their contribution to the history of the text is very slight; and one may say that from the time of Aristarchus onwards to the ninth century A.D. our interest in the history of the text shifts away from scholarship and criticism to the question of the physical transmission of the text. The general problem here is, of course, one which affects all ancient texts of any considerable length: the papyrus roll is not a very satisfactory means of recording texts of more than a modest length, and a complete text of the *Iliad* or *Odyssey*, even if more than one book were included in a single roll, would still require a considerable number of rolls. The evidence of the papyri suggests (it is still too fragmentary for certainty) that complete texts of either poem were very rarely to be found in private possession, as long as the roll was the standard format; and the difficulty was only overcome with the introduction of the *codex* (the book with pages) in the late first or early second century A.D.[40] The adoption of the codex entailed a great deal of activity among the copyists, but greatly improved the chances of survival for long works like the Homeric poems; and that chance was made even better by the introduction of parchment, which is more resistant than papyrus to the climatic conditions of the temperate zone and is easier to bind into volumes. Prepared skins of animals (especially sheep and goats) had been known to the Greeks as writing materials since a very early date (*cf.* Hdt. v. 58. 3); but papyrus was cheaper and for ordinary purposes more satisfactory, though the technique of preparing the skins is said to have been improved at Pergamum in the time of Eumenes II (195–158), whence the name περγαμηνόν. (The English *parchment* is a conflation of the French *parchemin* with the Latinized form *pergamentum*.) But the earliest known literary texts on parchment belong to the second century A.D.,[41] and the earliest Homeric texts on parchment are dated to the third century.

The use of parchment for codices enabled books to be produced with a much larger page than had been possible with papyrus; and it was found that the additional space might be used for illustrations,[42] or for marginal notes and commentaries. The practice of adding short notes between the lines ('paving the way'), and longer notes in the upper and lower margins or between the columns of the text, had begun in papyrus rolls.[43] These notes were for the most part unsystematic jottings, and indeed (as Allen has shown), if a long text in one of the papyrus bookhands, or in the uncial hands which were developed from them for use on parchment from the fourth century A.D. onwards, had been provided with full and systematic commentaries such as are known to us from minuscule manuscripts, the resulting volume would have been most inconveniently bulky. It seems likely therefore that the practice of treating the commentary as a substantive work, which goes back at least to the time of Aristarchus, remained the rule until the invention of the minuscule hand at the very end of the eighth century.[44] It is clear from the mediaeval scholia, from the commentaries of Eustathius, and from the remnants of the ancient lexica and etymologica [45] that the systematic commentaries and treatises of the great scholars from Aristarchus to Herodian were not regarded as sacrosanct works of literature; they have been combined and recombined until their original form is irrecoverable, and they have been abbreviated and summarized and excerpted until it is often extremely doubtful whether a view which we find ascribed to a given scholar can possibly have been held by him. None the less, we owe an incalculable debt to the scholars who, from the time of Herodian (second half of the second century A.D.) to that of Georgius Choeroboscus (about 600),[46] maintained the study of Homer in spite of all difficulties and preserved, in however fragmentary and unsatisfactory a state, the memory of such fundamental works as Didymus *On the edition of Aristarchus*, Aristonicus *On the Signs of the Iliad and Odyssey* (both dating from the Augustan period), Nicanor *On Punctuation* (about A.D. 130) and Herodian's *Prosody of the Iliad* (on accentuation — about A.D. 160). Without the first two in particular we should be unable even to attempt to reconstruct Aristarchus's contribution to Homeric studies.

Extracts from these four works, combined and summarized by an unknown scholar (some call him Nemesion, but the name adds nothing to our knowledge), and called in German *Viermännerkommentar* (abbreviated *VMK*; the French call it the *résumé des Quatre*), form one of the chief sources for that remarkable collection of ancient information about Homer which we know as the A Scholia to the *Iliad* (i.e. the various commentaries on the *Iliad* which are to be found in the early-tenth-century minuscule manuscript, *Venetus Marcianus* 454 (Pl. 5) known to editors of the *Iliad* as A). This is the earliest complete manuscript of either poem, and since its rediscovery in the Marcian library at Venice, to which it came in the fifteenth century from the library of Cardinal Bessarion, only to be forgotten until the late eighteenth century,[47] it has played a vital part in the constitution of the text of the *Iliad*, since it contains more information than any other manuscript about the readings preferred by Aristarchus. The history of its scholia has been studied most recently by H. Erbse, and the text of its prolegomena has been discussed by Severyns,[48] with results which seem to be of the greatest significance to to its proper appreciation as a witness to the text of the *Iliad*.

The first period of Byzantine scholarship was continuous with the

Graeco-Roman period, and was marked only by the ebbing of the tide of Greek studies alike in the Latin West,[49] in Syria, and in Egypt; the great centres from the time of Justinian (527–65) onwards were Constantinople and, to a lesser but still considerable degree, Salonica. In 717 the Arabs laid siege to Constantinople by land and sea, and it was not until late in 718 that the Isaurian emperor, Leo III, could force them to raise the siege and withdraw. The Iconoclast movement, which the Isaurians supported and which lasted from the time of Leo III until 843, was a period of complete stagnation, if not of actual persecution, for Classical studies. It was not until the empress Theodora and the patriarch Photius restored the icons to their old place in the worship of the Orthodox Church that it was possible to reform the educational system, and to restore the ancient writers to their proper place in the schools.[50] In the meantime, the introduction of the minuscule hand not long before 800 had created a demand for new manuscripts transliterated out of the old capital and uncial scripts [51]; and among those who were forward to meet the need Classical studies owe most to Arethas of Patrae (c. 862–932 or later). He was a pupil of Photius, and had imbibed his master's passion for literature and for the study of the ancient commentators; even as a deacon Arethas was an ardent collector of manuscripts, which he annotated with his own hand,[52] and there is no reason to think that his ardour was quenched when he became archbishop of Caesarea in Cappadocia (about 901) and presumably had even more money than before to spend upon the works of the best copyists — his last known acquisition is a volume of theology dated 932. No direct evidence connects the *Venetus A* of the *Iliad* with Arethas (it is certainly not one of the manuscripts which he annotated with his own hand), but Severyns has argued that it contains material which could only have come from a pupil of Photius, and that A is most probably a descendant of Arethas's own copy of the *Iliad*. It is almost certain in any case that the peculiarities of A's text are due not to inheritance from a very early (and perhaps even Alexandrian) manuscript, but to a learned recension by an almost contemporary scholar who had special sources of information about the work of Aristarchus; and it seems that it is methodically unsound to treat A (as editors since Wolf and Heyne have tended to do) as the most authoritative manuscript of the *Iliad*. It is certainly one of the most informative, but its differences from the traditional text seem to have a mainly negative value; they tell us rather what Aristarchus said in his commentary than what he had in his text.

The second period of Byzantine scholarship, which was ushered in by the fall of the Iconoclasts, was brought to an abrupt and terrifying end by the sack of Constantinople by those disreputable champions of Christendom, the warriors of the Fourth Crusade, in 1204. From the period

R

which preceded this hideous crime against civilization we have over a dozen manuscripts of the *Iliad*, including A and two others with important scholia,[53] and three manuscripts of the *Odyssey*, one with partial scholia,[54] a clear indication that the relative popularity of the two works remained much what it had been in the Graeco-Roman period. The chief scholars of this second Byzantine period who concerned themselves with Homer were John Tzetzes (*c.* 1110–*c.* 1180) and Eustathius of Salonica [a]; owing to our ignorance of the relations between the surviving manuscripts we cannot tell which, if any, of them retain traces of the work of these or other scholars. Allen, following Ludwich and Leaf, tried to bring order out of chaos by distributing the manuscripts of the *Iliad* and *Odyssey* into families, but he had to admit that his families were at best only statistical approximations; and a glance at the chart in which he has set out his conclusions about the manuscripts of the *Iliad* (*Homeri Ilias*, i, after p. 278) will show how far his families are from explaining the history of the text.[55]

The third period of Byzantine scholarship begins with the re-establishment of the Greek empire at Constantinople in 1261, and is marked by the work of such great scholars as Maximus Planudes (*c.* 1260–1310), Manuel Moschopoulos (*c.* 1265–*c.* 1316), Thomas Magister (1275?–1325?), and above all Demetrius Triclinius (1280?–after 1332), the only Byzantine scholar who deserves the name of textual critic in anything like the modern sense.[56] Moschopoulos compiled brief notes on *Iliad* i and ii; but there is no evidence that the critical activities of any of these scholars were directed to the text of Homer. A good many of the surviving manuscripts of the *Iliad* and *Odyssey* must have been written between 1280, when Planudes is first found at work, and 1340; but here again we are too ignorant about the relations of the manuscripts to one another to pick out the work of individual scholars, let alone to connect variations in the texts with any particular scholar or group of scholars. Not long after the death of Triclinius the flow of Greek texts and Greek scholars to the west, and especially to Italy, began; it was in the late fourteenth and fifteenth centuries that most of our manuscripts were copied, mainly in Italy and for Italian patrons, and we can identify some of the copyists and scholars, especially John Rhosus and John Lascaris, who were active in this work. But the Byzantine period really ends with the coming of printing; and for Homer a new age begins in 1488, with the printing at Florence by Demetrius Damilas, under the direction of Demetrius Chalcondylas, of the *editio princeps* of the *Iliad* and *Odyssey* (Pl. 6). Allen argued that the *Iliad* was printed from a manuscript of his *e* family, now lost (and perhaps destroyed by the printers), and the *Odyssey* mainly from a manuscript of his *g* family [57]; but he points out

[a] *Cf.* p. 226 above.

that Chalcondylas claimed to have made his own διόρθωσις, using Eustathius and the commentators to produce a readable text, and the facts which he reports go far to bear out Chalcondylas's claim. Further study might identify the manuscripts used by Chalcondylas, but at present we cannot go beyond what Allen has told us.

The history of the text since the introduction of printing is largely bound up with the development of scholarly opinion about the composition of the poems, and is dealt with in that connection in the next chapter. A list of editions (with dates) will be found in W. Schmid, *Geschichte der griechischen Literatur*, i (1929), 193, and a useful commentary on this list is provided by Allen (*Homeri Ilias*, i. 248-9, 258-72). Since 1929, the following critical editions have been published: Allen's *Iliad*, so often referred to above (1931), Mazon's *Iliad* in the Budé series (1937–1938), and P. von der Mühll's *Odyssey* (1946).[58] What is now needed, as will be abundantly clear from the foregoing account, is a thorough study of the mediaeval manuscripts with a view to constructing a history of the text from the ninth to the fifteenth centuries, as a preliminary to the preparation of new texts (and here, owing to the revaluation of A, the *Iliad* is in more urgent need of attention than the *Odyssey*).

NOTES TO CHAPTER 6

1. For the whole of this chapter G. Pasquali's study in *Storia della tradizione e critica del testo* [2] (1952), 201-47, is fundamental. Next in importance is P. Cauer, *Grundfragen der Homerkritik* [3] (1923), 9-135. Reference may also be made to W. Schmid, *Geschichte der griechischen Literatur* (*Handbuch der Altertumswissenschaft*, vii. 1) i (1929), 54-83, 129-73. For the Homeric Hymns see T. W. Allen, W. R. Halliday, and E. E. Sykes, *The Homeric Hymns* (1936), xi-lviii.

2. This is especially the case with the Byzantine manuscripts, to most of which modern methods of codicology have not yet been applied. For these methods in general, see R. Devréesse, *Introduction à l'étude des manuscrits grecs* (1954), and A. Dain, *Les Manuscrits* (1949); an example of the technique applied to the manuscripts of a single author is J. Irigoin's *Histoire du texte de Pindare* (1952).

3. Manuscripts of the *Iliad* are listed by T. W. Allen, *Homeri Ilias* (1931), i. 1 and 11-55; he mentions 190, ranging in date from the fifth to the eighteenth centuries, seven of which contain the *Odyssey* as well as the *Iliad*. See also P. Chantraine in P. Mazon, *Introduction à l'Iliade* (1942), 5-14. For manuscripts of the *Odyssey* see Allen, *BSR*, v. 1-84; he lists 75, from the tenth to the eighteenth centuries, including the seven already mentioned. Allen's work has been severely criticized; but without it the mediaeval tradition of Homer's text would be almost entirely unknown.

4. Latest list in R. A. Pack, *Greek and Latin Literary Texts from Greco-Roman Egypt* (1952); complete up to 1949 (with supplement, less complete, to 1951), it includes 381 items for the *Iliad* and 111 for the *Odyssey*, besides a large number of quotations in other authors and some 60 items which should be classified as indirect sources. The most important later additions to our knowledge of the text are V. Martin, *Papyrus Bodmer*, i.

(1954) and *P. Hibeh*, ii. 173. *Cf.* P. Collart in Mazon, *op. cit.* 39–73 (*Iliad*), *Rev. Phil.* 3ᵉ Sér. XIII. 291–307 (*Odyssey*).

5. For the *testimonia* to the *Iliad* see the critical apparatus to the editions of Allen (1931) and Mazon (1937–8); there is no satisfactory collection of those to the *Odyssey*. For the ancient quotations in general J. La Roche, *Homerische Textkritik im Alterthum* (1866) is still indispensable; J. Labarbe, *L'Homère de Platon* (1949) has discussed Plato's quotations. I have considered certain points of method concerning the use of ancient quotations and allusions in *Eranos*, liii. 125–40. Of the archaeological objects the most important are the so-called Homeric bowls (F. Courby, *Vases grecs à reliefs* (1922), 281–97, especially Nos. 16, 17) of the first half of the third century B.C. (*cf.* H. A. Thompson, *Hesperia*, iii. 451 ff., especially 457–8: *circa* 275). I owe the references to Courby and Thompson to Professor T. Dohrn of Cologne.

6. ἡ Σοῦδα, *i.e.* 'the fortress'. For a full discussion see F. Dölger, 'Der Titel des sog. Suidaslexikons' in *Sitzungsbericht d. Bayr. Akad.*, Phil.-hist. Kl., 1936, Heft 6.

7. The standard edition is still that by G. Stallbaum (1825–30, reprinted 1960). A new edition is urgently needed.

8. Originally published 1769; 2nd ed. by J. Bryant 1775, pp. 248–78.

9. The one exception is Glaucus's story of the document given to his grandfather Bellerophon by Proetus, king of Argos (Z 168–70); there is no suggestion that Glaucus himself or his contemporaries could read or write. Aristarchus had already commented on the illiteracy of Homeric society (Schol. A on Z 169, H 175); there is no evidence that he believed Homer himself to be illiterate.

10. Josephus, *contra Apionem*, i. 2. 12: φασὶν οὐδὲ τοῦτον ἐν γράμμασι τὴν αὑτοῦ ποίησιν καταλιπεῖν, ἀλλὰ διαμνημονευομένην ἐκ τῶν ᾀσμάτων συντεθῆναι.

11. Vol. i (1795), 40 ff.

12. E. R. Dodds in *Fifty Years of Classical Scholarship* (ed. M. Platnauer, 1954), 13 ff.; D. L. Page, *The Homeric Odyssey* (1955), 138–9.

13. *Cf.* A. B. Lord, *TAPA*, lxxxiv. 124–34, *The Singer of Tales* (1960), ch. vi; and C. M. Bowra, *Homer and his Forerunners* (1955), 5–13.

14. See M. Ventris and J. Chadwick, *Documents in Mycenaean Greek* (1956). Almost simultaneously with the publication of *Documents*, Professor A. J. Beattie launched an attack on the claim of Ventris and Chadwick to have deciphered the Linear B script; after the replies by Professor L. R. Palmer (*Gnomon*, xxix. 562–4) and Mr. Chadwick (*JHS*, lxvii. 202–4), this attack may reasonably be regarded as having completely failed.

15. *Cf.* H. L. Lorimer, *Homer and the Monuments* (1950), 128–9, 527; her answer to the much earlier dating preferred by A. Rehm, *Handbuch der Archäologie*, i (1939), 195–7, seems conclusive. Even Rehm admits (197) that there was a gap between the use of the Minoan script by Greeks and the Greek alphabet. A. J. B. Wace suggested (in the foreword to Ventris and Chadwick, *Documents*, xxviii–xxx) that literacy must have been continuous in Greece from the Late Bronze Age to the eighth century. *Cf.* R. Harder, *Kleine Schriften* (1960), 57–97.

16. His ἀοιδοὶ καὶ κιθαρισταί (*Theog.* 95) are not necessarily different people (*cf.* N 731 ἑτέρῳ κίθαριν καὶ ἀοιδήν, and B 594–600 where Thamyris has both ἀοιδή and κιθαριστύς to lose).

17. The names of three αὐληταί mentioned by Alcman are recorded by Athenaeus (xiv. 624 b = Alcm. fr. 112 Bergk); Alcman also mentions a κιθαριστάς as an accompanist (fr. 20. 2 Diehl). κιθαρῳδός and ῥαψῳδός occur first in Herodotus (i. 23; v. 67. 2), but in each case the context shows that performers of these types existed already in the seventh century. The nature of the rhapsode's performance is indicated by the fact that he held a wand (ῥαβδός) and not a musical instrument while performing; *cf.* the vase by the Cleophrades painter (BM E270, Beazley, *ARV*, 122, No. 13).

18. Eumelus of Corinth is said to have been contemporary with the founding of Syracuse (734 B.C.) and to have written a προσόδιον εἰς Δῆλον (of which two lines survive) for
the Messenians; this must have been before the end of the first Messenian war (c. 720).
Terpander, Callinus, and Archilochus all belong to the early years of the seventh century.

19. The chief sources for an account of the rhapsodes are: Schol. Pind. Nem. ii. 1
(ed. Drachmann, iii. 28-32), the disorganized remnants of a very well-informed discussion,
probably by Aristarchus, and Plato's Ion.

20. Schol. Pind. Nem. ii. l.c., which dates Cynaethus's first performance of 'Homer'
at Syracuse to the 69th Olympiad (504/0); for the correctness of the date cf. Wilamowitz,
Homerische Untersuchungen (1884), 259, n. 21, and H. T. Wade-Gery, Greek Poetry and Life
(1936), 56-78.

21. How long the Homeridae endured is not certain; the references to them in Plato
and Isocrates show that they were still active in the fourth century (though not necessarily
as rhapsodes), but the only later reference to them (Strabo, xiv. 645) is ambiguous, and
does not prove that the corporation still existed in his time.

22. For a concise summary of the dispute about the date and authorship of the Hipparchus see H. Leisegang, RE, xx. 2 (1950), 2367.

23. I have discussed the whole question of the 'Peisistratean recension', as it is called,
in TAPA, lxxxvi. 1-21. On Dieuchidas see CQ, n.s. ix (1959), 216-22.

24. Schol. A on Γ 230, Δ 273; Schol. B on B 557. Cf. Strabo ix. 394.

25. For examples known to Aristarchus cf. Lehrs, de Aristarchi studiis homericis ³ (1882),
233-8.

26. P. Hibeh, ii. 173 considerably increases the evidence for Archilochus's acquaintance
with the text of Homer, and strengthens the case for the view lately expressed by O. von
Weber (Die Beziehungen zwischen Homer und den älteren griech. Lyrikern, Diss. Bonn 1955,
106) that the earlier lyric poets 'imitated specific passages from Homer, which they already
had before them in the form in which we read them to-day'.

27. Schol. A on A 381 says that Theagenes read ἐπεί ῥά νύ οἱ φίλος ἦεν where our
manuscripts have ἐπεὶ μάλα οἱ κτλ.. (The whole passage was obelized by Aristarchus.)

28. W. Schmid, Geschichte der griechischen Literatur, iii (1940), 429, n. 1, is inclined to
put it nearer to 424 than to 421; G. Zuntz, The Political Plays of Euripides (1955), 89, n. 2,
93, puts it in 421, but gives no reasons.

29. See J. Labarbe, op. cit. (note 5, above).

30. See, for example, the works of A. Ludwich, Die Homervulgata als voralexandrinisch
erwiesen (1898), and G. M. Bolling, The External Evidence for Interpolation in Homer (1925),
The Athetized Lines in the Iliad (1944), Ilias Atheniensium (1950).

31. The value of these early revisions is vividly summed up in a story about Timon
preserved by Diogenes Laertius (ix. 113): Aratus asked Timon how he could obtain a
reliable text of Homer, and Timon replied 'Only if you come on the old copies and not
on those that have been revised already'.

32. Listed by La Roche, op. cit. (see note 5).

33. See especially M. van der Valk, Textual Criticism of the Odyssey (1949), and G.
Jachmann, Nachrichten v. d. Gesellschaft d. Wissenschaften zu Göttingen, Phil.-Hist. Kl. 1949,
167-224, in addition to the works of La Roche, Pasquali, Cauer, Sandys, and Bolling
already mentioned. Allen's chapter on the history of the text in Homeri Ilias, i. 194-216
begins with 300 B.C. See also my article, 'The Study of Homer in Graeco-Roman Egypt'
in Mitteilungen aus der Papyrussammlung der öster. Nationalbibliothek, n.s. v, 1956, 51-8.

34. Besides the editions of Antimachus and Euripides, already mentioned, the scholia
to Homer mention a number of editions by their place of origin (the so-called πολιτικαί,
sc. ἐκδόσεις). Of these the Massaliot is the most frequently quoted; then follow editions
from Chios, Sinope, Argolis, Cyprus, Crete, and Aeolis. Other editions are quoted as

ἡ κυκλική, ἡ ἐκ Μουσείου, ἡ πολύστιχος (on this see R. Cantarella, L' edizione polistica di Omero, 1929). Collective terms such as χαριέστεραι, ἀστειότεραι, εἰκαιότεραι, φαυλότεραι, κοιναί, δημώδεις also occur, but their precise meaning cannot be determined.

35. The Greek word for this is ἀθετεῖν; whence the terms 'athetesis', 'athetize'. The scholia use παραιτεῖσθαι as well as ἀθετεῖν.

36. The study of Aristarchus's contribution to Homeric studies was founded by K. Lehrs, De Aristarchi studiis homericis (¹ 1833, ² 1865, ³ revised by A. Ludwich 1882). Ludwich's own Aristarchs Homerische Textkritik nach den Fragmenten des Didymos dargestellt und beurtheilt appeared in 1884–5. Later works are A. Roemer, Aristarchs Athetesen und die Homerkritik (1912) and Die Homerexegese Aristarchs in ihren Grundzügen dargestellt (ed. E. Belzner, 1924); H. Erbse, 'Über Aristarchs' Iliasausgaben' (Hermes, lxxxvii. 275-303).

37. See P. Chantraine, Grammaire homérique, i ² (1948), ch. 1. J. Wackernagel's Sprachliche Untersuchungen zu Homer (1916) made a contribution of first-class importance to the establishment of this point; but his arguments have now been superseded in some vital respects (especially by the decipherment of Linear B), and should not be used any longer to support ancient allegations and modern superstitions about the 'Peisistratean recension'.

38. See C. D. Buck, The Greek Dialects (1955), 189-90.

39. Allen's editio maior of the Iliad gives all Aristarchus's signs for which there is evidence, but there are long passages without any signs at all (e.g., E 334-637), and the evidence is obviously incomplete. Examples : A 2 διπλῆ, 5 δ. περιεστιγμένη, 12-15 ἀστερισκοί, 29-31 ὄβελοι (Aristarchus did not use the κεραύνιον), B 192 ἀντίσιγμα ἐστιγμένον (to indicate that 203-5, which are marked with the σίγμα ἐστιγμένον, should follow this line), Θ 535-7 ἀντίσιγμα alone, 538-40 στιγμή alone.

40. The earliest fragment of a papyrus codex of Homer is P. Harris, 119 (Pack 669), part of a single leaf containing Λ 34-42 and 69-77, which is dated to the second(?) century A.D. Codices become common in the third century, and are the rule in the fourth. The earliest known parchment codex of Homer is P. Ryl. i. 53 (Pack 864) of the third century (the remains contain most of Odyssey xii-xxiv). On the codex in general see C. H. Roberts, Proc. Brit. Acad. xl. 169-204.

41. See Devréesse, op. cit. (note 2 above) 4, 11-16; he shows that parchment was in use for Greek documents about the end of the third century B.C.

42. For ancient book-illustration in general see E. Bethe, Buch und Bild im Altertum (ed. E. Kirsten, 1945), and K. Weitzmann, Illustrations in Roll and Codex (1947); the remains of an illustrated Homer of the fifth or sixth century A.D. are in the Ambrosian library at Milan (1019, F 205 inf.), and have been published in Ilias Ambrosiana (Fontes Ambrosianae, xxviii. 1953). R. Bianchi-Bandinelli, Hellenistic-Byzantine Miniatures of the Iliad (1955), has studied these pictures in detail, and dates them between 493 and 506 (cf. D. Talbot Rice, lxxvii. 351).

43. The Louvre papyrus of Alcman is a good example. Cf. D. L. Page, Alcman : The Partheneion (1951), 9-16.

44. Devréesse, op. cit. 31, puts it between 790 and 797.

45. See R. Langumier in Mazon, op. cit. (note 3), 74-88. T. W. Allen, 'The Homeric Scholia' (Proc. Brit. Acad. xvii. 3-31) is a handy guide to the possible sources of the scholia. More detailed works are : H. Erbse, Untersuchungen zu den attizistischen Lexika (1950), Beiträge zur Überlieferung der Iliasscholien (1960), and articles in Rh. Mus. xcv. 170-91 and Mnemosyne, 4 Ser. vi. 1-38; H. Gattiker, Das Verhältnis des Homerlexikons des Apollonius Sophistes zu den Homerscholien (Diss. Zürich, 1945); P. M. Privitera, Sicul. Gymn. n.s. v (1952), 1-8.

46. The date here given for Choeroboscus is very doubtful; P. Maas (Byzant. Ztschr. xxv. 359) wanted to date him in the ninth century A.D., and Erbse is now of the same opinion (Beiträge . . ., 106, n.1).

47. Its prolegomena were collated (very badly) by Siebenkees for Heyne's *editio princeps* or Proclus's *Chrestomathy* (1786), *cf.* A. Severyns, *Recherches sur la* Chrestomathie *de Proclos*, iii (1953), 21; the scholia, together with those of B (*Ven. Marc.* 453, of the eleventh century), were first published by Villoison in 1788.

48. See their works cited in notes 45, 47.

49. See especially P. Courcelle, *Les Lettres grecs en occident* ² (1948).

50. See J. M. Hussey, *Church and Learning in the Byzantine Empire 867–1185* (1937), F. Dvornik, *Photius et la réorganisation de l'académie patriarcale* (1950), R. R. Bolgar, *The Classical Heritage and its Beneficiaries* (1954), 59–90. B. Hemmerdinger, *Essai sur l'histoire du texte de Thucydide* (1955), 33–9, gives some ground for thinking that Classical studies may not always have been quite so badly off under the iconoclasts as is suggested in the text.

51. The earliest surviving Byzantine minuscule manuscript was completed on 7th May 835 (Leningrad State Library 219, of the Gospels); secular minuscule texts begin with the Oxford Euclid, written in 888 (Bodl. Dorville x. 1 infr. 2. 30); *cf.* Devréesse, *op. cit.* 32.

52. The earliest manuscripts which are known to have belonged to Arethas are both in the Bodleian Library: the Euclid already mentioned (note 51), and the *Clarkianus* 39 of Plato (895) — Devréesse, *op. cit.* 33, 94.

53. *Venetus Marcianus* 453 (eleventh century — B), Brit. Mus. Burney 86 (1059 — T, *i.e.*, Townleianus, after a former owner). The A and B Scholia were edited by G. Dindorf, *Scholia Graeca in Iliadem*, i–iv (1875–7), the T Scholia by E. Maass, *ibid.* v–vi (1887–8).

54. Two in Florence: Laur. 32. 24 (tenth–eleventh century — G), Laur. *conv. soppr.* 52 (eleventh century — F); one in Heidelberg: *Palatinus* 45 (1201–2), with scholia on Books i–vii. For the scholia to the *Odyssey* see G. Dindorf, *Scholia Graeca in Odysseam* (1855).

55. One of Allen's families (*h*) has a distinct individuality, which was recognized also by Ludwich and Leaf; it seems to connect remotely with the text, and rather less remotely with the scholia, of A, since the manuscripts which are assigned to it contain an unusually high percentage of Alexandrian readings. The oldest manuscript of this family (Allen's U 4) is of the twelfth–thirteenth century, and there is a possibility that the family may derive from a recension by Tzetzes, whom Severyns suspects of having produced a recension of the Proclean prolegomena to certain Homeric manuscripts; these prolegomena are found in a more complete form in A (Severyns, *op. cit.* 152–5).

56. See R. Aubreton, *Démétrius Triclinius et les recensions médiévales de Sophocle* (1949), especially pp. 17–23; A. Turyn, *The Byzantine MS Tradition of the Tragedies of Euripides* (1957); W. J. W. Koster, *Autour d'un manuscrit d'Aristophane* (1957).

57. For the *Iliad* see *Homeri Ilias*, i. 248 ff.; for the *Odyssey*, BSR, v. 63–5.

58. Critical questions are discussed in the commentaries on the *Odyssey* by W. B. Stanford (1947–8) and by J. Bérard, H. Goube and R. Langumier (1952), though neither edition is strictly a critical one.

CHAPTER 7

THE HOMERIC QUESTION

by J. A. Davison

Die Geschichte des Epos, das ist die homerische Frage. — WILAMOWITZ

Œuvres d'art, ces mondes à la fois achevés et inachevés. — JEAN WAHL

THE Homeric question is primarily concerned with the composition, authorship, and date of the *Iliad* and the *Odyssey.*[a] It is not possible to attain to certainty on any of these matters, because the external evidence is mostly vague and unreliable and the internal evidence is obscure and contradictory. Since so much depends on a proper understanding of the ancient evidence, it seems advisable to begin this article with as full an account as possible of the views which were held about the Homeric question in antiquity.

In the earliest period, down to the middle of the fifth century B.C., we must distinguish three main classes of references to Homer : (i) those in which he is named, (ii) those in which he is not named, and the Homeric connection is a matter of inference, and (iii) an intermediate class in which the reference is to 'a man of Chios'. In the first class, we have to make a further distinction between references of which the original wording is known, and those which are reported indirectly. Apart from two passages ascribed to Hesiod (*Certamen*, 213-14 Allen; fr. 265 Rzach), both of doubtful authenticity, direct references begin in the late sixth century with Xenophanes (frs. 9, 10 Diehl) and Simonides (fr. 32 Diehl) ; the indirect references begin with Archilochus (Homer composed the *Margites* — fr. 153 Bergk), include possible allusions by Callinus (Homer composed the *Thebais* — fr. 6 Bergk) [1] and Stesichorus (Homer on Helen — fr. 32 Bergk),[2] and become frequent in the late sixth and early fifth centuries. In the first half of the fifth century the references, both direct and indirect, in Pindar are of special importance.

The second main class of references also has to be subdivided, into (*a*) apparent quotations or adaptations of Homeric words and phrases, such as Alcman's borrowings from an *Odyssey* (frs. 16, 38, 39, 46, 80, 82, 106 Diehl) or the adaptation of *Iliad* xxii. 66-76 by Tyrtaeus (fr. 7. 21-30 Diehl), and (*b*) allusions to the subject-matter of the *Iliad* or *Odyssey*, whether in literature (*e.g.*, Alcman on Paris, fr. 73 Diehl) or in art (whether the persons represented are named, as in the Rhodian plate with ΜΕΝΕΛΑΣ

[a] On composition see also Ch. 3.

fighting EKTOP over the body of EYΦOPBOΣ (Pl. 28), or not, as in the
proto-Attic 'Ram Jug' ³ (Fig. 2).   As will be argued below, most of these
alleged references have little or no evidential value when taken separately ;
but when taken together and combined with the references to Homer
by name they create a strong impression that for the Greeks of the period
down to about 450 B.C. Homer was a real person who had lived at latest
in the early seventh century and had composed a large number of narrative poems of the highest quality which were still being recited by professional rhapsodes, and especially by a group of people who lived in

FIG. 2. The escape from Polyphemus : from a jug from Aegina, early 7th cent. B.C.

Chios and called themselves *Homeridae*, thus claiming to be the poet's
descendants.

This connection with Chios (first in Acusilaus, *FGH*, 2 F 2) gives
relevance to the references to 'a man of Chios' mentioned above.   There
are two of these: the famous passage in the *Hymn to Apollo* (169-73 ;
Thucydides iii. 104. 5 quotes it as a reference by Homer to himself) about
the blind man of Chios, and the probably fifth-century poem quoted by
Stobaeus (iv. 34. 28) and now included among the fragments of Semonides
(29 Diehl).⁴

By the early fifth century several different cities were already claiming
to have been Homer's birthplace, and conflicting accounts of his pedigree
were no doubt current ; we need not doubt Tatian's statement (*adv.
Graec.* 31) that a certain Theagenes of Rhegium, a contemporary of
Cambyses (*d.* 522), had found it worth while to write about the poetry,

pedigree, and date of Homer. The surviving fragments of Theagenes (collected by Diels-Kranz, *Fragmente der Vorsokratiker*, i, No. 8) tell us nothing of his views upon the Homeric question in the strict sense; for us, this branch of Homeric scholarship begins almost a century later in Herodotus's *History*. Herodotus, himself the nephew of a practising epic poet,[5] tackles the Homeric question from four points of view: Homer's date, his relation to other poets, his works, and the value of his poems as historical evidence.

On Homer's date, Herodotus professes to put forward new conclusions of his own: Homer lived not more than four hundred years ago (ii. 53. 2). At three generations to the century (*cf.* ii. 142. 2) this is equivalent to twelve generations, which is well within what Herodotus seems to regard as the historical period (Hecataeus, like Heropythus,[6] had fourteen human — that is, recorded — ancestors). Thucydides does not comment on Herodotus's view, except indirectly, by stating (i. 3. 3) that Homer lived long after the Trojan war. Secondly, Herodotus regarded Homer and Hesiod as contemporaries (ii. 53. 2), differing in this, it appears, from Xenophanes, who put Homer before Hesiod, and from others unspecified, who regarded Hesiod as the older (Xenoph. B 13 Diels-Kranz). In his opinion, too, the other poets who are said to be older than Homer and Hesiod were in fact more recent; and this may be taken as polemic against those who derived Homer's pedigree from Orpheus (*e.g.*, Pherecydes, Hellanicus, and Damastes — *FGH*, 3 F 167) or Musaeus (*e.g.*, Gorgias — Procl. 24 Severyns).[7] Thirdly, Herodotus is not only the first ancient author to mention the *Iliad* and *Odyssey* (ii. 116. 2, 4, iv. 29) by name as works of Homer; he argues in ii. 116–17 that the contradictions between the *Cypria* and the *Iliad* and *Odyssey* prove that the *Cypria* cannot be by Homer, and his doubts about the Homeric canon extend also to the *Epigonoi* (iv. 32). We cannot trace the development of this line of thought, apart from the possibility that the historian Hellanicus ascribed the *Little Iliad* to the Lacedaemonian Cinaetho (Schol. Eur. *Tro.* 822) [8]; it is certain only that by the latter part of the fourth century the *Iliad* and *Odyssey* alone of the major poems were still regarded as Homeric, and we do not know when the practice of assigning the rejected epics to such dim figures as Arctinus, Lesches, and Stasinus began. (Herodotus had certainly never heard of them, and it is very doubtful if they were known to Aristotle.) [9]

Herodotus's low opinion of Homer as a historical authority, implicit in the first chapters of his history, becomes explicit in his discussion of the Trojan war (ii. 113–18): Homer knew what had really happened to Helen in Egypt, but he preferred his own version as more suitable for epic poetry (116. 1). Thucydides agrees with Herodotus in finding Homer untrustworthy (i. 9. 4, 10. 3, ii. 41. 4). Otherwise, the study of

Homer in the fifth century seems to have been concerned mainly with details of interpretation (especially the meanings of difficult words) [10] and with the morality of the poems, the defenders of which seem to have found in allegory their best recourse. This sort of scholarship was practised not only by the philosophers and sophists, but also by the professional rhapsodes (of whose methods Plato gives us a perhaps not entirely fair picture in the *Ion*) ; both the linguistic and the moralizing-allegorical types of scholarship had an important influence on later Homeric studies, but do not concern the Homeric question directly.

The latter years of the fifth century were marked by a great revolution in the relations between Greek authors and their public — the spread of private reading as a pastime (first mentioned, it seems, in a fragment of Euripides's *Erechtheus* — 370 Nauck [2] — of about 424 B.C.), and the consequent development of an organized book-trade (first mentioned in the later Old Comedy; earliest datable reference Aristophanes's *Birds* 1288 of 414 B.C.). To the introduction of private reading we may ascribe not only the first appearance of texts of Homer ascribed to individuals (the so-called ἐκδόσεις κατ' ἄνδρα) such as the poet Antimachus and the younger Euripides, nephew of the tragedian, but also the appearance in the fourth century of a new kind of Homeric scholarship, which deals with the tradition of the text and the details of the narrative.

To the question 'How did the Homeric poems reach mainland Greece from Ionia ?' we have two fourth-century answers. One view is that the Spartan lawgiver Lycurgus had become acquainted with the poems during his travels (Ephorus even said that he had met Homer in Chios — Strabo x. 480-2) and had brought copies home to Sparta (Plutarch, *Lycurgus*, iv. 3-4, the source of which was apparently Heracleides Ponticus, *cf.* Aristotle fr. 611. 10 Rose) ; the other is that Hipparchus, son of the tyrant Peisistratus, was the first to bring the Homeric poems to Attica ([Plat.] *Hipparch.* 228 B). Neither story can be accepted at its face value, but they are not inconsistent, and each has something to be said for it : on the one hand, Laconian art and literature testify that epic poems were known in seventh-century Sparta, and on the other the study of sixth-century Attica art has shown that acquaintance with the *Iliad* at least came late to Athens.[11] Besides, the report about Hipparchus is coupled with the statement that he compelled the rhapsodes at the Panathenaea to recite Homer's poems 'according to the cues (ἐξ ὑπολήψεως), in order, as they do to this day'. The special position enjoyed by Homer at the Panathenaea in the fourth century is confirmed by the orator Lycurgus, speaking in 332 (*in Leocr.* 102) ; it is not surprising that he ascribes the law to 'your fathers' (ὑμῶν οἱ πατέρες) and not to a tyrant, but the vague phrase makes it impossible to be sure that Lycurgus believed the Panathenaic rule to be as old as the sixth century.[12] Nor does Diogenes Laertius's ascription to Solon (i. 57) of a decree that the works of Homer should be recited 'ἐξ ὑποβολῆς, that is to say that the second singer should begin where the first left off', fully confirm the sixth-century origin of the Panathenaic rule, since even if Diogenes here reports his authority accurately (which is far from certain), any ancient law may be ascribed to 'Solon'. We may, however, draw certain inferences from the report in the *Hipparchus*: (i) that there was something special about the Panathenaic rule, which suggests that at other rhapsodic contests competitors were free to select their own episode and handle it in their own way; (ii) that at the Panathenaea there was a prescribed text to which the competitors had to conform. This prescribed text could only have been imposed if it enjoyed a considerable degree of authority; and this authority may have been derived either from the literary merits of the text (as is suggested by Lycurgus), or from the source from which it had been obtained, or from a combination of both. When these inferences are combined with the archaeological evidence for the late appearance of the *Iliad* at Athens, and with the report (Schol. Pind. *Nem.* 2. 1 c Drachmann) that Cynaethus of Chios first recited Homer's poems in Syracuse in the 69th Olympiad (504/0),[13] it becomes probable that the institution of the Panathenaic rule was due to the introduction of the *Iliad*, and perhaps of our *Odyssey* as well, into Athens (these are the only poems in the pre-Herodotean Homeric canon which, so far as we can now tell, are at all likely to have given rise to such a rule), and that the arrival of the *Iliad* in Athens is to be dated to the latter part of the sixth century B.C., perhaps as part of a Peisistratid reorganization of the Panathenaea. In that case, both in the *Hipparchus* and in the scholiast to Pindar 'the poems of Homer' must be understood in fourth-century terms, and limited to works which were still included in the Homeric canon in that century, and not in the wider sense in which the sixth or early fifth century would have understood them.

The problem of the Panathenaic rule required a fairly full discussion because it seems that the ascription of it in the fourth century to a Peisistratid may have combined with later allegations of Peisistratid interpolations in the text of Homer to give rise in the Hellenistic age to the belief in the 'Peisistratean recension' of Homer, which had a far-reaching influence upon the *communis opinio* of educated men in the Roman world, and through them upon modern Homeric scholarship. We are thus brought to the second of the suggested fourth-century innovations in Homeric scholarship, the inquiry into the internal consistency of the Homeric text. This problem scarcely arises when men owe their acquaintance with literature to recitations and public readings; only when they have the text in their hands and can read it reflectively do they begin to perceive inconsistencies in the narrative. So far as we know, the first critic of Homer to make a real study of these inconsistencies was Zoilus of Amphipolis,[14] who was known as 'the scourge of Homer' from the violence of his criticisms, and who was doubtless the source of many of the cavils against Homer's narrative technique to which Aristotle replied in his Ἀπορήματα Ὁμηρικά.[15] A special feature of the inquiry into the internal consistency of Homer, the attack on the reliability of the Athenian text, seems to have been mainly due to historical and political motives, especially Megarian irredentism in reference to Salamis. Plutarch's life of Theseus (xx. 1) tells us that Hereas (a Megarian historian — FGH, No. 486) accused Peisistratus of omitting a line discreditable to Theseus from the text of Hesiod (Catal. fr. 47 Traversa), and of inserting a reference to Theseus into the Odyssey (λ 631). Diogenes Laertius (i. 57) seems to suggest that Dieuchidas (FGH, No. 485, cf. CQ, n.s. ix. 216-22) accused Peisistratus of foisting lines in praise of the Athenians into the Catalogue of Ships (B 546 καὶ τὰ ἑξῆς — presumably down to 558). The praise of the Athenians in these lines is certainly inconsistent with the undistinguished part played by them in the rest of the Iliad, but this is not by itself a very forcible argument against the text (and need not in any case concern Peisistratus). The ulterior motive of Megarian attacks on the Athenian text (and especially on the Catalogue) is made clear by Aristotle (Rhet. i. 1375 b 30), who tells us that the Athenians quoted the Catalogue (our next earliest authority, Strabo ix. 394, tells us that the lines were B 557-8) to prove that they had a better right to Salamis than the Megarians.[16] Strabo reports that some ascribed the interpolation to Solon (so πολλοί, according to Plut. Solon x. 1; ἔνιοι, according to Diog. Laert. i. 48; τινές, according to Schol. B on B 557), and others to Peisistratus. It would be almost superfluous to point out here that there is no question so far of a sixth-century Athenian 'recension' or 'redaction' of the text of Homer or Hesiod (the alleged interpolations are trivial in extent, and do not imply any serious editorial activity),[17] were it not that these very passages are still being used as evidence for a Peisistratean recension of Homer.[18]

Plato's Homeric criticism, being concerned mainly with the morality of the poems, is not relevant here, except in so far as it emphasizes the literary charm of the Homeric poems; and in view of the often captious criticisms of Zoilus and his successors, it is well to stress Plato's judgement of Homer's charm as reinforcing the judgement of Aristotle upon the Iliad and Odyssey as literature. Aristotle's preliminary studies are known to us only from fragments (see note 15); but his final judgement is preserved in the Poetic: the Iliad and Odyssey are as well composed as possible and are as nearly as possible the representation of a single action (1462 b 11). With this judgement in mind, echoed as it is by the opinion of the Alexandrian poets, and especially by Theocritus's words about the uselessness of attempts to rival the Chian singer (vii. 47-8, and see

Gow's note), it is not hard to see why attempts such as that which won for Xenon and Hellanicus the name of 'separators' (χωρίζοντες),[19] to push farther the analytical criticism of the Homeric canon by excluding the *Odyssey* from it (Procl. 102. 2-3 Allen), fell upon stony ground at Alexandria. Here Homer was all but universally accepted as the author of both the *Iliad* and the *Odyssey*; and the aim of the great Alexandrian scholars was to produce texts of the two poems which should be worthy of the poet's fame. This involved a careful study of all the attacks which had been made on Homer's text, whether for immorality or for bad logic, and it is not to be wondered at that these critics sometimes mistook their moral or aesthetic prejudices or their difficulties in interpreting Homer's words for arguments against the genuineness of a passage in the text which lay before them.[20] Even when Aristarchus had succeeded in establishing a text which later scholars generally accepted as authoritative, there remained a great many points which were hard to reconcile with the fundamental conception of Homer as a great poet, and many lines had to be 'athetized' (*i.e.*, retained in the text, but marked as for one reason or another difficult to explain). Of these athetized lines, those which seemed to be inconsistent either with their context or with other parts of the *Iliad* or *Odyssey* are of special importance in the study of the Homeric question; next come the lines which are inconsistent with references to the same transactions in the νεώτεροι (Aristarchus's study of whom has been shown to be of importance for our understanding of the relation of the *Iliad* and *Odyssey* to the cyclic poems)[21]; and thirdly, the repeated lines, which Aristarchus marked with a special symbol. Aristarchus dated Homer to the time of the Ionian colonization, which he put 140 years after the Trojan war (Procl. 101. 14, *Vit.* ii. 16-20 Allen), and expressed the view that Homer was an Athenian (the great grammarian Dionysius Thrax agreed with him — *Vit.* ii. 13, v. 7-8 Allen).

By the time of Aristarchus and Dionysius Alexandria was no longer the only centre of scholarship in the Greek world; Pergamum was its rival, and the rivalry often led to contradiction. Aristarchus having argued that Homer was an Athenian, and Attic influence being evident in the language of the second-century Alexandrian text of Homer, it would not be surprising if some Pergamene scholar revived the earlier attacks on the reliability of the Athenian text; and though the first evidence for the new attack is to be found in Cicero, who says of Peisistratus (*de Orat.* iii. 34. 137) *primus Homeri libros confusos antea sic disposuisse dicitur ut nunc habemus*, it seems to be now accepted that it originated with Asclepiades of Myrlea, who was active in Pergamum in the late second or early first century B.C.[22] Later references to this story, whether derived from Cicero or his source, are numerous (they are printed in full by Merkelbach, *op. cit.*), but only two are worth mentioning here : a scholiast on K 1 says that Peisistratus inserted the *Doloneia* into the *Iliad* when he was putting it together (this I believe to be the only specific example alleged in any ancient source of Peisistratus's editorial activities), and Aelian characteristically tries to reconcile the story about Lycurgus with that about Peisistratus, by saying (*Var. Hist.* xiii. 14) that Lycurgus imported the poems into Greece and that Peisistratus made the *Iliad* and *Odyssey* out of them.   Modern believers in the Peisistratean recension follow Wolf in combining with the passages which mention Peisistratus a remark by Josephus (*c. Apion.* i. 2. 12) : 'they say that not even Homer left his poems behind in writing, but that they were transmitted by memorization, and put together (later) out of the songs, and that they therefore contain many inconsistencies [διαφωνίαι]'.   In fact, this reference is on quite a different intellectual level from Aelian's lucubrations ; Josephus, like Horace, goes back in thought to the great Alexandrians, who had already pointed out most of the διαφωνίαι which bulk so large in modern Homeric criticism ; but whereas Horace finds these inconsistencies merely irritating evidence that even Homer can nod (*A.P.* 351-9), Josephus employs them for a serious controversial purpose, as helping to prove the superiority of Hebrew literature and civilization to those of Greece.   It should, however, be noted that Josephus is not here writing as an historian ; nor (*pace* Merkelbach) does he mention Peisistratus in this connection.

This survey of Homeric scholarship in ancient times may end by noting that not all the inconsistencies which had been pointed out by Zoilus and his successors could shake the faith of antiquity in the artistic unity and high quality of the Homeric poems, or in the historical reality of Homer.   The works of the great literary critics of the Augustan and later periods (*e.g.*, the treatise *On the Sublime* or Quintilian's sketch of Greek literature) are imbued with the same conviction on these points as informs the poor remnants of the great age of ancient scholarship which have been preserved in the lives of Homer, in the ancient commentaries and reference-books, in the Byzantine scholia, and in the works of such academic Robinson Crusoes as the patriarch Photius in the ninth century A.D., the compiler of the *Suda* (formerly known as Suidas) in the tenth, and the archbishop Eustathius of Thessalonica [23] in the twelfth.

We are now in a better position to understand the materials which were available to the first scholars who, in modern times, took up again the Homeric question, and which still have to be combined with the evidence obtained from more recently discovered sources of information.[24]   Thanks to such works as the *Ilias Latina* and those ascribed to Dares the Phrygian and Dictys the Cretan, and to references to him in Latin writers, Homer had continued to enjoy a great reputation in the

West during the almost Greekless Middle Ages; but his works were unknown to the Latins until the late fourteenth century, when Boccaccio, who had learned Greek from the Calabrian Leontius Pilatus, encouraged his master to produce Latin versions of the *Iliad* and *Odyssey*. Through Boccaccio these versions, together with a copy of the Greek text, reached Petrarch, who was engaged in annotating the Latin *Odyssey* when he died in 1374. Pilatus's versions were superseded in the fifteenth century by those of Lorenzo Valla (1407–57); and at about the same time the first translations of Homer into modern languages began to be made, although the great age of the translators did not begin until after the appearance of the first printed edition of Homer in 1488. Homer at once took his place as the leading Greek author in the new classical curriculum of the Renaissance,[25] and was assigned much the same primacy in the neo-classical literary criticism of the sixteenth and seventeenth centuries as he had enjoyed in the literary criticism of antiquity; if his authority was ever challenged by the neo-classicists, as it was by Vida and J. C. Scaliger, it was only in order to put Virgil upon the pedestal from which Homer had been pulled down.

On the other hand, the Renaissance was a great age of intellectual nationalism, in which strong arguments were put forward for the development of vernacular literatures untrammelled by the devotion to classical models recommended by the neo-classicists. The attack on neo-classicism was especially strong in France, where Joachim du Bellay had nailed the neo-classical colours to the masthead in his *Défense et illustration de la langue française* (1549), and led to the great literary controversy of the seventeenth century which is known as the 'quarrel of the ancients and the moderns'.[26] In this dispute attacks upon Homer naturally played an important part, and in the earlier stages of the controversy some of the most violent attacks were made by François Hédelin, abbé d'Aubignac (1604–76).[27] D'Aubignac had quarrelled furiously with Corneille and the supporters of classicism in the theatre, and had failed of election to the Academy; he therefore established his own 'Académie de M. l'abbé d'Aubignac', which enjoyed a considerable vogue among the modernists. In 1664 d'Aubignac delivered before this academy his *Conjectures académiques ou dissertation sur l'Iliade*, in which he attacked the Homeric poems for bad morality, bad taste, bad style, and inconsistencies in the conduct of the narrative, from all of which, combined with the ancient reports of Homer's illiteracy, he concluded that there had never been such a person as Homer, and that the *Iliad* and *Odyssey* were the patchwork creations of a late and incompetent editor.

Neither in France nor in England did the professional scholars take much interest in the dispute about Homer.[28] Compared with the dramatists, for example, the text of Homer seemed to be in a reasonably

good state, and the main difficulties of interpretation had apparently
been solved by the various ancient lexica, by Eustathius's commentary
(*editio princeps* by N. Maiorano, 1542–50), and by such scholia as had so
far become known, namely the so-called Didymus scholia, first published
by J. Lascaris in 1517, the Genevan scholia used by H. Estienne in his
Poetae Graeci principes heroici carminis of 1566,[29] and the so-called 'scholia
Aloysii Alamanni' (Alamanni was a Florentine poet and literary man of
the early sixteenth century; his scholia were copied from a MS. now in
the Vatican — Vat. graec. 2193), first published in 1689.[30] The historical
difficulties too seemed to have been solved by the *communis opinio* of late
antiquity (and it should not be forgotten that the scholars of the late
seventeenth and eighteenth centuries had a far more intimate acquaintance
with the late grammarians and lexicographers than is common to-day).
So Bentley may be taken to have expressed the consensus of scholarly
opinion in his own day when in 1713 he somewhat pontifically observed
in his *Remarks upon a late Discourse of Free-thinking* (vii; *Works*, ed. A.
Dyce, 1838, iii. 304): 'To prove Homer's universal knowledge *a priori*,
our author [*sc.* of the *Discourse*] says, *He designed his poems for eternity, to
please and instruct mankind.* Admirable again: *eternity* and *mankind*:
nothing less than all ages and all nations were in the poet's foresight.
Though our author vouches that he *thinks every day de quolibet ente*, give
me leave to except Homer; for he seems never to have thought of him
or his history. Take my word for it, poor Homer, in those circumstances
and early times, had never such aspiring thoughts. He wrote a sequel of
songs and rhapsodies, to be sung by himself for small earnings and good
cheer at festivals and other days of merriment; the *Ilias* he made for the
men, and the *Odysseis* for the other sex. These loose songs were not
collected together in the form of an epic poem till Pisistratus's time,
above ['about' — 1713 edition] 500 years after.' The debate upon the
artistic and literary merits of the *Iliad* and *Odyssey* was mainly carried on
by the literary men, especially Dryden and Addison, who, following the
more reasonable among the French literary critics, explained Homer's
divergences from modern taste and customs by appealing to history.
So when d'Aubignac's *Conjectures* were finally published in 1715 (almost
forty years after his death, such was the reluctance of even the most
advanced modernists among the French *savants* even to seem to sponsor
his nihilistic views), little notice was taken of them in France, and they
were not translated into English, as most of the works dealing with the
'Querelle' had been, and as the much less important *Dissertation critique
sur l'Iliade d'Homère* of Jean Terrasson was soon to be.[31]

Bentley's discovery that many difficulties in the scansion of the
Homeric hexameter could be removed by the assumption that certain
words had originally been spelled with the digamma was more influential

S

for the future of the Homeric question than his views about the date and composition of the *Iliad* and *Odyssey*. The date at which he made the discovery is not known, but Monk in the second (1833) edition of his life of Bentley (ii. 363) says that there is a hint of it in the *marginalia* to Bentley's copy of Collins's *Discourse of Free-thinking*, which suggests that he had had an inkling of it by 1713 (Barnes's edition of the *Iliad* had appeared in 1711 and had stimulated interest in Homeric scholarship); but Bentley's plan to edit the *Iliad* was not formed until 1726, and the digamma first appeared in print in 1732. Scoffed at in the discoverer's life-time (especially by Pope in the *Dunciad*), the digamma had to await the creation of a really scientific philology before it could be given its due weight in the development of the Homeric dialect and in the history of Homer's text.

In 1735 [32] Thomas Blackwell (the younger), Regius Professor of Greek and Principal of Marischal College at Aberdeen, published anonymously the first modern book by a professional scholar which is entirely devoted to Homer, under the title *An enquiry into the life and writings of Homer*. The popularity of this work (in spite of a devastatingly accurate judgement of it ascribed to Bentley) [33] is attested by the fact that a second edition was called for in 1736 and by Blackwell's publication in 1748 of a volume containing English translations of the many passages from ancient authors which he had quoted in the *Enquiry*. Blackwell set out to show that there was nothing supernatural about Homer's pre-eminence as a poet, but that the virtues of his poetry derived solely from the fact that he had been born into a state of society for which his poetic gifts were uniquely fitted. Blackwell discussed in considerable detail, and with a full mastery of the literary evidence available to him, the conditions under which Homer, the primitive bard, must be presumed to have worked; and alike through his book and through his teaching at Aberdeen he had a great influence upon the study of primitive literatures, not only in Great Britain (where he undoubtedly helped to pave the way for Macpherson's *Ossian*) but also abroad, and especially in Germany, where his work aroused the enthusiasm of Herder and Heyne

It was at least partly under Blackwell's influence [34] that the next major contribution to Homeric scholarship came to birth. Robert Wood (1717 ?–71) had in the fifties made a journey to Syria with two friends to study, on behalf of the Society of Dilettanti, the ruins of Baalbek and Palmyra; and he had taken the opportunity to study the poems of Homer in the areas where, he concluded from the internal evidence Homer must have lived and travelled, and in the places of which he wrote. Wood's duties in the Foreign Office, of which he became Under Secretary, prevented him from writing down the results of his inquiries into the history and geography of the Homeric poems until after 1763 a few very imperfect copies of his work were printed for private circulation in 1767, and it was not until 1769 that the official first edition of his *Essay on the Original Genius and Writings of Homer* appeared.[35] In this essay Wood not only discussed the geographical, historical, and social background of the poems (throwing in a damaging examination of Pope's translations), but argued strongly, though apparently without knowledge of d'Aubignac's work,[36] that Homer had been ignorant of writing, and that his works had been preserved for a considerable time by the use of memory. Wood's vivid descriptions, both geographical and social, his frequent appeals to the continuing practice of Near Eastern peoples, and his straightforward and charming style, made a great impression upon those who saw his work, and nowhere more than in Göttingen, where C. G. Heyne praised it highly in a review published in 1770, and encouraged C. F. Michaelis to translate it into German.[37] The work is interesting in itself, as the first of many attempts to bring geography and history to bear upon the elucidation of the Homeric problem, and it had a great influence upon the important school of Homeric studies which Heyne had created in Göttingen, and hence upon F. A. Wolf.

Like so many of the great English students of Homer, Wood was not a professional scholar; and it is probable that his work would have been less influential, had it not been complemented by the discovery in 1779 of the two Homer manuscripts in the Marcian Library at Venice (the *Veneti Marciani* 454 and 453, now known respectively as A and B).[a] Both have scholia, those of A being of unique value for the information which they give about the editorial work of Aristarchus and other scholars. The text of A, together with the scholia from both MSS., was published in 1788 by the French scholar, J. B. G. d'Ansse de Villoison.[38] The discovery of these MSS., and particularly of A, which not only contains the earliest complete text of the *Iliad* but also varies in many respects from the text known from other MSS., made a new critical edition of the *Iliad* imperative; and the scholia provided a new basis for the evaluation of the traditions about Homer and his methods of composition. Wolf had already expressed his agreement with Wood's theory of an illiterate Homer before Villoison's work appeared; and in reviewing Villoison in 1791 he asserted that the text and scholia of A proved that the Homeric poems had long been preserved by memory alone.

In 1795 Wolf published the first part of the introduction to his edition of Homer, under the title *Prolegomena ad Homerum I.* (Part II, which should have dealt with textual criticism, never appeared.) In this he argued that the Homeric poems had been composed orally about 950 B.C., when the Greeks were still unacquainted with writing, at any rate for

[a] For A see Pl. 5.

literary purposes, and handed down for about four centuries by oral recitation, during which period they had undergone many changes, some deliberate, some accidental; that after the poems had been written down they had been deliberately edited by people who wished to bring them more into harmony with the ideas of their own times about style and subject-matter; that in their present form both the *Iliad* and the *Odyssey* have an artistic unity, the *Odyssey* to an even higher degree than the *Iliad*; that this unity results from the work of the editors after the poems had been written down; and that, though most of the original poems out of which the *Iliad* and *Odyssey* were finally created should be ascribed to Homer himself, some at least were composed after his time by the Homeridae, following the lines which he had himself laid down.

Previous expressions of doubt about the authenticity of the Homeric poems had been passed over, either as mere *obiter dicta* or as the work of amateurs; but Wolf's closely reasoned and highly professional argument could not be so easily disregarded. The earliest reactions were violent, and bore an understandable resemblance to the letters which appear in *The Times* when the National Gallery exhibits a newly cleaned picture. Men's minds could not easily adjust themselves to the new light which had been so suddenly thrown on a familiar object; but in fact Wolf, by admitting the high artistic quality of the *Iliad*, and above all of the *Odyssey*, had met the most serious objection which could be brought against his theory, and it is scarcely too much to say that every serious attempt to grapple with the Homeric problem since 1795 has been forced to accept Wolf's essential conception of the *Iliad* and *Odyssey* as the products of evolution. Recognition of this fundamental fact has at times been hindered by the misleading classification of theories of the creation of the Homeric poems as either 'unitarian' or 'analytical', and especially by the use of the term 'unitarian' to include not only the always small and now almost non-existent band of fundamentalists (who believe that Homer evolved the *Iliad* and *Odyssey* from his inner consciousness), but also two different types of evolutionist: those who put 'Homer' about mid-way in the evolution of the poems and believe that his original conceptions have been marred by later interpolations on a considerable scale (these people we may call 'interpolationists'), and those who believe that the *Iliad* and *Odyssey* in substantially their modern form are themselves artistic unities and the culmination of the evolutionary process, whether they believe that the poems are both by the same author or not (for this last class I shall use the term invented by Professor Kakridis of Salonica, and call them 'neo-analysts'). This last term, clumsy though it may seem, has the technical merit of reminding its user that even a belief that both the *Iliad* and *Odyssey* are the work of a single 'Homer' may (and nowadays must) rest upon an analytical view of the poems.

The upshot of this is that all theories of the origin of the Homeric poems have now to be classified in two ways, according to the theorist's opinion of the aesthetic merits or demerits of the poems as we now have them, and according to the point in the evolution of the poems at which the theorist puts 'Homer'.

For most critics, 'Homer' stands at the point of greatest artistic merit in the evolution of the poems; but Wolf's theory is as peculiar in this respect, as (in their very different ways) are those of Lachmann, C. Robert, and Gilbert Murray, since he stresses the literary value of the poems in their present form, and yet puts 'Homer' at the beginning of the evolution; Homer, he says, began the weaving of the web, but others completed it. The consequences of Wolf's view were worked out to some extent by Heyne in his *Bemerkungen zum 24. Gesang der Ilias* (1802, in which year he also published his great edition of Homer, in which the so-called T Scholia [39] were first used). Heyne laid great stress on the wrath of Achilles as the clue to the pattern on which the Homeridae and their successors had built up the *Iliad*, and he suggested early Ionic lays as the source from which they had obtained their materials. Heyne thus became the chief of the 'lay-hunters' (*Liederjäger*), to whom the romantic terminology of the period opposed the 'unity-herdsmen' (*Einheitshirten*). The second class included not only the fundamentalists (mostly literary men with little knowledge of the scholarly questions involved), but also the interpolationists, of whom Richard Payne Knight may stand as an example, and at least one fore-runner of the neo-analysts in G. W. Nitzsch (on whom see note 44, below). Payne Knight's edition of the Homeric poems, published in 1820, is primarily an attempt to reconstruct the orthography of Homer, and secondarily an attempt to restore the unity of Homer's text by omitting as interpolations all such lines as seemed open to attack on linguistic or other grounds. Payne Knight's view of the importance of restoring the original orthography as an aid to understanding the text was sound in principle, and he made some true observations; but the evidence available to him was inadequate to support his attempt, and the same might well be said about his views on interpolation, were it not that he is still quoted as an authority on this point.[40]

The great battle between the *Liederjäger* and the *Einheitshirten* [41] was mainly fought, so far was any scholar in those days from doubting Wolf's judgement of the *Odyssey*, over the *Iliad*; and it was in the struggle to establish the true nature of the *Iliad* and its aesthetic value that most of the intellectual weapons were forged which are still employed by analysts of Homer. Perhaps the most influential of these was the principle of the inerrancy of great poets, on which most hostile analyses of the *Iliad* and *Odyssey* have since been based. Fallacious in itself, as the works of known great poets (above all Shakespeare) show, this principle has been rendered especially dangerous in Homeric studies by the confidence of most of its users in their ability to detect 'errors' in the Homeric texts. Composed at an unknown period, and in conditions and for purposes of which we know little, in a language which (it seems) the author himself did not always understand, the text of the Homeric poems would still present an almost impossible problem to the modern interpreter if he could be sure that the author was always working up to the highest standard which could be imposed upon him; but the problem is made even more difficult by the real nature of the Homeric poems as we have them, since they may fairly be described in words applied by Mr Michael Sadleir to the most Homeric of all nineteenth-century novelists, Anthony Trollope [42] : 'His work is often diffuse, straggling, wanting in elegance and finish; but when — as constantly — it is concerned to portray character, it shows a sort of second sense, an instinctive power of judging motive, a prescience of human inclinations' (137-8), or again, 'Trollope's novels . . . provide a sensual rather than an intellectual experience' (366). It is therefore not surprising that no two scholars analyse the Homeric poems alike, and that the more moderate critics seldom find difficulty in demonstrating the unreality of many of the objections urged by the extremists against the poetical value of the traditional text. But when all the unreal objections to the unity of the traditional text have been cleared away, there remain many anachronisms in language and in social customs, and inconsistencies in the narrative of the poems (whether internal, as between the *Catalogue of Ships* and the rest of the *Iliad*, or external, as between the *Iliad* and the *Odyssey*, or between Homeric and actual geography, as in the description of Ithaca), which have to be accounted for [a]; and it was in these early disputes between the *Lieder-jäger* and the *Einheitshirten* that most of them were pointed out, and attempts were made to account for them. Of these attempts, the most valuable were those which tried to give some account of the conditions and the purpose in and for which the Homeric poems might have been composed, and especially those which, starting from the extracts from Proclus's *Chrestomathy* preserved in the MS. A and in some others,[43] studied the cyclic poems and tried to build up some picture of the Greek epic poem in general. In this category, the principal names are those of W. Müller (*Homerische Vorschule*, 1824, ²1830), F. G. Welcker (*Der epische Cyclus oder die homerischen Dichter*, 1835–49), H. Düntzer (*Homer und der epische Kyklos*, 1839), and G. W. Nitzsch (*Meletemata de historia Homeri*, 1834–9).[44]

The early thirties saw two other important developments, the beginnings of Homeric papyrology with the publication in 1832 of the

---

[a] On all these topics see the relevant chapters of Part II.

Bankes papyrus (called after its discoverer, W. J. Bankes; it is now *P. Lond.* 114),[a] and the publication in 1835 of K. Lehrs's work on Aristarchus (*de Aristarchi studiis homericis*), which was the first of a long line of works which have combined with later discoveries of papyrus texts, both of the poems themselves and of commentaries, lexica, and paraphrases, to illuminate not only the methods of Alexandrine scholars but also the problems which confronted them.[b]

The use of the narrative literature of other races (and especially of the peoples of Northern Europe) as comparative material in the study of the conditions in which the Homeric poems had been composed led to the most serious attack which had yet been made upon the unity of the *Iliad*. Karl Lachmann (1793–1851) had applied the new analytical methods to the *Nibelungenlied*, which he had dissolved into a number of original 'lays', and, knowing that the Finnish national epic, the *Kalevala*, had been created out of a number of separate poems by the scholar-poet Lönnroth, he argued that the *Iliad* might have been created in a similar way. In two papers delivered before the Berlin Academy in 1837 and 1841, and published as *Betrachtungen über Homers Ilias* in 1847 (later editions 1865, 1874), he claimed to have identified eighteen separate and distinct lays, not necessarily by the same author, out of which our *Iliad* had been composed; of these the last two (our Books Ψ and Ω) were a later addition to the original *Iliad*, the composer of which was by no means a first-class poet.[45] Thus Lachmann found virtually no place for any poet who could be called 'Homer'. The full development of Lachmann's views was new when Grote began to work on the first volumes of his *History of Greece* (first edition 1846); in these he laid down the principle that there is no way of determining the relation of Greek heroic myths to historical reality, and in Part I (devoted to mythical Greece) he discussed the value of the various Greek epics as authorities for an account of mythical Greece (ch. xv) and devoted a long chapter (xx) to the Homeric poems as historical phenomena. Taking up a suggestion already made by G. Hermann ('De interpolationibus Homeri', *Opuscula*, v, 1832, 52 ff.), Grote argued that the *Iliad* was not, as Lachmann had suggested, the direct result of joining together short lays, but the expansion of a poem of considerable length (consisting of Books A, Θ, and Λ-X of our *Iliad*), which might be called the *Achilleid* and was the work of Homer, into our present *Iliad* by the insertion of Books B-H, I-K, and Ψ-Ω. Thus for Grote the evolution of the *Iliad* took place in three stages: the primitive lays, the truly Homeric period when the *Achilleis* and similar poems were being composed, and the post-Homeric period, to which our *Iliad* and *Odyssey* and the cyclic

---

[a] See Pl. 3.
[b] On Aristarchus and the Alexandrine editors see the preceding chapter.

epics belong. All these stages were complete, in Grote's view, before the time of Peisistratus, and he severely criticizes the believers in a Peisistratean recension.

Hermann had suggested that the evolution of the *Odyssey* might prove to have been similar to that of the *Iliad*; but this suggestion was not taken up until 1859, when A. Kirchhoff published the first edition of his *Odyssey* ([2] 1879, on which this account is based). He argued that the original *Odyssey* had contained only parts of Books α and ε, Books ζ-ι, and parts of Books λ and ν. To this a later hand had added the rest of Book ν and Books ξ and π-ψ, 296 (according to Aristarchus the end of the *Odyssey*), and had expanded the account of Odysseus's wanderings into something like the present form of Books ι-μ. Lastly came a reviser (*Bearbeiter*; here, as usually in German Homeric criticism, a term of abuse), who inserted an originally separate poem about Telemachus (the *Telemachy*), thus bringing Books α-δ and ο to their present form, added the rest of Book ψ and all Book ω, and made sundry minor insertions in the older parts of the poem. The last stage, Kirchhoff thought, was unknown to Eugammon when he wrote the *Telegony* (traditional date 568/4). Kirchhoff's arguments are not all subjective (he uses the discrepancies between manuscripts, and appeals to linguistic and other differences between the different parts of his text); but his main critical principle is the equivalence of 'old' and 'good', and much of his argument depends upon his belief that there is a decline in poetic quality from the high level of the original poem to the inartistic patch-work of the latest revision.

The result of the work of Grote, Kirchhoff, and the rest (whom we may classify as 'revisionists') was to establish it as an academic dogma, in the face of all non-academic experience since Pindar's time at least, that the *Iliad* and *Odyssey* as they stand are very poor poems, and that the shorter epics which the revisers had used as a foundation had conformed far more closely to the archetypal epic poem, and were alone worthy to be ascribed to 'Homer', even if they were in fact by different authors. So far there was little external evidence against which either the revisionists or the interpolationists could test their opinions as to the authenticity or otherwise of any suspected passage; and in the seventies the interest of Homeric scholars shifted either to the more or less historical study of the world described in the poems, including historical geography and social and cultural history, or to detailed study of the Homeric language. It is perhaps ironical that Heinrich Schliemann, who was to be the prime mover in the historical direction, was a complete fundamentalist; in 1870 his faith in the literal truth of the *Iliad* led him to begin excavating the mound of Hissarlik, which he had identified as the Homeric Troy, with the spectacular results which encouraged him to make trial excavations at Mycenae in 1874 and at Tiryns in 1876; his detailed excavations at Mycenae were begun in 1876, but Tiryns had to wait until 1884. Schliemann contributed little directly to the discussion of the Homeric question, but his indirect influence has been very great, and began to be exerted very soon. Though the appearance in 1871 of the first of E. Buchholz's three volumes on *Die homerischen Realien* may have been a coincidence, it is hardly doubtful that the publication by B. Niese in 1873 of the first serious study of the *Catalogue of Ships* as a historical document [46] was due to the interest in Homeric geography and history which Schliemann's discoveries had aroused. Homeric archaeology in the true sense was not created until W. Dörpfeld joined Schliemann in 1882; its first real monument is the first edition of W. Helbig's *Das homerische Epos aus den Denkmälern erläutert* (1884, [2] 1887), which long remained a standard reference book.[47] Grote's doctrine of the separation of mythical and historical Greece now began to be challenged, and the agreement between Schliemann's finds (especially in the matter of weapons) and many passages in the Homeric poems seemed to provide a conclusive test for distinguishing older passages in the poems from later accretions. On the linguistic side, the work of such scholars as Buttmann and Ahrens on the Greek dialects enabled younger scholars to throw light on the evolution of the Homeric language, and paved the way for August Fick's gallant, and often unfairly depreciated, attempt to reconstruct the original Aeolic *Odyssey* and *Iliad* (*Die homerische Odyssee*, 1883; *Ilias*, 1886). The results of the linguistic study of Homer were summed up and developed in D. B. Monro's *Grammar of the Homeric Dialect* (1882; the syntactical sections of the second edition, published in 1891, have not been completely superseded, even by P. Chantraine's *Grammaire homérique* II of 1953).[48]

After his work on the *Catalogue*, Niese extended his inquiries into the historical background of Homer to cover the general problem of the evolution of Homeric poetry (*Die Entwickelung der homerischen Poesie*, 1882); and it seems that disagreement with Niese's entirely fundamentalist views was one of the motives which inspired U. von Wilamowitz-Moellendorff (1848–1931) to write his *Homerische Untersuchungen* of 1884. The first part of this deals with the composition of the *Odyssey*, and the second with the history of the epic and its transmission. In the first part, Wilamowitz argues that our *Odyssey* (except for some even later interpolations) was put together by 'a not very gifted patch-worker' (*ein gering begabter Flickpoet* — p. 228), who lived in Old Greece not earlier than 650, and who used three poems as a basis for his work: (i) a poem on Odysseus's victory over the suitors, which had been composed a short while before by a poet who used (ii) the *Telemachy* (Books β–δ 619, o 80–π, parts of ρ–τ) and (iii) the 'elder *Odyssey*' (Books ε–ξ with other parts of ρ–τ. Of these (ii) and (iii) were Ionian, of much higher poetical quality than (i); and (iii) was already known to Archilochus and the author of the *Theogony*. The 'elder *Odyssey*' was itself a composite poem, in which three earlier poems were used: (1) and (2) on Odysseus's wanderings, of which (2) supplied his visits to the Lotus-eaters, Polyphemus, the underworld, and Calypso, and (3) on the recognition of Odysseus by Penelope (after which Odysseus killed the suitors). Of these, (1) and (3) originally belonged to longer poems which cannot now be reconstructed; (2) was complete in itself. From these three poems, together with additions from cyclic epics (*e.g.*, the *Nostoi*, *Cypria*, and *Little Iliad*) and out of his own head, an editor (*Redactor*) produced the 'elder *Odyssey*', and then came the *Bearbeiter*, who muddled together the 'elder *Odyssey*', the *Telemachy*, and the *Victory of Odysseus*, along with tasteless additions of his own, into a younger *Odyssey*, out of which later interpolators produced the *Odyssey* as we have it to-day.

In this first part Wilamowitz had distributed his censures on *Redactor*, *Bearbeiter*, and interpolators with a really staggering confidence alike in the linguistic, historical, and textual evidence for the date of given passages and in the soundness of his own judgement of their poetical value; but in the second part he handled the problems involved in the evolution and transmission of the Greek epics generally with a scholarship which makes the *Homerische Untersuchungen* still one of the indispensable works in any Homeric library, and his final chapter, entitled 'Retrospect and Prospect' (*Rückblick und Ausblick*), may stand as a classic statement of the Homeric problem as it appeared in 1884 to the most brilliant of the younger scholars of that day. Wilamowitz later revised (and somewhat simplified) his views of the evolution of the *Odyssey* (*Die Heimkehr des Odysseus*, 1927), but he never departed from his fundamentally revisionist view of our *Odyssey* as an incompetent patchwork, further deformed by later interpolations; and most of the studies of the *Odyssey* which have been published in Germany since 1884 [49] have followed more or less closely the pattern set by Wilamowitz, though they differ from him, and also from each other, in their views about the number of stages in the process, the number and lengths of the various older poems used, and the poetical value of given passages. But all agree that the *Bearbeiter* (usually known nowadays as 'B') was thoroughly incompetent and surpassed in stupidity only by the interpolators.

The nineties were mainly a period of consolidation and preparation for new advances [50]; the most important contribution to the discussion of the Homeric question was the first edition of Paul Cauer's summing-up of the various aspects of the problem, in his *Grundfragen der Homerkritik*

(1895; [2] 1909, [3] 1923). Of rather more than passing interest, partly for its later influence in Britain (especially on such popular works as T. E. Shaw's translation of the *Odyssey*), and partly for its interesting comments on the language and narrative technique of the poem, is Samuel Butler's *The Authoress of the Odyssey*, (1897, [2] 1922). So far as the *Iliad* is concerned, the Homeric scholarship of the nineteenth century is summed up in the second edition of Leaf's *Iliad*; his view of the evolution of the *Iliad* is essentially that of Grote, and his commentary remains indispensable.

In 1901 appeared what, so far as I know, is still the only book by a professional archaeologist which attempts to explain the composition of the *Iliad* systematically with the help of archaeological evidence. In his *Studien zur Ilias* C. Robert analysed the various types of armament used by the heroes, and argued that passages with 'Mycenaean' armament (large shield, no body-armour) must be older than those with 'Ionic' armament (round shield, breast-plate, greaves); this he combined with a linguistic argument, provided by F. Bechtel, about Aeolic and Ionic strata in the Homeric dialect, and by using these two scales produced an original *Iliad* of about 3000 lines in the Aeolic dialect and with Mycenaean armament, which had been expanded in three main stages, partly by the inclusion of eight separate poems (*e.g.*, the *aristeiai* of Aeneas and Diomede, the killing of Hector) and partly by the addition of specially composed episodes, into a really unified *Iliad*, of such a character that even a number of later additions (the *Catalogue of Ships*, the *supplicatio* in Z, Books K, N, Ψ, and Ω) served only to enhance its unitary character. Robert must therefore be classed as an interpolationist, but his recognition of the existing *Iliad* as an artistic whole of high quality puts him into a different category from the other interpolationists.

Not long after the publication of Robert's book, the influence of recent advances in anthropology, and especially of Frazer's *Golden Bough* (1890, [2] 1900), began to make itself felt in Homeric studies, at first through the new light which it seemed to throw on Greek religion (Jane Harrison's *Prolegomena* appeared first in 1903),[51] and then through Gilbert Murray's Harvard lectures on 'The Rise of the Greek Epic', first published in 1907 (later editions 1911, 1924, 1934). In this book, Murray used not only all the standard evolutionary arguments, but also arguments drawn from the higher criticism of the Bible, from the new Aegean archaeology, from papyrology and from anthropology, to prove that the *Iliad* and *Odyssey* were to be regarded as traditional books in much the same sense as the historical books of the Old Testament, and that they had been evolved by an almost unconscious process through the work of generations of rhapsodes and revisers (who were especially concerned to soften the barbarities of the original poems), and had indeed not taken their final form until the second century B.C. There is no room in this argument for any individual Homer; and, except for Murray's high opinion of the poetic quality of the existing *Iliad* and *Odyssey* (which he shares with Wolf, Grote and his followers, and Robert), his basic theory is as nihilistic as d'Aubignac's or Lachmann's.

Murray's demonstration of the logical conclusion to which both revisionism and interpolationism lead severely shocked his contemporaries, and it is not surprising that the first full-length reply came from a 'unitarian', the first since Nitzsch to take up a neo-analyst position. In 1910 D. Mülder published his *Die Ilias und ihre Quellen*, in which he set out to prove the following points: (1) the *Iliad* is a unitary poem, composed on a unified plan, (2) the many incontestable inconsistencies result from the peculiar task which a truly poetical personality has set itself, (3) the *Iliad* stands at the end, not the beginning, of a long literary evolution, (4) its sources are works produced during that evolution, (5) these sources were not 'lays' in the Lachmannian or any similar sense, (6) only a few of them had any connection with Troy, (7) the transference of these non-Trojan tales to a Trojan context formed a considerable part of the work involved in composing the *Iliad*, and (8) work of this kind could not result from accident (by which he seems to mean interpolation, especially of the kind postulated by Robert) or from organic development (where the reference is presumably to Murray) or from the work of a *Bearbeiter* — it demands a poet. Of these eight principles, only the first four and the last are essential to the theory,[52] and of these (1), (2), and (8) were anathema alike to the revisionists (whether they preferred the more complicated analyses of a Kirchhoff or Wilamowitz or simpler theories such as Grote's) and to the interpolationists, while (3) and (4) mortally offended the fundamentalists. The heavy attacks on Mülder by his contemporaries have tended to discredit him; and yet to-day it seems that his five essential principles pointed to an escape from the deadlock to which the conflicting views of scholars brought Homeric criticism in the first quarter of this century.

It is therefore convenient (and, I hope, legitimate) to consider Homeric scholarship since 1910 under six headings, derived from Mülder's principles.

I. The artistic unity of the poems has been proclaimed by almost every literary critic of importance since Aristotle, and is supported not only by the opinion of ordinary readers (a fact emphasized from different points of view by books such as E. Drerup's *Das Homerproblem in der Gegenwart* and J. A. Scott's *The Unity of Homer* of 1921, J. T. Sheppard's *The Pattern of the Iliad* of 1922, and A. Rüegg's *Kunst und Menschlichkeit Homers* of 1948), but also by recent researches into the composition of the poems, whether they deal with one or other poem as a whole, or with

problems of detail.[53]   As a result of these and other studies, a belief in
the unitary plan of the Homeric poems can now be firmly based upon
the evidence for design which both poems provide.

II. We have next to grapple with the problem of the inconsistencies
in language, equipment, religion, and social customs, as well as those in
the narrative.   To do this, it is essential to begin by studying the case for
the prosecution, as it is presented by the revisionists, among whom
Wilamowitz must take pride of place (*Die Ilias und Homer* of 1916 and
Die Heimkehr des Odysseus of 1927 are classics of Homeric scholarship),[54]
and the interpolationists, especially G. M. Bolling (*The External Evidence
for Interpolation in Homer* (1925), *The Athetized Lines of the Iliad* (1944),
Ilias Atheniensium (1950 — an attempt to reconstruct the Peisistratean
text)) and Miss H. L. Lorimer (*Homer and the Monuments* (1950)).   Many
of the counts in the indictment are unreal,[55] but even after all the un-
realities are removed, no amount of self-deception on the part of believers
in the unity of the poems can alter the fact that a serious case remains for
them to answer; and the question is whether it is possible to show that
these inconsistencies are compatible with the purpose for which the poem
was planned.[56]   In the sixth and fifth centuries, at least, the Homeric
poems were recited at periodical festivals by professional singers or
rhapsodes competing for prizes (Hdt. v. 67, Plat. *Ion*) ; and at Athens
these competitions were so regulated that the poems had to be recited
in sequence ([Plato] *Hipparch.* 228 B).   Earlier poetical competitions (not
necessarily for heroic poetry) are mentioned, both at festivals (Delos —
Hymn to Apollo 149-50) and at the funerals of great men (Chalcis — Hes.
W. & D. 654-9).[57]   It is thus at least possible that the Homeric poems
were originally composed for the purpose for which they were used in
historic times — to be the text for rhapsodes in a public competition.[58]
Only so, it seems, would it be possible to gather a continuing audience
for the minimum time which would be necessary for the performance of
a complete poem (with relays of reciters the *Iliad* would require three
full days, the *Odyssey* not much under three days).   In that case some,
at least, of the inconsistencies, especially those in the narrative, can be
explained as the sort of things which do occur in works intended for
popular entertainment [59] (ἀγωνίσματα ἐς τὸ παραχρῆμα ἀκούειν, in
Thucydides's terminology) — either the audience would not notice them
or would not care if they did, or they were what the audience expected
in tales of mediaeval chivalry.   That the poet should have admitted such
lapses may lower him in critical eyes; but no poet can be popular for
long who writes over his audience's head,[60] and in any case we must
allow for the dual nature of works of art.   The element of perfection in
the Homeric poems (Jean Wahl's 'monde achevé') is there for the person
who reads them at about the speed at which they were intended to be

performed (hence the importance of Ronsard's sonnet, referred to in note 25); the imperfections (the 'monde inachevé') become visible only when the poem is read slowly and dissected under the academic magnifying-glass. Other inconsistencies, especially those in language or equipment, are due to the nature of the epic language, which is the product of a long professional tradition and deals largely in formulae and similes [61]; the formulae especially tend to preserve many linguistic and cultural fossils, much in the same way as modern English preserves many forgotten quotations and dead metaphors.[a]

III. That the *Iliad* and *Odyssey* are the products of a long literary evolution is accepted to-day by every serious scholar, and since in them the evolution of the Greek epic poem may be said to have 'attained its nature', they may be regarded logically as the end of that evolution. The remote date at which the evolution must have begun is attested by the fossil forms in the epic language (Arcado-Cypriot and Aeolic words and forms; words which seem to be used in different, even contradictory, senses; irrelevant formulae; and so on),[b] by the metre,[c] by the persistence of Mycenaeanisms in armament, domestic equipment, social customs, and even (though less obviously) in religion,[d] by the allusions to a surprisingly wide range of myths, many going back into the Mycenaean period (or even earlier),[62] and by what we can learn from the poems themselves (and especially from the *Odyssey*) about professional bards, their training and their relations with their public, in what we may call 'pre-Homeric' times.[e] The 'Homeric' language then was not used, and the myths were not told, for the first time in the *Iliad* and *Odyssey*; and this has important consequences for any attempt to prove the early existence of our *Iliad* or *Odyssey* from incidental occurrences in early poems, and especially in elegy, of short phrases which also occur in the *Iliad* or *Odyssey*, or to prove the early existence of any particular epic poem from representations of its known subject-matter in early art. A short phrase, even a whole line, may be simply an epic formula [63]; a scene which seems to illustrate heroic life on a vase or brooch or shield-strap or comb, even if it can be identified with absolute certainty, need not necessarily illustrate any poem known to us — Phoenix in the *Iliad* (I 524-5) is our witness that the heroes who lived before Agamemnon had their *vates sacri*, whose works may well have been known to late Geometric artists.

IV. This leads us to the question of the sources of the *Iliad* and *Odyssey*; here again all the works of the evolutionists are relevant, and among them we may note especially C. Robert's attempt to establish

[a] On the formulaic style *cf.* Ch. 5, pp. 184-8.
[b] See Ch. 4.   [c] See Ch. 1, pp. 19-25.
[d] See Chs. 14-22.   [e] *Cf.* Ch. 5, pp. 182-4.

objective criteria by which the different strata in a poem can be distinguished. Internal evidence gives us some idea of the material on which 'Homer' worked; the *Odyssey* speaks several times of οἶμαι ('paths'), which are either collections of stories or longish continuous poems from which some part can be extracted, to be sung in hall after dinner, and the components of such an οἴμη are once called κλέα ἀνδρῶν ('tales of men' — θ 73-4), a phrase which looks back to two passages in the *Iliad* (I 524-5 τῶν πρόσθεν . . . κλέα ἀνδρῶν | ἡρώων and 189, where Achilles sings them to the φόρμιγξ [64]). It was presumably in these οἶμαι, knowledge of which was a monopoly of professional bards (θ 480-1), that the stories were preserved which formed the basis for the *Iliad* and *Odyssey*; and both poems make it clear that their stories were already known in essentials to the audience. Thus attempts to analyse the sources of the Homeric epics [65] operate mainly with pre-Homeric epic poems, and with them we return to something very like Grote's view of the *Iliad*; and Focke has argued cogently that the *Odyssey* too is an expansion (by a poet of talent, though not perhaps of genius) of an original *Odyssey* which was by a great poet.[66] We must suppose that the cyclic poems were formed in the same way, out of pre-Homeric οἶμαι; it is thus natural that many *motifs* are common to the Homeric poems and to one or other of the cyclic epics.

V. No one, that I know of, now believes that the *Iliad* or the *Odyssey* was created by joining together 'loose songs' into 'a sequel of songs and rhapsodies' in such a way that the original components could be simply uncoupled from one another and resume an independent existence. All the researches into the relative chronology of the various elements in the poems show that 'older' and 'younger' elements (whether archaeological, linguistic or social) interlock (perhaps the best example is the occurrence of the unquestionably ancient boar's tusk helmet in K, a book in which the language is characteristically modern and even 'post-Odyssean'). We may therefore deny that the *Iliad* and *Odyssey* were created directly out of lays in the Lachmannian sense; but we cannot deny that there are blocks which seem to be closely inter-connected, and may have originally formed parts of separate οἶμαι (or even κλέα ἀνδρῶν), as for example Γ-Ε, Η-Θ, Κ, and ι-μ.[67]

VI. Mülder's conclusion, that the *Iliad* (and, by legitimate extension, the *Odyssey*) can have been created only by a poet, and not by a *Bearbeiter*, by evolution, or by accident, depends for its cogency on one's own estimate of the poetic value of the plan and its accomplishment. The question is no longer whether the poems are composite, but whether the composition is good and the pieces of which it is composed are well chosen, well shaped, and well arranged — mosaic can be a great art, and even the humble patchwork quilt may be beautiful. In judging this aspect of the poems, it is well to stress the way in which the story is told ; the arrangement is not what mediaeval critics called the *ordo naturalis* ('Begin at the beginning, go on to the end, and then stop'), but the much more complex *ordo artificialis*. Formally, the *Iliad* (the real title of which must have been *The Wrath of Achilles*) deals with only a few days, relatively speaking, in the tenth year of the siege of Troy. Using this short episode as his framework, the author has built up around it by means of reminiscences and prophecies almost the whole story of the Trojan war from the marriage of Peleus and Thetis [68] down to the establishment of the Aeneadae at their town in the Troad as Priam's successors ; thanks to these reminiscences and prophecies, together with the tales and anecdotes about past events elsewhere in the heroic world (Elis, Aetolia, Thessaly, Lycia, etc.), the main narrative is displayed against a background of past history, and also put to some extent in perspective by occasional reminders to the audience of what has happened since those days.[69] The *Odyssey* follows a similar, though somewhat simpler, plan ; it is noteworthy that it almost never overlaps the *Iliad*, although it fills several gaps left by the *Iliad* between the death of Hector and the sack of Troy. In both these poems a sense of narrative strategy is shown which is paralleled in Greek literature only by Herodotus, and in Latin is approached only by the *Aeneid* ; nothing like it is found again in literature until the Renaissance, and then only in one or two poems, of which *Paradise Lost* perhaps comes nearest to the Homeric standard. It does not seem that any of the modern heroic poems which are invoked by the believers in the comparative method [70] shows anything like the narrative strategy of the *Odyssey*, not to mention the *Iliad* ; the more elaborate modern poems may qualify for the title οἴμη, but they are not fully-developed epic poems. It is on the narrative strategy and the character-drawing (both unsurpassed in later times) of the Homeric poems that the claim of their author (or authors) to a place among the great poets finally rests. We cannot say that the same person composed both poems,[71] but there can hardly be a doubt that each was given its present form by a single person with all the resources of a professional bard at his finger-tips, or that the author of the *Odyssey* was intimately acquainted with the *Iliad*.

Two points still await consideration : the date of the poems, and the question of writing. The belief in the artistic unity of our *Iliad* and *Odyssey* can rest only upon the assumption that the textual tradition of the two poems is at least as reliable as that of Pindar ; and this can be true only if (*a*) the poems were preserved in writing from the moment of composition by some self-perpetuating corporation (such as the Homeridae), (*b*) the copy brought to Athens in the sixth century was obtained from that corporation (if so, it would explain the authority

PLATE 5

MS Venetus Marcianus 454. Early-tenth-century MS of the *Iliad* with the ancient *scholia*.
Height of page $15\frac{1}{2}$ in.

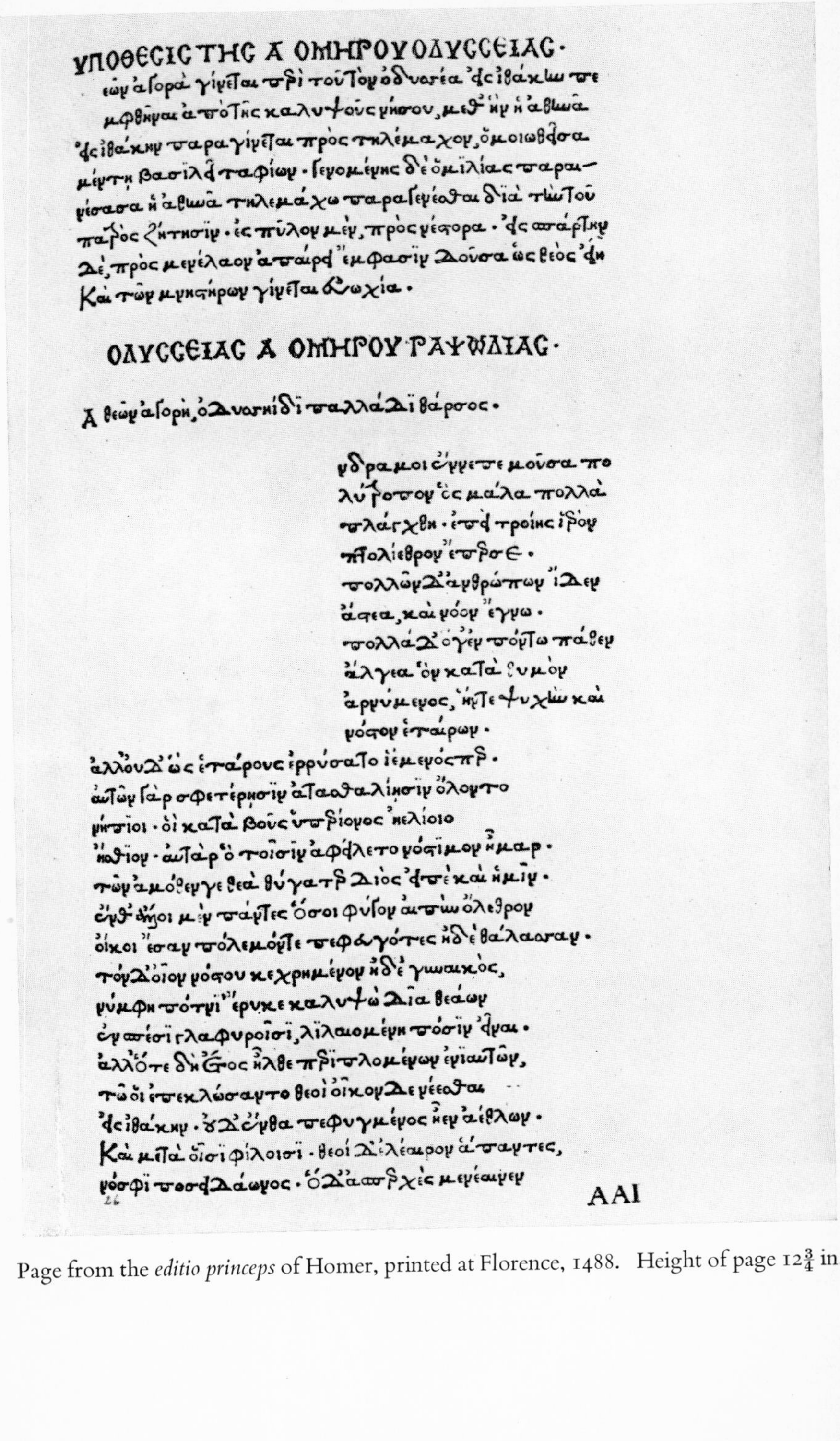

PLATE 6

ΥΠΟΘΕΣΙΣ ΤΗΣ Α ΟΜΗΡΟΥ ΟΔΥΣΣΕΙΑΣ·

ἐῶν ἀγορὰ γίνεται περὶ τοῦ τὸν ὀδυσέα ἐς ἰθάκην τε
ἐμφθῆναι ἀπὸ τῆς καλυψοῦς νήσου, μεθ᾽ ἣν ἡ ἀθηνᾶ
ἐς ἰθάκην παραγίνεται πρὸς τηλέμαχον, ὁμοιωθεῖσα
μέντη βασιλεῖ ταφίων· γενομένης δὲ ὁμιλίας παραι-
νέσασα ἡ ἀθηνᾶ τηλεμάχῳ παρασκευάσασθαι διὰ τὴν τοῦ
πατρὸς ζήτησιν· ἐς πύλον μὲν, πρὸς νέστορα· ἐς σπάρτην
δὲ· πρὸς μενέλαον ἀπάρα ἐμφασίν δοῦσα ὡς θεὸς ἦν
καὶ τῶν μνηστήρων γίνεται εὐωχία·

ΟΔΥΣΣΕΙΑΣ Α ΟΜΗΡΟΥ ΡΑΨΩΔΙΑΣ·

Α θεῶν ἀγορή, ὀδυναί ἰδὲ παλλάδι θάρσος·

ἄνδρα μοι ἔννεπε μοῦσα πο-
λύτροπον ὃς μάλα πολλὰ
πλάγχθη· ἐπεὶ τροίης ἱερὸν
πτολίεθρον ἔπερσε·
πολλῶν δ᾽ ἀνθρώπων ἴδεν
ἄστεα, καὶ νόον ἔγνω·
πολλὰ δ᾽ ὅ γ᾽ ἐν πόντῳ πάθεν
ἄλγεα ὃν κατὰ θυμόν,
ἀρνύμενος, ἥν τε ψυχὴν καὶ
νόστον ἑταίρων·
ἀλλ᾽ οὐδ᾽ ὣς ἑτάρους ἐρρύσατο ἱέμενός περ·
αὐτῶν γὰρ σφετέρῃσιν ἀτασθαλίῃσιν ὄλοντο
νήπιοι· οἳ κατὰ βοῦς ὑπερίονος ἠελίοιο
ἤσθιον· αὐτὰρ ὁ τοῖσιν ἀφείλετο νόστιμον ἦμαρ·
τῶν ἁμόθεν γε θεά θύγατερ διὸς εἰπὲ καὶ ἡμῖν·
ἔνθ᾽ ἄλλοι μὲν πάντες ὅσοι φύγον αἰπὺν ὄλεθρον
οἴκοι ἔσαν πόλεμόν τε πεφυγότες ἠδὲ θάλασσαν·
τὸν δ᾽ οἶον νόστου κεχρημένον ἠδὲ γυναικός,
νύμφη πότνι᾽ ἔρυκε καλυψὼ δῖα θεάων
ἐν σπέσσι γλαφυροῖσι, λιλαιομένη πόσιν εἶναι·
ἀλλ᾽ ὅτε δὴ ἔτος ἦλθε περιπλομένων ἐνιαυτῶν,
τῷ οἱ ἐπεκλώσαντο θεοὶ οἶκόνδε νέεσθαι
ἐς ἰθάκην· οὐδ᾽ ἔνθα πεφυγμένος ἦεν ἀέθλων·
καὶ μετὰ οἷσι φίλοισι· θεοὶ δ᾽ ἐλέαιρον ἅπαντες,
νόσφι ποσειδάωνος· ὁ δ᾽ ἀσπερχὲς μενέαινεν

26   ΑΑΙ

Page from the *editio princeps* of Homer, printed at Florence, 1488.   Height of page 12¾ in.

which it obviously enjoyed), (c) the Panathenaic text was scrupulously preserved from excisions or interpolations (the conditions of its use would presumably guarantee that), and (d) the text which was victorious over all competitors in the second century B.C. was an accurate copy of the Panathenaic text. Not one of these things can be proved; but none is impossible, or even improbable, and if they are true, it follows that the text of the poems, as reconstructed by the normal processes of textual criticism from the Byzantine MSS. and checked with the papyri of the period after 150 B.C., must be taken to be as accurate a representation as is now attainable of the original text as it was first written. From this text, there cannot be any rejection of passages as interpolations or revisions; what is in it must be accepted as it stands, and either explained or admitted to be inexplicable with our present knowledge. In that case the *terminus post quem* for the composition of the *Iliad* will be the latest datable archaeological object mentioned in it. The archaeologists have still to determine the identity and date of this object, but it will be surprising if the suggested *terminus post quem* is found to lie after, or many years before, 700 B.C. The *terminus ante quem* for the *Odyssey* seems to be, at latest, the founding of Naucratis (Rhys Carpenter, *op. cit.* 100), *i.e.* *circa* 620.[72] Between these two extremes, to account for the universal belief in pre-Alexandrian times that both poems were by the same man, a single working life-time should cover their creation. In any case, if we put the creation of the *Iliad* and *Odyssey* at the end of the eighth or in the first half of the seventh century, all difficulties about the use of writing in their composition disappear, and there is no gap to be accounted for between the Homeric poems and the earliest surviving lyric and elegiac poetry of the late eighth and seventh centuries. The earlier literature has perished, either because it was not committed to writing or (perhaps more probably) because it was out-classed and to some extent swallowed up by the new poetry of the early seventh century.

The theory thus advanced seems to me to come nearer to satisfying the requirements of the evidence now available than any other; but, like all theories, it is only provisional, and may be destroyed by the discovery of new evidence or by the reflections of other minds upon the existing evidence. The 'revolutions of learning' are not (*pace* Dr. Johnson) merely circular, keeping the human mind 'in motion without progress'. In the Homeric scholarship of the last three centuries we may watch the progressive application to the old problems of new types of evidence and new methods of interpretation. To this progress all the scholars whom I have named, and many whom I have not named, have made their several contributions; and even apparently retrograde movements have sometimes proved to be the starting-point for new advances. 'Other men have laboured and ye are entered into their labours.'

T

NOTES TO CHAPTER 7

1. The reference to Callinus is due to a reasonable emendation by Sylburg. I have discussed these and some other passages (including Semonides fr. 29 Diehl) in *Eranos*, iii. 125-40.

2. It is a legitimate inference from what we know of Stesichorus's *Helen* that the poem to which he referred treated Helen's matrimonial adventures less charitably than do the *Iliad* and *Odyssey*.

3. Rhodian plate (British Museum) : Rumpf, *Malerei und Zeichnung* (1953), 36. Ram jug (Athens, Nat. Mus. 2612) : *ibid.* 25 ; Beazley, *Development of Attic Black-Figure* (1951), 9-10.

4. See H. Fränkel, *Dichtung und Philosophie des frühen Griechentums* (1951), 275, n. 13 (his 'Fg. 28' is a misprint for 'Fg. 29').

5. Panyassis, who wrote a *Heracleia* in fourteen books and 9000 verses. Halicarnassus was also the home of Pigres, brother of Artemisia, who produced an elegiac *Iliad* and wrote the *Margites* (*Suda*, *s.v.* Πίγρης (π 1551 Adler)) and the *Battle of Frogs and Mice* (Plut. *Mor.* 873 F — Mal. *Hdt.* 43). The testimony of the *Suda* is made doubtful by its mention of the *Margites*, which Aristotle regarded as Homeric (*Poet.* 1448 b 30, *Eth. Nic.* vi. 1141 a 14), and by its failure to decide whether the Artemisia in question was the heroine of Salamis or the wife of Maussolus. (For a possible fragment of the *Margites*, very un-Homeric in appearance, see *Oxyrhynchus Papyri*, xxii, No. 2309.)

6. On Heropythus see H. T. Wade-Gery, *The Poet of the Iliad* (1952), 8-9, Pl. I, App. I.

7. The reference can hardly be to the authors of the 'cyclic' epics, of which the *Cypria* and *Epigoni* were certainly, and the other poems most probably, still regarded as Homeric by Herodotus's contemporaries.

8. The reference to Hellanicus depends upon a reasonable conjecture by G. Hermann ; it is possible, but not very likely, that the Hellanicus referred to may be the Alexandrine scholar to be mentioned below.

9. How little Hellanicus's ascription of the *Little Iliad* to Cinaetho affected later tradition may be seen from the 'Homeric bowl' from Anthedon (F. Courby, *Vases grecs à reliefs* (1922), 286, No. 8) which explicitly ascribes the *Little Iliad* to Lesches. Another bowl not listed by Courby, but discussed by A. Severyns, *Le Cycle épique dans l'école d'Aristarque* (1928), 403-5, seems to ascribe the *Nostoi* to Agias. H. A. Thompson, *Hesperia*, iii. 451 ff., especially 457-8, dates these bowls about 275 B.C. Phanias (? = Phaenias of Eresus, Aristotle's pupil) is said to have put Lesches before Terpander but after Archilochus (Clem. Alex. *Strom.* i. 21. 131. 6).

10. See now H. Erbse, *Hermes*, lxxxi. 163-96.

11. See K. F. Johansen, *Iliaden i tidlig graesk kunst* (1934) and J. D. B.'s review (*JHS*, liv. 84-5). See also the references indexed under *Homer, Iliad, Odyssey* in Beazley's *Development of Attic Black-Figure*, which seem to prove that the earliest scenes which must be from the *Iliad* appear about 530.

12. For the shortness of Athenian historical memory *cf.* F. Jacoby, *JHS*, lxiv. 37-46. I have discussed the whole question of the 'Peisistratean recension' in *TAPA*, lxxxvi. 1-21.

13. For the correctness of the date see Wilamowitz, *Homerische Untersuchungen* (1884), 259, n. 21, and H. T. Wade-Gery in *Greek Poetry and Life* (1936), 56-78. 'Homeric' poems were certainly known in Sicily before 504, *cf.* note 2 above.

14. For the ancient references and fragments see *FGH*, i, No. 71.

15. Fragments in *Aristotelis fragmenta*, ed. V. Rose (1886), 142-79.

16. For a similar example of 'text-slinging' by the Athenians *cf.* Hdt. vii. 161. 3 (referring to B 553-4). Aristotle gives no indication of date or circumstances.

17. The nearest parallel is the crime alleged against Onomacritus (Hdt. vii. 6. 3). Much

worse accusations are made against Cynaethus (Schol. Pind. *Nem.* 2. 1 c, e Drachmann), but one never hears of a 'Cynaethean recension'.

18. *Cf.* R. Merkelbach, *Rh. Mus.* xci. 23-47; his conclusions are accepted by P. von der Mühll, *Kritisches Hypomnema zur Ilias* (1952), ix, and by D. L. Page, *The Homeric Odyssey* (1955), 135, n. 32, but the theory seems to be no better grounded now than it was when Grote demolished it in 1846 (*History of Greece*, Part I, ch. xxi; Everyman edition 2. 261-70).

19. Xenon is known, it seems, only from this reference and from the title of Aristarchus's monograph *Against Xenon's Paradox* (Schol. A on M 435). *Suda, s.v.* Πτολεμαῖος (π 3035 Adler), tells us that this Hellanicus had been taught by Agathocles, who was himself a pupil of Zenodotus; *cf.* Gudeman, *RE*, viii (1913), 153-5, *s.v.* Hellanikos 8. References to the χωρίζοντες are fairly frequent in the A Scholia to the *Iliad* from B 649 onwards.

20. On the subjective element in Alexandrian criticism see M. van der Valk, *Textual Criticism of the Odyssey* (1949); attacked by G. M. Bolling, *AJP*, lxxi. 306-11, his views have been accepted in principle by von der Mühll, *op. cit.* (above, note 18) 11.

21. See Severyns's important but neglected book already referred to (above, note 9). I owe my knowledge of this book to Dr. van der Valk, who read this chapter in draft and made many helpful comments and suggestions.

22. For Asclepiades see *Suda, s.v.* (a 4173 Adler), Wentzel, *RE*, ii (1896), 1628-31, *s.v.* Asklepiades 28); B. A. Müller (Diss. Leipzig 1903). He was first tentatively identified as Cicero's source by G. Kaibel (*Abh. d. kgl. Ges. d. Wiss. zu Göttingen*, Phil.-Hist. Kl. N.F. ii. 4, 1896, 26), who argued from an allusion in *Suda, s.v.* Ὀρφεύς (ο 657 Adler).

23. On the Lives see especially T. W. Allen, *Homer, The Origins and Transmission* (1924), chap. i, and W. Schadewaldt, *Legende von Homer* (1942). On the sources of Eustathius see H. Erbse, *Untersuchungen zu den attizistischen Lexika* (1950), *Beiträge zur Überlieferung der Iliasscholien* (1960), 122-73.

24. The best account in English is still that by M. P. Nilsson, *Homer and Mycenae* (1933), chap. i; for the period before 1885 the account in Jebb's *Introduction to Homer* [2] (1887), chap. iv, is useful. Sir John Myres, *Homer and his Critics* (ed. D. Gray, 1958) contains much of interest. The best account in any foreign language is that by W. Schmid, *Geschichte der griechischen Literatur*, i (1929), 133-48, 192-5 (bibliography); for the period up to 1924 it can be supplemented from G. Finsler, *Homer*, i [3] (1924), 71-224 (the section on the years 1912-24 is by E. Tièche). Finsler's *Homer in der Neuzeit von Dante bis Goethe* (1912) is valuable for the earlier periods. The literature published since 1929 is discussed by A. Lesky, *Die Homerforschung in der Gegenwart* (1952), a reprint of articles published in *Anz. f. Altertumswiss.* in 1951-2 (additions thereto, *ibid.* vi (1953), 129-50, viii (1955), 129-56, xii (1959), 129-46. H. J. Mette, *Lustrum* i (1957), 7-86 (and additions in later vols.) provides a useful catalogue, but his comments are less reliable than Lesky's.

25. We may perhaps see the result of Jean Dorat's teaching, in which Homer played a great part, in Ronsard's sonnet, 'Je veux lire en trois jours l'Iliade d'Homère' (*Oxford Book of French Verse*, No. 63), *cf.* P. de Nolhac, *Ronsard et l'hellénisme en France* (1921), 52-84 (for Dorat, especially 69-73 for his interest in Homer), 125-9 (for Ronsard and Homer).

26. See H. Gillot, *La Querelle des anciens et des modernes en France* (1914).

27. See C. Arnaud, *Les Théories dramatiques au XVIIᵉ siècle : étude sur la vie et les œuvres de l'abbé d'Aubignac* (1888), especially Part I, Book I (biography) and Book II, chap 2, sec. 2 (on the *Conjectures*). Wolf refers to the abbé in complimentary terms (*Prolegomena*, cxiii, n. 84); Payne Knight mentions him, with his name deformed to 'Hedlin' (*Carmina Homerica*, 6), and then he goes practically unmentioned until Finsler drew attention to his work in *Homer in der Neuzeit*. V. Magnien republished the *Conjectures* with a good introduction in 1925; his dates differ rather from Arnaud's (he puts the composition of the *Conjectures* about 1670 and the author's death about 1673).

28. See especially M. L. Clarke, *Greek Studies in England 1700–1830* (1945), chap x, and D. M. Foerster, *Homer in English Criticism* (*Yale Studies in English*, 105, 1947).

29. J. Nicole, *Les Scolies genevoises de l'Iliade* (1891), identified Estienne's *vetus codex* as Genavensis 44 (Ge) ; on the Ge scholia see H. Erbse, *Rh. Mus.* xcv. 170–91. The *scholia minora* (including those of 'Didymus') are being re-edited by V. di Marco.

30. The Leipzig scholia (Lipsiensis 32 = Li) were first used in Lederlin and Bergler's edition of the *Iliad* (1707) ; parts of the Leiden scholia (Leidensis Vossianus gr. 64 = Le ¹) were published by Valckenaer in 1739.

31. Partial translation by F. Brerewood 1716, complete translation 1722. On Terrasson see *Biographie universelle*, xlv (1826), 172.

32. Vico's views on Homer, especially Book III ('Dalla discoverta del vero Omero') of his *Principi di scienza nuova* (published in 1730) are interesting as an anticipation of later analytical criticism. Though Professor L. A. Stella refers to them in her book, *Il poema di Ulisse* (1955), they seem to have had almost no influence upon the development of Homeric studies. For a summary see B. Croce, *The Philosophy of Vico* (tr. R. G. Collingwood, 1913), 183–96.

33. Monk's *Life*, ii (1833), 367, n. 3 : 'Of which book [sc. the *Enquiry*] it is said, but I know not on what authority, that Bentley observed, "when he had gone through half of it, he had forgotten the beginning ; and when he had finished the reading of it, he had forgotten the whole"'.

34. Wood refers to the *Enquiry* by name three times : *Essay* (1775 edition), 99, note *d*, 117, 295–6.

35. Even of this, it is said, only seven copies were printed (Nichols, *Literary Anecdotes*, iii. 81). One of these was sent on Wood's instructions to J. D. Michaelis in Göttingen (Foerster, *op. cit.* 110, n. 5). On Wood see now T. J. B. Spencer, *Journ. of the Warburg and Courtauld Institutes*, xx. 75–105.

36. He names Boileau, Mme Dacier and Boivin as Homer's chief defenders, and La Motte, Perrault, Fénelon, and Fontenelle as his chief detractors (1775 edition, 144, note *e*).

37. C. F. Michaelis, son of J. D., the translator : Foerster 111. The translation appeared with Heyne's review as a preface in 1773 ; in 1775 Jacob Bryant published a new edition of the *Essay* with revisions and the addition of *A Comparative View of the Ancient and Modern State of the Troade*. Wood had meant to make this the core of his book — it is named first on the title-page of the 1767 printing, but it is absent from the only known copy of that printing (formerly in the Grenville Library, now in the British Museum). In 1778 Michaelis published a pamphlet of *Zusätze und Veränderungen wodurch sich die neue Ausgabe von . . . Woods Versuch . . . von der alten auszeichnet*. Wolf, who quotes Wood by the 1775 edition (*Prolegomena*, xli, n. 8), was a student at Göttingen until 1779.

38. See C. Joret, *D'Ansse de Villoison et l'hellénisme en France* (1910). On the textual tradition of the Venetian scholia see H. Erbse, *Mnemosyne*, 4 Ser. vi. 1–38, *Beiträge zur Überlieferung der Iliasscholien* (1960).

39. These are the scholia to the MS. known after an eighteenth-century owner as the Townleianus (now Brit. Mus. Burney 86). For the great importance of this MS. to the student of the history of the Homeric scholia see Erbse, *opp. cit.* (note 38).

40. *Orthography* : cf. P. Chantraine, *Grammaire homérique*, i ² (1948), ch. 1. *Interpolations* : see for example G. Jachmann, *Symbola Coloniensia* (1949), 46, n. 64.

41. For details see L. Friedländer, *Die homerische Kritik von Wolf bis Grote* (1853) ; R. Volkmann, *Geschichte u. Kritik d. Wolfsche Prolegomena zu Homer* (1874).

42. The references are to the 1945 edition of *Trollope : a Commentary*.

43. See now A. Severyns, *Recherches sur la* Chrestomathie *de Proclos*, iii (1953).

44. Nitzsch was already known for his 'unitarian' (almost neo-analyst) commentary, *Erklärende Anmerkungen zu Homers Odyssee*, vol. i of which appeared in 1826. His *Sagen-*

poesie der Griechen (1852–9) was important in the period between Grote and Kirchhoff.

45. Lachmann's *Iliad*, or something very like it, was published by A. Köchly, *Iliadis carmina XVI restituta* (1861).

46. B. Niese, *Der homerische Schiffskatalog als historische Quelle betrachtet* (1873); among its successors are W. Leaf, *Homer and History* (1915), T. W. Allen, *The Homeric Catalogue of Ships* (1921), V. Burr, Νεῶν Κατάλογος (1944), K. Marót, 'La Béotie et son caractère hésiodique' (*Act. Ant. Hung.* i. 261-320), G. Jachmann, *Die homerische Schiffskatalog u. die Ilias* (1958), D. L. Page, *History and the Homeric Iliad* (1959).

47. On weapons it was soon succeeded by W. Reichel, *Homerische Waffen* (1894, [2] 1901), but in other respects it was replaced only by H. L. Lorimer, *Homer and the Monuments* (1950).

48. The first edition of Leaf's *Iliad* appeared in 1886; besides a school edition of the *Iliad*, Monro published an annotated edition of *Odyssey* xiii-xxiv (1901), which completed the edition of the *Odyssey* begun by W. W. Merry and J. Riddell (i-xii, 1876). Monro's volume contains a masterly series of appendices (289-488) on the Homeric question.

49. *E.g.*, O. Seeck, *Die Quellen der Odyssee* (1887), E. Bethe, *Homer*, ii (1922), E. Schwartz, *Die Odyssee* (1924), P. von der Mühll, *RE*, vii A (1940), *s.v.* Odyssee, R. Merkelbach, *Untersuchungen zur Odyssee* (1951). D. L. Page, *The Homeric Odyssey* (1955), is a revisionist of the school of Kirchhoff.

50. The chief new publications of the decade, apart from Cauer's, were: Leaf's *Companion to the Iliad* (1892), W. Schulze's *Quaestiones epicae* (1892), J. van Leeuwen's *Enchiridion dictionis epicae* (1894), L. Ehrhardt's *Die Entstehung der homerischen Gedichte* (1894), and P. Kretschmer's *Einleitung in die Geschichte der griechischen Sprache* (1896). A. Ludwich's important edition of the *Odyssey* (i-xii, 1889; xiii-xxiv, 1901), which is still not superseded as an authority for the text, and his *Iliad* (1902-7), which remains second in importance to T. W. Allen's *editio maior* of 1931, may also be mentioned here.

51. In this year began the long series of works on the *Odyssey* by V. Bérard: *Les Phéniciens et l'Odyssée* (1903-4, [2] 1927), *Introduction à l'Odyssée* (1924-5, [2] 1933), *Les Navigations d'Ulysse* (1927), *La Résurrection d'Homère* (1930).

52. The fifth may be called 'flogging a dead horse'; the doctrine of 'saga-transference' (*Sagenverschiebung*) contained in the sixth and seventh points may form part of any evolutionist theory, and was soon taken up and developed by the revisionist Bethe.

53. The tide began to turn against the destructive analysts in 1929 with the publication of W. Schmid's *Geschichte der griechischen Literatur*, i; his account of Homer (83-195) strongly emphasized the artistic unity and importance of the poems. In 1930 it was followed by C. M. Bowra's *Tradition and Design in the Iliad* (a pioneer work of first-class importance), W. J. Woodhouse's *The Composition of the Odyssey*, J. L. Myres's *Who were the Greeks?* (a valuable store-house of information), and the first part of Milman Parry's 'Studies in the Epic Technique of Oral Verse-Making' (*Harv. Stud. Class. Phil.* xli. 72-147; Part II appeared *ibid.* xliii. 1-50). M. P. Nilsson's *Homer and Mycenae* (1933) combines the results of all these three works with his own unrivalled knowledge of all matters affecting Homer. More recently, W. Schadewaldt's *Iliasstudien* (1938) and F. Focke's *Die Odyssee* (1943) are of vital importance for the understanding of the plan of the poems. Of the detailed studies, the most important are: G. Scheibner, *Der Aufbau des 20. und 21. Buches der Ilias* (1939), U. Hölscher, *Untersuchungen zur Form der Odyssee* (1939), F. Klingner, *Ueber die ersten vier Bücher der Odyssee* (1944), the discussion of the topography of the Trojan battlefield in J. Cuillandre, *La Droite et la gauche dans les poèmes homériques* (1944), the chapter on character-drawing (iv) in F. Robert, *Homère* (1950) and W. Mattes, *Odysseus bei den Phäaken* (1958). W. B. Stanford, *The Ulysses Theme* (1954), deserves mention here for its emphasis on the consistency of Homeric character-drawing.

54. Other important revisionists within this period are: for the *Iliad*, E. Bethe, *Homer,*

i (1914), E. Schwartz, *Zur Entstehung der Ilias* (1918), P. Mazon, *Introduction à l'Iliade* (1942), P. von der Mühll, *Kritisches Hypomnema zur Ilias* (1952 — see my review in *Gött. Gel. Anz.* 208, 1954, 38-45); for the *Odyssey*, the scholars listed above (note 49).

55. One of the worst stumbling-blocks, the allegation that the composer of T did not know of the attempted reconciliation in I, seems now to have been cleared away by D. E. Eichholz (*AJP*, lxxiv. 137-48). On Athena's lamp see R. Pfeiffer, *Stud. It.* xxvii/xxviii. 426-33 (= *Ausgewählte Schriften* (1960), 1-7).

56. This is where the principle of 'poetic contradiction', emphasized by J. T. Kakridis, *Homeric Researches* (1949), 8 and *passim*, comes in.

57. The occasion of the contest to which Thamyris looked forward with such confidence (B 597) is not stated, but the possibility that the Muses might be among the competitors suggests the funeral games of a major hero.

58. See H. T. Wade-Gery, *The Poet of the Iliad* (1952), 14-18; he suggests the Panionia on Mt. Mycale. In a paper summarized in *Proc. Class. Assoc.* xlvi. 25 I arrived independently at conclusions very similar to Wade-Gery's, and suggested the Delian festival. Wade-Gery's view is supported for the *Iliad* by N 403-5, mine for the *Odyssey* by ζ 162-7. But see now A. B. Lord, *The Singer of Tales* (1960), esp. ch. v.

59. One might instance the anachronisms in *Ivanhoe*, the simultaneous blossoming of the orchard and ripening of the strawberries in *Emma*, the unexplained resurrection of Lady Glenlivat in *The Newcomes*, or the letter in *Ayala's Angel* which turns up undamaged in Papa's desk after being torn up and put into the waste-paper basket.

60. Compare the remark ascribed by Mr. A. Alvarez (*New Statesman and Nation*), 11th December 1954, in a review of *Autumn Sequels*) to Mr. Louis MacNeice: '(On the air) you can get away with anything so long as you entertain'.

61. On the general nature of Homeric language see especially J. Wackernagel, *Sprachliche Untersuchungen zu Homer* (1916), K. Meister, *Die homerische Kunstsprache* (1921), and M. Leumann, *Homerische Wörter* (1950). For the formulae see Milman Parry, *L'Épithète traditionnel dans Homère* and *Les Formules et la métrique d'Homère* (both 1928), W. Arend, *Die typischen Szenen bei Homer* (1933), and Miss D. H. F. Gray, *CQ*, xli (1947), 109-21. For the similes see H. Fränkel, *Die homerischen Gleichnisse* (1921), A. Severyns, *Homère*, iii (1948), 153-64, W. Schadewaldt, *Von Homers Welt und Werk* ² (1951), 130-54, R. Hampe, *Die Gleichnisse Homers und die Bildkunst seiner Zeit*.

62. On anachronisms see especially Miss Lorimer, *op. cit.*; her work is supplemented on armament by H. Trümpy, *Kriegerische Fachausdrücke im griechischen Epos* (1950 — to be used with caution, *cf.* Miss Gray's review in *JHS*, lxxiv. 189-90), on religion by M. P. Nilsson, *The Minoan-Mycenaean Religion* ² (1950), on tactics by E. Delebecque, *Le Cheval dans l'Iliade* (1951), and on metal-working by Miss Gray, *JHS*, lxxiv. 1-15. On mythology see especially M. P. Nilsson, *The Mycenaean Origin of Greek Mythology* (1932); J. T. Kakridis, *Homeric Researches*, treats the background of the *Iliad* with interesting use of modern Greek folk-tales and ballads; K. Meuli, *Odyssee und Argonautika* (1921) is valuable for Odysseus's adventures. Rhys Carpenter, *Folk-tale, Fiction and Saga in the Homeric Epics* (1946) takes the evolution of the *Odyssey* so far back in time as to escape criticism. For the use of non-Greek, especially oriental, material see G. Germain, *Genèse de l'Odyssée* (1954), L. A. Stella, *Il poema di Ulisse* (1955), 85-149, C. H. Gordon, *Hebrew Union College Annual*, xxvi. 43-108, and T. B. L. Webster, *From Mycenae to Homer* (1958). Hampe's paper on Nestor (in R. Herbig, *Vermächtnis der antiken Kunst*, 1950, 1-70) is interesting on Pylos and the Aeolids, K. Reinhardt's *Das Parisurteil* (1938, now in *Von Werken und Formen*, 1948, 11-36) goes far beyond its nominal subject to throw light on Homer's handling of myths in general.

63. The apparent quotation of Z 146 in what passes as Semonides fr. 29 Diehl is a good example. Even if the fragment is really by Semonides (which is far from certain), the line

quoted is proverbial, and was certainly not invented for its place in the *Iliad* (note the ambiguity of γενεή).

64. Achilles is the only Achaean hero whom Homer credits with the ability (peculiar to Paris among the Trojan leaders) to play a musical instrument. Homer's ἀοιδοί sing their οἴμη-extracts to a stringed instrument played by themselves; they know nothing of unaccompanied recitation in the manner of the rhapsode. *Cf.* W. Schadewaldt, *Von Homers Welt und Werk* ² (1951), 54 ff.

65. H. Pestalozzi, *Die Achilleis als Quelle der Ilias* (1945), E. Howald, *Der Dichter der Ilias* (1947), and W. Schadewaldt, *op. cit.* (note 64), 155-202, deal with the *Iliad* from this point of view. On the cyclic poems see Bethe's *Homer*, ii ² (1929), 149-389, and W. Kullmann, *Die Quellen der Ilias* (1960).

66. Focke effectively criticizes the earlier revisionists, from Kirchhoff to Schwartz and Wilamowitz, and confutes in advance (he wrote in 1938, though his book did not appear till 1943) von der Mühll's *RE* article of 1940. Schadewaldt's views on the *Odyssey* have to be reconstructed from his 'Die Heimkehr des Odysseus' (*Von Homers Welt und Werk* ³ (1960), 375-412), 'Der Prolog der Odyssee' (*Harv. Stud. Class. Phil.* lxiii (1958), 15-32), 'Neue Kriterien zur Odyssee-Analyse' (*Sitz.-Bericht Akad. Heidelberg,* Phil.-hist. Kl. 1959, 2) and *Hermes* lxxxi (1959), 13-26. He may be classified as a 'revisionist'.

67. Favoured by Wilamowitz, this theory has been revived in different forms by G. Jachmann, *Symbola Coloniensia* (1949), 1-70 and H. J. Mette, *Der Pfeilschuss des Pandaros* (1951). On I see Margarete Noé, *Phoinix, Ilias und Homer* (1940), with Kakridis's reply (*Homeric Researches*, chaps. i and ii); for K see now M. van der Valk, *Mnemosyne*, 4 Ser. v. 277-8. On Odysseus's adventures see A. Lesky, *Thalatta* (1947), 149-87, K. Reinhardt, *Von Werken und Formen* (1948), 52-162 and W. Mattes (above, note 53). Like the *Catalogue of Ships* (for which see note 46 above), λ is a special case; it has been studied by van der Valk, *Beiträge zur Nekyia* (1935).

68. H. J. Rose, *Humanitas*, iii. 1-5, seems to have proved that Ω 23-30 does not refer to the conventional story of the Judgement of Paris. Homer ignores the golden apple and the connection of Helen's abduction with the marriage of Peleus and Thetis, with all its attendant chronological difficulties.

69. This *Mehrschichtigkeit* is well emphasized by Pestalozzi, *op. cit.* (above, note 65). On the proportions of the various parts of the narrative J. L. Myres's articles in *JHS* (*Iliad* : lii. 264-96 ; *Odyssey* : lxxii. 1-19) are of interest.

70. See especially C. M. Bowra, *AJA*, liv. 184-92 and *Heroic Poetry* (1952), and my own article in *Gymnasium*, lxi. 28-36.

71. That the *Iliad* and *Odyssey* are by the same author is made hard to maintain by arguments such as those of A. Heubeck, *Der Odyssee-Dichter und die Ilias* (1954), D. L. Page, *The Homeric Odyssey* 149-57, and W. Schadewaldt (in the papers listed in note 66).

72. See R. M. Cook, *JHS*, lvii. 227-37. We cannot date Alcman accurately, nor would it help much if we could, since it is not at all certain that the poem about Odysseus which he knew (see p. 234 above) was the same as ours.

AUTHOR'S POSTSCRIPT TO CHAPTER 7

The text of this chapter was originally written in the summer of 1953, and has been little changed since; the notes were revised in 1955, when I was working on the chapter dealing with the transmission of the text, and again in proof. Of the older works which I have read since 1955, two claim special mention:

C. Rothe, *Die Ilias als Dichtung* (1910) and *Die Odyssee als Dichtung und ihr Verhältnis zur Ilias* (1914).

Had I known Rothe's books sooner, I should have taken pleasure in recording his sympathetic attitude to the poems as works of literature, his independence of the shibboleths fashionable among Homeric scholars in the early years of this century, and the sound judgement which puts him among the few scholars whose work on Homer retains more than a merely historical interest. Like Andrew Lang in this country and Dietrich Mülder in Germany, Rothe was always swimming against the stream; and I regret that I learned of his works too late to give him the place which he deserves in the foregoing survey of certain aspects of Homeric scholarship.

PART II

THE PICTURE AND THE RECORD

§A: The Setting

§B: The Rediscovery of the Heroic World

§C: Social Culture

§D: Material Culture

§A: THE SETTING

CHAPTER 8

THE PHYSICAL GEOGRAPHY OF GREECE
AND THE AEGEAN

by N. G. L. Hammond

GENERAL CHARACTERISTICS

THE Mediterranean climate is temperate, and the cycle and character of the seasons are constant. The stabilizing factor, which mediates between the cold of Europe and the heat of Africa, is the influence of the Mediterranean Sea. In winter it draws the rainy westerlies from the Atlantic; in summer, when the heat belt moves northwards from Africa, it attracts the dry cooling north-easterly winds, the Etesians of antiquity. In the lowlands the Etesians deposit no moisture and impose a summer drought, which lasts in Greece and Sicily for four months. The winter rains fall in heavy showers and are succeeded by warm sunshine. The climate and the constancy of the seasons favour agriculture; the winter sun and summer drought admit of a long period of germination and growth, and the dates of sowing and harvesting in modern Boeotia are those recorded by Hesiod. The vine, fig, and olive mature best in the long drought, the olive being peculiar to the Mediterranean zone, and where the soil is suitable cereals and vegetables flourish. Moreover, the mountainous areas of Greece with their less arid climate support sheep and goats, which are kept for milk, butter, and cheese rather than for meat. These products provide the basis of a healthy diet; and the preponderance of sunshine, combined with the mildness of winter and dry heat of summer, facilitates an open-air life and stimulates the energy and health of the population.

The Mediterranean Sea divides into several basins, of which the most favoured for summer navigation is the Aegean. Out at sea the Etesian winds are constant, and near the coast onshore and offshore winds blow at evening and morning, and the seas are so thickly studded with islands that the beacon signals of Troy's fall leaped easily across the Aegean. By day the navigator rarely loses sight of land, and by night the bright stars are a reliable guide. Through most of the Aegean there were neither tides nor currents to deter the early mariner, and the seas offered an abundance of fish, especially the tunny; from the skill of the fisherman developed the arts of trade, piracy, and naval war. Under such favourable conditions the Aegean was a good nursery of seafaring in the Minoan Age of Crete, and the tradition of sail still lives in the caïques of modern Greece. When the Greek peoples crossed the Mediterranean basins, they found a similar climate in many parts of its coasts and islands — South Italy, Sicily, Cyrenaica, Syria, Cyprus, Asia Minor, the Bosporus, and Thrace — and they were able to establish the same mode of life there as in the homeland. Thus trade, migration, and colonial expansion encountered fewer physical difficulties than in other parts of the world.

THE GREEK MAINLAND [1]

There are wide variations of climate within the Greek peninsula. They are due to the Balkan land mass, the high altitude of the mountainous spine of Greece, and to the watershed dividing west from east Greece, which obstructs the rainy westerly winds. North Greece experiences the hard continental winter, and central Greece forms a transitional zone leading to the mild Mediterranean winter which prevails in Attica and in the periphery of the Peloponnese; and within this gradation the mountain masses carry the continental climate south to the highlands of Arcadia. The high watershed precipitates the greater part of the winter rains on west Greece, so that the annual rainfall of the western lowlands is almost double that of the eastern lowlands; for instance, Ambracia has 42·6 inches and Pagasae 21·6, Patrae 26·5 and Athens 16·0, Pyrgos 33·8 and Tiryns 20·0. This wide variation in climate endows each canton with an individual character; any invading people from the north passes by gradual stages from the full continental to the full Mediterranean climate. The mountain system imposes a further distinction between west Greece and east Greece. Not only does the high and almost continuous watershed divide west from east but the subsidiary ranges in the west are differently aligned from those of the east. The west Greek ranges are parallel to the high watershed, and the most westerly of them forms the western coast of Greece, the whole system tending south-south-east. As a result ports on the west coast are cut off from the interior, and the main overland routes run north and south; these routes lead into the gulfs of Ambracia and of Corinth, where the sea has broken through the mountain system. These gulfs tend to centralize the export of goods from the western land-areas. The east Greek ranges run eastwards from the main watershed, being in general parallel one to another and at right angles to the main watershed. An area enclosed between two such ranges presents an open face and its overland routes lead down towards the sea, which in turn has encroached on the valleys and formed an indented coast line. The eastern Greek states turned therefore to seafaring and exploited the favourable conditions of the Aegean basin; on the other hand, the ranges running eastwards were a barrier to overland routes from north to south and so made sea communications more desirable.

The geological structure of Greece has not been fully surveyed, but the broad lines are clear. The western Greek ranges are of limestone; on leaving the mainland they are continued in the outer Aegean islands along the line of Crete and Rhodes and form the adjacent coast of Asia Minor. The high watershed is composed partly of limestone and partly of volcanic rock, especially serpentine, which reappears sporadically in some Aegean islands, for instance Aegina, Melos, Thera, and Nisyros. The eastern Greek ranges are partly limestone and partly crystalline, the latter containing marble and minerals, and the continuation of these ranges forms the islands of the central Aegean basin and the opposite coast of Asia Minor. Between these ranges and the alluvial plains there are beds of *flysch*, which consist of sandstone, marl, slate, and conglomerate, and the soil formed from them; these beds, which are hilly and fertile, are wider in east Greece than in west Greece and endow some Aegean islands with fertile tracts. The effects of such geological formations on the individual cantons will be illustrated by the following survey.

NORTH-WEST GREECE

The four limestone ranges and the narrow valleys of flysch squeezed between them give *Epirus* a deficiency of arable land, but the heavy rainfall and continental climate fit it for pastoral life. In antiquity it was famous for cattle, horses, sheep, and goats. The western faces of the mountains are denuded by erosion, but the eastern faces are thickly forested with oak, pine, and fir. The natural centre of mountainous Epirus lies in the plateau of Ioánnina, beside 'wintry Dodona'. This plateau is formed by a central subsidence in a broad belt of limestone. It is drained by underground funnels called *katavothrai*, which give out their copious water at lower altitudes in strong springs called *kephalovrisia*. Such springs form the headwaters of the rivers Thyamis, Acheron, and Lourós. The high watershed and the parallel range to the west are drained by the great rivers Aous and Achelous, the former flowing north to the Adriatic and the latter south to the Gulf of Ambracia. While communication between the western coast and the interior is difficult, the coastal plains of Buthrotum and of the lower Acheron enjoy the Mediterranean climate and are rich in olives, cereals, and winter pasture. The Gulf of Ambracia forms the maritime outlet for central Epirus; its north shore is rich in olives, cereals, fruit, and winter pasture. In Homeric times *Thesprotia* appears to have comprised both the Acheron plain and the Ambraciote plain.

While the main overland routes run south to Ambracia, there is only a narrow passage along the east shore of the Gulf through *Amphilochia* into *Acarnania*. The latter shares the general character of Epirus; and its overland routes also run south, through lacustrine basins and along the lower Achelous to the Gulf of Corinth. It is less deficient in arable land, which centres on Stratus and Oeniadae. The peninsular outline of Acarnania makes its climate transitional between those of Epirus and south Greece; but the Acarnanians like the Epirotes were not a seafaring people, and they tended to lag behind South Greece in level of culture.

NORTH-EAST GREECE

Macedonia is ringed round by mountain ranges except towards the sea. The inner slopes of these ranges fall into upland plateaus of flysch, extensive and fertile, which are shut off one from another and also from the coastal plain by less lofty mountain ranges; these upland plateaus form the cantons of Upper Macedonia, which drain either into lakes or into the rivers Axius, Lydias, and Haliacmon. These break through the ring of mountains enclosing Lower Macedonia, a rich alluvial plain, to enter the Thermaic Gulf. In climate Macedonia is continental, with bitter north winds in winter and heavy heat in summer; rich in timber, cattle, horses, sheep, cereals, and vines, its trade-routes converge upon the coastal plain and the Thermaic Gulf. Two shores of the Gulf are Mediterranean in climate: the promontories of Chalcidice and the coastal zone of Pieria. The former is rich in olives, fruit, and timber suitable for ship-construction, and its hinterland grows fine cereals. The latter has the same products, and its highlands are densely forested with beech and conifer; dominated on the south by the sheer precipices and towering peaks of Olympus (9570 ft.), Pieria was regarded as the playground of the gods.

The routes from Macedonia into *Thessaly* either pass high over the passes of the Pierian and Cambunian ranges or follow the Vale of Tempe, shaded by plane-trees. Originally a vast lake, of which the waters were released when Olympus was sundered from Ossa, the level plains of Thessaly are enclosed by a ring-wall of mountains; the lowest of these separates the plains from the sea. The ring-wall of mountains, and especially the coastal range of Ossa and Pelion, shut out the influence of the sea from the inner plainland; both in climate and in character it is continental rather than Mediterranean, with a hard winter and hot summer and a surplus of cereals grown in its deep rich soil. The winter pastures, too, support fine herds of horses, cattle, and sheep, and the mountains are extensively forested. The whole plain is drained by the Peneus and its tributaries but is divided by foothills into four districts:

Pelasgiotis, Hestiaeotis, Thessaliotis, and Phthiotis, with respective centres at Larissa, Tricca, Arne, and Thebes. Phthiotis contains fertile coastal plains, facing the Pagasaean Gulf and the strait of Euboea, which are Mediterranean in climate and products; the northern shore also and the slopes of Pelion are rich in olives, fruit, nuts, and timber. The Gulf with its narrow outlet, resembling the Gulf of Ambracia, was the cradle of the 'Argo', built of timber from the Thessalian mountains; but the Thessalians of classical times were an agricultural people, whose exports were handled by southern Greeks.

CENTRAL GREECE

The southward route from Thessaly leaves Pharsalus in Phthiotis and climbs a high pass over Mt. Othrys to descend into the valley of the Spercheus. The lower valley of this fast-flowing river is captured by the long Maliac Gulf. The small alluvial plain by its mouth forms the district *Malis*, of which the capital is Lamia; soft in climate and fertile, it is dominated by the forested slopes of the upper valley and of the parallel ranges to north and south. In antiquity the Malians were unable to master the pastoral tribes of these hills, the Aenianes and Oetaeans. The range to the south is formed by Oeta (7060 ft.) and Cnemis; its eastern declivities overlook the narrow gates of Thermopylae, leading to *Locris*, a narrow district facing the Euboean Channel and containing small fertile plains at Thronium and Opus. The other route southwards from Malis climbs high over the flank of Oeta into the small plateau of *Doris*, which collects the headwaters of the Cephissus. A windy and wintry plain, it gains importance from its position, for from it radiate the route through Amphissa to the Corinthian Gulf and the route down the Cephissus valley into *Phocis* and Boeotia. The greater part of Phocis is formed by the limestone masses of Mt. Parnassus (8061 ft.); at high altitudes it is forested with conifers and affords summer pasture, but the lower slopes are mainly barren or sparsely covered with the prickly scrub 'garigue'. The west side of the mountain overlooks the narrow valley of Amphissa, and the south side falls in sheer precipices into a rift, running west and east, which contains the route from Lebadea in Boeotia to Itea on the Corinthian Gulf. On the north side of the rift and at the foot of the cliffs, the sanctuary of Delphi commands the western exit of the route, which then drops down to the sacred olive-groves of Cirrha. Between the rift and the Gulf is an area of broken and intractable limestone. The richest part of Phocis is the Cephissus valley, narrow but well-watered, with arable land and good pasture; its towns, such as Daulis, are set on the spurs of Parnassus and look out over the plains of Boeotia.

Boeotia, like Thessaly, is ringed by mountains except towards the south-east and is mainly fertile plainland. Its two main plains are separated by an outlier of Mt. Helicon; on the lower slopes are situated Ascra and Thebes. Into the northern plain, the centre of which is Orchomenos, the river Cephissus empties its silt-laden waters, for which the only exit is afforded by *katavothrai*; if these are blocked, the Lake Copais forms and floods. In the Late Bronze Age the Lake was successfully drained, and the very fertile soil raised cereals and pasture. The southern plain, with a heavy and rich soil, is drained by the Asopus, which enters Attica before reaching the sea. The climate of the plains resembles that of Thessaly, torrid in summer and raw in winter, for they are cut off by mountains from the sea. Boeotia was famous for cereals, horses, cattle, and sheep, to which are added to-day rice and cotton. Although Boeotia has littorals on the Straits of Euboea and on the Corinthian Gulf, it was in classical times an agricultural area.

The above districts are defined by cultivable areas; they are separated one from another by mountainous zones. These zones are dotted with villages, which win a frugal living from livestock, summer-sown cereals (mainly maize), nuts, and vegetables; the hardy villagers trade with the plains and form a reservoir of population, on which the cities draw. In antiquity they were organised as hill-tribes, such as the Orestae, Athamanes, Aenianes, Dolopes, and Eurytanes, prone to brigandage and formidable as light-armed troops. The largest zone is formed by the continuous range of *Pindus*. The central point in the range is Mt. Lacmon, whence rise the Aous, Arachthus, Achelous, Peneus, and the southern tributaries of the Haliacmon; between the headwaters of the Peneus and Arachthus the least difficult route between Thessaly and Epirus climbs over 5000 feet. The mountains north of Lacmon are mainly serpentine in formation. Soft in contour, rich in springs, and soil-covered, they are clad in virgin forest of beech, conifer, oak, and sweet chestnut, where the bear is still extant, and they contain wide areas of Alpine pasture. On the west of the serpentine formations, precipitous limestone masses carry coniferous forest and a lesser amount of pasture. To the south of Lacmon the limestone belt is of great width, and the serpentine appears only on the eastern fringes in isolated outcrops. A route more difficult than that north of Lacmon joins the Spercheus valley to the Gulf of Ambracia (passing through *Agrapha* and *Amphilochia*). The timber of these areas is only slightly exploited, but the pastures form the summer feeding-ground of myriads of sheep, valuable for milk-products, skins, and wool. They winter in the lowlands we have described, the shepherds and their families being nomadic. To the south the range is cut by the long Corinthian Gulf.

The southern mountains and the coastal belt form the districts of

PLATE 7

Greek landscape : cultivated plain and barren mountains (Sparta and Taÿgetus)

PLATE 8

Aetolia and *Ozolian Locris*, of which the hinterland is pastoral and continental in its winter climate and the lowland, facing the sea, is Mediterranean in climate and products. The most fertile land surrounds Lake Trichonis in Aetolia and Amphissa in Locris. The two areas resemble Achaea across the Gulf in climate and in lack of a natural centre, for each narrow valley runs into the Gulf and is cut off from its neighbours.

ATTICA AND MEGARIS

On crossing the ranges of Cithaeron and Parnes (4636 ft.) one enters abruptly into the full Mediterranean climate of Megaris and *Attica*, both being peninsular and containing less high mountains. The chief product of Attica is the olive, to which the thin arid soil is suited; the vine and fig are less important, and there is insufficient pasture for stock-farming. The central plain of Athens is limited by three separate mountains, Parnes, its limestone summits bearing coniferous forest, Pentelicus, scarred by marble quarries, and Hymettus, whose western slopes of limestone are bare save for thyme and other bee-nurturing herbs. The lower slopes and the hill country of the coasts carry evergreen woods, especially the stunted Mediterranean pine, tapped for resin. From the central plain easy routes lead to the smaller plains of Eleusis, Marathon, and the Mesogaea; the first grows wheat, the others mainly barley. Poor in agricultural resources, Attica was enriched by silver mines at Laurium and by the possession of natural harbours facing the Saronic Gulf, which leads to the Cyclades, similar in climate and in terrain. *Megaris*, controlling the Isthmus, has a port on either Gulf and grows vines and olives. Megara lies between a barren limestone outcrop and a small coastal plain, where vegetables are grown. Its poverty is compensated for by its strategic position.

PELOPONNESE

The central mountainous area of the Peloponnese forms the district *Arcadia*, set within a ring of high mountains, which is drained by the Alpheus River breaking its way westwards to the sea. High in elevation and remote from the sea, its climate is continental, and its products are cattle, sheep, horses, asses, and pigs rather than cereals; the best arable land is in the basins of Megalopolis, Tegea, Mantinea, Lake Stymphalus, and Lake Pheneus, which also afford rich pasture. The north of Arcadia is formed by Mt. Erymanthus and Mt. Cyllene (7792 ft.), of which the northern slopes carry fine forests of oak and conifers; these belong to the district *Achaea*, rich in vines, olives, and fruit but deficient in arable land for growing cereals. The best harbour in its long coast is Patrae, west of the narrows, and separated from east Achaea by Mt. Panachaeus.

U

From the south of Arcadia start the three parallel ranges of Ithome (3730 ft.), Taÿgetus (7903 ft.), and Parnon (6355 ft.), which form the promontories of Acritas, Taenarum, and Malea. The central range of Taÿgetus and the mountain-system of Arcadia divide the Peloponnese into western and eastern halves. The heavier rainfall of the western areas, almost double that of the eastern, extends up the shores of the Corinthian Gulf; this rainfall makes possible the growing of the currant-grape, which is the main export of modern Greece, and supplies the western areas with better pasture and more extensive forests.

In particular *Messenia* combines the advantages of higher rainfall with a southerly latitude. This makes it the richest district in vines, olives, and figs, to which are added pasture for stock and alluvial plains for cereals in the Pamisus valley and on the west coast. In position, however, it is remote from the main currents of Greek trade; its overland communications through the ring of mountains are not easy, and the value of its southern ports is impaired by the stormy promontories enclosing the Messenian Gulf. The best harbour lies on the west coast at Pylos. Well-sheltered and sandy-beached, it forms an important station in the circumnavigation of the Peloponnese, but its importance declines when trade passes through the Isthmus of Corinth. To the north, *Elis* is better placed for trade by sea with the Ionian islands and the Gulf of Corinth. It is unique among the western areas in having an extensive coastal plain open to the sea, known as Coele-Elis. Low-lying and swampy, the plain provides excellent pasture for horses, cattle, and sheep and also raises cereals; on the rising ground the currant-grape is extensively grown, and the highlands of Mt. Erymanthus are clad with forests of oak and conifer. The cantons of south Elis are Pisatis, watered by the lower Alpheus, beside which stands the sanctuary of Olympia, and Triphylia, with a narrow coastal plain and large area of mountain. As a whole Elis is more pastoral than agricultural, and little given to seafaring. Both Messenia and Elis are rich in evergreen woods of the 'maquis' type (including laurel, myrtle, arbutus, ilex, and juniper). These give the hill-country a fresher and softer appearance than in other parts of Greece.

Land-communication between west and east Peloponnese is difficult and discourages overland trade. The shortest pass, from the Messenian plain over Taÿgetus to Sparta, can be traversed in one day but is not very suitable for pack-animals. Less difficult but longer routes lead from Messenia and Elis to the plateau of Megalopolis, and thence either to the head-waters of the Eurotas in Laconia or via Tegea towards the Gulf of Argos. Thus Megalopolis and Tegea occupy important strategic positions.

In the eastern Peloponnese, *Corinthia* controls both the land-route to Central Greece, which in antiquity followed the flank of Mt. Gerania rather than the edge of the Scironian cliffs, and also the four-mile neck of Isthmus, on which a paved way was made for hauling ships from Gulf to Gulf, before the Canal of Corinth was cut. The site of ancient Corinth, with its massive rock-citadel, is suited for trade by sea and land and for purposes of war. Much of its territory is barren or sparsely wooded limestone; the more fertile areas (in western Corinthia) are occupied by extensive vineyards of the currant-grape and produce also wheat and barley. Between Corinthia and Achaea, the small district of *Sicyonia* has a fertile coast and wooded hill-country; its southern frontier is formed by the small upland district *Phliasia*. The route from Corinth to *Argolis*, passing east of the shrine of Nemea, is not difficult for pack-animals and enters the upper Argive plain, which is overlooked by Mycenae. In shape and climate Argolis resembles Attica; but the range of Arachnaeus (3510 ft.) separates it into two parts, the Argive plain and environs facing the Argolic Gulf, and the cantons of Epidauria, Troezenis, and Hermionis facing the Saronic Gulf. The latter, rich in vegetables, fruit, and olives, trade more readily with Aegina and Athens than with Argos; the former is a more self-sufficient unit, growing autumn-sown cereals in the plain, olives, figs, and vines on the foothills, and summer vegetables and maize in the swampy land round Lerna and Tiryns, which also provides pasture for horses and cattle. The plain, brown and withered in the arid summer, faces the Cretan sea; for mountains form its landward sides.

The routes from Argolis and Arcadia into *Laconia* unite at Sellasia and enter 'hollow Lacedaemon', set between the dark cliffs of Taÿgetus and the barren spurs of Parnon. In the arid summer the small plain, watered by springs from Taÿgetus and ringed by olive-groves (Pl. 7), has the fertility and charm of an oasis. A broad limestone ridge separates the plain from the swampy delta of the Eurotas, which provides pasture for horses but is devoid of harbours. The south-western part of Laconia grows excellent olives; of the eastern part the slopes of Parnon are barren except towards the coast where woods of Mediterranean pine face the sea, and the lowlands contain pockets of arable land productive of cereals and figs. The centre of Laconia lies at Sparta in hollow Lacedaemon, withdrawn from the sea; for the Laconian Gulf, enclosed by the storm-breeding promontories of Taenarum and Malea, does not encourage seafaring, and land-communication with the ports of the east coast is difficult. Thus ancient Sparta turned to conquest rather than trade, in order to offset her deficiency in arable land.

IONIAN ISLANDS

As the circumnavigation of the Peloponnese was dangerous, sea-borne trade was drawn to the Corinthian and Saronic Gulfs and the

Isthmus states.   The approaches to each Gulf are set with islands.   The Ionian islands are the peaks of a submerged limestone range of the Western Greek type.   *Ithaca* consists of two such peaks, linked by a low isthmus, and contains only two pockets of arable land, one in the north and the other near Ithaca town (Pl. 8).   The rest of the island, with little water and little pasture, produces an export of olives.   The population is less concerned with agriculture than seafaring, for which it is well placed; for its harbour on the east coast and its inner position among the islands establish it on the coasting route from the Gulf to the north-west.   *Cephallenia*, the largest of the islands, is primarily agricultural, producing vines, cereals, olives, and fruit and raising sheep, goats, and pigs.   Its high peaks (5380 ft.), dominating its neighbours, were once clad in forests of *Abies cephalonica* and its slopes with 'maquis' woods, of which now little remains.   Its main export is wine and currant-grapes.

To the south *Zacynthus* is rocky but well watered; wheat is widely grown, the vine takes precedence over the olive, and sheep and goats are pastured on the island, on which there are remains of extensive woods. Its capital and ports face Elis, which it resembles in terrain and products. To the north *Leucas* is separated from Acarnania by a shallow channel, which periodically requires dredging to admit of navigation; the inner passage is preferred because the white cliffs of Cape Leucate breed stormy weather.   Producing sufficient cereals for home consumption, Leucas exports olives, wine, fish, and salt.   *Anti-Paxos* and *Paxos*, lacking water but rich in olives, form stepping-stones towards *Corcyra*, whose eastern capital and port control the channel facing Epirus and form the point of departure for the stormy passage past the Acroceraunian range to the Adriatic and South Italy.   With the highest rainfall and densest rural population in Greece, Corcyra exports olives, wine, and fruit and imports cereals and winter fodder for stock.   The chain of Ionian islands affords a more direct route and better ports than the mainland coast; in consequence, they attract sea-borne trade and act as middlemen to the mainland.

AEGEAN ISLANDS

In the same way the long island of *Euboea* acted as a maritime centre for the adjacent mainland, towards which the ports of Chalcis and Eretria face.   Despite the irregular currents of the Euripus Channel, the coasting route followed the Channel rather than face the storms off the east coast of Euboea.   Well forested with pine and sweet chestnut and rich in pasture, Euboea is also productive of cereals (mainly wheat), vines, and olives, and its southern tip contains deposits of marble, lead, and zinc. The Lelantine plain, facing the Euripus, is the wealthiest part of the island.   In the Saronic Gulf rocky *Salamis* lies in a recess, west of Peiraeus, but *Aegina* has a central position; it grows good figs, olives, and some cereals, and possesses a small sheltered harbour facing west.

The *Cyclades*, terminating to the south-east in Anaphe and Amorgos, form extensions of the ranges of Euboea and Attica, the group from Andros to Naxos containing marble deposits and the southerly islands being partly volcanic, like south Aegina and the Methana peninsula of northern Argolis. In antiquity gold and silver were mined at Siphnos. All the islands are mountainous and resemble Attica in climate, in production of olives and wine, and in deficiency of cereals; Naxos and Melos alone have sufficient pasture to export cheese. The centre of the Cyclades lies in Delos and Syros, both important markets at different periods. To the south, the outer Aegean islands form an extension of the Western Greek range, swinging in a semicircle to join the Carian Coast. *Crete*, the largest Greek island, is divided throughout its length by a high range with only two gaps. The northern part has more rainfall and possesses much better ports; Crete therefore looks more to the island-studded Aegean than to the open Libyan sea. Its balance of trade to-day is favourable, the main exports being currants, wine, olives, fruit, nuts, hides, and timber. The richest arable land is the plain of Gortyn and Phaestus; north of this a gap in the range leads to Knossos in rolling hilly country and to the port of Iráklion (Heracleum). This area is the natural administrative centre of the island, but land-communications are difficult, whether to the upland plateaus, productive of cheese and cereals, or to the western plain of Cydonia and eastern plain of Sitía. Of the original forests of deciduous and evergreen oak, pine, cedar, and cypress there are scanty remnants to-day, mainly in the west. The cypress was particularly important in antiquity for ship-building.

From Crete *Anti-Cythera* and *Cythera* lead towards Laconia, and *Casos*, *Carpathos*, and *Rhodes* towards Caria. The latter group enjoys a favoured climate, the heat of the long summer being alleviated by westerly winds. Casos being deficient in water is dependent on fishing. Carpathos exports olives, wine, and fruit and imports cereals, Rhodes exports olives, wine, fruit, vegetables, and honey and raises a considerable quantity of cereals. The key to the Aegean is held by Rhodes; it lies at the end of the chains of islands which lead from the Peloponnese, Central Greece, and the Hellespont, and its two harbours of Rhodes and Lindus face east towards the coastal route for Cyprus, Syria, Palestine, and Egypt. Mt. Atabyris (4067 ft.), a conspicuous landmark for mariners, bears the remnants of coniferous forest and cypress, which were used for shipbuilding.

To the south-east *Cyprus* lies outside the Aegean. By its strategic position it controls the approaches to the coasts of Cilicia and Syria, and its numerous small harbours form an important stage in the coasting route from Egypt to the Aegean. Its natural wealth was a further attraction in antiquity; rich in copper and in timber for ship-construction, especially cedar, cypress, and pine, it grew sufficient cereals to export and was famous for its figs and fruit. The main exports to-day are the locust-bean, potato, currant, cotton, silk, and fruit, while it has to import cereals. The climate, as in Crete, is more hot and arid in the south than in the north, and the population is mixed, the Greek-speaking element forming to-day about four-fifths.

To the north of Rhodes a belt of islands girdles the Asiatic coast, affording a direct route and acting as emporia to the mainland. The richest are *Lesbos* and *Chios*, the former in olives, wine, figs, and timber, the latter in wine, figs, and mastic gum; both grow a considerable quantity of cereals, and their mountains carry forest and pasture. *Samos*, less well watered but well wooded, is more suited to the vine, olive, and fruit-trees, especially the locust-bean; *Icaros*, which exports cattle and honey, links Samos to the Cyclades, the route from Attica to Samos being the shortest crossing of the Aegean. The islands further south, dominated by *Cos*, have little cultivable land and win their living from the sea.

In the north Aegean the promontory of Pelion is continued in the *Northern Sporades*, limestone outcrops with little fertile land, some olives, and a seafaring tradition; for *Sciathos*, *Peparethos*, and *Scyros* possess excellent harbours. Between them and the Hellespont lie the islands of *Lemnos*, *Imbros*, and *Tenedos*. Lemnos and Imbros are mainly covered in fertile sandstone flysch, the former producing cereals and wine, the latter timber and cattle. Tenedos exports wine and raises some cereals. The best harbour in the group is that of Lemnos. Finally, *Samothrace* and *Thasos* lie towards the Thracian coast. Samothrace, with its granite peak (5577 ft.) and forbidding coast, is thickly forested and exports only timber, cheese, and fruit. Thasos is rich in olives, fruit, wine, sheep, and honey, and exports timber from its forests of pine, fir, oak, and chestnut. With its temperate climate, natural harbours, and mineral wealth, it attracted colonization and was in a position to exploit trade with Thrace.

THRACE AND THE TROAD

The climate of Thrace is predominantly European, for only the sheltered sections of its coast experience the temperate influence of the Mediterranean. While the highlands are heavily forested, the lowlands and plains are rich in cereals, especially wheat, and in grazing for horses, cattle, and sheep; in addition to these products, nuts, figs, and wine are exported, the strong wine of Maroneia being especially famous. In antiquity Thrace was rich in gold and silver; the main deposits were in the area of Mt. Pangaeum, and gold was also washed in the Hebrus River of eastern Thrace. Despite its natural resources Thrace rarely achieved any national unity, for overland communications are difficult and the greater part of its coast is devoid of harbours; it has therefore tended to fall under the control of neighbouring land powers whether in Europe or Asia. South-east Thrace resembles the Troad in climate and in strategic control of the Hellespont. Both areas are exposed to the violent north winds from the Black Sea; these winds bring a heavy annual rainfall (30 inches), but their coldness is tempered by the warmth of the Aegean, Troy for example being much warmer than Constantinople.

The entry from the Aegean to the Black Sea is rendered difficult for ships under sail by the prevalence of the northerly winds and by the southbound current, usually four knots strong in the Bosporus and two and a half knots strong in the Hellespont; the sailor is therefore dependent on free access to harbours in the Straits. The Thracian coast of the Helles-pont is formed by steep limestone bluffs which contain some sheltered coves for anchorage but hinder movement by land along the shore. The Asiatic coast consists of a low foreshore of silt, deposited by the current at the Hellespont, and a background of sloping hills. The only obstacle to movement along this coast is offered by the limestone spur north-east of Troy, and the water offshore being shallow is less affected by the current. In contrast to the Thracian Chersonese, the Troad (bounded by the rivers Aesepus and Caïcus) is a fertile area, for which the copious springs and streams of Mt. Ida (5740 ft.) provide water; the alluvial plains are rich in cereals and in pasture for horses, cattle, and sheep, while the hills are wooded, especially with the valonea oak, and the mountains carry the remains of coniferous forests. Here the bear, deer, boar, wolf, and jackal are still extant, and the lion and panther were known in antiquity; birds too are abundant, especially the crane and stork. The richest fisheries of the Aegean world are located in the exit of the Black Sea, where vast shoals of mackerel and tunny move towards the Aegean from August to October. On the coast of the Troad extensive beds of murex are exploited for the production of purple dye. These factors combine to make the Troad a rich area in its own right, and, when it controlled both the sea-borne traffic between the Aegean and the Propontis and the overland trade between East Thrace and the Asiatic hinterland, it was able not only to increase its own revenues but to exercise an important influence on the Greek world.

CONDITIONS IN THE LATE BRONZE AGE

Throughout its history Greece has suffered a progressive deforestation, which has reduced its mountain slopes to barrenness and its rivers to dry torrent-beds in summer. In the Late Bronze Age, when the forest cover extended into the plains, there was less arable and more pastoral land. As a result meat was more plentiful and vegetable substitutes less important ; man was more of a nomad and a hunter, for wild game was prolific ; and areas suitable for settlement were more limited. To-day eighteen per cent of the land surface is cultivable, and the proportion must then have been less. The forests conferred some advantages : timber was available for fuel and building, the pine, cedar, and cypress supplied material for ships, and the valonea oak provided acorns as food for pigs and even for men, as well as dye and tanning extract. Throughout its history, too, Greece has suffered from a growing deficiency in cereals. This is partly due to the increase in population, which turns to trade and industry in order to cover the deficiency ; cereals are then displaced by more exportable articles such as the currant-grape, tobacco, rice, cotton, citrus, potato, and locust-bean, all introduced since classical times. This development has altered the balance in cereals, Cyprus for instance exporting cereals in antiquity which it now has to import. Even so, the general deficiency in cereals was always a factor in causing over-population, which has been a recurrent phenomenon under settled conditions in Greece.

In the Late Bronze Age it is probable that the margin of safety for an expanding population was smaller than in classical times. With less land under the plough and with a pastoral economy, which was not reinforced by the rise of industry and the development of wide overseas trade, the Bronze Age Greek turned in time of famine to freebooting by land and sea. For this the Aegean offered ready access to the mainlander and islander, and its innumerable coves and small sandy beaches offered shelter to their light craft. And across the Aegean lay lands with a similar climate and with richer resources in cereals, minerals, and accumulated wealth.[a]

NOTE TO CHAPTER 8

[1. Reference should be made throughout to a good classical atlas or map of ancient Greece, *e.g.*, *Murray's Small Classical Atlas* or *Murray's Handy Classical Map* of Greece (both ed. G. B. Grundy).

Books of Greek travel and topography are too numerous to list here. Among recent works whose illustrations give a good impression of scenery as well as monuments are —

Lord Kinross and Dimitri, *Portrait of Greece* (1956).

Robert Liddell, *Aegean Greece* (1954), and *The Morea* (1958).

A. A. M. van der Heyden and H. H. Scullard, *Atlas of the Classical World* (1959). (This has excellent photographs of landscape, including air views.)]

[a On food and agriculture in Homer see Ch. 20.]

CHAPTER 9

LANDS AND PEOPLES IN HOMER

by Helen Thomas and Frank H. Stubbings

i. INTRODUCTION

In addition to what the epics have to tell us of the political and physical geography of the Aegean area we may piece together from them some account of the whole world as known to the Greeks at the time when the poems were composed. The information they contain must have come from a variety of sources, including sailors' stories, folk-tale, and saga, as well as the poet's own observation; and the composite picture which these elements make up, though in parts merely fantastic, is yet generally consistent. Hardly anywhere is it a detailed picture; for ethnological and geographical data are never more than incidental to poetry, and we shall not find much in Homer about the manners and customs either of Greeks or of other peoples. Even of languages we learn little; for it better suits the progress of the story in epic, as in drama, to ignore the barriers of tongues and not to intrude the interpreter into an heroic parley. Herodotus may have been called ὁμηρικώτατος, judged as a historian; but Homer is no Herodotus, and the ethnographical excursus has no place in *Iliad* or *Odyssey*. Homer's world is revealed to us as it were in passing.

The earth seems to be conceived as a circular plane, surrounded by the stream of Oceanus, the source of all waters,

$$ἐξ οὗ περ πάντες ποταμοὶ καὶ πᾶσα θάλασσα$$
$$καὶ πᾶσαι κρῆναι καὶ φρείατα μακρὰ νάουσιν. \qquad (Φ 196-7)$$

Out of Oceanus rises the sun, and sinks again into it, as do most of the stars, except for the Great Bear, which

$$οἴη \ . \ . \ . \ ἄμμορός ἐστι λοετρῶν Ὠκεανοῖο. \qquad (Σ 489)$$

There are no words in Homer for the points of the compass, but the four winds have names, and their characteristics are differentiated. East and west are indicated by the periphrases πρὸς ἠῶ τ' ἠέλιόν τε ('towards the dawn and the sun') and πρὸς ζόφον or ποτὶ ζόφον ἠερόεντα ('towards the (misty) gloom'). Such phrases are necessarily approximate, and it is well in discussing questions of Homeric geography to remember that they refer to *sectors* rather than *points* of the compass.

283

The sea lies at the centre of the known world, and the more familiar parts of it (*e.g.*, the Hellespont) have particular names. The Black Sea, however, seems to have been unknown to Homer,[1] and in the *Odyssey*, once we are out of sight of western Greece, the Mediterranean stretches for uncharted distances to west and north. *Omne ignotum pro magnifico*: Odysseus's wanderings, however factual their ultimate source, however firmly stated the exact number of days' sail between the ports of call, show how insubstantial was Homer's knowledge of the lands beyond the western horizon.

The real, inner world of Homer consists of the Greek mainland and islands and the other countries fringing the Aegean. Within this area take place, Odysseus's adventures excepted, not only the main events of *Iliad* and *Odyssey* but practically all other events related or alluded to in either poem. In this area the Greeks of the epic are thoroughly at home. The names of rivers and mountains are common currency, their character-istics known, and their peculiarities noted.[2] Homer mentions all the large mountains south of Macedonia by name, except for Pindus, the Cretan Ida, and Tymphrestus; and of the rivers he names the Alpheus, Asopus, Boeotian Cephissus, Achelous, Spercheus, Peneus (and some tributaries), and Axius. Some parts of the Aegean area Homer clearly had seen with his own eyes, including the plain of Troy[3]; western Greece, one may surmise, he knew only from hearsay, for even the ancients had difficulty in interpreting his references to the Ionian islands.[a] But, on the whole, there is a clear and consistent conception of the main features of the Aegean lands, and of their mutual relation. There are, however, a few surprising inconsistencies which provoke the questions how far the background is part of the saga, handed down with it, and how far it was supplied by the poet from the circumstances of his own day.

It appears to be a general characteristic of epic poetry that major events of saga have firm local attachments; and in Greece there is a solid basis for these attachments, since it has been demonstrated that the places richest in heroic legend were also centres of the Mycenaean civilization.[4] It can hardly be doubted therefore, that the basis of Homer's geography is traditional; but we must not be surprised to find in similes and other parts of the poems not integral to the tradition that the geographical background is occasionally later.

ii. THE GREEKS, THE TROJANS, AND THEIR ALLIES

The primary document for the study of Homeric geography is that part of *Iliad* ii known as the *Catalogue of Ships*. This is of unique value as

[a] See below, Ch. 13 (iii).

describing the political geography of Greece at a period for which other written records — even since the decipherment of the Linear B Script — tell us next to nothing.   In it are parallel lists of the Achaean contingents which sailed to Troy and of the Trojans and their allies — a gazetteer of Achaean Greece, and a conspectus of the foreign nations north and east of the Aegean.   Fierce controversy has raged over the date of the *Catalogue*, some scholars holding it to be later, some earlier, than the rest of the *Iliad*.   The view adopted here is that it is a factual record of great antiquity, an integral part of the traditional tale of Troy, incorporated (perhaps in parts *verbatim*) into the *Iliad* to serve as a list of *dramatis personae*.[5]   The Greek catalogue (lines 494-759), which describes the various contingents by numbers of ships, may originally have belonged to an earlier stage in the tale of Troy describing the muster at Aulis; other scholars regard it as an adaptation of a national list of the Achaean dominions, pointing out that certain details — *e.g.*, that Thessaly comes last — are best explained on this assumption.

It is common ground among those who believe in the antiquity of the *Catalogue* that it belongs to the last part of the Bronze Age, the end of the Mycenaean period; that is, to the late 13th or early 12th century B.C. (This fits very well with one of the traditional dates, 1183, for the fall of Troy.)   Those who do not have made much of discrepancies between the *Catalogue* and the rest of the poems,[6] but their arguments have been largely disproved.   It is generally accepted that here and there the Homeric poems do contain references to objects and conditions which can be dated as far back as the 14th century B.C., but these cannot be used to invalidate the historicity of the *Catalogue*.

GREECE AND THE GREEKS

The Trojan War was to some extent a conflict between east and west; but as Thucydides rightly observed, Homer does not draw that distinction which the classical Greeks did between Hellenes and βάρβαροι; indeed he does not even use the word βάρβαροι — according to Thucydides because the Greeks on their side had as yet no established national name. But although it may be true that the Greeks before Troy were somewhat less conscious of social or cultural unity than the Greeks who faced the Persian at Plataea, the point should not be pressed.   Their unity was clearly more than a mere offensive alliance.   Ἕλληνες is admittedly in Homer still a local name, proper only to the people of a part of Central Greece; but the names of Argives (Ἀργεῖοι), Danaans (Δαναοί), and above all Achaeans (Ἀχαιοί) — with the occasional Παναχαιοί to stress their oneness — are applied collectively to all the people of Greece from northern Thessaly to Crete, from Cephallenia to Rhodes.   It is presumably because their common cultural characteristics were taken for

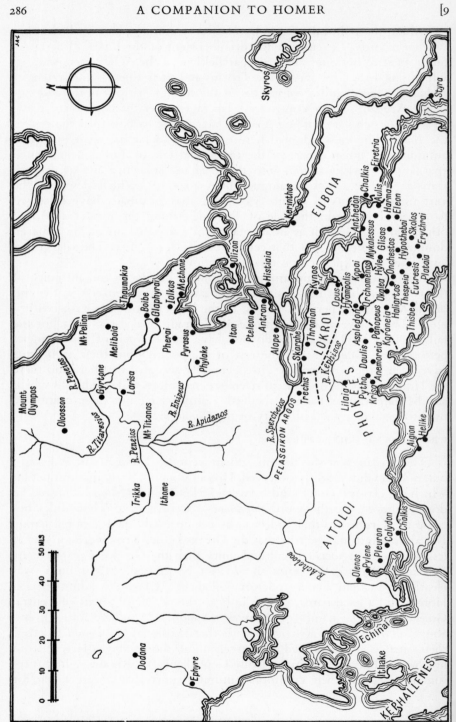

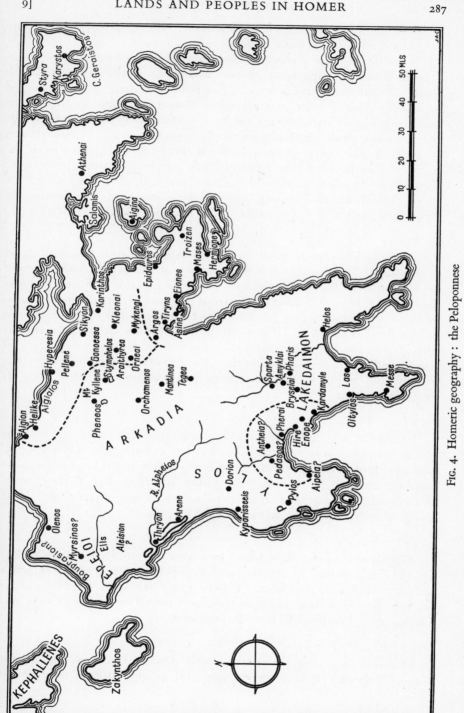

Fig. 4. Homeric geography : the Peloponnese

granted that they are nowhere described : all, apparently, speak one
language and hold the same customs and religion.

None the less, the Achaeans have their local divisions, and the *Catalogue* indicates the importance of these, and of the loyalties associated with
them. The divisions are not racial, but political rather, and are arranged
in a geographical order, starting from Boeotia, possibly because Aulis
was the point of assembly for the fleet. After covering central Greece
the list turns south *via* Attica to the Peloponnese, which it describes in
roughly circular order, coast-wise, from east to west. From Elis in the
north-west it passes to the Ionian islands and their adjacent mainland;
then across the sea to Crete and the Southern Sporades, and finally back
to the mainland, to Thessaly. It will be convenient to examine the
separate entries of the list in order. (For maps see Figs. 3 and 4.)

(i) *Boeotia*

Twenty-eight towns are named, of which four are mentioned again
in the *Iliad*. The most remarkable omission is Thebes, represented only
by Hypothebai, the lower town. This is a valuable indication of the
date of the *Catalogue*, for we know, from Δ 406 and from all later versions
of the Theban cycle, that its citadel, the Cadmeia, fell to the Epigonoi
before the Trojan War. There are at least fifteen known Mycenaean
sites in Boeotia, but none, except Thebes, on an impressive scale. This
corresponds well enough with the *Iliad's* picture of a province rich
enough and populous (its fifty ships had 120 men in each) but no
longer important.

(ii) *Orchomenos*

Politically separate, the neighbouring Boeotian state of Minyan
Orchomenos has only two named towns but a contingent of thirty ships.
The wealth of heroic Orchomenos was proverbial (I 381) and is archaeo-
logically attested, for a somewhat earlier age than that of the Trojan
War, by the remains of a frescoed palace and a magnificent tomb, and
above all by the drainage works of Lake Copais.

(iii) *Phocis*

Eight towns are listed, of which two were famous, Pytho (*i.e.*, Delphi)
for the 'rich shrine' of Apollo, and Panopeus as the scene of Tityos's
attempt on Apollo's mother. Phocis sent forty ships to Troy. It is
known that Delphi and many of the places round about (*e.g.*, Crissa and
Cirrha) were inhabited in late Mycenaean times.

(iv) *Locris*

Homer knows only the eastern Locris, described here as over against
(πέρην) Euboea. It sent forty ships. Of its eight towns only one is

mentioned again in the *Iliad*, Opoeis, the home of Patroclus's father. Like the Locris of historic times it seems to have been an undistinguished state, famous only as the home of the lesser Ajax. As yet few Mycenaean sites are known in this area.

(v) *Euboea*

This large island, the majority of whose seven towns were still in existence in historic times, also sent forty ships. Euboea in general and Chalcis in particular was inhabited from quite early Mycenaean times, but not thickly. Its southern cape, Geraistos, is mentioned by Nestor (γ 177) in his account of his *nostos*.

(vi) *Attica*

The only town mentioned is Athens, the δῆμος Ἐρεχθῆος, with a contingent of fifty ships. This is one of the most difficult passages to reconcile with a belief in the Mycenaean reference of the *Catalogue*. There are at least seventeen Mycenaean sites in Attica, the majority lasting well into the 13th century or even later. Perhaps, therefore, we should accept as historical the tradition that the *synoikismos* of Attica was due to Theseus in early heroic times — i.e., not later than the 13th century. Otherwise, the omission of Eleusis is strange, from whatever period the *Catalogue* dates, since it was more or less continuously inhabited from the third millennium and was famous in myth. In one passage (N 685 ff.) the Athenians are distinguished from their neighbours by the name of Ionians; but doubt has been cast on the genuineness of these lines (see below, p. 299). The 'strong house of Erechtheus' at Athens, which in η 81 is mentioned as a haunt of Athena, is probably to be identified in certain Mycenaean remains beneath the older temple of Athena on the Acropolis.

(vii) *Salamis*

This small island sent twelve ships under the greater Ajax. It has produced Mycenaean and sub-Mycenaean remains.

Megara is not mentioned, and the Megarid was probably included in Homeric Boeotia: Nisa, one of the *Catalogue* towns, is perhaps the same as Megarian Nisaea.

(viii) *Argos*

Before discussing the state of Argos, with which the *Catalogue* begins its Peloponnesian section, a few words must be said about the other meanings attaching to the word Ἄργος. In B 108 Agamemnon is said to rule over many islands and all Argos —

πολλῆσιν νήσοισι καὶ Ἄργεϊ παντὶ ἀνάσσειν,

a context in which Ἄργος appears to mean the Greek mainland. A similar meaning is to be seen in the many passages in which characters are said to perish (or to be in danger of perishing) 'far from Argos' (I 246; δ 99; ω 37, etc.). Elsewhere (e.g., δ 174) Argos apparently denotes the Peloponnese as distinct from the more northerly Ἑλλάς (on which see (xix) below); indeed Argos and Hellas are mentioned together (e.g., a 344; δ 726, 816; o 80). With the adjectives Ἀχαϊκόν and Ἴασον Argos is more definitely limited to the Peloponnese, while the Πελασγικὸν Ἄργος (B 681) is certainly the Spercheus valley (see below). Ἄργος ἱππόβοτον in the Iliad is simply a metrical variant for Ἄργος meaning Greece; in the Odyssey it is used impartially of the Argive plain and the Argive kingdom (e.g., γ 263; o 239, 274). The original meaning of the word is generally believed to have been 'plain'; like ἤπειρος it came easily to be used as a proper noun.

In the Catalogue the Argive kingdom is given nine towns and eighty ships. It covered part of the Argive plain (including Argos itself and Tiryns), the whole of the Argolic Akte from the Saronic Gulf south and westwards, and the island of Aegina. All this area is rich in Mycenaean sites, one, Tiryns, being of the first importance.

(ix) *Mycenae* (outside the *Catalogue* always singular, Μυκήνη)

This, the personal kingdom of the commander-in-chief, appropriately provides the largest number of ships, one hundred, and his followers are 'the most numerous and the best'. From Mycenae, in the north-eastern corner of the Argive plain, it stretches northward to include the whole Corinthia, the hill country between the Arcadian mountains and the Corinthian Gulf, and 'all the Aigialos' — that is, the coast as far as Aegium or even farther, in the later Achaea.

Many Homeric scholars have quarrelled with these two sections of the *Catalogue*, taking particular exception to the division of the Argive plain between two separate dynasties.[7] This division is, however, borne out by other passages in the *Iliad*. In Δ 376, for example, Agamemnon describes how the Argive ruler Tydeus had come on an embassy to solicit support for Polynices in the first war against Thebes. T. W. Allen pertinently remarks that you do not send embassies to your own country. There was no doubt a time when, as recorded by the legends of earlier generations, Mycenae, Tiryns, and Argos were united, under the Perseid dynasty: there is a reminiscence of these days in the mention (O 638 f.) of Periphetes of Mycenae, whose father was the herald of the last Perseid Eurystheus, who had his capital at Tiryns. But at that time Corinthia was independent under the Aeolids ruling at Ephyre (which is probably the Mycenaean predecessor of Corinth), as we learn from Glaucus's story in Z 152 ff. There is no intrinsic improbability in supposing that during the last century of Achaean power the domain of Mycenae shifted northwards.

At all events, nothing like the kingdom described in the *Catalogue* was known at any later stage of Greek history. Classical writers — Euripides for example — tended to confuse the heroic kingdoms, and to place Agamemnon's capital at Argos; Homer alone, uninfluenced by later history or earlier legend, preserves the distinction between them. The architectural magnificence and the wealth of Bronze Age Mycenae amply bear out the *Catalogue's* statement that it was the capital of the Great King of the Greece we rightly call Mycenaean; it is proper to presume that his kingdom too was as described. The area in question has numerous Mycenaean sites: besides the remains at Mycenae itself, the most impressive testimony to its supremacy is the great road system, still in places well preserved, radiating north, south, and east from the acropolis. And is it mere coincidence that Achaea has produced only *late* Mycenaean remains, not long antedating the Trojan War?

(x) *Lacedaemon*

The kingdom of Menelaus provided sixty ships from ten towns, of which those that can be identified were all in the Eurotas valley, near its mouth, or in the Tainaron peninsula. Sparta, Amyclae, and Helos were important places in classical times also, though only Amyclae can confidently be said to have kept its situation unchanged after the coming of the Dorians.

The extent of this kingdom is difficult to gauge, especially on the west. In I 149 ff. Agamemnon offers Achilles seven towns — Καρδαμύλη, Ἐνόπη, Ἱρή, Φηραί, Ἄνθεια, Αἴπεια, and Πήδασος — which ancient and modern scholars alike locate round the coast of the Messenian Gulf. All were

$$\text{ἐγγὺς ἁλός, νέαται Πύλου ἠμαθόεντος,}$$

i.e., bordering on the kingdom of Pylos (see below), and they seem to be named in order from east to west. Kardamyle, which has kept its name to the present day, is less than twenty miles north of Oitylos (now Vitylo), the most westerly Lacedaemonian town mentioned in the *Catalogue*; in classical times it belonged to Laconia. Pherai can hardly be other than the classical Pharai, which occupied the site of Kalamata castle (now also known to be a Mycenaean site). The princes of Pherai were descended from the river Alpheus (E 544 f.), and their political position appears ambiguous. When, in the *Odyssey* (γ 488 and ο 186), Diocles of Pherai appears as host to Telemachus on his journeys between Pylos and Sparta, he seems to be an independent prince; his sons were killed at Troy, but we are not told in whose contingent they served. It

x

has recently been suggested that the seven towns, under the dynasty of Pherai, constituted a small buffer state between Pylos and Lacedaemon, subject only to the overlordship of Mycenae, but this does not explain how Agamemnon should have been free to dispose of it at will to Achilles. Another passage in the *Odyssey* seems to imply that part at least of this area belonged to Lacedaemon (φ 13 ff.); Odysseus's great bow and its arrows, says the poet, were a present to him as a very young man from Iphitus, whom he chanced upon in Lacedaemon, when they met in Messene in the house of Orsilochus (father of Diocles).[8]

To the north there was, as in classical times, Arcadia. East and south, the barren promontory and dreaded cape of Malea doubtless belonged to Menelaus; but the island of Cythera perhaps did not. When Agamemnon, on his *nostos*, was carried away as he approached Malea,

$$\text{ἀγροῦ ἐπ' ἐσχατιὴν ὅθι δώματα ναῖε Θυέστης}$$
$$\text{τὸ πρίν, ἀτὰρ τότ' ἔναιε Θυεστιάδης Αἴγισθος,} \quad (δ\ 517\text{-}18)$$

it is difficult not to agree with Allen [9] that it was to Cythera that he was carried. If so, the island would have been a 'dower house' of Mycenae. Its chief town (K 268) was called Skandeia.

(xi) *Pylos*

Nestor's kingdom of Pylos has nine cities and provides ninety ships. It is thus the second largest in the Peloponnese, and the pleasant garrulity of Nestor makes it perhaps the most familiar of all. To the south-east, as we have seen, it reached the Messenian Gulf, to the east it marched with Arcadia. To the north it bordered on Elis, land of the Epeians, with whom in Nestor's youth the Pylians were constantly at war. The Alpheus flowed through it (E 545), but in some reaches formed the frontier, since Thryon, 'the ford of the Alpheus' (B 592), can hardly be other than the Thryoessa of Λ 711-12, which was also on the river and on the Pylian frontier.

By historic times the Pylian kingdom had faded from the map; its boundaries were unknown, the position of its capital city a matter of scholarly dispute. There were two towns called Pylos, one in Elis, the other in Messenia by the Bay of Navarino, known to all from Book IV of Thucydides; but Strabo, convinced that neither of these sufficiently answered to Homeric data, especially to the timetable of Telemachus's journeys in the *Odyssey*, proposed to look for Homer's Pylos in Triphylia. Until 1939 there seemed much to be said for Strabo's theory, both on the internal Homeric grounds and because a suitable Mycenaean site had been excavated in 1909 at Kakovatos. Since 1939, however, excavations at Epano Englianos, about six miles north of Messenian Pylos, have revealed an undoubted Mycenaean capital with a splendid palace, and an impressive series of royal tombs have been found in the area.[a] This can hardly be other than Homer's Pylos, and the name occurs with frequent prominence on the series of inscribed tablets, the archives of its last days, found in the palace. It may be only coincidence that the tablets, like the *Catalogue*, list nine principal towns in the Pylian kingdom; for their names are not those of the *Catalogue* and Pylos itself is not one of the nine.

(xii) *Arcadia*

The land-locked Arcadians went to Troy in sixty ships provided by Agamemnon. They came from seven towns, none of which is mentioned again in Homer but which include the familiar names of Mantinea, Tegea, Orchomenos, and Stymphalos. Tegea and Orchomenos at least were inhabited in Mycenaean times. When Nestor was a young man (H 132 ff.) the Arcadians and Pylians were at war

$$\epsilon\pi' \ \dot{\omega}\kappa\upsilon\rho\dot{\omega} \ \text{K}\epsilon\lambda\dot{\alpha}\delta o\nu\tau\iota \ . \ . \ .$$
$$\Phi\epsilon\iota\hat{\alpha}\varsigma \ \pi\dot{\alpha}\rho \ \tau\epsilon\dot{\iota}\chi\epsilon\sigma\sigma\iota\nu, \ \text{'I}\alpha\rho\delta\dot{\alpha}\nu o\upsilon \ \dot{\alpha}\mu\phi\dot{\iota} \ \dot{\rho}\dot{\epsilon}\epsilon\theta\rho\alpha.$$

Might Keladon be an earlier name for the Ladon? Homer gives us little help in defining the boundaries of Arcadia; it would be dangerous to assume, because the places mentioned are rather to the north and east, and the country itself is $\dot{\upsilon}\pi\dot{o} \ \text{K}\upsilon\lambda\lambda\dot{\eta}\nu\eta\varsigma \ \ddot{o}\rho o\varsigma \ \alpha\dot{\iota}\pi\dot{\upsilon}$, that it extended less far on the west than in classical times.

(xiii) *Elis*

This state is defined as much by districts and landmarks as by towns. There are four Eleian commanders, each with ten ships, from 'Bouprasion and holy Elis' [? districts], 'within the limits of Hyrmine and outlying Myrsinos' [? towns], 'of the Olenian rock, and Alesion' [? a hill]. These names recur in Nestor's tales (Λ 756 ff. and Ψ 631): from the former passage it appears that Bouprasion, the Olenian rock, and Alesion were not very far from the Pylian frontier. We do not know whether or not the whole of the north-west corner of the Peloponnese as far as Agamemnon's Aigialos was under Eleian sovereignty. At least one Ithacesian, Noemon, owned land for stud-farming there, and he was probably not exceptional (δ 635). The rarity of towns in this part of Homeric Greece corresponds to a scarcity of Mycenaean sites. The absence of any mention of Olympia, the sole glory of historic Elis, is to be remarked: few Mycenaean remains have been found there either.

From Elis it was but a short sea-crossing to the other Epeian kingdom, Dulichion and the sacred Echinae isles.

[a] See Ch. 13 (iv).

(xiv) *Dulichion and the Echinae*

This is another of the entries in the *Catalogue* which have provoked heated controversy.[10]   Both as a political entity and as a place-name Dulichion had vanished by the classical age and in modern times the references to it in the *Odyssey* have drawn it into the vortex of the Ithaca question.[a]   The rest of the *Iliad* does nothing to expand or illuminate the brief entry in the *Catalogue*.   From the *Odyssey* it is clear that Dulichion was an island (ι 22-4), fertile (ξ 335), and large (it produced fifty-two suitors for Penelope, almost as many as the other three islands put together).   This agrees with the *Catalogue's* forty ships.   The barren Echinades are unlikely to have contributed much to this total, and it is reasonable to suppose that the island kingdom had a considerable περαία, probably on the Acarnanian coast.

(xv) *The Kephallenes*

Odysseus's contingent — a small one of twelve ships — comes from the trinity of islands, Ithaca, Samos or Same (*i.e.*, Cephallenia), and Zacynthus, with some also from the near-by mainland (line 635: οἵ τ' ἤπειρον ἔχον ἠδ' ἀντιπέραι' ἐνέμοντο).   Of the other places listed, Strabo (452) says Krokyleia and Aigilips were in Acarnania.   Mycenaean remains are fairly common in all three islands.   Like Ajax, Odysseus owed his celebrity not to the size of his kingdom but to his personal qualities.[b]

(xvi) *The Aetolians*

This people, occupying approximately the same area as their descendants of classical times, send forty ships from five towns including Pleuron, Calydon, and a coastal Chalcis, perhaps to be identified with a place of that name mentioned in ο 295.   Two notable heroes of an earlier generation, Tydeus and Meleager, were at home in Aetolia (Ξ 116, I 529 ff.) and Pleuron and Calydon were already famous cities in their day.   Excavation too has shown that they were important in very early Mycenaean times.   The name of the Homeric ruler, Thoas, may be connected with the (identical) older name of the great Aetolian river, the Achelous.

Of the rest of north-west Greece Homer says very little.   The peoples here were probably barbarians, who would naturally take no part in the expedition against Troy and whose relations with their Achaean neighbours were slight and spasmodic.   Dodona, already famous as an oracle (*cf.* Π 233 ff.; ξ 327; τ 296 ff.), belonged politically to Thessaly (see (xx) below).   It was accessible through the kingdom of Thesprotia, whose ruler Pheidon is called ἥρως by Odysseus and merited the title by

---

[a] See Ch. 13 (iii).

[b] For further discussion of Odysseus's kingdom see Ch. 13 (iii).

his civilized and helpful behaviour to travellers (ξ 316 f., 331 ff.). Odysseus had a friend in a Thesprotian Ephyre (on or near the river Acheron) [11] who supplied him with poison to tip his arrows (α 259, β 328). Other less civilized characters also were placed by Achaean fancy on this part of the mainland, like the king Echetos, βροτῶν δηλήμονα πάντων (σ 85), with whom the suitors threatened the unhappy Irus.

Having thus reached one of the limits of the Achaean world, the *Catalogue* leaves the west and turns to the Aegean islands.

(xvii) *Crete*

The large Cretan contingent of eighty ships comes from seven named cities (the most famous are Knossos, Gortyn, and Phaistos) and from others, unnamed, of the many implicit in the *Catalogue*'s adjective ἑκατόμπολις. (τ 172 ff. speaks of 90 only.) Excavations at Knossos and elsewhere have shown that by the Homeric age the great days of Crete were long past. Successive shocks, earthquake or invasion, devastated the great Minoan cities and palaces, and after 1400 B.C. Crete was little more than a backwater, if a prosperous one, off the main stream of Mycenaean culture. The epithet ἑκατόμπολις may be a reminiscence of days long past, like Ariadne's dancing-floor (Σ 591-2). Nearly all Odysseus's fictitious adventures (ψευδέα πολλὰ . . . ἐτύμοισιν ὅμοια) start in Crete. From his tales we learn of the island's mixed population (see p. 299 f. below); of Amnisos, port for Knossos, and its sacred cave of Eileithyia (rediscovered in modern times by the Greek archaeologist Marinatos, and mentioned in the Knossos tablets); of the steep rock in the Libyan sea which kept the southerly gales off Phaistos; and of the far-seen ὄρεα νιφόεντα, which to the modern sailor too loom welcome and lovely above the empty Cretan sea. Homer knew Crete to be the most southerly of Greek lands; it was but four days' sail from there to Egypt,[12] and Crete was the only land seen on Odysseus's alleged journey from Phoenicia to Libya.

(xviii) *Rhodes; Syme; Nisyros, Krapathos, Kasos, Kos, and the Kalydnai*

Rhodes, which sends nine ships, has three cities, Ialysos, Lindos, Kameiros, just as in classical times. The *Catalogue* informs us that their ruler Tlepolemos was a son of Herakles; but it cannot follow from this, as is often alleged, that the Rhodians of the *Catalogue* were Dorian Greeks.[13] Tlepolemos himself had come to Rhodes as an exile from Greece, but need not have been the founder of Achaean rule there; in fact excavation has shown that Minoan and Mycenaean settlers had been installed at Ialysos and elsewhere since the 16th century B.C. Rhodes is not mentioned again in Homer; nor is Syme, which sent three ships. The rest of the islands — the Kalydnai presumably being the smaller members of the group — provided thirty ships between them. Their leaders too, Pheidippos and Antiphos, were descendants of Herakles. Kos is mentioned again in Ξ 255, where we hear that Herakles himself was once driven thither by the spite of Hera. This island had important Mycenaean and, earlier, Minoan settlements. Mycenaean remains are known also from Krapathos (Karpathos) and Kalymnos.

(xix) *Phthia and Pelasgic Argos*

Thessaly (this name is post-Homeric) comes last, perhaps because it was the latest acquired of the Achaean dominions. Here, as in the western Peloponnese, the Homeric and classical pictures are in strong contrast. The coming of the Dorians, which according to Greek tradition drove the Pylians overseas, similarly swept away the nine baronies which in the *Catalogue* occupy the Thessalian plain, and replaced the Myrmidons in the Spercheus valley by Aenianes (doubtless descendants of the Enienes, subjects of Guneus, who in Homer occupy north-west Thessaly) and Malians. Very few of the towns of classical Thessaly were built over Bronze Age sites.

Achilles, son of Peleus, commanded fifty ships manned by warriors from his father's kingdom of Pelasgic Argos, from the three towns Alos, Alope, and Trachis, and from Phthia and Hellas. These were known as Μυρμιδόνες . . . καὶ Ἕλληνες καὶ Ἀχαιοί. Alos cannot be certainly located; but Alope and Trachis both lay near the shores of the Maliac Gulf, and it is sufficiently indicated by Achilles's prayer to the Spercheus (Ψ 142 ff.) that the Spercheus valley was the heart of his kingdom, *i.e.*, Πελασγικὸν Ἄργος. The Μυρμιδόνες seem to be the nucleus of Achilles's force, as appears from those parts of the *Iliad* (such as the *Patrocleia*, Π) in which they and their leaders are most prominent.

The terms Phthia and Hellas cannot be clearly defined. There is good reason to regard Phthia as a regional rather than a political name. Though Achilles's home was Phthia (*e.g.*, A 154-6; I 253) his people are not called 'Phthioi', a name which does not occur except in N 686, 693, 699, a passage suspected on other grounds. It is there applied to the contingents of Podarkes and Medon, who, according to the *Catalogue* (see (xx) (*a*) and (*c*) below) came from the districts north and south of the Gulf of Pagasae. Leaf [14] set out to discredit the Thessalian sections of the *Catalogue* by assuming that Homeric Phthia belonged exclusively to Peleus and was co-extensive with the later Achaia Phthiotis — which makes nonsense of most of the Thessalian entries. We should regard the name rather as analogous to the modern Macedonia, geographically defined, capable of evoking nostalgia and other emotions, but at no time in its history a political entity.

As to Hellas, two things suggest that it was adjacent to Phthia, and to the south of it. Phoenix, leaving his father's home at Eleon (presumably the Boeotian town of that name) fled from and through Hellas to Phthia (I 447 ff., esp. 478-9). His statement that he *left* (λίπον) Hellas seems to imply that that name even included Eleon (in what was later Boeotia). The part of 'Hellas' between Eleon and Phthia contains the separate kingdom of Locris (see (iv) above) whose ruler Ajax

$$\text{ἐγχείη . . . ἐκέκαστο Πανέλληνας καὶ Ἀχαιούς.}$$

Here Πανέλληνας apparently marks him out as a local champion, Ἀχαιούς as a national one.

Peleus, then, ruled over the Spercheus valley (Πελασγικὸν Ἄργος, a part of the larger region of Phthia), and an undefined area of Hellas to the south. The Dolopes, who inhabited a distant corner of Phthia (ἐσχατιὴν Φθίης, I 484), in the kingdom of Peleus, may or may not have been outside the Spercheus valley; perhaps the allusion to them refers to a different age from that of the *Catalogue* (*cf.* p. 299 below).

(xx) *The rest of Thessaly*

Eight baronies or petty princedoms occupy the plain of Thessaly and its surrounding hills as far as Tempe; the power of one apparently extended over Pindus to include Dodona. But the transference and duplication of place-names and the wanderings of peoples — not to mention the 'adjustments' of later writers, usually in the interests of ruling families in search of heroic pedigrees — made it difficult for the ancients, and make it still more so for ourselves, to define their boundaries.

(*a*) The sons of Iphiklos (forty ships and five towns) have been placed, probably rightly, along the south-western side of the Gulf of Pagasae.

(*b*) The domain of Eumelos (eleven ships and four towns) is fixed for us by the mention of Iolkos (now Volo, one of the few places in Thessaly to have been in continuous habitation from the remotest times) at the head of the Gulf, Lake Boebeis, and Eumelos's capital at Pherai (mentioned also in δ 798).

(*c*) Philoctetes (seven ships and four towns) probably owned the east side of the Gulf. His power must have extended over the coastal strip on the Aegean side of Pelion and Ossa, for the site of Meliboea, one of his towns, has been discovered on the sea-coast under the south-eastern foothills of Ossa.

(*d*) Inland, the sons of Asklepios (three towns and thirty ships) had their capital at Trikka, the modern Trikkala, on the Peneus at the western end of the great plain (the classical Hestiaeotis). We are not told who provided the ships for these land-locked princes.

(*e*) East of this, and defined by two towns and two natural features, was the domain of Eurypylos (forty ships) centring upon the junction of the rivers Enipeus and Apidanos with the Peneus.

(*f*) The Lapiths (five towns and forty ships) held an area extending from Oloosson (now Elassona), among the mountains on the Macedonian frontier, to the Larisa district and the Dotian plain. In earlier days they had ranged more widely and had driven their traditional enemies, the centaurs, from Mt. Pelion across the Pindus.

(*g*) Guneus of Kyphos and his subjects, the Enienes and Perrhaibians (twenty-two ships and two towns), must have lived about the headwaters of the Peneus, since it is in this 'barony' that Dodona is included.[15]

(*h*) Finally, the Magnetes under Prothoos (forty ships, no towns mentioned) lived 'about the Peneus and leafy Pelion' — *i.e.*, in the later Magnesia on the east coast. Their northern boundary was probably the Vale of Tempe.

This whole area is little mentioned by Homer outside the *Catalogue*. In general, most of his references to northern Greece concern natural features rather than towns : correspondingly, Mycenaean sites, though not lacking, are thinly spread, especially to the west. Beyond Thessaly, Macedonia was in hostile, Paeonian, hands. Mycenaean objects have been found in Chalcidice and the Axios valley, but this need imply no more than trade contacts similarly attested for Troy itself. In any case Macedonia was always, until it grew into a great power in the fourth century, rather on the fringe of the Greek world.

Much more surprising omissions from the political geography of Homeric Greece are the Cyclades, the Northern Sporades, and the large islands off the Asia Minor coast ; with the exception of Delos and Scyros, these are mentioned only as landmarks. The poet obviously had a clear conception of their positions ; and sailors to-day, leaving Troy for Greece, would doubtless debate like Nestor and Menelaus whether to sail

$$καθύπερθε \ Χίοιο \ . \ . \ . \ παιπαλοέσσης$$

or

$$ὑπένερθε \ Χίοιο \ παρ' \ ἠνεμόεντα \ Μίμαντα.$$

The majority of the islands are shown by archaeology to have been inhabited in Mycenaean times ; but perhaps it is a historical fact that they took no part in the war. It seems to have been the neutrality of Scyros that made it a suitable place to send the young Neoptolemus, out of the way of the perils of war (T 326). Whether the inhabitants were Achaeans is nowhere stated.[16] Delos, like Delphi, was already sacred to Apollo.

The names of Lesbos, Tenedos, Lemnos, Imbros, and Samothrace, recur with some frequency in the *Iliad*. Lesbos and Lemnos are both referred to as having been conquered by the Achaeans, and were clearly non-Greek in population. (Lemnos was partly so even down to classical times.) Lesbos is ruled by one Makar — an un-Greek name; and the inhabitants of Lemnos, the Σίντιες, are specifically called ἀγριοφώνους (θ 294). These Σίντιες are always mentioned in connection with Hephaestus, whom they had taken up after his long fall from heaven; and presumably some special cult of the fire-god was localized in their island. Samos and Icaria are not mentioned at all by Homer.

Throughout the *Iliad* and *Odyssey* the same background of Greek political geography is assumed which is detailed in the *Catalogue*; and practically no local divisions of Greeks are mentioned which do not occur in it. There is an apparent exception in the Kouretes, whose attack on Aetolia and siege of Calydon is recalled by Phoenix (I 529 ff.); but he belongs to an older generation, and is talking of a time before the Trojan War, when the political set-up was different. Similarly he speaks of a different dynasty (the family of Oineus) as ruling in Aetolia; and the name of the Dolopes, whom he mentions as inhabitants of Phthia, may perhaps have disappeared by the age represented in the *Catalogue*.

In all the *Catalogue* there is no reference at all to Dorians or Ionians, the two great groups by which Greeks were so commonly classified in historical times. In fact those two names only occur once each in the whole of the two epics. The Ionians are mentioned in N 685 ff.:

> ἔνθα δὲ Βοιωτοὶ καὶ Ἰάονες ἑλκεχίτωνες
> Λοκροὶ καὶ Φθῖοι καὶ φαιδιμόεντες Ἐπειοί,
> σπουδῇ ἐπαΐσσοντα νεῶν ἔχον, οὐδ᾽ ἐδύναντο
> ὦσαι ἀπὸ σφείων φλογὶ εἴκελον Ἕκτορα δῖον,
> οἱ μὲν Ἀθηναίων προλελεγμένοι.

Several arguments combine to suggest that this passage is an interpolation, perhaps designed to support the Athenians' claim to be the leaders of the Ionians. The name Φθῖοι does not occur elsewhere in Homer; nor do the adjectives ἑλκεχίτωνες and φαιδιμόεντες. The latter is an odd word-formation; and the reference in the former to the long-flowing *chiton* characteristic of the classical Ionians appears to be an anachronism, besides being out of place in describing warriors.

The one reference to Dorians occurs in the important description of the peoples of Crete in τ 172 ff.:

> ἄλλη δ᾽ ἄλλων γλῶσσα μεμιγμένη· ἐν μὲν Ἀχαιοί,
> ἐν δ᾽ Ἐτεόκρητες μεγαλήτορες, ἐν δὲ Κύδωνες,
> Δωριέες τε τριχάϊκες, δῖοί τε Πελασγοί.

Here again, interpolation has been suspected; but there is less positive support for such a suggestion, and the mention of Dorians remains a puzzle. Usually they are explained, like the Pelasgians in the same line, as intrusive elements superimposed upon an autochthonous pre-Achaean population of Eteocretans and Kydonians. The Eteocretans are mentioned here alone in Homer; the Kydonians occur also in γ 292, where they are localized on the river Iardanos, apparently in the south-west of the island. The present passage is in any case remarkable as the only definite mention in Homer of such a heterogeneous mixture of peoples and languages within Achaean lands. The *argumentum ex silentio* is notoriously unsound; but this exceptional reference to a variety of peoples and tongues in Crete does suggest that in the remainder of Greece in the Heroic Age there were not such marked differences of language or population.

In any case, these isolated references to Dorians and Ionians do not disturb the general chronological consistency of the epic picture of an essentially pre-Dorian Greece, the Greece of the closing century of the Late Bronze Age.

THE TROJANS AND THEIR ALLIES

If we may believe the words put in the mouth of Agamemnon (B 123 ff.) the Trojans proper, the inhabitants of Troy, did not number even one-tenth of the Achaean force who besieged them; but they were supported by numerous allies of many different nations and languages —

πολλοὶ γὰρ κατὰ ἄστυ μέγα Πριάμου ἐπίκουροι,
ἄλλη δ' ἄλλων γλῶσσα πολυσπερέων ἀνθρώπων   (B 803-4)

—and these are all duly enumerated in the *Catalogue*. In the usual epic manner, little is said here or elsewhere of the characteristics of the Trojans. That they are not of Achaean speech is perhaps to be assumed, though it is not stated. Perhaps the most distinctive feature actually mentioned is the prominence of the bow as a Trojan weapon. Paris carries a bow (though he has sword and lances as well); and there is a foreign touch about the leopard-skin he wears over his shoulders (Γ 17). Pandaros also, who leads the Trojans of Zeleia in the foothills of Mt. Ida, is a noted archer: his bow is of horn, and his arrows are tipped with iron. And when Menelaus is struck by an arrow Agamemnon at once assumes that it was shot by a Trojan or a Lycian, someone τόξων εὖ εἰδώς (Δ 196 f.). In many respects, however, it seems that the Trojans differ little from the Achaeans. They are used to the same rules and customs of warfare, and — whether by epic convention or by a tacit identification of similar cults — they are represented as worshipping at least some of the Greek gods. Menelaus, proposing a truce, bids the Trojans sacrifice a black and a white lamb to the Earth and the Sun, while the Achaeans will make a like sacrifice to Zeus; and here there is perhaps a deliberate suggestion of difference. But elsewhere (E 9 f.) we hear of a priest of Hephaestus among the Trojans; there is a temple of Apollo in their city; and another of Athena, containing an image of the guardian goddess of the city, to whom Hecuba offers a robe of many colours.

The peoples north and east of the Aegean were all allies of Troy, actual or potential enemies of the Achaeans; and nothing more strikingly demonstrates the early date of the whole cultural reference of the *Iliad* than the complete absence of any mention of Greek colonies on the Asia Minor coast. The Trojan catalogue (*i.e.*, B 816-77) appears to represent the knowledge of Asia Minor current in Greece before the Ionian migration, and the sum of that knowledge is remarkably small. There is more information to be found in the rest of the poem (*e.g.*, B 459 ff.; Υ 390-2; Ω 614 ff.), in which we may perhaps see the increased familiarity of the poet's own day. The *Odyssey*, of course, has little to say about the east, though it adds something to the *Catalogue's* scanty notice of the Kikones.

The Troad alone is treated on anything like the same scale as the Greek entries in the *Catalogue*; the rest of the allies are listed in three groups, the last in each group being said to come τηλόθεν — 'from afar'. Few of them figure with more detail than their ethnic name, the name and descent of their leader, and a single town or landmark. In spite of the work that has been done [17] to illuminate these scanty references, the whereabouts of several of these peoples remains vague; no frontiers are mentioned, and it is often impossible to guess whether, and where, their territories touched one another. Even their relative importance cannot be gauged, since there was no Trojan muster-roll of ships (Some of the allies, of course, *e.g.*, Asios of Arisbe, came by land.) After the Trojans, the Lycians take the second largest part in the war, and we are told that both Thracians (near neighbours) and Phrygians (who had specially close relations with the Trojan ruling house) had lately sent reinforcements (K 434; N 793-4). In the following paragraphs the entries of the Trojan *Catalogue* will be examined in order. (See the map, Fig. 5.)

(*a*) *The Troad.*—Six separate contingents are listed, Hector's Trojans, πολὺ πλεῖστοι καὶ ἄριστοι, naturally taking pride of place. Next come Aeneas and his Dardanians: the evidence suggests that Dardania was inland, the middle valley of the Scamander. Perhaps the Dardanians had no towns, but only villages, since we learn (Υ 216) that Dardanus 'settled' (κτίσσε) Dardania, while Troy was a built city (πεπόλιστο). Other Trojans were led by Pandaros from Zeleia by the river Aesepos, 'under the extreme foot of Ida'. Another passage (Δ 91 and 103) confirms that Pandaros lived by the Aesepos (always a Trojan stream, as in M 21), but in E he is twice said to be from Lycia. Leaf [18] sees no difficulty in finding a branch of Lycians settled so far north: he points out that the Lycians proper called *themselves* Termilai,[19] and concludes that the

Lycian name has no special ethnic connotation. Nilsson, on the other hand, thinks that Pandaros was really a Lycian, but by a misunderstanding metamorphosed into a Trojan leader with a home in the Troad.[20]

The next two groups have no racial name. The first, under two sons of Merops, came from Adresteia, Apaisos, Pityeia (on the site of the later Lampsacus) and Mt. Tereia, places near the north-east coast of the Hellespont. Five other Hellespontine towns are named as the home of the next contingent, including the familiar pair Sestos and Abydos. Their leader Asios is to be distinguished from Hestor's Phrygian uncle of that name. But if not Trojans, these people were closely linked with Troy; one of Hector's cousins lived at Perkote (O 548) and a half-brother, Demokoon, at Abydos, where Hector also had a guest-friend, Phainops (Δ 499 and P 584).

Finally, there are the 'tribes of the Pelasgians' —

τῶν οἳ Λάρισαν ἐριβώλακα ναιετάασκον—

under Hippothoos and Pylaios. Attempts have been made to locate these Pelasgians either in Europe, as neighbours of the Thracians, or (by Strabo) far away in Aeolis. In earlier passages, however (440 and 604), Strabo refers to a Larisa near Hamaxitos (a small classical town a few miles north of Cape Lekton in the S.W. Troad); and Leaf has described a suitable site for identification with this Larisa. This seems the most likely position for the Pelasgians' city, and Strabo's reasons for rejecting it (Strabo 620) need not detain us. There is no room for Pelasgians in Europe between Troy and the Thracians, whose country, we are told, reached the Hellespont; and a southward excursus of 100 miles (to Strabo's choice) at this point of the *Catalogue* does not seem consonant with its general arrangement. Whether these Pelasgians are to be connected with those of Crete (p. 300 above), both being remnants of a once widespread race, is a matter of speculation.

The rest of the southern Troad is omitted from the *Catalogue*, but some of its towns are mentioned in other parts of the *Iliad* as among those which Achilles had sacked earlier in the war. (He claimed twenty-three such conquests in all: I 328-9.) They include Thebe Hypoplakie, the home of Andromache (A 366 ff.); Lyrnessos, where Achilles captured Briseis; and Pedasos on the river Satnioeis. The positions of all these are somewhat vague, and known only by inference. Pedasos and Lyrnessos are mentioned together in a passage (Υ 90 ff.) which implies they both lay near the Trojan Mt. Ida. They were inhabited by the Leleges, whose king Alteus was the maternal grandfather of the Trojan hero Lycaon. Some of the Leleges fought on the Trojan side along with the Pelasgians (K 428). Thebe 'under Mt. Plakos' lay, according to Strabo, in the plain of Adramyttium. Its people were Kilikes (Z 397), but

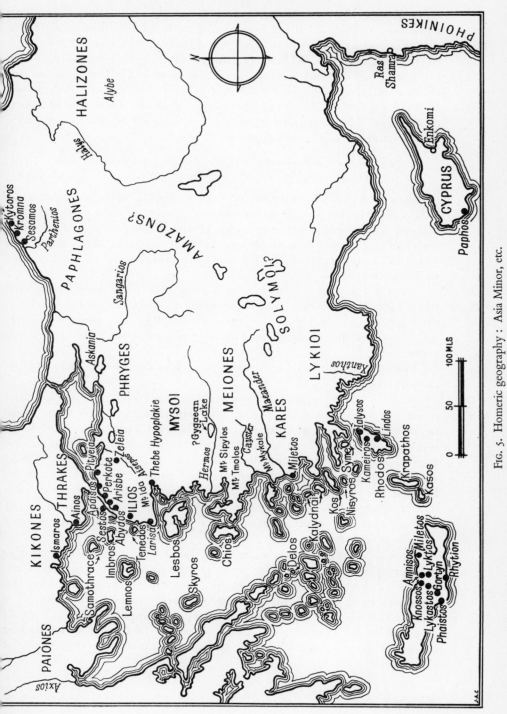

FIG. 5. Homeric geography: Asia Minor, etc.

in view of Strabo's statement, and of B 691, which links it closely with Lyrnessos, these can hardly have anything to do with the historical Cilicia.

Next come the European allies, listed from east to west.

(b) *The Thracians.*—These are distinguished by the epithet ἀκρόκομοι, carry long spears, and are famous as horsemen. They inhabit an area defined only by the Hellespont, but later we learn that one of their two leaders came from Ainos, near the mouth of the Hebrus; and their country probably extended even some way west of that, since Hera, *en route* from Olympos to Lemnos,

> σεύατ' ἐφ' ἱπποπόλων Θρηκῶν ὄρεα νιφόεντα . . .
> ἐξ Ἀθόω δ' ἐπὶ πόντον ἐβήσατο.   (Ξ 225 ff.)

(c) *The Kikones.*—Of these we are told only their leader's name. Odysseus, however, began his adventures by sacking their town Ismarus, famous (as Polyphemus learnt to his cost) for the potency of its wine. This fact has suggested an identification of Ismaros with Maroneia, which had a similar reputation. The Kikones may have formed a coastal enclave in Thracian country.

(d) *The Paeonians.*—This race of archers came from Amydon and the river Axios (modern Vardar). It is useless to speculate on the extent of their country, though we may guess that if they had been immediate neighbours of the Achaeans in Thessaly, Homer would have said more about them.

The next group of allies consists of two only, coming from northeast of Troy.

(e) *The Paphlagonians.*—If lines 853-5 are rejected [21] we have no clues about the Paphlagones except the statement that they came from 'Enetai, where is the race of wild mules'. Wherever Enetai may have been, we may probably accept, as implied in the three lines mentioned, that Paphlagonia came down to the Black Sea, as in historic times. Wild asses or onagers — Aristotle calles them 'mules' — used formerly to breed in the central highlands of Asia Minor; so the country may also have extended a good way inland. A touch of local colour in E 583 tells us that the Paphlagonian leader Pylaemenes had chariot reins decorated with ivory.

(f) *The Halizones.*—Alybe, whence this people came, is described as 'the birthplace of silver'. The word appears to be a transcription of the Hittite word for the 'land of the Halys', which fits well enough, since the Halizones must be beyond (*i.e.*, east of) Paphlagonia. The country of the river Halys was a province of the Hittite empire, which before its downfall about 1200 B.C. was the chief source of silver for the ancient world. This, at least, is a possible, though not a certain, interpretation of this section of the *Catalogue.*[22]

It is possible that the Paphlagonians and Halizones were conceived as lying in a line running north from Troy, following the general direction of the Hellespont. Otherwise it is hard to understand why they were not combined with the next group, which also lie roughly to the north-east.

(g) *The Mysians.*—For the Mysians the *Catalogue* gives no more than their leaders' names, but their position in the list puts them between Troy and Phrygia. Elsewhere (Ω 278) we get the scrap of information that they gave Priam a fine yoke of mules: did they perhaps draw on the same source as the Paphlagonians?

(h) *The Phrygians.*—The Phrygians' city Askanie is perhaps to be placed near Lake Ascania, in the region of the later Nicaea, no great distance inland from the Propontis. Their territory probably extended some distance south of this, since Π 719 suggests that the Sangarios flowed through Phrygia, and again in Γ 184 Priam tells how he had been the ally of the Phrygians when they were campaigning on the Sangarios against the Amazons. Such a position agrees with the statement that Priam's kingdom was bounded on one side by Lesbos and on the other by Phrygia and the Hellespont.

The final group of Trojan allies, the Maeonians, Carians, and Lycians, are less obscure; they represent in order the remaining parts of western Asia Minor, proceeding southwards from Troy. Between Troy and the first of them, however, is a gap, into which some would very tentatively put the country of the Κήτειοι on the slender grounds that their leader Eurypylos was the son of Telephus, ruler of Teuthrania, which was in this area. The Κήτειοι are in fact, only mentioned once, in λ 521. According to tradition Eurypylos came late to the war (like Neoptolemus on the Greek side), which might account for the non-appearance of the Κήτειοι in the *Catalogue*. But even in antiquity scholars were somewhat mystified by this people, some regarding them as a division of the Mysians, others rejecting them from the text and adopting readings not involving a proper name. In modern times their name has been tentatively connected with that of the Hittites, but this is highly speculative.

(i) *The Maeonians.*—The leaders of the Maeonians were children of the Gygaean Lake (Γυγαίη λίμνη) and came from under Mt. Tmolus. The lake is unidentified, but they perhaps lived in the region of Sardis. From E 43-4 and Υ 385, 390-2, we can add the names of two Maeonian towns, Tarne and Hyde, to the rivers Hermos and Hyllos. So much information about an area eighty miles inland in a hostile country is surprising; and like the simile of birds by the Caÿster (B 461) and Achilles's reference to the rock-sculptures of Mt. Sipylos (Ω 615), some of its detail may be due to Homer's personal knowledge.

(j) *The Carians.*—The Carians are described, uniquely, as βαρβαρό-φωνοι, and it is perhaps a further mark of their outlandishness that one of their leaders, Amphimachos, went to the war bedecked with golden ornaments like a girl (B 872). Their country lay around Miletus, Mt. Mycale, and the river Maeander, all readily identifiable, and Mt. Phthires, which is not. Compared with other allies of the Trojans they are clearly defined, and indeed this area had long been very familiar to the Greeks. Important Mycenaean remains have been discovered at Miletus, though little has been published on them; and Caria was close to the Mycenaean settlements in the Southern Sporades. It is striking, however, that after Miletus had become one of the greatest cities of Greece she should still figure in the national epic on the enemy side. The only likely explanation is that the *Catalogue* is presenting historical fact.

(*k*) *The Lycians*. The Lycians from the river Xanthus, though the most remote of the Trojan allies, play a remarkably prominent part in the *Iliad*, especially in Books M and Π; and the frequent phrase Τρῶες καὶ Λύκιοι suggests that they are, in fact, next to the Trojans themselves in importance. To the Achaeans they were, though distant, by no means unknown. Their leaders Sarpedon and Glaucus were both grandsons of the Achaean hero, Bellerophon, who had been exiled to Lycia from Greece, and after accomplishing many perilous tasks had won the hand of the Lycian king's daughter. The story is told (Z 153 ff.) by Glaucus when challenged by Diomede to state his name and pedigree before engaging in single combat, and it leads to a scene of unexpected recognition. There was an ancient friendship between the grandfathers of the two heroes, and indeed the link goes back a generation more, for Bellerophon's father had himself married a princess of Lycia. Two further interesting facts about the Lycians emerge from the story: that with them descent was matrilineal (Sarpedon has precedence over Glaucus as being the son of Bellerophon's *daughter*, Laodameia); and that like the Achaeans they were acquainted with the art of writing.

In spite of all this, the only known geographical feature of the Lycians' country is the river Xanthus — enough to identify it roughly with the historical Lycia, but not enough to show how it compared with it in extent.

(iii) THE REST OF THE WORLD

The allies of Troy do not include the whole population of Asia Minor, but the epics have scarcely anything to say of the remainder. The Solymoi, against whom Bellerophon once fought, may have been near neighbours of the Lycians. Strabo remarks in passing that they lived in Pisidia. The Amazons, with whom Priam too had fought as an ally of the Phrygians, on the Sangarios front, are so firmly implanted in Greek literature that it is hard to believe that these female warriors do not represent a real people of central Anatolia; the theory which identified them with the Hittites, romanticized by legend, has met with little favour, but deserves serious consideration.

We hear little of the other countries of the eastern Mediterranean. Cyprus was in historical times mainly Greek in culture if not in population; but how far this was so in the heroic age we cannot tell from Homer. No Cypriot contingent is mentioned in the *Catalogue*, but the king of the island, Kinyras, had sent to Agamemnon an ornamental cuirass as a complimentary present when he heard of the preparations for the expedition against Troy (Λ 20). This is the only allusion to Cyprus in the *Iliad*. In the *Odyssey* we hear (δ 83) that Menelaus had touched there in the course of his νόστος; so too (according to one of his invented yarns) had Odysseus (ρ 442). But there is nothing to show whether the Cypriots were reckoned as Achaeans or foreigners; there is a passing allusion to the precinct of the Greek goddess Aphrodite at Paphos (θ 362) — but is she truly Greek?

Menelaus had been to Syria also: the country is called Φοινίκη, and the people Φοίνικες (Phoenicians) or Σιδόνιοι (men of Sidon). They are famed as sea-traders and as craftsmen: Menelaus had brought away, as a present from his royal host, a *krater* of silver with a gold rim; another such *krater* was offered as a prize in the funeral games for Patroclus (Ψ 740); and we hear also of Sidonian textiles, brought to Troy by Paris (Ζ 290). Phoenician seamen appear to have been familiar in Greek waters, both as traders and as pirates.[a]

Along with the Sidonians, Menelaus mentions the Αἰθίοπες and the Ἐρεμβοί. The latter have been tentatively identified (on the suggestion of Strabo 41) with the Arabians, but we can only guess; the Aithiopes possibly belong to Palestine. They are, however, on the borderline between fact and fiction; they are divided into two groups, both in lands remote, at the rising and the setting of the sun (22 ff.). The eastern Aithiopes, however, seem usually implied; but of their manners and customs we only know that they offer many hecatombs of sheep and bulls to the immortal gods — a point which apparently interests Poseidon especially (*cf.* Ψ 205). Archaeology has shown that the Palestinian coasts were, in fact, known to Mycenaean traders in the period before the Trojan War; but it appears from the epic's references to the Aithiopes that such knowledge had been mostly forgotten.

Egypt is mentioned in the *Iliad* only once (Ι 382), when Egyptian Thebes is cited as typical of extreme wealth. Isolated as this reference is, it is interesting as preserving a memory of the Late Bronze Age, before Thebes had been superseded by Memphis as a centre of Egyptian power. The picture in the *Odyssey* is a little fuller. Menelaus had stayed there long enough to acquire great riches himself; and sure enough the country

[a] On Phoenicians in Homer see also Ch. 22.

Y

figures in Odysseus's fictitious adventures also. He had gone there (he says) with a raiding expedition, and gives a brief picture of the country's broad and fertile fields, tempting enough to a pirate band; but they went too far, and in next to no time the whole countryside was full of soldiery, horse and foot (ξ 245 ff., ρ 425 ff.). The incident is slightly drawn, but well illustrates the wealth and power of the Egyptians. It is too of some importance historically, since it seems to involve a memory of the raids made on Egypt by 'Peoples of the sea' in the early twelfth century B.C., which we know of from Egyptian records, and in which Greeks perhaps really did take part.[23]

Libya completes the tale of these lands of adventure, mentioned briefly (δ 85 ff.) as a country of flocks and herds, fabulously rich in dairy produce, where there are three lambing seasons in the year.

Peoples to the north of Greece are barely named; but it would be wrong to suppose that Homer's geography stopped short at Thrace. This is clear enough when he lifts us up into the stratosphere with Zeus, as he turns his gaze from the warring Trojans to take a bird's-eye view of the horsemen of Thrace, the Mysians, the Hippemolgoi (some nomad tribe of horse-breeders beyond the Danube, we may suppose) and the unidentified Abioi, 'most righteous of men' (N 5 f.). West of Greece the world of the epics soon fades into the mists of unknown seas. The exact home of the Taphians, who appear in the *Odyssey* only, is not clear; they appear to be near neighbours of Ithaca, but as they are not in the *Catalogue* are probably non-Achaean. They are described as φιλήρετμοι, sea-faring folk, and in several places the reference is to Taphian pirates. The father of the suitor Antinous had got into trouble by being associated with them (π 426); and Eumaeus the swineherd had bought a slave of them, probably some unfortunate fellow kidnapped on one of their raids. Elsewhere we hear of more peaceable trade, their ruler Mentes (or rather Athena in the guise of Mentes) says he carries a cargo of iron, which he hopes to exchange for copper from Temese (α 182 ff.). The location of Temese is unknown: some would identify it with the later Tempsa in Bruttium — likely enough in the context; others suggest Tamassos in Cyprus.

Scheria, the isle of the Phaeacians, where Odysseus was so richly entertained on the last stage of his wanderings, has since ancient times been identified with Corcyra (*e.g.*, in Thucydides i. 25). This people too are great seafarers, very wealthy, and as highly civilized as the Achaeans themselves. Formerly they had dwelt

ἐν εὐρυχόρῳ Ὑπερείῃ,

ἀγχοῦ Κυκλώπων   (ζ 4-5)

— a statement which may enshroud some fact of history, but we cannot now elucidate it. The Phaeacians are highly romanticized; but the Cyclopes belong wholly to the world of fairy-tale, along with the Aeolian Isle, Calypso, Circe, the Sirens, Scylla and Charybdis, and the oxen of the Sun. Later writers (e.g., Strabo 22 ff.) fixed Circe and the Sirens near Naples, Scylla and Charybdis in the Straits of Messina, and the Cyclopes on Mt. Etna. Although similar enthusiasts [24] in modern times have produced a wide variety of identifications in the western Mediterranean for many of Odysseus's earlier ports of call, a review of the later adventures encourages scepticism: Thrinakie and Ortygia might be anywhere; Circe (to judge from her family tree) has connections with the Black Sea; the Planetae may even have been imported whole-sale from the familiar tale of the Argo — 'Αργὼ πασιμέλουσα (μ 70). Yet we cannot say that these apparently mythical places and peoples were not in Homer's belief real enough, though little known. The country of the Arimoi,

$$\text{ὅθι φασὶ Τυφωέος ἔμμεναι εὐνάς,} \qquad \text{(B 783)}$$

may be only Sicily, with its conspicuous volcano Aetna. The Pygmies, against whom the migrating cranes are supposed to direct their southward flight, may even be the real Pygmies of Africa, vaguely known by indirect accounts. We cannot dismiss the Laestrygones without wondering whether Achaean mariners may not have heard of real cannibals in their wanderings, οὐκ ἄνδρεσσιν ἐοικότες ἀλλὰ Γίγασιν, in some land far north of the Mediterranean, where 'the paths of day and night are near to one another'. And if they had, it would not be difficult for them to believe also in the Cimmerians, at the very edge of the world, dwelling by the streams of deep-flowing ocean in perpetual darkness.

NOTES TO CHAPTER 9

1. Rejecting B 853-5 as an interpolation: see T. W. Allen, *The Homeric Catalogue of Ships* (1921), 156 ff.

2. E.g., Ταΰγετus, περιμήκετος; and the phenomenon noted in B 752 ff.

3. On the Troad see W. Leaf, *Troy*; Rhys Carpenter, *Folktale, Saga and Fiction* . . . 35-8, 45-6; A. W. Kinglake, *Eöthen*, chap. iv *ad fin.*

4. M. P. Nilsson, *Mycenaean Origin of Greek Mythology.*

5. *Cf.* T. W. Allen, *op. cit.* 34-5. For other views, W. Leaf, *Homer and History*, and Rhys Carpenter, *op. cit.*, who believes the *Catalogue* to describe the political divisions of Greece in the age of Pheidon of Argos. A re-investigation of the *Catalogue* by V. Burr (*Klio*), Beiheft ixl [= xlix], Neue Folge, Heft 36 (1944)) confirms the Mycenaean origin. For a fuller discussion of the *Catalogue* and its relation to the rest of the *Iliad* see now D. L. Page, *History and the Homeric Iliad* (1959), ch. iv (published after the present chapter had gone to press).

6. See especially W. Leaf, *Homer and History*, chaps. iii–vi. The theories of E. Mireaux, *Les Poèmes homériques*, are generally disbelieved by archaeologists. The discrepancies are carefully examined by Page, *op. cit.*

7. Especially W. Leaf, *Homer and History*, chap. vi. But *cf.* Page, *op. cit.* 127 ff.

8. On the identification of the seven towns see *BSA*, lii. 231 ff.

9. *Op. cit.* 68.

10. W. Leaf, *Homer and History*, chap. vi; T. W. Allen, *op. cit.* 82 ff., and references there.

11. It appears to be quite distinct from the Ephyre of B 659, Z 152, which in ancient times was identified with Corinth.

12. ξ 252 ff. In γ 318 ff., however, Nestor speaks of a sea so great that even birds do not cross it within one year (ὅθεν τέ περ οὐδ' οἰωνοὶ αὐτόετες οἰχνεῦσιν), apparently referring to Menelaus's return from Egypt (δ 571 ff.). The inconsistency can be explained on the assumption that the two accounts are of different date, and that the southern sea was not always so familiar. Alternatively, Nestor is just making the most of his story, and implies that birds which cross the sea to Egypt (on their annual migration) do not return till the following year because it is so long a journey.

13. Strabo (653) is very clear on this.

14. *Homer and History*, 110 ff.

15. On the location of the curious natural phenomenon described in B 752–5 see T. W. Allen, *op. cit.* 133 ff.

16. The Skyros conquered by Achilles (I 668) is probably a different place — in Phrygia according to the Scholiast.

17. W. Leaf, *Troy*, *passim*; Allen, *op. cit.* 147 ff. and references there.

18. *Op. cit.* 181–2.

19. Herodotus i. 173, vii. 92.

20. *Mycenaean Origins of Greek Mythology*, 57 ff.

21. *Cf.* note 1 above.

22. *Cf.* T. W. Allen, *op. cit.* 159–61.

23. See L. A. Stella's article in *Archaeologia classica*, iv. 72 ff.; also her *Il poema di Ulisse* (1955), 41 ff.

24. Notably Victor Bérard, *Les Phéniciens et l'Odyssée*, and *Dans le sillage d'Ulysse*, which richly illustrates the poem's Mediterranean setting, whether the identifications are accepted or not.

CHAPTER 10

AEGEAN LANGUAGES OF THE HEROIC AGE

by A. J. Beattie

GREEK began as a dialect of the Indo-European parent language, probably in east central Europe and probably in the third millennium B.C. Like other groups of Indo-European speakers, the proto-Hellenes separated themselves from an original state or cluster of communities and migrated in search of new lands. The route and duration of this movement are uncertain, but from archaeological evidence it seems that the Greeks reached Greece early in the second millennium, perhaps by sea from Asia Minor rather than by land from the north. From the speech of their early settlements classical Greek emerged after a development of a further thousand years. The purpose of this chapter is to bridge the gap in Aegean linguistic history between this first Hellenic immigration and classical times.

i. AEGEAN LANGUAGES IN THE CLASSICAL AGE

Such an investigation must start from the situation in the historical period, and account must be taken, first, of the distribution of classical Greek and the barbaric languages and, secondly, of dialect division within Greek (see the map, Fig. 1).

Asia Minor.—The early Greek cities in Asia Minor formed a coastal chain from the Troad to Pamphylia and extended into the main river-valleys. Various native languages were spoken in the hinterland, and these were by no means extinct in the Greek cities. The most important were, from north to south, Phrygian, Mysian, Lydian, Carian, and Lycian. All of these disappeared in early Christian times, leaving few records, and the nature of each is to some extent in dispute. Lydian, Carian, and Lycian are often regarded as an 'Anatolian' group of languages, distantly related to Hittite and to other languages spoken in Central Asia Minor in the second millennium and, like Hittite, derived from a mixture of non-Indo-European tongues with the speech of Indo-Europeans who entered Asia soon after 2000 B.C.[a] It has long been held, however, that Phrygian is of direct Indo-European descent, forming part of a Thraco-Phrygian group, and that it was introduced from Europe to Asia towards the close of the second millennium. Similarly, the

[a] *Cf.* p. 323 below.

Mysians are thought to be Thracians who reached Asia about the same time. But Phrygian in classical and post-classical times shows a complex form. Apart from parallels with Greek, which may be explained as due to long association with the Aeolians, it has a strong Asiatic element, which should perhaps be regarded as basic and not as a mere accretion to the features which resemble Thracian. It is noteworthy also that Mysian was thought by Herodotus (i. 171, *cf.* Strabo, xii. 4. 564, xii. 8. 572) to be akin to Lydian and Carian, although according to the current modern theory it should have had a pronounced Thracian character.

Thrace and Macedonia.—In Thrace and Macedonia, Greek colonies (founded much later than those of Asia) were likewise confined to the coast. From the Hellespont to Chalcidice most of the inhabitants spoke Thracian, which was certainly Indo-European, but distinct from Greek. Although the unity of the Thraco-Phrygian group is not beyond doubt, Thracian penetration into Asia (particularly Bithynia) during the immediately pre-classical period must be accepted. In Macedonia the situation is obscure. According to Greek tradition, the people were related to the Dorians (Hdt. i. 56, etc.; *cf.* Strabo, vii. 1. 321, vii. 7. 326); and among the extant Macedonian words parallels with Greek, and particularly with West Greek, do exist. Probably, however, many of the Macedonians were non-Greek in race and speech; in both respects they may have been related to the Illyrians in the west.

Illyria and Epirus.—The Illyrians dwelt in the Pindus mountains and along the Adriatic coast, and their settlements extended through Epirus to the borders of Thessaly and Aetolia. Their language was Indo-European also, perhaps closest to Thracian, but at any rate strongly differentiated from Greek.

Greece and the Islands.—The remaining Aegean lands, namely mainland Greece and the islands, were Greek-speaking in classical times. There is proof, however, of non-Greek speech on two islands on the periphery.

Lemnian.—Lemnos only became Greek when it was captured by the Athenians under Miltiades (Hdt. vi. 136 f.; *cf.* Thuc. iv. 109). Its previous inhabitants are called variously Tyrrhenians, Pelasgians, or Minyans. One Lemnian stele of the sixth century, in fact, bears inscriptions in an un-Hellenic language. These cannot be translated, but words and phrases show affinity with the Tyrrhenian (Etruscan) of Italy. Lemnian is thought to be a branch from the same stem as Etruscan, which was no longer spoken in sixth-century Asia, but (according to tradition) had been carried to Italy from the Lydian coast by a mass migration, perhaps between 1000 and 800 B.C. Etruscan must then be added to the pre-classical languages of Asia. This creates a new problem; for although Etruscan shares some features with Lydian, etc., the nature of its relationship with these tongues is obscure.

Eteocretan.—In Crete, there are two non-Greek inscriptions from Praisos and a third from Hierapytna, all of the late fifth or early fourth century. Each is fragmentary and hard to decipher. The language is usually called Eteocretan (a name borrowed from Homer, τ 176) because Praisos, according to tradition, was not affected by the early Hellenization of Crete (Hdt. vii. 170 f.). While it has no obvious relationship either with the Asiatic languages or with Lemnian, such connections are not impossible. (Attempts have been made, however, to link Eteocretan with Messapian and Venetic, which are normally recognized as trans-Adriatic dialects of Illyrian.)

The Greek dialects.—The Greek-speaking area is divided into local dialects, which may reflect conditions in an earlier age. Here it is enough to note that the division indicates for the immediately pre-classical period the eastwards expansion of the Greeks towards Asia. There are three roughly parallel bands across the Aegean; an *Aeolic* band, from Thessaly and Boeotia, through Lesbos to Mysia and Lydia; an *Ionic*, from Attica and Euboea through the Cyclades to Lydia and Caria; and a *Doric*, from the Peloponnese through Thera, Crete, Rhodes to Lycia and Pamphylia. The Doric band is interrupted, however, by two dialects in *Arcadia* and *Cyprus* which form a group akin to Aeolic and Ionic. The fact that Arcado-Cypriot characteristics occur also among the Doric dialects, notably Pamphylian, suggests that Doric may be overlaid on an earlier dialect-group which reached from the Peloponnese to Cyprus; but this hypothesis is not free of difficulty.

Lastly, in the mountains of central Greece, especially towards the west (Aetolia, Phocis, Locris), there are dialects which resemble Doric and are unlike Aeolic, Ionic, and Arcado-Cypriot. Accordingly these dialects and Doric (and perhaps also Macedonian) may be classed together under the term 'West Greek', and a period of early unity may be postulated for them. The other groups are termed 'East Greek'.[a]

ii. THE DARK AGE

The conditions described above were the product of the Greek Dark Age, a period which covers roughly the sub-Mycenaean and Geometric phases of Aegean culture. Its remote limit is fixed by the Dorian invasion (about 1100 B.C.), which completed the downfall of Mycenaean political power and replaced the Achaean princes of the Peloponnese and the southern islands by a West-Greek ruling caste. The political and economic changes of the next five centuries were inevitably accompanied by far-reaching linguistic developments. Some trends are obvious; for example, the regression of Asiatic speech in the east Aegean before

[a] The characteristics and interrelation of the dialects are discussed in Ch. 4 (ii)., pp. 84 ff.

the advance of the Aeolian, Ionian, and Dorian colonists. In the Greek lands, moreover, the political separatism of the Dark Age must be held partly responsible for the plethora of local dialects in the sixth century. But to assess the full scale of linguistic change induced by the Dorian invasion, we must turn to the Mycenaean or Heroic Age which preceded it.

iii. AEGEAN LANGUAGES IN THE HEROIC AGE

Most of our information concerning this era is derived from the Homeric poems. Although these attained their final form towards the end of the Dark Age, they retain elements which are peculiarly Mycenaean. The most important passage of this kind is the *Catalogue of Ships* (B 484 ff.), where the realms of the Achaeans and of the Trojan coalition are listed.[a]

The Achaean Empire.—The Achaean boundaries were much narrower than those of classical Greece. They included only central and southern Greece and the southern islands. The Thessalian plain as far as Oloosson is held by Achaeans, but their northern frontier is undefined; and although there is an Achaean route to Dodona, the people there, if perhaps Achaean in speech, are probably beyond the pale. North of the Corinthian gulf and in the Western Isles there are Achaeans, but in the remoter parts of this area the claims of Taphians and others are more than dubious. It is in the Aegean islands, however, that the limits of Achaean power are most noticeable. Apart from Euboea and other coastwise islands, only Crete, Rhodes, and the Southern Sporades send contingents to Troy; neither the Cyclades nor the cities of the Asiatic coast figure in the *Catalogue*. The very name 'Ionian' is as rare in epic as that of the Dorians. It appears at least possible that most of the Ionian regions of later times were either not Achaean at all or, if subject to the Atreidae, were peopled for the most part by non-Achaeans. In the north, Lesbos is hostile territory (I 129, etc.) and neither this nor any neighbouring island can have been Achaean.

Asia Minor.—On the Asiatic seaboard, Maeonians, Carians, Lycians, and other Trojan allies were in full possession and their languages of Anatolian pattern prevailed. It is regrettable that Hittite records contemporary with the Heroic Age throw little light on conditions in this area. Of the later languages, Lydian must in any case be discounted as a dialect which only acquired importance in the Dark Age: its place in Homer is filled by the Maeonians (see Hdt. i. 7). Achaean settlements are only possible in the extreme south-west and there only on a small scale; this much may be read into legends of ancient wars in Lycia and Cilicia (*e.g.*, Z 152-211). If, as is now believed, the state called in the

[a] *Cf.* Ch. 9 above, with maps (Figs. 3 to 5).

Hittite records *Arzawa* lay in these south-western parts of Asia Minor, then such Achaean settlements would have been surrounded by speakers of Luvian, an Indo-European language closely akin to Hittite. Luvian may have been in some degree an ancestor of the Lycian tongue. Otherwise the only Eastern colonies of Achaeans which may be postulated are in Cyprus (Λ 21 f.; ρ 442 f.).

Trojan.—The identification of the Trojan language is especially difficult. Some scholars on the basis of personal names would associate it with Thraco-Phrygian or even Illyrian, but strictly Asiatic connections are just as likely. Phrygians from the Trojan hinterland appear in the anti-Achaean alliance, but are not more closely associated than others with the Trojans. A passage in the Homeric Hymns (which has no claim to great antiquity) indeed draws a distinction between Phrygian and Trojan speech (*Hom. Hymn.* v. 113 f.). Some scholars who think that the Greeks came through Asia to the Aegean are inclined, on account of the similarity between Middle Helladic culture and the contemporary culture in Troy, to suppose that there may have been Greeks in the Troad at least for some part of the second millennium. So Priam might have spoken Greek. It would be improper, however, to connect this hypothesis with the fact that Homer does not distinguish the Trojan language from Greek. That need be no more than a literary convention.

The North Aegean.—Of the peoples of Thrace it is enough to say that none of them can be Achaeans. All were Trojan allies, and some at least may have spoken Thracian; but some may have been more nearly akin to the Trojans (if these were non-Thracian). The Lemnian language may be imagined to have had a wider currency in Heroic times, not only in the northern islands but on the adjacent Asiatic and Thracian coasts. And it is possible that this language is a descendant of the Trojan tongue.

The Cyclades.—In the Cyclades and east central islands, if these were not fully Achaean, speech of the Carian type may have been the norm. This would be in keeping with Greek tradition concerning Carians and their kinsmen the Leleges in this region (Hdt. i. 171; Thuc. i. 4, 8).

But the profusion of legends forbids not merely definite identification of peoples and languages in any part of the north and east Aegean but also the assumption that only one language or people is to be assigned to any single district. We must be content to recognize merely a linguistic pattern broadly similar to that of the historical period.

iv. THE LANGUAGE OF THE ACHAEANS

Hittite and Egyptian records of the Achaeans.—Before the language of the Achaeans is considered, notice must be taken of the contemporary records of the Hittite and Egyptian kings and also of the later inscriptions of the rulers of Kara Tepe in Cilicia. These tend to confirm the existence of Homer's Achaean Empire as a small but aggressive power, at times dominant in the Aegean.

In the second half of the fourteenth century, the Hittite King Muršiliš had dealings in south-west Asia with a state called *Aḫḫijawa*, which, despite all objections raised, can only be the Homeric Ἀχαίϝα, Ἀχαιϝοί. There is, moreover, a king named *Antarawaš*, whose dominions included *Lazpa*. Later the Hittites were in relations with his son and successor *Tawagalawaš*. Father and son have been identified with two mythical kings of Orchomenos named Ἀνδρεύς and Ἐτεοκλῆς (archaic Ἐτεϝοκλέϝης) and *Lazpa* with Λέσβος. *Milawanda*, where their interests met those of the Hittites, is perhaps Μιλύας in Pamphylia or Μίλητος in Caria. Phonetically there is not much against these equations and their mere accumulation lends them some plausibility. They involve, however, the assumption of a pre-Atreid empire centred on Boeotia and a conquest of Lesbos before the Trojan war. Neither of these things is particularly probable, and in any case there seems to be no good reason for associating *Antarawaš* and *Lazpa* with *Aḫḫijawa*.

Hittite-Achaean relations were apparently maintained in the following century. The Achaeans were active in the direction of Lycia, Pamphylia, Cilicia, Cyprus, and the Phoenician coast. In the middle decades the Hittite Tutḫaliaš had to defend himself in southern Asia against *Attariššyaš*, 'a man of *Aḫḫijawa*'. The latter is not the king of *Aḫḫijawa* and therefor not Ἀτρεύς, as has been suggested; this equation would in any case be unacceptable on phonetic grounds.

At the end of the thirteenth century the Egyptians refer to *Aqaiwasha* in the characteristically Achaean role of lending military aid to a rebel Libyan prince. They make no other mention of Achaeans, but two possible references occur to the closely associated name Δαναοί. One of these, dated 1379 B.C., refers to a northern land called *Danuna*; this, as the Kara Tepe documents seem to show, was located in the Cilician plain, but whether the Achaean Δαναοί were Asiatics who migrated thence to Greece or people from Greece who migrated to Cilicia is at present beyond the limits of conjecture. The other, describing a warlike migration which about 1200 B.C. destroyed the Hittite Empire and nearly penetrated into Egypt itself, speaks of *Danawa* among the invaders. The hordes in question may have originated among Indo-European peoples in the Balkans but certainly included native peoples of western Asia Minor. This movement led directly to the rise of the Phrygians and Mysians and may have contributed a century later to the fall of the Achaeans. But the appearance of Δαναοί here might indicate an Achaean element in league with the barbarians.

The language of the Achaeans.—From these references, the chief linguistic fact that emerges is the Achaean name. Now, the Greeks in the classical age and later assumed, not unnaturally, that 'Achaean' is equivalent to 'early Greek'. Yet the name itself is not Indo-European, and even the place-names, ethnics, and personal-names of the Hittite records, if they are correctly identified, are, with the exception of Ἐτεοκλῆς, of a non-Greek type. These facts alone are a caution against a simple equation with Greek.

Achaean Greek.—That Greek *was* spoken in the Achaean territories is supported by the absence of evidence of any large-scale Indo-European immigration into Greece after or during the late Bronze Age. The only movements of Aegean peoples at this time are purely local, the latest being the Dorian invasion, which involved no more than the intrusion into the Peloponnese of Greek tribes hitherto domiciled on the northern border of Central Greece. The first coming of the Greeks must be referred to more distant times.[a]

The nature of Achaean Greek is perhaps to be inferred from the distribution of the classical dialects and from the Dorian legend. All or most of the West Greek dialects must have been beyond the proper influence of the Achaean king. Achaean speech must, accordingly, be the source of the remaining dialect-groups — Arcado-Cypriot, Aeolic, and Ionic. It was formerly thought that the Ionians were the first Greeks to arrive in the mainland, and that they were subsequently driven eastwards and partly overrun by an influx of Achaeans and Aeolians, who were in turn swamped by Dorians. The first part of this theory is based mainly on the confused legends concerning early Ionians in the Peloponnese, referred to, for example, by Herodotus (i. 145-6) and Strabo (viii. 1. 333). The objections to it are that, while it recognizes the relationship between Arcado-Cypriot and Aeolic, it exaggerates the difference between them and Ionic, and it does not fit the Homeric world, where there is no room for an Ionian element of the kind supposed. The only Homeric reference to Ionians is in N 685, where the following lines show that Athenians are meant. The alternative is to recognize Ionic, Arcado-Cypriot, and Aeolic as alike descended from Achaean (the Ionians having according to legend reached the islands not only from Attica, Euboea, and Boeotia but from the northern Peloponnese also) and the development of Ionic as later than both the Trojan War and the occupation of the islands.

In the Heroic Age, the dialect division of later centuries cannot have been fully developed. We may postulate, however, that the foundations of Aeolic were laid in Achaean speech north of the Isthmus, those of Arcado-Cypriot (together with related elements embedded in Doric)

[a] *Cf.* Ch. 12.

in Achaean of the Peloponnese, and those of Ionic in a combination of both effected in a new environment.

Other Achaean languages.—Was Greek the *only* language of the Achaeans? One passage in the *Odyssey* (τ 172 ff.) suggests, at least for Crete, a complicated situation. It describes Crete as an island of ninety cities and of many tongues mingled one with another. Five peoples are named — Eteocretans, Kydonians, Pelasgians, Achaeans, and Dorians. Even if Dorians are dismissed as a post-Mycenaean addition, the others probably date from Heroic times. And even if Achaean be Greek and Eteocretan be both the language of Praisos and that of the Minoan civilization, the remaining languages, Cydonian and Pelasgian, are unlikely to be identical with or even closely related to either of them.

Evidence of a different order appears in the Homeric reference to certain objects by a 'divine' as well as by a 'mortal' name (A 403; B 813-14; Ξ 291; Υ 74; cf. κ 305; μ 61). Synonyms are a recognized sign of linguistic mixture. Moreover, a language ousted from common use by another sometimes retains currency as a sacral or learned language. It is, therefore, tempting to see in these Homeric expressions a memory of non-Greek speech surviving through religious sanction. Even if this was the origin of the distinction, however, it is not possible to identify the language in question; for either the divine name or the mortal name, or both or neither, appear to be good Indo-European Greek or non-Greek at random.

Mycenaean Greek.—Direct evidence of the speech of the Heroic Age is provided only by documents in the Linear A script, found in south and east Crete (but hardly at all at Knossos) and the Linear B script, which occurs at Knossos and also at Mycenae, Pylos, and other mainland sites. Attempts to interpret the documents as Hittite having failed, and other hypotheses which aimed at establishing some sort of connection with Etruscan, or, more vaguely, 'Pelasgian', having little prospect of success, a good many possibilities remained: *e.g.*, an inflected language related to Carian or another dialect of the Asiatic coast, or even a completely unknown language. But in the light of the archaeological theories now prevailing the most obvious possibility is Greek.[1]

The non-Greek languages of Praisos and Lemnos impose caution against any general assumption of homogeneity. Even if the people of the Achaean principalities were predominantly Greek-speaking, their rulers might have been foreigners speaking a foreign tongue. The variegated ancestry of the heroes in legend, together with their unintelligible names, might point to this conclusion. Alternatively, if the rulers spoke Greek, their lieutenants and servants might have continued to use the idiom of an older civilization. In parts of Crete it is even conceivable that Greek rulers might have spoken a non-Greek language, taken over from the native population, as a *lingua franca*. These are mere possibilities, and want of evidence prevents their becoming anything more; but while the Cretan hieroglyphs as well as the Linear A and Linear B scripts remain unintelligible none of them can be ruled out.[a]

V. BORROWED ELEMENTS IN GREEK

Certain features of the classical Greek language must be added to the external evidence already adduced. Apart from its Indo-European structure and vocabulary, Greek contains distinctive elements which can hardly be pure innovations. They must be borrowings from another language or languages, either non-Indo-European or Indo-European in another tradition. Their occurrence in all or most classical dialects guarantees their antiquity. While in theory it is possible that large-scale borrowing took place during the migration from the north, there is no evidence for this and correspondence with other Aegean languages obliges us to seek the sources of borrowing in the Aegean after the migration.

The clearest evidence is in vocabulary, both in complete words and in formative elements.

Place-names.—Many Greek place-names are not explicable as Indo-European and must either have been in use when the first Greeks arrived or have been introduced by other peoples, such as the Minoans, after this date. The geographical extension of these names does not agree with that of Greek speech at any time. Important in this category are place-names with the suffixes -ινθος / -υνθος, -ανθος and -ασσός, -ησσός / -ηττός: Κόρινθος, Σάμινθος, Ἀμάρυνθος, Ἐρύμανθος; Παρνασσός, Κνωσσός, Ὑμηττός. These have many parallels in south-west Asia: Ἴσινδα, Κάρυνδα, Ἀλάβανδα; Ἁλικαρνασσός, Ἀθανασσός. They can also be compared with identical forms in Thrace and north-west Asia, however (Ὄλυνθος, Πέρινθος, Λυρνησσός, etc.), and although the -νθος suffix is plausibly derived from the Indo-European adjectival suffix -ent-, -ant-, through an Anatolian medium, its exact history is still uncertain. Other suffixes have a narrower range, *e.g.*, -ωτός associated with central Greece and Epirus, -στός chiefly with central Greece and the north Aegean, -ήν with Crete and the Gulf of Sunium. There are also place-name roots with similar peculiarities:

σαμ-: Σάμη, Σάμος, Σαμικόν, Σάμινθος, ? Σαμόρνα, ? Σμίνθος;
(α)μυκ-: Μυκῆναι, Μύκονος, Ἄμυκλαι, Μυκάλη, Μυκαλησσός;
γαργ-: Γαργηττός, Γάργαρα, Γαργαφία.

Divine names.—Secondly, the names of many Greek gods are non-

[a] For a fuller account of these scripts and of Ventris's decipherment of Linear B see Ch. 23; on Mycenaean Greek, Ch. 4 (ii).

Indo-European. They were apparently adopted from the pre-Greek population or from neighbouring peoples. Of Homer's deities only Ζεύς and Ἔως have names which are certainly Greek. Some others have parallels in Asia Minor, e.g., Ἄρτεμις, as does also the post-Homeric by-name of Dionysus, Βάκχος. The name Ἀπόλλων (and that of his mother Λητώ, perhaps Carian *lada*, 'woman') may be Asiatic. Occasionally, associated myths and the distribution of cults suggest a specific origin. Hephaestus is connected with Lemnos and his name has a northerly cast; Eileithyia (Ἐλευθώ, etc.) is limited to Crete, the Peloponnese and east-central Greece, and might be a Minoan deity. Many other names, such as Ἀφροδίτη, Ἑρμῆς, Δη-μήτηρ are wholly or partly non-Greek.

Personal names.—Thirdly, in the Homeric poems and in other early tales, there are personal names which have no reliable explanation, e.g., Ζῆθος, Βῶρος, Λαέρτης, Νέστωρ, Ἄδρηστος (cf. Strabo, vii. 7. 321). While the Indo-European compound type (Ἀριστόδημος, Σοφοκλῆς, etc.) which in the Classical Age is standard, does appear in Homer, it is not predominant there. There are, on the other hand, names derived from place-names (Γουνεύς, Ἄβας, Ἰδαῖος) which are common in the Heroic Age but less frequent later. Moreover, some which are speciously Greek in the last resort resist analysis (Πηνέλεως, Ἀγαμέμνων); this suggests the possibility that they are Grecized foreign names. Now, although personal names are no indication in themselves of the nationality of their owners, they must indicate some fusion of languages in earlier times. Since in the Heroic Age the Greeks had been only a few centuries in Aegean territory and we have other evidence of linguistic mixture, it is possible that some of the heroes may have owed their names to non-Greek forebears within a generation or two of their own lifetime.

General vocabulary.—The true measure of indebtedness, however, is not in proper names, but in words of common currency. There are many early loan-words covering a variety of human activities. The test of their foreignness is in their phonetic and syllabic structure and in the absence of parallels in Indo-European languages; cognate words rarely survive in the sparsely attested Aegean languages. It is accordingly difficult to assess the number and range of the loan-words, for in many cases no verdict can be given. It is reasonably certain, however, that the Greeks at the time of borrowing were inferior in material civilization and probably also in political status to the people who used the language or languages of origin. Typical examples are:

Political and social organization: ἄναξ, βασιλεύς, πρύτανις (Etruscan *purθne*, 'magistrate'), ὀπυίω (Etruscan *puia*, 'wife').

Religious belief and ceremony: θεός, ? ἱερός, τιτάν, γίγας, θίασος, διθύραμβος, ἴαμβος, λυκάβας.

Dress, armour, weapons : χιτών, χλαμύς, ἀρβύλη, θώρηξ, ὑσσός, ξίφος.
Metals and metal products : σίδηρος, κασσίτερος, χαλκός, δέπας, λέβης.
Pottery : λήκυθος, ἀρύβαλλος.
Buildings and furnishings : πύργος, θόλος, θριγκός, ἀσάμινθος.
Flora : σῦκον, σίδη, μίνθη, τερέβινθος, ῥόδον.

Among many alien words adopted into general vocabulary, a striking instance is φίλος related to Car. bilis, 'his own', suus, in which sense it is often used by Homer.

As with place-names, non-Greek suffixes were applied to stems of Indo-European origin. The elements -ινθος, -ανθος, -ισος, -ασος, common in place-names, occur also in common words which are evidently hybrids : ἕλμ-ινς (-ινθος), ἄκ-ανθος, πέτ-ασος, τάμ-ισος. The suffixes -εύς and -ίσκος are also suspected of such an origin, and the expansion of the -κ- element in the Greek aorist and perfect tenses, which among other Indo-European languages is found only in Phrygian and Latin, has been attributed to Anatolian influence.

Syntax.—It is more difficult to trace alien features in classical syntax. It seems possible, however, that the Greek fondness for emphatic and other particles rests on Aegean models. In particular, the antithetic sentence-structure marked by the balance of μέν . . . δέ . . . has a direct parallel in Etruscan, where an enclitic -m appears in this role. This -m may also occur in the Lemnian inscriptions, while Thessalian Greek has a μέν . . . μά . . . combination which seems close to the Etruscan.

Phonetics.—The speech-sounds of Greek are a simplified version of the Indo-European sounds. Although most of the Indo-European vowel distinctions are maintained till the fifth century, the consonants are greatly modified by the disarticulation and loss of the continuants y, s, w, in most positions in the word or phrase, and by a tendency to shift to the front of the mouth the point of articulation of stop consonants when they were originally followed by the front vowels i, e, or by the dental continuants, y, s. Phonetic changes are, as a rule, further advanced in the East Greek dialects, i.e. in those which were in earlier contact with Aegean speech. There is accordingly a possibility that such East Greek features as the change of ty to s or of ti to si may be historically connected with similar phenomena in the Anatolian languages, including Hittite. Again, the Ionic vowel-change ā to ō, together with the not dissimilar development -ans-, -ons- to -ais-, -ois-, in Lesbian, certain kinds of Doric, and Theran, may have its source in Lydian and Carian pronunciation.

vi. THE ESTABLISHMENT OF GREEK

Date of borrowings.—Examples of borrowing, especially in vocabulary, could be multiplied if isolated features of the local dialects were taken into account. It is important, however, to exclude from consideration of early influences on Greek any elements which may have entered the language during the Dark Age; these are particularly common in Lesbian, Eastern Ionic, and other dialects which were in close contact with barbaric speech in that period, and sometimes found their way into mainland Greece from them. If only those borrowings are considered which are rooted in Greek from early times, and if a time is sought when Greeks were in close contact with alien speech and when, in addition, Greeks were culturally dependent on other peoples, then it becomes clear that large-scale borrowing must be referred to a period beyond the Dark Age, to the Heroic Age at the latest, and perhaps even earlier. While it is impossible to attach a date to all loan-words, it is a reasonable criterion that elements which occur both in pre-Greek place-names and in general vocabulary should be assigned to a very early stratum, the remotest parts of which may be co-eval with the Hellenic immigration.

At one time attempts were made to single out borrowings from Eteocretan, Pelasgian, Lelegic and other unknown or hypothetical languages. This procedure is now acknowledged to overstep the limits of available information; not enough is known of these languages to enable us to detect faint reminiscences of them in Greek. It has, therefore, become fashionable to speak generally of 'Aegean' linguistic features as opposed to those inherited directly from Indo-European, and of an 'Aegean' substrate in the Greek nation. This is a convenient term, provided that it is not assumed to imply homogeneous conditions in the pre-Greek Aegean. Neither linguistic survivals nor other sources guarantee the existence of a single language or even a single group of dialects opposed to Greek. Indeed it is noticeable that where a cognate of any loan-word is known it cannot be quoted from more than one of the non-Greek languages.

The Pre-Mycenaean Age.—Of all the languages hitherto discussed, the language of Minoan Crete and the assumed Anatolian language of the Cyclades were clearly in a position to influence Achaean speech in Heroic times. The former, as the medium of a rich and powerful civilization, may be thought likely to have enriched Greek with political terms, names of artifacts, etc.; the latter, whether related to the Cretan language or not, might account for apparently Carian or Lydian features. Further analysis, however, necessitates consideration of the pre-Mycenaean Age, the period from *c.* 1800 to *c.* 1500 B.C. This also is a Dark Age which, apart from the baffling Minoan writings, has neither historical records nor linguistic documents. There is much archaeological evidence and a kaleidoscope of early legend. But to reconcile and interpret these two sources in terms of race and language is a Herculean task. Here it is only necessary to indicate certain key problems.

The Greek immigration and rise to power.—About the nineteenth century B.C. the immigrant Indo-European Greeks came into contact with Aegean cultures far superior to their own. In some five centuries or more they advanced to political domination in the Aegean and to mastery of the technical arts. The Mycenaean civilization thus created combined elements of diverse origin, the chief being the Minoan culture and that other 'Middle Helladic' culture which is associated with the 'grey Minyan' ware of north-west Asia Minor and mainland Greece. How this mixture was achieved is unknown.[a]

The Minoan contribution can be defined with some confidence. Minoan objects are found in Greece, and they may perhaps be related not only to legends concerning Minos himself but also to the tales of Phoenicians and Cadmeans (*e.g.*, Hdt. v. 56 f.), which generally deal with events long before the Trojan War. It thus appears that *after* the arrival of the Greeks but *before* they rose to great political power, there was in mainland Greece a period of strong Minoan cultural and economic influence and we may trace to this time such Minoan influence as was exerted on the Greek language.

The originators, or carriers, of the 'grey ware' culture are more difficult to identify. It is commonly supposed nowadays that they were Greeks. The likeness between their pottery and the grey ware of Troy need not imply that they had an Anatolian origin, but only that the Helladic and the Trojan grey ware cultures derive from a single source. The route by which the Helladic grey ware people entered Greece is not known, but since there is little or no trace of their culture in Greece north of Olympus, it seems likely that they came by sea from the north-east Aegean. They established themselves on the Greek mainland at the expense of the Early Helladic people, who were apparently of Asiatic origin.

Alternatively, it is possible to suppose that the Greeks were immigrants with Balkan affinities penetrating into north and central Greece at the end of the Early Helladic period. There is, however, little or no archaeological evidence for such an invasion, and, if it were assumed, we should have to infer that the bearers of the grey ware culture were *Asiatics* coming from the Hellespontine area. Then, apart from the absorption of the Early Helladic occupants, the history of the mainland between 1800 and 1400 B.C. would have to be regarded as a triangular contest among three strains, in the course of which the Greeks assimilated the superior cultures of both the Minoans and the grey ware people and finally destroyed the political power and nationality of both.

This theory would make it tempting to discover the racial and linguistic character of the 'grey ware' people in the Pelasgians and other

[a] The archaeological evidence is discussed in Ch. 12.

northern peoples of legend, and perhaps even in the Hellespontine and Lemnian Pelasgians of Herodotus (i. 56 f.; *cf.* Thuc. i. 3, iv. 109). Thus a Pelasgian-Lemnian-Etruscan unity might be constructed, and a key found to the puzzling linguistic ties between Greek and Etruscan. But for the present the opinion that grey ware and Greek go together must be held to prevail.

To these problems there can be no certain solution at the present time. But the salient fact which emerges from the shadowy picture is the rapid advance of Greek between the nineteenth and twelfth centuries to become the dominant language of the Aegean. At some time in this period the Achaeans passed over from the mainland to Crete and seized power in Knossos and the other centres of Minoan culture. Presumably linguistic pockets remained in their wake, on the mainland as well as in the islands; the last of these pockets, in Crete, survived till classical times. In the elimination of these non-Greek languages, the Dorian invasion must have been of decisive importance. By flooding the south Achaean lands with a new race of conquerors, not, perhaps, very numerous but destined to establish themselves permanently, the invasion confirmed Greek as the language of that region and ultimately set in motion a new wave of Greek-speaking colonists towards Asia Minor.

NOTE TO CHAPTER 10

1. Ventris's decipherment of Linear B as Greek of a type related to Arcadian is now supported by many scholars but is, in this writer's judgement, mistaken. Recent attempts to decipher Linear A as Greek, Akkadian, etc., are equally without value. Some account of these matters is given in Ch. 4 (ii) and Ch. 23 by writers who accept Ventris's claims.

§B: THE REDISCOVERY OF
THE HEROIC WORLD

CHAPTER II

THE HISTORY OF HOMERIC ARCHAEOLOGY

by Alan J. B. Wace

THE Alexandrian and other ancient critics treated the Homeric Question as a literary problem with some historical implications. They knew or thought they knew the Homeric sites and they accepted Homer's picture of the life of the heroes as a reasonable description of the great days of long ago. When in the eighteenth century the modern criticism and study of the *Iliad* and *Odyssey* began, scholars were still more concerned with the literary aspect of the poems and less with the historical and archaeological. Some travellers endeavoured to locate the site of Troy, the identity of which with the Greco-Roman Ilium had been doubted or denied since late Roman times; the general attitude, however, to the Homeric descriptions of life and its surroundings was that they were mainly poetic. Mycenae and Tiryns were known and so was Ithaca, then universally identified with the island which the classical Greeks had known as *Ithake* (in modern times *Thiaki*), but these were regarded as the settings for romantic stories. Practically no one believed that the world of Homer had any real basis of fact. The interpretation of Homer was based on literary or grammatical considerations, with occasional assistance from history or geography, but archaeology was never invoked. Indeed archaeology, especially Aegean archaeology, the archaeology of prehistoric or pre-Homeric and Homeric Greece, had not yet been born. This state lasted really until 1870 when Schliemann began his excavations at Hissarlik, which he correctly believed to be the site of Troy. Later Schliemann was the first to excavate the sites of Mycenae (1876) and Tiryns (1884), which no one had hitherto thought of as capable of throwing light on Homeric questions. Similarly he was also the first to explore Ithaca and Orchomenos archaeologically (1868 and 1880).

The new turn given to Homeric study by Schliemann can now hardly be realized, for we have become so much accustomed to the archaeological approach. Schliemann said with absolute truth that he had discovered a new world for archaeology. The foundation of Schliemann's work was his strong faith in Homer and his belief that the life and characters depicted by Homer had had a historic reality. This was the spirit with which he worked. In spite of the ridicule and of the fantastic theories to which he was once subjected both by scholars and by amateurs the greatness of his work is now triumphantly recognized by the majority of learned opinion. Occasionally attempts are made to resurrect some of the old theories, but Schliemann's fame as the founder of the science of Aegean archaeology and as the first excavator of the site of Troy is unshakably established.

The royal Shaft Graves at Mycenae, which, following the indications of Pausanias, he discovered in 1876, are still the richest archaeological find ever made in Greece. In 1884 with Dörpfeld as his lieutenant he discovered the prehistoric palace at Tiryns. In his first flush of enthusiasm Schliemann identified what he had found as truly Homeric. Thus the second city of Troy which really belongs to the Early Bronze Age (much too early for Priam), was for him Priam's city and the treasure he found in it Priam's treasure. The princes buried in the royal graves at Mycenae were for him Agamemnon and his companions. Similarly the palace at Tiryns was required to conform to what Homeric commentators then thought should be the plan of the Homeric house, a purely hypothetical plan concocted academically in their studies. The progress of research in Aegean archaeology, which Schliemann initiated, now tells us that these early enthusiastic identifications of his must be modified. Just after Schliemann's death in 1890 Dörpfeld showed that the sixth city of Troy, in view of the presence of Mycenaean pottery in its ruins, and its massive walls, could more probably be identified as Priam's Troy. Now the results of the new American excavations show that Priam's city was the first stage of the *seventh* settlement (Troy VIIa). The princes of the royal shaft graves at Mycenae flourished in the sixteenth century B.C., nearly four centuries before Agamemnon. The plan of the palace at Tiryns, although it is in its last stage probably more or less contemporary with the age of Homer's heroes, has been much misunderstood.

Schliemann's work has been continued by a host of successors. In Greece Tsountas and other Greek scholars have worked at Mycenae, at Vaphio near Sparta, at Thebes, in Attica, in Euboea, in the Cyclades, in Cephallenia, and in Thessaly. Foreign scholars have excavated at Pylos, Mycenae, Tiryns, Boeotian Orchomenos, Asine and Midea (Dendra) in the Argolid, Aphidna in north Attica, Kakovatos in Triphylia, at Argos, in Corinthia, in Messenia, in Thessaly, in Macedonia, in Melos, Ithaca, and Rhodes. In Crete Evans, by his work at Knossos, where Schliemann had once hoped to excavate, revealed the Minoan civilization, and other scholars, Greek and foreign, have excavated in that island at Phaistos, Ayia Triadha, Mallia, Tylissos, Pseira, Mochlos, Pachyammos, Gournia, Vasiliki, Palaikastro, Zakro, Amnisos, in Mesara, in Lasethi, and at many other

sites (see Fig. 6).   Scholars of many nations by their excavations throughout the island of Cyprus, along the western and southern littoral of
Asia Minor, and down the coasts of Syria and Palestine, have thrown
much light on the eastern contacts of the Minoan and Mycenaean cultures.   In Egypt Petrie, by his work at the city of Akhenaten at Tell el
Amarna, has provided a definite date (*c.* 1370–1350) for the Mycenaean
pottery found there, and other scholars working elsewhere in the same
country have helped much in chronological questions.

In addition to the actual work of excavation, other scholars have devoted much attention to studying the objects found in exploration of the
Aegean sites in relation to Homer's account of life in the Heroic Age.
They have endeavoured to see how far the life, manners, customs, and
objects described by Homer correspond with archaeological discoveries

FIG. 6. Principal Bronze Age sites in Crete

and have tried to arrive at some idea of the date when the Homeric
epics would have been composed.

From the results of the actual excavations, and the discussions of the
excavated objects in connection with Homer, scholars have been able to
recreate for us the history of pre-Homeric Greece, even while the written
documents remained undecipherable, and so to provide a background
against which our modern study of Homer should be staged.   As
explained, not all who have shared in this work have been archaeologists
and in consequence some of the archaeological evidence has been misunderstood.   On the whole, however, the archaeological evidence shows
that Homer's world was a reality and Homeric critics who have worked
on this basis have much facilitated the interpretation and understanding
of Homer.   Archaeology has brought to Homeric criticism a much-
needed element of common sense by supplying material facts.   Naturally,
we cannot expect the civilization described by Homer to agree in every
respect or even in most of its aspects with what we know of Mycenaean
culture.   It is, however, undeniable that there is in Homer much of the

Mycenaean civilization, and that there is some that is post-Mycenaean. There is inevitable argument about some of the things referred to by Homer — whether they are descriptions of objects Homer actually knew, whether they are reminiscences of Mycenaean culture, or whether they are post-Mycenaean.   One difficulty is that much of the evidence is unfortunately negative, and this is unsatisfactory.   The lack of archaeological illustration of an object in the epics does not necessarily mean that such an object never existed.   Another difficulty is that we do not necessarily know whether a word used by Homer to describe something had the same meaning to him as to later Greeks of the classical or post-classical age.   Homer, in some respects, was as remote to the Alexandrian critics as he is to us, and in some respects even more remote, because the Alexandrians had no knowledge of the Aegean civilization.   This consideration about the use and meaning of words has especial force when applied to subjects like dress or arms.   We know that as regards these two topics English words given as names to some article of dress or armament have not always had the same meaning, or implied the same shape or use. A skirt of the mid-eighteenth century was very different from the knee-length skirt of the 1920's.   The British army still practises musketry drill, but no longer uses muskets.   The word gun has several connotations. An eighteenth-century pistol is very different from an automatic pistol of to-day which in some circles is referred to as a gun.   We must be careful, therefore, not to assume that Homer meant by a word exactly what Plato or Thucydides meant.   We should not strike out as an interpolation any passage in Homer because the mention or description of an object does not agree with our assumptions of what it should be or with the object to which that name was applied in classical times.   Further, as regards the results of excavations we must remember that no excavation can be exhaustive, and many surprises undoubtedly await us.   For many assumptions have accumulated around the interpretation of the text of Homer and its relation to Aegean archaeology, and we must not allow them to obscure our estimation of the evidence.

Homeric criticism since the middle of the nineteenth century has acquired two distinct aspects, a literary which continues the old tradition, and an archaeological which has grown up since 1870 when Schliemann began work.   The two aspects cannot really be separated.   Homeric archaeology must base itself on the text of Homer as well as on the material objects found in excavations.   On the other hand literary criticism cannot afford to neglect archaeology and the light thrown by archaeology on ethnology and geography.   Above all, in dealing with any branch of Homeric studies we must be on our guard against unwarranted assumptions even if sanctified by long tradition.

Troy and Ithaca are, of course, the two great Homeric sites, for they are the settings for the principal parts of the *Iliad* and of the *Odyssey*. Mycenae too is naturally closely associated with them as the seat of Agamemnon's confederacy and the principal cultural centre of Greece in the Late Bronze Age. The next chapter, on Greek prehistory, gives a general conspectus of the evolution of culture in the Aegean area down to the end of the Bronze Age. This is followed by a chapter summarizing the results of the archaeological exploration of the four main Homeric sites individually and the questions which archaeology has helped to solve as well as those which it has as inevitably raised.

Archaeology has had a stimulating effect on Homeric study as a whole. It has given a reality to the text of Homer which cannot be ignored and it has encouraged 'unitarians' in their belief, especially when linked with the comparative study of epic, which is a recent development.

There have, it is true, been some scholars who have endeavoured to use archaeological evidence in support of a disruptive criticism of Homer, rejecting some passages as archaeologically impossible, or as late in date, and therefore interpolated. But the general effect of archaeology can be best seen in the contrast between the generally 'separatist' tendency of mid-nineteenth-century Homeric criticism, before Schliemann, with the present tendency, which is in the main unitarian. A major contribution of archaeology to Homeric studies has been the growing belief that the first immigration of a Greek-speaking people into Hellas took place at the beginning of the Middle Bronze Age (soon after 2000 B.C.). The corollary of this, that the Mycenaeans were Greeks, has recently received positive proof by the decipherment of their writing, which is in Greek. This brings Homer and Mycenae ever closer together in our studies, and eliminates what might previously have been a possible objection to the view that a continuous epic tradition existed from the Late Bronze Age onwards. That view was originally based on the demonstrably Mycenaean character of features in the culture depicted in Homer. Indeed, some objects mentioned by him belong to a period before the Trojan War, and had dropped out of use before the end of the Bronze Age. Now that we see clearly in the Mycenaean tablets the origins of archaic features in Homeric Greek, and as the contents of the tablets increase the list of things in the Homeric picture which are recognizable as Mycenaean, the reality of a long poetic tradition before Homer becomes more and more apparent: we may even conclude that epic had already begun in the Mycenaean Age itself.

NOTE TO CHAPTER 11

[The relevant literature will be more specifically cited in subsequent chapters. For a general account of Schliemann's work see C. Schuchhardt, *Schliemann's Excavations* (trans. E. Sellers, 1891). His life has been written by Emil Ludwig, *Schliemann of Troy* (Engl.

edition 1931); but nothing better describes his consuming enthusiasm than his own auto-biographical introduction to his *Ilios* (1880). For a brief narrative of Sir Arthur Evans's career see Joan Evans, *Time and Chance* (1943).

Some idea of the progressive effects of archaeology on Homeric studies may be gained from the following:

W. Helbig, *Das homerische Epos aus den Denkmälern erläutert* (1886).

C. Tsountas and J. I. Manatt, *The Mycenaean Age* (1897).

A. Lang, *The World of Homer* (1910).

M. P. Nilsson, *Homer and Mycenae* (1933).

H. L. Lorimer, *Homer and the Monuments* (1950).

J. L. Myres (ed. D. H. F. Gray), *Homer and his Critics* (1958).]

CHAPTER 12

THE EARLY AGE OF GREECE

by Alan J. B. Wace

In Egypt history begins with the dawn of the Bronze Age, for there we have written records which stretch back to that period, and events are datable in terms of our own era. For Greece and Crete we do possess, it is true, a growing number of written documents, and they can now be read; but they do not contain records of events, and consequently the history of Bronze Age Greece can only be reconstructed by archaeological methods, from the results of excavation. By studying the sequence and stratification of remains, especially the pottery, at ancient sites the archaeologist can at least interpret the general progress of human culture, even though the stages of the progress are undated except in relation to each other; and if connections between different areas are discernible from the remains, the archaeological sequences of these areas can then be arranged in parallel columns, according to their points of contact. Fortunately, such connections are traceable at various points between the Bronze Age Aegean and Egypt. Datable Egyptian objects sometimes occur in Greece or Crete, or objects from Greece or Crete may be found in a datable context in Egypt, and thus the prehistory of the Greek world can be pegged at a few points to an 'absolute' chronology, and the duration of intervening periods be roughly assessed, even though we may know nothing of historical events. Such methods have within the last eighty-five years enabled us to push back far into the third millennium B.C. the beginnings of Greek history, which it was formerly the fashion to trace back only as far as a well-developed phase of the Iron Age.

Indeed, modern students, before the development of archaeology, showed little curiosity and perhaps excessive agnosticism about the earliest civilizations of Greece; but the classical Greeks themselves always preserved and cherished lively traditions, in local legend and above all in epic poetry, of a glorious and heroic period long before their own time. The trouble with such traditions, resting ultimately on a long period of oral transmission, is that they are for a variety of reasons subject to distortion and to fanciful accretions which eventually obscure the boundaries of true historical legend, folk-tale, and myth. Yet the classical and post-classical historians of Greece, though they disagreed as to the extent to which the old traditions deserved credence, never in any case doubted

that there was at least a core of history in them. The more modern
historian of Greece, for fear of what might be rotten about the core,
preferred usually to reject the whole. The archaeological approach, to
which this rejection has now given place, provides a testing of the truth
or probability of legend. The testing process is independent of legend;
yet recourse to it was prompted in the first place by belief in the essential
reliability of Greek tradition. Schliemann dug at Troy and Mycenae
because he believed the Trojan War really happened. The success of his
work established the relevance of Greek prehistoric archaeology, and it
has continued as a study in its own right. The archaeological account
of Greek prehistory, here summarized, has been built up independently
of the traditions, and therefore in what follows little direct reference will
be made to them.

The Bronze Age in the countries of the Aegean has been divided into
three stages, Early, Middle, and Late, which correspond roughly with the
Early, Middle, and Late Kingdoms of Egypt. For the Neolithic Period
and the Early and Middle Bronze Age the chronological correspondences
with Egypt and other neighbouring lands can be established only in very
general terms; but for the Late Bronze Age we have better contacts with
Egypt, giving an 'absolute' dating which may be regarded as approximately correct. For the Greek mainland the archaeological periods of
the Bronze Age are called Early, Middle, and Late Helladic; for Crete
they are called Early, Middle, and Late Minoan; and for the Cyclades
Early, Middle, and Late Cycladic. At Troy the nine successive settlements identified by Schliemann are still, though modified in detail by
later excavations, the basis of the archaeological sequence. Of these
settlements, those numbered I to V cover the Early Bronze Age, and VI,
VIIa, and VIIb1, the Middle and Late Bronze Ages.

It is natural to look for the beginnings of Greece and the Greeks on
the mainland of Greece, for it was there that the people who called themselves Hellenes evolved the brilliant civilization which has led the progress
of the world. The first definite inhabitation of Greece which we know
opens in the Neolithic Period. Remains of this period have been found
all over the Greek mainland, although certain districts such as Thessaly
have been more explored than others.

The Neolithic Age on the mainland was originally divided into two
main periods, A and B. Now it is proposed, following the current
fashion, to divide it into three stages, Early, Middle, and Late. Period A
covers the Early and Middle stages, while the much shorter Period B
begins at the end of the middle stage and continues through the late
stage. The Neolithic culture begins quite abruptly, and there are so far
no indications of its origin. The earliest stage so far known goes back
well before the beginning of painted pottery. To trace its development

we rely mainly on the remains of pottery, which are plentiful; but from the first there are also axes and hammers of stone, and implements of obsidian, which since its source is Melos indicates that its users had sea-borne contacts. Houses were rectangular in plan, built of crude brick or of wattle and daub on low stone foundations.

The settlements were usually placed near some good permanent source of water, a spring or perennial river for preference. Many seem to have been established on low mounds in the plains. In other cases small isolated rocky eminences at the edges of the foothills were chosen. There are no definite signs of defensive walls of this date. The bones of oxen, sheep, goats, and swine suggest that this people had already domesti-cated some animals, while the use of deer horns for hafting stone weapons and for light hammers shows that they were also hunters. Of their intellectual development we can say nothing, though the existence of a fertility cult, common among primitive peoples, has been conjectured from the female figurines which are found in their settlements.

Since the Neolithic culture appears comparatively suddenly, and since the use of Melian obsidian implies that these people were sailors it has been suggested that they came to Greece from elsewhere, some Near Eastern country; but no certain archaeological links have yet been established.

The B Period is marked by changes in the pottery and some other artifacts which have been interpreted as indicating fresh influences from Asia Minor and the Nearer East; again attempts have been made to identify Danubian and Central European elements, and it has been asserted that the striking 'Dimini' pottery of this phase was imported from the Ukraine. But nothing is certain, and for the present an agnostic attitude is preferable.

The Neolithic culture of Crete, which is the first indication of human inhabitation of that island, seems to show very little, if any, connection with that of the mainland. If the depth of the deposit at Knossos is any guide, the period lasted for some considerable time, and can be sub-divided into three stages which show signs of gradual evolution. At first the people seem to have lived in rock shelters and caves. Later small two-roomed huts with stone foundations are found and towards the close of the period houses of crude brick or wattle and daub on stone foundations with several small rooms and central hearths are known. The pottery does not show any likeness to that of the mainland. The Neolithic people seem to have entered Crete from the east end of the island and then to have spread over central Crete. Few signs of Neo-lithic inhabitation of western Crete have yet been found. Stone tools and weapons, obsidian knives, and terracotta figurines rather different in type from those of the mainland accompany the pottery. Some of the obsidian is Melian, but other obsidian seems to come from the small island of Gyali (ancient Hyale), which lies between Cos and Nisyros. In this, and in the distribution of the remains within Crete, we may perhaps see a hint that this people came from western Asia Minor across the island bridge of the Southern Sporades.

On the mainland the close of the Neolithic Period is marked by the appearance of a new kind of pottery and the abandonment of many of the Neolithic sites, which presumably indicates the advent of a new people into Greece. Though some sites were re-occupied by the new-comers, they seem to have preferred to choose new ones. The settlements so far known seem to be thickest along the eastern and south-eastern coasts of Greece and this suggests that the Bronze Age people came across the Aegean Sea through the islands from the western or south-western coasts of Asia Minor. It has been noted that in the region where the Bronze Age settlements are thickest, place names of types generally assumed to be non-Hellenic also occur most frequently. These are the names ending in -ινθος, -σσος or -ττος, and -ηνη, as Κόρινθος, Παρνασσός, Ὑμηττός, and Μυκήνη. Some words that were current in classical Greek, especially plant names, belong to the same group : τερέβινθος or κολόκυνθος for instance, and words such as λαβύρινθος and ἀσάμινθος. These names and words seem likely to be a legacy from the Early Bronze Age. At this time the people of the mainland (Early Helladic) seem, if we can judge by their pottery and their other artifacts, to have been related to the Early Cycladic people of the islands and to the Early Minoan population of Crete (see Fig. 7). These can be regarded as three parallel branches of the same race, and they presumably were in fairly frequent communication with one another. Some scholars believe that on their first arrival on the Greek mainland the Early Helladic people lived, on some sites at least, together with the Neolithic folk and that thus for some little time the two cultures coexisted; but there is no definite evidence of this. Nevertheless, it is not to be supposed that the invaders completely exterminated the existing population, and doubtless the Early Helladic people of Greece became, in the course of time, a blend of the two races.

The culture of the Early Helladic people is very different from that of the Neolithic folk. Though few actual bronze implements have been found there is no doubt that this was a metal-using age. Gold and silver were both known as well as lead and copper. At first the favourite metal for tools and weapons was an almost pure copper or copper with natural alloys. Later, bronze artificially produced became the common metal. The pottery in its shapes shows the influence of metal, noticeably in the so-called 'sauceboat', a typical shape of which examples in gold are known (Fig. 7, a, d). The characteristic feature of the pottery is the use of a

FIG. 7. Early Bronze Age vase-types, Asia Minor and the Aegean

(a) Troy II (gold) ; (b) Isbarta (borders of S. Phrygia and Pisidia) ; (c) Alaca
Höyük (copper) ; (d) Early Helladic (Tiryns) ; (e) Early Helladic (Lerna) ;
(f) Early Cycladic ; (g) Early to Middle Cycladic (Phylakopi in Melos) ;
(h) Early Cycladic ; (j, k) Early Minoan (Pyrgos in Crete)

(Scale, approx. : (a) 1 : 3, (b) 1 : 5, (c) 1 : 9, (d) 1 : 5, (e-g) 1 : 6, (h) 1 : 9,
(j, k) 1 : 6)

lustrous paint usually dark brown in colour. A fair idea of an Early Helladic settlement is provided by the site Zygouries, a little south of Corinth (see map, Fig. 25). The houses are roughly rectangular and have two or more rooms. They seem to have been constructed of crude brick or wattle and daub on stone foundations. They were grouped together closely into small villages, through which run narrow winding lanes roughly cobbled. Obsidian remained in use and also heavy stone hammers, but as yet Early Helladic artifacts (apart from pottery) are too little known for us to reconstruct the general manner of life. Early Helladic graves are so far represented by two groups of rock-cut chamber-tombs and rock-shelter ossuaries.

In the islands the development of Early Cycladic culture seems to have run on similar lines but with certain differences due to local conditions. Vessels of stone, especially of the island marble, were in common use, and the skill in working this material is also shown in marble figurines, usually of women, of a stylized fiddle-shape. In the early phases of the period incised patterns were popular on the pottery, and the most characteristic shape is a peculiar shallow dish known as a 'frying-pan' (Fig. 7, h). Among the designs used on this ware the spiral is common, and representations of ships remind us that like all islanders these people were natural seamen. Towards the end of the period vases ornamented with patterns in lustrous brown or black-brown paint make their appearance and among these a beaked jug is a favourite shape (Fig. 7). Double axes in bronze are a well-known feature and, of course, obsidian knives. The usual form of grave is a cist built of four slabs of stone and roofed with another. Sometimes the graves are small roughly circular constructions of stone slabs laid in courses corbelled inwardly to cover the centre space.

In Crete, at the transition from the Neolithic to Early Minoan civilization at the beginning of the Bronze Age, the population seems to have been reinforced by fresh drafts of people from the Asiatic side, no doubt people akin to the Early Cycladic and Early Helladic newcomers. It seems, however, to have been subject also to influence from the south, from Egypt and Libya, since objects have been found in graves in the southern part of central Crete which indicate connections with those parts of Africa. Perhaps, as has been suggested, refugees from the western Delta fled to Crete from Egypt when Menes united Upper and Lower Egypt by conquering the Delta, or else at the end of the Third Dynasty when Khasekhemui reasserted his rule over the north-western Delta. Egyptian contact is indicated by the presence of ivory, by fragments of stone bowls, and by the introduction of certain patterns, and above all by a definite rise in the general development of civilization.

The first Early Minoan pottery is gradually evolved from the latest

Neolithic. Other wares show analogies with the Early Helladic wares of the mainland (*cf.* Fig. 7). Stone bowls were popular and are the Cretan parallels to the marble bowls of the Cyclades, though their shapes often betray strong signs of Egyptian influence. In architecture great progress was made. In southern Crete there are the great circular stone-built ossuaries of Mesara (often erroneously called *tholoi*), the many burials and funeral offerings in which show that they remained in use right down into the succeeding Middle Minoan period. In east Crete there are houses of many rooms, built on more than one story, and the planning of tombs in this area reflects house-architecture in their elaborate subdivision into a number of separate rooms. The great variety in decorative arts points to extensive foreign contacts. For example, engraved seals and signets (mostly from the south) suggest Egyptian influence, while in the north marble figurines point to intercourse with the Cyclades. Altogether, the progress of civilization in Crete was much more rapid than in the islands or on the mainland, though we cannot say why. Perhaps a basic difference between the Neolithic populations of the two regions was partly responsible ; perhaps the cause lies in the cultural impulses (and possibly immigration too) from Egypt and Libya, where civilization had already attained a higher standard.

On the Greek mainland the Middle Bronze Age opens with another archaeological change which is interpreted as indicating the arrival of yet another racial element. On the sites so far excavated where Middle Helladic remains have been found succeeding Early Helladic strata there is a clear division, apparently representing deliberate destruction, between the two. Some sites seem to have been abandoned and not re-occupied. In the Middle Helladic strata an entirely new type of ware appears for the first time in Greek lands, called 'Minyan Ware' because it was first recognized by Schliemann at Orchomenos in Boeotia, famous in antiquity as the home of the Minyan tribe. The most usual category is a monochrome grey ware with shapes that show strong metallic characteristics and are wheel-made — the first indication of the use of the potter's wheel in Greece. The two favourite shapes are a tall wide-bodied goblet with a ringed stem, and a drinking cup with two handles standing high up above the rim (Fig. 8). Both shapes are angular in profile and perhaps with their grey colour imitate vessels of silver. The vases have a carefully smoothed surface, almost soapy to the touch. In some districts the same shapes occur in a rather different ware of red clay with a highly burnished black (or occasionally brown) surface. Much more like the true grey Minyan are the yellow and yellow buff varieties which become commoner as the period advances. Minyan ware, which presumably was introduced by the newcomers, is accompanied by a pale yellowish green or buff ware decorated with linear patterns in matt black paint (Fig. 8).

This matt-painted ware resembles the contemporary pottery of the Cyclades but there is no reason to regard it as a Cycladic import, for from its fabric and varieties, it was clearly made in the various districts of the mainland. Just as the matt-painted Middle Cycladic ware developed out of the Early Cycladic painted pottery, so this matt-painted ware may on the mainland represent a survival and development of the patterned Early Helladic wares. The coexistence of Minyan and matt-painted ware may thus be the archaeological reflexion of the mingling of two racial

Fig. 8. Middle Helladic pottery-types
(*a*) Matt-painted jug, from Mycenae ; (*b, c*) Minyan ware, from Korakou
(Scale about 1 : 5)

strains, the Early Helladic, which in its turn had incorporated whatever survived of the Neolithic population, and the Middle Helladic. From the beginning of the Middle Bronze Age right down to the classical period there is no archaeological break which can be read as indicating the arrival of a new racial element. Even at the transition from Bronze Age to Iron Age the evolution of material culture is continuous, and no new features occur which might suggest a racial change. Thus, if neither the Neolithic nor the Early Helladic people can be regarded as Greek, we must accept the newcomers of the Middle Helladic period as the first Greeks in Greece. We shall see later that there are several aspects of their culture which seem to show Hellenic characteristics. In any case, as we know from their writing, the Mycenaeans had Greek as their

PLATE 9

(b) Grave *stele* from Grave Circle B, Mycenae (cut to serve as socket for another *stele*); relief of lions and warrior. About 24 in. × 42 in.

(a) Grave Zeta in Grave Circle B, Mycenae. Late M.H. period.

PLATE 10

(*a*) Knossos : Grand Staircase of the Domestic
Quarter

(*b*) Knossos : magazine with *pithoi* (store-jars) and floor-cists

language; and the Mycenaean civilization is sufficiently continuous with that of the Middle Helladic people for us to believe that they too were Greek. Naturally they had absorbed other elements, the survivors of the Neolithic and Early Helladic populations, and inevitably were still to be affected by other influences, both racial and cultural, such as the Minoan, which reached them from neighbouring lands. We cannot regard the classical Greeks as a pure race; but no race is strictly speaking

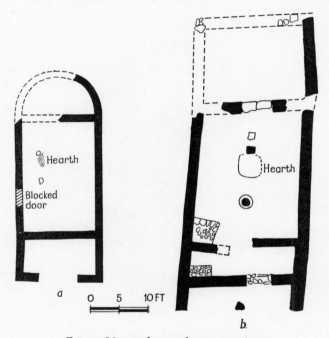

FIG. 9. *Megaron* house-plans at Korakou
(*a*) Middle Helladic ; (*b*) Late Helladic

pure. We may well bear in mind also the principle which Isocrates says was demonstrated by Athens, that διάνοια means more than mere γένος. The brilliant Mycenaean culture for which the Middle Helladic culture paved the way was the first flowering of the Greek genius.

This we may adopt as our creed; Greek art and culture did not suddenly spring out of the earth about the beginning of the first millennium B.C., but evolved slowly, despite setbacks, through many long centuries from the opening of the Middle Bronze Age onwards, and expressed themselves in many brilliant phases — Mycenae, Athens, Alexandria.

The Middle Helladic period is marked in architecture by a well-defined type of house, an early form of the so-called *megaron* (Fig. 9).

2 A

This is a long and rather narrow-fronted building. At the entrance end the long side walls may project so as to form an open porch, from which one enters the main room, which has a central hearth. Behind the main room is another, separated by a cross-wall with a central doorway. This is often used as a storeroom. The graves of this people are as a rule cist graves built of stone slabs or crude brick (Fig. 10). Sometimes they are small shafts sunk into the ground. It is a type of grave which has numberless varieties but the general characteristics remain the same. The bodies

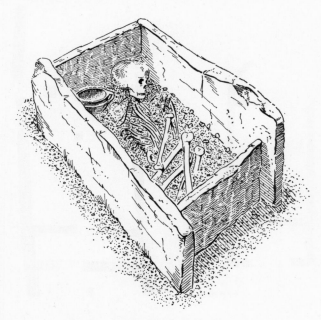

Fig. 10. Middle Helladic cist-grave

were usually laid in the contracted attitude and had few, if any, grave goods. At Malthi in Messenia and probably at Argos and Mycenae the settlements possessed defensive walls, but it is not yet clear whether this was usual. In fact few Middle Helladic settlements have yet been explored. The progress in civilization of the people can best be read in the pottery. Minyan ware as the period advanced becomes more elegant and gradually the grey varieties give way to yellowish or pale buff wares. In the matt-painted ware also the shapes become more refined and the patterns begin to show floral and curvilinear motives and birds are a favourite subject. At first there are no definite signs of contact with outside regions. Presently in the full Middle Cycladic period Minyan ware is found in Melos (at Phylakopi) and other islands of the Cyclades.

Although in the later phases of the Middle Bronze Age Cycladic (Melian) vases are found at Knossos few, if any, definite signs of direct contact between the mainland and Crete at this time have as yet been observed. But as Cycladic pottery now shows Cretan influence, perhaps Cretan influences filtered through the Cyclades to the mainland. We must remember, however, that much of the mainland is still unexplored. In Laconia, for instance, which lies nearer Crete than most districts, no site of this period has been excavated. Towards the end of the Middle Helladic Period some varieties of pottery appear which seem to reflect the influence of the polychrome styles of Middle Minoan Crete. There are vases covered with a dull lustrous black paint on which floral or curvilinear designs are rendered in white and red. Some vases, both large (such as big-bellied, beaked jugs) and small, of a polished red-brown fabric, display polychrome (purple-red, black, white) designs in which birds and griffins often play a part. A few actual Cretan sherds have been found in Argolis (at Asine and Lerna) and in Aegina, but they are rare. Even at Mycenae there are few Cretan imports, the most noticeable being a small vase of Knossian faience from one of the graves in the Middle Helladic Grave Circle recently found. At one site in Leucas in western Greece small Middle Helladic graves have been found grouped within stone circles (see Chapter 13 (iii)). These are small versions of the great Grave Circles of Mycenae. Of these, that found by Schliemann within the walls of the acropolis belongs to the first phase of the Late Helladic Period; the other, explored in 1952–4, is of the last phase of Middle Helladic. The graves in this circle (Pl. 9 a is one of the earlier ones) range from shallow rock-cut graves to deep shaft graves and are elaborate, perhaps royal, versions of the ordinary cist and other graves of the age. In contrast to the ordinary graves they are rich in funeral offerings and a number of them had been reopened after the first interment for the burial of other persons presumably of the same family.

In the pottery the main feature which illustrates the development is the use of a lustrous instead of a matt paint for the dark on light wares, and the replacement of grey Minyan ware by yellow buff ware which, as the brief phase of polychromy fades away, begins to be decorated with a semi-lustrous paint which is the forerunner of the first stages of 'Mycenaean' pottery. In short there is, so far as our evidence goes, no definite line where we can say this is the end of Middle Helladic and this the beginning of Late Helladic. There is an obvious period of transition between Middle and Late Helladic when the earlier characteristics can be seen gradually giving way to the later (cf. Figs. 11, 12).

By the end of the Middle Helladic period culture was advancing rapidly. The people, who, we believe, were of Greek race, learned quickly. They adopted many features from Crete which they developed and im-

proved in their own way. They used long swords and daggers with
ivory pommels. They used golden cups and golden ornaments. As their
pottery shows, they possessed artistic tastes and the construction of the
royal shaft graves shows they were able craftsmen. Further, the presence
of grave *stelai* carved in low relief above the royal graves is the first revelation of actual stone sculpture on the Greek mainland (Pls. 9, *b*; 33).

Whence the people which introduced Minyan ware to the Greek
mainland came we do not know. There is no culture similar to theirs

FIG. 11. (*a*) Jar from Zakro, early L.M. I ; (*b*) Jar from Shaft Grave Beta, Mycenae,
transitional M.H./L.H. I

(Scale about 1 : 4)

anywhere in the Balkan Peninsula north of Greece nor in the Nearer
East generally is there, with one exception, any sign of likeness. The
exception is Troy. There in the culture of Troy VI, which stands at the
beginning of the Middle Bronze Age, the characteristic pottery is a grey
'Minyan' ware, and has no resemblance to the pottery of any neighbouring region. There is, however, a difference in the two cultures. In the
Middle Helladic period inhumation was the rule, but in Troy VI cremation was practised by the end of the period. In spite of this it is possible
that the people of Troy VI and the makers of Minyan ware on the Greek
mainland came originally from the same general region, but the home
of this people, whom we believe to be the first Greeks, remains obscure.

It is just conceivably possible that they may have come from some region north of the Black Sea, a region sometimes suggested as the home of Aryans. They may have descended into the Nearer East by a route similar to that taken by the later Cimmerians. One branch may have occupied the Troad and another have skirted the coast line of Thrace and Macedonia and have finally reached Greece. This is conjecture, for we have no definite knowledge on this subject.

In the Cyclades the Middle Bronze Age showed great development. There is, however, no archaeological break between Early and Middle Cycladic: the later period evolves gradually and naturally from the earlier. The usual pottery is a simple wheel-made ware, at first decorated with linear patterns in matt black or brown paint, which are followed by curvilinear and floral designs often rendered in black and red on the light ground. It is possible that these designs were to some extent due to the influence of the contemporary floral patterns of Middle Minoan Crete; certainly Middle Minoan pottery was imported to Melos. In the same strata much Minyan ware was also found as well as local imitations. There is thus no doubt that although Melos and probably the other islands as well were in close contact with Crete and much under its influence, there was at the same time active intercourse with the mainland. In this period the simple one-roomed or two-roomed huts gave way to larger houses. The settlement at Phylakopi in Melos has a defensive wall. Though undoubtedly flourishing, the culture of the Cyclades did not reach the same height as that of Crete and at the same time it lacked the impulse of the new race which made Minyan ware and transformed the character of the Greek mainland.

In Crete during the Middle Bronze Age civilization made most remarkable progress. The first Cretan palaces were built and grew from comparatively simple beginnings into large, wide-spaced, many-roomed mansions. By the end of the period they were equipped with all the luxuries of the age, including bathrooms and an elaborate drainage system, and bright fresco decoration on the walls. A hieroglyphic system of writing was introduced. The magazines and storerooms suggest an efficient administrative system. The terracotta figurines show that women's dress was highly sophisticated. Their best pottery of the Middle Minoan period shows a superb fabric of egg-shell thinness with well-composed designs of a floral and of an abstract character painted in red and white on a black ground. The shapes of the vases, many of which were made under the influence of metallic prototypes, display great feeling for form as well as brilliance of execution. In minor arts, notably in gem-engraving, the Middle Minoan lapidaries show a skill which has rarely been surpassed. A fine and sensitive feeling for artistic design goes hand in hand with superb craftsmanship. One art which the

Cretans especially practised in the latter part of the Middle Minoan Age was the making of faience. To the close of this age belongs the group of faience objects from the Temple Repositories of the Knossian palace. These comprise figurines of a goddess holding snakes and of her votaries, small representations of seashells and fish, and delicate small vases adorned with plastic flowers. (One of these last, as mentioned above, found its way overseas to Mycenae.) It was at the close of this period that Crete as exemplified by the Knossian palace reached perhaps the height of its

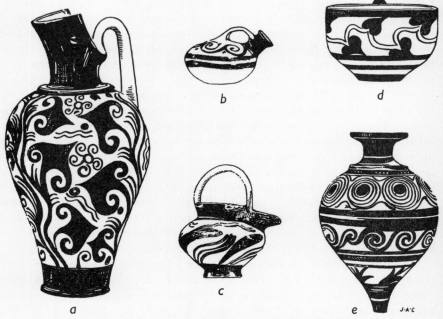

FIG. 12. Helladic (a–c) and Minoan (d, e) pottery of the Shaft Graves period
(a) from Shaft Grave I, Mycenae ; (b, c) from Grave III of the extra-mural cemetery, Mycenae ; (d, e) from Gournia, Crete
(Scale about 1 : 4)

culture, and the same rich culture flourished also at Phaistos and other centres. Although it had not penetrated the Greek mainland it seems to have dominated the islands. In its last phase it reached Rhodes and Minoan pottery of the latest Middle Minoan style has been found in a settlement near Ialysos. We cannot yet define the limits which Middle Minoan culture reached, but we do know that Middle Minoan pottery was carried as far as Cyprus and Ugarit (Ras Shamra) on the Syrian coast (see map, Fig. 5) and that it penetrated to Egypt during the Middle Kingdom. Similarly some Middle Kingdom Egyptian objects have been found in Crete and these mutual contacts give us reasonable clues for dating.

The last phase of the Middle Minoan period is interrupted by the destruction of palaces and towns in some great disaster. It was probably an earthquake and may have been connected with the volcanic convulsion which about this time (to judge by the evidence of the pottery found beneath the lava) split the island of Thera in two and buried the settlements on it. But the Late Bronze Age in Crete sees a quick reestablishment of the palaces, which were rebuilt even more splendidly than before. In pottery (cf. Figs. 11, 12) the *dark on light* style of decoration, in lustrous paint, replaces the *light on dark* and great feeling is shown in the floral patterns. Spiral designs were also popular. The hieroglyphic system of writing develops into a linear script (known as Linear A).[a] Gem-engraving and the making of stone vessels, especially vases of steatite carved in low relief (Pl. 12, *a*) show the taste for artistic detail. Architecturally the palaces and large houses are rambling structures created round a central court. Constant features are well-built staircases and extensive galleries of magazines with tall storage jars for supplies of all kinds both dry and liquid (Pl. 10). In the floors of the magazines were stone-lined cists to hold metal and other treasures. The floors were paved with cement and stucco. Gypsum was a favourite material for decorative facings, but had to be protected from the weather. The walls were covered with frescoes among which naturalistic scenes of flowers and foliage and animals (especially birds) were popular (Pl. 11, *a*). Broadly speaking, this first phase of the Late Minoan period represents an elaboration and perfection of the preceding Middle Minoan culture.

On the mainland, as already stated, there is at the end of Middle Helladic a more remarkable kind of transformation, in which the earlier culture develops very rapidly, adopting and adapting many features from Minoan Crete to produce the Late Helladic civilization familiar under the name of Mycenaean. The character of the Minoan borrowings makes it clear that the change took place about the beginning of Late Minoan; and the brilliance of the resultant first phase of Late Helladic is amply illustrated by the treasures found by Schliemann in the royal Shaft Graves in the Grave Circle within the acropolis of Mycenae. These graves are perhaps little separated in date from those of the other grave circle already discussed; but while the others still show strong Middle Helladic characteristics these look forward into the developed Mycenaean civilization. The royal personages buried in these graves wore an abundance of gold ornaments on their persons and on their clothes. The excavator collected from the bodies of the three women in the third shaft grave seven hundred gold discs decorated with various patterns, bees, rosettes, cuttle-fish,

[a] See Ch. 23.

Fig. 13. Gold objects from the Shaft Graves at Mycenae

(*a*) Sword-hilt; (*b*) Diadem; (*c*) Goblet ('Nestor's cup'); (*d*) Fluted cup; (*e*) Face-mask; (*f*) Bowl of 'Minyan' shape; (*g*) Miniature jug. ((*a*) from Grave Circle B; the rest from Grave Circle A) (All to a scale of roughly 1 : 3)

spirals. The dead wore masks, diadems, and other ornaments of sheet
gold. The scabbards, hilts, and pommels of their long bronze swords
and daggers were decorated with gold.
They used rings of gold whose bezels
bore elaborately engraved scenes. They
drank from vessels of gold and silver
(see Fig. 13). They used ivory and
amber which, as imports from east and
north, hint at the extent of their relations abroad. They had large cauldrons
and jugs of bronze (Fig. 14). Apart
from these indications of actual wealth
their treasures reveal a wonderful
artistry. The delicate engraving of the
gems and signets, the chasing and em-
bossing of the gold and silver cups, the
carving of the ivories, the daggers (Fig.
15) inlaid with scenes in gold, silver,
and *niello* prove beyond all doubt that

FIG. 14. Bronze *krater* from Shaft
Grave V. (Height *c.* 20 in.)

these Late Helladic rulers had indeed master craftsmen. Their pottery
(Fig. 12), which imitates metal in its forms, is well made and is decorated
with great taste. It is an advanced form of yellow Minyan ware orna-

FIG. 15. Inlaid decoration on a dagger from the Shaft Graves : lion-hunt
(Drawn from a facsimile ; very slightly reduced)

mented in the current Cretan fashion with curvilinear and naturalistic
floral patterns painted with a thick lustrous paint on the carefully smoothed
yellow-buff surface of the vases. Spiral designs were especially popular.
In dress the men wore simple tunics or loin cloths. The women wore the
long flounced and pleated Cretan skirt with an open-fronted bolero jacket.

We know all too little about the architecture of this time, for the houses and palaces of the period were destroyed or changed to make way for those of the succeeding periods. But we can be sure that the craft of building was not being neglected; for before the close of this first phase the first *tholos* tomb had been built, though the full development of such tombs belongs to a later phase.[a] What it was that gave the new impetus to the civilization of the mainland and opened the way to Minoan influences at the beginning of Late Helladic I has yet to be satisfactorily explained. The theory, sometimes put forward, of a Minoan conquest or colonization of the mainland can hardly be maintained in the face of many strongly non-Minoan features in the Shaft Grave burials — the form of grave, the grave-stelai with their representation of chariots, the non-Minoan choice of subjects of hunting and fighting in the decorative arts, the use of gold face-masks, and the physical type which these portray. At the same time it is difficult to accept all of these as a natural indigenous growth without some fresh stimulus provided by the influx of a further wave of people, perhaps cognate with the existing population of the mainland, into both Greece and Crete. Such an event might well open up the channels of trade and cultural intercourse between the two areas.

However it began, the assimilation of Helladic and Minoan civilizations proceeded apace. In the second phase of Late Minoan, in many ways one of the most brilliant in Crete, Knossos, which seems to have been always the most important centre of life in the island, appears to become separated from the other centres, Phaistos, Mallia, and the east of the island. (The west throughout seems not to have shared the Minoan culture to the same extent as central and eastern Crete.) The features which mark off Knossos at this time from the rest of Crete at the same time hint at closer connection with the mainland. The closeness of contact is well shown by the so-called 'Palace Style' of vases (Fig. 16). This in Crete occurs practically only at Knossos, but an almost identical style on the mainland occurs at almost every known centre and the mainland vases are always of local fabric, not imported from Crete, though the naturalistic floral and marine patterns which so lavishly adorn them are of obviously Minoan inspiration. The 'Ephyraean' style, which is undoubtedly of mainland origin, is copied in Crete at Knossos (Fig. 16). The Knossian frescoes show in their subjects a shift of interest from the world of nature to the world of man, which finds a closer parallel with the spirit of mainland art than with, say, the frescoes of Phaistos. The Linear B script, which now develops, is in Crete peculiar to Knossos and the Knossian tablets resemble those of the mainland rather than those of other Cretan sites. Like the mainland tablets they are written in Greek.[b] The Throne Room of Knossos (Pl. 11, *b*) has its counterparts on the

---

[a] *Cf.* below, p. 350 f.; also Fig. 49, and Pls. 17, 18 *a*.   [b] See Ch. 23.

FIG. 16. L.H. II and L.M. II pottery

(a) Palace style jar, from Berbati ; (b) Palace style jar, from Knossos ; (c) Ephyraean
goblet, from Korakou ; (d) Ephyraean goblet, from Knossos ; (e) L.H. II *alabastron*,
from Mycenae ; (f) L.M. II *alabastron* (of stone), from Knossos
(Scale : (a, b) c. 1 : 10, (c–e) c. 1 : 4, (f) c. 1 : 7)

mainland, at Tiryns, Mycenae, and Pylos,[a] but not in Crete. In the throne room area at Knossos stone *alabastra* were found like two from chamber-tombs at Mycenae; but the *alabastra* of painted pottery, even if this vase-shape originated in Crete, are much more characteristic of the mainland at this date than of Crete, where they are best known at Knossos (Fig. 16). In architecture the *tholos* tomb, essentially a mainland type, makes at this time an isolated appearance in the neighbourhood of Knossos. It thus seems clear that, whatever the reason, Knossos at this period was in close connection with the mainland, and whereas the current of influence previously flowed from Crete to the mainland there was now influence in the reverse direction as well. Does this imply merely that mainlands fashions became popular at Knossos, or that in Crete Knossos at least became politically subject to the mainland? The Aegean vases of this date which have been found in Egypt are practically all of mainland fabric. At this time too mainland influence ousts Cretan from Phylakopi in Melos and Ialysos in Rhodes, and it is not impossible that the mainlanders should at the same time have spread to Crete. At the end of the Late Minoan II phase Knossos was destroyed and the brilliant Minoan culture was eclipsed. We cannot tell what the cause was. It may have been due to another disastrous earthquake (but there are reasons against this). It may have been due to an attack by enemies from the mainland of Greece. Of, if the suggestion that during the Late Minoan II phase Knossos at least was under the suzerainty of the mainland is admissible, the destruction of Knossos may have taken place in a revolt of the Cretan population against mainland overlords. Alternatively it may have occurred in an attempt by the mainland to suppress a representative who tried to assert his independence. Although the palace of Knossos was then wrecked and the power of Crete definitely weakened, it was partially reoccupied in the subsequent Late Minoan III phase and the culture of Crete retains a 'Minoan' character, though it never regains it splendour. As on the mainland, the style of pottery indicates a simplification and a standardization. There is less skill, but the traditions of earlier Minoan art are still to some extent recognizable. Thus Minoan culture may be said to have continued until the end of the Bronze Age when, like the Helladic culture of the mainland, it gradually and naturally evolved to yet another stage.

Late Helladic II is, as already indicated, the mainland counterpart of Late Minoan II, equalling it in wealth and splendour. Many Minoan fashions appear in architecture; and the walls of the palaces and large houses were adorned as in Crete with bright and spirited frescoes. Unlike the Cretans, the mainland architects developed in the *tholos* type of tomb an almost equally imposing abode for the dead. This kind of tomb

[a] *Cf.* Ch. 13 (ii), (iv).

(alternatively known as a beehive-tomb) is in essence a stone-lined version of the rock-cut chamber-tomb (Fig. 48, p. 482), which gradually became popular in Late Helladic I and remained the regular type of ordinary burial-place through Late Helladic II and III. The *tholos* is a circular underground vault approached by an open passage cut horizontally into a hillside (*cf.* Fig. 49). Its architectural possibilities lay in the method of lining it with corbelled horizontal courses of stone converging to a point at the top so as to produce a walled chamber shaped like an old-fashioned skep beehive. These tombs, and many even of the ordinary rock-cut chamber-tombs, were filled with a rich assortment of funeral offerings, painted vases of excellent fabric, carved ivories (*cf.* Pl. 27, *a*), weapons and implements of bronze, vessels and rings and ornaments of gold (Pl. 12, *b*), engraved signets, amber beads, Egyptian scarabs, which all tell of the wealth of the age. The pottery shows the influence of metal vessels and, as stated, delights in imitating the elaborate Cretan fashions. During the period, however, a revulsion sets in and a return is made towards the restraint and simplicity of the local styles which is especially marked in the goblets known to archaeologists as 'Ephyraean ware'. These are well-formed, two-handled, stemmed goblets of fine yellow-buff polished fabric on which patterns are rendered in a reddish brown or blackish lustrous paint. The patterns are rosettes, flowers, the argonaut, or the octopus, all simply drawn and limited to one unit on each side of the vase. Two other vase shapes become popular at this time, the stirrup-jar and the *alabastron*, both of which seem to have originated in Crete, but then to have been adopted on the mainland, where they became far more popular than they ever were in Crete.

With the third phase, Late Helladic III, which is subdivided into three stages a, b, and c, we reach the climax of the Mycenaean civilization. Since its remains form the topmost stratum on the excavated sites we have a much clearer idea of this period than of its predecessors. To this age belong the large palaces known at Tiryns, Mycenae, Pylos, Thebes.[a] These have well designed state halls (*megara*) with columned porticoes, vestibules, and large central hearths, and wide courts before them. The floors and walls were covered with gaily painted frescoes, among the subjects of which men and women are shown in processional friezes, in scenes of war, or engaged in the chase and sport. The palaces are well planned with long corridors off which lead rooms for various purposes, including shrines with movable painted stucco tables for offerings. These are truly royal residences. There are also private houses in which the *megaron* is again a central feature, in one case fronting a colonnaded courtyard. Staircases descend to basements or ascend to upper stories. Every house, especially in a site like Mycenae which is built on sloping hillsides,

[a] See Ch. 13 (ii), (iv).

possessed a basement where stood large storage jars for oil, wine, or grain and also stocks of large stirrup-jars in which liquids were perhaps packed for sale.[a] Some buildings contained rooms with stocks of unused vases both painted and unpainted. Both houses and palaces were built

FIG. 17. The citadel of Tiryns, restored

according to plans carefully laid out. The same applies to the *tholos* tombs, especially the finest of them all, the Treasury of Atreus at Mycenae, which shows that the builders of the period possessed not only good artistic taste but also a sound knowledge of construction and engineering. The Cyclopean walls of Mycenae (Pl. 19, *a*) and Tiryns (Fig. 17), the dykes of Copais, and the changing of the course of a stream at Tiryns are works of this age. The terracing and levelling of sites was another feature of the period. The Lion Gate and the sculptured friezes and

[a] *Cf.* Ch. 17, p. 491.

FIG. 18. Mycenaean pottery

(*a–d, f*), L.H. IIIa ; (*e, g–j*), L.H. IIIb. (Vases *a, d, f* are from Rhodes ; *e* from Mycenae ; the rest from Attica)

(Scale : (*c*) 1 : 3 ; rest about 1 : 5)

columns from the Treasury of Atreus indicate a taste for monumental sculpture. Amber is no longer found, but ornaments of gold and carved ivory, which probably came from Syria, are still plentiful. The inscribed clay tablets from Pylos and Mycenae show that writing and reading were not merely known but used in the everyday keeping of accounts. Further inscriptions, on stirrup-jars, show that this degree of literacy was not confined to Mycenae and Pylos but prevailed at other centres such as Orchomenos, Thebes, Eleusis, and Tiryns. It is obvious that it would have been useless to inscribe stirrup-jars to indicate their contents or ownership unless the men who handled them could read the inscriptions. The pottery of the period (Fig. 18) is of excellent fabric and is decorated with patterns which have become standard or conventional and are simplifications of those popular in the preceding phase. A novel feature

FIG. 19. L.H. IIIb *krater* from Cyprus. (Height 14 in.)

in one class of the pottery is the use of figures of men and women, chariots, bulls, and other animals, perhaps inspired by the frescoes of the palaces, as the main decoration of large vases (Fig. 19, *cf*. Pls. 30, 37, *a*). Late Helladic pottery is spread widely about the Nearer East and is especially common in Cyprus. It is found also at Troy, at Miletus, in Cicilia, in Syria and Palestine, in Egypt, and even in southern Italy and Sicily. Eastward trade is also attested by Egyptian and other Near Eastern objects found on Mycenaean sites in Greece. In Egypt Late Helladic III pottery is commoner than Minoan, and it is the same elsewhere: pottery of Late Minoan fabric found abroad is rare, but that of Late Helladic fabric is common.

It has already been observed how both Minoan and Helladic influences

PLATE II

(*a*) Fresco from the House of Frescoes, Knossos (restored). Late Minoan I. Height *c.* 2 ft.

(*b*) Knossos : the Throne Room (frescoes restored). Late Minoan II

PLATE 12

(a) The 'Harvesters Vase'. Black steatite, carved in relief; Late Minoan I (from a replica). Diameter $4\frac{1}{2}$ in.

(b) Gold cup with repoussé design of octopus, etc., from Dendra. Late Helladic II. Diameter $7\frac{1}{4}$ in.

affected Phylakopi in Melos towards the end of the Middle Bronze Age. In the Late Bronze Age the situation gradually changes. At first Late Minoan and Late Helladic pottery occur, as imports, in almost equal quantities, alongside attractive local wares which imitate the current Minoan fashions in decoration. But as the period progresses the Cretan element becomes weaker, and by the opening of the third phase (Late Cycladic III) the mainland influence predominates, and Late Helladic III pottery continues to be imported to Melos to the very end of the Bronze Age. The settlement of Phylakopi has a strong defensive wall, but the houses are rather cramped and on the average not large. Most noticeable is a 'palace' which, though possessing a *megaron* of mainland type, has some Cretan features. It is decorated with frescoes, among which a splendid composition of flying fish stands out. The cemeteries have unfortunately been looted by tomb-robbers, so that we are ignorant of the burial customs of the place. Nor do we know how far Phylakopi is typical of the culture of the Cyclades, as it is practically the only site yet excavated. At Rhodes, however, we know that by Late Helladic III times Minoan influence had, as in Melos, wholly given way to Mycenaean.

Down to the end of the period called Late Helladic IIIb the general advance of culture on the mainland seems to have been remarkably peaceful and prosperous. The Greek legends tell us indeed of wars within Greece — that of the Seven against Thebes was the most famous (*cf.* Δ 376-410; E 800-8) — but there seems to have been little or no danger from abroad. Only the royal residences, the citadels of Mycenae and Tiryns, were fortified; and at Mycenae at least, large and wealthy houses outside the walls were apparently occupied in security. The presence of pottery and other objects from their workshops in fifty different lands shows that the Mycenaeans were bold traders and sailors, though they have left us few representations of their ships. They both rode and drove horses, and used chariots, though probably not cavalry, for war. They built roads and causeways and culverts.[a] They were clearly well organized for peace and for war. The archive room at Pylos is evidence of an efficient central administration. It was a highly organized and civilized society and the spirit we can read in its remains and monuments displays the same sense of ordered thought and plan which we recognize in the monuments of classical and later Greece. We can see the same feeling at work in the Treasury of Atreus as in the Parthenon. The progress recently made in deciphering their inscribed tablets has now come to support and confirm the belief that this people really was Greek. Abroad, Mycenae had become a power to be reckoned with; that much might be inferred from the evidence of pottery finds alone; but it is also pretty certain that it is the Greeks who are referred to in Hittite records

[a] *Cf.* Ch. 22.

of the thirteenth century B.C. under the name of *Aḫḫijawa*, a word which may be equated with the Homeric 'Αχαιϝοί. The sphere of influence of these Achaeans met and at times conflicted with that of the Hittites; and there may, of course, have been other clashes with foreign states of which we have now no record. In later Greek tradition what stood out was the great war against Troy immortalized in the epics. In the light of archaeological evidence there is nothing improbable in the picture of Agamemnon, king of Mycenae, heading a pan-Achaean host against Troy and a number of Asiatic allies. Troy was always alien to the Mycenaean civilization, though there is evidence of trade contacts throughout the

Late Helladic age; and the settlement known as Troy VIIa was certainly sacked at a date shortly before the end of Late Helladic IIIb, which corresponds closely enough with the early twelfth-century date given by most ancient authorities.[a]

It was the last great enterprise of Mycenae. Though Troy fell, the success led to no Greek expansion; rather the reverse. Perhaps other

FIG. 20. L.H. IIIc bowl of 'Close Style', from Mycenae. (Diam. *c.* 3½ in.)

foes were already pressing. The culture of the last Mycenaean period, Late Helladic IIIc, is impoverished. The chamber-tombs are not so rich in funeral offerings, and the pottery displays a simplification of pattern and less care in execution. (There is an exception in one class, the so-called 'Close Style', occurring in some of the latest deposits at Mycenae. This shows good design and fine drawing: neat friezes of birds are characteristic in its decoration (Fig. 20).) In the last phase of the Helladic culture ornaments of glass, often covered with thin sheet gold, were much in use. These perhaps were made for people who could not afford ornaments of real gold. It was during this phase of Late Helladic culture that Mycenae and the other principal centres on the mainland were finally destroyed. There was an interruption in the way of life, for the chamber-tombs which had continuously served several generations are now no longer used. The interruption is generally attributed to the Dorian Invasion, which was not the incoming of a new race, but the immigration of a fresh wave of Greek-speaking people. For a time the Greek world was in a state of flux. The political predominance of Mycenae was ending. The old order was giving way to a new order. The Iron Age was succeeding that of bronze. The inhabitants of Greece, the Greeks, passed through another transitional period during which the

[a] *Cf.* Ch. 13 (i), esp. p. 385 f.

character of their culture underwent further evolution.

The end of the Bronze Age on the Greek mainland, in Crete, and in the islands came with the destruction of Mycenae and the other great centres of the culture of the period. Mycenae was captured by enemies, looted, and destroyed by fire. The same fate seems also to have fallen upon the other principal foci of culture about the same time. Tiryns perished by fire and Nestor's palace at Pylos also fell in a great conflagration. There does not seem to have been a universal cultural break, for in Attica and elsewhere it has been observed that a class of pottery called sub-Mycenaean develops naturally out of the Late Helladic IIIc wares. There is no sudden introduction of a new style. The old style evolves and about the same time we observe that inhumation in some places begins to give way to cremation and iron weapons and tools begin to replace bronze. Then the sub-Mycenaean pottery in its turn is transformed into Protogeometric. The Protogeometric develops into Geometric pottery and the Iron Age is then fully established and the first stage towards the evolution of classical Greek culture is visible. This slow transformation is best observed in Attica, as far as our present evidence goes, and Attica is a vital area because the Athenians claimed that Attica was never overrun by the Dorians. In other areas, Thessaly, the islands, Argolis, something of the same evolution can be seen and it is only to be expected that as exploration proceeds, further evidence will come to light from other regions of the Greek mainland. The Dorian invasion, to which the destruction of the last strongholds of Mycenaean Greece is usually attributed, was associated by the Greeks with the 'Return of the Heraclidae', dated by Thucydides some eighty years after the Trojan War. These 'children of Herakles' were the descendants of an earlier Mycenaean dynasty (of which Herakles is the most famous figure in legend) who had been exiled from their kingdom in the Peloponnese when the Pelopids came to power. This had happened before the Trojan War: Agamemnon was a Pelopid (cf. B 100–8); but according to Homer there were princes of the Heraclid line still ruling in the Aegean at the time of the War (Tlepolemos in Rhodes, for example: see B 658–70 and 676–80). The association of Heraclids and Dorians emphasizes that what happened at the end of the Bronze Age was not really an alien conquest; and archaeology seems to confirm that the Dorians did not introduce anything new in material culture. It can now no longer be maintained, for example, that the Protogeometric or Geometric style in pottery was a Dorian innovation or that they introduced iron. Knowledge of iron seems to have come from the east; the Geometric style evolves by a natural process from the latest Mycenaean or sub-Mycenaean pottery. What we know of the transitional period is derived principally from the excavation of graves: inhabited sites are rare, and have not yet attracted archaeologists. Yet the important fact already emerges that although the Bronze Age sites went under in a political upheaval more serious than such later events as the Ionian Revolt, the Macedonian supremacy, or perhaps even the Roman Conquest, there was cultural and racial continuity. It is no longer possible to assume that the first Greeks were Achaeans who arrived in Hellas just before the Trojan War or Dorians who overthrew the declining Mycenaean civilization. Greeks had, in all probability, entered Greece by the Middle Helladic period. No doubt they were reinforced and even modified by fresh drafts of cognate people from time to time — perhaps, for example, in Late Helladic I, certainly at the time of the Dorian invasion. But these in no case produced the kind of cultural or racial change that might have resulted if, say, the Gallic invasion of 279 B.C. had overrun Greece.

It is the lack of evidence about the Geometric period, particularly evidence from inhabited sites, which has in the past caused some scholar to assume a more fundamental kind of change between the Bronze and Iron Ages, and to describe the period as a 'dark age'. Transformation there certainly was, and civilization unquestionably fell below what had been known in the great period of the Mycenaean palaces. But present archaeological knowledge suggests that both historians and archaeologist have picturesquely exaggerated the effects of the transformation scene and so obscured the origins of the Hellenic people and the essential continuity of culture on the Greek mainland from the Middle Bronze Age right into the Classical period and even later.

APPENDIX: CHRONOLOGY

The Bronze Age in Greece is prehistoric because we have no written records of the period which will give absolute dates for it. If we wish to assign absolute dates to any phase of the Greek Bronze Age we can only do so by archaeological comparison with Egypt. In Egypt in the Bronze Age we have a fairly accurate system of dating for the New Kingdom and a not unreasonable system of dating for the Early and Middle Kingdoms. Recently some German scholars have tried to reduce the dating for the Early and Middle Kingdoms, but their views have not been generally accepted. Our earliest direct Greek source for dates in the Heroic Age is the *Marmor Parium* or 'Parian Chronicle' of 264/3 B.C. otherwise we have to rely on post-classical authors quoting earlier sources of whom the most famous is Eratosthenes. The *Marmor Parium* gives us date of 1209 B.C. for the sack of Troy; a number of later writers agree more or less with Eratosthenes (whom one specifically quotes) in dating the event at or near 1183 B.C. Some French scholars have lately proposed abandoning the traditional early twelfth-century date and placing the

Trojan War much earlier, about 1370 B.C., but the archaeological evidence from Troy and Mycenae does not support this suggestion.[a]

The Late Helladic I and II vases found in Egypt in contexts of the early 18th Dynasty (from 1580 B.C. onwards) and those of Late Helladic III found at Tell el Amarna in the ruins of Akhenaten's city (c. 1370–1350 B.C.) give us approximate dates for the Late Bronze Age in Greece. The Middle Bronze Age in Crete can be dated approximately by similar but rather vaguer contacts with Egypt. The islands show points of contact with Crete in the Middle and Late Bronze Ages through pottery found in the strata of Phylakopi in Melos and through some Melian vases found in a Middle Minoan III context at Knossos. There are indications of Cretan influence on the mainland in the Late Minoan period, and of mainland influence on Knossos in the second phase of the same period. Middle Helladic pottery is found at Phylakopi in Melos in the same strata in which Middle Minoan vases are found. So from these and other similar contacts the archaeological sequences can be correlated and a chronological system can be constructed. The system, however, should not be regarded as accurate, but only as approximate. It is impossible to achieve accuracy and any system must inevitably be subject to fluctuation as fresh evidence is discovered. The earlier the date, of course, the more the uncertainty and the greater the margin of error. The simplified chronological table on the following page is based on considerations such as those given above and may be regarded as reasonable for all practical purposes.

[a] On the date of the Trojan War cf. Ch. 13 (i), ad fin. For a handy account of the Marmor Parium see Sir J. Forsdyke, Greece before Homer, 50 ff.

AEGEAN CHRONOLOGY

B.C.

4000 + ?	Neolithic Period
3000±	Beginning of Early Bronze Age
	Early Helladic pottery from middle of Troy I to Troy V
	Trojan vase (Troy IV) at Lerna in Early Helladic stratum
	Early Minoan contacts with Early Dynastic Egypt
1900±	Beginning of Middle Bronze Age
	Middle Minoan contact with Egypt (Twelfth Dynasty)
	Middle Minoan contact with Melos
	Middle Helladic contact with Melos
	Late Middle Minoan contact with Ialysos (Rhodes)
	Early Royal Graves at Mycenae, late Middle Helladic
1600±	Minoan influence on mainland begins
	Eruption of volcano at Thera; great earthquake at Knossos
1550±	Beginning of Late Bronze Age
	XVIIIth Dynasty in Egypt
	Late Helladic I vases in Melos and Rhodes
	Royal Graves at Mycenae (Schliemann), L.H. I
	Late Helladic vases (L.H. I-II) in Egypt
	Minoan influence on mainland continues
1500	Beginning of Late Bronze Age II
	Late Helladic I-II vases in Crete, Egypt, Melos, Rhodes, Levant
	Late Helladic II influence on Knossos
	Aegean (Late Minoan, Late Helladic) objects illustrated i$\mathbb{n}$ Egyptian tombs
1425±	Beginning of Late Bronze Age III
	Late Helladic IIIa
1408	Amenhotep III
1400±	Destruction of Knossos
1370–1350	Amarna Age
1340±	Late Helladic IIIb [a]
	XIXth Dynasty in Egypt
1210±	Late Helladic IIIc
	XXth Dynasty in Egypt
	'Peoples of the Sea' (including Achaeans) invade Egypt
	The Trojan War
1100±	Return of Heraclidae and Dorian Invasion
	Fall of Mycenae
1100	Transition to Iron Age
	Sub-Mycenaean
	Protogeometric
1000	Geometric Period begins

[a] This phase is usually considered to begin c. 1300. For an exposition of Prof. Wace higher date see BSA, lii. 220 ff. [F. H. S.].

NOTE TO CHAPTER 12

[There is unfortunately no up-to-date general survey of Greek prehistory in English. H. Bossert, *The Art of Ancient Crete* (English edition 1937), is essentially a picture-book, and valuable as such; it gives full references to sources, and covers Mainland Greece and the islands as well as Crete. For admirable new illustrations with a short text see S. Marinatos and M. Hirmer, *Crete and Mycenae* (1960). In German there are good accounts of the subject by F. Matz in Otto-Herbig, *Handbuch der Archäologie*, vol. ii (1950), and *Kreta, Mykene, Troja* (1956) in the series *Grosse Kulturen der Frühzeit*; the latter has excellent illustrations.

For Minoan civilization see J. D. S. Pendlebury, *The Archaeology of Crete* (1939).

For Mainland Greece the following will serve as an introduction to more specialized study :

A. J. B. Wace and M. S. Thompson, *Prehistoric Thessaly* (1912) (for the neolithic period) ;

S. Weinberg in *Hesperia*, vi. 487 ff. (for the neolithic of southern Greece) ;

H. Goldman, *Excavations at Eutresis* (1931) (an E.H. type-site) ;

J. Caskey, reports on excavations at Lerna in the Argolid, in *Hesperia*, xxiii. 3 ff. ; xxiv. 25 ff. ; xxv. 147 ff., 175 ff. ; xxvi. 142 ff. ; xxvii. 125 ff. ; xxviii. 202 ff. (important E.H. and M.H. site) ; and for supplementary excavations at Eutresis, *Hesperia*, xxix. 126 ff. ;

C. W. Blegen, *Korakou* (1921) (for M.H.) ;

A. J. B. Wace and C. W. Blegen, 'The pre-Mycenaean Pottery of Mainland Greece', in *BSA*, xxii. 175 ff.

On Mycenae, Pylos, and Ithaca, also Troy, see Ch. 13 below and notes thereto.

For Melos, T. D. Atkinson and others, *Excavations at Phylakopi in Melos* (Soc. for the Promotion of Hellenic Studies, Supplementary Paper no. 4 (1904) ; and *BSA*, xvii. 1 ff.

On pre-Hellenic architecture :

E. Bell, *Pre-hellenic Architecture in the Aegean* (1926) ;

A. W. Lawrence, *Greek Architecture* (Pelican History of Art, 1957).

On Mycenaean pottery :

A. Furumark, *The Mycenaean Pottery* and *Chronology of Mycenaean Pottery* (1941).]

CHAPTER 13

THE PRINCIPAL HOMERIC SITES

(i) TROY

by Carl W. Blegen

HISTORY OF THE SITE AND ITS EXCAVATION

IN the extreme north-western corner of Asia Minor, less than four miles inland from the Aegean Sea and only some three and a half miles from the southern shore of the Dardanelles, lies the ancient site called Hissarlik (Fig. 21). It occupies a natural elevation which forms the western terminus of a long plateau that descends gradually from the east and, though of no great height, dominates at the same time a broad flat plain extending westward to the line of hills bordering the sea, and a smaller tributary valley lying toward the north. Through the latter flows a sluggish stream known as the Dümrek Su, which most modern students take to be the Homeric Simoeis; while at the far side of the western plain a considerable river winds northward to empty into the straits, its modern name, Menderes Su, probably representing a modification or corruption of the ancient designation Scamander.

For a citadel the position was admirably chosen with reference to ancient strategy and economy. Standing far enough back from the shore to be safeguarded against a sudden piratical raid or an unexpected hostile attack, the stronghold was yet sufficiently near to maintain control over traffic moving through the straits, and was no doubt able to exact tribute from all shipping that passed. Furthermore, it sat almost astride one of the old land-routes coming from western Anatolia to the crossing that led over the narrow Hellespont to the European side. The long-continued importance and prosperity of the settlement that grew up on this spot may, in large part, safely be attributed to its command of this early crossroad of trade and communications by land and by sea.

First noted in the early years of the 19th century by Maclaren,[1] who thought it might be the site of Troy, the mound of Hissarlik for a long time received relatively little attention from other travellers and explorers. For most of the distinguished classical scholars of the day accepted as established the view that Troy had stood on Balli Dagh, a lofty hill rising above the Scamander some six miles farther to the south near the village of Bunarbashi.[2] Frank Calvert, who lived many years in the Troad and knew the country well, believing that Maclaren's identification was correct, ventured to dig a trial trench at Hissarlik in an attempt to determine the character of the remains, but his test was too small to give decisive results.   Calvert, however, showed the place to Schliemann,

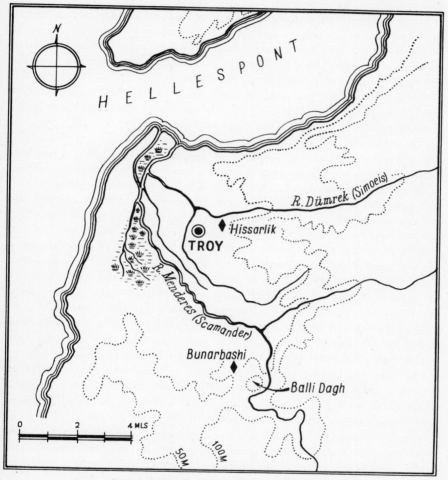

FIG. 21. Map showing the situation of Troy

who in 1868 had carried out some explorations at Balli Dagh and had been convinced by the insignificance of the ancient remains unearthed there that Troy was to be sought elsewhere; and it is to Heinrich Schliemann that we must award the credit for the definite discovery and identification of the site of Troy at Hissarlik.

Beginning in 1870 and operating on a large scale, Schliemann, in a series of campaigns spread over the next twenty years, excavated the greater part of the mound, bringing to light remains of massive walls, houses, and other structures, and a wealth of objects of numerous kinds, demonstrating conclusively that the site had been occupied for a long period of time by a powerful citadel which had passed through many successive stages marked by destruction and rebuilding. The steady advance of the excavations and the corresponding progress in the interpretation of the remains unearthed are well illustrated in the successive volumes of reports which Schliemann published with exemplary promptness: *Troy and its Remains* (1874), *Ilios* (1881), and *Troja* (1884). In the last-named work he was able to distinguish seven superposed layers of remains which he called 'cities'; and in the second from the bottom he believed he could recognize the Troy of Priam.

Doubts cast by critics on the correctness of his observations and explanations led to the resumption of digging in 1890 when a series of fresh discoveries made it apparent that a startling revision of his dating of the layers was necessary. Schliemann himself, dying in December of that year, did not live to see these new views tested; but his assistant and collaborator, Professor Wilhelm Dörpfeld, who had joined him in 1882, was enabled to continue the excavations in 1893 and 1894 with brilliant success, revealing the imposing fortification walls and the great houses of the sixth layer from the bottom, which by the evidence of abundant imported pottery was seen to be contemporary with the strongholds of Mycenae and Tiryns. A systematic account of the results, incorporating in its two volumes all that had so far been learned at the site, was published by Dörpfeld and his assistants in 1902 under the title *Troja and Ilion*. It was now established that there were nine principal layers, and the sixth in chronological order was held to be Priam's Troy. During the ensuing thirty years no further digging was done at Hissarlik; but in 1932 an American expedition, sponsored by the University of Cincinnati, and under the general direction of Professors W. T. Semple and C. W. Blegen, with the generous consent and support of Professor Dörpfeld and of the German Archaeological Institute, began a new investigation, which was only completed after seven annual campaigns in the summer of 1938. In this undertaking the whole problem of the stratification was independently re-examined; each layer was subject to a fresh and thorough study, and all material recoverable was collected. Much new evidence was thereby unearthed to illustrate the state of civilization attained in each period, to follow the development of culture from period to period, and to provide a basis for a more definite dating than was heretofore possible (*Troy* i, ii, iii, iv, Princeton, 1950, 1951, 1953, 1958).

GENERAL CHARACTER OF THE REMAINS

The mound itself, of irregularly oval shape, has a length of about 225 yards from east to west and a breadth of approximately 175 yards from north to south. Before excavations were made the summit of the hill rose some 104 feet above the level of the plain at its northern foot, or about 130 feet above the sea. The underlying ridge of soft limestone accounts for fifty-six feet of the elevation, and the balance was composed of earth, walls of buildings, stones, together with miscellaneous rubbish and débris, which had gradually accumulated to a depth of nearly fifty feet as a result of long-continued human habitation. In the central area this deposit was once at least ten or fifteen feet higher; but in Hellenistic and Roman times, when the citadel had become a sanctuary, the whole top of the hill was sliced off in order to permit an open, level, rectangular precinct to be laid out about the Temple of Athene.

The vast mass of débris was not a single accumulation of uniform character; when trenches were dug through it, a study of the scarp, or one vertical side of the cutting, revealed many clear lines of demarcation dividing the deposit into a series of layers. Nine major divisions of this kind have been recognized, each of which was seen to be further subdivided into minor strata varying in number from two or three to ten or even more. The nine layers, which must represent a like number of successive periods of occupation, differed considerably in thickness, ranging from four to fourteen feet, with an average of some six feet. The relative depth of a layer is, however, by itself no safe criterion for estimating the duration of the period it represents, since other evidence has to be taken into account.

The accumulation of so enormous an amount of rubbish on a site continuously inhabited calls for some explanation. The problem has often been discussed elsewhere, and here it will suffice to mention only two of the many contributory factors. In the first place, it must be remembered that the houses within the citadel were for the most part erected with a superstructure of crude brick resting on stone foundations and supporting a heavy roof of wooden beams, clay, and thatch. The serious damage or destruction of the roof by storm, earthquake, or fire, frequent scourges in the ancient world, would speedily cause the walls thus exposed to collapse into a heap of broken and dissolved brick. As the clay was now too much mixed with rubbish to be serviceable again, the survivors of the disaster merely flattened out the heap of ruins, brought in fresh material from clay-beds in the neighbourhood, and built a new house at a higher level over the old. Destruction of this kind, affecting the whole settlement, is clearly recognizable in each of the layers from the first to the fifth, and it usually resulted in raising the ground-level by three to five feet. In the second place we may note that floors in these houses were made of clayey earth trodden down until hard. Housekeeping was untidy, and when refuse accumulated to an offensive degree, instead of sweeping it out the occupants merely laid a new floor of fresh clay above the old. In some buildings at Troy a dozen or more successive pavements of this kind account for a rise of two or three feet in the level of the floor during one and the same period.

The nine main layers that can be distinguished in the deep deposit have been numbered from I to IX, beginning with the lowest, and the settlements they represent are usually designated as Troy I, Troy II, Troy III, etc. Schliemann called them 'cities', but this was an unfortunate misnomer, for only the last of all, Troy IX, the Hellenistic and Roman Ilion, can properly be called a city in the modern sense of the word. The earlier establishments, certainly from I to VII, were apparently fortified strongholds, or castles, in which a chieftain, prince, or king had his residence, surrounded by his court, officials, and garrison, while the general population of the district, depending for its livelihood on agriculture, lived in small villages and hamlets scattered about the countryside and only took refuge inside the citadel in times of danger.

The layers from I to VII produced no contemporary written records, nothing to indicate even that writing was known (although such negative evidence is by no means conclusive). A reconstruction of the history of the site must thus depend on a detailed study of the remains discovered in each stratum. These remains comprise the ruins of buildings represented by walls and foundations, together with miscellaneous objects of many different kinds, of metal, stone, bone and ivory, shell, glass-paste, wood, and terracotta, among which by far the most numerous are the fragments of broken pottery.

Troy I.—Troy I, the earliest settlement to be established on the hill, with its first buildings founded on native rock, was a small citadel surrounded by a massive fortification wall of rough unworked stones (Pl. 13, *a*; and see plan, Fig. 22). The enclosure was hardly more than 300 feet long and 240 feet wide. About one half of the wall has been traced still standing to a height of more than eleven feet, and in some places immensely thick. An important gateway, in the middle of the south side, was flanked by two projecting rectangular towers, and traces of similar towers suggest that there was probably another gateway on the east. The wall has a sloping exterior face, but this is evidently only the lower part which once supported a high vertical breastwork of crude brick difficult to scale. Troy I was a period of long duration, with some ten or twelve successive phases marked by superposed strata. The fortification wall described belongs to one of the middle phases, but vestiges of an earlier and a later fortress of the same kind were recognized.

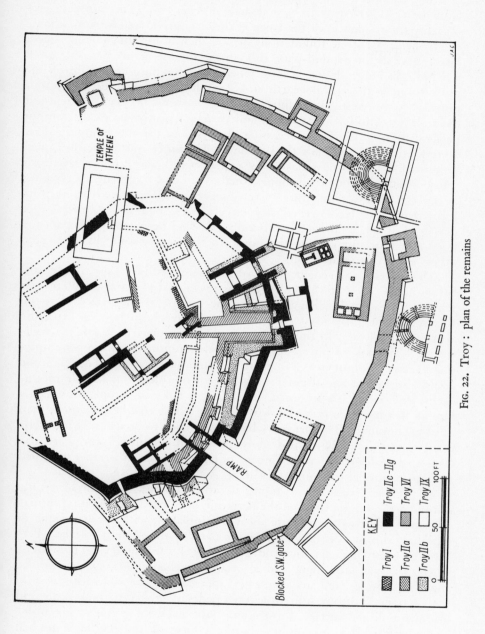

FIG. 22. Troy : plan of the remains

KEY

Troy I
Troy IIa
Troy IIb
Troy IIc–IIg
Troy VI
Troy IX

0   50   100 FT

TEMPLE of ATHENE

RAMP

Blocked S.W. gate

Within the citadel, apparently rather widely spaced, stood several large houses, perhaps ten or a dozen, or even more in number, presumably the residences of the ruler of the stronghold and his subordinate chieftains. The stone foundations of one such house, uncovered almost intact, give us the ground-plan, though the superstructure of crude brick is wholly lacking. It was a long rectangular building consisting of one great room with central hearth and a single doorway leading out to a portico at the west. It is thus a typical *megaron* in plan, the earliest example yet known in Anatolia, and clearly a prototype of the famous palace of Troy II. Two successive pivot-stones for the swinging door were found in place beside the opening. The inner end of the room had been used as a kitchen, indicated by a small hearth about which lay much refuse of animal bones, fish bones, shells, etc., and fragments of cooking pots. No traces of furniture were observed except for two stone platforms that may have served respectively for a bed and a bench. Six graves of infant children were found; two had been buried beneath the floor and four just outside the house to the north, some in small jars, others merely in shallow pits.

Though an antecedent stage of the same culture, apparently still belonging to the Late Stone Age, was revealed by a trial excavation at Kum Tepe, a small village-site near the mouth of the Scamander, the first settlers at Troy itself seem already to have been familiar with the working of metal. In the deepest stratum was unearthed a fairly well-shaped fish-hook of pure copper, and other remnants of copper implements came to light here and there throughout the whole layer. Stone could also be cut and dressed; and one of the most remarkable monuments discovered is a large *stele* (Pl. 13, *b*) of flaky limestone, on which a human face has been carved in low relief in a style that betrays more than a little schooling. The *stele* may have been made to be set as a tombstone over a grave. Fiddle-shaped idols, celts, and a hammer-axe were also fashioned of stone. A crude figurine of terracotta shows a rather unskilled attempt to model the human form.

A necklace made by stringing together a series of small birdbones illustrates the simple tastes of the period in personal adornment. Numerous small whorls of terracotta show a familiarity with the technique of spinning, almost as it prevails in some parts of Asia Minor to-day. Perhaps the most characteristic product of Troy I is its pottery. The potter's wheel was yet unknown, and all wares are handmade. Open bowls, cups, beaked jugs, and jars (Fig. 23, *a*) appear in a variety of forms, usually with flattened bottom, sometimes on a pedestal, relatively thick walls, and brightly polished surface, most commonly black, or greyish-, greenish-, or brownish-black in colour. In the course of the period a gradual change from sharply angular to rounded profiles may be followed.

Occasionally on rims appears a plastic representation of human features, and incised linear decoration is fairly common.

From its very beginning Troy was thus laid out as a royal stronghold, with considerable open space, where the populace might take refuge inside the walls in times of danger. There is some evidence that smaller houses were also built outside the fortified enclosure. This early settlement was repeatedly damaged or destroyed, and as often rebuilt, until the accumulated strata of débris attained a depth of some fourteen feet. The final destruction, the most violent of all, accompanied by fire which has left a thick deposit of charred débris, led to the rebuilding of the whole citadel on a larger scale, which we may regard as the beginning of Troy II.

Troy II.—Troy II, represented by seven successive strata of remains, was likewise a period of long duration. The new fortification wall was more massive than its predecessors, and enclosed a much larger area of ground. Within the period it was twice reconstructed, each time with a considerable enlargement of the enclosure, which eventually attained a length of nearly 400 feet and a width of almost as much. The well-known walls revealed by Schliemann along approximately three-quarters of the entire circuit, and which he at first thought to be those of Homeric Troy, still stand in some places to a height exceeding twenty feet, with a thickness of ten to fifteen feet and more. These walls, too, have a sloping outer face, but the upper part, in some places preserved, was built up vertically in crude brick to an adequate height for defence. In its final form the citadel had two monumental gateways, one on the south-west approached from outside by an ascending ramp (Pl. 14, *a*) paved with huge flat stone slabs, and one on the south-east, constructed with projecting antae and a double portico in a startling anticipation of the classical Greek propylon (see plan, Fig. 22).

Within the citadel were many houses of great size, the largest and most magnificent of which, in the middle of the hill, is generally identified as the palace of the king. Like most of the others, it is a true *megaron*, with a deep porch fronting on a court and opening into a long rectangular chamber which had a central hearth. The *megaron* has deep foundations of large stones, on which rests a stone socle that supported the superstructure of crude brick and a flat roof. Some of these edifices, which were erected in the third phase of Troy II, were succeeded in the later phases of the period by smaller houses more closely crowded together. In the final phase the whole citadel once again fell a victim to a devastating fire, which reduced the settlement to ruins. The haste with which the inhabitants departed, without delaying to collect their treasured possessions, may be deduced from the fact that almost every house of this phase, when excavated, has yielded objects of gold, which the vast amount of débris heaped up by the catastrophe seems to have prevented the survivors from recovering. Most of the 'treasures' found by Schliemann came from this stratum; and in the gold diadems, necklaces, bracelets, ear-rings, and small ornaments by the thousands, as well as in the numerous goblets and other vases of silver and gold (*cf*. Fig. 7, *a*), and in the weapons and vessels of copper and bronze, one can see vividly how prosperous the settlement had become and how greatly the arts and crafts had been developed during the time of Troy II.

The working of stone likewise attained remarkable skill, and among the most beautiful and artistic objects recovered by Schliemann must be mentioned four splendid hammer-axes adorned with fine carving, veritable masterpieces of prehistoric craftsmanship, three made of a greenish jade-like stone and one of lapis lazuli. The material is not of native Trojan provenience, and the weapons may have been imported from the east. Two small lion heads carved in crystal are also of considerable artistic merit. Innumerable whorls of terracotta, many bearing a decoration of incised patterns filled with white matter, show that spinning was carried on intensively; and from the traces of a loom observed in one house it is clear that weaving was a household industry. Handles of bristle brushes were also made of terracotta. Though copper was frequently employed, bone was still used freely for implements and tools, and was often carved for ornaments as well as for fiddle-shaped idols.

The potters of Troy II did not lag behind the other craftsmen in enterprise and progress: the invention (or adoption) of the potter's wheel, which may be assigned to the second phase of the period, revolutionized the ceramic industry, and henceforth hand-made pots gradually declined in importance, while wheel-turned vases almost reach a stage of mass production. The new technique naturally led to innovations in the shapes of vases; shallow plates and flaring bowls (Fig. 23, *e*) now become very common, and curving profiles almost completely displace the angular. Capacious goblets with two sturdy handles (*cf*. Fig. 23, *a*) and slender cylindrical cups, Schliemann's *depas amphikypellon* (Fig. 23, *c*) present characteristic forms, and large jugs appear with human features modelled in relief on their high necks or on their cylindrical lids (Fig. 23, *b*, *d*). Colours range from black to buff and red.

The culture of Troy II was clearly evolved from that of Troy I without a break in continuity. But the Second Settlement greatly surpassed the First in power and material wealth, under the influence of which is apparent a corresponding rise in the conditions of living. The general character of the settlement implies a fairly well-regulated social organization with several grades of class distinctions. The common people still lived in small houses or huts clustered about the fortress or grouped together in rural communities favourable to agricultural pursuits. The jewellery and the many other gold objects that have been brought to

PLATE 13

(b) Carved *stele* from Troy I

(a) Fortification wall of Troy I

PLATE 14

light, presumably constituting no more than an insignificant remnant of the real aggregate of the valuables once possessed by the inhabitants in this period, must clearly reflect a very considerable accumulation of wealth in actual gold.   How and whence so great a quantity of it was acquired are questions that cannot be answered with complete certainty. The bulk of the population, as already implied, no doubt eked out a living by tilling the soil and perhaps by raising cattle; but such early agriculture can hardly have led to the heaping up of large fortunes in precious metals.   The rivers of the Troad may have contributed their share of golden sands, and it is not impossible that the working of ore-bearing deposits on Mt. Ida yielded its hard-earned quota.   But some additional source of income must be postulated, and we shall surely not go wrong in concluding that it sprang from the fortunate situation of the citadel itself in a position where it dominated a cross-road of traffic both by sea and by land and was able to levy tolls of some kind on those who passed.

   Troy III.—Troy III, which was built over the ruins after the final destruction of Troy II by fire, carries on the development of the same civilization without interruption and with little perceptible change.   The new settlement was larger than its predecessor, and its houses spread out over the mound of débris covering the buried remains of the earlier fortress walls.   Coincident with the evident growth in population and the increase in the number of houses constructed on the citadel, we note that the whole establishment seems to have been laid out in an orderly manner, and a suggestion of a town-plan emerges more clearly.   Main streets and branching lanes divided it into irregular blocks of houses.   No proper defensive wall has been identified, but there can be little doubt that such a wall existed, and that the Third Settlement retained the traditional character of a fortified stronghold.   Some of the houses were large and well built, with high walls of solid stone masonry instead of crude brick; they seem to have been divided into small rooms by narrow partition walls of clay or brick, and no real example of a *megaron* has been recognized.   It may be that some social change had occurred, perhaps associated with the burning of Troy II, by which the upper class had lost some of its wealth and power while new forces were rising from the lower ranks.

   Precious metals are rare in the deposits of the Third Settlement, but, as shown by several crucibles, copper continues to be used, along with stone and bone for tools and implements.   A great increase in the number of bones of deer may indicate some advance in methods of the chase. Idols of marble are fairly common, and horn was also sometimes utilized for crude figures of this kind.   Distinctive of this period are some clumsy figures of four-legged animals in terracotta.   Spinning and weaving were

2 C

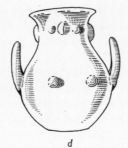
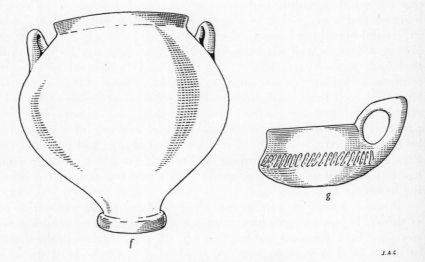

FIG. 23. Pottery types from Troy

(*a*) Two-handled tankard (Troy I-II) ; (*b*) Lid of face-pot (Troy II) ; (*c*) *Depas* (Troy II) ; (*d*) Face-pot (Troy II) ; (*e*) Bowl (Troy II) ; (*f*) Burial-urn (Troy VI) ; (*g*) Cup of knobbed ware (Troy VIIb)

(Scale : *c.* 1 : 6)

familiar occupations in each household, as one may conclude from the presence of numerous terracotta whorls, many decorated with incised patterns, and loom weights of clay. The potters seem to have worked more to supply utilitarian demands than for aesthetic purposes, on the evidence of countless flaring bowls of careless workmanship and numerous heavy jugs and jars of coarse ware. But they were capable of finer products, too, which we may see in an extensive series of well-modelled face-pots and face-lids and in many highly polished, thin, slender goblets, with two handles, of the form to which Schliemann applied the Homeric term *depas amphikypellon*. These vessels, and in fact all the pots of Troy III, are unmistakably the direct descendants of prototypes which had already been evolved during the time of the Second Settlement (*cf.* Fig. 23, *b-d*), from which it is indeed hardly possible to distinguish them; and in this unbroken ceramic tradition we have clear evidence of the essential continuity of Trojan life from period to period.

After having passed through three or four chronological phases, recorded by superposed strata of débris, which accumulated to a depth of some six feet, Troy III came to its end in some unknown manner, not by fire; the inhabitants evidently had time to salvage their belongings of chief intrinsic value, for no considerable 'treasures' were found in the excavation of the ruins.

Troy IV.—Troy IV begins with the construction of a new settlement over the mounting débris. It was greater in extent than Troy III, though it appears to have had approximately the same town-plan. The new streets in some instances certainly followed the lines of the old, and the system of dividing the establishment into blocks of houses seems to have survived. The town was almost surely fortified; sections of its massive wall have probably been correctly recognized on the eastern and southern sides of the mound, although the exact course of the circuit has not been determined. In some parts of the citadel many small houses were crowded closely together, with party walls separating them one from another. One such house, in a row of three or four, consisted of a fairly large rectangular chamber, with an anteroom and a porch opening on a street, and the others were similar. In each, frequently in a corner, was a hearth or a small domed oven of crude brick or clay. The old style of building prevails, with low stone walls supporting a superstructure of crude brick.

Metal is still limited mainly to copper, which is used along with stone and bone for pins, awls, chisels, and other implements. Small marble idols are fairly common, and loom weights of stone occur. Spindle-whorls of terracotta are often decorated with patterns formed by incised lines filled with white matter. Among other characteristic objects of terracotta are some brushes, or brush-handles, like those of Troy II, riddled on one face with tiny punched holes presumably for the insertion of bristles. The pottery of the Fourth Settlement shows a direct continuity with that of Troy III, although clearly affected by a certain progress and change. Flaring bowls become extremely rare, face-pots appear occasionally, but in much conventionalized style, and the two-handled goblet, the *depas amphikypellon*, occurs infrequently. A new type of cup makes its début, and in somewhat coarser ware there is evidence of an innovation in the use apparently of straw for tempering.

The deposit of débris that can be attributed to Troy IV has a total depth varying from six to nine feet. In one area five subdivisions are clearly discernible in the strata, elsewhere only three. The end of the settlement was brought about by some cause that has not been determined.

Troy V.—In Troy V the steady enlargement of the area occupied by the settlement is continued, and the new citadel spreads out beyond the limits of its predecessor. It was again undoubtedly a fortified stronghold. The stratigraphic evidence along the south edge of the hill indicates that there must have been a wall, although the circuit cannot be clearly traced. Within the enclosure were many houses, some of relatively complex plan, divided into several rooms. The masonry of the period has a style of its own. The walls are remarkably thin, constructed with a certain trimness and precision that one cannot fail to notice in their plumb stand, regular alignment, and careful articulation at corners. A socle was made of unworked smallish flat stones laid with care, supporting a superstructure of crude brick; and both faces of a wall were coated with a thick plaster of yellowish clay. Hearths, both trough-shaped and of the flat circular type, and free-standing domed ovens are common; and occasionally in an angle of a room one finds a substantial seat or bench built of stone and clay. The hard-packed earth floors seem for the most part to have been kept in a fairly clean-swept state, and no great deposit of rubbish, rich in objects, was brought to light.

Metal objects recovered from this layer are insignificant, including merely a few pins and bits of other tools of copper, and perhaps of bronze. Idols were still made of marble and other stone, and stone implements continued to be used. Many of the spindle-whorls of terracotta are extremely well made. In the field of pottery the ceramic tradition inherited from the preceding age is still followed, and there is no sharp break in development; but a general improvement in technique is apparent, and a fine ware, coated with red, attains a high quality. Among the most characteristic vessels is a shallow curving bowl bearing a large cross painted in broad red bands on the interior or the exterior or both, and a deeper bowl with angular profile.

It is clear that the culture of Troy V is evolved from what had gone before, and there is no sign of any break in continuity. Four successive strata observed within the layer, which had a thickness of five to six feet, indicate that the Fifth Settlement passed through as many chronological phases. What brought about its final destruction or abandonment it is impossible to say; but from the fact that no great quantity of charred débris has been found anywhere it seems safe to conclude, at all events, that a general conflagration was not the cause.

Troy VI.—With Troy VI we come to the greatest and most powerful of all the citadels that successively occupied the site. Widespread changes of many kinds indicate the arrival of a vigorous new stock which imposed its domination over the old in political as well as cultural matters. In economics, too, the impact was doubtless great: among other things the newcomers brought with them the horse, previously unknown at Troy. The period itself must have been a lengthy one, for along the eastern and southern flanks of the hill it has left an accumulation of débris more than seventeen feet deep in which eight strata can be distinguished. There is some evidence to show that at least three successive fortresses were erected one after the other within this time. The last in the series, which may be attributed to the late phases of the settlement, and which itself exhibits three or more chronological stages of construction, still stands in a fairly good state of preservation (Pl. 15), and can be followed through some two thirds of its total course of nearly 600 yards about the site. Except for a small remnant it is missing on the north, along the edge of the hill, where it was subjected to serious depredations in Greek and Roman times and where Schliemann's early excavations may have removed what little, if any, still remained.

The masonry varies somewhat in different parts of the wall, especially in the size of the stones used, the technique of jointing, and the degree of batter, the eastern, southern, and western sections each having a style of its own. But through most of its extent it is a monumental structure from thirteen to fifteen feet thick, and it was originally from twenty to thirty feet high. The outer face, usually marked by characteristic shallow vertical offsets at intervals of roughly thirty feet, has a batter, sometimes with an inclination as great as one in three; but this slope was restricted to the lower part of the wall, and the upper, built either of stone or of crude brick, rose vertically high above it. The material of the lower part consists of a hard limestone which for the visible portions was carefully squared and dressed and laid in regular courses; and the southern section, with its closely fitted blocks and almost perfect jointing, has a quality rivalling that of the best classical Greek work. Four gateways have been found, on the east, south, south-west, and west respectively; there may have been a fifth on the north, and a small postern led into the great tower at the north-eastern angle. The East and the South Gates were each flanked and defended by a massive, projecting, rectangular tower.

Within the citadel, which had a length of some 225 yards from east to west, the ground rose toward the centre in a series of broad steplike terraces, perhaps four in number. The uppermost was almost certainly occupied by the palace of the king; and ranged about it in a radiating fashion on the descending terraces were numerous large houses, spaciously distributed, with no attempt to utilize all available ground. These were presumably the residences of the king's mother and sons, perhaps also of councillors and other officials of high standing in the state. Only the buildings on the lowest terrace, and to a slighter extent on the second from the bottom, escaped destruction in the ancient levelling operations already mentioned, as a result of which the palace and its immediate neighbours have completely vanished. The lowest terrace provided room without crowding for at least fifteen such buildings. Seven of them, together with one on the next higher level, have been uncovered and in each case found sufficiently well preserved to give a general idea at least of the ground-plan. Three of these houses have been compared with a *megaron* in arrangement; two others have a single axial row of interior pillars and an entrance on one long side; one has two rows of stone column bases, five in each row; one is a simple rectangular building with no trace of partitions or interior supports; and one is a complex structure of three or more rooms. There is thus no little variety in these buildings, but with their massive construction and careful execution, which show that they were designed to last for a long time, they testify to the architectural skill of their builders as well as the substantial wealth and important rank of their occupants. The citadel is clearly still a royal stronghold as it was in the time of Troy II.

Contemporary with the last phase of this citadel is the only early cemetery that has yet been brought to light in the neighbourhood of the site. It lay some 550 yards to the south of the acropolis, at the southern edge of the adjacent plateau. A town wall of Hellenistic or Roman date passed directly through the area, and various other later activities further contributed to the disturbance and destruction of the ancient burial ground. Nevertheless, remains of some 200 urns (Fig. 23, *f*) of various shapes and sizes were brought to light, including twenty which still contained ashes, charred fragments of human bones, remnants of simple ornaments, and a few small pots. The bones are those of adults as well as of children; and the discovery makes it certain that the custom of cremation was known and practised in the time of Troy VI.

The Sixth Settlement has yielded little in the way of jewellery and ornaments, but it is certain that gold, silver, and electrum were skilfully used for such purposes. Bronze weapons, spear-heads, knives, arrowheads, etc., as well as sickles and chisels have been found; and it is worth noting that real bronze has now supplanted copper. Vessels, various implements, and beads of stone show that the technique of stone-cutting was highly developed. Bone and ivory were likewise delicately worked for small receptacles, seals, ornaments, etc.; while beads of glass-paste and faience represent the simpler fashion of jewellery.

In the pottery of the period an entirely new fabric, grey Minyan ware, makes its appearance in abundance. It is the same kind of ware that marks the advent of the Middle Helladic Period on the Greek mainland; and it is likely that both areas were overrun at about the same time by invaders in the same folk-movement and probably of Hellenic stock. At Troy red-coated ware of native Trojan descent with a long history on the site survives for a time. It may have had some influence on the later development of grey Minyan ware, though the latter largely maintained its own repertory of forms. From the ceramic evidence it appears that we must postulate the survival of some native elements, so that the continuity of culture on the site was not altogether broken.

Along with the pottery mentioned a great many fragments of imported Mycenaean ware (*cf.* Fig. 24, *a–c*) came to light, and it was from this fact that Dörpfeld concluded that the Sixth Settlement must be contemporary with the strongholds of Mycenae and Tiryns, and must, therefore, be identified as the Troy of Priam and the Trojan War.

There are, however, no signs of a general destruction by fire such as one might properly expect in the ruins of a town captured in war and sacked by the conquerors. On the other hand, investigations along the eastern and southern sides of the citadel, wherever the latest strata of Troy VI still lie undisturbed, have revealed huge masses of stones fallen from the upper part of the fortification wall and from the neighbouring houses and terraces (Pl. 14, *b*). The débris seems far too extensive to have been pitched over wantonly by the hand of man, and, considering other supplementary evidence, we may safely conclude that the end of Troy VI was brought about by a severe earthquake, which rendered the houses uninhabitable and caused serious damage to the superstructure of the fortress itself.

Troy VIIa.—Troy VII, as differentiated by Dörpfeld, includes the remains of two successive settlements differing considerably in character, and logically entitled to separate numbering, though called by him VII [1] and VII [2]. We use the terms VIIa and VIIb.

Troy VIIa represents the reconstruction of the citadel after the seismic disaster. In culture it marks no appreciable change from what had gone before, and its ceramic and other products are with few exceptions almost indistinguishable from those of the late Sixth Settlement. Dörpfeld, therefore, recently suggested that it might be more appropriate to call this stage VIb rather than VIIa; but the latter designation has

J.A.C

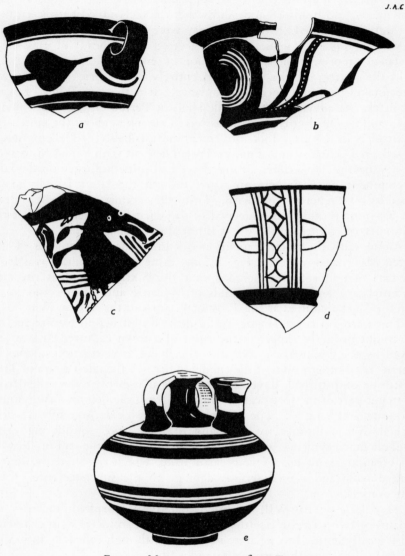

FIG. 24. Mycenaean pottery from Troy

(*a, b*) L.H. I–II, from Troy VI (middle) ; (*c*) L.H. IIIb, from Troy VI (late) ; (*d*) L.H.
IIIb, from Troy VI/VIIa ; (*e*) L.H. IIIb, from Troy VI (late)
(Scale : *c.* 1 : 2)

been retained in order to avoid confusion, since it conforms to the one that appears in Dörpfeld's standard publication. New houses were built everywhere over the site in a characteristic masonry in which is combined the use of rough unworked stones along with many fine squared blocks obviously recovered from the heaps that must have lain in abundance beside the damaged walls of the Sixth Settlement. The fortification wall itself continued to serve as the main defence of the town, apparently with some rebuilding, where necessary; and some of the earlier gateways still provided access to the citadel. The houses within the latter, for the most part rather small or divided into small rooms, were closely crowded together, occupying virtually all space available. In almost every house are found groups of huge storage jars, often six feet high, varying from a few to ten or a dozen or sometimes even more in number. They were set deeply in the ground under the floor so that the mouth of each vessel, usually covered by a stone lid, emerged only a few inches above the level of the pavement; and they were, of course, installed for the storage of liquid and dry provisions (Pl. 16, *a*). The abrupt and general adoption throughout the settlement of this innovation in the method of conserving food supplies might be taken to imply that some particular emergency was anticipated; and since the state of the ruins (*cf.* Pl. 16, *b*) indicates that the whole citadel, after a relatively short existence, was in fact destroyed by a devastating fire, with suggestions of accompanying violence (human bones lay unburied in the streets just inside the South Gate and were also found in two houses), we may infer that it was a hostile attack that was feared. Some fragments of imported Mycenaean pottery (*cf.* Fig. 24, *d*, *e*) and associated local imitations show that the settlement was in general contemporary with an early stage of Furumark's ceramic style IIIb when pottery of IIIa had not yet ceased to be used.

Troy VIIb.—Once more the town was reconstructed, and in Period VIIb new houses again speedily sprang up throughout the acropolis. Many spread out over and beyond the great wall of Troy VI and VIIa, which in some places was now largely buried in debris. It is uncertain whether or not a new supplementary fortification was erected at some points outside the earlier circuit; but the old South Gate, at all events, still maintained its rôle as one of the principal entrances to the town. The houses, which are for the most part small and unpretentious, usually exhibit a characteristic peculiarity of construction marked by the use of rough orthostates of no great size in the lowest courses of their walls. Many of these houses follow closely the lines and plans of their fore-runners of Period VIIa, and a certain continuity is undeniable. It is most strongly indicated in the initial phase of Troy VIIb, during which the pottery and other products differ little, when at all, from those of Period

VIIa. But in a second phase a startling ceramic change may be noted in the sudden appearance of *Buckelkeramik*, or knobbed ware (Fig. 23, *g*). With its primitive-looking, hand-made, black-polished vessels, in forms and fabric wholly unrelated to anything hitherto made at Troy, it has been thought to show an unmistakable kinship with a kind of pottery well known in the lower basin of the Danube, and in central Europe, where it has been named from its principal place of discovery 'Lausitz Ware'. Whether this view is correct or not — there are some chronological difficulties — there can be no doubt that the evidence implies a folk-movement of some kind, and we must infer that a new cultural, if not racial, element, whatever its provenience, established itself in the settlement at Troy. Its complete domination was perhaps only temporary; for a considerable body of Trojans of native stock probably survived. How long the period lasted is unknown. The destruction of the settlement was occasioned by a disastrous fire which raised up a heap of burned and blackened debris, and the site may thenceforth have stood unoccupied a long time.

Troy VIII.—The scanty architectural remains of Troy VIII offer little information regarding the state of the citadel. The fortification wall, built mainly of smallish rough stones, seems to have followed pretty closely the course of its monumental predecessor, on which it is in some places directly founded. Some scattered pieces of smaller walls, noted here and there, indicate that houses stood both within and without the fortress, but only one is well enough preserved to give us the ground-plan of such a building. On the south-western slope of the hill outside the citadel two small sanctuaries have been uncovered, each a walled precinct without a temple, but enclosing an altar, or rather a series of successive altars. The abundant pottery recovered here supplies the best record of the historical development occurring within the period. In the early phases grey and buff wares occur and it is likely that they are evolved from the fabrics that had survived to the end of Period VIIb. But there is virtually nothing that can be dated to a time earlier than the close of the eighth century. The new culture is purely Hellenic, and most of the pottery belongs to distinctive East Greek categories, possibly made at Troy itself; but there are also a few pieces representing Attic and Island styles. Orientalizing ware makes it appearance in considerable quantities. The bulk of the material again forms a class by itself, of East Greek affinities; but other styles are well exemplified, including the Protocorinthian, Corinthian, and Rhodian. Some sherds of black-figured ware of Corinthian and Attic fabric have likewise been recognized. At the same time monochrome grey and buff wares, now much refined and Hellenized, still point to the persistence of a native element of population at Troy.

The Hellenization of the site seems to have led to no great results, for there is little evidence that Troy blossomed out as an important Greek city state. A few sherds, including a number in the red-figured style, indicate that some form of activity was still carried on here and there on the hill in the fifth and early fourth centuries, perhaps in connection with a sanctuary or a temple; but there is little trace of real habitation, and we can only conclude that the site had been virtually abandoned. It is not impossible that the bulk of the population was for some reason induced to move away to a new situation elsewhere in the neighbourhood; that they still retained their name and entity as a state is, however, shown by the fact that the Ilians are recorded in the Athenian tribute lists as having been charged with an assessment of two talents.

Troy IX.—Late in the fourth century, after some encouragement from Alexander, and under the protection of Lysimachos, an entirely new settlement was founded on the site. It bore the name Ilion, and from the beginning it was an urban establishment extensive enough to be called a city. The old acropolis was now in large part given over to the sanctuary of Athene, while the town was laid out below it spreading far to southward and eastward over the adjacent plateau, which was enclosed by a fortification wall said by Strabo to have had a length of forty stades. Ilion had a long subsequent history; with many vicissitudes of fortune it maintained its existence through Roman times at least until the end of the fourth century of our era. Since no real break in cultural continuity is manifest within this lengthy period, the whole of it is here included under the designation Troy IX. Beginning as a Hellenistic foundation, granted various privileges by the successors of Alexander, it gradually developed, probably without a change of population, into a small provincial town of the Roman empire. Thoroughly sacked and destroyed by Fimbria in 86–85 B.C., it was some time later rebuilt, partly through the help and favour of Julius Caesar and the Emperor Augustus. Exemption from tribute and other privileges, first conferred by these patrons, were renewed by many other emperors down to the third century after Christ.

The remains of the town exhibit almost everywhere two main strata, the earlier of Hellenistic date, the later probably representing the rebuilding after the destruction by Fimbria. The whole plateau is covered with the ruins of houses, some small, others large and rather pretentious; only a few have been examined at all. Near the southern foot of the acropolis lay an open rectangular agora, bordered by colonnades, with a large palaestra beside it toward the west. Built up against and over the south wall of the earlier citadel have been found several structures, the most important being (from west to east) a small stadium associated with a sanctuary, a small theatre or odeum, and a *bouleuterion*. A vast theatre was built in a natural hollow below the north-eastern angle of the acropolis. On the latter lay the sanctuary of Athene, a huge rectangular precinct, surrounded by colonnades, in which stood the temple and a large altar.

CHRONOLOGY

Chiefly on ceramic evidence the chronology of the successive settlements has now been fairly well determined in relation to the Aegean system established by Sir Arthur Evans and others. Thus in broad terms Troy I, II, III, IV, and V fall in the Early Bronze Age; the first half of Troy VI in the Middle Bronze Age; the second half of VI together with Troy VIIa and VIIb in the Late Bronze Age.

Numerous fragments of imported Early Helladic pottery are found in all the early layers from after the middle of Troy I to Troy V inclusive. The predominant occurrence of grey Minyan ware in the deeper strata of Troy VI and the appearance somewhat later of matt-painted ware give further fixed points for sequence dating. In the upper strata of Troy VI imported Mycenaean pottery makes its appearance in increasing quantities, Late Helladic I and II being somewhat scantily represented in the middle strata, Late Helladic III much more abundantly in the final phases (see Fig. 24).

The Mycenaean sherds from the cemetery and from the 'earthquake layer' (Phase VIb) represent predominatingly Furumark's style of Mycenaean IIIa with an appreciable admixture of IIIb. If these categories may be taken as having real chronological value, the destruction of Troy VI by an earthquake must accordingly have taken place when pottery of Mycenaean IIIb was beginning to displace that of IIIa.

In Troy VIIa imported Mycenaean ware is relatively scarce, falling short of local imitations in quantity. Most of this material belongs to Mycenaean IIIb, but it is still accompanied by a good many pieces of IIIa. No certain examples of Mycenaean IIIc were found in this context. Troy VIIa seems thus to have lived out its life before the appearance of Mycenaean IIIc. Fragments of characteristic Cypriot bowls in 'White Slip II Ware' have come to light in the upper stratum of Troy VI as well as in the layer of Troy VIIa, and support the general synchronism.

A few sherds of Mycenaean ware of the so-called 'Granary Class' have been recovered along with other fragments in the style of Mycenaean IIIc in the deposits of Troy VIIb1 and VIIb2.

The foregoing brief analysis of the ceramic evidence gives a good basis for sequence dating which, however, pending further progress in the study of Mycenaean pottery, cannot with accuracy be translated into terms of absolute years. Meanwhile for convenience our current views (almost wholly conjectural for the divisions of the Early Bronze Age) are recapitulated in the following table:

Troy I	3000–2600
II	2600–2300
III	2300–2200
IV	2200–2050
V	2050–1900
VI	1900–1300
VIIa	1300–1250
VIIb	1250–1100
VIII	700–350
IX	350 B.C.–A.D. 400

FOREIGN CONTACTS

A study of the imported pottery is interesting from another point of view. It comes from the west in all periods. Indeed there are few easily recognizable indications of close contact with central Anatolia at any time, or of specific imports from that region. Although the conclusion is based on negative evidence and therefore subject to revision, it looks as if the foreign relations of the site were always primarily with the Aegean (Cyprus may be counted as part of the Aegean world), and there can be ... doubt that there was considerable seaborne traffic in the waters b... ...reece and the coast of Asia Minor from the middle of the E... ...e down to Hellenic times. The settlements along th... ...oughout their early history thus seem to have had ... ... outlook; and it is not impossible that their ... ...some degree of racial kinship with the bearers ... ...cladic, Early Helladic, and perhaps Early ... ...ot to deny that there were contacts with ... ...Mesopotamia, maintained probably by ... ...ian littoral.

...ELIGION

In th... ... said regarding the religion of the pe... ... so many centuries; and, indeed, the ... ... t best scanty and particularly difficul... ... In dealing with the early layers from ... ...her frequent occurrence of small figu... ...ne, sometimes of bone or terracotta. ... ...mblance to an analogous group of ob... ...bundance, at Aegean sites, especially in ... ...ably indicate at least a superficial general similarity in the household cults of the two regions. The stone *stele* of the First Settlement which, with its remarkable sculptural representation of a human face, we have ventured to interpret as a sepulchral monument, may likewise, or alternatively, have possessed some religious significance; and two accompanying stone slabs, each bearing on one surface a series of worked bowl-like depressions, must surely be regarded as tables of offerings, rude and simple forerunners of the more elaborate and elegant altars of this kind best known from Minoan Crete. Analogous furniture in such a case might well imply analogous ritual. For the Early Bronze Age little more can yet be said with safety.

When we come to the Sixth Settlement, however, we are confronted by monumental remains which look as if they may have been designed to serve religious ends. Most striking are the monolithic pillars, rectangular in shape, originally at least four, possibly five in number, which were set up in a row along the outer face of the tower flanking the south gate. A similar block was also erected in a corresponding position beside the western gate. Utilitarian purposes appear to be excluded, and we can hardly regard these monoliths as other than objects of worship in a pillar-cult, which finds analogies not only in Crete, but throughout the remoter regions of the Near East. A small circular stone pavement, laid near the centre of the southern tower itself, might conceivably have served as a platform about an altar; if this conjecture is right, the altar must have been supported on two columnar legs, for faintly discernible rounded traces, left by a difference in weathering, indicate that a pair of columns stood close together on a stone base. If they were real pillars of some height, and not merely low supports, they might themselves have stood as symbols in a cult. No temple or shrine could be certainly recognized among the buildings of the Sixth Settlement discovered within the citadel. But the Pillar House, named from its axially placed rectangular piers, recalls by its plan, with three small rooms or compartments at its western end, the shrines and temples of Babylonia and Assyria; the resemblance may be fortuitous, but it is not impossible that this great structure had some provision for a cult.

Evidence that cremation was practised in the time of Troy VI has already been mentioned; but the cemetery yielded no further information with a recognizable bearing on religion. For the later periods nothing is known that sheds any light on cult and worship until we come in the Eighth Settlement to the establishment of two purely Hellenic sanctuaries, enclosing altars, but no temples, on the south-western slope outside the citadel. The cults have not been specifically identified, though one may be a shrine of Cybele. The noted temple of Athene, with its broad rectangular precinct occupying the centre of the acropolis, must clearly be attributed to Troy IX, though it may have had an earlier history going back into the preceding age from which no certain remains survive. In its focal position on the citadel it may well, like the temple of Athene at Mycenae and the temple of Hera at Tiryns, be the direct descendant of the principal palace-cult of pre-classical times.

TROY, HOMER, AND THE TROJAN WAR

In this chapter we have used the name Troy freely and without hesitation; but, in view of past controversies, the question of the identification of the site deserves some further mention. It is really a very simple problem, so simple that most of the lengthy discussions have missed the main point and lost themselves in a maze of unessential detail. In the Homeric poems and in the entire body of relevant Greek tradition Troy is a royal stronghold, the seat of a mighty king and the capital of the whole region of north-west Asia Minor. The site at Hissarlik is just such a citadel. With its monumental fortification walls of the Sixth Settlement it takes a worthy place alongside the similar castle of Mycenae; and its succession of earlier fortresses, renewed in period after period, shows clearly that its royal character is continuous from its first foundation. In its strategic position controlling navigation through the straits as well as traffic on an important land-route it is the key site which dominates the Troad. Intensive exploration throughout the region has revealed numerous subordinate settlements, villages, and hamlets, in which the agricultural populace lived, but not the slightest trace of another comparable stronghold. There is no room for another. Meticulous examination and testing of all the minor topographical details mentioned in a great poem, written down some six or seven hundred years after the events with which it deals, may be an interesting academic exercise, but it surely has no value for this particular problem. For who can determine what is derived from enduring tradition and what is due to the creative imagination of a great poetic genius? Mathematical computations of the exact area of the citadel and conjectural calculations of the possible number of the inhabitants are likewise futile so far as the identification of the site is concerned. There is no alternative site. If there ever was a Troy (and who can really doubt it?), it must have stood on the hill at Hissarlik.

It remains only to determine in which one of the many layers at Hissarlik are to be recognized the ruins of Priam's Troy. Schliemann's early attempts to identify the citadel in layers III and II were shown to be incorrect by his final campaign of 1890; and it was Dörpfeld, after his discovery in 1893 and 1894 of the magnificent walls of the Sixth Settlement with associated Mycenaean potsherds, who put forward the view, which has since prevailed, that Troy VI was the Homeric citadel.

The recent excavations, however, have made it clear that the Sixth Settlement was brought to its end by an earthquake and not by the hand of man. When we find that Troy VIIa, which immediately followed Troy VI, with continuity of culture and a re-use of the great fortification walls, was actually destroyed in a great fire, which apparently brought violent death to more than one human victim, it does not seem too bold to draw the logical conclusion. The agreement is too striking to be merely casual. Troy VIIa must surely be the Troy of Priam and Hector. Certain peculiarities of the settlement have been noted suggesting that it was crowded with people taking refuge within the walls, and that unusual supplies of food had been accumulated and stored in almost every house.

The exact date of the Trojan War has not been determined. The Greeks of classical and later times failed to reach full agreement on the subject. The conventional view going back to Eratosthenes and others places it in the early years of the twelfth century (1193–1184 B.C.). The Parian Marble assigns the capture to 1209–1208 B.C. Other computations, likewise based on calculations of genealogies, thrust the event back nearly half a century (Herodotus : ± 1250 B.C.), or even a whole century and more (Duris of Samos : c. 1334–1333 B.C.).[3] Our own conclusion, represented in the tentative chronological table, favours the general date given by Herodotus.

NOTES TO CHAPTER 13 (i)

The principal literature from Schliemann onwards is cited in the text.

1. Charles Maclaren, *Dissertation on the Topography of the Plain of Troy* (1822) ; and *The Plain of Troy described* (1863).

2. That the Troy of heroic times was not on the same site as the classical Ilion was first propounded by Demetrius of Skepsis in the second century B.C. His views are quoted by Strabo (592 ff.). Its supposed identification at Balli Dagh, which had a wide vogue in the nineteenth century, was due to Chevalier, *Description of the Plain of Troy* (Edinburgh, 1791). A useful summary of the arguments will be found in C. Schuchhardt, *Schliemann's Excavations* (Eng. edition 1891) chap. ii, pp. 17–32.

3. For a recent discussion of the ancient evidence see Sir J. Forsdyke, *Greece before Homer : Ancient Chronology and Mythology*, chap. 4. See also D. L. Page, *History and the Homeric Iliad*, chap. 2.

(ii) MYCENAE

by Alan J. B. Wace

HISTORY OF THE SITE

HOMER knew Mycenae as the seat of the realm of Agamemnon, but there is naturally no account of it in either *Iliad* or *Odyssey* since the scene of action lies elsewhere. Whenever mentioned it is spoken of as well

PLATE 15

Fortification walls of Troy VI

PLATE 16

(a) Troy VIIa : *pithoi* for food-storage set in the floor of a house

(b) Fallen masonry of Troy VIIa

PLATE 17

Doorway of the Treasury of Atreus, Mycenae

PLATE 18

(a) The Treasury of Atreus at Mycenae

(b) Remains of Mycenaean bridge-abutment near Mycenae

known and the adjectives applied to it are appropriate to its position as a royal stronghold. It is 'rich in gold', 'broad-streeted', 'well-built', and it was obviously regarded as a fortress of wealth and power. The site of Mycenae has always been known. Pausanias visited it in the second century A.D., and left a description of the 'Cyclopean' walls and Lion Gate which identify it beyond all doubt; they have remained visible to every later traveller or archaeologist from Leake and his predecessors onwards. Gell in 1810 and the French Expédition de Morée in 1830 made the first plans of the area and afterwards Schliemann and Steffen carried out other surveys of its ruins. From 1876 and 1886 onwards the excavations of Schliemann, Tsountas, and others have shown how extensive these ruins are and have revealed to us the brilliance of its civilization.

The site owes its importance to its natural position (see sketch-map, Fig. 25). It stands on a limestone peak between two high mountains at the western foot of the Arachnaeus range, the mountain backbone of Argolis. It overlooks the fertile Argive plain and has easy access to the sea, so that, with the neighbouring fortress of Tiryns, it could command the landfall of the sea routes coming from the south and south-east. At the same time it controls the roads that lead northwards through the mountains towards Corinth and central Greece. Its position was strong for both military and economic purposes; it could check the passage of hostile forces or levy dues on traders with caravans. The plain provided good cornland, and grazing for cattle and horses, thus meriting the Homeric adjective ἱππόβοτον. The main weakness of the citadel was lack of water, but this was overcome towards the end of the Bronze Age by extending the walls of the acropolis eastwards and bringing to a secret underground cistern outside them a constant supply of water from the perennial spring that rises rather less than half a mile to the east of the Lion Gate. Within the citadel there are one or two wells, but these can never have been a permanent source of water. The walls of the citadel, which is by nature not easy of access, are exceptionally massive and when in all their original strength must have been practically impregnable to the assaults possible in that age. This powerful fortress was well fitted to become the centre of a mighty realm which embraced most of Greece and the islands,

$$\pi o\lambda\lambda\tilde{\eta}\sigma\iota\nu\ \nu\dot{\eta}\sigma\sigma\iota\sigma\iota\ \kappa\alpha\grave{\iota}\ ^{\prime\prime}A\rho\gamma\epsilon\ddot{\iota}\ \pi\alpha\nu\tau\grave{\iota}\ \dot{\alpha}\nu\dot{\alpha}\sigma\sigma\epsilon\iota\nu.\qquad\text{(B 108)}$$

The enterprise and adventurous spirit of her people carried the arms and trade of Mycenae to most of the shores of the Nearer East.

Although the site was inhabited from Early Bronze Age times at least, this earliest settlement seems to have been unimportant. Mycenae first began to flourish with the Middle Bronze Age when the first Greeks, it is believed, came to Hellas. Then the summit of the citadel was surrounded by a defensive wall, part of which survives on the north-west

2 D

side.   There are other broken walls of this period below the palace ruins
and in the area of the Prehistoric Cemetery within and without the walls. To
the end of this period belongs the Grave Circle (Fig. 27, **E**), containing the

FIG. 25. Map of Argolis and Corinthia, showing the situation of Mycenae

tombs of over twenty princes and princesses, found in 1951 by the Greek
Archaeological Service immedately to the west of the *tholos* tomb called
by archaeologists the 'Tomb of Clytemnestra' (**G**). Earlier in this period a
large area at the western foot of the acropolis began to be used as a cemetery.   Within the citadel it covers the space now occupied by the Ramp
House, South House, and Warrior Vase House, the Grave Circle (**N**)
discovered by Schliemann, and the 'Granary'; outside the citadel, it

covers a considerable area, perhaps as far as the new Grave Circle, but its limits in this direction have not yet been defined. This cemetery continued in use until the end of Late Helladic II. Then it was cut into two portions by the building of the Lion Gate and the Cyclopean Wall. After the royal graves had become a sacred *temenos* (*cf.* Fig. 29) the rest of the portion within the walls was built over. The portion outside the walls also seems to have been built over, but with buildings of no importance.

From the later years of the Middle Bronze Age and the early years of the Late Bronze Age Mycenae, which had now fallen much under the cultural influence of Crete, began to prosper and grow larger and more important. Until the end of Late Helladic I the princes who ruled Mycenae had been buried with all their treasures in the rich Shaft Graves found by Schliemann. It was probably at the very close of this phase that the earliest *tholos* or beehive tomb,[a] the Cyclopean Tomb, was built. This new type of tomb replaces the Shaft Graves for royal burials; and the change may reflect a change of dynasty. In the next phase (Late Helladic II) Mycenae was already a powerful state and her overseas influence spread widely.

After the fall of Knossos about the beginning of Late Helladic III, Mycenae reached the zenith of her power and wealth. Then the Lion Gate and Cyclopean walls of the acropolis were built. On the summit of the citadel and covering practically the whole area of the original fortress of the Middle Bronze Age stood a great palace equipped with all the refinements and luxuries of the age. Doubtless, important buildings had already stood on this area in Late Helladic II; but the Late Helladic III building activity was such that little trace of them can now be found. With the construction of the Cyclopean citadel walls the building of larger houses on the slopes of the ridges to the west was much extended. It seems certain that at this time the private citizens of Mycenae lived in separate settlements set on the hills and ridges lying westward from the acropolis. In Late Helladic III, especially in its first and second stages (Late Helladic IIIa and b), many of the houses built on terraced slopes on the ridge west of the Lion Gate (Fig. 27, L), must, from their size, have been the residences of nobles or wealthy merchants. If we can judge by these houses, Mycenae at this period must have been most prosperous and peaceful, secure from attack by enemies. The tablets found in these houses indicate that the Mycenaeans had reached a comparatively high standard of literacy. During this time were built the largest and finest of the *tholos* tombs including those known as the Treasury of Atreus and the Tomb of Clytemnestra. It was the period of greatest achievement in the civilization of Mycenae. At the end of this phase disaster came. Most of the large houses outside the citadel

[a] For the type see Fig. 49 below, p. 483; also Pls. 17, 18, *a*.

were looted and then destroyed by violent fires. The citadel, however, was untouched. There seem to be no signs of invasion by enemies from overseas or by barbarian tribes. On the other hand it is possible that Mycenae at this time was ravaged by civil war. The legends tell us of a bitter feud between Atreus and his brother Thyestes for the throne, and it is not inconceivable that in some such contest one of the rivals, failing to dislodge the other from the citadel, plundered and destroyed all the buildings lying outside it, especially the houses of the rich. Perhaps, too, on this occasion the *tholos* tombs were ransacked by mercenaries in the service of one of the rivals. Mycenae recovered from this disaster, but never apparently regained its former height of peace and prosperity. Yet, though already past its prime, it was this Mycenae whose ruler Agamemnon early in the twelfth century led the Greek host against Troy. Towards the end of the Bronze Age, at the end of the twelfth century B.C., the traditional date of the return of the Heraclidae and the Dorian Invasion, Mycenae was captured by enemies, plundered, and burnt. This political revolution changed the career of Mycenae. When the site was reoccupied in the early Iron Age she never recovered her former status owing to the shifting of political power to Argos. Some of her traditions remained, for a temple of Athene rose on the site of the shrine of the palace of the Atridae.

Mycenae continued to exist as a small city state independent of Argos and loyally sent her contingents to fight for Greece at Thermopylae and Plataea. She thus aroused the jealousy of Argos, and about 468 B.C., when Sparta was too distracted by her own misfortunes to intervene, Argos took the opportunity to compel the Mycenaeans to submit. The inhabitants were scattered and the walls were dismantled. The shrines were left to fall into ruin.

In the third century B.C. Mycenae was again inhabited, but this time as a dependency (a *kome*) of Argos. The Cyclopean walls were repaired and the temple on the summit of the citadel was restored. Many small houses grew up within the walls. Outside the citadel a lower town was laid out and enclosed with walls running along the ridge to the west enclosing a large part of the western ridge (see Fig. 26). A theatre was built above the *dromos* of the long-forgotten *tholos* tomb which archaeologists have nicknamed the Tomb of Clytemnestra. A fountain house called Perseia was built outside the Lion Gate and water led to it from the spring to the east of the citadel. This town existed for some few centuries, but was apparently already in ruins when Pausanias visited it in the second century A.D. A few broken lamps suggest, however, that some inhabitants still lingered on until the fourth century A.D. Thereafter the site seems to have lain desolate until archaeology once again revived the glories of the Homeric stronghold.

THE MONUMENTS

The monuments of Mycenae fall into two groups, those within and those without the acropolis. Outside the acropolis (see sketch-map,

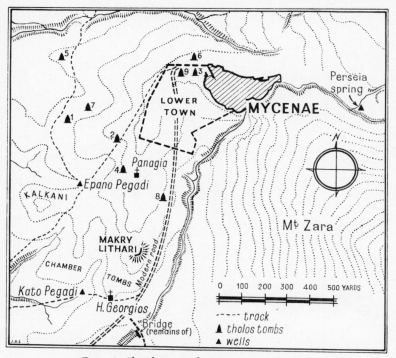

FIG. 26. Sketch-map of Mycenae and vicinity

Fig. 26) lie the nine *tholos* tombs which form one of the great features of Mycenae. They all belong to the Late Bronze Age and they divide into three groups. The first group begins just before the end of Late Helladic I and covers the first part of Late Helladic II. The second group was built in the second half of Late Helladic II. The third group, which includes the finest of all, the Treasury of Atreus (Pls. 17, 18, *a*), and the so-called Tomb of Clytemnestra, was built in the first two stages of Late Helladic III. The ridges which slope down westward from the acropolis are honeycombed with rock-cut chamber-tombs which belong to the three successive phases of the Late Bronze Age. On the crests of the ridges were a number of isolated unwalled settlements where the ordinary civil population lived. The history of some of these seems to go back to the Early Bronze Age. Among them lie two sources of water.[a] The

[a] Nowadays called *Epano Pegadi* and *Kato Pegadi* — 'Upper Well' and 'Lower Well'.

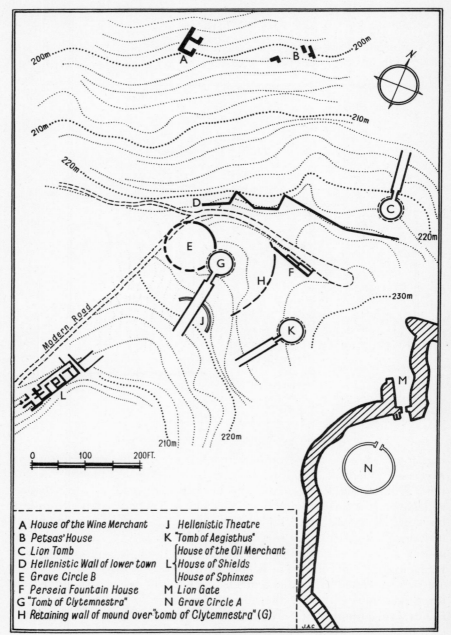

FIG. 27. Mycenae : area N.W. of the citadel

A House of the Wine Merchant
B Petsas' House
C Lion Tomb
D Hellenistic Wall of lower town
E Grave Circle B
F Perseia Fountain House
G "Tomb of Clytemnestra"
H Retaining wall of mound over "tomb of Clytemnestra" (G)

J Hellenistic Theatre
K "Tomb of Aegisthus"
L {House of the Oil Merchant / House of Shields / House of Sphinxes}
M Lion Gate
N Grave Circle A

richest of the settlements seems to have been that which lay on the ridge above the Treasury of Atreus. Round it lie the finest chamber-tombs (see Fig. 48 below, p. 482), for it would seem that each settlement had its own cemetery of chamber-tombs at the foot of the ridge on which it stood. The chamber-tombs were family tombs and were used by successive generations over a long term of years. They were reopened from time to time on the occasion of the death of a member of the family. A striking monument is the ruined bridge (Pl. 18, *b*) which carried across a ravine the main road leading from Mycenae to Prosymna, the Argive Heraeum. This is one of the many roads radiating from Mycenae which emphasize its character as a capital.

On the north end of the ridge where lies the Treasury of Atreus runs the line of the Hellenistic town wall which was built outside the acropolis on the reoccupation of Mycenae in the third century B.C. On the one side it ran to the north-west angle of the citadel and on the other it ran across a valley to the south-west angle of the Cyclopean walls (see Fig. 26). Within the area of the Hellenistic town (see Fig. 27) lie two monuments of the period, the theatre (J) which was built across the *dromos* of the Tomb of Clytemnestra (G), and the Perseia Fountain House (F), the ruins of which lie on the backbone of the ridge between the theatre and the Lion Gate. In the same area lies the newly found Middle Helladic Grave Circle (E), which is in all probability what was shown to Pausanias as the site of the tombs of Clytemnestra and Aegisthus, who were buried according to tradition outside the acropolis because they were not thought worthy of burial within. The lower slopes of this same ridge, which runs westwards from the Lion Gate, were occupied by large houses built on terraces. On the south side (at L) are the House of the Oil Merchant and two adjoining houses, the House of Shields and the House of Sphinxes, close to the entrance to the Tomb of Clytemnestra; on the north slope lie the ruins of several houses, that which Mr. Petsas found in 1950 with storerooms full of unused pottery (B) and the Cyclopean Terrace complex with the House of the Wine Merchant (A). The road that led up to the Lion Gate may have passed the House of the Sphinxes, the House of the Oil Merchant and the House of Shields, and the entrances to the *tholos* tombs named after Clytemnestra and Aegisthus (G, K), and then proceeded by zig-zags, supported by still visible Mycenaean terrace walls, up to the court before the Lion Gate (M).

The acropolis itself (see plan, Fig. 28) is surrounded by a massive Cyclopean wall built of gigantic unhewn blocks of limestone. The Lion Gate (A), however, with the bastion thrown out on its west and the short stretch of wall on the same line to the east of it (Pl. 19, *a*), is built in ashlar with large blocks of conglomerate. The same construction can be observed at the postern gate (R) in the middle of the north wall and

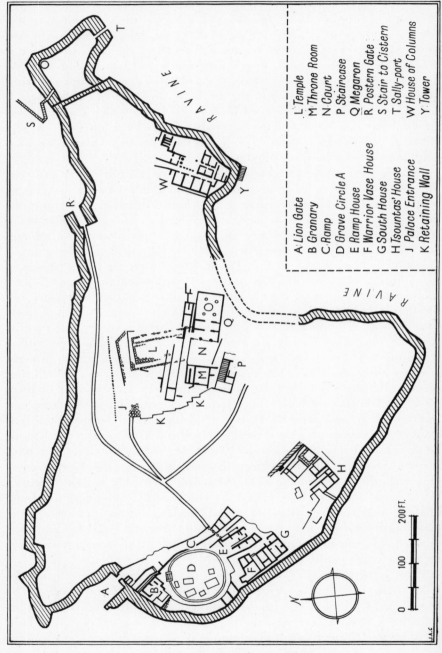

A Lion Gate
B Granary
C Ramp
D Grave Circle A
E Ramp House
F Warrior Vase House
G South House
H Tsountas' House
J Palace Entrance
K Retaining Wall
L Temple
M Throne Room
N Court
P Staircase
Q Megaron
R Postern Gate
S Stair to Cistern
T Sally-port
W House of Columns
Y Tower

Fig. 28. Mycenae : the citadel

in a massive tower (Y) on the south-eastern side overlooking the precipitous ravine which guards the citadel on the south.   Patches of Hellenistic
repairs can be seen in the bastion, in the western wall (the so-called Polygonal Tower), and at the north-east corner.   The whole of the north-
east part is an addition (though still of Mycenaean date) to the original
fortress, and the joints between the older and the later work can be seen
clearly on both the northern and southern sides.   One object of this
north-eastern extension was to afford easy access to the secret subter-
ranean cistern which lies just outside its northern wall.   At its south-
eastern corner a small sally port (T) was provided to help repel attacks
from the east.

Within the citadel just beyond the entrance from the Lion Gate lies
the famous Grave Circle (D) found by Schliemann, which, with its
double wall of standing slabs and stately entrance (Pl. 19, b and Fig. 29),
protected the tombs of the kings who ruled Mycenae in Late Helladic I.
Above this towers the Ramp (C), the base of the roadway which led up to
the palace on the summit.   By the side of the Grave Circle lie the Granary
(B) and the ruins of several large private houses, the Ramp House (E), the
South House (G), and the Warrior Vase House (F).   A little farther away
is 'Tsountas's House' (H), which the latest researches have shown to be a
shrine with a priest's house attached.   By its side a stepped street mounts
to the upper part of the citadel.   On the western slope of the acropolis
lie the ruins of houses both of the Bronze Age and of the Hellenistic
period.   Against the northern wall of the citadel in the latest period of
Mycenae was built a large chamber with a roof in the form of an inverted
V which has a superficial likeness to the galleries at Tiryns.   It is not,
however, built in the thickness of the Cyclopean Wall, but against its
inner face.   On the eastern side of the acropolis lie the ruins of more
houses of the Bronze Age and of Hellenistic date.   Among them are the
ruins of a large private house of Late Helladic III, the House of Columns
(W), which has a large *megaron*, a colonnaded court, and an extensive
basement (*cf.* Fig. 50, p. 492).

On the summit of the citadel (see plan, Fig. 28) lie the ruins of the
palace, which seems to have occupied almost all of the area of the original
Middle Bronze Age stronghold.   The entrance was at the north-west
corner (J) and a passage ran along the west side on top of a retaining
wall (K, K).   From this two parallel corridors ran upwards to the higher
part of the palace on the summit, which has been much denuded and is
overlaid by the construction of the later Greek temple (L).   The foundations of the temple are themselves now much dilapidated, but show that
it was built first in Archaic times and supported on the north by a high
terrace wall standing on the edge of a steep rock.   Its south end, where
there seems to have been an altar of the Archaic period adorned with

MYCENAE
SKETCH RESTORATION
OF GRAVE CIRCLE
JUST AFTER COMPLETION

FIG. 29. Grave Circle A at Mycenae; reconstruction drawing by Piet de Jong

sculpture in relief, projected over the ruins of the court of the palace. This court (N) formed the centre of the state apartments, which were approached from the south by a grand staircase (P; Pl. 20, *a*) leading up from a special entrance. On the west of the court lay the throne room (M) and on its east the *megaron* (Q) with its porch and vestibule. In the centre of the *megaron* four columns surrounded a raised hearth of painted plaster (Pl. 20, *b*). From the north side of the *megaron* a short stairway led up through a lobby to the domestic quarter of the palace, which included a bathroom in the form of a stepped tank. The palace was laid out on a series of terraces over the whole summit and had more than one storey, for there is clear evidence of an upper floor above the throne room. The walls of the palace were decorated with bright frescoes (*cf.* below, Fig. 51, and Pl. 30) and the court, *megaron*, and throne room had floors of painted stucco. Like all the other Mycenaean buildings within the walls it had been destroyed by a violent fire and seems to have been first thoroughly plundered. This disaster apparently took place at the close of the Bronze Age (Late Helladic IIIc, towards the close of the twelfth century B.C.).

THE HEROIC TRADITION

Although Mycenae's greatness was gone, her heroic traditions survived and were still vivid in the days of Pausanias, and all the monuments he saw can now be identified. He saw the treasuries of Atreus and his sons, as the *tholos* tombs were called, the Cyclopean Walls and the Lion Gate, the Perseia Fountain House, the graves of Agamemnon and his companions within the walls (in Schliemann's Grave Circle), and the graves of Clytemnestra and Aegisthus without the walls (in the Middle Helladic Grave Circle found in 1951–2). The 'tomb of Atreus' shown to him was probably the mound of earth raised over the dome of the *tholos* tomb called by archaeologists 'The Tomb of Clytemnestra'. Although we now know that the royal graves in the Grave Circle found by Schliemann were not the graves of Agamemnon and his companions, but some three centuries older, yet we must recognize the strong traditions which persisted at Mycenae. The grave *stele* found by Schliemann with a chariot scene (*cf.* below, Pl. 33) perhaps marked what tradition described as the grave of Agamemnon's charioteer Eurymedon. In other graves, Pausanias was told, lay Cassandra and her twin infant sons. In the Third Shaft Grave Schliemann discovered the remains of three women, and two infants wrapped in gold. Is this mere coincidence? If not, then the traditions from earlier times must indeed have been strong. It is only natural that the names of long dead and forgotten royalty should have been abandoned in favour of those well known in

legends. It is the same with the Grave Circle without the walls, presumably the spot traditionally said to be the burial place of Clytemnestra
and Aegisthus. The graves themselves belong to the Middle Bronze
Age and so are some four centuries older than Clytemnestra. The
princes laid in them were presumably the predecessors of those buried in
Schliemann's Grave Circle, but not so wealthy or powerful.

NOTE TO CHAPTER 13 (ii)

[For a fuller account of the site, its history and excavation, see A. J. B. Wace, *Mycenae:
an Archaeological History and Guide* (Princeton, 1949), which contains a good list of the
earlier literature.

For excavations since 1939 see *BSA*, xlv, xlvii-lii; *PAE*, 1950, 194 ff.; 1951, 192 ff.;
1952, 427 ff.; and G. E. Mylonas, *Ancient Mycenae* (1957).]

(iii) ITHACA

by Frank H. Stubbings

Not only the situation of Ithaca has been called in doubt by various authors, but even
the virtue of the chaste Penelope. — E. DODWELL, *A Classical and Topographical Tour through
Greece*, 1819.

ITHACA. This island retains its ancient name. — *Admiralty Mediterranean Pilot*, 1929.

THE ITHACA QUESTION

The question of the identification of the Ithaca of the *Odyssey* has
produced one of the most notorious learned controversies of this century.
This is not because of the absence of a definite tradition, but because of
doubts cast on the truth of the tradition in modern times. The island now
called Ithaki [a] is amply proved by finds of coins and inscriptions to have
borne the same name Ἰθάκη from classical to Roman times. Nor did the
ancients have any doubt that this was the home of Odysseus: he was
frequently portrayed, as the local hero, on coins of the island, and an
inscription of the third century B.C. refers both to a shrine of Odysseus
and to games called Odysseia.[1] Strabo clearly accepts the tradition,
though he does admit that there are difficulties in understanding Homer's
references to the lands constituting the realm of Odysseus:

οὐ γὰρ εὐκρινῶς ἀποδίδωσιν ὁ ποιητής, οὔτε περὶ τῆς Κεφαλληνίας, οὔτε
περὶ τῆς Ἰθάκης καὶ τῶν ἄλλων πλησίον τόπων, ὥστε καὶ οἱ ἐξηγούμενοι
διαφέρονται καὶ οἱ ἱστοροῦντες (Strabo x. 2. 10).

[a] Ἰθάκη, sometimes corrupted locally to Θιάκη. The transliteration *Ithaki* is used here
to avoid ambiguities.

Most travellers and investigators down to the time of Schliemann accepted Ithaki as the Homeric Ithaca. Schliemann's investigation of the island in 1868, in the first enthusiasm of his archaeological career, was unfortunately incomplete; but he had no hesitation in 'identifying' practically all the features of Ithaca mentioned in the *Odyssey*.[2] He visited the island again ten years later, and planned to conduct further excavations there with W. Dörpfeld after he had completed his work at Troy. This was prevented by Schliemann's death in 1890.

When Dörpfeld visited the island in 1897 he found himself unable to accept all of Schliemann's conclusions, and in particular believed that the town and palace of Odysseus should be sought in the north, and not in the centre, on Mt. Aetos. It was with this definite object of unearthing the home of Odysseus that Dörpfeld began his excavations in Ithaki in the spring of 1900, but after less than two months' work he abandoned the search. Meanwhile, from study of the Homeric evidence, he had formed the opinion that Ithaca must be identified with the modern Lefkas, the classical Leucas. This theory had very far-reaching implications, and produced storms of protest. Dörpfeld, however, stuck to his guns, and thenceforward devoted his energies to the elaboration of his theory, and to excavation in Lefkas. His final account of his investigations and of the whole controversy was published in 1927 in *Alt-Ithaka*. Dörpfeld's opponents endeavoured to refute him chiefly on the ground of the correspondence of the Homeric description of Ithaca with modern Ithaki, and paid too little attention to the acquisition of further archaeological evidence to support their case. This defect has, however, since been to a considerable extent remedied, and we are now in a position to consider the problem more fairly on both types of evidence.

ITHACA IN HOMER

At once the most important and the most obscure passage of Homer referring to Ithaca is ι 21-7, where Odysseus is describing his island home to Alcinous. The difficulties of the passage were already felt in antiquity, for Strabo comments on them at some length and refers to the views of earlier commentators. His explanation must be considered first, since no modern theory is entirely independent of it. The passage runs:

21 ναιετάω δ' Ἰθάκην εὐδείελον· ἐν δ' ὄρος αὐτῇ
22 Νήριτον εἰνοσίφυλλον, ἀριπρεπές· ἀμφὶ δὲ νῆσοι
23 πολλαὶ ναιετάουσι μάλα σχεδὸν ἀλλήλῃσι,
24 Δουλίχιόν τε Σάμη τε καὶ ὑλήεσσα Ζάκυνθος—
25 αὐτὴ δὲ χθαμαλὴ πανυπερτάτη εἰν ἁλὶ κεῖται

26 πρὸς ζόφον, αἱ δέ τ' ἄνευθε πρὸς ἠῶ τ' ἠέλιόν τε—
27 τρηχεῖ', ἀλλ' ἀγαθὴ κουροτρόφος.

Homer here implies that Ithaca is one of a group of four islands, the other three being Dulichion, Same, and Zacynthus. On the map (Fig. 30) we find a group of three considerable islands, Zacynthus, Ithaki, and Cephallenia, with a possible fourth in Leucas, which is only separated from the mainland by very shallow lagoons with an artificial channel for the passage of ships. Strabo did not reckon Leucas among the four Homeric islands. This is what he says of it:

This [Leucas] was in old times a peninsula of Acarnania, and the poet calls it 'a peninsula of the mainland' — meaning by 'mainland' the land opposite Ithaca and Cephallenia. . . . In Leucas was Neritos, which Laertes says he captured (451 f.).

The last sentence refers to ω 377-8:

οἷος Νήρικον εἷλον, ἐυκτίμενον πτολίεθρον,
ἀκτὴν ἠπείροιο, Κεφαλλήνεσσιν ἀνάσσων.

Leucas, in short, was not an island in Homer's time, and is referred to by Homer as something else. Strabo (*ibid.*) further states that Leucas became an island when the Corinthians cut the canal through the isthmus, that is about 650 B.C., when the city of Leucas was founded.

Of the three undoubted islands Strabo naturally identified Ithaca and Zacynthus with the islands still so called. Same he identified with Cephallenia, on the east coast of which there was and remains to-day a town called Same or Samos. For lack of a fourth island it has sometimes been supposed that Dulichion was the western peninsula of Cephallenia, called in later times Pale. Strabo (456) mentions this view; moreover, Pausanias (vi. 15. 7) mentions that he saw a statue at Olympia dedicated by the people of Pale, 'formerly the Δουλίχιοι', and Hesychius has an entry 'Dulichion: a city of Cephallenia'. Strabo, however, rejected this identification because in the *Catalogue of Ships* Dulichion is referred to with the Echinades as being under the rule of Meges, while the Κεφαλλῆνες are led by Odysseus (B 625, 631-4). The objection seems sound; for it is unlikely from their relative position that Pale and the Echinades would form a political unity. Strabo consequently identifies Dulichion with one of the Echinades, called in his time Δολιχά, 'situate opposite Oeniadae and the mouth of the Achelous'.

Line 25 of the passage under consideration appears at first sight to call Ithaca both χθαμαλή, 'low', and πανυπερτάτη, 'highest of all'. Strabo comments on the apparent contradiction that 'they explain it rather well'. 'They' — presumably the ancient commentators on Homer — understand χθαμαλή to mean πρόσχωρον τῷ ἠπείρῳ, 'close to the mainland', and take πανυπερτάτη with πρὸς ζόφον, that is, 'farthest of all towards the

FIG. 30. The Ionian Islands

north', making πρὸς ἠῶ τ' ἠέλιόν τε mean 'towards the south'. To justify this explanation of ζόφος and ἠώς Strabo quotes κ 190 ff. :

ὦ φίλοι, οὐ γάρ τ' ἴδμεν ὅπῃ ζόφος οὐδ' ὅπῃ ἠὼς
οὐδ' ὅπῃ ἠέλιος φαεσίμβροτος εἶσ' ὑπὸ γαῖαν
οὐδ' ὅπῃ ἀννεῖται,

saying that here all four points of the compass are indicated, in the order N, S, W, E.

Thus what Odysseus says, according to Strabo, is this:

I dwell in Ithaca the far-seen island. In it is a mountain called Neriton, thickly wooded and outstanding; and round about lie many islands, very close one to another, Dulichion and Same and wooded Zacynthus. Ithaca itself is close to the mainland and lies in the sea farthest towards the north; the rest lie at a distance, towards the south.

This is a consistent explanation of the passage, but there are certain objections to it. First, it gives a quite unparalleled meaning to χθαμαλή, and in fact Strabo's own expression ἐξηγοῦνται δὲ οὐ κακῶς suggests that it is more ingenious than convincing. Secondly, the explanation of ζόφος and ἠώς is unsatisfactory. The words mean literally 'gloom' and 'dawn' and in Homer normally indicate west and east. The passage Strabo adduces in support of his explanation more probably refers to only two points of the compass, west and east. Thirdly, the identification of Dulichion among the Echinades has been questioned. Let us examine these points in order.

1. The phrase αὐτὴ δὲ χθαμαλὴ κεῖται occurs again in κ 196, describing Circe's island as seen from high above; but it seems impossible that the phrase can mean the same in both places. The word χθαμαλή may, however, mean 'low' in both passages. Ithaki is not in fact a low-lying island, but mountainous, with steep-to coasts; and the adjectives applied to Homer's Ithaca — κραναή, τρηχεῖα, παιπαλόεσσα [3] — imply the same. It has, however, been pointed out by Victor Bérard [4] that, as seen by some-one approaching from the south or south-east, Ithaki does seem low by contrast with the very high mountains of Cephallenia behind it. It is from this aspect that Ithaki would be familiar to most of the ancient Greek world, and Bérard urges that the whole of the passage now under discussion is written from this standpoint.

2. If we accept this view it also makes possible a less strained inter-pretation of πρὸς ζόφον. It is quite reasonable in describing the position of Ithaki relative to the rest of Greece to say that it is 'farthest away to-wards the gloaming' (i.e., the west or north-west). It might be argued that Cephallenia is just as far away, and farther; but as it extends a good deal farther south than Ithaki it is reached from Greece sooner. It is then possible to interpret πρὸς ἠῶ τ' ἠέλιόν τε, which means literally 'towards the dawn and the sun', as 'towards the east and south'. The words then describe the position, relative to Ithaca, of Dulichion to the east as well as of Zacynthus and Same (Cephallenia) to the south.

3. In the enumeration of the suitors (π 247-51) Dulichion is men-tioned together with Same and Zacynthus; and in another passage refer-

PLATE 19

(*a*) Mycenae : the Lion Gate

(*b*) Mycenae : Grave Circle A, from the south

PLATE 20

(a) Mycenae : staircase in the palace

(b) Mycenae : the *megaron*

PLATE 21

(*a*) Ithaca : Polis Bay and the Ithaca Channel, looking south

(*b*) Ithaca : Gulf of Molo

PLATE 22

(*a*) Pylos : *propylon*, court, and *megaron* of the palace, from the S.E.

(*b*) Pylos : the *megaron* from the N.W., with oil-magazine in the foreground

ring to the suitors (α 245-8) the four islands are again grouped together, three of them in the stock line

Δουλιχίῳ τε Σάμῃ τε καὶ ὑλήεντι Ζακύνθῳ.

Dulichion thus appears to be one of a group of four islands, but it is not at once clear whether a political or a geographical group is intended. Bérard and others have assumed that all four were ruled by Odysseus; but this is contradicted by the *Catalogue of Ships* (B 625-30), which says that the men from Dulichion and the Echinades were led by Meges, who commanded a contingent of forty ships in all. Odysseus himself led only twelve ships to Troy (B 631-7), so that it is not necessary to suppose that he ruled so large a kingdom. Nor need it be thought that such an account of his forces is incompatible with the fame of Odysseus as portrayed in the *Odyssey*. Ajax is another hero of great personal distinction who yet commanded only a small force of twelve ships (B 557). The *Odyssey* states further that Dulichion produced fifty-two of the suitors of Penelope, against twenty-four from Same, twenty from Zacynthus, and twelve from Ithaca itself (π 247-51). This suggests that it was an island of considerable size and population. Finally, it is described as πολύπυρος and ποιήεις — 'producing much corn' and 'grassy' (π 396).

From such evidence it is difficult, if not impossible, to identify Dulichion. The phrase Δουλιχίοιο 'Εχινάων θ' ἱεράων (B 625) does not make it impossible that Dulichion was one of the Echinades; but none of these islands seems large enough or could well be called πολύπυρος or ποιήεις. An ingenious solution is that the Dulichion of Homer has, like some of the smaller Echinades, become attached to the mainland through the silting up of narrow and shallow waters at the mouth of the Achelous. The present conformation of the mainland does not, however, suggest that any *large* island has become attached to it within measurable time.

Bérard proposes as an alternative the island Meganisi, a little to the south-east of Leucas. It is larger and more agricultural than any of the Echinades, but his arguments are unconvincing.

Several other scholars, notably T. W. Allen,[5] have suggested that Dulichion was Leucas (modern Lefkas, Santa Maura). Leucas fits the description of Dulichion, and may well have been the chief component of a maritime confederacy (the realm of Meges) which also included Meganisi and the Echinades and perhaps parts of the mainland. Such a state, as Allen says, might raise forty ships and produce fifty-two princes to woo Penelope. This, if we must revise Strabo's account, is perhaps the most satisfactory way of doing it. But there are still snags ahead.

THE LEUCAS THEORY

If Leucas is included among the four islands then Ithaki cannot be called πανυπερτάτη πρὸς ζόφον, but Leucas can. Therefore Leucas must be the Homeric Ithaca. This is the basis of Dörpfeld's theory. For the other islands, he identifies Same with Ithaki and Dulichion with Cephallenia.

To prove his theory Dörpfeld seeks first to show that Leucas was in Homeric times an island. Not only Strabo but Livy and Pliny too state that in earlier times it was a peninsula. Dörpfeld holds, however, that Leucas has a naturally insular character. Bérard just as firmly declares that Leucas has all the characteristics of a peninsula. Gustav Lang has adduced the evidence of an ancient harbour-mole at the north end of Drepano Bay (perhaps constructed by the Corinthian colonists) which is now two to three metres under water, to show that the sea-level has, in fact, risen since ancient times. Dörpfeld accepts this fact, but does not consider it affects the insular nature of Leucas. All such argument, in short, fails to produce anything more conclusive than the common-sense view of Leake that Leucas was never 'more of a peninsula nor less of an island than it is at present'.[6] Our acceptance or refusal of Dörpfeld's theory must depend rather on the extent to which Leucas fits the Homeric description of Ithaca and the extent to which such correspondence can be supported by the archaeological evidence.

We might accept that Leucas lies πανυπερτάτη πρὸς ζόφον, even without believing Dörpfeld's ingenious theory that ζόφος has its normal connotation of 'west' and that the ancients supposed this western coast and the adjacent islands to lie in a line west-east and not north-south.[7] It cannot, on the other hand, be said that the other islands lie 'around' or 'on either side of' Leucas, as implied in ἀμφὶ δὲ νῆσοι πολλαί. The vexed word χθαμαλή Dörpfeld interprets 'close to the mainland', following Strabo, and thinks it a strong point in favour of his theory, that Leucas is in fact close to the mainland. No parallels, however, can be found for such a meaning. In connection with this barely insular situation of Leucas, Dörpfeld says that the line

$$\text{οὐ μὲν γάρ τί σε πεζὸν ὄ́ιομαι ἐνθάδ' ἱκέσθαι}$$
$$\text{(α 173; ξ 190; π 59, 224)}$$

addressed to strangers arriving in Ithaca would be nonsense unless Ithaca *could* be approached on foot. He will not allow it to be conscious humour, as in

$$\text{οὐ γὰρ ἀπὸ δρυός ἐσσι παλαιφάτου οὐδ' ἀπὸ πέτρης. (τ 163)}$$

A further check on the relative position of Ithaca may be found in the Homeric references to the island of Asteris. In δ 669 ff. Antinous asks the assembled suitors to give him a ship so that he may waylay Telemachus on his return from Pylos.

ἐν πορθμῷ 'Ἰθάκης τε Σάμοιό τε παιπαλοέσσης

— 'in the strait of Ithaca and craggy Samos'. This is agreed to, and later (842 ff.) the poet describes more exactly where the suitors laid their ambush. From these passages we see that Asteris is a small rocky island lying 'in the midst of the sea' in the strait (πορθμός) between Ithaca and Same. Further, it contains λιμένες ἀμφίδυμοι, which most commentators translate as 'twin harbours'. If we accept Ithaki as the ancient Ithaca and Cephallenia as Same, the πορθμὸς 'Ἰθάκης τε Σάμοιό τε obviously must be the Ithaca channel, towards the northern end of which there is actually a rocky islet, now called Δασκαλειό, from which any vessel coming up the broad sheet of water to the south (see Pl. 21, *a*) would be clearly visible. This island is usually accepted as the Homeric Asteris. It is, however, too small to afford cover for a ship of any size, and has no harbours. Moreover, Antinous describes, after the ambush has failed, how the suitors had kept a continual watch 'on the windy heights' (π 365), which again suggests a larger island. Bérard points out that on the coast of Cephallenia a little north of Daskalio there is the excellent natural harbour of Phiskardo, which may even be called ἀμφίδυμος, since it is divided into two bays. He proposes, therefore, temptingly, that we should read ἐπὶ for ἐνὶ — '*by* it there are twin harbours'. The 'windy heights' also he would locate on this coast instead of on the island. But the discrepancies are best attributed to the fact that Homer was writing an epic, not a guidebook.

To identify Ithaca with Leucas makes it difficult to find a suitable Asteris. It seems doubtful whether the sea between Leucas and Ithaki (Dörpfeld's Ithaca and Same), which is almost as broad as it is long, could be called πορθμός, which usually means a *strait*; and the island Arkudi, which Dörpfeld claims is the Homeric Asteris, is only in a vague sense 'between' Leucas and Ithaki (μεσσηγὺς 'Ἰθάκης τε Σάμοιό τε).[a] Arkudi is stated to be provided with λιμένες ἀμφίδυμοι on either side of the little peninsula of Podi, in the south-east of the island; but these beaches, while better than anything on the bare rock of Daskalio, could shelter only the smallest of boats.[8]

We must now consider the Homeric evidence as to the general physical character of Ithaca. When Odysseus is describing the island to Alcinous (ι 21 ff.) the only single feature of the island he mentions is Neriton — a conspicuous wooded mountain; and he adds that the island is τρηχεῖα, ἀλλ' ἀγαθὴ κουροτρόφος — 'rugged, but a good nursery for heroes'. Such a description would suit either Leucas or Ithaki. This brief impression, however, is supplemented later in the *Odyssey*. Athene, in disguise, is replying to Odysseus's inquiries, on awaking in Ithaca,

[a] See map, Fig. 30.

as to what land it is :

> ἦ τοι μὲν τρηχεῖα καὶ οὐχ ἱππήλατός ἐστιν,
> οὐδὲ λίην λυπρή, ἀτὰρ οὐδ᾽ εὐρεῖα τέτυκται.
> ἐν μὲν γάρ οἱ σῖτος ἀθέσφατος, ἐν δέ τε οἶνος
> γίγνεται. αἰεὶ δ᾽ ὄμβρος ἔχει τεθαλυῖά τ᾽ ἐέρση.
> αἰγίβοτος δ᾽ ἀγαθὴ καὶ βούβοτος· ἔστι μὲν ὕλη
> παντοίη, ἐν δ᾽ ἀρδμοὶ ἐπηετανοὶ παρέασιν.   (ν 242 ff.)

Most of this would apply equally well to either Leucas or Ithaki at the present day, but to neither exactly. In particular there is not much timber in either, though that may be due to centuries of deforestation. The points which in Dörpfeld's view favour Leucas are that it is better watered and produces more corn than Ithaki. But it is well to observe that the general tone of this passage is : 'Ithaca is a narrow and rugged island, *but . . .*'. Consequently the tale of Ithaca's resources may well be somewhat idealized. The salient point about Ithaca whenever it is mentioned in the *Odyssey* is its mountains and its rocks. Most striking is the speech of Telemachus to Menelaus at Sparta, asking not to be given horses as a parting present : he says that not only are there no proper roads in Ithaca to use horses on, but there is no pasture for them to live on; which is true of all the islands, *but of Ithaca more than any* (δ 605 ff.) This seems to weigh heavily against Leucas, which has much more flat land than Ithaki.

There is one more serious objection to the Leucas theory, that the supposed transfer of the name Ἰθάκη to the island now bearing it cannot be satisfactorily accounted for. Dörpfeld holds that the change took place in the period of migrations after the Trojan War associated by tradition with the coming of the Dorians. He assumes that the inhabitants of Ithaca (modern Leucas), being pushed out by the invading Dorians, removed to Same (modern Ithaki) and gave to it the name of their old home. In this move they would probably have expelled from Same some of the previous inhabitants, who crossed the Ithaca channel to found a new Same on the coast of Dulichion (now Cephallenia).[9] This theory seems possible only if the *Odyssey* is, as Dörpfeld thinks, to be dated to the twelfth century B.C., before the Dorian invasion and the consequent transference of names. Even so, it would be surprising that when so many traditions of this period of migrations survived in classical times there should be no mention of the change or transference of the name of an island so famed as Ithaca. Dörpfeld claims that there is such literary evidence in the *Catalogue of Ships*, which he holds to be of later date and to represent post-Homeric political geography. The realm of Odysseus is described as follows :

> αὐτὰρ Ὀδυσσεὺς ἦγε Κεφαλλῆνας μεγαθύμους,
> οἵ ῥ᾽ Ἰθάκην εἶχον καὶ Νήριτον εἰνοσίφυλλον,

καὶ Κροκύλει' ἐνέμοντο καὶ Αἰγίλιπα τρηχεῖαν,
οἵ τε Ζάκυνθον ἔχον, ἠδ' οἱ Σάμον ἀμφενέμοντο,
οἵ τ' ἤπειρον ἔχον ἠδ' ἀντιπέραι' ἐνέμοντο.   (B 631-5)

Here only three of the four islands, Ithaca, Same, and Zacynthus, are mentioned; and Dulichion is placed elsewhere in the *Catalogue* as part of the kingdom of Meges. Dörpfeld, however, says that all four are mentioned. He pretends that Ἰθάκη here means the post-Homeric Ithaca, modern Ithaki; and that the Homeric Ithaca is denoted by the name Νήριτον, formerly the name only of the chief mountain, now applied to the whole island. This seemed to Dörpfeld the more natural, to others a perverse interpretation of the words

Ἰθάκην . . . καὶ Νήριτον εἰνοσίφυλλον.

They more probably refer only to the one island, Ithaca, and are so explained by Strabo (452 *ad fin.*).

THE TOPOGRAPHY OF LEUCAS

(See map, Fig. 31)

Numerous attempts have been made to identify, either in Ithaki or in Leucas, the actual scenes and places described in the *Odyssey*. The inquiry may even be of practical assistance to the archaeologist, but if we are to draw any conclusions from such topographical fancies we must subordinate them to the factual evidence of excavation.

We can best weigh Dörpfeld's identification of sites in Leucas by recalling the events of the story. The Phaeacians put Odysseus ashore in Ithaca at the 'harbour of Phorcys', which is carefully described:

Φόρκυνος δέ τις ἔστι λιμὴν ἁλίοιο γέροντος
ἐν δήμῳ Ἰθάκης, δύο δὲ προβλῆτες ἐν αὐτῷ
ἀκταὶ ἀπορρῶγες, λιμένος ποτιπεπτηυῖαι,
αἵ τ' ἀνέμων σκεπόωσι δυσαήων μέγα κῦμα
ἔκτοθεν· ἔντοσθεν δέ τ' ἄνευ δεσμοῖο μένουσι
νῆες ἐΰσσελμοι, ὅτ' ἂν ὅρμου μέτρον ἴκωνται.   (ν 96 ff.)

This harbour Dörpfeld finds in the bay of Syvota, in the south-east of Leucas. It is a long narrow inlet, sheltered, like the harbour of the poem, by steep headlands either side of the entrance. The harbour of Phorcys is further distinguished by a cave, situated ἐπὶ κρατὸς λιμένος, and sacred to the Nymphs:

ἄντρον ἐπήρατον, ἠεροειδές,
ἵρον Νυμφάων, αἳ νηιάδες καλέονται.
ἐν δὲ κρητῆρές τε καὶ ἀμφιφορῆες ἔασιν
λάϊνοι· ἔνθα δ' ἔπειτα τιθαιβώσσουσι μέλισσαι.

ἐν δ' ἱστοὶ λίθεοι περιμήκεες, ἔνθα τε νύμφαι
φάρε' ὑφαίνουσιν ἁλιπόρφυρα, θαῦμα ἰδέσθαι.
ἐν δ' ὕδατ' αἰενάοντα. δύω δέ τέ οἱ θύραι εἰσίν,
αἱ μὲν πρὸς Βορέαο καταιβαταὶ ἀνθρώποισιν
αἱ δ' αὖ πρὸς Νότου εἰσὶ θεώτεραι, οὐδέ τι κείνη
ἄνδρες ἐσέρχονται, ἀλλ' ἀθανάτων ὁδός ἐστιν.　　　(ν 102 ff.)

The stone bowls and jars of this description, and the looms on which the
Nymphs weave, must be, in plain prose, stalactite formations. But
Greece, a limestone country, is riddled with stalactite caves, many of
them sacred in ancient times to the Nymphs or other divinities. Dörpfeld
found no less than five around Syvota Bay; and since the exact meaning
of ἐπὶ κρατὸς λιμένος is disputed, it is hard to choose among them by
position. None has the two entrances of Homer's cave, nor is there the
requisite running water. There is, however, a spring close to the sea
at the head of the bay, and Dörpfeld conjectures that the Cave of the
Nymphs may have been here, but that its entrance has been blocked and
hidden by the rise of the sea-level since ancient times.

To return to the story: Odysseus hides in the cave the treasures which
he has brought as gifts from the Phaeacians, and then sets out to find the
swineherd Eumaeus. He takes a rocky path over hills and through
woods —

$$προσέβη\ τρηχεῖαν\ ἀταρπόν,$$
$$χῶρον\ ἀν'\ ὑλήεντα\ δι'\ ἄκριας\ —\ \ \ \ \ \ \ \ (ξ\ 1\text{-}2)$$

and finds Eumaeus, as Athene said he would,

$$πὰρ\ Κόρακος\ πέτρῃ\ ἐπί\ τε\ κρήνῃ\ Ἀρεθούσῃ\ —\ \ \ \ \ (ν\ 408)$$

'by the rock Korax, above the spring Arethusa'. The site of Eumaeus's
pig farm is also stated to be περισκέπτῳ ἐνὶ χώρῳ (ξ 6), which is sometimes taken to mean 'in an *open* place'. Dörpfeld, probably more correctly, understands 'in a *sheltered* place', deriving περίσκεπτος from
σκέπω, and points to two sheltered valleys close above Syvota, to the
west. He attempts no exact location of the abode of Eumaeus, but
identifies Korax and Arethusa with a cliff and spring near the village of
Evgiros. He calls attention to the various place names in the district
which recall that pig-keeping flourished there until not very distant
years, notably Syvota (Σύβωτα) itself, and Choirospilia (Χοιροσπήλια),
a large cave near Evgiros, which was shown by excavations to have
been used as a habitation from Neolithic times right through the Bronze
Age.[10]

While Odysseus is with Eumaeus, Telemachus arrives in Ithaca from
Pylos. Athene had given him sailing directions, so that he should avoid
the suitors lying in wait at Asteris: he was to sail by night, keeping his
ship 'well out from the islands', and as soon as he struck land in Ithaca to

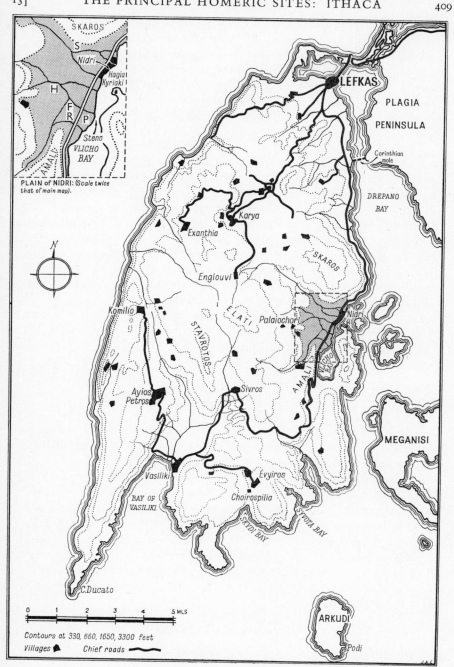

FIG. 31. Map of Lefkas

go ashore, sending his ship on to the town, and then make his way up to
Eumaeus, whom he was to send to Penelope to announce his safe return
(ο 28-42). As he arrives from the south, his landing-place must be in
the south of the island, and within easy reach of Eumaeus. Dörpfeld
accordingly places his landing at Skydi bay, west of Syvota; the ship
then sails on round the coast to the harbour of Vlicho. By this course it
would in fact avoid passing close to Arkudi, the Asteris of the Leucas
theory.

The town and palace of Odysseus are placed by Dörpfeld in the low
plain of Nidri on the west side of Vlicho bay. The only objection to this
is that it seems to leave too short a distance between the town and
Eumaeus. Telemachus arrives early in the morning, and Eumaeus, sent
off at once to the town, does not return till evening, having spent all day
on the double journey, only stopping long enough to deliver his message
to Penelope (π 150, 452 ff.) The journey from the region of Choirospilia to Nidri and back would, however, only take some six hours.
(Dörpfeld argues that it was a winter day, so that Eumaeus could not
have more than six or seven hours for the journey; but in Mediterranean
latitudes winter days are not so short as that!)

Outside the town there was, in the description of the *Odyssey*, a
'built fountain' (κρήνη τυκτή) surrounded by poplar trees, where 'the
chill water flowed down from on high out of the rock' —

> ἀμφὶ δ’ ἄρ’ αἰγείρων ὑδατοτρεφέων ἦν ἄλσος
> πάντοσε κυκλοτερές, κατὰ δὲ ψυχρὸν ῥέεν ὕδωρ
> ὑψόθεν ἐκ πέτρης· βωμὸς δ’ ἐφύπερθε τέτυκτο
> νυμφάων.
>   (ρ 205 ff.)

Dörpfeld considers that ὑψόθεν ἐκ πέτρης implies that the water was
brought down the hill by an aqueduct; and he did actually discover a
pipeline leading from a spring at Palaiochori in the hills west of Nidri
down towards the plain. The lower stretches of this pipeline have
disappeared, so that it is not known where the ultimate fountain was.
The pipes are of two periods, the earlier ones being of a very simple
tapered shape, fitting one into the other with no collar at the joint.
Dörpfeld supposes these to date from the Bronze Age, and points for
parallels to water systems at Mycenae and Knossos.[11] There is, however,
no close similarity, and dating of this aqueduct remains conjectural.

EXCAVATIONS IN LEUCAS

When Dörpfeld began excavating in Leucas in 1901 he had already
decided on most of these identifications, and his attention was therefore

chiefly directed to looking for the town and palace of Odysseus in the Nidri plain (see map, Fig. 31, inset). Trial trenches dug in 1901–3 showed that the plain was extensively inhabited in the Bronze Age, and in subsequent campaigns between 1905 and 1910 numerous graves of the same period were discovered. The most important are the rectangular grave-complex F towards the south-east, the Grave Circle S at the foot of Skaros in the north, and the thirty-three grave circles (the 'Royal Graves', R) near Steno, in the extreme south-east of the plain. Near the last were found remains of a large building (Building P) which Dörpfeld supposed was the palace of Odysseus. Apart from this, and certain house walls on the slope of the hill Amali to the south, traces of Bronze Age buildings are scanty. At the site called Sotiros, in the west of the plain, a sanctuary of the classical period was discovered beneath the buried ruins of a Byzantine church, and at a lower level was a rich deposit of sherds indicating that the sanctuary had a predecessor in the Bronze Age. A similar continuity of tradition was found at the chapel of Hagia Kyriaki on the east side of the entrance to Vlicho bay; Bronze Age remains lay under a deposit of classical sherds and votive terracottas from a shrine of the Nymphs.

The Settlement Remains.—There have been frequent destructive changes in the course of the torrents that flow through the Nidri plain, so that apart from some five whole pots [12] the Bronze Age stratum contains only scattered sherds. The remains of walls also, both in the plain and on the slope of Amali, are too much damaged for us to recognize any clear type of house. Building P [13] could not be fully excavated; but one thick and well-built wall some forty metres long seems to imply a building of considerable size, if it is indeed the wall of a building, which cannot be proved.

The Bronze Age sherds are plentiful but all badly damaged by the action of water. Besides innumerable fragments of large vessels of coarse ware, there are finer wares, both plain and painted, which resemble in their shapes the Early Helladic pottery of the mainland. At Amali appears a Middle Helladic ware which is a local variety of Minyan. There are also a very few sherds of painted Mycenaean (Late Helladic III) from here and from Skaros. In general, however, Mycenaean pottery was lacking. In the absence of more substantial finds it is difficult to date at all accurately the settlements represented.

Grave Circle S [14] lies at the foot of Skaros, to the north of Nidri. It consists of a wall of rough stones, about 0·75 m. thick, enclosing a circle some twelve metres in diameter. Only three or four courses of the wall were preserved. Within the circle were thirteen graves, and a fourteenth in an 'annexe' built against the circle to the north-east. All but two were cist-graves. Since the graves lie at various levels, some actually higher than the wall, it appears that the whole space inside the circle around and above the graves was filled with earth, probably heaped up in the centre to form a low barrow or tumulus. The skeletons lay on a floor of sand or pebbles (never of stone slabs) in the contracted posture. Generally there was one skeleton in each grave, though some contained more. Probably the circle may be regarded as a family cemetery, used over some length of time. The grave furniture usually consisted of a pot or two, and sometimes a few tools or other objects of bronze or stone. The pottery is all unpainted, and mostly of a grey or blackish clay; some is hand-made, some wheel-made, and similar to Minyan. The finds as a whole belong to the Middle Helladic period.

Grave-mound F [15] lies on the south side of the plain, and to the north-west of Steno. In form it is a rectangle, 9·20 by 4·70 metres, enclosed by a wall half a metre high, built of flat limestone slabs set on edge, packed on the inside with earth and stones, and weighted on top with horizontal slabs. At the south-west corner an annexe of similar construction was added at a later date. This contained two graves, the main rectangle eight. All but one were cist-graves, and the manner of burial and the contents of the graves were similar to those of Grave Circle S.

One grave contained a copper spearhead of a peculiar form, almost exactly paralleled in a Middle Helladic grave at Sesklo. With it was a dagger-shaped bronze knife with silver rivets to fasten the blade to the handle. These were the only objects of metal except for two ear-rings, one of silver and one of bronze, in another grave. Coarse and fine pottery appear together, the fine ware having a grey or yellow surface like Minyan. The most notable shape is the Minyan *kantharos*. Such pottery is typical of an advanced stage of Middle Helladic. In mainland Greece it is found with matt-painted ware and the earliest products of Late Helladic, but these do not occur here. The graves must be dated somewhat later than those of Grave Circle S.

The Royal Grave Circles. [16] — West of Building P at Steno was a group of thirty-three grave circles similar to S. The whole group must cover a long period, but the graves show a uniform culture, and the relative order of construction of the circles can be inferred only from the way in which one is built against another. The two largest, which lie at the south-western edges of the group, are probably also the latest.

The circles vary in diameter from 2·70 to 9·60 metres, but most measure between 4·50 and 6·50 metres. The outer walls are constructed of flat white limestone slabs, laid in courses, sometimes on a pebble foundation, and are nowhere preserved to a height of more than 0·60 metres. The inner space is filled with one or two layers of large pebbles, among which the graves are placed. Probably a mound of earth was heaped over each circle. In practically every circle which was excavated there was found, generally under the pebble layer, an oval space about one metre by two, covered with a thick layer of charcoal. These appear to be the places where corpses were cremated before burial, since in two circles fragments of the same objects were found both in the burnt patch and in the graves. There is no white ash, but only charcoal, with sometimes quite large pieces of wood recognizable among it, which seems to confirm that the pyre was quenched (cf. Ψ 250) before the complete incineration of the corpse, as may be inferred from the completeness of the skeletons in many graves.

The graves are of four types: (a) *pithos*-burials, the remains being enclosed together with the grave-gifts in a large earthenware *pithos* about a metre high; (b) cist-graves, as in S and F; (c) 'walled graves', that is, rectangular pits lined with a walling of stone, like the Shaft Graves of Mycenae (this type is rare and occurs in the latest circles); (d) plain inhumation; this also is infrequent, but in one circle the chief grave is of this sort.

The contents of the graves are, on the whole, richer than those of S and F: for this reason, and because of the grandiose lay-out of the whole group and its nearness to the supposed palace, Dörpfeld dubbed them Royal Graves. The sum total of finds, however, is not so great as might be expected from the number of grave circles. Some of them had been partly destroyed by time and water, some robbed in antiquity, and some it was not possible to excavate completely.

The finds include five necklaces of gold beads, most of them of a type which occurs also in later, Mycenaean contexts, and also several gold earrings, and other ornaments. Most striking are the casings of two dagger handles. One of these was found in a *pithos*-burial, the other in the cremation-deposit of one of the circles. The former is decorated with simple geometrical patterns, including the running spiral so frequent in Middle and Late Helladic art. Five bracelets of silver were found in all: one is a simple circlet of wire with overlapping ends; the others have several spiral coils, with the ends knobbed.

The metal weapons and tools are not of bronze, as in Grave Circle S, but of almost pure copper. Five swords were found, and fragments of a sixth. All were in the cremation-deposits, not the graves themselves, and are badly damaged by fire. They are of two types, one short and broad, the other longer and narrower, with a marked rib down the blade. In one grave both types occur together. The narrow type is the commoner at Mycenae, and in southern Greece generally, and possibly originates in Crete. There were also twelve daggers, and various other tools. The excavators consider that the metal weapons and tools as a whole are related to finds from the Cyclades and from Troy II. They are more primitive than the bronzes from F and S and those from Sesklo, and therefore should not be dated later than early Middle Helladic. Small tools of flint and obsidian are common, and one grave contained forty-eight flint arrowheads, of a shape known from Sesklo.

All the pottery from the Royal Grave Circles is hand-made. Most of it is of a polished red ware found also at Building P and elsewhere in the plain. The finds at the cave Choirospilia showed that in Leucas this ware occurs first in the Neolithic Age, and continues well into the Bronze Age.

The characteristic red ware from these graves has its nearest parallels in Early Helladic pottery. The excavators suggest that it continues in Leucas right down to the Late Helladic period; but although it is probable that in so remote a part of Greece as Leucas progress was slow, there is no positive evidence for such dating. The parallels for the other finds, where determinable, are Middle Helladic; and since there is no matt-painted or Minyan ware (although the latter is known in Leucas from Amali) the graves should not be dated very late in the Middle Helladic period. In any case we are not justified in ascribing the finds to a Mycenaean society and culture.

THE TOPOGRAPHY OF ITHAKI

(See map, Fig. 32)

Those who have stuck to the traditional Ithaca may be divided into two camps, some putting the town and palace of Odysseus on Mt. Aetos, beside the central isthmus of the island, others in the north near the modern village of Stavros. The former is the older view, and was held by Gell [17] and Schliemann, who supposed that the ancient town-walls on the slopes of Aetos, being partly of polygonal masonry, were prehistoric. That is not so; and Aetos is moreover unsuitable by its position relative to the other sites. The spot usually pointed out for the 'rock Korax and the spring Arethusa' is in the south-east of Ithaki, at the edge of the plateau of Marathia. Here is an impressive sheer cliff, below which a spring (Perapigadi) discharges its waters down a steep gully to the sea. At no great distance to the south lies Port Andri or Hagios Andreas, the most southerly port in the island, where Telemachus must have landed on his return from Pylos. These places, as Homer tells, were a good half day's journey from the town; but the distance from Hagios Andreas to Aetos is not nearly so much. Nor can we, with the town at Aetos, find an Asteris where the suitors could waylay the homecoming ship. The only island in the 'channel of Ithaca and Same' — the Ithaca Channel — is Daskalio, well towards the northern end. For these reasons Leake

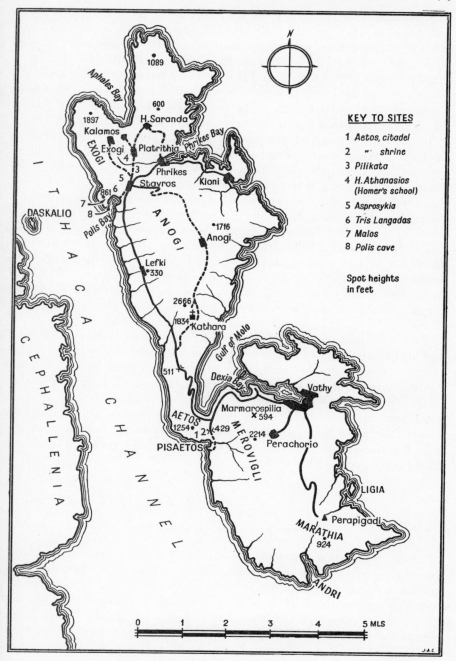

FIG. 32. Map of Ithaca

suggested that the Homeric town lay in the north above the bay which is still (though we cannot tell since when) called Polis (Pl. 21, *a*). In Ithaki itself excessively local patriotism has produced strong advocates of both views, and attempts have been made to discover all the Homeric landmarks in each half of the island. A Korax and Arethusa have been found at Kalamos in the north as well as in the south, and Mt. Neion has been identified with both Exogi in the north and Merovigli above Vathy. More objective investigators, however, mostly place the town near Polis. It is also generally agreed that the Harbour of Phorcys is to be identified with some part of the mountain-girt Gulf of Molo (Pl. 21, *b*), on the inner arm of which lies the modern capital Vathy. Various 'caves of the Nymphs' have been discovered in the neighbourhood, some of them collapsed or imaginary, none remarkably like Homer's, except perhaps Marmarospilia, which lies some 180 metres above the sea on the hills behind Dexia bay. This is a stalactite cave with two entrances, the main one to the north, the other, to the south, a mere hole in the roof which could not be used as an entrance unless, as Homer says, by gods. Besides Andri, Polis, and Vathy, there remains one more harbour, which like them is dignified by mariners with the title of 'Port' : this is Phrikes in the north-east. It may be identified with the fourth Homeric harbour, Rheithron.

We have thus disposed of all the chief landmarks of Homer's Ithaca, and at the same time of all the main features of present-day Ithaki. This complete and satisfactory setting for the story has been arrived at independently by a number of scholars — Leake, Bérard, G. Lang, Pavlatos [18] — all with personal knowledge of the island; and anyone who visits Ithaki and re-reads the relevant parts of the *Odyssey* will need little imagination to fit the events and characters to the setting in the same way. It is for the archaeologist to discover whether the actual remains in Ithaki correspond with the Homeric story.

EXCAVATIONS IN ITHAKI

Aetos.—The ancient town walls of Aetos have long been noticed, and are mentioned by Gell and Leake. They enclose a considerable area extending from the summit down the east slope of the hill to the col which lies above the Gulf of Molo on one side and Pisaetos bay on the other. The masonry is partly isodomic, partly polygonal. Schliemann conducted a small excavation in the walled enclosure on the summit, in the belief that it was the site of the Homeric palace. It appears, however, from his description that vases which he found there were not

earlier than the classical period.[19]   Subsequent investigations confirm
that the town is classical, and the pottery associated with the walls is
mostly of the fifth century B.C.[20]   On the col, however, remains of much
earlier date have been found.   This site was noticed in 1904 by the Dutch
archaeologist Vollgraff, who found sherds dating from Geometric to
Roman times.[21]   Excavations of the site by the British School at Athens
between 1931 and 1934 and again in 1938 revealed remains of a small
temple with rich deposits of pottery and votive offerings ranging from
Protogeometric to Corinthian.   Close by were found confused masses of
stones mixed with numerous sherds of Protogeometric pottery and some
Mycenaean.   The absence of any house plan or household objects led the
excavators to conclude that these were the remains of funeral cairns.   The
Mycenaean sherds include kylix stems and stirrup-jar fragments.   They
bear an affinity with late Mycenaean from Cephallenia, and belong to
the very end of the Late Helladic III period.   Most of the pottery from
the 'cairns' site, however, is transitional between Mycenaean and Protogeometric.   There is no definite evidence of habitation there in
prehistoric times.[22]

Pilikata.—The hill Pilikata, near the modern village of Stavros, is
probably the most suitable site for an early settlement in Ithaki.   It lies
between the mountain masses of Anogi and Exogi, and commands three
valleys sloping down to the bays of Aphales to the north, Phrikes to the
east, and Polis to the south-west.   Gell mentions considerable ancient
walls surrounding a summit above Polis, probably Pilikata; but now
only a few blocks remain in position.   Dörpfeld examined the site super-
ficially in 1900 but found only Hellenic sherds; Vollgraff in 1904 excavated some late houses on the site, and in the course of his work noticed
'pre-Mycenaean' sherds; but the first systematic excavation was undertaken by Heurtley of the British School at Athens in 1930–1.[23]   The line
of the circuit wall was traced, and assigned from the evidence of sherds
to the Bronze Age.   Various blocks built into modern walls and houses
appear to come from some ancient building, which may also have been
of the prehistoric period, since no Hellenic or later sherds were found
in the region.   In six areas which were excavated masses of jumbled
stones were found and sherds of Early Helladic pottery.   In two of the
areas Minyan also appeared, and in one of these a little Mycenaean too.
The Early Helladic pottery is closely allied to mainland Early Helladic,
particularly that of Corinthia.   Most of the normal shapes are there,
but 'fruitstands' are rare.   The Minyan ware is more nearly related to that
of central Greece.   The Late Helladic III sherds are few, and were found
'in shocking condition'.   They include kylix stems, and are perhaps of
the thirteenth century B.C.   A few Mycenaean sherds were also found at
the near-by sites of Hagios Athanasios (popularly called 'Homer's School')

and Asprosykia. In view of the scarcity of Middle Helladic and Late Helladic, Heurtley suggested that Early Helladic ware continued in use (as Dörpfeld supposed for Leucas) until Late Helladic times, and was never completely superseded by Mycenaean. Another possible explanation is that the site of the Late Helladic settlement was elsewhere.

Tris Langadas.—There are ancient walls on the acropolis Malos, which rises steeply above the north-west side of Polis bay, but they are not earlier than the classical period.[24] The slopes of the Polis valley were examined both by Dörpfeld and by Vollgraff without result; but a Mycenaean site was discovered at a spot called Tris Langadas on the north slope in 1937, and excavated by Miss Benton of the British School at Athens in the following year.[25] The site lies on steeply-sloping ground, and has been much disturbed by deep terracing for vineyards. Remains of a fairly large building were found, but it was impossible to recover any house plan. A great deal of Mycenaean pottery was found, which, though in bad condition, was the best in quality so far found in Ithaca, and the earliest. Near the main site were remains of another rectangular building, and of three superimposed apsidal buildings. Mycenaean sherds were found with all of these, but the apsidal buildings possibly date back to an earlier period. Slight as are these remains, they are yet the best evidence so far of settlement in this part of Ithaki in the Mycenaean (Late Helladic III) period, and it is natural to associate them with the story of Odysseus.

The Cave at Polis.—Equally important in its relation to Homer is a cave-shrine of the Nymphs on the north-west side of Polis bay. The site was first discovered in 1868 by the owner of the land, one Loizos, who found a bronze sword and spear, an inscribed flute, various coins, and a stone slab with an inscription to Athene. Schliemann on his first visit to Ithaki purchased most of these objects, and records the statement that they had been found in a tomb. In 1873 Loizos dug again and found pots and a bronze tripod.[26] Dörpfeld noticed the site, but did not excavate it. Vollgraff, digging there in 1904, found pottery ranging from Mycenaean to Roman; but although this was the first Mycenaean to be found in Ithaki he failed to appreciate the importance of the site, and it was not scientifically explored until Miss Benton's excavations of 1930–2.[27]

The sea has risen in level since ancient times and invaded the floor of the cave, and the roof has at some period collapsed, but in spite of these obstacles it was possible to excavate a rich stratified deposit of pottery and votive offerings ranging from the Bronze Age to the first century A.D. A number of inscribed sherds prove that the cave was sacred to the Nymphs, and a fragment of a terracotta mask of the first or second century B.C., inscribed ΕΥΧΗΝ ΟΔΥΣΣΕΙ — 'a votive offering to

PLATE 23

(*a*) Pylos : the palace bathroom, etc., from the N.E.

(*b*) Pylos : the Queen's apartments

PLATE 24

(*a*) Pylos : older wing of the palace

b

c

d

(*b*) Pylos : painted floor-decoration. (*c*) Gold seal, from a beehive-tomb at Pylos.
(*d*) Gold and *niello* inlay from a cup (prob. of silver), from the palace *propylon*, Pylos

Odysseus' — shows that it was associated also with Odysseus.[28]   In the Late Helladic III stratum were remains of a pavement, which suggests that the cave was a shrine even at that date.   The Late Helladic III pottery is of a very late style, possibly as late as the twelfth century, the most striking pots being kylikes with ringed stems of a type peculiar to Ithaki.[29]   The most remarkable of all the votive objects found are twelve bronze tripod-cauldrons of the ninth to eighth centuries B.C. (Fig. 33). These, though imperfectly preserved, are of very beautiful workmanship, and indicate that the shrine was of considerable importance at that period. It seems certain that this shrine helped to inspire the description of the Cave of the Nymphs in the *Odyssey*.   Possibly the cave of Marmarospilia, above Vathy, was also in the poet's mind; we have seen that it suits the story well in position and form.   But as the Polis cave is proved to have been connected in historical times with the legend of Odysseus, it is even possible to see in the bronze tripods the 'originals' of those which Odysseus in the poem brings home from Phaeacia.   They are not of the Mycenaean period, but probably older than the writing of the *Odyssey*, and sufficiently remarkable as works of art to have acquired a traditional association with the local hero.   Even their number fits. Alcinous and his twelve fellow-rulers (θ 387 ff.) each gave Odysseus 'a great tripod and a cauldron' (ν 13).   In the Polis cave were remains of twelve tripods: the thirteenth had been found previously by Loizos.

We have, then, evidence of continued habitation in Ithaki not only in the Early and Middle Bronze Age, but right down to the end of the Mycenaean (Late Helladic III) period, which corresponds to the heroic age depicted in the Homeric poems.   The remains suggest a culture undoubtedly in the Mycenaean sphere, but towards the edge of it, an outpost of the Mycenaean world.   A little farther, in Leucas, we can so far see nothing that reflects the Mycenaean civilization.   Ithaca was culturally as well as geographically πανυπερτάτη πρὸς ζόφον.   The transitional (sub-Mycenaean and Protogeometric) remains at Polis and at Aetos link the Bronze Age to the historic period of Greece, so that the traditions of Odysseus which undoubtedly existed in Ithaca during classical and Roman times may well have survived in unbroken line from the time of the hero himself.

As to topography, Homer appears to have drawn on local knowledge of the island (whether acquired at first-hand we cannot tell): for the correspondence between the poem and the actual topography is too remarkable for coincidence.   Some things, admittedly, do not fit; but they are not too great to be due to that licence permitted to poets (but not to archaeologists) of varying, transferring, and combining details to suit an artistic purpose.

2 F

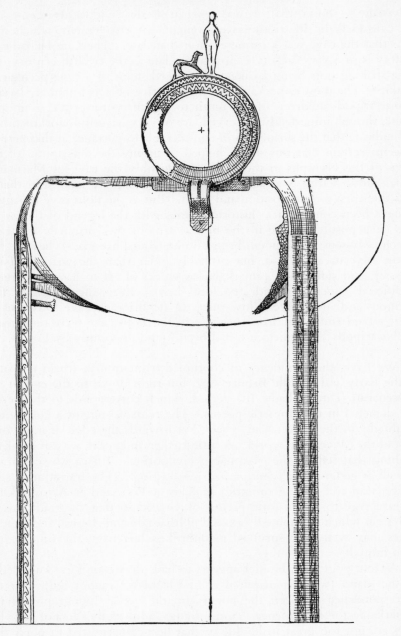

FIG. 33. Tripod-cauldron of the Geometric period from Polis.   (Height *c.* 3 ft.)

NOTES TO CHAPTER 13 (iii)

1. *Cf.* S. Benton in *BSA*, xxxv. 53 f.
2. See *Ithaque, le Péloponnèse, Troie* (Paris, 1869).
3. κραναή five times, τρηχεῖα twice, παιπαλόεσσα once. *Cf.* W. Dörpfeld, *Alt-Ithaka*, 101.
4. *Les Phéniciens et l'Odyssée* (1902–3), ii. 412.
5. *The Homeric Catalogue of Ships*, 86 ff.
6. Livy, xxxiii. 17; Pliny, *N.H.* iv. 1. 5; Dörpfeld, *op. cit.* 68–9, 268; Bérard, *op. cit.* ii. 422 ff.; G. Lang, *Untersuchungen zur Geographie der Odyssee* (1905); W. M. Leake, *Travels in Northern Greence* (1835), iii. 19.
7. Dörpfeld, *op. cit.* 87 ff. *Cf.* Myres in *Greece and Rome*, xii. 34-5.
8. Dörpfeld, *op. cit.* 98 ff. with Taf. 7 and Blg. 4-5.
9. *Op. cit.* 136 ff.
10. Excavations published *op. cit.* 330 ff.
11. *Op. cit.* 196 ff.
12. Illustrated *op. cit.* Blg. 58 b 1-4; 58 c 1-2.
13. Plan and section, *op. cit.* 119, 201.
14. Plan and illustrations, *op. cit.* Taf. 14 and Blg. 33.
15. Plan, etc., *op. cit.* Taf. 15, fig. 16 (p. 214), Blg. 34.
16. Plans, etc., *op. cit.* Taf. 13, figs. 17-21, Blg. 35-44.
17. Sir W. Gell, *Geography and Antiquities of Ithaca* (1807).
18. N. Pavlatos, Ἡ ἀληθὴς Ἰθάκη τοῦ Ὁμήρου (Patras, 1901), and Ἡ πατρὶς τοῦ Ὀδυσσέως (Athens, 1906). The latter includes translations of G. Lang, *op. cit.* and L. Salvator, *Wintertage auf Ithaka.*
19. *Ithaque, le Péloponnèse, Troie,* 29.
20. *Cf.* W. A. Heurtley in *BSA*, xxxiii. 25.
21. *BCH*, 1905, 147.
22. Excavation reports in *BSA*, xxxiii. 22 ff.; xliii. 1 ff.; xlviii. 255 ff.
23. *BSA*, xxxv. 1 ff. *Cf. Antiquity*, ix. 410 ff. In *BSA*, xl. 9 f. Heurtley argues for the identification of Pilikata as the site of the palace of Odysseus; but see also S. Benton in *BSA*, xliv. 307 ff.
24. *Cf.* Dörpfeld, *op. cit.* 147.
25. *BSA*, xl. 10. A full account has not yet been published.
26. N. Pavlatos, Ἡ πατρὶς τοῦ Ὀδυσσέως, 149. *Cf.* S. Benton in *BSA*, xxxv. 46.
27. Reports in *BSA*, xxxv. 45 ff., xxxix. 1 ff.
28. *Cf.* S. Benton in *Antiquity*, x. 358 ff.
29. *BSA*, xxxix. 13 with pl. 8.

Note on maps. — The best large-scale map of Lefkas is that in W. Dörpfeld, *Alt-Ithaka*, ii, pl. 2, from surveys of 1905 and 1910 (scale 1 : 100,000). Fig 31 is based on this and other maps in *Alt-Ithaka.*

For Ithaca the only map from a proper survey seems to be the British Admiralty Chart, which gives little detail inland but has served as the basis for most subsequent maps. Of these the best are those of J. Partsch in *Kephallenia und Ithaka* (*Petermann's Mitteilungen*, suppl. vol. xxi, no. 98 (Gotha, 1890)), and Dörpfeld, *op. cit.* ii, pl. 5, which follows Partsch. Both are on a scale of 1 : 125,000. Fig. 32 is based on Partsch, supplemented by Greek maps, by the detail-maps of the *BSA* excavation reports, and by personal observation.

(iv) PYLOS

by Carl W. Blegen

GREEK tradition has it that the palace of the Neleids in western Messenia was captured and destroyed in the course of the Dorian Invasion some two generations or slightly more after the fall of Troy. The capital of

FIG. 34. Sketch-map to show the situation of Pylos

Neleus and Nestor certainly vanished from the sight and ken of men, and in the classical period no vestige of it was known. Speculation concerned itself with the problem of recognizing the exact place where the town had stood. (See the map, Fig. 34.) By the time of Strabo in the first century B.C. three different theories had been evolved.[1] One held that Pylos had occupied a citadel close beside the sea, and this was generally identified with Koryphasion, known to the Messenians in the fifth century as Pylos, about which later clustered a Hellenistic and Roman settlement also called Pylos. Another view maintained that the palace of Nestor lay some distance inland among the foothills of Mt. Aigalion. The third guess, propounded by the ὁμηρικώτεροι as Strabo calls them, placed the lost site far to the north near the Alpheios River in the district of Triphylia. Strabo himself found this theory most plausible of the three.

Modern topographers and historians up to the first decade of the current century were generally inclined to believe that Pylos was to be sought in south-western Messenia not far away from Navarino Bay. Dörpfeld's discovery in 1907 of three *tholos* tombs, along with remains of a fairly large building on an adjacent hill, near Kakovatos, led him to the conviction that the problem was at last definitely solved and that Pylos must be recognized in the newly-discovered Triphylian site, lying not far from Olympia, some fifty geographical miles to the north of Navarino Bay. Dörpfeld's arguments attracted several ardent supporters to his view, though there was relatively little discussion of the question.[2]

The excavation by Kourouniotis of a fine Mycenaean *tholos* tomb near Traganes in 1912 drew attention again to south-western Messenia. A second tomb of the same type, not far from the first, was discovered and cleared in 1926 by Kourouniotis, who likewise observed superficial remains indicating the existence of several other similar sepulchres in the vicinity.[3] The presence in the district bordering the Bay of Navarino of so many Mycenaean *tholoi*, which most archaeologists take to be royal tombs, encouraged an intensive exploration of the neighbourhood in a search for the corresponding royal palace. In a trial excavation carried out in 1939 by a joint expedition of the Greek Archaeological Service and the University of Cincinnati such a palace was actually found among the foothills of Mt. Aigalion on the flat top of a high ridge now called Epano Englianos, some four miles to the north of Navarino Bay.

In nine seasons of systematic excavation undertaken since 1952 the greater part of the palace itself has been uncovered,[4] and some evidence obtained for the surrounding lower town. In size, in plan and in the style of its architecture, in the quality of its painted floor designs and frescoes, in the character of the objects found on the floors, and in its relatively good state of preservation this new palace takes a worthy place alongside those that have long been known at Mycenae and Tiryns.

The building was destroyed about 1200 B.C. in a tremendous fire that laid the whole complex in ruins, and the site was never reoccupied by habitations. Since the walls in large part still stand to a height of three or four feet or more the entire ground plan is remarkably well preserved.

The Messenian palace (see the plan, Fig. 35) comprises two administrative and residential units, a fairly large workshop, and a wine
magazine, the whole covering an area some one hundred and twenty
yards long from east to west and sixty-five yards wide and filling the
south-western end of the Epano Englianos ridge. Belonging to the
residential quarters is what we take to be an early wing of modest size on

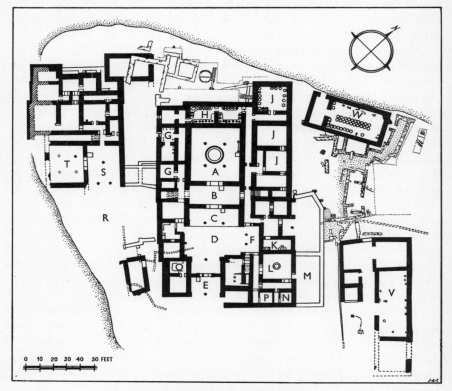

FIG. 35. Pylos : plan of the palace

the south-west, as well as a much more pretentious later block in the
centre. The latter, forming the core of the complex, contains the apartments of state : a *megaron* of the classic Mycenaean type with a Throne
Room (**A**), a Vestibule (**B**), a Portico (**C**), and a Court (**D**), which was
entered from the south-east through a small but elegant *propylon* (**E**).

In its plan this gateway (see Pl. 22, *a*), designed to present a single
column *in antis* in each facade, offers a startling anticipation of the classical
Hellenic *propylon*. The Court to which it gives access, nearly twenty-
three feet deep, was bounded on the north by a stoa with a two-columned
front (**F**).

The main Portico had two columns *in antis* beyond which a large doorway led into the Vestibule. The latter had a lateral doorway opening to the north-east on a corridor and a stairway that ascended to an upper story. There was probably a similar doorway leading to a corridor and a stairway on the south-west. Straight ahead towards the north-west one could pass through a broad doorway into the Throne Room (see Pl. 22, *b*, where it is viewed from the inner end).

The Throne Room, some forty-three feet long and thirty-seven feet wide, the ceiling and roof of which were supported by four wooden columns, still contains a well-preserved central circular hearth, thirteen feet in diameter, made of stucco and rising some ten inches above the stucco floor of the room. The vertical edge, a narrow shelf-like step, and a broad border around the central fireplace bore painted decoration showing a symbolic flame pattern, a sawtooth design, and a broad running spiral in three or more colours. The floor of the Throne Room was divided by paired incised lines into chequerboard squares measuring about forty-three inches on a side. Each square was brightly decorated with painted patterns, all abstract designs except in one square on the north-eastern side of the hearth, where a large semi-realistic octopus appears. This is the second square directly in front of a rectangular recess in the floor against the north-eastern wall, obviously the place where a built-in throne had once been installed. The octopus, on which the king must have looked, presumably had some symbolic meaning. Whether the throne was made of wood, ivory, stucco, stone, or some other material has not been determined, but it was roughly of the same size as the throne at Knossos, which it may have resembled. In the floor beside the Messenian throne is a basin-like hollow from which a shallow channel leads to a second similar depression some six and a half feet distant to the north-west. This may have been intended to provide a convenient place for the king to pour libations without getting up from his seat of state.

The walls around the four sides of the Throne Room were coated with fine plaster which bore wall paintings in several registers in a variety of colours. Behind the throne there seems to have been a composition of protecting griffins somewhat like the scene familiar from Knossos. Beyond, to the south-east, on the same wall, was a male figure playing a lyre and apparently charming a large birdlike creature — perhaps a reflection of some tale connected with Orpheus or Apollo (Fig. 36).

A gallery ran about the four sides of the Throne Room. It was held up by the four fluted columns of wood; set on stone bases, they also supported probably a clerestory for light and air as well as the roof. This lantern rose directly over the hearth and there is evidence that an outlet for smoke was provided by a chimney made of large cylindrical sections of terracotta pipe.

On each side of the *megaron*, accessible from a corridor, were ranged suites of chambers: waiting rooms and pantries (**G**) containing many thousands of pots of twenty or more different shapes on the south-west; magazines (**H**) with *pithoi* fixed in stands, for olive oil, directly behind the Throne Room (Pl. 22, *b*); and on the north-east large and small store-rooms in varying combinations (**J**). Also on the ground floor near the eastern angle of the palace is a bathroom (**K**) with larnax-bath built in against a wall and two large jars, presumably for water, set into a high clay stand in the corner toward the south-west (Pl. 23, *a*). The living

FIG. 36. Fresco of lyre-player from Pylos

quarters of the royal family were evidently in the upper story above the north-eastern storerooms.

The easternmost corner of the building is occupied by what seem to be the special apartments of the queen and her ladies (Pl. 23, *b*). From the stoa (**F**) on the north-east side of the entrance court a corridor leads to an approximately square hall (**L**) with a central hearth. From this there is private access to a small enclosed court (**M**) which when excavated was full of fallen blocks from the destruction of the palace. Beyond this hall on the south-east, and separated from it by a corridor, are two small rooms. That in the very eastern corner (**N**) had its stucco floor adorned with a painted pattern of squares in which octopus motifs alternate with groups of dolphins or fish, the whole being surrounded by squares of abstract pattern (Pl. 24, *b*). In the other (**P**), which appears to have been a lavatory, were found the fragments of a number of large stirrup-jars.

To the south-west, beside the propylon that formed the main entrance, are two small chambers (Q; and see Pl. 22, a), the contents of which revealed them to be the repositories of the economic archives of the palace. Here were found more than a thousand inscribed clay tablets and fragments of tablets, bearing writing in the Linear B script. The inner room, provided on three sides with a clay bench or shelf, was evidently the store-room, while the outer perhaps served also as the office of the accountants and book-keepers if not indeed of the tax collector. The language of the tablets, as discovered by Michael Ventris, is an early form of Greek.[a]

The roof of the central insula was presumably flat, probably built in a series of two or three terraces with the *megaron* rising highest and no doubt surmounted by a rectangular or rounded lantern.

The south-western, and evidently the older, residential wing of the palace (Pl. 24, a) — not yet fully exposed — was separated from the other by a stucco-paved court (R), which could be reached through an ascending ramp or passage from a large exterior court outside the *propylon*. The early insula contains at least two halls of considerable size (c. twenty-three by thirty-two feet). One (S) has a façade with two columns *in antis* looking out on the court, and a single axially-placed interior column to support ceiling and roof. This may have been designed as an antechamber leading to a throne room of similar dimensions farther to the south-west (T), which probably had four interior columns. Both apartments were decorated with brightly coloured wall paintings in the fresco style. Behind these rooms of state to the north-west are corridors, small pantries and storerooms, and remains of one or more stairways that mounted to an upper story.

To the north-east, on the opposite side of the central block, and separated from the latter by a stucco-paved ascending ramp, is what may be called the Palace Workshop (V), a fairly large building containing seven or more rooms and probably only one storey high. Tablets and sealings found on the clay floors refer to leather goods, perhaps elements of harnesses, parts of chariots, and to 'manpower owed' presumably to the state. Many crushed vases were likewise recovered here.

Farther to the north-west, along the steep edge of the site, is another separate building (W), evidently a magazine in which wine was stored in large earthenware jars. Remains of at least thirty-five *pithoi*, which had been arranged in rows, survive, and beside them, here and there, were found numerous clay sealings, some of them bearing incised the symbol which in the Linear B script designates wine.

The entire summit of the hill, which was apparently not enclosed within a fortification wall, seems to have been reserved for the use of the

[a] See Ch. 23, and Pls. 39, 40.

king together with his family and staff.   On the slopes below the palace
ruins of modest walls and abundant fragments of Mycenaean pottery
indicate the existence of a lower town where the common people lived.
It was of considerable size, though the full extent of the settlement has
not yet been determined.

Three stone-built *tholos* tombs have been excavated: one less than a
hundred yards to the north-east of the palace site, another perhaps a hundred and fifty yards to the south of the hill, the third beside the modern
highroad about one kilometre farther southward.   All had been plundered
or in part disturbed in ancient times, but the intruders had overlooked
many items of gold, silver, bronze, ivory, amethyst, and amber, and in
one tomb five or six burial pits beneath the floor were found untouched.
The quality and quantity of the objects recovered may be taken to show
that the tombs had originally been rich in their funeral gear (*cf.* Pl. 24, *c, d*).
In their first use all three *tholoi* antedate the building of the palace.

Greek tradition records the names of several local kings in western
Messenia, but the only family credited with the wealth and political power
one must attribute to the builders and occupants of the palace at Epano
Englianos is that of the Neleids.   Coming down from Thessaly Neleus
and his sons arrived and established themselves at Pylos some two generations before the Trojan War and their descendants held on to the palace
until they were driven out by the Dorians some two generations after the
fall of Troy.   The evidence of the objects found on and below the floors
indicates that the palace at Englianos was built when pottery of Mycenaean IIIb was being used and was destroyed in a holocaust at a time when
the ceramic style of Mycenaean IIIb had not yet been superseded by that
of IIIc.   The equation of this sequence dating with terms of absolute
years is not yet certainly established, but in accordance with some current
views, we might provisionally take the period to extend from about 1300
to 1200 B.C.   It can hardly be mere coincidence that Greek tradition and
archaeological chronology agree so closely.   Numerous smaller Mycenaean settlements have been discovered in a widespread distribution
throughout the whole Pylian region; but nowhere has a second key site
been found that could challenge domination with the palace at Englianos.

In the *Iliad* and the *Odyssey* Pylos is regularly called sandy.   It has
been argued that this epithet could not properly be applied to a site that
lies some three miles inland from the sea.   This is an arbitrary subjective
argument.   Many of the Mycenaean sites known to us seem to have been
chosen because they were far enough away from the shore to be secure
from sudden piratical raids.   In any event, hardly more than an hour's
walk from the palace at Englianos, and wholly subject to its control, are
extensive beaches with deep soft sand stretching for miles along the coast,
amply justifying the Homeric epithet.   It was at some such distance from

the sea and not at the very beach that King Nestor's palace stood, as recorded in the *Odyssey*. When evening descended and the festival to Poseidon came to its end, the royal company, with Telemachus as a guest, set off for the palace which lay remote enough from the seashore for refreshment and libations to be in order when the *megaron* was reached.

NOTES TO CHAPTER 13 (iv)

1. Strabo, 339.
2. See Dörpfeld's articles in *AM*, xxxii. vi ff. ; xxxiii. 295 ff. ; also K. Müller in *AM*, xxxiv. 269 ff.
3. *AE*, 1912, 268 ; 1914, 99 ff. ; *PAE*, 1925/6, 140 f.
4. Preliminary reports in *AJA*, xliii (1939), 557 ff. ; lvii (1953), 52 ff. ; lviii. 27 ff. ; lix. 31 ff. ; lx. 95 ff. ; lxi. 129 ff. ; lxii. 175 ff. ; lxiii. 121 ff. ; lxiv. 153 ff.

§C: SOCIAL CULTURE

CHAPTER 14

POLITY AND SOCIETY
(i) THE HOMERIC PICTURE

by George M. Calhoun

THE study of Homeric society invites by its very difficulty, but tends unfortunately to become involved with the Homeric Question and so to be dominated by sterile theories of composition. Investigators have too often taken up their problems with conclusions already formed, like explorers seeking El Dorado or the fabulous empire of Prester John. During a great part of the last century the goal was commonly the discovery of an 'original' state of society, or of religion, or government, which could be connected with the hypothetical kernel of the *Iliad*; more recently it has been the Empire of Agamemnon. The general result has been a substitution of deduction for induction and the consequent development of a pseudo-criticism which at times violates the first principles of sound historical method; perhaps the most flagrant violation has been the practice of stigmatizing as 'late' or 'interpolated' passages which are fully attested in the tradition but do not square with the hypothesis of the critic. It is a *sine qua non* of sound method to deal fairly with all that the tradition attests, since there is at present no other primary datum, and to prefer a reasonable explanation of difficulties or contradictions to excision or emendation. Purely objective interpretation is, humanly speaking, almost impossible, but it can be closely approached by exploring all possibilities honestly and patiently without dogmatic insistence upon one or another to the exclusion of the rest.

It is essential to keep always in mind that a creation of the poetic imagination, cast in a highly developed conventional verse-form, cannot be dealt with as if it were a sober historical record or a mere compilation of information. Little can be said for the type of criticism, unfortunately all too common, that fails to take account of the conventional use of numerals, of ornamental epithets, and of other formulary elements whose incidence is determined largely by metrical and artistic considerations; or makes no allowance for exigencies of the plot; or proceeds upon the assumption that the poet tells everything he knows upon a given subject every time it comes up, and cannot know anything that is not to be found somewhere in the poems.

Over against the peculiar difficulties of using the Homeric poetry as a source may be set its peculiar advantages. Perhaps the greatest is its disinterestedness, the absence of a didactic or protreptic element; it is pure story-telling, and the poet, as Eratosthenes wisely observed, aims to entertain, not to instruct. No theological doctrine is advanced in the Olympian scenes and the Phaeacian Utopia serves no tractarian purpose; both, since they derive ultimately from human experience, may be drawn upon in an attempt to recreate the life of the poet's time.

What is most needed is thorough and accurate knowledge of the poems, conjoined with the sort of common sense that would be used in the study of a modern author. This can be better attained by reading Homer and consulting the literature of criticism than by reading the literature of criticism and consulting Homer, though the latter method has still its devotees.

THE POLIS

The theoretical and general terms used so freely in discussions of Homeric social and political conditions are not in Homer. It is doubtful whether an instance can be found of πόλις with anything like the connotations of the familiar phrase 'the Homeric Polis'. In Homer a πόλις, like πτολίεθρον or ἄστυ, is simply a town, an aggregation of buildings, often fortified on a hill or other easily defensible position. Yet the fact that the people represented in the poems normally live together in πόλεις is fundamental. It is not accidental that the first two and the longest scenes from human life on the shield of Achilles are of two πόλεις, or that a traveller is habitually asked his name, his πόλις, and his family.

The town is consistently distinguished from the rural area belonging to it (ἀγρός, ἔργα), and its entire territory, rural and urban together, is termed δῆμος or γαῖα. The former word may also designate the inhabitants of the territory, and in some passages may be taken to mean either land or folk or both. When a person in Homer speaks of the land of his fathers (πάτρη, πατρὶς γαῖα), he means ordinarily the land belonging to his πόλις. The fact that the town contains the residence of the king and the place of assembly (ἀγορή) suggests that each town with its country-side is a political unit, not necessarily autonomous; since the people of both town and country belong to this unit, which is the *polis*, the name of the town is often the name of the entire territory or of the *polis* in its political sense.

The simplest form of the *polis*, then, is a single town with its surrounding territory. But some kings are rulers of more than one town (*e.g.*, o 412 f.; I 149 ff.; δ 174 ff.). Even without going into the difficult historical and geographical problems of the *Catalogue*, it is clear that the Homeric state may be expected ordinarily to contain several towns, each with its proper territory. That in which the king resides will normally be the political centre of this larger state, and its agora the place of general assembly. In regions where there are extended areas of arable land with few natural barriers, political units will tend to be larger; in less fertile regions, cut up by hills and mountains, they will be smaller.

To return for a moment to the shield of Achilles, all scenes which are not drawn from the life of the *polis* are of activities closely connected with the household. This again is significant, for the household is a second fundamental fact in Homeric life. The warrior or traveller in a far country longs to return to his οἶκος and to his native land, οἰκόνδε φίλην ἐς πατρίδα γαῖαν. Practically all connotations of the English words 'house' and 'home' have already become attached to οἶκος in Homer, and in some passages it suggests the whole complex of the establishment — family proper, servants, possessions, the 'estate' in general (*cf.* β 44 ff.; α 397 ff.). As the individual belongs to a household and to a *polis*, so the *polis* is an aggregation of households. There are elements in its organization which point to the existence of intermediate kinship groups, but everywhere in the poems the two salient facts are the *polis* and the household.

Within the territory of the *polis* the settlement of the population, as far as is known from the poems, is what might naturally be expected where life is predominantly agricultural and pastoral. In regions suited for grazing there will be remote steadings, like that of Eumaeus, with buildings and enclosures for flocks and herds. Scattered through the countryside will be isolated dwellings, like that of Laertes, surrounded by orchards and vineyards. Where arable lands are far from town, agricultural workers as well as herdsmen may be settled on them (Ψ 832-5). But in the main the habitations of the various family groups tend to cluster in the towns, whence the workers go out daily to the fields, as do modern villagers, or on more distant expeditions for woodcutting and other necessary occupations. Though a family with large possessions may have a number of steadings throughout the countryside for tending its flocks and herds, its vineyards, and more distant cornfields, the principal dwelling will be in one or another of the towns. Members of the king's council seem usually to reside in the political centre.

The inhabitants stand in differing relations to the state; there are in general three elements — slaves, resident aliens, and the 'folk', those who in modern parlance would be termed citizens.

Slaves, commonly called δμῶες, δμωαί, seem always to be the property of individuals; those attached to the household are apparently thought of as belonging to the head of the family. They are acquired by capture, or by purchase, or are born of slave parents. There is no reference to serfage, although ἐπάρουρος in λ 489 is often wrongly so interpreted. What proportion of the population was not free cannot be estimated even approximately, but it seems to have been not large.

Resident aliens appear to be relatively few. The typical instances are of exiled homicides, like Patroclus, Medon, or Lycophron (Ψ 86; N 695; O 430). The permanent resident in a *polis* not his own is properly μετανάστης, but some opprobrium seems to attach to the word, which occurs only twice, both times in a derogatory sense (I 648; Π 59). The alien permanently domiciled as well as the passing traveller may be called ξεῖνος.

With slaves and aliens eliminated, a residue is left of free native inhabitants who evidently constitute the bulk of the population. They are the folk, λαός, λαοί, δῆμος, Pylians, Phthians, Myrmidons, etc., etc., members of the *polis*, citizens. Attempts to discriminate a tall, blonde, 'Achaean' ruling class from a shorter, darker, 'Pelasgian' subject population have not succeeded. There is in fact no evidence in the poems of a cleavage within the *polis* in language, race, or fundamental political status; in all these respects the Homeric state appears to be a homogeneous unit organized under a simple type of monarchy. Where institutions are rudimentary and law almost non-existent, citizenship is not the precise legal concept it later becomes. It is not defined positively or explicitly in the poems, but only negatively and by implication in references to aliens and slaves. Thus the θῆτες (Φ 444; λ 489; σ 357), who seem to be landless freemen working for hire, possibly include impoverished native families; they appear to be an indeterminate element, intermediate between folk and slaves.

KING, COUNCIL, ASSEMBLY

It is often remarked that the Homeric state contains the germ of every type of government later found in Europe, of monarchy in the king, of oligarchy in the council, and of democracy in the assembly of the folk.

The duties, powers, and prerogatives of the βασιλεύς are exhibited particularly in the persons of Agamemnon, Odysseus, and Alcinous. In the case of Agamemnon a highly controversial question at once arises. Is he merely the richest and most powerful of the Achaean kings, chosen for that reason to serve as commander-in-chief of a joint expedition against Troy ? or is he the ruler of an Achaean Empire, a king of kings, and are the other kings his vassals ? The controversy cannot be settled here. It can merely be pointed out that the arguments in favour of a *Grosskönigtum* involve in a number of passages arbitrary insistence upon one of several equally tenable interpretations. For example, Agamemnon's refusal to give up Chryseis despite the outcry of the army is held to prove that his power is absolute. But this ignores the fact that the girl is his private, individual property, and when he refuses to accept the ransom he is represented merely as declining, somewhat ungenerously, to make a personal sacrifice. When Paris does the same thing in a very similar situation (H 345 ff.), no one assumes that he is an emperor and the Trojan allies his vassals, for here no thesis is to be upheld and the passage is approached without preconceptions. When Agamemnon is said to rule over many islands and all Argos (B 108), Argos is taken to mean the whole of Greece, though it may equally well be taken in another of its meanings. ⌈When the Achaeans shout approval of Diomede's fiery speech, rejecting the Trojan proposal for peace, and Agamemnon says to the herald, 'You yourself hear the word of the Achaeans, the manner of their reply, and so it seems good to me', Agamemnon is said to be giving the royal sanction, since he alone has the power of decision.⌋ From the point of view of simple common sense, however, his words seem to be merely assent (ἐμοὶ δ' ἐπιανδάνει οὕτως, H 407). The implications of Agamemnon's offer (I 149) to give Achilles seven cities to rule and of Peleus's action (I 483) in making Phoenix ruler of the Dolopes, in a part of his kingdom, are substantially the same, but no one proposes on that account to elevate Peleus to the rank of *Grosskönig*. Contrariwise, Alcinous, who ought by rights to be made super-king over the twelve other glorious kings in Scheria, since it is he who issues orders and makes decisions (*e.g.*, η 317 f.; θ 390 f.), is reduced to no more than the executive officer of an aristocratic board of magistrates. The reason here is that too often the primary aim of those who study political conditions in the *Odyssey* is to devise arguments for the 'lateness' of the poem. With astounding complacency this theory disregards the well-known fact that in both poems the title βασιλεύς is freely bestowed upon others than kings of states, and the less known but equally important fact that of all the many titles later given to magistrates in the aristocracies not one is ever used in Homer.

One or another of the hypotheses connected with the Great King of Mycenae or with the various theories of composition may in the future be proved true, perhaps from external sources yet to be discovered, possibly from new interpretations which will meet such objections as have been noted; but in the present state of our knowledge they must be kept strictly on the plane of hypothesis and regarded as no more than conjecture, as yet unsupported by satisfactory proof. As a matter of critical method, in the absence of external evidence which might outweigh the unity of the tradition, an interpretation which will suit all cases in both poems is to be preferred. For that reason it may be profitable to ask whether the internal evidence, fairly interpreted, is not entirely compatible with the view that in both poems the political background is a simple tribal monarchy. This hypothesis is followed provisionally in the present sketch of the Homeric state.

In war and in peace the king is the leader and ruler of his folk. It is

2 G

his duty to think constantly of their welfare (B 24 f.) and not to lead them into disaster (B 233 f.); the general responsibility for good order and well-being in the state is his (τ 109 ff.); if he is gentle and kindly, like a father, not harsh and arbitrary, his people owe him grateful loyalty (β 230 ff.). His authority falls far short of autocracy; he commonly consults his council of elders, and discussion of his plans before the assembly of the folk is not unusual. Yet in the last analysis the responsibility and the power of decision seem to be his. That the king had judicial functions is often denied, but it is the most reasonable explanation of the reference to Minos judging disputes of the dead (λ 568 ff.) and of the king's connection with the θέμιστες (I 98 f.). The king enjoys the special favour and protection of Zeus; this is undoubtedly a heritage from the patriarchate and in no way implies a doctrine of divine right. On the human side he has various prerogatives and perquisites, often comprehended in the broadly inclusive concept of τιμή and sometimes in γέρας (e.g., λ 175, 184 ff.). In war a special portion of the booty, γέρας in the stricter sense, is set aside for him by the army before the general division, and similarly in an apportionment of lands among the folk he, like the gods, has a special domain (τέμενος) reserved for him prior to the assignment of lots (κλῆροι) among the generality of the folk (M 310 ff.; Σ 550 ff.). His people give him presents and pay him dues (I 155 f.), and at the feast he has a seat of honour, a special portion of meat, and a full cup of wine (M 311). Traders coming to his land make him rich gifts (Ψ 744 f.). As Telemachus sagely remarks, it is not at all a bad thing for a man to be a king; quickly his house becomes wealthy and his person more honoured (α 392 f.). Out of his revenues the king probably has to meet the expense of dining the members of his council and also his personal retinue in the great hall of his palace, and, of course, he has to maintain a considerable household. In public feasts and sacrifices on festal occasions the victims are probably provided by the folk. Succession to the throne is normally, but not invariably, hereditary (α 386-96). The abdication of Laertes is often cited as proof that the retirement of superannuated kings was usual (λ 187 ff.). However, it should not be forgotten that the presence of Laertes in the palace would not suit the plot of the *Odyssey* and his withdrawal is at least as likely to be a matter of artistic convenience as a reflection of actual usage; Peleus, Idomeneus, Priam, and notably Nestor, have not relinquished their thrones. Delegation of military command to a son in the prime of life is another matter.

Though Agamemnon's council at Troy comes at once to mind as the most impressive portrayal of the βουλὴ γερόντων, it cannot safely be taken as typical. Whether Agamemnon be regarded as king of kings or merely as commander-in-chief, his council represents a large number of states, it is primarily a military staff of leaders attached to their several contingents, and its number and personnel are affected by the wish to bring in the great heroes of tradition. Again, in the *Odyssey*, the plot makes it impossible to portray Odysseus in a normal relationship with his council. Curiously enough, the ordinary peacetime functioning of the council seems to be most faithfully represented in the Phaeacian utopia, on the borders of fairyland. When Odysseus enters the great hall of the palace, he finds Alcinous at table, surrounded by the leaders of the Phaeacians (ἡγήτορες ἠδὲ μέδοντες), who are in the act of making the customary last libation before retiring (η 136 ff.). The amazed silence which falls upon the company is broken by the oldest and wisest of the elders, their best speaker; after the discussion which follows the company retires. In the morning Alcinous and his guest go out to the *agora* and sit in the seats of smoothly wrought stone, where presently they are joined by the Phaeacian leaders, evidently the larger gathering of elders proposed by Alcinous the night before; at the same time the folk throng into the *agora* to behold the visitor. In all the subsequent feasting and celebration the king is accompanied by the Phaeacian leaders, with the folk making up the background (θ, ν 1 ff.). So in the tale of Eumaeus the king goes out after dinner with his retinue to sit in the *agora*, where the folk hold their talk (ο 466 ff.); in the *Iliad* too the leaders of the Achaeans drink wine of the *demos*, or wine of the elders, at the royal board (δήμια πίνουσιν P 249 ff.; γερούσιον οἶνον Δ 259 f.). What is important is the constant association of the king from day to day with the members of his council; they live near him, dine in his hall, and ordinarily need not be specially convened for deliberation. The *gerontes* are often called βασιλῆες and in general are accorded the same titles and the same epithets as the king. Their duties, powers, and prerogatives are very like the king's, upon a somewhat lower plane, and it is probably correct to think of them as sharing in the royal functions and privileges by virtue of the personal relationship in which they stand to the ruler. Organization of the council seems to be very informal, its number and personnel depending upon the wishes of the king, with probably the practical limitation that he will be inclined to choose men of marked ability or prowess, or those who are heads of important kindreds. Men of this type, whether or not they are members of the council, will have each his retinue of attendants and comrades (θεράποντες, ἑταῖροι), his heralds, and his individual γέρας, conferred upon him by the folk (η 149 f.).

When occasion demands, the folk are called together at the instance of the king or of another prominent person to listen to discussion by the king and members of his council. The first to speak is usually the eldest of the *gerontes* or the king, and a younger man, like Diomede, is likely to begin with apologies. In the *Iliad* the Achaean assembly is, of course, the muster of the army; assemblies of the Trojans, like those in the

Odyssey, include also men too old for war. The will of the folk is expressed by shouts of assent or dissent and on one occasion by instant concerted action (B 142 ff.; *cf.* ω 463 ff.). It is a mistake to under-estimate the latent power of the Homeric assembly for the sole reason that often it merely ratifies one or another of the proposals put forward by king or elders; a modern parliamentary body may habitually approve the reports of its committees without any implication that it lacks power to alter or reject. Decisions of the assembly are normally by acclamation. This means that debate goes on until a proposal is made which evokes applause from all or from a decided majority; when that takes place, the business of the meeting is over and it breaks up, usually at the rising of the king and council. There has, however, been much speculation in regard to details of these assemblies.

It is commonly assumed that the folk in Homer constitute a plebeian mass, ruled over by a nobility of birth claiming divine descent. To this view there are serious objections, notably the conspicuous absence from both poems of specific terms for nobility of birth, of the antonyms of these terms, of words for ancestors and descendants, of the words later used in connection with the aristocratic γένη, and the appellations later given to the lower classes. All this cannot well be mere coincidence, and it needs to be explained before the theory of a Homeric nobility of birth can be accepted.[a] What is found in the poems, clearly expressed, is a distinction between kingly and powerful families and the folk, between persons of eminence and the generality of freemen, such a distinction as might be looked for in a simple tribal organization where all are thought of as belonging to the same stock.

JUSTICE AND LAW

On the shield of Achilles (Σ 497) the folk of the city at peace are gathered in the *agora*. Here a quarrel has arisen and two men are dis-puting about the price of a man slain; both are desirous of a settlement, and the *gerontes*, sitting in the seats of smoothly wrought stone, are in the act of giving their judgements before a tumultuous throng, while heralds try to keep order. Probably no two experts agree completely in their interpretations of this celebrated passage, but most would accept what is said above. What is fundamental is that folk and *gerontes* are in the *agora*, and the latter are performing functions which accord with the title

---

[a] [On the other hand nobility of birth is frequently emphasized, not merely by stock epithets (διογενής, διοτρεφής, δῖος) and by the use of patronymics (Πηλείδης, ᾿Οϊλιάδης, etc., or more fully, as, *e.g.*, ᾿Ευρύμαχος, Πολύβου πάϊς), but also by specific comment on the recognizable characteristics of speech and behaviour among the nobly born (*e.g.*, δ 611; δ 62-4). — *Ed.*]

δικασπόλος. This brings to mind at once the man who gets up and goes to supper from the *agora*, where he has been deciding quarrels of litigants (μ 439 f.), and the less agreeable picture of men who by violence make crooked decisions in the *agora* and drive out justice (Π 386 ff.). It is evident that primitive self-help, private war, and the blood-feud are being displaced by simple, practical methods of settling disputes peaceably. When members of a community habitually frequent the *agora*, the principals in quarrels and feuds are bound sooner or later to come face to face; there is always the possibility of violence, but the *agora* is a place for talk and there at hand sit the *gerontes*, men of authority and wisdom; disputes are referred to them for decision.

There is, of course, no written law in Homer, and no positive law in the stricter sense of definite prescription by a sovereign power. But decisions by the *gerontes* upon the basis of custom and of common notions about right and wrong tend to create a body of unwritten substantive law, δίκαι or collectively δίκη (Π 542, 388), which will influence future decisions. The δικασπόλοι ἄνδρες, king and *gerontes*, are likewise guardians of the θέμιστες (Α 238 f.). These may be understood as authoritative pronouncements, ordaining what is customary and right in a given situation. The source of law in Homer is custom, expressed in these decisions and pronouncements.

To describe the content of this customary law would be in the main merely to repeat what is known about the state and the family. But something should be said more particularly about rights connected with persons and property and remedies against their violation. All rights of individuals, including ownership of property, seem to be conditional upon membership in a family. Each member of a family within the *polis* has his τιμή, the price set upon his person or rights, and this the head of the family can demand as compensation for an injury (τιμή, ποινή). So the alien resident is ἀτίμητος because no price is set upon his person or his rights; not being included in a family he has no legal status. The alien guest (ξεῖνος), however, can claim protection under the custom of hospitality, and the slave has a certain status as property.

The scattered hints relating to ownership of property cannot be fitted into the framework of modern legal doctrine. The poet is more interested in possession than in ownership. Usually he speaks as though the property of the family belonged to its head, but Penelope has a slave and and orchard apparently her own (δ 736 f.). Laertes seemingly has yielded ownership of the family property to Odysseus, but has kept his country place; within it, however, are fruit trees and vines that belong, nominally at least, to Odysseus, having been given him in childhood (ω 336 ff.). Probably possession is what counts, as in a modern family, where a minor child has his own personal belongings, though in law all is the property of his parents. It may be safely taken for granted that any adult male, even though not head of a family, will be *de facto* owner of certain things — his arms, articles he has himself made, booty he has taken in war, including perhaps slaves, prizes he has won, the horses that draw his chariot, his pet dogs, and similar personal belongings. He may even have a house of his own, like Paris and Hector. In regard to tenure of real property there is little evidence and much uncertainty of opinion. The gift of a *temenos* by the folk certainly conveys full title to the individual; the *temenos* of a god, though used in common acts of worship, is probably thought of as the god's property. Ordinary allotments of land among the folk (κλῆροι) are by some believed not to constitute ownership, but if they do not it is difficult to understand the use of ἄκληρος (λ 490) and πολύκληρος (ξ 211) in the sense of 'poor' and 'rich', and the general possession of orchards and vineyards suggests long continued, if not permanent, tenure. Sites of family dwellings apparently belong to the heads and pass to the heirs. In one instance, two men are said to be disputing about a boundary ἐπιξύνῳ ἐν ἀρούρῃ (M 422), and this has been taken to refer to the 'common-field' type of communal holding. But it is not certain that more is implied than adjacent holdings in an area of ploughland, and there is no other information on the subject. Even in regions used for grazing stock, the construction of permanent steadings suggests at least private use, if not private ownership, of the land.

Succession is in the male line, without primogeniture, and division of the paternal estate among sons is by lot (ξ 208 ff.; cf. O 189 ff.; E 158); it is possible that the principal dwelling of the family was excepted from the partition, as in the division between the sons of Kronos Earth and Olympus remain common to all (O 193). Bastards apparently have no heritable rights but may receive portions as gifts (ξ 210).

The state does not concern itself with punishment of offences against individuals, which are regarded as private wrongs, to be dealt with by the families of the persons involved. Homicide is not a crime, nor a sin, but a private wrong, and the shedding of human blood does not, as later, involve ceremonial pollution. A slayer ordinarily goes into exile to avoid retaliation from the kindred of the victim, but need not do so if the nearest of kin will accept wergild (I 632-6). The notion of justifiable homicide is to be seen faintly in the formal warning addressed by Telemachus to the suitors (α 376-80 = β 141-5). Acts which injure the entire community directly may be punished directly, by mob action, and death by stoning is not unknown (π 424 ff.; Γ 56 f.).

HOME AND FAMILY

In the fundamental human relationships the Homeric family is not unlike a well-to-do country family to-day in a community where agriculture and stock-raising are the economic basis of life. There will be normally man and wife, sons and daughters, perhaps other relatives and a guest or two, with male and female attendants and slaves. Married sons and daughters with their children may remain in the parental home, though the households of Aeolus and Priam are certainly not to be taken as typical; however, daughters often leave the family at marriage (*e.g.*, δ 5 ff.; ο 367) and married sons may, like Hector and Paris, have their own dwellings (Ζ 242, 313). Where there is a concubine, her children seem to be treated like those of a wedded wife (ξ 202 ff.; Ε 70 f.; *cf.* Θ 283 f.). If the head of the house is a powerful chieftain, his hall will be the resort of a personal retinue of comrades and retainers who are entitled always to sit at his table; if he is king of a *polis*, his entourage will include the members of his council and probably some of their retainers. It is difficult to assign a precise status to the personnel of these retinues, since words like ἑταῖρος and θεράπων range as widely in their connotations as do 'comrade', 'companion', or 'attendant'. The homes and families described in the poems are those of kings or distinguished chieftains; there were doubtless many humbler households made up of only the immediate family, with perhaps a slave or two.

The little scenes of daily life within these groups of men, women, and children, bound together by various ties of kinship or association, lead from infancy to hoary age. There is the new-born babe put in his grandfather's lap to be given a name (τ 399 ff.); the mother keeping the flies from her sleeping baby (Δ 130 f.); the little child catching at her hurrying mother's dress and begging tearfully to be carried (Π 7 ff.); the infant Achilles who will not eat unless Phoenix takes him on his lap and feeds him, who dribbles wine upon his kind friend's tunic (Ι 485 ff.). And boys — little boys playing in the sand on the seashore (Ο 362 ff.), or fighting over their knucklebones, once with fatal result (Ψ 85 ff.), or being kidnapped by their nursemaids (ο 465 ff.); older lads helping in harvest or making music at the vintage (Σ 554 ff.); the young Odysseus, on a visit to his grandparents, joining the boar-hunt and almost getting killed (τ 428 ff.); Achilles, in young manhood, and Patroclus, aiding their fathers in the sacrifice and in the reception of guests (Λ 771 ff.); the brothers of Nausicaa, unhitching the mules and carrying in the newly-washed clothes (η 4 ff.); scene after scene through youth and the prime of life to the old age of a Nestor, or Phoenix, or Laertes.

Women have their separate quarters but are not kept in strict seclusion. Nausicaa, though she has her meals apart, served by her old nurse (η 7 ff.), seems in general to have much freedom. Arete and Helen sit in the great hall with the men after dinner or supper, and Penelope comes in when she is in the mood; apparently the ladies dine in their own apartment and join the gentlemen as they sit at wine after dinner, reversing modern usage. Visits are made to kinsfolk or neighbours (Z 376 ff.); women come out to watch passing wedding processions (Σ 495 ff.); young people of both sexes mingle in the tasks and merrymaking of the vintage and in the village dances (Σ 567 ff., 593 ff.).

The guest is treated most graciously, for hospitality is a cardinal virtue. Many of the most charming scenes in the *Odyssey* are between host and guest. When the weary traveller arrives, he is greeted cordially by the master of the house, or a son, courteously relieved of his weapons, given a bath and a change of clothing, and regaled with the best the house affords in the way of food and drink. Only when his hunger is satisfied is he asked who he is. During his stay he is offered the best of everything and shielded from violence or rudeness, and when he takes his leave, rich gifts are bestowed upon him. The bond of guest-friendship created by even a single visit may link families for generations (Z 215 ff.).

Slavery at best is an evil thing, but the lot of the slave in a Homeric household has its pleasant features. There is much evidence of mutual affection and esteem between master and servant; Eumaeus as a lad is treated as one of the family and in his later years is a valued friend; Eurycleia too is loved and respected. It is significant that throughout the poems the word δοῦλος, though evidently well known, is definitely avoided; this is clearly because of its connotations and is the more striking because Homer is not given to euphemism. We may perhaps infer that slaves were usually treated with some consideration by the poet's contemporaries. On the other side of the picture is the poor woman wearily grinding meal (υ 109 ff.), the savage punishment of Melanthius and the faithless maidservants (χ 465 ff.), and Eumaeus's bitter word, that slavery takes away half of a man's goodness (ρ 322 f.).

There are scenes where all the household join in work or play in a joyous spirit, where ploughmen quaff the honey-sweet wine at the end of the furrow, where a bountiful feast is made ready for the reapers, where the vintage is brought in with music and merriment (Σ 541 ff.).

RELIGION AND MYTHOLOGY

Throughout the *Iliad* and the *Odyssey* the world of humankind is surrounded and interpenetrated by a supernatural realm, swarming with gods and other beings who influence the lives of mortal men in matters small and great. To discover how the poet and his hearers thought of these gods is a difficult problem, and it is only in terms of this problem that we can speak of 'Homeric religion'. Proposed solutions have differed widely, and it has even been maintained that Homer's gods are so wholly mythological and artistic that nothing can be learned from the poems about the religion of the times in which they were composed.   This paradox, virtually a *reductio ad absurdum*, seems to be an intrusion of modern habits of thought into a very ancient world, for it rests on distinctions and classifications of which the poet and his hearers were almost certainly unaware.   Few who have prayed and worshipped with Homer's men and women will be disposed to allow it any real validity.

It is true that Homer's gods are figures of ancient myth, that they are used for artistic purposes, and that this usage is already thoroughly conventionalized.   But these are only partial truths.   There are still other aspects of the gods under which they may be present to the mind of the poet and his hearers.   They may be conceived as supreme rulers of the universe, arbiters of human destiny, defenders of moral values, as personifications of natural forces or phenomena or of ideas or feelings or impulses to human action, or they may be no more than a picturesque expression of impersonal agency.   What is important is that these aspects of divinity are not kept separate in the poet's mind, each in its appropriate pigeonhole, but are always potentially present to his imagination and that of his hearers in a complex of ideas which is continually changing, shifting, dissolving, and re-forming, in accordance with the varying moods and purposes of the artist.   This makes it difficult to extract from the text a series of definite conclusions which may be neatly indexed and put by for a systematic exposition of Homeric religion.   Yet there is in the poems much valid evidence regarding what men have been told by others about the gods, what they themselves feel about the gods, and what they do about the gods.

What men of the Homeric age have been told about the gods can be learned in a general way from numerous brief references in the poems to tales of gods and heroes.   These references are for the most part purely incidental, and so expressed that they would be meaningless were not the audience, as well as the poet, already familiar with the tales.   There are also stories told at greater length which seem to be taken from a stock of ancient legend already known to the audience.   In addition, scattered through both poems, are many common folk-motifs found in the *Märchen* of every land and time.   When all of this material is considered as a whole, it shows that a wealth of myth and folk-tale was thoroughly familiar to Homeric audiences; this represents a mingling of myth, saga, and popular tale, but much of it is divine mythology in the proper sense, having to do with the gods and their relations with one another and with mankind.   Homer did not compose theogonies, but he took them for granted.

After Zeus and his brothers had dispossessed Kronos and the older gods (Ξ 203 ff.), they divided the Universe, as an inheritance, by lot. The broad heaven fell to Zeus, the hoary sea to Poseidon, and to Hades the dark and misty realm of the dead; earth and Olympus were to be held in common (O 187-93). Olympus, however, is the abode of Zeus, and here, men say, the gods have their eternal seat, in a bright radiance undimmed by cloud or storm, having delight all their days, living in ease (ζ 42-6; Z 138). Zeus is never called 'king' of the gods (βασιλεύς) in either poem, but appears to be conceived as the head of a patriarchal household (*paterfamilias*, οἴκοιο ἄναξ) which includes most of the greater gods, the so-called Olympians. Except for Hera, his sister and wife, these are mostly his sons and daughters, Athene, Artemis, Aphrodite, Apollo, Hephaestus, Hermes, Ares, Hebe. Lesser deities, such as the Muses, the Horae, Iris, or Charis and Themis, attend upon the Olympians in various capacities, or assemble in the halls of Zeus at the word of the Father much as human retainers wait upon a mortal chieftain.

When Zeus called the great assembly of the immortals to prepare the climax of the *Iliad*, all the gods came, says the poet, all the rivers save Oceanus, and all the nymphs who haunt the groves and fountains and grassy meadows (Υ 4 ff.). Rivers and nymphs are representative of the thronging hierarchies of minor divinities, like the Nereids (Σ 38-49), who dwell in the grotto of Nereus beneath the waves; Oceanus and Tethys, Proteus and Eidothea, Leucothea, Circe and Calypso, Eos, Helios, Aeolus, keeper of the winds, with his sons and daughters; the Winds, Zephyrus, Boreas, and their brethren. Then there are the Eileithyiae, goddesses of childbirth; Ate, goddess of ruin, followed haltingly by the Litae (Prayers); the Erinyes, and all the gods of the dark realms below, with the Titans, the elder race of gods, fettered in the murk of Tartarus in bonds of adamant.

With few exceptions, greater and lesser divinities alike are described as radiant and beautiful immortal beings in human form. In this anthropomorphic aspect they differ from humankind chiefly in two respects, in being ageless and deathless for all time to come, and in possessing a certain divine power, magical and supernatural, which makes them infinitely potent as compared with men. Most of the lesser divinities have their special functions, and the Olympians likewise have their several spheres of influence, their functions, and prerogatives; many gods of all classes, from Zeus the Father down to the woodland nymphs, are personifications of natural elements or forces, or of abstract ideas, or possibly, like Hermes, of material objects. But in Homeric times the matter was not so simple as that. Eos was the dawn, but she was at one and the same time the goddess who loved Tithonus, who had her home and dancing places in the isle Aeaea, who drove her steeds each morn from the stream of Ocean up the eastern sky (ε 1 f.; μ 3 f.; ψ 241 ff.). Scamander, called by the gods Xanthus, a son of Zeus, appears now as simply a river and now as an anthropomorphic god who rises up from the midst of himself, as it were, to cry out to Achilles; the modern reader finds it hard to say when he is the god and when the river in spate, but the ancient hearer was not so troubled, for Scamander was always to him at once god and river. The Winds feast in the castle of Zephyrus and stand up when a lady enters (Iris the rainbow) and are mildly flirtatious; but a moment after they are driving a scud of cloud before them and raising huge billows on the sea (Ψ 192 ff.). Hephaestus is at once the somewhat comical figure of A and θ, the glorified craftsman of Σ, the holocaust of Φ, and the flame over which men broil their meat (B 426).

What men felt about the gods can likewise be learned from the poems, at least in general outline. An important difference has been observed between the poet's own narration and the speeches of his characters in the matter of references to the gods. In the narrative individual gods usually are named, and indefinite expressions, like θεός or θεοί, are uncommon; but in direct quotations, in which the first person is used, the reverse is the case, names of gods are relatively infrequent and references are usually in general terms. The poet is supposed to know what god did this or that and can name him, but his characters ordinarily cannot. When they are reporting what they have been told about the gods, repeating some old tale of the past or referring to a characteristic function of a god, they can supply the names; but when they are telling of their own experiences they commonly speak of the gods in the most indefinite terms, often letting Zeus stand for the gods in general. A distinction of this kind suggests strongly that the poet is influenced by actual observation of the men of his own time and that in consequence the speeches of his characters offer useful clues to what men felt about the gods. In these speeches anything and everything is ascribed to divine agency, from the most trifling occurrence or a bit of luck to an overwhelming catastrophe, from a casual whim or fancy to a decision of the gravest moment. Evidently men were conscious of much in their experience that could not well be explained in terms of purely human activity or physical causes; having been told from childhood of the gods in all the divers guises in which they were represented in tradition, they naturally attributed to divine agency what could not otherwise be understood. This feeling of being constantly surrounded and controlled by higher powers is very close to the primary connotations of *religio*.

What men did about the gods is told in the poems, circumstantially but incompletely, for references to religious ceremonies are usually incidental. This is not without its advantages to the student of religion, for the incompleteness of the data is compensated by their objectivity. Every household, apparently, offered frequent sacrifice to Zeus Herkeios at the altar which stood in the court; the head of the house officiated and was attended by his sons or other younger men or lads (Λ 772 ff.;

χ 334 ff.). Similar sacrifices might be offered to any god at any time when something came up that fell within that deity's province, or after some special manifestation, or in payment of a vow (*e.g.*, γ 380-4, 418 ff.). It can be said fairly that every meal was a sacrifice and an act of worship, and every sacrifice a meal. The beef on which Agamemnon dines with his council before Troy is a sacrifice to Zeus, offered with due ceremony and prayer (B 402 ff.; H 313 ff.), and so also when Alcinous dines in Scheria (ν 24 ff.). The swineherd Eumaeus makes an offering to all the gods at the start of dinner, and a full portion is set aside for Hermes and the nymphs (ξ 420 ff.). When Achilles sits down to meat with his guests, he bids Patroclus sacrifice to the gods, and the latter casts an offering into the flame (I 219 f.). Libation preceded, accompanied, and concluded the potations at dinner, and might be made at any indication of its propriety; Odysseus appears in the hall of Alcinous at the moment when the diners are pouring a last libation to Hermes before retiring, and at once when he has made his appeal a libation is poured to Zeus the protector of suppliants (η 136 ff., 163 ff.).

These are some of the acts of worship that are a part of daily life, but there are others of a more special sort. If one lives near a river, he makes frequent offerings to the god (Ψ 144 ff.; Φ 131 f.); if near a mountain, to Zeus (X 170); if on the seacoast, to Poseidon (γ 5 ff.); and few live far enough removed from the grottoes and groves and springs where dwell the nymphs to neglect due homage to these gracious beings (ν 349 f., 355-60; ρ 205-11). Such rites as these range from the simplest worship of local deities by individuals to collective festivals where important periodic sacrifices are offered to the greater gods, as to Poseidon at Helice (Υ 403 ff.; Θ 203 f.). Truces and treaties and even solemn engagements between individuals involve religious ceremonies and usually offerings to the gods by whom the oaths are sworn (Γ 264 ff.; T 249 ff.).

When acts of worship are performed elsewhere than at home, it is in places associated with the gods to whom homage is being paid, and here will be found altars, sacred precincts, or perhaps temples of simple design (*e.g.*, Θ 48; ζ 291, 321 f.; η 81). Where there are not such local associations, as may well be the case with the greater gods, altars or temples are likely to be placed near the centre of the *polis*, the *agora*, where is the dwelling of the king; so the Achaeans at Troy raise altars to the gods in the centre of the camp where is their *agora* (Λ 806-8; Θ 222 f., 249 f.), and in the citadel of Troy are several temples (E 445 ff.; Z 87 ff., 269 ff., 297 ff.; H 82 f.; *cf.* B 549; I 404; ζ 10, 266). Whenever any of these places of habitual worship acquires unusual sanctity and the rites there performed become especially important, the heads of the communities or families with which they are associated will naturally be increasingly occupied with religious functions. Here probably is the origin of the

Hellenic priesthood, so unlike the hierarchies of the orientals. Every king is celebrant and priest for his folk (ἱερεύς, ἀρητήρ), every head of a household for its members, but those to whom it falls to conduct the rites at places of especial sanctity come to be thought of primarily as ἱερῆες and ἀρητῆρες, and so become priests rather than kings or simple chieftains. Chryses and Maron are called priests of Apollo, no doubt, because there are shrines of great holiness in Chryse and in Ismarus, towns which are especially protected by Apollo (A 11, 23, 370; ι 197-201). In Troy are a number of temples and a number of priesthoods (e.g., E 9 f., 77 f.; Z 300; Π 604; cf. I 575).

Where worship is so important in the life of the individual, the family, and the state, it must be that the great majority of men believe in the gods to whom they pray and sacrifice. And this worship is offered in every instance to the same gods who appear in the myths to which the poet refers and also as *dramatis personae* in the poems, to Zeus, Apollo, Athene, Poseidon, and the other Olympians, the Homeric deities *par excellence*, or to nymphs or rivers. In view of this relatively abundant evidence, it is nothing short of absurdity to maintain that Homer's gods are purely figures of art and story, and that the men and women he knew did not believe in them, but in other gods none of whom he so much as mentions. The puzzling problem of the relation between the later Hellenic religion and that described in Homer cannot be solved piecemeal, nor by such logic as this.

Men believed that the gods revealed their purposes to human beings by portents, or through omens or oracles. Special portents are relatively more common in Homer than in later literature; the habitual observation of omens and consultation of oracles less so, the Greeks having apparently not yet developed their systematic techniques and habitudes so highly as later. But it must be kept in mind that the two latter practices belong to ordinary life and are likely to be mentioned only incidentally, while special portents are part of the divine entourage of the epic hero and artistically useful for enhancing grand effects. Yet even so omens and oracles seem less important than in the classical period.

Homeric notions of the hereafter are closely connected with concepts that relate to the mind and soul of the living person. The living body contains the ψυχή, which is the vital principle and possibly something more; the θυμός, which seems to be the passionate and spirited element; the νόος, which is mind and thought. The ἦτορ and the φρένες, as well as the κραδίη (K 93 ff.; α 353), are seats of these immaterial entities and by common metonymy may become their synonyms. When a living creature is slain, the ψυχή leaves the body and, in the case of human beings, goes to the realm of Hades, where it resides as an εἴδωλον of the dead and is called either εἴδωλον or ψυχή with no apparent difference of meaning.

Ordinarily it does not have φρένες, which seems to mean no more than that disembodied spirits lack something which living men have, for, despite the lack, the shades are able to remember their past lives, to converse rationally, and to react emotionally (Ψ 65 ff.; λ 51 ff., 387 ff.; ω 15 ff.). Their voices are the same as in life, easily recognizable by friends, though generically, as ghosts, they play their part and go twittering and squeaking like bats.[a]

The pale, dank realm of Hades and Persephone is thought of sometimes as below the earth, sometimes as beyond the stream of Ocean in the darkling West. Efforts of critics to divide and classify what the poet says about the condition of the dead and to arrange the data in neat subdivisions, each logically coherent and corresponding nicely to a particular stage in religious evolution, have failed signally. To those who are not critics, this is not surprising, since common sense reminds us that the popular tales and myths upon which the poet drew and the common notions about ghosts vary infinitely, and this not only for different times but for different localities as well. Homer was not constructing a system of doctrine on immortality, but composing poetry; he took what he wanted where he found it, and if the epic formulas suited the situation and the verse and gave the effect he was after, he was not troubled by inconsistencies in topography or theology. So the visit of Odysseus to the nether regions finds its topography in the old tales of marvellous adventure, its motivation in the ritual of necromancy; both are forgotten when they have served their purpose, which is to introduce the famous gallery of mythological portraits and the colloquy with the heroes who fell at Troy.

What perplexes the historian of religion, as well as the Homeric critic, is that so much in Homer seems more advanced and more civilized than the religious notions and practices found centuries later in the golden age of Greek culture. There is the comparative freedom from superstitious terrors and tabus, from fear of ghosts and demons; the unquestionable absence of any feeling that the shedding of human blood brings pollution and of ritualistic purifications; the silence of the poet in regard to hero worship and the sort of crude, savage cult found almost everywhere in historic Hellas; the general tone of humanism and self-reliance that pervades the worship and the prayers of the Homeric hero. How this is to be related to what is known about popular Hellenic religion in historic times is part of a greater problem which is still unsolved.

RELIGION AND ETHICS

At first glance it seems that religion has little or nothing to do with

---

[a] On the attitude to death and the dead see also Ch. 16.

ethics in Homer. Punishment for evildoing is scarcely to be expected from gods who themselves commit almost every crime in the calendar. Nor can a pattern of righteous living be sought in the trivial and ignoble characters of the Olympians, whose freedom from death and from real suffering keeps their passions engaged on a mean and petty level; only Zeus, torn between his love for Sarpedon and his duty of carrying out the decrees of Fate, once almost ceases to be a god and rises to the tragic heights of human sorrow and fortitude (Π 431 ff.). This incompleteness in the divine character is reflected in the worship which is so often no more than barter of offerings for supernatural aid or favour (Δ 43-9, 101 ff., 119 ff.; Χ 168-72; Ψ 546 f., 768 ff., 862 ff.; Ω 33 f., 66-70; cf. ν 355 ff.; τ 363-9; φ 265 ff.). Even the punishments seen by Odysseus in Hades are without ethical implication; it happens that three of the six mythological celebrities who are presented have in one way or another injured gods and are being tortured by way of reprisal. There is nothing here of reward and punishment for good or bad living, nor any hint of the esoteric doctrines later associated with the mystery religions. The judgements of Minos likewise are simply decisions in disputes among the shades (λ 568 ff.). A single reference, in the *Iliad*, to punishment of perjurers after death is connected with an oath in which the powers of the underworld are invoked, and seems not to imply any doctrine of general retribution (Γ 278 f.). When the gods punish perjury, it is as a direct offence against themselves, a breach of contract rather than of morals.

All in all, the gods appear to be little concerned with questions of right and wrong. But these are primarily the gods of mythology and popular tale, who retain the characteristics with which they were endowed by the semi-savage imagination of a primordial past. It is different with the rulers of the cosmos, those higher powers men feel about them on every side guiding human destiny; an underlying conviction that these powers are on the side of right and justice shows itself here and there in casual observations. The reverent, god-fearing spirit (νόος θεουδής) is linked with the virtue of hospitality and opposed to the fierce and lawless violence of barbarous peoples (ζ 120 f. = ι 175 f. = ν 201 f.; θ 575 f.; cf. ι 269). In the realm of the god-fearing king nature is lavish of her bounty and the folk prosper under his wise and just sway (τ 109-14). Gods go about the cities of men in manifold disguises, noting the ordered justice or the violence of mankind (ρ 485-8). The blessed gods, says Eumaeus, love not cruelty (σχέτλια ἔργα), but value justice and decency (ξ 83 f.). Zeus is roused to fury by men who give crooked judgements in the *agora* and drive out justice, caring not for the wrath of the gods (Π 386-8). Anger of the gods is referred to in connection with the refusal or neglect of funeral rites (Χ 358; λ 73), the brutal conduct of the suitors in the home of Odysseus (β 66), the murder of a guest (φ 28).[a] It is worth noting that the offences which invite divine reprobation are precisely those for which human justice in a simple society will be least likely to offer adequate remedies — neglect of the dead, injuries to suppliants or guests, the perversion of justice. Religion enters the field of morals where secular custom does not suffice.

In the main, however, the moral standards of Homeric society are based on human and social sanctions, on men's feeling of what is decent and right and what is not, on αἰδώς and νέμεσις (N 121 f.). Though *aidôs* is primarily one's own feelings of restraint, and *nemesis* a feeling of disapproval in the minds of others, the two are so intimately connected that they may be regarded as aspects of the same feeling. *Aidôs* enjoins respect and courtesy towards elders and superiors, kindness to inferiors, or humane treatment of a fallen foe, or forbids the warrior to forsake his comrades in battle. *Nemesis*, reinforcing or engendering *aidôs*, restrains from unworthy or extravagant actions of many sorts; often it finds expression in the voice of the folk, δήμου φῆμις, φάτις, whose spokesman Τις, 'the man in the street', is fond of moral comment. Moral injunctions and prohibitions may be in the forms θέμις — οὐ θέμις, καλόν — οὐ καλόν, δίκαιον — οὐ δίκαιον, ὡς ἐπιεικές — οὐδὲ ἔοικε, οὐ κατὰ κόσμον: this or that is, or is not, usual, good, fair, decent, in order, etc., etc.; it is, or is not, 'done'. And here the moral code enters the field of good manners and of custom.

The constant appearance of these phrases is alone enough to refute the mistaken belief that there is in Homer no morality; there is much, but it is different from that of moderns. The virtues that centre in Christian humility are absent or little esteemed, and their place is taken by qualities, later summed up in μεγαλοπρέπεια, that Christian ethics tends to regard as vices; when the poet uses the words μεγαλήτωρ, μεγάθυμος, δαΐφρων, his tone is of approval. Yet with all allowance for differences, for the conventions of heroic epic and the actual state of society, virtues and vices in Homer are not entirely unlike those of to-day; they can easily be determined from the ornamental epithets, from the situations which call forth moral pronouncements, and, best of all, from the words and acts of the characters. The man who is generously endowed with virtues is καλός or ἐσθλός or ἀγαθός, the κακός is he in whom the virtues are deficient and vices predominate. Besides the more personal qualities, there is clear recognition of what may be called the social virtues, particularly in the case of kings or chieftains who are responsible for the welfare of their folk.

---

[a] [In one passage (I 497 ff.) Phoenix is made to say that the anger of the gods may be averted by a transgressor by means of prayer, libation, and sacrifice. — *Ed.*]

ETHICS, MANNERS, AND CUSTOM

Although some moral principles are so often expressed in the poems that they have become formulas, ethics is in general less a matter of precept and doctrine than of behaviour in practical relationships with other persons and with society. So the reciprocal rights and obligations involved in every relationship — husband and wife, parent and child, master and servant, chieftain and retainer, king, councillors, and folk, host and guest, suppliant and protector — all are definitely established in a code of manners created by long custom. For manners, now thought of as an agreeable accessory of life, less important than law or religion or government, were all-important and all-inclusive in a time when positive law did not exist and religion was only beginning to be concerned with morals. The man who knew how to conduct himself in each of these relationships, who had *savoir-faire*, who to-day would be termed a 'gentleman', was δίκαιος and he followed the 'way' of doing things that was δίκη and θέμις.

There is no end to learning about Homeric manners, for they are in all the actions, the speeches, and the soliloquies of all the characters — in Achilles's anxiety for the aged Peleus, in Telemachus's reluctance to send his mother away, in Helen's remorse and Penelope's faithfulness, in the mutual affection and esteem between Eumaeus and the family he serves, in the bond between Achilles and Phoenix, in the deference invariably shown to Nestor. Manners prescribe that the king take the advice of his council, and that in so doing he invite them to a meal and sacrifice. Manners assure the guest and the suppliant of hospitality and protection, so making possible travel or sojourn in alien lands and cementing friendships between families from father to son. No better cross-section of Homeric life can anywhere be found than the scenes of hospitality on which the poet is prone to linger — Achilles with Priam or the Achaean envoys, Telemachus receiving Athene or Theoclymenus and being received by Nestor or Menelaus, the colloquy of Diomede and Glaucus, Odysseus in the hall of Alcinous and the exquisite scene of his leavetaking.

Manners crystallized into custom constitute a great force in the life of Homer's world, a major element in what later was called Hellenism.

MARRIAGE

On the shield of Achilles, the first of two typical scenes in the city at peace shows weddings and feastings. Brides are being escorted from their homes; torches blaze, the hymeneal song is sung, and dancers pirouette to the strains of flutes and lyres; the women of the town stand in their doorways and look on in wonder. Similar scenes greet Tele-

2 H

machus upon his arrival in Sparta. Menelaus is giving a double wedding feast; his son is marrying a maiden of Sparta and his daughter is taking her departure for the home of her future husband, Neoptolemus. The great hall is filled with banqueters, relatives, and neighbours; in their midst the minstrel sings to the lute, while two tumblers lead the dance (δ 1-19). Two principal elements appear clearly, the feast and the procession from the home of the bride to that of the groom; both are characterized by music, dancing, and abundant good cheer. So at the wedding feast of Peleus and Thetis, where all the gods were present, Apollo had his lyre and probably sang (Ω 62 f.).

The gifts spoken of in connection with marriage are oftenest given by the bridegroom to the bride's father (ἕδνα, cf. Π 178, 190; Χ 472; Λ 243; θ 318 f.; λ 281 ff.; ο 231 ff., 367; Ι 146, 288; Ν 365 ff.), but several passages point to gifts from the bride's father or kin (Χ 50 f.; β 132 f.; cf. α 277 f. = β 196 f.; β 53 f.). The former suggest the bride-price and primitive marriage by purchase, the latter the dowry so common in the historical period. Attempts to establish two separate stages of development, corresponding to two strata of composition, have not been more successful than other like efforts of the higher criticism, and there is really nothing against the possibility that gifts of both types were made. Two passages in which ἕδνα seem to be gifts from the bride's family have been discussed since ancient times and no entirely satisfying conclusion has been reached (α 277 f. = β 196 f.). Since Thetis was a ward of the gods (Ω 59 ff.), the gifts of the immortals to Peleus are probably thought of by the poet as coming from the bride's kin. The suitors give presents directly to Penelope, at her suggestion (σ 275 ff.), in what must have been an exceptional situation, and Aphrodite gives a wimple to Andromache (Χ 470). It is not unlikely that weddings were occasions for gifts all round and rigid classification as difficult as it would be to-day. The religious ceremonies, including the sacrifices at the feasting and the singing of the nuptial hymn, were intended primarily to secure to the bridal couple the favour of the gods; marriage was not a sacrament of religion, but a contract between families.

(ii) HISTORICAL COMMENTARY

by T. B. L. Webster

THE preceding section of this chapter gives a picture of Homeric society as a unity, the sort of picture that a Greek of the classical period might have drawn of the Heroic Age. It is, however, becoming increasingly possible to date the different elements in this picture and to say that here

Homer has preserved a Mycenaean memory, whereas there he is thinking of his own times. Many new archaeological finds have been made in the last twenty years, and Dr. M. G. F. Ventris's discovery in 1952 that the Linear B script on thousands of clay tablets from Knossos, Pylos, and Mycenae was used for writing Greek has consequences which we are only beginning to appreciate.[1]

On the one hand then we have part of the palace archives of Knossos in the late fifteenth and Pylos in the late thirteenth century and the picture of Mycenaean, post-Mycenaean, and early Greek polity which can be deduced from archaeological remains and literary sources; on the other hand we have the knowledge that our *Iliad* and *Odyssey* is the final product of a long tradition of poetry which has preserved stories, atmosphere, and phrasing of all dates from at least the fifteenth century to the eighth. If I may use an image to explain the problem as I see it, a constellation appears to the naked eye as a significant pattern of similar stars but to the astronomer as a random collection of stars of different magnitude situated at very different distances from the earth. So far Homer has been considered as a constellation. Now the individual stars must be examined with all the evidence at our disposal. It must be emphasized at the outset that the attempt is provisional, since much of the evidence is very new and the inadequacy of the Mycenaean syllabary and the difficulties of a language many centuries older than our Homer interpose two layers of fog which are hard to penetrate.

The ruins at Knossos, Mycenae, or Pylos immediately suggest a strong government on a considerable scale, and this impression is reinforced by the immense detail of the records preserved in the tablets. Moreover the likeness of the tablets from different sites to each other in form, drafting, language, and writing shows that procedure must have been the same in fifteenth-century Knossos and thirteenth-century Mycenae and Pylos; the same characters are also used on the rather different documents from Tiryns, Thebes, and Eleusis. This is in strongest contrast to the wildly divergent alphabets of the little cities of Greece in the eighth century and later. The common procedure is evidence for an interconnected Greek world like the world of Agamemnon and his Greek allies, in which the Mycenaean palaces ruled their distinct territories but also formed part of a larger unity. It is too early to say yet how we should interpret the women or men from Corinth, Pleuron, Zacynthus, Crete, Lemnos, Miletus, Knidos, etc., who appear on the Pylos tablets; they may be allies, captives, or refugees, but at least they are evidence for some connection between Pylos and these places. The tablets show nothing to contradict the Homeric picture of a major expedition led by the ruler of the most powerful state, to whom the other states owed some sort of allegiance.

Within Pylos and Knossos the tablets show an organization based on allegiance to the ruler, which has left traces in Homer but was greatly different from the *polis*, if we mean by *polis* a state which is essentially an organization of free citizens, even if in early times certain families played a predominant rôle and many citizens had only a minimum of rights. The recent excavations in Chios have revealed a small town at Emporio, which was apparently founded by the beginning of the eighth century and lasted until the end of the seventh. About fifty houses were discovered grouped round an acropolis, containing a large house and a temple of Athene (which survived long after the settlement was abandoned). This seems to be the kind of unit of which the state in Homer's own time was composed, a temple and a great house and a number of small houses. The government of such a state was in the hands of the aristocratic owners of the big houses, and the states could themselves be linked together in a common council. Further development towards the *polis* in its classical sense came from various causes: the new hoplite army which meant that a larger number of citizens of moderate means claimed a voice in affairs, the growth of trade at the expense of agriculture, and so on. Our Homer lived at the time when this transition was taking place.

The architectural feature which distinguished the classical *polis* from this earlier aristocratic state was the *agora* on which life now centred rather than on the acropolis, and the whole city, not only the acropolis, had its wall; the aristocratic state differed from the still earlier Mycenaean state in having no single great palace which dwarfed all other buildings, and in having the chief shrine outside instead of inside the great house. In Homer *agora* normally means 'assembly', but it seems to have its classical sense in two similes (Π 387; μ 439) and the description of the city on the shield of Achilles (Σ 497); these passages are on linguistic and other grounds likely to belong to the eighth century, when the classical city was coming into existence. Scheria was founded as a *polis*: Nausithoos drove a wall round the city and built houses and made temples of the gods and divided the fields (ζ 9); it has an *agora* on either side of the fair Poseideion. But illogically Alcinous has a Mycenaean palace. Old and new are juxtaposed, as so frequently in the battle scenes. If we consider the temples in Homer, we have at one end of the time scale 'Athene entered the palace of Erechtheus' (η 81), which has long been recognized as Mycenaean (the same sort of relationship between god and mortal is implied for Zeus and Minos in τ 178), and at the other end we seem to have something much more like a classical temple in the temple of Apollo at Delphi (I 404), and the temple of Athene at Athens (B 549). To these last may be added as probably eighth-century fiction the temple of Athene at Troy (Z 87 f.) and the temple of Apollo at Troy (E 446).

For Mycenaean times themselves, however, a distinction should probably be drawn between the cult which was actually carried on in the ruler's palace and other cults, which had their own places : the cave of Eileithyia at Amnisos is mentioned in the *Odyssey* (τ 188) and has been excavated ; a Knossos tablet (Gg 705) [a] lists an offering of honey to Eileithyia at Amnisos.   Moreover the tablets record a 'Daidaleion' in Knossos (Fp 1, 3), which corresponds to 'all the gods' and 'the priestess of the Winds' in a list of recipients of oil, and at Pylos (Tn 316) a *Posidaiion* and a *Diwion*, in which golden objects are offered to Poseidon and Zeus respectively.   To house such offerings, these must have been buildings, however simple, and it is therefore possible that the temple which Chryses roofed (A 39) and the grove of Apollo in which the priest Ismaros lived (ι 197) are Mycenaean memories.[b]

The organization of the Mycenaean state centred on the palace.   The tablets give some evidence about military organization, classes of citizens, land tenure, and obligations.   Where this organization can be detected in our Homer we have to try to distinguish between reminiscences of Mycenaean times and survivals into Homer's own time.   A Pylos tablet (Er 312) gives the amount of corn sown in the *wanakatero temeno* and the *rawakesijo temeno*, the *temenos* of the *wanax* and the *temenos* of the *lawagetas*. We have already noticed that when Athene enters the palace of Erechtheus (η 81), she behaves as the archaeologists expect a Mycenaean goddess to behave ; she lives with the ruler.   We now learn that the Mycenaean ruler was called *wanax* and had a *temenos*.   After Homer *temenos* is only used for the precinct of a god and *wanax* is only used as the title of a god. To this statement about *wanax* there are two significant exceptions, which prove the rule : (1) *wanax* is used of rulers in poetry dependent on Homer, (2) *wanax* is used of rulers in Cyprus, where many elements of Mycenaean language survive.   The words *wanax* and *temenos* suggest that the Mycenaean ruler was divine, and Homer remembers this when he calls him *wanax* and gives him a *temenos* (*e.g.*, Alcinous in ζ 291) or says that he was honoured as a god.   Thus Sarpedon tells Glaucus (M 312 f.) : 'all look on us as gods and we have a *temenos*'.   By Homer's own time the *wanax* and his *temenos* had vanished, just as the royal palace had vanished : where there was still a single ruler, he was called *basileus* and the aristocrats might be called *basilêes* or *basileidai* ; the *basileus* also is found in the Mycenaean texts and will be considered in due course, but there is no hint that he was in any way divine.

The people in Homer who are 'regarded as a god' or 'honoured as a god' fall into three main classes : (1) *wanaktes* : *e.g.*, Thoas, *wanax* of all Pleuron and steep Kalydon (N 218), and Alcinous (η 11).   Royal women

---

[a] For the system of reference to the tablets used here and elsewhere see p. xxix.

[b] For further discussion of religion and cult-places see Ch. 15.

may also be 'regarded as gods', particularly Arete (η 71), and the adjective *wanasewija* (Ta 711) suggests that Pylos had a *wanassa* as well as a *wanax*. (2) Priests: Dolopion, priest of Scamander in E 78, and Onetor, priest of Zeus in Π 605. In Pylos (Tn 316) Drimios, the priest of Zeus, receives an offering of gold like Zeus and Hera, who are named immediately before him, and in Knossos the priestess of the winds receives offerings (Fp 1; Fp 13). (3) Great warriors: *e.g.*, Achilles (I 155), Hector (X 394, 434). On the Pylos tablet (Er 01, now 312) the first and larger *temenos* belongs to the *wanax*, the second and smaller *temenos* belongs to the *lawagetas*, the commander of the army. There are traces of this relationship between *wanax* and military leader in Homer: Priam and Hector, Agamemnon and Achilles (I 155), Oineus and Meleager (I 578), Iobates and Bellerophon (Z 173, 194), perhaps also Sarpedon and Glaucus (M 312 f.). In the eighth century such people would have been aristocrats, but nothing suggests that they would have been divine or honoured as gods.

When Agamemnon offers Achilles seven cities (I 149 ff.), whose rich inhabitants will honour him as a god, these inhabitants also οἱ ὑπὸ σκήπτρῳ λιπαρὰς τελέουσι θέμιστας. This is a unique use of *themis* for 'due', and it is Mycenaean. Chadwick has pointed out that on a tablet from Knossos (As 821) *themis* and *opa* represent two different kinds of 'due', although we cannot say what the distinction between them is. *Opa* has derivatives: *opawoneja* (KN Fh 339) is perhaps the headquarters of those who pay *opa*; *anopasija* (PY Ea 805) is 'freedom from *opa*' and *opawon* (Fn 03, now 324) is 'one who pays *opa*'. In view of the use of *opa* at Knossos it is interesting that five of the six Homeric occurrences of *opawon* refer to Cretans, *e.g.*, H 165, 'Idomeneus and the *opawon* of Idomeneus, Meriones'. The sixth is Phoenix, who is called the *opawon* of Peleus (Ψ 360). The terminology recalls Phoenix's autobiography (I 483 πολὺν δέ μοι ὤπασε λαόν): 'he made me rich, and made many soldiers payers of *opa* to me, and I dwelt in the far end of Phthia as *wanax* of the Dolopes'. Peleus established Phoenix as a local *wanax* as Agamemnon hoped to establish Achilles; the difference is that Achilles was certainly to be established for his military prowess: he would therefore have been more like the *lawagetas*. If we take the two Phoenix passages together, we find that Peleus received *opa* from Phoenix and Phoenix received *opa* from his *laos*. Presumably service could be demanded instead of dues, as appears from various passages in Homer where military service is rendered or commuted (*cf.* N 669, Ψ 297, Ω 400).

In the Phoenix passage the formula ὤπασε λαόν has its full feudal sense: elsewhere it merely means 'allotted troops' for a particular operation, and the verb may mean no more than 'to give'. *Laos* means 'troops' as in the Mycenaean title *lawagetas*, which survives in such phrases as ἡγήτορα λαῶν (Υ 383). But by Homer's time *laos* could be used of the common people generally (it occurs so in similes, Λ 676, P 390). Another Mycenaean military survival is the phrase ὄρχαμε λαῶν (Ξ 102, etc.); ὄρχα, 'command', is found in the headings of a series of tablets which appear to give dispositions for watching the coast (PY An 519, 654-7, 661); the tablets are divided into sections which approximate to the following form: (a) 'Command of X at Y', (b) list of men by name, many of whom are known from other tablets; possibly they are owners of chariots, (c) small detachments of troops, e.g., 'kekide [probably some particular kind of troops], 10 men, Kyparissians 20 men', (d) 'and with them the equeta PQ'. Equeta, which becomes in classical Greek ἑπέτης, has been convincingly explained as the equivalent of 'count' (Latin, comes); they are the companions of the wanax, and are nobles, for several of them have adjectival patronymics attached to their names. The word equeta only survives in Homer in a verbal formula ἕσπετο, which is often used of heroes accompanying their troops (e.g., Σ 234). The function is described by the word ἑταῖρος in Homer. We know that the equeta had chariots (PY Sa 787, 790) and it seems to me possible that the honorific ἵππότα or ἱππεύς applied by Homer to Peleus, Nestor, Tydeus, Oineus, and Patroclus may be a confused reminiscence of the old title equeta. However that may be, Homeric formulae consisting of name with adjectival patronymic, e.g., Τελαμώνιος Αἴας, Νέστωρ Νηλήϊος, are memories of Mycenaean titles, which are older than Πηληϊάδης Ἀχιλεύς, Λαερτιάδης Ὀδυσσεύς, etc.

Some of the men who are named in sections A and B of the coast-watching tablets recur on two other tablets, which were written by a single hand and therefore belong together (Sn 64; An 218). Their precise meaning is unclear but they group the men in four classes: (1) basileuontes, (2) men with ktoinai, (3) men liable for contribution (?), (4) men without ktoinai. The men in sections A and B of the coast-watching tablets recur in all four classes, so that all are presumably people of some importance. We can say something more about the first two classes at any rate.

It is surprising to find a number of basileuontes. Possibly a distinction should be drawn between the participle basileuontes and the noun basileus: these six men would then exercise the functions of a basileus without having the title; they have other titles, moropa and korete, of which the former possibly means a holder of a moira or large portion of land and the latter is possibly religious (cf. zakoros, etc. in classical times), although other interpretations have been suggested. For the basileus himself we have considerable evidence: four men have the title basileus after their names; one of these has also a geronsia (body of seniors), and this allows us to identify three more men, who have a geronsia, as 'kings' (it should be noted in passing that these geronsiai are the only evidence that the tablets provide for councils in Pylos); five men have a *basileia*, which may very well mean royal house. Thus we have evidence for twelve 'kings' and six men exercising the functions of 'kings'. Phaeacia had twelve kings and the *wanax* Alcinous was the thirteenth (θ 390 f.), but the coincidence of numbers is probably merely a chance. It is, however, clear that the multiplication of 'kings' in the *Odyssey* and in Hesiod is not a late development. What happened may have been something like this: when the great Mycenaean palaces were sacked, the divine *wanax*, in whose house the goddess lived, vanished; the many 'kings' were left, and the nearest they got to divinity was to have the goddess living just outside their houses, as at Emporio. One might become pre-eminent (βασιλεύτερος or βασιλεύτατος — I 69, 160) and then we speak of monarchy, and if he succeeded in establishing a dynasty, the ruling family might be called *basileidai*, but often probably the nobles were still called 'kings' as long as the aristocratic city lasted. The later associations of *basileus* as a single supreme monarch were very much influenced by the supreme position of the Persian King.

The second class of men on the Pylos tablet (Sn 64) are the 'men with *ktoinai*'. *Ktoinai* were portions of land, and the word survived in Rhodes as the name for a local division. In Pylos these portions were of two kinds, one of which are called *ktimena*, the other *kekemena* (see the E tablets *passim*). The distinction seems to be between private land and common land. Among the Hittites, as L. R. Palmer has pointed out, the 'men of feudal service' hold the private land and 'the men of the tool' (craftsmen) hold the common land. In Pylos by the time that the tablets were written it seems that such a system has become blurred; men may hold a *ktoina* of the common land as a private portion, and craftsmen may hold private land. But the distinction still exists because small holdings of the common land are held 'from the people' (*damos*). The men who hold private land are called *ktitai* in contrast to other members of the population, *ktoinoochoi* as landholders, and possibly *telestai* as paying feudal dues (*cf.* I 156). In Pylos the *ktoinoi* both of private and of public land are further subdivided on an elaborate leasehold system; of this no trace survives in Homer, but it is tempting to see a trace of the original distinction between private and common in B 546 οἳ δ' ἄρ' Ἀθήνας εἶχον, ἐϋκτίμενον πτολίεθρον, δῆμον Ἐρεχθῆος. Perhaps the *ktitai* of the Pylos tablets are the original settlers, since they are contrasted with *metaktitai* (An 610), which would correspond to μετανάστης in Homer (I 648, *cf.* β 65, where περικτίονας is explained by περιναιετάουσι); these 'after-settlers' may perhaps belong to the third and fourth classes of the tablet from which we started.

In Pylos the small holding of common land is held 'from the *damos*', which has therefore some sort of personality. It is at least possible that the *damokoros*, who is known in Pylos (On 300; Ta 711) and Knossos (L 642; X 7922) is the responsible official; the only possible trace of such an official in Homer is in the title δημογέρων (Γ 149, Λ 372), which is twice used of Trojans and to Homer probably meant no more than 'an elder of the land'. We cannot be certain whether the *damos*, which grants holdings in Pylos, is the *damos* of the whole territory of the *wanax* or whether (as I am slightly inclined to believe) each town has its own *damos*; in either case the extension of meaning to 'land' and so to 'country' (*e.g.*, Π 437; θ 390) is easy. On one tablet (Un 718) *damos* is listed with the *wanax*, the *lawagetas*, and a religious community as making an offering to Poseidon, and here we seem to have the meaning of 'commons' as opposed to the ruler, since there is some reason to suppose that it includes the 'settlers' as well as the holders of common land (*cf.* B 198, Λ 704). In Mycenaean times the *damos* presumably also had to render services in return for its rights in the common land and Homer sometimes remembers this (*e.g.*, P 250, η 150), but by his own time the whole system of common land and services had vanished; the small free-holders (*cf.* O 498) are, however, still called *demos* in contrast to their aristocratic rulers, and it is they who turn out to beat off a marauding lion (Υ 166, in a simile) or gather in the *agora* to watch a murderer being tried (Σ 500, on the shield of Achilles).

One word connected with *demos* remains to be considered, δημιοεργός which only occurs twice in Homer (ρ 383, τ 135), and in both cases denotes a welcome kind of stranger — herald, singer, seer, doctor, or carpenter. He is not a local craftsman but an expert from outside.[a] The word does not occur on the tablets and it is questionable to what extent the tablets give evidence of full-time craftsmen. The list of workers with special crafts is impressive: smiths, fullers, potters, tailors, armourers, goldsmiths, shipbuilders, masons, bakers, woodcutters, grainkeepers, bath-attendants, seamstresses, wool-carders, etc. But in the rather full records of smiths it is noticeable both that the allocation of bronze is small and that some eighty of the names are known in other connections. This may be chance; but, if so, the number of people with the same name is remarkable. It may be more correct to think of men and women with special skills that can be exercised when needed rather than of full-time craftsmen. These special skills were acquired by training. In Knossos (Ak 781, etc.) older women apparently train younger women, just as Eurycleia claims to have trained the women in Odysseus's household (χ 421 f.): 'there are fifty bondwomen in your house, whom we teach to do their work, to card wool, and to endure slavery'. More specialized skills seem in Pylos to have been under the patronage of particular gods, as in classical times. I think we should consider together *potinijawejo*

---

[a] See also p. 537.

kakewe (smiths of Potnia, Jn 310/4), *Atemito doero* (slave of Artemis, Es 650/5), Μενέλαος ἀρήϊος (Γ 339), θεράποντες Ἄρηος (Β 110, etc.), δμῶος Ἀθηναίης (carpenter, Hesiod, *Op.* 430), ἐσθλὸν θηρητῆρα· δίδαξε γὰρ Ἄρτεμις αὐτή (Ε 51). Here are three types of relationship between skilled man and patron god : slave of a god, belonging to a god, taught by a god. The last explicitly mentions teaching in the past, the first two may imply it. In Homeric as in classical times craftsmen have their patron gods, whom they honour with offerings and who guide their work. The phraseology which we have examined implies some special relation-ship between the apprentice and the god of the craft, which existed in Mycenaean times and survives in the terminology of Homer and Hesiod ; that the smiths of Potnia are apprentices seems likely, as they are listed separately after the other smiths ; but we cannot say in what sense they belonged to Potnia.

Most of the crafts and skills remained unchanged from the Mycenaean period until Homeric times, and when they are described in similes, as many of them are, Homer is likely to be thinking of his own day.[a] Some-times we can prove this : the technique of colouring ivory does not seem to have been invented before the ninth century (Δ 141 f.) ; iron as a useful material is not much earlier, and therefore the simile of the smith tempering iron (ι 391-3, *cf.* Δ 485) is likely to be drawn from contemporary life ; so too are Hephaestus's preparations to work on the shield (Σ 468 f.), which, it has been claimed, have no relation to Mycenaean inlay technique.[2]

It may be regarded as certain that in Homeric times, as earlier and later, the women of the household did the spinning and the weaving, ground the corn, and prepared the food, and it is not surprising that, where the women on the Mycenaean tablets have adjectives describing their activities, these activities can be for the most part paralleled in Homer. But, when Homer gives Odysseus fifty women slaves (χ 421), he is imagining a royal household far bigger than any that is likely to have existed in eighth-century Ionia but far smaller than the royal household of thirteenth-century Pylos : there, according to my reckoning, 347 women, 240 girls, and 159 boys are listed in Pylos itself, and 322 women, 152 girls, and 122 boys elsewhere in the kingdom. Two other points may be noted in which Homer preserves memories of Mycenaean palaces. When a Homeric hero arrives he is bathed and anointed by slave women ; this again is out of scale with what we know of life in Ionia, but the Pylos tablets record 37 women who are labelled 'bath-pourers', and a terracotta bath with a large jar beside it to hold oil has been discovered in the palace. Secondly, the princely gifts which visitors receive and the luxury articles such as Penelope's chair (τ 55) are Myce-naean memories ; in Pylos the Ta tablets list tables, chairs, and footstools

[a] On crafts, etc. see also Ch. 21.

inlaid with ivory and other precious material, which were apparently gifts presented at the installation of a *damokoros*. Penelope's throne, inlaid with ivory and silver, was made by an artist called Ikmalios; the name may well be connected with the Cypriot ἰκμάω 'to strike', and may therefore be a Mycenaean 'speaking' name, like the smith's name Mnasiwergos at Pylos (Jn 431/3).

A modern scholar has said of Homeric religion that the spirit of *do ut des* permeates man's dealings with the gods. The same is likely to have been true of Mycenaean religion, and if we can accept the suggestion that the Pylos tablets show something of the preparations to avert a military attack which destroyed the palace, these preparations included the collection of gold from the different communities (Jo 438) and the offering of gold vessels and men and women to various gods in their sacred places (Tn 316). Other offerings listed in the tablets include honey, oil, grain, cheese, wine, and animals; these could all be paralleled in classical times. On one tablet (PY Un 1189) *Peleia* (probably the dove goddess, who is perhaps the classical Aphrodite) receives a cow, a ewe, a hog, and two sows; it will be remembered that Odysseus was told to sacrifice to Poseidon on his last journey a ram, a bull, and a hog. The offerings seem to be much the same, and the names include many of the gods and goddesses with whom we are familiar: Zeus, Hera, Poseidon, Athene, Enyalios, Paieon, Ares, Artemis, Eileithyia, Hermes, Dionysus, Demeter, Erinys, Themis, the winds. The absence of Apollo is probably due to chance. Paieon is still independent of Apollo, as he is in Homer; and Enyalios is still independent of Ares, as he is in many passages of Homer. But syncretism has already started, as Athene on one tablet (KN V 52) is called Athene Potnia, whereas elsewhere Potnia is independent, and may well be a neutral name for a pre-Greek goddess. Several Knossos tablets mention offerings sent to the Daidaleion, the (?) shrine of Daidalos; Daidalos was, therefore, perhaps a god, but in Homer has become a man (Σ 592). Similarly, if the name *qerasija* of the Knossos tablets is rightly interpreted as Tiresias, he also lost his divine status in the intervening centuries. Iphimedeia was a goddess in Pylos; Homer knows her as the wife of Aloeus, who bore Otos and Ephialtes to Poseidon (λ 305). Erinys and Eileithyia are singular and independent in Knossos; in Homer they are sometimes plural, and the Eileithyiai are sometimes daughters of Hera; this again is a degrading. The process of systematizing the pantheon may well have been due to early contact with the East. We have evidence that Mycenaeans could understand the language of Ugarit and of the Hittites, and both knew the myth of successive divine rulers, who appear in Greek mythology as Ouranos, Kronos, Zeus; in Homer this is already a known story to which the poet can allude as he needs it.

The resemblance between Mycenaean religion (in so far as the tablets reveal it) [a] and classical religion is far more striking than the differences. Here, as in some other departments of life such as agriculture and home industries, we can speak of survival, and there was no difference for Homer between past and present. In other respects the Mycenaean world, notably the divine *wanax* with his great palace and luxurious possessions and the whole system of allegiance, was part of the story and therefore survived in poetry, although it had long ceased to belong to present-day experience. Sometimes the scale was reduced to make the past credible; sometimes, notably in descriptions of fighting, new equipments and methods were introduced without wholly ousting the old. Always the poets were aware of their contemporary world and introduced it where they could into the stories as well as into the similes. But the similes were the natural place for modern elements because the purpose of the similes was to illustrate the heroic past in terms of the known present.

NOTES TO CHAPTER 14 (ii)

1. For a full account of the discovery, with texts of the most important tablets and a commentary on them, see M. G. F. Ventris and J. Chadwick, *Documents in Mycenaean Greek* (1956), to which the reader is referred for detail.

2. D. H. F. Gray, 'Metal-working in Homer', *JHS*, lxxiv. 1 ff. For another view see Ch. 21.

[For another view of the historical background of Homeric society, and a different estimate of the relevance of the Mycenaean documents, cf. M. I. Finley, *The World of Odysseus* (revised edition, 1956), and *Economic History Review*, 10 (1957), 128 f.]

[a] See Ch. 15 for further statement of the archaeological evidence, including the tablets.

CHAPTER 15

RELIGION

by H. J. Rose

APART from what Homer himself tells us,[a] our information concerning the religion of Greek lands in early times comes mainly from archaeology, to a less extent from analysis of certain myths, sacral names, and fragments of ritual, which without the help of modern excavations would be nearly, if not quite, unintelligible. So far as the Minoan culture in Crete is concerned, the archaeological material may be classified as follows:

(1) sanctuaries and holy places, shown to be such by the presence of votive offerings and other cult-objects;

(2) statuettes (there are no large statues of early date), objects known or reasonably supposed to be sacred symbols, altars, and other implements of cult;

(3) representations in art of scenes of cult;

(4) graves and their contents.

Light is thrown on the significance of these finds, and of those on the mainland, by:

(1) the ritual and legends of cult-places where the worship, continuing to historical times, shows non-Greek features, explicable as survivals from the Minoan age, coming down (at least in the case of the mainland) through the Mycenaean culture;

(2) the functions of deities whose names have formations characteristic of the pre-Hellenic language, notably the suffixes -νθ- and -να, such as Hyakinthos, Athena.

Putting all these indications together we may legitimately conclude that the Minoans, and it would seem also the pre-Hellenic inhabitants of Greece proper, practised a religion differing widely from that which we find depicted in the Homeric poems, yet influencing it and possessing features which long survived the culture or cultures in which they originated.

Beginning then with the archaeological material, the first and perhaps most easily recognizable form of sanctuary is the sacred cave. Of these there were many, both on the mainland and in Crete, some indeed surviving in sacral use to this day, as the sacred grotto of the Virgin Mary (Panayía Khrisospiliótissa) on the Acropolis at Athens. Perhaps the most

[a] See Ch. 14 (i), pp. 442-50.

famous is the cave of Psikhró in Crete, often identified with the Dictaean Cave of ancient tradition, the birthplace or nursery of Zeus. Discovered by peasants in 1888, it yielded from time to time interesting finds till at length it was properly excavated by the British School in 1900.[1] It is double, the inner sanctuary being apparently in the upper part; the finds are of various dates from M.M. (with a little doubtful material which seems earlier) to Geometric. Exploration of another cave, near the summit of Mt. Ida, which is the one usually associated with Zeus by the classical writers, shows that it was not used in Minoan times at all.[2] Other caves on the same mountain were used as early as, or even earlier than, M.M.,[3] but the objects found in them, being mostly pieces of pottery, tell us little of the character of the deities worshipped. There is, however, a rock shelter at Petsofa near Palaikastro which has yielded a number of terracotta models of parts of the human body, strongly suggesting that the deity worshipped there was a healer and that the objects are either thank-offerings for cures or prayers (or charms) intended to bring such cures about.[4] The little sanctuaries or *lararia* found in secular buildings, the most noteworthy of which is the Shrine of the Double Axes in the palace at Knossos,[5] have given us several figurines of deities; of these the most interesting is the 'Snake Goddess', from a repository, probably not a shrine, though it has been called the Central Palace Sanctuary, at the same place.[6] She is one of the many goddesses who form a prominent feature in Minoan cult as we know it, and the fact that she is entwined with serpents hints, if we may use an analogy from classical Greek cult supported by similar phenomena elsewhere, that she was rather of the earth, possibly even of the underworld, than of the heavens. An overwhelming preponderance of the figures found and supposed with any reasonable plausibility to be divine is female, and the impression that goddesses formed a principal object of worship is strengthened by the frequency with which pottery models of dresses, such as we know from Minoan art to have been worn by ladies, are found in shrines and repositories.[7] This indicates that in that age, as in classical Greece (for instance, at Dodona),[8] it was customary to offer clothes to the goddess, if only in this symbolical form. If actual garments were also dedicated, as they may have been, they, of course, have long ago rotted away.

But commoner than any figures of the kinds described are two symbols, one of which has yet to be certainly explained. The first is the so-called 'horns of consecration', whereof we have innumerable examples, painted and modelled,[9] representing in ways which vary from fully realistic to highly conventional the long, outward-curving horns of a bull, one of the breed which we know from art to have been common in Minoan Crete.[10] This at least is the usual explanation, and it seems adequate. The horns would thus correspond to the *bucrania* of classical art, representations of the horns and skull of a sacrificed beast, which in turn symbolize the real skull and horns, hung up in the holy place partly because they were sacred and the property of the deity, partly to remind him of the piety of his worshipper. It is easy to conceive that such a symbol could pass into a conventional indication that the place was holy. The other symbol is the double axe, distinguishable from ordinary axes intended for practical use (of which a number have been found) by its size, often very small, its material (gold, thin bronze, lead, soft stone, etc.), and its constant occurrence, whether in the round, painted, or carved, in places obviously holy from the presence in them of other cult-objects. It has been variously suggested that the axe was originally a thunderbolt, as indeed it seems to be elsewhere, in the hands of more than one Asian god, or that it was a sacrificial implement which in time had acquired a holiness of its own; but the only thing certain is that it did have a religious meaning and, like the horns, commonly marks a sacred place or object.[11]

Both from Crete and from the mainland comes evidence of aniconic worship, the visible objects of it being often either sacred trees or pillars which may plausibly be explained as conventionalizations of tree-trunks, though they may also be a particular form of sacred stones, a common object of cult in Greece and elsewhere.[12] Naturally, no specimens of actual trees survive, but apart from other evidence we know from Theophrastus [13] that in his time there was a plane tree near Gortyn which, unlike others in the neighbourhood, never shed its leaves, and that under it Zeus was fabled to have lain with Europa. Theocritus again knows of another plane near Sparta which was venerated as Helen's tree.[14] Both these are instances of a tree either actually worshipped or at any rate treated with deep respect, and connected with one whom we have good reason to suppose a pre-Hellenic goddess. That these planes were in early times the actual centres of cults is likely when considered in connection with the other evidence given below. Perhaps the best example of what seems to be a venerated pillar is the relief over the famous Lion Gate at Mycenae (Pl. 25, a), which shows a free-standing column flanked by figures of lions whose forepaws rest on its base while their heads, now lost, seem to have been turned towards the spectator, whether in vigilant guard or because the column was too holy for them to gaze at.[15] There is abundant evidence from art of reverence paid to similar columns, having no architectural function because they support nothing, and it goes to show that in this respect Crete and the mainland did not differ. What sort of divinities were supposed to inhabit or haunt these columns we do not know.

In dealing with cult scenes on signets and other works of art, it is, of course, necessary to interpret the artists' symbolism. As we have as yet no Minoan literature available, this cannot be done with certainty and a large margin of error is quite inevitable. For example, a ring found at Mycenae [16] shows a seated woman holding what looks like a disk (mirror ?) with a handle. Before her stands another woman in an attitude which is reasonably interpreted as one of adoration, since it is much the same as that of figures elsewhere which are shown approaching sacred objects (pillars, double axes, etc.). Neither figure at all suggests a statue; the seated woman therefore seems to be a visible goddess. Shall we say that she is a priestess personating or possessed by the deity, or that the artist would indicate that the goddess is really present, though the eye of flesh may see only the little shrine which stands behind

FIG. 37. Minoan gold ring (Athens, National Museum)

her ? Neither supposition is impossible nor without parallels from the cults and sacred art of other peoples; the latter is perhaps the more generally adopted. Another and very interesting series of seal-engravings deals with sacred trees, or at all events trees possessed of some mysterious power in Minoan and also, it would seem, in Mycenaean belief.[17] The general design is much the same in all, though details differ quite widely. One or more persons are shown in attitudes which can hardly be anything but poses in a vigorous and perhaps ecstatic dance. They grasp at trees or other large plants and seem to be tearing or plucking their leaves,

FIG. 38. Minoan gold ring (Iraklion Museum)

branches, or fruit (Fig. 37). On other representations [18] the figures stand or move quietly, and the attitude of their hands is not one of plucking; they seem rather to be tending the plants, perhaps removing dead leaves or the like, or gently touching them as if to share in their good influences (Fig. 38). It has been argued by Delatte [19] that in the former kind of representations the figures are gathering the plants with due ceremonial and that the dancing is part of a ritual, parallel to, if not actually historically connected with, that known to have been used by herbalists of much later

PLATE 25

(a) Limestone relief over the Lion Gate, Mycenae

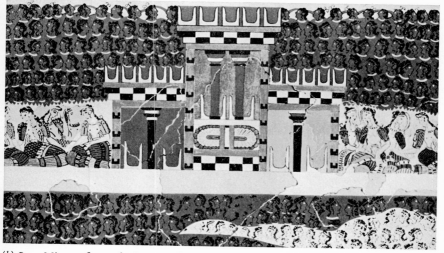

(b) Late Minoan fresco depicting a shrine. Height of building in the original about 6½ in.

PLATE 26

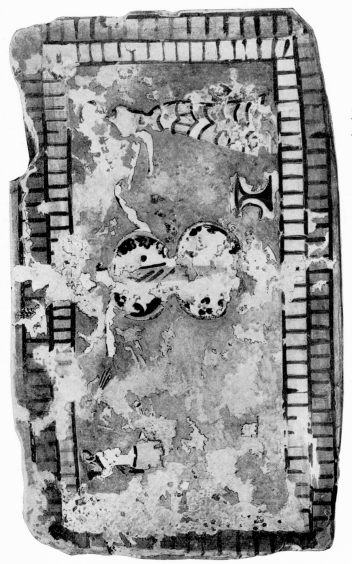

Painted limestone plaque from Tsountas's House, Mycenae.   Length $7\frac{1}{2}$ in.

times. On either interpretation, that of Delatte or the more usual one that the persons in question are worshipping the plants, we have corroboration of the existence of trees and the like which are in some way sacred, or magical.

Another piece of evidence given by art is the existence, not indeed of elaborate temples, but of little shrines and small sacred enclosures. Thus the plants in one of the scenes mentioned above have a sort of railing or low wall about them; another stands on what seems to be a little stone platform, while a worshipper approaches with uplifted hand.[20] Yet another is shown growing

FIG. 39. Gold signet ring from Mycenae

out of something like an elaborate flowerpot elevated on a pedestal (Fig. 39); adoring women approach from both sides. A fourth (Fig. 40) shows three women coming to a kind of gateway or pylon, apparently purely sacral, for it does not form part of a wall; it is crowned with the 'horns of consecration'. Two of the women are making reverential gestures, apparently to the pylon. That this derives from a well-known form of megalithic monument, the trilithon, and is in its turn somehow connected with the various sacral gateways of later date whereof the Roman *iani* are

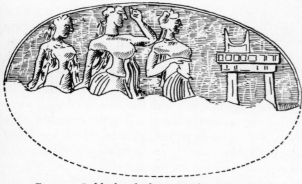

FIG. 40. Gold-plated silver ring from Mycenae

perhaps the best known, is not unlikely, but proof is as yet lacking. That small buildings which might be called temples did exist seems highly probable from such monuments as the gold-leaf model from Mycenae (Fig. 41) showing an erection divided into three rooms (*cellae* ?) marked as sacred by the 'horns of consecration' which surmount them and perhaps also by the birds (see below) which perch on two of them; the piece of gold leaf from Volo [21] representing a stone or brick building which

2 I

perhaps (for the leaf is damaged) was originally surmounted by the horns; and not least the wall painting from Knossos (Pl. 25, *b*) [22] which when complete seems to have represented a building not unlike the one from Mycenae. These shrines might well, if indeed they are the small and unpretentious affairs they seem to be, admit of being 'roofed', *i.e.*, built, by one man, if that is the meaning of A 39 (εἴ ποτέ τοι χαρίεντ' ἐπὶ νηὸν ἔρεψα); it is, of course, quite possible that Chryses there means simply that he superintended or ordered the building. They are scarcely larger than, if as large as, the temple of Athene at Troy in Z 269 ff., 297 ff. This has room inside for Theano the priestess to enter and lay a robe on the knees of the goddess, which is generally taken to imply a cult-statue of something like life-size. Our representations of temples, Knossian or other, have no indication of any kind of idol within.

FIG. 41. Gold ornament depicting a shrine or temple, from the Mycenae Shaft Graves. (Height *c.* 3 in.)

It was mentioned above that one of the temples in question had birds perching on it. This is far from being an isolated phenomenon in Minoan and Mycenaean art. Thus, an idol from Gazi in Crete [23] has two birds on its head together with 'horns of consecration'. At Knossos, a curious piece of M.M. II pottery, apparently a conventionalized representation of a shrine, is surmounted by birds.[24] Birds perch upon two little gold-leaf figures of a naked woman from Mycenae [25] (presumably a goddess), and on the double axes in the scene of libation on the famous sarcophagus from Ayia Triadha.[26] If we remember that Athene in the *Odyssey*,[27] and both she and Apollo in the *Iliad*, more than once take bird-shape, it will appear in no wise improbable that these birds are epiphanies of deities, manifesting themselves to Minoan, or Mycenaean, worshippers at their shrines or on their cult-images or other sacred objects. Another characteristic of Cretan art is the rather frequent appearance of monsters, which, however, seem to be subordinate figures, guardians for instance of a sacred pillar, heraldically balancing one another as supporters, like the lions at the gate of Mycenae.[28] There is no evidence that they were

adored as gods, though they may be supernatural beings attendant on
the greater deities. Their oriental origin is highly likely, as we know
that Minoan Crete had dealings with the Near East. If any survival of
them lingers into classical times it is to be found in occasional grotesque
but formidable figures such as the Minotaur, of
which indeed a not improbable prototype has been
found at Knossos (Fig. 42).[29]

But the most characteristic representations of
beings known or supposed to be divine are anthropomorphic. Of these, goddesses predominate, but
gods are occasionlly found. The latter are often
armed. A signet from Knossos (Fig. 43) shows a
woman worshipping before a pillar ; in the middle
of the gem, near the pillar and apparently descending through the air, is a rude representation of
what seems a naked man, holding something like
a spear in his outstretched right hand. It seems
reasonable to explain this as a god coming to visit
his emblem and the little shrine with a tree appearing over the wall which stands beyond the pillar. A
gem from Kydonia (Fig. 44) indicates a tendency
to assimilate gods to the better-known goddesses.

FIG. 42. The 'Minotaur'
seal, from Knossos

A male figure, naked except for a loincloth, stands between two mon-
strous creatures, a winged goat and a demon of some kind. He has his
hands against his chest, much in the attitude familiar from female idols,
which very commonly press their hands against their breasts. Another

FIG. 43. Gold signet ring from Knossos

god whose attitude recalls that of a goddess comes from Aegina. A gold pendant [30] shows him between two water-fowl, which he grasps by the necks. It is very reminiscent of the representations of the Lady of Wild

FIG. 44. Gem from Kydonia

Things (see below). Incidentally, it may be mentioned that some male figures are rather ambiguous, and may represent either gods or mortals. For example, one signet [31] shows a male figure stooping to help a female to climb out of a pit or hollow in the ground; it is hard to determine whether this is the emergence of an earth-goddess from her element, assisted by some attendant deity, or her epiphany to a human worshipper, or a purely human scene, perhaps mythological, although the existence of scenes from myth in Minoan art is generally, perhaps too dogmatically, denied.

Goddesses are of several types, and there is no reason whatever to assume that they are merely different or local forms of one goddess, or that their functions are closely alike. Often the divine figure is distin-

FIG. 45. Amygdaloid gem from Mycenae

guished from a human being only by the fact that she is plainly being adored by other figures; as already mentioned, it is conceivable that she is human, a priestess or other woman possessed by or temporarily incarnating (or even personating) the goddess. Such is the tall central figure on a signet now at Copenhagen,[32] who stands with outstretched arms between adoring figures; or the similar one in the centre of two signets (one at Iraklion and the other at Athens) already illustrated in Figs. 37, 38.

The only strong indication that these are really supernatural beings is that they are shown on a somewhat larger scale than the worshippers, and even this is not conclusive; Virgil's Sibyl looked bigger when her inspiration came upon her.[33] However, it may be taken as practically certain that a goddess is supposed to be present in some way. In other representations, there is no room for doubt. It is certainly not a mortal woman, even an inspired one, who is depicted on a ring from Amari in Crete,[34] sitting between two lions and stretching out a hand, apparently to caress one of them. Everything, including the attitude of the beasts and the pedestal-like throne of the goddess, suggests that she replaces, so to speak, a sacred pillar. Several representations of this goddess, or at least of goddesses in similar attitudes and with the like attendant beasts, have been found (Fig. 45), as also (see above) one or two which suggest that she had a male consort of a nature like her own (Fig. 46). We may think of her as more or less resembling Rhea-Cybele, with power over the wild and the creatures inhabiting it; hence for want of knowledge of her Minoan name, she is referred to as the Πότνια Θηρῶν, the Lady of Wild Things. Another, perhaps similar,

FIG. 46. Lentoid gem from Kydonia

FIG. 47. Seal impression from Knossos

goddess is shown on the very familiar seal-impression from Knossos (Fig. 47). A hieratically stiff figure, clad in the flounced Minoan skirt, stands, holding a spear or staff in her outstretched right hand, on what seems to be a conventional representation of a mountain. She has lions for her supporters, one on either side of the mountain, a shrine crowned with 'horns of consecration' behind her and an adoring woman in front. An extremely interesting monument is a painted tablet of limestone from Mycenae (Pl. 26), showing a goddess (not a god, for such parts of the body as can be seen are white, the regular convention for female flesh in Minoan-Mycenaean as in classical Greek art), half-hidden behind a figure-of-eight shield of Mycenaean type. Here we may very well have to do with Mycenaean and not Cretan religion. For the association of goddess and shield we may compare the relation between Hera and the 'shield of Diomedes' at the Hekatombaia or Heraia at Argos,[35] but a nearer parallel, probably arising from actual historical connection, is the armed Athene of classical times. The shielded goddess, being worshipped by some warlike Mycenaean king or baron, has herself become war-like,[36] as Athene did in her own city, where her pre-Hellenic name and the existence of Mycenaean remains on the Acropolis combine to indicate that she was the castle-goddess. But to return to Cretan cult, we find the Minoans worshipping several types of goddess and apparently more than one god; we further see that there is no sign of any god being their supreme divinity. If there was one, it was no doubt a goddess. So far, there is little or no disagreement; the further conclusion sometimes drawn that the society of those days was matrilineal is quite unfounded as far as our evidence goes. A goddess may be worshipped, even as chief deity, by a people of any sociological structure; we simply do not know how the Minoans reckoned descent.

Graves of undoubtedly Minoan date tell us comparatively little, both because of their rarity, at least in M.M. times, and owing to the scantiness of their contents.[37] Of anything like a Minoan hero-cult we lack evidence, and to judge by what we have, even the ordinary and widespread tendance of the dead with offerings of food and the like at the graves was but slight, if it existed at all.[a]

Legends and ritual which show traces of non-Hellenic influence meet us at various points both in Crete and on the mainland. Their most remarkable feature is the occurrence of a figure naturally interpreted as a kind of embodiment of the springing up, maturing, and fading of vege-tation, a dying god who is annually reborn. That this contrasts sharply with Olympian immortals need hardly be pointed out; yet traces of such a deity are clearly to be seen in the myths attached to more than one classical cult. A good example is Hyakinthos of Amyclae, whose name,

[a] This is more fully discussed in Ch. 16.

with its suffix -νθ- and its absence of a Greek root, shows him pre-Hellenic.[38] In classical times he is represented as a boy loved and accidentally killed by Apollo, but his festival has features hardly to be interpreted from hero-cult and the decorations on the throne of Apollo at Amyclae showed his entrance into heaven and represented him as bearded. The fact that at the Hyakinthia there was a tabu on cereal food suggests that he was connected with the fruits of the earth. But more than once we find a god actually represented as a baby abandoned by his mother and reared either by a supernatural being, such as a nymph, or by some beast which suckles him. The Cretan 'Zeus' is the best known but by no means the only instance, and that he was important is indicated by the Greeks' identifying him with their own chief god, although they were much puzzled by the existence of what was alleged to be his tomb.[39] He is nurtured either by the goat Amaltheia and by bees, or by nymphs who feed him with milk and honey.[40] In Greece proper, we have the baby god Sosipolis at Elis, who was said to have been brought by his unknown mother to the forefront of the Elean army on the day of battle, when he turned into a serpent and made the enemy flee in terror.[41] Direct evidence for such gods in Crete is hardly to be found in our archaeological material, however. There is indeed a Knossian seal-impression in which a naked child sits under a horned sheep, but the beast is as much like a ram as a ewe and the child certainly is not sucking but merely sitting up.[42]

It remains to consider the much-discussed 'Hymn of the Kouretes'.[43] Late though it is (about 200 B.C.), this curious document has been plausibly thought to preserve very old ritual. In it, Zeus is hailed as the 'greatest *kouros*', *i.e.*, young man, and invited to 'leap' (beget ?) for the increase of blessings ranging from full wine-jars to peace and order. Such an invocation is understandable as a rite of fertility presided over by a somewhat vague deity, perhaps a 'projection' of the performers themselves, the young men of the community. It furnishes also a far from impossible explanation of the common myth that the Kouretes danced in armour about the infant Zeus to drawn his cries. It is, however, by no means certain that the origin of the hymn and the rite is prehistoric; direct evidence is lacking.

Passing now to Mycenaean religion, we have in addition to the sources listed above for Minoan cult the recent decipherment by Ventris and Chadwick and their associates of the Linear B tablets. If we take the interpretations offered as approximately right, these documents furnish most welcome information, although far from a complete picture of Mycenaean affairs, religious or other, since the tablets are not very numerous, represent but a few sites, and mostly are very brief in contents, mere lists of land-holders and enumerations of contributions of one kind

or another, men liable for service in various capacities or employed about
the palace, and so forth.　In fact they are very summary archives.　They
do, however, tell us not a little concerning gods and goddesses and throw
some light on their worship.　This would seem to have been quite highly
organized.　We hear, as might be expected, of priests and priestesses
(*e.g.*, PY Eo 247, Eo 224),[a] also of a person or persons, probably always
feminine, described as *ka-ra-wi-po-ro*, interpreted as κλαϜιφόρος, in other
words either a priestess who had charge of a temple or other holy place
(the κλαϜιφόρος is associated with a priestess on PY Eb 317) or something
like a Roman *aedituus*.　But we also find that sundry deities owned not
inconsiderable propety.　Thus on PY Tn 316 [44] we have a list of gold
objects presented to deities, and also men and women.　Concerning these
we may suppose that they become slaves of their divine owners, for the
expression 'slave' (male or female) 'of the god' or of some named deity
is fairly common, and it would appear that through these slaves land
could be owned by the god or goddess; *e.g.*, in PY Es 650. 5 we read
a-te-mi-to do-e-ro e-ke to-so-de, i.e., Ἀρτέμιτος δοῦλος ἔχει τοσόνδε,
'Artemis's slave has the following amount', and then comes a statement
of what seems to be the allowance of seed-corn issued to him.　It is
parallel to line 1 of the same tablet, in which a man's slave is in a like
position.　Some deities again had in their service skilled work-people,
whether free or slaves; PY Un 249 for instance presents us with a certain
Philaios, who was *po-ti-[ni]-ja-we-jo a-re-pa-zo-[o]*, interpreted as
'unguent-boiler to the Mistress'.

　　The deities include a number of goddesses, not all known as such in
classical times.　The 'Mistress' may be Athene (*a-ta-na po-ti-ni-ja*, KN
V 52), though it would be hasty to assume that she is always so.　Artemis
we have already met with; *e-ra* occurs several times and seems to be
Hera; *e-re-u-ti-ja* seems to be Eleuthia (Eileithyia).　We also find in the
difficult text PY Tn 316 someone called, apparently, *pe-re-(i)-ja*, which
if it is identical with πέλεια would seem to make her a dove-goddess;
another styled *ma-na-sa* (?) *po-si-da-e-ja*, an otherwise unknown consort
or cult-partner of Poseidon, it would appear; and a third, *i-pe-me-de-ja*,
who can hardly be anyone but Iphimedeia, familiar in myth as the mother
of Otos and Ephialtes (*cf.* λ 305).　*Di-u-ja*, on the same tablet, pretty
certainly derives her name from that of Zeus and to this extent is parallel
to Dione.　KN Fp 1 mentions an offering to *e-ri-nu*, which suggests the
name Erinys, and Mr. Chadwick informs me that in a tablet published
by Blegen (*AJA*, lx, pl. 46, fig. 18) he reads *ma-te-re te-i-ja*, i.e., ματρὶ
θείᾳ.　This, if it indeed means 'to the Mother of the Gods', is astonishing
for so early a monument, but I incline to interpret it as 'to Mother
Theia', again indicating actual cult of one whom we know from Hesiod

　　　　　　　　　[a] For the system of reference to tablets see p. xxix.

(*Theog.* 135, 371) and Pindar (*Isth.* v. 1) as a mythological person, one of the Titans.

Gods become relatively numerous and important in these records, which give us a large proportion of the familiar classical pantheon. Zeus is several times mentioned and we hear of his priest at Pylos (PY Tn 316, *di-ri-mi-jo di-wo i-je-⟨re ?⟩-we*, which would be in Latin *Drimio Diali flamini*). Poseidon is a leading figure in Pylian worship, as might be expected. Enyalios occurs on KN V 52. Apollo has yet to be found, for we must not assume that he is identical with Paieon (*pa-ja-wo-[ne ?]*, KN V 52), seeing that the two are separate in Homer (E 401, 899, 900). Ares is perhaps present by implication, for an otherwise unknown man on PY An 656. 6 is described as *a-re-i-jo*, apparently Ἀρήιος, whether that means that he claimed descent from the god or simply that he was war-like. Another very doubtful identification is that of Hephaestus, for the name *a-pa-i-ti-jo*, which might be Hephaestion or Hephaistius, is slender evidence when we remember the history of the god. Very surprising for chronological reasons is the fragment from Pylos, Xa 06, which reads clearly *di-wo-nu-so-jo*, hardly to be rendered otherwise than by Διωνύσοιο.

Little less unexpected are the traces of a calendar. KN Fp 1 speaks of a month Deukios in which certain offerings are made to some of the deities mentioned above and a 'priestess of the winds', *a-ne-mo i-je-re-ja*, is spoken of. KN V 280 reads almost like an early forerunner of the Roman calendars, for in it several days have the entry *o-u-ki te-mi*, naturally interpreted as οὐκὶ θέμις, in other words N (*nefastus*).

Thus we have evidence, scrappy but suggestive and highly interesting, of two pre-Homeric strata of religion [a] : the Minoan, carried by a people not of Indo-European speech or antecedents, and the Mycenaean or Achaean, belonging to the Greek-speaking invaders. Neither is identical with the Homeric picture, but both, especially the latter, have influenced it and the subsequent Greek cults alike. That very numerous problems remains to be solved is self-evident, but we may perhaps claim with some confidence that we now possess the main outlines of the religious history of pre-classical times in the Greek world.

NOTES TO CHAPTER 15

The most important work is M. P. Nilsson, *The Minoan-Mycenaean Religion and its Survival in Greek Religion*, second edition, Lund, 1950 (*M.M.R.*). Others are cited in the notes.

1. *BSA*, vi. 94 ff.; *M.M.R.* 62.
2. *M.M.R.* 64.
3. *M.M.R.* 65-7.

    [a] On their syncretism *cf.* Ch. 14 (ii) p. 461.

4. *M.M.R.* 69 f.

5. *M.M.R.* 78 ff.; *P. of M.* ii. 332 ff.

6. *P. of M.* i. 500 ff. and frontispiece; *M.M.R.* 83 ff.

7. *M.M.R.* 86.

8. The dedication of clothes to Iphigenia at Brauron (Eur. *I.T.* 1464 ff.) is hardly parallel, for those were the clothing of women dead in childbirth.

9. *M.M.R.* chap. v.

10. For a fine representation in the round of such a bull's head see *P. of M.* ii. 527 ff. fig. 330.

11. *M.M.R.* chap. vi, where other explanations are mentioned. It is remarkable that it is often shown in art carried by women, probably priestesses or worshippers, and that the deity worshipped is regularly female, though divinities of thunder are regularly male.

12. For abundant examples of Greek aniconic cult see M. V. de Visser, *Die nicht menschengestaltigen Götter der Griechen*, Leiden, Brill, 1903, 1 ff., 55 ff.

13. *Hist. plant.* i. 9. 5, *cf.* ii. 3. 3.

14. Theocr. xviii. 43 ff., where see Gow's commentary.

15. Often reproduced, see for instance (Sir) A. J. Evans, *Mycenaean Tree and Pillar Cult* (London, Macmillan, 1901 = *JHS*, xxi. 99 ff.), 59 (157), fig. 35. This monograph is still valuable for the whole subject, though it should now be supplemented by *M.M.R.* chaps. vii, viii, which summarize much information not available in 1901.

16. Evans, *op. cit.* 92 (190), fig. 64.

17. Examples in *M.M.R.* 266 ff., and discussion in the text, *ibid.*

18. For instance, Evans, *op. cit.* 84 (182), figs. 55, 56.

19. A. Delatte, *Herbarius*, ed. 2 (Paris, Droz, and Liège, Faculté de Philosophie et Lettres, 1938), 7 ff. with figs. 2-13, *q.v.* for additional examples to those mentioned in n. 17. He further (p. 13) suggests a connection with Asia, which in itself is not unlikely, but many details of his interpretation are still uncertain.

20. Evans, *op. cit.* 87 (185), fig. 59.

21. *M.M.R.* 174, fig. 79, from *AE*, 1906, pl. xiv.

22. *M.M.R.* 175, fig. 80. It is unfortunate that none of these representations gives any clear indication of scale, such as human figures standing outside the building might furnish. The Knossos fresco does indeed show the heads of a crowd projecting above the temple, but it is not clear whether they are supposed to be standing or sitting. The general impression conveyed is that these are quite small buildings.

23. *M.M.R.* 100, fig. 24, with n. 61 for earlier publications.

24. *M.M.R.* 87, fig. 17.

25. *M.M.R.* 333, figs. 154 A, B, from Schliemann, *Mykenae*, p. 200, figs. 267, 268.

26. *M.M.R.* 330; R. Paribeni in *MA*, xix. 5-86, with illustrations, whence A. B. Cook, *Zeus*, ii. 516 ff. and pl. xxviii. That the scene is rather a Cretan artist's representation of Achaean ritual than anything purely Minoan seems to have grown more and more probable since it was mooted by M. P. Nilsson in Κρητικὰ Χρονικά, iii. 14.

27. γ 371 f., χ 240, α 320; H 58 f., E 778, and ε 51 are less certain. *Cf. M.M.R.* 491 ff.

28. *M.M.R.* 368 ff.

29. *Cf. P. of M.* ii. 763, fig. 491, where a cynocephalus is suggested.

30. *M.M.R.* 367, fig. 177, from Marshall, *Cat. of Jewellery in Br. Mus.* 54, pl. vii, 762.

31. Evans, *P. of M.* iii. 458, fig. 319; Delatte, *op. cit.* 12, fig. 13.

32. *M.M.R.* 280, fig. 140. This seems to be the only certain example of male worshippers, though, for instance, the so-called 'armed god and seated goddess' on the Mycenaean signet (Evans, *Tree and Pillar Cult*, 77 (175), fig. 51) might be taken to be a human warrior receiving advice from a female deity — a pre-Homeric Tydeus or Diomede with a precursor of Athene, perhaps.

33. Virg. *Aen.* vi. 49 ff., *maiorque videri | nec mortale sonans, adflata est numine quando | iam propiore dei.*

34. Evans in *JHS,* xiv. 66, fig. 56.

35. I. R. Arnold in *AJA,* xli. 436 ff.

36. M. P. Nilsson, *Die Anfänge d. Göttin Athene,* in *Kgl. Danske Videnskabernes Selskab, Hist.-Phil. Medd.* iv. 7 (Copenhagen, 1921) ; *M.M.R.* 344 f., 490 ff.

37. *M.M.R.* 299.

38. The *loci classici* are Pausanias iii. 19. 3 ; Athen. 139 d ff. *Cf. M.M.R.* 556 ff.; M. J. Mellink, *Hyakinthos* (Utrecht, 1943).

39. *M.M.R.* 553 ; see the whole chapter.

40. *E.g.,* Callim. *Hymn.* i. 46 ff.

41. Pausanias vi. 20. 2 ff.

42. Evans, *Tree and Pillar Cult,* 31, fig. 17 ; *P. of M.* i. 515, fig. 373.

43. Found at Palaikastro in 1904, see *BSA,* xv. 339 ff., whence Diehl, *Anthol. Lyrica,* ii. 279 ; Powell, *Collectanea Alexandrina,* 160 ; discussed in J. E. Harrison, *Themis,* ed. 2, chap. i ; *M.M.R.* 546 ff.

44. The author makes no pretence of expertise here. His knowledge is entirely second-hand, derived partly from M. G. F. Ventris and J. Chadwick's *Documents in Mycenaean Greek,* partly from sundry articles on the subject, especially A. Furumark in *Eranos,* lii. 18-60 ; L. R. Palmer, *ibid.* liii. 1 ff. ; and, of course, the fundamental general accounts given by Ventris and Chadwick in *JHS,* lxxiii. 84-103 and Sterling Dow in *AJA,* lviii. 77-129.

[Now see also the article by W. K. C. Guthrie, *Bulletin of the Institute of Classical Studies* (London), 6 (1959), 35 f.]

CHAPTER 16

BURIAL CUSTOMS

by George G. E. Mylonas

SINCE the days of Schliemann, scholars have been pointing out that the burial customs described in the *Iliad* and in the *Odyssey* contain elements which are in disagreement with the evidence obtained from the excavation of Mycenaean sites. More recent excavations, especially those at Mycenae, Prosymna, and Troy, have reduced the margin of disagreement to such an extent that a new study of the evidence, both literary and archaeological, promises to lead to a satisfactory reconciliation of the differences and to the conclusion that the Mycenaean customs provided the tradition from which the epic descriptions were drawn.

The *Iliad* and the *Odyssey* contain but few accounts of burials, but they are sufficient to furnish a clear picture of the customs, beliefs, and patterns of behaviour in Homeric times. We have the group burial of the Greeks and Trojans (H 331 ff. and 424 ff.); the burial of Eetion (Z 416 ff.); of Sarpedon (Π 678 ff.); of Patroclus (Σ 315 ff., Ψ 6 ff. and 128 ff.); of Hector (Ω 580 ff., 707 ff.); of Achilles (ω 43 ff.); of Phrontis (γ 284-5); of Elpenor (λ 51 ff., μ 11 ff.). In addition we find scattered in the poems a few references to the death of Agamemnon, Aegisthus, Antilochus, Ajax, and the suitors of Penelope. The description of the burial of Patroclus is the most complete and on it are based the statements usually made regarding the Homeric burial custom.

It seems clear that the loss of a dear one caused an outburst of grief and lamentation accompanied by tearing of the hair, strewing of 'dark dust' over head and face, and even lying and rolling in the dirt (Σ 22 ff.; X 405 ff.; Ω 161 ff.). The actual funeral rites, however, began with the washing and anointing of the body (Π 669; Σ 350; Ω 582), the closing of the eyes and the mouth (λ 425-6; ω 296), considered as the γέρας θανόν-των, the clothing of the corpse, the πρόθεσις or lying-in-state on the bier, and the formal lamentation (Π 670 and 680; Σ 315 ff.; Ω 719 ff.). In the funeral of Patroclus these acts were followed by a feast and processions of the Myrmidons in military array around the body of their comrade (Ψ 6 ff.). In the case of Hector the lamentations and *prothesis* lasted nine days and nights (Ω 784); in that of Achilles seventeen days and nights (ω 63-4).

This long *prothesis* of the corpses of the main heroes of the *Iliad* would seem to indicate that some form of elementary embalming was practised occasionally. The actions of Thetis, Apollo, and Aphrodite, who treated the corpses of their favourite heroes — Achilles, Sarpedon, and Hector — with ambrosia and ἀμβρόσιον ἔλαιον and thus kept their bodies ἔμπεδα until burial, seem to reflect that practice. The comrades of Patroclus filled his wounds with ἀλείφατος ἐννεώροιο and thus protected it against an early disintegration (Σ 351).[1] But complete embalming seems to be unknown to the Homeric heroes. The verb ταρχύω, used three times in the *Iliad* (Π 456, 674; H 85), which might be taken to imply such a custom, is proved to have been used in the sense of 'giving proper burial'.

The feast was an essential part of the burial rites. The feast in honour of Patroclus was held before the cremation ceremonies; that of Hector after (Ψ 29; Ω 801 ff.). Whether or not the holding of the feast before the funeral was normal or was imposed by the description of the games which followed the burial of Patroclus cannot be determined; the fact, however, remains that the burial feast was a required rite, for even Orestes gave a funeral feast for his mother and Aegisthus after their death (γ 309-10).

The burning of the body formed the central rite of the burial. Patroclus's body was placed on the pyre decked with the locks of his comrades and was covered with the fat of animals; around his bier were placed the carcasses of those animals, two-handled jars filled with oil and honey and the newly-slain bodies of four horses and of two of the nine dogs raised by Patroclus. This was followed by the slaying of twelve Trojan captives (Ψ 128-77). Hector's body, still dressed in the φάρεα left by Achilles, was placed on the pyre (Ω 785-7) and Achilles's body was burned 'in the raiment of the Gods and in abundance of unguents and sweet honey' (ω 67-8). Even though Elpenor was a humble warrior his body, dressed in his armour, was burned amid lamentations (μ 12-15). In a similar fashion Eetion was burned bearing his armour (Z 418-19).

The significance of the objects, animals, and men burned along with the bodies has to be considered next. It has been pointed out that in the case of Eetion and of Elpenor the armour was burned with the bodies, while both Hector and Patroclus were placed on the pyre without their armour. The simplest explanation of this is to be found in the fact that both Patroculus and Hector had lost their armour in battle. The poet explains that Achilles burned the corpse of Eetion dressed in armour because he σεβάσσατο τό γε θυμῷ; it was an act of pity of a magnanimous chieftain towards an adversary who had lost everything in honourable combat and who had seen his seven sons slain on the self-same day. It seems, therefore, reasonable to conclude that in normal cases the armour of a warrior was burned with his body.

It is customary to see a sacrificial act in the burning of the animals on the pyre of Patroclus.[2] This I believe not to be true. Some of the animals placed on the pyre were slain to provide the fat with which the body was covered and which was intended to speed its cremation; that seems to have been the purpose of their immolation and not an act of sacrifice. The horses and dogs formed part of the belongings of the dead and, like any other of his possessions, were placed on the pyre to give pleasure and comfort to the departed in his passage to Hades. If the sacrifice of animals was part of the burial ritual we should expect to find the rite performed at least in the burial of the warriors who had fallen on the Trojan plain and who were given burial under a truce. The honey and oil, contained in the two-handled jars, were also intended to give comfort to the departed in his long journey, and I believe that they were placed there as a result of a custom which postulated a long journey to the nether world, a journey for which supplies were necessary; a custom which must go back to the rite of inhumation.

The immolation of the twelve Trojan youths, often taken to be a remnant of a barbaric ritual that had become obsolete and that demanded human sacrifices over the grave of a hero, is explained by the poet as ποινὴν Πατρόκλοιο Μενοιτιάδοιο θανόντος (Φ 28; cf. Σ 91-3, 336-7, etc.). Thus it should be placed in the same category as the killing of an enemy in revenge for a friend lost. To avenge the death of a friend or kinsman by killing his slayer or an opponent of equal or even of lower rank was a common Homeric practice (P 34-5, 538-9; Ξ 470, and especially 482-5).[3] Achilles considered himself responsible for the death of his friend; he therefore tried to atone for his error and at the same time to avenge the death of his friend by inflicting the greatest possible punishment on the Trojans (cf. Σ 98-9, 329-42; T 321 ff.). Deiphobus's statement that he killed Hypsenor, son of Hippasos, first to avenge the death of Asios and then to provide to his friend a πομπόν — 'one to escort him on his way' (N 414 ff.), seems to explain both the killing of the Trojans and the true meaning of the gifts placed on the pyre; these were to provide for the journey to the House of Hades. The calling of the name of the departed and the pouring of libations while the corpse was being burned seem to be another rite illustrated by Achilles (Ψ 217-21). Both were stopped as soon as the body was consumed by the fire. Then the end of the cremation rites was reached; the smouldering fire was extinguished with wine and the bones were collected and placed in an urn. Over the pyre an earthern τύμβος was erected and a stele was placed — the γέρας θανόντων (H 86-91, 336; Π 457; Ψ 245; δ 584; λ 74 ff.; μ 13; etc.). The τύμβος had no relation to the state of the psyche in the lower world and its only purpose was to attract the attention of the generations of men yet to be born (ἐσσομένοισι πυθέσθαι) and thus to keep alive the memory and especially the κλέος of the departed (H 87-91). Games held in honour of the dead completed the burial ceremonies (Ψ 257 ff. ; see also Ψ 630-1). By then the *psyche* — whatever we may wish to understand by that term — had descended Ἄϊδος εἴσω, there to stay without clear self-consciousness, like an εἴδωλον, neither feeling nor desiring anything. All its associations with the world of the living had ended. For it is reasonable to suggest that the Greeks of the epics believed that at death the *psyche*, abandoning the body, proceeded towards the House of Hades, but could not mingle with the other denizens of Erebus ; that it was kept away from the realm of shadows until the corpse was given proper burial (Ψ 69 ff.) ; that the *psyche* remained sentient as long as the body remained unburied. τὰς τῶν ἀτάφων ψυχάς, remarks Aristonicus (on Ψ 104), Ὅμηρος ἔτι σωζούσας τὴν φρόνησιν ὑποτίθεται. Once the body was properly buried, and in the poems once the body was destroyed by fire, the *psyche* was no longer tied to the world of the living.

In contrast to the anxiety expressed for the cremation of the body is the apparent indifference to the fate of the bones of those who perished far from their native land. These could be left in hostile soil, and consequently at the mercy of surviving foes, or anywhere on the way, and no one seems to have wished his bones to be returned to his native land. It is true that Nestor in the *Iliad* (H 334 ff.) advises Agamemnon to burn the dead a 'little way from the ships that each man may bear their bones home to their children, whenso we return again to our native land'. But long ago Aristarchus had rejected the lines, ὅτι οὐ διὰ τοῦτο ἐκαίοντο, ὅπως τὰ ὀστᾶ κομίσωνται, ἀλλὰ συνηθείᾳ, and these lines certainly are in opposition to the general practice as illustrated by the poems. For in the *Iliad* and the *Odyssey* we find no effort on the part of the living to take the cremated remains of their friends and relations home. Thus the ashes and bones of Patroclus, Achilles, Antilochus, and Ajax and of the warrirors of *Iliad* H were left in foreign, hostile soil. We may also recall that when Achilles boasted that he would load his ships with the booty he had accumulated and with all his belongings, he did not even mention the bones of comrades fallen in battle (I 356 ff.). It seems clear that the destruction of the flesh and the sinews formed the important part of the burial ; that the sinews and flesh were believed to tie the *psyche* to the world of the living and to prevent its admission to the circle of the phantoms ; that the bones had no significance after they were deprived of the flesh and sinews which covered them.

It is generally agreed, and it has become apparent from our discussion, that cremation was the sole method of burial employed by the Homeric people. The bodies of Patroclus, of Hector, of Achilles, of Eetion, of Elpenor, and of the warriors in the seventh book of the *Iliad* were so

disposed of.   References to cremation are numerous throughout and even
the bodies of the warriors who perished by the darts of Apollo were
cremated : αἰὲν δὲ πυραὶ νεκύων καίοντο θαμειαί (Α 52).   It is not clear
what kind of burial was given to Phrontis, the pilot of Menelaus (γ 284-5),
and the friends of Penelope's suitors merely carried the bodies from the
halls of Odysseus and θάπτον ἕκαστοι (ω 417).   The verb θάπτειν used in
that instance would perhaps give the impression of inhumation ; but in

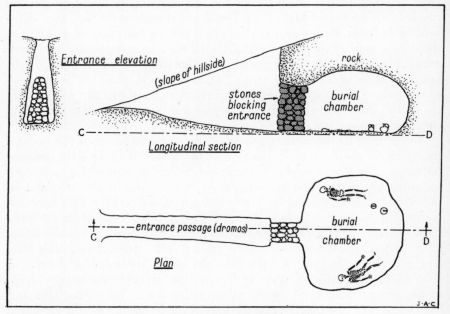

FIG. 48. Mycenaean chamber-tomb

the *Iliad* and the *Odyssey* it was used to indicate cremation : θάπτε με
ὅττι τάχιστα, pleads Patroclus, and his corpse is burned as he wished
(Ψ 71).   Elpenor begs not to be left ἄθαπτον, ἀλλά με κακκῆαι (λ 72-6)
and Odysseus θάπτει him, which is further explained ἐπεὶ νεκρός τ' ἐκάη
(μ 13).   Yet we have a few references to 'bones rotting in the rain'
(α 161 ; cf. μ 45).   These references, however, could be explained by the
assumption that the bodies of the heroes involved, through inability to
perform the proper rites, were left unburied on hostile soil, like those
of Odysseus's comrades in the land of the Kikones.   It is reasonable therefore to conclude that cremation was the only mode of burial described or
mentioned in the *Iliad* and the *Odyssey*.

     If from the epics we turn to the actual remains of prehistoric Greece
we shall find, I believe, that the evidence of the poems agrees more fully
with that provided by the late Mycenaean period.[4]   The remains teach

us that inhumation was the only mode of burial in that period. The dead were placed in family graves; those in chamber-tombs (Fig. 48) were usually placed on the floor, more seldom on a platform or bench built or cut out of the rock. Around them gifts were laid; among them predominate drinking cups, vessels meant to contain liquids, and storage jars apparently filled with supplies. In some graves at Prosymna, for example, jars were found still covered with tightly-fitting lids; and in Tomb 530 at Mycenae two *alabastra* were full of a greasy earth which on

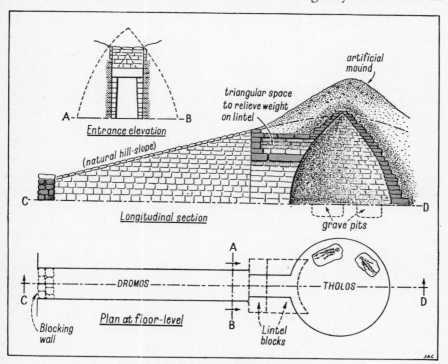

FIG. 49. Mycenaean beehive-tomb

analysis showed definite traces of oil. Weapons and occasionally the tools of the deceased were also placed with him. After every burial the door of the grave was walled up and its *dromos* was filled in. The filling in of the *dromos* necessitated the placing of markers over the graves for identification purposes. Sometimes these were regular *stelai*, more commonly they seem to have been boulders. The *stelai* over the Shaft Graves at Mycenae are well known; and more were discovered in 1952 in the new Grave Circle there (Pls. 9, *b*, 33). Examples at Eleusis and Mycenae (*cf.* Pl. 29, *b*) respectively prove that the use of *stelai* persisted from late in Middle Helladic till the end of the Mycenaean period. In the case of the beehive-tombs additional earth was heaped over the *tholos* (*cf.* Fig. 49), so that from a distance they must have shown up as mounds, which in at least some cases were made more conspicuous by a low wall running round the base. Thus the practice of χεύειν χυτὴν γαῖαν over a grave was not foreign to the Mycenaeans. Around the grave a funeral feast was held, and it is possible to deduce that before blocking the door of the grave a toast in farewell to the dead or a libation in his honour, followed by the shattering of the goblet against the door of the tomb, formed part of the burial ceremonies.

The most striking characteristic, perhaps, of the burial customs of the Mycenaeans appears to be the disrespect shown to the bones of ancestors. As a rule they were swept against the walls of the graves, or piled with some of their belongings in cists cut in the floors, and occasionally bones and pottery and other belongings were thrown out into the *dromos*. This disrespect contrasts strongly with the reverence exhibited and the care shown to the bodies when they were laid in the grave and it can be explained only if we assume that the Mycenaeans, like the Homeric people, believed that the spirit of the departed was sentient and still in the world of the living as long as the flesh was in existence; that the moment the flesh was dissolved and the body was transformed into a pile of bones it no longer dwelt in the grave, that it could not reappear; that then the spirit had descended into its final abode never to return and was not interested in the actions of relatives whose lives it could no longer influence. And so the bones could be swept aside or even thrown out with impunity.

Finally we may note that the Mycenaeans were in the habit of erecting cenotaphs in honour of friends or relatives who had perished in foreign lands, as can be proved by Grave 2 at Dendra and perhaps by Tomb 528 at Mycenae. With less certainty we can assume that funeral games were customary and that the chariot scenes depicted on Mycenaean *stelai* are representations of chariot races held in honour of the deceased. Perhaps we should add that the existence of a general cult of the dead in Mycenaean times cannot be proved by the available evidence. At Menidi sacrifices were made in the *dromos* of a Mycenaean beehive-tomb from Geometric to classical times; but the practice does not extend back to the Mycenaean period itself. What happened here seems rather to be that the tomb was discovered some centuries after its construction and use, and 'identified' as the grave of a hero, who was subsequently honoured as such. In a similar way certain Helladic tombs discovered by the writer at Eleusis appear to have been identified in early classical times as the burial places of the seven heroes (less Amphiaraus) who fought against Thebes and were according to tradition buried in Attic soil. These graves were consequently surrounded by a wall and respected as a historic precinct, even down to the time of Pausanias (Pausan. i. 31. 1). Again, a cult was held over a number of graves at Prosymna (thirteen out of fifty graves explored) and perhaps in the *dromos* of the Tomb of Clytemnestra and above Tomb 520 at Mycenae. However, that practice dates from Late Geometric times and could not be considered as a survival of a practice current in the Mycenaean period. Other similar instances could be quoted; but though they illustrate the archaic and classical Greeks' interest in the heroic age and their religious veneration of the heroes, they are not evidence for any cult of the dead among the Mycenaean Greeks. Nor is there any clear evidence for it in Minoan Crete, despite the Temple Tomb at Knossos and the interpretation sometimes put on scenes painted on the famous sarcophagus from Ayia Triadha. The latter, which are unique in Minoan and Mycenaean art, show offerings being carried towards a small but richly decorated building, outside which stands a robed man in a stiff attitude; but their interpretation is obscure. Though some sort of ritual seems implied it is quite uncertain whether (as has been suggested) the stiff figure represents a dead man receiving posthumous honours. In one instance only, in the Grave Circle at Mycenae, we may possibly have a cult. That it lasted for a brief period only is indicated by the fact that the altar in the Grave Circle was covered up at the time of the levelling of the circle area and of the construction of the parapet wall. This cult, moreover, can be attributed to external, Egyptian-Minoan, influences and to the belief in the superhuman qualities of a benevolent king which were continued even after his death. In a similar manner some of the heroes of the *Iliad* and the *Odyssey* — Menelaus and the Dioscuri — were destined not to share the common lot of mortals and were assigned special places away from the House of Hades (δ 561 ff.; λ 300 ff.). Homer refers also to sacrifices offered to Erechtheus, the benevolent ruler of Athens (B 547 ff.).

The comparison of the burial customs described in the Homeric poems and those followed by the Mycenaeans will disclose the differences and similarities existing between the two. Of especial importance is that the basic conception of what happens to the spirit once death has brought life to an end seems to be essentially the same in both instances. The Homeric heroes raised a τύμβος over the area of the pyre; in a similar manner earth was poured over the *tholos* and in the *dromos* of the graves which enclosed the corpse of a relative. The *stele* was the γέρας θανόντων; it was also the common means used by the Mycenaeans to identify their graves. Personal belongings and food supplies were burned with the body of Patroclus; in a corresponding manner such were placed in the graves of the Mycenaeans. Supplies and gifts were not given to the dead after cremation in the epic story; similarly after the decay of the flesh no provisions were laid in the Mycenaean graves and even the original furnishings were scattered. In both we find libations poured in honour of the dead; in both we find cenotaphs built for those who perished away from home. It seems that in both cases a funeral feast and funeral games formed part of the ritual.

The most striking difference in the burial customs of the Mycenaeans and of the people described in the poems is that inhumation was the only mode employed by the prehistoric people in the mainland of Greece while cremation was the mode employed by the Homeric heroes. The Homeric custom cannot agree with reality because, as has often been pointed out, cremation was never universally practised in Greece but went alongside inhumation. For the Mycenaean period the only verified case of cremation is that discovered by Blegen in Tomb XLI at Prosymna. Cremations are, however, now reported from the cemetery of Porto Rafti in Attica, belonging to the closing years of the Mycenaean era. Miss Lorimer has pointed out [5] that at Athens in the Protogeometric cemetery of the Kerameikos cremation was the sole mode of burial; she has attributed the burials to Achaean refugees who were established in that city after the Dorian invasion, and has advanced the view that these cremations could have formed the Homeric background. However attractive that suggestion may be, it is difficult to reconcile with all the facts: inhumation continued to prevail at Asine, Tiryns, Mycenae, and the territory around these sites, where presumably a good many Achaeans remained even after that invasion; we cannot be sure of the complete prevalence of cremation in Attica in Protogeometric times, since we seem to have both inhumation and cremation at Eleusis; and we are unable to explain how the refugees were able to influence the native Athenians to abandon abruptly their ancestral custom of inhumation and to adopt cremation. The sudden change could be due to other causes, such as plague conditions, as in the Peloponnesian War. The rather un-impressive Protogeometric cremations certainly could not have inspired the magnificent description of Patroclus's funeral; and the cremation burials of Athens are not associated with the erection of τύμβοι and στῆλαι, which in Homer are considered as the γέρας θονόντων. It seems to us, then, that the Protogeometric burials of Athens could not have formed the source from which were drawn the Homeric descriptions.

At Halos in Achaea Phthiotis, where in the early Iron Age inhumation was practised, a number of tumuli have been excavated, one of which covered sixteen funeral pyres of the eighth century; and at Colophon tumuli were associated with cremation burial in a Geometric cemetery of perhaps similar date. But the isolation of these instances makes it at present impossible to define their relation (if any) to Homeric usage. Miss Lorimer has indeed suggested that at Halos (in Achilles's own country) there might be imitation of Homeric practice. The same might

be said for Colophon; but this would take us into the field of conjecture. It would be equally hazardous to suppose that the practice at
Colophon (not, so far as present knowledge goes, paralleled elsewhere in
Ionia) was familiar to Homer, and therefore projected by him into the
heroic scene.

We may now remark that the burials described in the poems in some
detail take place beyond the mainland of Greece, on hostile soil and during
a military campaign. Phrontis was buried in Greece, but no details of
his burial are given. The same holds true in the case of Penelope's suitors
(γ 284-5; ω 417). In the *Iliad* and the *Odyssey* we have but two references to cremation which may be taken to apply to the mainland of
Greece. In the *Odyssey* (λ 218 ff.) we find Anticleia explaining 'the
appointed way with mortals when one dies. For the sinews no longer
hold the flesh and the bones together, but the strong might of fire
destroys these, as soon as the life leaves the white bones. . . .' The
statement can be construed as indicating that cremation was the mode
of burial, but it can also be considered as a summary of the practices
described in the *Iliad*. Again, Phoenix's assertion that the Calydonian
Boar πολλοὺς δὲ πυρῆς ἐπέβησ' ἀλεγεινῆς (I 546) can be taken as a set phrase
which may or may not reflect actual conditions in Greece proper. At
best, both statements are doubtful and cannot prove definitely the existence
of the custom of cremation in the mainland during the period represented
by the poems.

There can be no doubt, however, that the Trojans of Priam and the
members of Agamemnon's expeditionary force, while in the Troad,
practised cremation. We are now in a position to assert that as far as the
Trojans are concerned the poems seem to agree with reality. For the
excavations of the University of Cincinnati, under the direction of Prof.
Blegen, have proved that the inhabitants of Troy VI practised cremation.[a]
Taking into consideration the conservatism which dominates burial
customs, we can assume with a degree of certainty that the custom was
continued to the days of Priam. We may further assume that the
Mycenaean Greeks of Agamemnon met with the custom in the Troad
and that they adopted it as the most expedient and appropriate in their
circumstances. Their beliefs about the disposition of the dead would in
no way be violated by the adoption of the foreign custom; for it brought
about in a faster way the release of the spirit obtained previously by the
gradual and rather long process of natural decay. Conservatism, the
existence of ancestral sepulchres and even the limited supply of wood
could have forced them to revert to the older custom of inhumation after
they returned home. Thus the use of cremation by the Homeric heroes
can be explained and an answer can be advanced for the question raised

[a] *Cf.* Ch. 13 (i).

by the evidence obtained in all the excavated Late Mycenaean cemeteries.

Our survey, we believe, has shown that the similarities of burial customs existing between the Mycenaean and the Homeric world are many and weighty and that the main difference, the contrast of inhumation practised in the former and of cremation held in the latter, can be reconciled in a satisfactory manner. It seems therefore reasonable to conclude that the Mycenaean and Trojan burial customs of the Late Bronze Age provided the tradition which was followed by the poet or poets of the *Iliad* and the *Odyssey*.[6]

NOTES TO CHAPTER 16

1. For the meaning of ἐννεώροιο see S. Marinatos in *Studies presented to David M. Robinson*, i. 131-2.

2. Rohde, *Psyche* (transl. Hills), 45, n. 12, maintains the sacrificial character of the 'proceedings at the *rogus* of Patroclus'. For the opposite view *cf.* von Fritze, *De libatione veterum Graecorum*, 71 ff.

3. *Cf.* S. E. Bassett, 'Achilles's Treatment of Hector's Body', *TAPA*, lxiv. 41 ff.

4. For the archaeological evidence the following excavation reports are important:

Asine: O. Frödin and A. W. Persson, *Asine, Results of the Swedish Excavation 1922-30* (1938).

Dendra: A. W. Persson, *The Royal Tombs at Dendra near Midea* (1931) and *New Tombs at Dendra* (1945).

Mycenae: C. Tsountas, Ἀνασκαφαὶ τάφων ἐν Μυκήναις, in *AE*, 1888, 119 ff.

A. J. B. Wace and others, in *BSA*, xxv. 103 ff. (for Grave Circle A) and 283 ff. (for the *tholos* tombs).

A. J. B. Wace, *Chamber Tombs at Mycenae* (1932) (= *Archaeologia*, lxxxii); and *Mycenae* (1949), esp. ch. iv.

G. E. Mylonas, *Ancient Mycenae* (1957) (for Grave Circle B).

Messenia: N. Valmin, 'Tholos Tombs and Tumuli' in *Corolla Archaeologica Principi Gustavo Adolpho dedicata* (1932), 216 ff. = *AIRRS*, ii).

Prosymna: C. W. Blegen, *Prosymna, the Helladic Settlement preceding the Argive Heraeum* (1938), esp. ch. vi.

Vapheio: C. Tsountas, Ἐρευναὶ ἐν τῇ Λακωνικῇ καὶ ὁ τάφος τοῦ Βαφειού, in *AE*, 1889, 136-7.

Troy: C. W. Blegen, *Troy*, iii.

5. H. L. Lorimer, *Homer and the Monuments* (1950), ch. iii. 1.

6. For further discussion of funeral rites, etc., see:

G. E. Mylonas, 'Homeric and Mycenaean Burial Customs', *AJA*, lii. 56 ff.

'The Figured Mycenaean *Stelai*', *AJA*, lv. 134 ff.

'The Cult of the Dead in Helladic Times', in *Studies presented to David M. Robinson*, i. 102 f.

§D: MATERIAL CULTURE

CHAPTER 17

HOUSES AND PALACES

by Alan J. B. Wace

IT is strictly speaking incorrect to speak of the Homeric *house* because Homer nowhere gives any definite information about the house of an average man. Practically the only dwelling he mentions other than the homes of kings and princes is the hut of Eumaeus, the swineherd. He is represented as living a solitary and rather primitive life, for he was a slave, among the swine he watched. We have allusions to the palace of Priam with quarters for fifty sons and fifty daughters-in-law, to say nothing of possible nurseries for grandchildren like Astyanax; the palace of Troy, however, is fanciful and romantic as Homer wished his hearers to imagine it. The palace of Alcinous again is the dwelling of an ideal monarch and is equipped with magic contrivances such as anyone of Homer's audience might have liked to possess. Circe's home is the abode of a sorceress, Polyphemus's cave is the den of a barbarous giant. There is no need to multiply instances. Homer mentions three palaces in the *Odyssey*; that of Odysseus in Ithaca, that of Nestor at Pylos, and that of Menelaus at Sparta. The allusions to the two latter are few, those to the other are many. We must remember that Odysseus's palace in any case is not the house of the average man, but that of a king or prince. It is a second-class palace, too, for Telemachus, used to the palace at Ithaca where geese waddle about the court littered with dung heaps, is amazed at the sight of Menelaus's home, a first-class palace. His reactions are those which a Trollope character might have who comes from the shabbiness of Belton Castle to the glories of Gatherum.

Homer being a poet does not, of course, describe the home of Odysseus in detail. He assumes that his audience is familiar with the appearance of a royal or princely dwelling and therefore that his allusions to this or to that feature will be understood. His hearers would naturally believe him to be referring to the kind of house they would at once imagine as fit for a hero and as one which could be inhabited. They would also naturally allow for agglutinative grandeur as in the palace of Priam, with accommodation for a family of really royal and heroic size. They would equally discount the supernatural, necessary in the house of a king like Alcinous who lived happily for ever with a devoted wife and a beautiful daughter.

The early-nineteenth-century commentators on Homer assumed that in Homeric lands the houses never had more than one storey and that the men and women occupied separate quarters in a rather oriental manner. There was no evidence to support such assumptions, which incidentally disregard Homer's mention of staircases. After Schliemann's excavation of the Mycenaean palace at Tiryns in 1884 the Homeric commentators, once they had been convinced that the ruins were not Byzantine, immediately began to interpret them in the light of their own belief of what a Homeric great house should be. They also paid no attention to the clear evidence of staircases and basements. Even modern writers like Miss Lorimer have not been able to cast off the shackles of old assumptions and have failed to take advantage of the information derived from the House of Columns at Mycenae (Fig. 50). Since then the palace at Pylos, probably Nestor's palace, has been excavated, and other private houses at Mycenae have been explored.

A passage in the *Iliad* (Z 316) referring to the house of Paris gives it a triple division : οἵ οἱ ἐποίησαν θάλαμον καὶ δῶμα καὶ αὐλήν. This seems to mean the private or domestic rooms such as bedrooms and storerooms, the reception rooms, and the court with perhaps a *propylon* or gatehouse. There is no hint in this passage that these rooms were all on one floor, and none of the other passages in the *Iliad* or *Odyssey* referring to houses or palaces gives any indication that they were on one floor only. On the contrary, in both the *Iliad* and the *Odyssey* there are many references to ascents to an upper storey or descents to basement rooms. This agrees with what we know of Mycenaean houses and palaces. The palaces of Mycenae, Tiryns, and Pylos all had more than one floor. The private houses excavated at Mycenae not only have basements, but also undoubtedly had upper storeys. In the *Iliad* (Z 288) Hecuba descends to a storeroom where clothes were kept.[1] In the *Odyssey* (β 337) Telemachus goes down to a storeroom where gold and bronze were kept, clothes in chests, oil, and *pithoi* of wine set in a row along the wall. The key of this was kept by Eurycleia, the housekeeper. Also in the *Odyssey* (o 99) Menelaus and Helen go down to a basement storeroom to pick out presents for Telemachus. Thus the evidence of the excavations of Mycenaean houses and that of Homer agree.

It is reasonable therefore to believe that Homer in referring to the houses or palaces of Odysseus, Nestor, and Menelaus had in mind buildings not unlike those which have been excavated at Tiryns, Pylos, and Mycenae. How Homer obtained this knowledge of such buildings is another question which is irrelevant to the present study. The references to the various parts of the house given in the *Odyssey* can be illustrated reasonably by the plans of the Mycenaean palaces just mentioned. Perhaps the large house on the eastern side of the citadel of Mycenae called the House of Columns illustrates the simple palace of Odysseus better than the elaborate palaces of Pylos or Tiryns. This house (see plan, Fig. 50) stood just behind the tower near the south-eastern angle of the citadel on a broad terrace partly artificial. It seems to have been the residence of some well-to-do person, a noble or high official perhaps. The entrance (A) lies on the north. The main threshold, of conglomerate, is set back between two *antae* whose corners were formed by two blocks of the same stone. From the threshold a corridor floored with cement (B) leads into a court which had on the west a row of five columns and on the east a row of three columns. On the north side of the court are two large column bases which belong to the porch (C) or αἴθουσα of the main room of the house. The porch led over a conglomerate threshold into a vestibule or πρόδομος (D). The vestibule in turn led into the main room or μέγαρον proper (E). This, unfortunately, is much ruined and none of its internal arrangements can now be determined. In its east wall there is a small doorway (F) which gave access to a corridor (G). From this corridor a small staircase (H) led to an upper storey. The doorway (F) thus apparently was a private means of communication with the *megaron* from the domestic rooms of the house approached by the staircase (H). The corridor (G) seems to have turned at right angles southwards into another corridor (K) which would have led into the arcade (L) on the east side of the court. This plan would have provided a separate exit from the domestic quarter to the court and thence to the main entrance. It would meet all the requirements of the account in the *Odyssey* (χ 126-38) which tells how Odysseus sent Eumaeus to guard a corridor by which the suitors and Melanthius might have sent word to friends outside while Odysseus was covering the main door of the *megaron*.

On the south side of the court a heavy conglomerate threshold (M) led to rooms which were above the basement and on the same level as the court. There was probably yet another storey above this, but no certainty about it is now obtainable.

From the south-west corner of the court a ramp (N), which was perhaps once covered by a flight of wooden stairs, leads to a basement. This contained five rooms at least. One of these which opened to the outside contained *pithoi* set against the walls as Homer describes (β 337 ff.). Another which opened indoors had contained a series of large stirrup-jars, one of which was inscribed (*cf.* Pl. 39, *a*). Both these storerooms had thresholds of conglomerate. The house was excavated by Tsountas in 1892, but no account of it was ever published and so practically no further details are known about its interior arrangements or equipment. It is reasonable, however, to assume that the house of Odysseus as

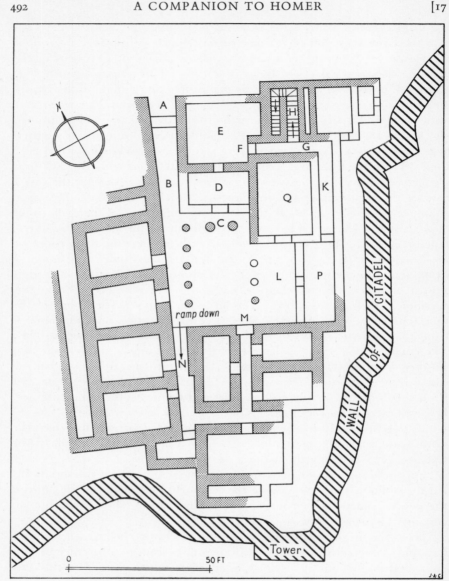

Fig. 50. Plan of the House of Columns, Mycenae

visualized by Homer resembled it in plan. We can now examine in
more detail some of the features of the Homeric great house.

Θάλαμος, *Thalamos.*—Homer, who was a poet, does not always keep
to one meaning for this word. In its simple use it seems to be applied to
a room which is private, can be kept locked, and is not open to visitors.

In this sense it is used for Penelope's room upstairs and for storerooms, both in the basement and upstairs. In a general sense it can be applied, as in the passage in the *Iliad* already quoted (Z 316), to the special domestic quarters of the house, the family part of the house as opposed to the reception rooms. It can thus be used in much the same way as the English word 'room', and mean bedroom, storeroom, and in short any kind of room. In Odysseus's house Penelope's *thalamos* (τ 53) was on the upper floor near the *megaron*. The *thalamos* where the bow was kept was apparently upstairs (φ 8) and in it lay κειμήλια of gold, copper, and iron. Telemachus transferred the arms from the *megaron* to a *thalamos* (τ 17) and also fetched arms for his father from a *thalamos* (χ 109). Melanthius goes to a *thalamos* which seems to have been upstairs (χ 142) to get arms for the suitors. It is possible that all these passages where arms are concerned relate to one room (see χ 140), probably upstairs, which was the armoury. It was apparently not the room where the bow was, because Penelope had the key of that room, while the door of the room with the arms does not seem to have been locked, since Telemachus obtained access to it without asking his mother or anyone else for the key. The basement storeroom of which Eurycleia had the key (β 337) is also called a *thalamos*. The bedroom of Penelope and Odysseus was also a *thalamos* (ψ 192). Menelaus and Helen sleep μυχῷ δόμου ὑψηλοῖο, but when Menelaus gets up in the morning he goes ἐκ θαλάμοιο. We imagine therefore that the bedroom of Helen and Menelaus was in some inner private or domestic part of the house.

Θόλος, *Tholos*.—This, which to judge by its name was a round construction of some kind, is mentioned only in the *Odyssey* (χ 442, 466) as being in the courtyard of the house of Odysseus. We have no clue to its purpose and no archaeological evidence for it up to the present. Thus in default of satisfactory evidence either literary or archaeological it remains inexplicable.

Κλῖμαξ, *Klimax*.—This as applied to a house in Homer means staircase and not ladder. Homer clearly imagines his characters as going up and down stairs (α 362, τ 602). The palaces and houses excavated at Mycenae, Tiryns, and Pylos all had staircases and upper floors. The same is true of Cretan palaces and houses. So the old idea that Homeric houses had only one floor must be abandoned. A staircase is an essential feature of a Homeric house.

Λαύρη, *Laure*.—This is mentioned only in one passage (χ 128, 137) and from the context seems to mean a passage or corridor. It led apparently from the side door (see 'Ορσοθύρη) of the *megaron*, to the court. It appears to have been narrow, because it could be defended by one man. It could thus well be applied to the corridor in the House of Columns at Mycenae which goes from the back of the eastern arcade of the court

(L, P) along (K, G) the side and back of the room (Q) to a side door (F) in the east wall of the *megaron* or hall. This passage in the House of Columns well suits the requirements of the *Odyssey*. It leaves the *megaron* by a side door and its exit into the east side of the court could easily be watched by anyone at the main entrance (C) of the *megaron*. From the side door (F) of the *megaron* access to any rooms above could easily be obtained by the staircase (H) in the side corridor (G). We need not imagine that every Homeric house had such a λαύρη, but Homer gives one to the house of Odysseus for the purposes of his tale.

Μέγαρον, *Megaron*.—The best translation of this word is probably 'hall'. In its simple usage it seems to mean a large reception room or dining hall. In this use it is applied to the great hall of Odysseus's house where the suitors congregate and feast and where their slaughter takes place (α 365; χ 127). It is in fact the centre of the palace, the principal living room analogous to the great hall of a mediaeval English manor house or the dining hall of an Oxford or Cambridge college. From this it comes to denote the whole residence or great house, a sense in which it is frequently used in the plural (Α 396, 418; ρ 569). So too the English *hall* can be used to denote the whole residence, as in the names of some manor houses or colleges, like Haddon Hall or Trinity Hall. The Mycenaean analogy to the Homeric *megaron* is complete. In each of the great Mycenaean palaces, at Mycenae, Tiryns, and Pylos, there is a great hall on one side of the court.[a] This has a porch, αἴθουσα, a vestibule, πρόδομος, and a dining Hall with a hearth in the centre, μέγαρον. A similar arrangement occurs in smaller houses as in Tsountas's House and the House of Columns at Mycenae. Homer assumes that his audience was familiar with this kind of arrangement. Visitors are given beds in the αἴθουσα (γ 399; δ 297 f.), but Odysseus even when disguised as a beggar sleeps in the vestibule, πρόδομος (υ 1). The *megaron* seems to be derived from the Middle Bronze Age house and its development is well illustrated by the Middle and Late Helladic houses excavated at Korakou and other sites (*cf*. Fig. 9).[2] There is good reason also to believe it to have been the prototype of the classical Greek temple.[3] Certainly there are correspondences of form, and temples are known at some places to have arisen on the sites of Mycenaean palaces. The so-called temple built in the *megaron* at Tiryns, however, is not a classical temple but a simple and partial reconstruction of the great *megaron* after it was first destroyed.[4]

Μεσόδμαι, *Mesodmai*.—In the two passages where this word is used it is closely connected with the walls of the house: τοῖχοι μεγάρων καλαί τε μεσόδμαι (τ 37; υ 354). Whether the word has the same meaning as the classical μεσόμναι known from Attic building inscriptions is uncertain. Aristarchus identified the *mesodmai* as spaces between the columns,

[a] For plans of the Mycenae and Pylos palaces see Figs. 28, 35. For Tiryns *cf*. Fig. 17.

but there is no reason to accept his explanation. From the use of the word in the two passages it is clearly an expansion of τοῖχοι. A possible explanation is that it refers to the timber framework which supported the crude brick superstructure of Mycenaean house walls.[5] The word could then denote either the timber framework itself and so parallel that of the classical *mesomnai*, or else the masonry interspaces between the vertical and horizontal beams of the timber framework. A possible objection to this is that when the walls were finished and covered with

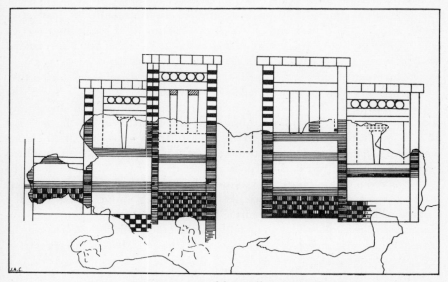

FIG. 51. Reconstruction of fresco illustrating a building.
(Width in the original *c.* 20 in.)

plaster or stucco the timber framework would be invisible. It might, however, have been picked out as in some English black and white building or in some Mycenaean frescoes to give a pattern to the walls (*cf.* Fig. 51). In any case the phrase καλαί τε μεσόδμαι seems obviously an expansion or almost a synonym of the word τοῖχοι.

Μυχός, *Mychos*.—This word seems to mean 'recess' or 'corner'. In the passages in the *Iliad* referring to the tent or hut of Achilles in the camp before Troy it seems to apply to the two inner or back corners of the main and probably only room. In these corners Achilles and Patroclus slept (I 663 ff.). In the *Odyssey* (δ 304) Helen and Menelaus sleep μυχῷ δόμου ὑψηλοῖο, but we should not imagine that the host and hostess of a house so grand that it astonished Telemachus slept in the inner corners of the dining room. Moreover, Menelaus (δ 307 ff.) next morning when he gets out of bed and dresses goes ἐκ θαλάμοιο. So we can take μυχῷ δόμου to mean 'within the house'. So Menelaus and Nestor sleep μυχῷ δόμου and Andromache weaves μυχῷ δόμου. The superlative μυχοίτατος, 'inmost' (φ 146) confirms the generic use of μυχός. We cannot press the meaning too closely and try to distinguish between μυχῷ μεγάροιο and μυχῷ δόμου and say that the first refers to the actual back corners of the hall while the latter means deep within the house. In the Homeric hymn to Hermes (l. 252) μυχοὺς μεγάλοιο δόμοιο means, as we should say, 'the depths of the great house'. So we can assume that μυχός can have a special meaning 'inner corner' or 'recess' and a generic meaning 'depths' or 'within' and for this latter sense we may compare μυχῷ "Αργεος ἱπποβότοιο. Our translation of μυχός must therefore be governed by the context. It is not a specialized word denoting a specific type of room or part of the house.

'Ορσοθύρη, Orsothyre.—This, from the passage in the Odyssey (χ 126, 132, 333) where it is mentioned, was obviously a side door from the megaron leading to the domestic portion of the great house and also giving access to a narrow corridor leading past the front door of the megaron and so to the outside world. This is clear from a passage in the Etymologicum Magnum (634. 1); 'the orsothyre is a little door through which one ascends to the upper floor or women's quarters'. The side door (F) of the megaron of the House of Columns leads into a narrow corridor (G) which gives access to the staircase (H), to the storey above, and also to the eastern colonnade (L) of the court. From this one can go past the main door of the megaron and so reach the west colonnade of the court, the entrance passage, and the front door of the house. If this interpretation is correct we have an archaeological illustration of an orsothyre which satisfies the Homeric requirements, and there is no need to look further.

Οὐδός, Oudos.—The thresholds in the house of Odysseus are described as of stone and as of wood. The wooden thresholds are of oak, δρύινοι and ash, μείλινοι. In the Mycenaean palaces at Mycenae and Tiryns and also apparently at Pylos the main thresholds are of stone. The same holds true for the House of Columns at Mycenae where some basement thresholds even are of stone. On the other hand, at Mycenae the basement thresholds in the South House, the House of the Warrior Vase, the House of the Oil Merchant, and the House of Sphinxes were of wood. In Tsountas's House some thresholds on the upper floor were of stone and some, in the basement, of wood. This evidence suggests that in first-class positions the thresholds were of stone and that in second-class positions (as in basements) the thresholds were of wood. Thus we need not lay unnecessary emphasis on the stone and wooden thresholds in the house of Odysseus, which was a second-class palace. In such a 'palace' we should expect the important doors to have stone thresholds (as in the megaron, υ 258) and the less important doors to have wooden thresholds

(ϕ 43), though the position of the wooden threshold in ρ 339 is not clear. It was presumably not at an important doorway or a beggar would not be permitted to sit there.

'Ῥῶγες, Rhoges.—This word is a *hapax legomenon* (χ 143) and has not yet been satisfactorily explained. One view was that they were narrow windows or loopholes looking into the *megaron* from a staircase leading to an upper storey. Another view was that they were openings in the *megaron* wall between the ends of the roof beams above the architrave, somewhat like open metopes, and that by scrambling up to them a man could pass through to the upper floor and so to the storeroom. Jebb long ago pointed out the absurdity of these views. How could Melanthius scramble through a narrow window or a metope opening with twelve sets of spears, shields, and helmets (χ 144) ? Homer's words ἀνέβαινε ἐς θαλάμους 'Οδυσῆος ἀνὰ ῥῶγας μεγάροιο imply that there were storerooms on the floor above the *megaron*; and Melanthius suggests (χ 141) that Odysseus and Telemachus had moved the arms from the *megaron* to a storeroom. 'Ῥῶγες, therefore, must presumably refer to some means of reaching the upper floor from the *megaron*. In the palace at Pylos there seem to have been balconies or galleries round the *megaron* supported by the four columns which surrounded the hearth. If Melanthius could reach such a balcony he would presumably have access to the rooms or *thalamoi* (bedrooms, storerooms, and so on) which were on an upper floor at the same level as the balconies. Can ῥῶγες then mean 'openings', *i.e.*, openings over the balustrades of balconies looking down to the hearth and the central part of the *megaron* ? Even so to reach the balconies a man would have to swarm up one of the columns and he would not find it easy to climb down again with a heavy load of arms, though he could, of course, have passed them over the balustrade of the balcony to the suitors below. We can only admit that there is at present no satisfactory interpretation or illustration for ῥῶγες.

NOTES TO CHAPTER 17

1. Leaf *ad loc.* says Hecuba comes down from an upper floor 'to the θάλαμος or treasure chamber on the ground floor at the back of the house', but gives no authority except the plan in E. Buchholz, *Die homerische Realien*, which is based on assumptions.

2. C. W. Blegen, *Korakou*, 76 f. ; H. Goldman, *Excavations at Eutresis*, 33 f.

3. H. Payne, *Perachora*, i. 38 ff.

4. Blegen, *Korakou*, 130.

5. Wace, *Mycenae*, pls. 24 *a*, 108 *b*.

[For other recent discussions of the Homeric house see :
D. H. F. Gray, 'Houses in the *Odyssey*', in *CQ*, xlviii (1955), 1 ff.
L. R. Palmer, 'The Homeric and the Indo-European House', in *Transactions of the Philological Society*, 1948, 92 ff.]

CHAPTER 18

DRESS

by H. P. and A. J. B. Wace

HOMERIC dress is not so simple a subject as might be expected. There are several inherent difficulties which have no easy solution. Much has been written on Homeric dress,[1] about it and around it, but there is little true agreement among the commentators, who show a great tendency to stray away from the real point, and a considerable lack of common sense.

Homer nowhere describes in detail the dress of men or women. He assumes that his hearers thought of his characters as clothed, but he is not dress-conscious. We do not know whether he considered his characters as wearing the dress of the 'heroic' period or what we should call 'contemporary costume'. In any case without knowing the date of the composition of the *Iliad* and *Odyssey* we do not know what 'contemporary costume' would be. Since so much of the Mycenaean culture has been preserved in Homer we might expect the elaborate dress of Mycenaean women to appear in the *Iliad* or *Odyssey*. On the contrary no women's dress in the Homeric poems seems as yet to have any suggestion of Mycenaean dress as far as we can tell. The words φᾶρος, πέπλος, χιτών, χλαῖνα, are used to describe garments, but we do not know what the garments were like or whether they had any relationship to classical Greek garments with the same names. We know, if we consider for a moment the history of English dress, that words like 'skirt', 'hose', 'waist-coat', imply very different garments at different periods. The man's hose of 1600 were quite unlike those of 1900. A woman's skirt of 1700 was a very different garment from a skirt of 1925. Was a garment to which the name πέπλος was applied always the same in shape and appearance? Finally we must remember that ancient materials had a narrow loom width. The one large piece of classical linen that has survived is about 0·50 m. wide, which is the average loom width of home-woven, hand-woven materials made in Greek villages to-day. The average loom width of English linen of about 1600 was nineteen inches, not far off half a metre. No silks, linens, woollens, and cottons exceeded that width before the introduction of the power loom. Consequently we must think of ancient Greek garments, Homeric or classical, Mycenaean or post-Mycenaean, as composed of material basically narrow with all that that

PLATE 27

(b) Ivory plaque from Delos.   Height c. 5 in.

(a) Ivory group of two ladies and a child ; L.H. II (?).   Height c. 2¾ in.

PLATE 28

Hector and Menelaus, fighting over the body of Euphorbos. Illustration of *Iliad* xvii, on an early-sixth-century plate, probably Rhodian. Diameter *c.* 15 in.

PLATE 29

(*a*) Late Mycenaean warriors ; from the L.H. IIIc Warrior Vase (from Mycenae).
Height of figures *c.* 7 in.

(*b*) The Warrior *Stele*, from Mycenae. (Painted on a plaster-coated limestone *stele*.)
Height of portion illustrated *c.* 27 in.

PLATE 30

Fresco from Mycenae showing warriors and horses. (Figures about 6 in. high in the original)

involves.   Even with a simple, straight garment a sewing together of
several widths would be necessary.   Artists both ancient and modern
rarely make any conscious attempt to indicate accurately how their
subjects' costumes are made.   The sculptors of the Parthenon, Reynolds,
and Sargent are all alike in this.

There is a formula in Homer which occurs twice and sets out clearly
the distinction between men's and women's dress.   It is applied to
Odysseus and Calypso (ε 229 ff.) and to Odysseus and Circe (κ 542 ff.)
when they dress in the morning.   The former passage runs:

> αὐτίχ' ὁ μὲν χλαῖνάν τε χιτῶνά τε ἕννυτ' Ὀδυσσεύς.
> αὐτὴ δ' ἀργύφεον φᾶρος μέγα ἕννυτο νύμφη,
> λεπτὸν καὶ χαρίεν, περὶ δὲ ζώνην βάλετ' ἰξυῖ
> καλὴν χρυσείην· κεφαλῇ δ' ἐφύπερθε καλύπτρην·

The χιτών is always assumed to be an undergarment and the χλαῖνα
an outer garment.   We need not necessarily suppose that the order in
which they are mentioned is the order in which they are put in.   We
have an analogy in English writers, who are apt to say 'He put on his
coat and waistcoat'.   We know well that this phrase does not give the
order in which the garments were put on.   So the order of χλαῖνα and
χιτών has no ulterior meaning.   There are many passages in which the
two garments are mentioned as a man's dress (e.g., ο 331, 338, 368).
Nausicaa, however, gives Odysseus a χιτών and a φᾶρος to wear (ζ 214).
After the slaughter of the suitors Eurycleia (χ 487) proposes to dress
Odysseus in a χλαῖνα and χιτών, but Eurynome after she has bathed him
puts on him a φᾶρος and a χιτών (ψ 155).   Agamemnon wears a φᾶρος
(Β 43).   A φᾶρος and a χιτών were provided for Hector's body (Ω 588).[2]
Are we to assume that the use of φᾶρος in these passages is a slip of the poet
or of some copyist, or is it possible that a man could wear a φᾶρος, which
in ordinary Homeric usage is a woman's garment?   It is too much to
imagine that φᾶρος and χλαῖνα are synonymous, for a woman never
wears a χλαῖνα.

What a χλαῖνα was we do not know.   It is usually translated 'cloak'.
The word survived into classical times as the name of a garment, but again
we do not know what kind of a garment a classical χλαῖνα was.   In
Homer a χλαῖνα could be used also as a covering in bed.   For instance
Eurynome puts a χλαῖνα over Odysseus when he is sleeping in the vestibule of his house.   Helen orders χλαῖνας to be provided for Telemachus
and Peisistratus when they sleep in the vestibule of Menelaus's palace
(δ 299).   Achilles too provides χλαῖνας for Priam's bed (Ω 646).   This
does not imply, however, that a χλαῖνα also means a blanket, but simply
that a garment could be spread over a sleeping man to give extra warmth.
Even to-day travellers in cold climates or in winter may spread overcoats

2 L

or dressing gowns over themselves in bed for the sake of extra warmth in unheated inns. A χλαῖνα could be single or double and apparently when put on was fastened by a buckle or brooch (K 134), but these simple facts do not help towards its identification. Odysseus (τ 225 ff.) describing his own dress says he wore a double χλαῖνα (fastened with the gold brooch which commentators always assert is non-Mycenaean, although the subject of its decoration — a lion seizing a deer — has analogies in Mycenaean art) and a specially fine chiton. In the absence of any more definite information about a χλαῖνα we cannot tell what sort of outer garment it was and it is useless to try to identify it either in Mycenaean or in early Iron Age representations.

A χιτών is apparently the basic garment of a man, for it is the one garment which Telemachus takes off when he goes to bed (α 437). The fact, however, that there is no mention of anything being worn under the χιτών does not necessarily mean that there was no undergarment. Writers of all ages never

FIG. 52. Mycenaean man's dress, from a fresco. (Height of original c. 8 in.)

or rarely speak of their characters' underclothes. A χιτών is assumed to have been usually of linen and to have been a kind of sleeveless tunic. There is no proof of this, but if it was a tunic it may well have resembled the garment worn by men in the frescoes of Mycenae and Tiryns (Fig. 52).[3] We can imagine that χιτῶνες differed in quality and in decoration. The word χιτών is generally believed to be non-Greek in origin[4] and it seems odd that the name of the Homeric Greeks' basic garment should be a foreign word. It need not necessarily have always been of linen any more than a skirt to-day is always of one material only. There is no evidence that it was worn under the armour, but when Athene takes off

her woman's dress and puts on her father's equipment she first puts on a
χιτών and then dons the armour over it. It is hardly likely that a Homeric
hero would wear his armour without any garment between it and his
skin. It used to be supposed that any mention of a θώρηξ in Homer
was an interpolation.[a] It is true that no θώρηξ has yet been found at any
Mycenaean site, but the word and its ideogram occur in the Linear B
tablets. Thus the interpolation theory falls to the ground. The very adjective χαλκοχίτωνες too implies the wearing of some kind of body
armour. So a hero may well have worn a linen or a woollen χιτών and
over it a bronze one.

What is presumably a woman's normal dress is briefly described in
the passages already quoted about Calypso and Circe. The main garment
is called φᾶρος[5] or πέπλος (E 734; σ 292) and it apparently required
fastening, for that given to Penelope by Antinous (σ 292 f.) had twelve
buckles, clasps, or brooches.[6] It is usually assumed from the use of the
word κατέχευεν in E 734, where Athene takes off her garment, that it
was fastened on the shoulder and that Athene simply undid the shoulder
fastening (whatever it was) and let the garment fall at her feet. She must
first have removed the girdle which is not mentioned in that passage, but
which both Calypso and Circe wear. Hera (Ξ 170 ff.), when she dresses
in her best to beguile Zeus, first washes and scents herself and then does
her hair. Next she puts on — presumably not over her head — a garment
which Athene had made for her. It is not clear whether Athene was the
weaver or the dressmaker or both. At any rate the phrase τίθει δ' ἐνὶ
δαίδαλα πολλά implies that it was decorated. In such passages we must
be careful not to translate δαίδαλος and ποικίλος and their cognates as
referring to embroidery. In spite of his translators and commentators
Homer never mentions embroidery. The decoration of such a garment
(probably of linen, for adjectives applied to it include λεπτόν and χαρίεν)
would most likely be by means of inwoven panels of tapestry work [7]
(σημεῖον is the later Greek word used for them and tessera the Latin) like
those in the garments of Hellenistic and Roman date found in Egypt.
What Hera's dress was like we do not know, but it had fastenings on the
breast, κατὰ στῆθος περονᾶτο. It was thus possibly similar to the πέπλος
given by Antinous to Penelope. It was girt at the waist, for Hera like
Calypso and Circe puts on a girdle. She inserts earrings and finally
puts on a κρήδεμνον, a head-dress.[8] This word is also applied (γ 392)
to the cap which covers the top of a wine jar. Miss Lorimer mistrans-
lates it lid, but to judge by the clay caps of oil jars found at Mycenae
it was a cap of clay put over the stopper and spout and stamped with a
seal.[9] It thus corresponded to the caps of lead foil often put over the
corks and tops of wine bottles to-day. A woman's κρήδεμνον was thus

---

[a] Cf. pp. 506-10, with note at end of Ch. 19.

probably a head-dress which hung down all round the head to the neck
or even lower and which could easily be pulled in front of the face as
Penelope does when she enters the *megaron* where the suitors are (α 334).
It would have corresponded to the φακιόλι of the modern Greek country-
woman.

We thus see that the dress of women in Homer has little likeness to
the elaborate dress of Mycenaean women as shown in the frescoes (Fig. 53),

FIG. 53. Mycenaean woman's dress, from
a fresco at Thebes. (Height of original
c. 5 ft.)

FIG. 54. Mycenaean wo-
man's dress, from the
Warrior Vase. (Height
of original *c.* 8 in.)

ivories (Pl. 27, *a*), and other works of art. Almost the only Mycenaean
women whose dress might be regarded as at all resembling the Homeric
are those of the Warrior Vase (Fig. 54). Their dress is, however, so
summarily rendered that it cannot be relied on for details. It differs any-
way from the elaborate flounced skirt and open jacket worn by the
Mycenaean women of the frescoes and ivories and gold rings. The
Warrior Vase is probably later in date than the frescoes and the ivories.
Had there been a change of fashion ? We know little or nothing about
any changes in dress dictated by fashion in Greek or Roman life, although
we know that under the first centuries of the Roman Empire there were

successive changes of fashion in hair-dressing. It is usually assumed that the dress of Greek women never changed throughout classical times. To us, accustomed to frequent changes in women's fashions, this seems almost incredible. Would not Cleopatra have thought Aspasia's dress old-fashioned ?

If the actual dress of Mycenaean women seems to have no analogies in Homer, Mycenaean jewellery or costume accessories such as earrings, necklaces, and pins, both of ivory or bone and of metal (gold, silver, bronze) do find Homeric parallels although we cannot, of course, say how far Homeric jewellery is Mycenaean. For instance, amber necklaces (usually of L.H. II date) are known in Mycenaean tombs and in Homer (σ 296).

So far then as we can tell from our present knowledge Homeric dress is unrepresented in Greek art, Mycenaean or post-Mycenaean, and there is little profit in trying to identify Homeric dress in the representations we possess until we can fix with more certainty the date of the composition of the *Iliad* and of the *Odyssey*.

NOTES TO CHAPTER 18

1. The latest detailed discussion is that of Miss H. L. Lorimer, *Homer and the Monuments*, 336 ff.

2. A φᾶρος could also be used as a shroud (Σ 353, β 97, ω 147 f.) and for sails (ε 258). In these cases it may simply mean a piece of woven material.

3. *Cf.* G. Rodenwaldt, *Tiryns*, ii, pls. i, xi, 4, 5; *BSA*, xlviii, pl. ix *a*.

4. Lorimer, *op. cit.* 370.

5. The word φᾶρος occurs in the Linear B tablets: Ventris and Chadwick, *Documents*, 314 ff.

6. P. Jacobsthal, *Greek Pins*, 102, says that πόρπη and περόνη are used indiscriminately in Greek.

7. Miss Lorimer's statement (*op. cit.* 374) that embroidery is the only way of decorating linen is, of course, mistaken.

8. Leaf and Bayfield's account and sketch of Hera's dress (Ξ 178 ff., note *ad loc.*, and sketch on p. 638) are unconvincing. Would a goddess with a blanket wrapped round her have had enough feminine charm to fascinate Zeus ? Would her glamour have enchanted even a Homeric commentator ? In any case the dress could not have been woven in one piece, but must have been made up of two or more widths sewn together.

9. *Cf. BSA*, xlviii. 13.

CHAPTER 19

ARMS AND ARMOUR

by Frank H. Stubbings

IN Greek vase-paintings and sculptures of the classical period the heroes of old are depicted with such arms and armour as were familiar to the artist and his public in the contemporary scene (*cf.* Pl. 28). Nor is this un-archaeological attitude peculiar to classical Greece; it could be paralleled in almost any representation of the Trojan War down to the Renaissance (*cf.* Pl. 2), when archaeology began, and when the introduction of firearms drew the first clear line between ancient and modern warfare and weapons. Until then, helmet, cuirass and greaves, shield, sword, spear, and bow were, in varying form and subject to varying fashion, the recognized equipment of civilized warriors anywhere; the warfare of one age was broadly intelligible to another, and anachronisms of detail in art did not result in any essential misrepresentation. In the main, Greek poetry shows the same unconcern for historical exactitude as the pictorial arts; and if the Greek epic were entirely an imaginative fiction it might well have been no exception in this respect. Artistically, 'period' details are a non-essential; and even though the heroes of the Trojan War had for the later Greeks a historical reality, it is not likely that Greek hearers or readers of Homer would have been very sensitive to inconsistencies of a kind that might trouble a modern film-goer or reader of historical novels. But the Homeric epic is a product of tradition as well as of original poetic genius; and the strength of the tradition, rather than the historical intentions of the poet, has resulted in the epic picture of the heroic warrior preserving some details which belong to the Mycenaean period alone, and which might even have seemed obscure or odd to a Greek of the classical age. Indeed we can now see that the force of the tradition has occasionally itself produced anachronisms, and of an unusual kind: some details of military equipment in Homer may actually belong to a period *anterior* to that of the Trojan War. Recognition of these Mycenaean features, late or early, has, of course, come about through discoveries of actual remains and contemporary representations of Mycenaean arms and armour. Such discoveries also show that, although the epic tradition has for the most part preserved only so much about arms and armour as was readily understandable in post-heroic times, it has nevertheless very rarely, if ever, superimposed upon the

heroic scene any post-Mycenaean features to make it more easily understood or more 'up-to-date' in public estimation.

The Homeric warrior's typical equipment may best be understood
from the descriptions of arming for battle which occur at four places in the
Iliad. We have the arming of Paris for his single combat with Menelaus
(Γ 328-38), of Agamemnon at the beginning of his ἀριστεία (Λ 15-46),
of Patroclus in the borrowed arms of Achilles (Π 130-44), and of Achilles
himself in the truly heroic arms newly made by Hephaestus (Τ 367-91).
Although these passages vary in detail — especially in the description of
particular weapons or pieces of armour — they follow the same basic
pattern, which had probably long been part of the epic poet's stock-in-
trade, and which indeed includes some standard repeated lines. First,
the hero puts on his greaves; next his cuirass — this presumably comes
after the greaves because it would hamper bending movements; then
his sword, slung by a baldric or cross-belt from the shoulder; next he
takes his shield — this too would be slung from the shoulder; finally
the crested helmet. Then he picks up his spears or lance, and is ready
for the fray. This is the bare outline; much detail (explicit and implied)
can be added, partly from the arming-scenes themselves, partly from
other passages in the poems. How much corresponds with the
archaeologist's picture of heroic armour?

GREAVES

Our examination may begin with the greaves — not inappropriately,
since ἐϋκνήμιδες is the most frequent epithet of the Achaeans in Homer,
used thirty-one times in the *Iliad* and five times in the *Odyssey*. Even
the Greekless are aware that the Achaeans were 'well-greaved'. If the
epithet is of long standing in epic (as its frequency suggests) it is likely
that κνημῖδες were a distinctive feature of the Achaeans. Neither the
Egyptians nor any of the foes depicted on their monuments of the Late
Bronze Age wear them. They are, however, usual in Mycenaean frescoes
of the L.H. III period, and in a few other representations such as the
Warrior Vase and Warrior *Stele* (Pl. 29). It has been sometimes assumed
that κνημῖδες must be made of metal, that metal greaves were unknown
in Mycenaean times, and that all references to greaves in Homer (including
the word ἐϋκνήμιδες) must therefore be 'intrusions' from a period after
the introduction of hoplite armour in the early seventh century. But the
word κνημίς has in itself no metallic connotation; it is simply a shin-
piece, and could well be made of leather (or even canvas?) — such,
presumably, were the galligaskins (ῥαπταὶ κνημῖδες) worn by Laertes in
his vineyard (ω 228-9). Moreover, the Homeric text does not normally

imply that warriors' greaves were of metal: the adjective χαλκοκνήμιδες is used once only (H 41), and Achilles's greaves of fine tin (if that is what ἑανοῦ κασσιτέροιο means) are, of course, meant to be exceptional — they are the work of Hephaestus. The standard description of greaves in the arming scenes is ἀργυρέοισιν ἐπισφυρίοις ἀραρυῖαι.

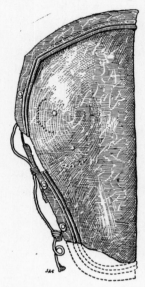

We do not know what ἐπισφύρια were; the suggestion of a flap or projection to cover the ankle (σφύρον) is not borne out by any known greaves or representations, whether Mycenaean or later, and they are more likely to have been decorative — conceivably rims of silver round the lower edge of the κνημίς. As to Mycenaean greaves, their usual material is again uncertain. In the frescoes they are coloured white, which may be a matter of artistic convention, or of realism. If the latter, the material is likely to be leather or some woven fabric, and the colour would account for the choice of the white metal tin for Achilles's greaves. Bronze greaves of Mycenaean date are extremely rare: a fragmentary pair from Enkomi in Cyprus are preserved in the British Museum (see Fig. 55); and to these may be added the remains of another pair recently identified in the Cyprus

FIG. 55. Mycenaean bronze greave. (Length *c.* 11½ in.)

Museum. The only example so far known from Mainland Greece was discovered in 1953 in a L.H. III tomb near Khalandritsa in Achaea [a]; others, probably Minoan, but of unknown provenance, are in the Iraklion Museum (unpublished). In the published examples the bronze is quite thin, and may have had a backing of leather or other fabric; they were fitted to the leg by a wire lacing down the back edges.

THE THOREX OR CUIRASS

As with κνημῖδες, it has in the past been argued that all Homeric mentions of a θώρηξ or cuirass are 'late' or 'intrusive'. The argument rested on false or untested premisses: first that θώρηξ means a 'breast-plate', tacitly assumed to be of metal; second, that metal cuirasses were unknown in Greece before the development of hoplite arms and tactics. Like κνημίς, the word θώρηξ has etymologically no inherent metallic connotations. For this reason the translation 'breast*plate*' should be avoided. ('Cuirass' is satisfactorily ambiguous: as worn by the Horse Guards it is of steel; but by derivation it denotes a protection of leather,

[a] But see note at end of chapter.

Lat. *corium*, Fr. *cuir*.)   As to the existence of metal or metal-covered cuirasses in heroic times, it is true that as yet no actual remains are known to archaeology, but the example of greaves (above, p. 505 f.) and the helmet (below, pp. 513 ff.) should nowadays be sufficient warning against making deductions from negative evidence.[a]   The antiquity of the word was already attested (though not accurately datable) by the existence of a derivative verb θωρήσσεσθαι, common in Homer, meaning simply 'to put on one's armour'; and recently it has been proved, by its identification on the Pylos tablets, that θώρηξ is at least as old as the twelfth century. What is more, the Homeric references to body armour as of bronze are so frequent and so well embedded in the poems as to suggest that they are part of the epic tradition.   'Bronze-shirted', χαλκοχίτωνες, is an epithet applied no less than twenty-four times to the Achaeans, as though it described a distinctive characteristic; no other people or tribe are so called more than twice.   The supernatural armour made for Achilles by Hephaestus (Σ) could, of course, be of nothing less than bronze; the bronze θώρηξ adorned with an edging of tin, given as a prize to Eumelos (Ψ 560 ff.), is again something special; but other quite ordinary θώρηκες are described as 'brightly-gleaming' (λαμπρὸν γανόωντες Ν 265) and 'newly scoured' (νεόσμηκτοι Ν 342); πολυδαίδαλος (which possibly though not certainly implies a metallic glitter) is almost a 'standard' epithet (Γ 358; Δ 136; Η 252; Λ 436); and the twice-used αἰολοθώρηξ also seems to imply metal.   To deduce the material of the θώρηξ from its efficacy or otherwise in protecting this or that hero against a wound seems too speculative a mode of inquiry.   It is, however, perhaps legitimate to infer from the epithet λινοθώρηξ, used only in the *Catalogue*, of the Lesser Ajax and the Trojan Amphios (Β 529, 830), that at any rate a linen cuirass (presumably padded or quilted) was something unusual in the heroic scene as known to tradition.   Later references to linen θώρηκες show that they were in historical times known to the Greeks only as something exotic.   As to the exact form of the Homeric θώρηξ, the poems cannot be said to help us much.   There are various references to wounds inflicted through the γύαλον θώρηκος, and an ancient commentator (Schol. A on Ε 99-100) explains that the γύαλα were the convex front and back plates of the cuirass.[b]   There is no strong reason for doubting this; yet if the γύαλα are simply the two halves of a metal breastplate of the seventh- or sixth-century type it is odd that in one passage (Ο 530) a θώρηξ is specifically described as γυάλοισιν ἀρηρότα, as though this were abnormal.   In this passage, moreover, the account of

---

[a] Since this chapter went to press, a bronze θώρηξ of Mycenaean IIIa date has been discovered in a chamber-tomb at Dendra (Argolid).   See note at end of chapter.

[b] In classical Greek γύαλα is used of 'hollows' of the landscape; also of a metal bowl: see Liddell and Scott.

how the owner came by this particular θώρηξ also implies that it was something unusual. Possibly (but this remains a conjecture) the explanation is that the γύαλα were plates or overlays of bronze attached to a θώρηξ of leather or some other material; and that this use of bronze was something fairly new. How much of the body the θώρηξ or its γύαλα protected is not absolutely clear. In one notoriously difficult passage (Δ 132-6) an arrow pierces through Menelaus's belt (ζωστήρ) and then καὶ διὰ θώρηκος, as though the belt lay over the θώρηξ. The line in question, καὶ διὰ θώρηκος πολυδαιδάλου ἠρήρειστο, is a formula used in several places, and it is conceivable that in using it here the good Homer has nodded. Yet elsewhere weapons piercing through the γύαλον θώρηκος inflict wounds in the abdomen (N 506-7; P 313-14) as well as in the shoulder (E 99, 189) and the chest (N 587). The natural inference is that the θώρηξ is understood to extend somewhat below the belt; but we cannot be sure.

Though not actually called θώρηξ, it must be some similar kind of protective clothing which is referred to by the phrase στρεπτὸς χιτών, 'plaited shirt' (E 113, Φ 31). This is worn on both the Greek and the Trojan side. According to Aristarchus, the phrase refers to chain-mail; but from one passage (Φ 31), where Achilles binds his Trojan prisoners with 'the straps which they wore on their στρεπτοὶ χιτῶνες', something of plaited leather seems not unlikely.

That some form of cuirass actually was worn in Late Mycenaean times is certain. We see it in the well-known representations on the twelfth-century Warrior Vase and Warrior *Stele*, in which the warriors wear a short jerkin coming down to about waist-level, not confined by a belt but standing rather stiffly away from the body; it appears to be a quite separate article from the 'kilt' that appears below it (Pl. 29). The material of neither is clear from the pictures, nor is it certain whether both are of the same stuff. There seems nothing to support the theory that the white spots on the garments represent discs or studs of metal attached to a cuirass of, say, leather. In any case the drawing is crude, and the distribution of spots inconsistent. In earlier representations, in the frescoes, warriors wear a thigh-length tunic all in one piece, drawn in at the waist by a belt, and pretty certainly of the same material as their greaves, like which it is coloured white. In the Mycenae fresco of men and horses (Pl. 30) the neat dotted lines that run in regular patterns across two of these tunics strongly suggest stitching, as though the garment were of leather or some quilted woven fabric. If the latter, these warriors are perhaps what epic would have called λινοθώρηκες.

Tablets from Knossos (*c.* 1400 B.C.) list, along with chariots and horses, items which from the ideogram used are pretty certainly tunic-length corslets, and a similar ideogram was current at Pylos about 200 years later. There the corslet has what appear to be short sleeves, and is generally accompanied by a helmet (Fig. 56). These corslets are on other Pylos tablets called *to-ra-ke* (*i.e.*, θώρᾱκες). Neither at Knossos nor at Pylos is the material certain, though in some cases at Knossos it appears that an ingot of bronze was an alternative 'issue' to the corslet. At Pylos the *to-ra-ke* are in a number of instances described as having so many *o-pa-wo-ta* (*op-aworta*, perhaps from ἀϜείρω, and meaning 'things appended' or 'attachments'), *e.g.*, 'twenty large, ten small', or sometimes 'twenty-two large, twelve small'; and it has been suggested that these are metal reinforcements of the corslet. Though such metal reinforcements are not definitely recognizable in Mycenaean art, nor represented by

a   b

FIG. 56. Linear B ideograms for *thorex* and helmet

tangible remains from Mycenaean contexts, they were certainly used in the Near East from the fifteenth century B.C. onwards in the form of small plates or scales of bronze arranged in rows. It is improbable that this type of corslet would have been quite unknown to the Aegean. Indeed something of the kind seems to be remembered in the Homeric description of Agamemnon's cuirass in Λ 19-28. This was a gift from King Kinyras of Cyprus, sent when he heard of the projected expedition against Troy. As a work of unusual art it is described in detail:

> τοῦ δ᾽ ἤτοι δέκα οἶμοι ἔσαν μέλανος κυάνοιο,
> δώδεκα δὲ χρυσοῖο καὶ εἴκοσι κασσιτέροιο·
> κυάνεοι δὲ δράκοντες ὀρωρέχατο προτὶ δειρὴν
> τρεῖς ἑκάτερθ᾽, ἴρισσιν ἐοικότες . . .   (Λ 24-7)

The materials, tin, gold, and κύανος (probably some sort of enamel, or *niello*), and the figured decoration, remind us of Mycenaean metalwork with decorative inlays in the style of the Shaft Grave daggers (Fig. 15, p. 347) or the silver bowls (rather later in date) from Dendra and elsewhere, though the application of such a technique to so big an object as a cuirass must be due simply to the poetic exaggeration natural to heroic epic. The word οἶμοι, literally 'paths', must here mean 'stripes' or 'bands', which may be imagined running horizontally across the θώρηξ. Their number tempts comparison with the *op-aworta* of the Pylos tablets. In a wall-painting in the tomb of the Pharoah Ramses III corslets of scale-armour are actually depicted with the scales coloured in horizontal stripes of yellow, red, green, and blue, and Miss Lorimer may well be right in proposing to identify the θώρηξ of Agamemnon as of this foreign type. (Incidentally, if it was, it would be a tunic-length garment; and in Λ 234 we learn that Agamemnon's θώρηξ did have a belt, made of silver.) Since Cyprus was in Mycenaean times in frequent contact with the countries bordering the eastern end of the Mediterranean, a mail-shirt of the kind would be a possible and appropriate gift for Kinyras to send to another monarch on the eve of a great campaign. But from the Pylos and Knossos tablets it now seems likely that something similar was a familiar fashion among the Mycenaean Greeks themselves.

THE SHIELD

The two words for shield used in Homer — σάκος and ἀσπίς — perhaps originally denoted separate types: the ἀσπίς is commonly ὀμφαλόεσσα, 'bossed', and πάντοσ' ἐΐση, 'round'; the σάκος is often μέγα τε στιβαρόν τε, 'large and stout', ἑπταβόειον, 'made of seven ox-hides', and several times ἠΰτε πύργος, 'like a tower'. That they do not borrow each other's adjectives suggests that the σάκος was not, like the ἀσπίς, round in shape with a characteristic boss; but it does not prove that an ἀσπίς could not be large, or made of hide; and there are definite exceptions to the general distinction, as with the shield of Achilles, which though undoubtedly round in shape is almost always called σάκος, or that of Periphetes, called an ἀσπίς although it is not the round type. It seems, then, that the two words had by Homer's time become assimilated; and the remaining vestiges of distinctive meaning may well be accounted for by the persistence of the useful metrical formulae such as κατ' ἀσπίδος ὀμφαλοέσσης and σάκος μέγα τε στιβαρόν τε. There are, however, other indications in the epic that not all shields referred to are to be understood as of one kind; and we can observe in some passages clear traces of an early Mycenaean type which was perhaps going out of fashion among the Greeks, if not actually out of use, by the time of the Trojan War. This has two forms, both depicted on the 'Lion-hunt' dagger blade (Fig. 15) and on other objects found in the Mycenaean Shaft Graves. The less familiar form has straight sides and bottom, and a curved top, and forms roughly a half-cylinder, protecting the body from the neck to below the knee. Better known, because it persists in Mycenaean art as a decorative motif after it has ceased to appear in actual fighting scenes, is the 'figure-of-eight' shield. It has been satisfactorily shown that this was made of ox-hide stretched on a frame made probably of pliant wood. Seen from the front it has the characteristic 8-shape (cf. Pl. 27, b); in profile it shows a strong convex curvature, both vertically and horizontally. Both these types of shield were hung from a strap or baldric running over the left shoulder and under the right arm; when in use, a limited amount of manœuvring with the left hand was probably possible ; and when not in use they could be swung round behind the back. Reichel, who first recognized this early type of shield in Homer, and who took it to be typical of the whole Mycenaean period, assumed that any shield suspended from the shoulder by a τελαμών or baldric must be of this kind. This was an error ; but nevertheless there are other Homeric references to shields which can still be explained only in terms of the early Mycenaean body-shield. Periphetes, for example, turning to run away, trips against the rim of his shield, which reached to his feet —

> στρεφθεὶς γὰρ μετόπισθεν ἐν ἀσπίδος ἄντυγι πάλτο
> τὴν αὐτὸς φορέεσκε ποδηνεκέ᾽, ἕρκος ἀκόντων.   (Ο 645-6)

The shield of Hector, too, in one passage reaches from neck to ankles, as the figure-of-eight shield would :

> ἀμφὶ δέ μιν σφυρὰ τύπτε καὶ αὐχένα δέρμα κελαινόν,
> ἄντυξ ἣ πυμάτη θέεν ἀσπίδος ὀμφαλοέσσης.   (Ζ 117-18)

The 'black hide' is appropriate for a figure-of-eight shield ; yet it is a little odd that in the next line (cf. Ν 192) it is called ὀμφαλόεσσα, an epithet that seems rightly to belong to *round* shields ; and indeed Hector's shield is elsewhere actually called πάντοσ᾽ ἐΐση (Η 250 ; Λ 61 ; Ν 803). Miss Lorimer also points out that the body-shield belongs on the Greek rather than the Trojan side. Perhaps we have here a piece of conscious archaism which has misfired because Homer, aware from the epic tradition of these outsize shields, did not appreciate that their shape too was peculiar. The shield of Ajax, the legendary type of the mighty warrior, must generally be understood as of this kind, particularly because the formula φέρων σάκος ἠΰτε πύργον is used of him alone (Η 219 ; Λ 485 ; Ρ 128). In Ξ 402-5 Ajax is struck by Hector's spear on the chest, where the baldrics of his sword and shield were 'stretched' —

> τῇ ῥα δύω τελαμῶνε περὶ στήθεσσι τετάσθην
> ἤτοι ὁ μὲν σάκεος, ὁ δὲ φασγάνου ἀργυροήλου—

and the leather straps save him from a wound. It has been acutely pointed out that this probably implies the straps crossed each other, as they would with a body-shield slung in the usual way ; and that Ajax was not wearing any cuirass, which only came into use when shields became smaller and more mobile. For Ajax, then, the picture of early Mycenaean equipment is consistent. If in his duel with Hector the phrase μέσσον ἐπομφάλιον does for a moment suggest a round shield it is still astonishing to what an extent the epic tradition has preserved a true picture of usages apparently as old as the fifteenth century B.C.

It seems to have been in L.H. III that the Mycenaeans adopted a new type of shield, smaller and approximately round in shape, best illustrated on the Warrior Vase from Mycenae (Pl. 29, *a*). On one side of the vase we see warriors on the march, lances shouldered, with their shields held or slung on their left; on the other side other warriors advance to the attack, lances raised, with their shields brought round to the front, and now seen in profile. The artist is not strong in perspective, nor has he shown how in either case the shield was supported; but in the action scene there is on the inner face of the left-hand man's shield a small hand-grip, clearly drawn. As he is not actually holding this grip the shield must have been slung from the shoulder by a τελαμών, like the older type: the handgrip would serve for manœuvring the shield in battle, not for carrying. The vase appears to be very roughly of the time of the Trojan War, so that this un-glamorous picture could be regarded as a contemporary portrayal of the well-greaved Achaeans. Their shields can hardly be held to correspond entirely with any Homeric description: though roughly round, their shape at the bottom edge scarcely justifies the epithet πάντοσ᾽ ἐΐση, and they are certainly not ὀμφαλόεσσαι. Miss Lorimer has, however, demonstrated that, whatever their shape, shields with a single handgrip, supported by a τελαμών, remained in use until the adoption of hoplite armour about 700 B.C., and it is clearly some variety of this type that is usually implied in Homer. Again, shields with a prominent central boss were certainly known in the Eastern Mediterranean in the Late Bronze Age, though our first positive evidence for them in Greece comes from an early Iron Age grave in the Kerameikos at Athens.

As to material, the figure-of-eight shield was certainly of ox-hide, though we may doubt whether the real thing ever required all the seven hides of the epic ἑπταβόειον. Whether later Mycenaean types were ever faced with metal, in a way that would justify Homeric epithets such as παμφαῖνον, παναίολον and the like, we simply do not know. In favour of the theory that these epithets are not long-standing elements of the epic tradition it has been argued that they are less obviously embedded in metrical formulae than some phrases already mentioned. In any case it would be rash to assume that shields of only one shape or material were in use among the Greeks who fought at Troy; and any variety existing in the original tradition would facilitate its 'contamination' by features more appropriate to a later age. There is consequently, as Miss Lorimer says, 'little hope that by examining the epic we should be able to discriminate between traditional matter incorporated by the poet and original descriptions of the warfare of his own day. Many formulae may be ancient; they would remain as applicable as on the day when they were first coined.'

It remains to say something of the shields of Achilles (Σ) and Agamemnon (Λ 32-40). The shield of Achilles is a masterpiece of supernatural art for which we must not expect to find material parallels in any age; but it is like more normal shields in being round, made in layers (πέντε δ' ἄρ' αὐτοῦ ἔσαν σάκεος πτύχες Σ 481) and fitted with a *telamon*. Its decoration with many elaborate figured scenes inlaid in precious metal would seem to be in general a poetic expansion on heroic scale of an art which was known by tradition (and is now even better known by examples) to have been practised in heroic — that is, Mycenaean times. But, however fascinating the possible speculations as to the arrangement of the decoration, the description is too poetical in character for it to be reliably related to any particular style or system of iconography. As well try to assign to its precise period the Grecian urn of Keats's ode.

The shield of Agamemnon (Λ 32-40) is simpler, and more easily visualized. Round it ran ten circles of bronze, and on it there are twenty ὀμφαλοί of white tin, and in the middle one of κύανος, which is specially elaborated:

> τῇ δ' ἐπὶ μὲν Γοργὼ βλοσυρῶπις ἐστεφάνωτο
> δεινὸν δερκομένη, περὶ δὲ Δεῖμός τε Φόβος τε.

This reminds one strongly of the early archaic votive bronze shields from the Idaean Cave in Crete. They are decorated with figures in relief, arranged in concentric zones round a projecting central boss in the form of a grotesque animal mask. On one, the 'Hunt Shield', the zone next to the boss is chiefly occupied by two fierce-looking beasts, which should probably be understood as personifications of such powers as Δεῖμος and Φόβος. Such a work as this might perhaps have been in Homer's mind when describing the shield of Agamemnon. Unfortunately the Cretan shields are not very closely datable; nor do we know if they are the earliest of their kind. We do know that personifications of ideas like Eris and Phobos were familiar in art by the seventh century; but we cannot say how early the practice began. Possibly Homer has been influenced here by something of his own day; yet the decorative use of tin and κύανος, as elsewhere, harks back to Mycenaean art.

THE HELMET

There are four words for 'helmet' in Homer: κόρυς (used as often as forty-six times), κυνέη (twenty-eight times), τρυφάλεια (fifteen times), and πήληξ (ten times). We may disregard for present purposes στεφάνη, which though three times used with reference to a helmet shows by its obvious derivation that it does not *per se* denote a piece of head-armour but only something crowning or encircling the head. The other four words, though it is, of course, likely that in origin they had distinguishable connotations, perhaps even referring to different *types* of helmet, seem to us virtually interchangeable in meaning as used in the epic, and one particular helmet may be described by several of them within a few lines. Such assimilation of meaning is probably bound up with the fact that the four nouns in their various cases are seldom metrically equivalent — *e.g.*, if a dative singular were required, the poet's choice between κυνέη, τρυφαλείη, and πήληκι, might be governed mainly by metrical convenience. It does, however, appear that, where a form of κόρυς and κυνέη are metrically both possible, κόρυς is more usual; and the relative infrequency of τρυφάλεια and πήληξ may imply that their meaning was more specialized than that of either κόρυς or κυνέη. We should note too that the word κόρυς is so far the only word for helmet found in the Mycenaean Greek of the Pylos and Knossos tablets.

A number of epithets — χαλκήρης, φαεινός, and others less specific — show that the hero's helmet was commonly, if not always, envisaged by the poet as of metal, or at least plated with metal; it gleams in the sun, it rings as it or its wearer falls or is struck (*e.g.*, N 341; Π 105, 794). From the use of epithets like χαλκοπάρηος and κροτάφοις ἀραρυῖα we can see that the poet thought at least sometimes in terms of a helmet with side-plates to protect the cheeks. Others — ἵππουρις, ἱπποδάσεια, ἱππόκομος, indicate that it has a crest or plume of horsehair, the λόφος ἱππιοχαίτης that frightened Hector's baby son (Z 469); and this crest is specifically mentioned in a stock formula of the arming scenes:

> κρατὶ δ' ἐπ' ἰφθίμῳ κυνέην εὔτυκτον ἔθηκεν
> ἵππουριν, δεινὸν δὲ λόφος καθύπερθεν ἔνευεν.

Certain other epithets of helmets are obscure, especially ἀμφίφαλος, τετράφαλος, and τετραφάληρος, and their meaning was already debatable in ancient times. Since φάλαρον in classical Greek denotes the metal-plated cheek-piece of a horse's head-stall, the Homeric τετραφάληρος may mean 'with four metal plates' — but not, presumably, four cheek-pieces — and this would suit also the use (once only, in Π 106) of the noun φάλαρα. Clearly ἀμφίφαλος and τετράφαλος mean 'with two φάλοι' and 'with four φάλοι', but it is not so clear from the passages where the noun occurs by itself what a φάλος is, though it must be of metal, since the adjective λαμπρός can be applied to it (N 132 and Π 216). An ancient equation of φάλος with φάλαρον does in fact make quite good sense wherever φάλοι are mentioned, if we take them to be simply the metal plates of a helmet. On some of the Pylos tablets helmets are listed as having four *op-aworta* (? 'plates' — *cf.* on the θώρηξ, p. 509 above); but the cheek-pieces are mentioned separately as *pa-ra-wa-jo* (= παραϝja, Hom. παρηά). Some scholars, however, explain φάλος as some sort of horn or projection such as is known on various kinds of Late Bronze Age helmet in the eastern Mediterranean area, and is pictured on the famous late Mycenaean 'Warrior Vase'. This, however, suits only some of the

PLATE 31

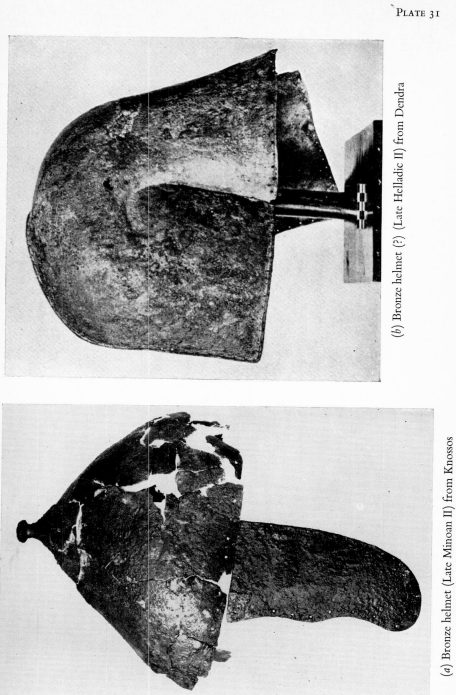

(b) Bronze helmet (?) (Late Helladic II) from Dendra

(a) Bronze helmet (Late Minoan II) from Knossos

Plate 32

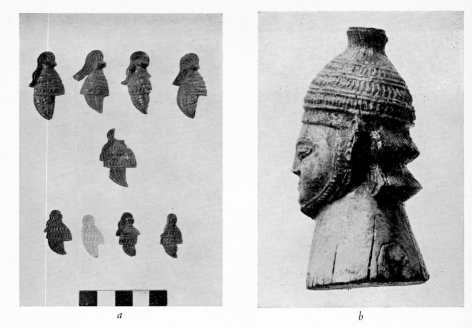

a   *b*

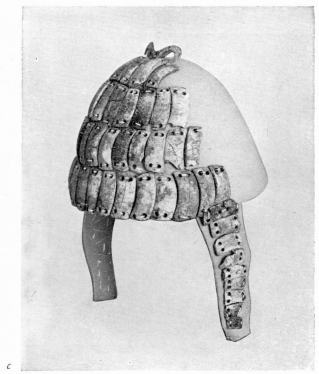

c

(*a*) Ivory inlays representing boar's-tusk helmets, from Mycenae. (*b*) Ivory relief of man wearing boar's-tusk helmet, from Mycenae. (*c*) Reconstruction of boar's-tusk helmet, from fragments found in a chamber-tomb at Mycenae

PLATE 33

Stele V from Grave Circle A, Mycenae.   About 4 ft. 4 in. × 3 ft. 6 in.

PLATE 34

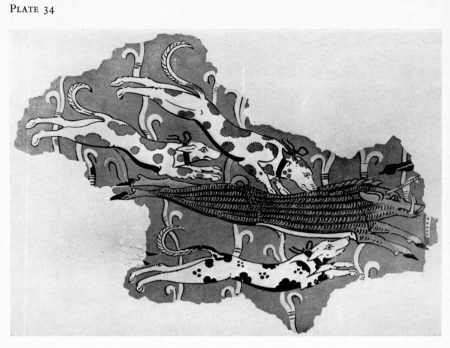

(*a*) Fresco from Tiryns, depicting a boar-hunt.   Width *c.* 17 in.

(*b*) Threshing (in the Argolid)

passages where a φάλος is mentioned; and another ancient explanation, that it is the holder for the crest, suits even fewer of them.

The word τρυφάλεια may very plausibly be explained as originally an adjective, applicable to κόρυς or κυνέη, which has come to be used as a noun. Its original meaning would then be the same as τετράφαλος. In the poems, however, it is already noun enough to be itself qualified by adjectives, notably the obscure epithet αὐλῶπις, which is used of no other object. It appears to be derived from αὐλός, a tube. According to Hesychius it describes a helmet with a visor, restricting the vision, as through a tube; according to the scholiast it means that the helmet has a tube-like holder for the crest. An αὐλός is once mentioned as part of a helmet, in P 297, where reference to a tubular crest-holder is possible and suitably gruesome, but not obvious.

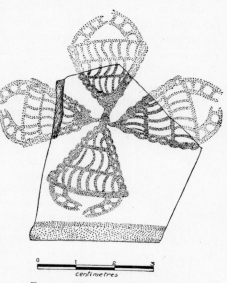

FIG. 57. Vase-motif of helmets

That such difficulties of explanation arose in antiquity suggests that the terms are traditional, and refer to features unfamiliar in the helmet-types of historical times. Whether these features belong specifically to the Mycenaean period or not we cannot be sure; but reference to archaeological evidence now available at least shows that in other respects the helmets of the epics do not present any characteristics which were unknown in Mycenaean Greece. Helmets of bronze, once thought to belong only to historic times, are now known definitely to have existed in the Mycenaean period, though there is at present no certain means of telling how common they were. Apart from a cheek-piece from a tomb at Ialysos in Rhodes (now in the British Museum), probably of L.H. III date, two only are preserved, one found in a beehive-tomb at Dendra in the Argolid and datable to L.H. I-II, the other in a L.M. II chamber-tomb near Knossos (Pl. 31). Both are of thin bronze, and clearly had a lining of some stoutness. That from Dendra protects the whole head, coming down at the back and sides almost to shoulder-level, and probably had a crest trailing behind from an attachment near the front.[a] Representations in Mycenaean art

---

[a] Cheek-pieces of another have been found at Dendra since this went to press. But see note at end of chapter.

show no parallels, though something a little like it (and even more like a classical Corinthian helmet) appears on the Minoan 'Boxer Vase' found at Ayia Triadha in Crete. The shape of the Knossos example, however, a conical helmet with a knob on top, pierced vertically for the crest (*cf.* αὐλῶπις), and two separately made pendent pieces to protect ears and cheeks, is much more frequent in Mycenaean art — in fresco (Pl. 30), in ivory-carvings (Pls. 27, *b*, 32, *a*, *b*), on engraved gems, and sometimes painted as a decorative motif on pottery or other objects from the fifteenth century onwards (Fig. 57). In these representations there is sometimes a clearly distinguishable piece to protect the back of the neck, a feature not preserved (if it ever existed) in the Knossos example.

Most of the representations, however, despite the correspondence of shape, do not depict helmets of bronze. Their surface is divided into horizontal bands, often themselves divided by a series of curved vertical lines. It was Reichel who first recognized that in these we have an illustration of the helmet lent by Meriones to Odysseus and precisely described in K 261-5 :

ἀμφὶ δέ οἱ κυνέην κεφαλῆφιν ἔθηκε
ῥινοῦ ποιητήν· πολέσιν δ' ἔντοσθεν ἱμᾶσιν
ἐντέτατο στερεῶς· ἔκτοσθε δὲ λευκοὶ ὀδόντες
ἀργιόδοντος ὑὸς θαμέες ἔχον ἔνθα καὶ ἔνθα
εὖ καὶ ἐπισταμένως· μέσσῃ δ' ἐνὶ πῖλος ἀρήρει.

Pieces of boar's tusk cut and pierced for attachment to such helmets (Pl. 32, *c*) have been found in a number of Mycenaean graves in mainland Greece, and once in a L.M. III grave in Crete. From the representations and remains it appears that the boar's-tusk helmet was already used in the Shaft Grave period; but some have doubted whether it remained in fashion to the end of the L.H. III period. In many of the representations, moreover, it appears along with the old-fashioned figure-of-eight shield (*e.g.*, Pl. 27, *b*). (It is interesting that both figure-of-eight shield and boar's-tusk helmet come to be used by L.H. III as decorative motifs, in many cases without forming part of a pictorial representation.) Homer's close description of such a helmet must be due to an epic tradition rather than to post-Mycenaean survival of an actual helmet; and his account of the past history and ownership of the helmet in K 266-70 is the more appropriate if the object seemed to him (as it may possibly have been in fact) unusual and old-fashioned at the date of the story's action.

Whether helmets of similar shape in bronze remained in use to the end of L.H. III we do not at present know. One side of the Warrior Vase shows helmets which are certainly different in form, a simple hemispherical cap with a hedgehog-like outline presumably representing some sort of fore-and-aft crest. The helmets on the other side are also usually regarded as of a new type, though apart from the apparent absence of cheek-pieces the difference from the earlier shape may be due to clumsy drawing, especially as regards the crest-holder.

THE SWORD

Of the sword comparatively little need be said. Of the three words for sword in Homer, ξίφος 'continues to be used throughout antiquity to denote in verse and prose alike an object which in essentials remained the same' (Lorimer). In quoting an ancient testimony that ἄορ and φάσγανον are respectively Arcadian and Cypriot words, Miss Lorimer remarks that this, if true, should imply that they are survivals from Bronze Age Greek, and since she wrote this the decipherment of Linear B tablets has shown that φάσγανον actually was current in Mycenaean times. It is never found in classical prose, and its survival in poetry was presumably due entirely to the influence of an epic tradition that had begun while it was still an everyday word. In the tablets ξίφος also occurs, but it cannot be shown that the two words refer to different types of sword. (If this were ever true, it might be that ξίφος was originally the narrow rapier-like weapon known in early Mycenaean contexts, φάσγανον the broader slashing-sword which came into fashion only in late Mycenaean times.) ἄορ, if correctly derived from the root of ἀείρω, merely denotes the sword as being slung from the shoulder by a baldric or τελαμών. In Homer one hero's sword can be described by all three words; and such limited descriptions of sword-fighting as there are do not give any precise picture of either the shape of swords or the manner of sword-play. Homer will not (pace Ion the rhapsode in Plato) teach you swordsmanship, whether as practised in the Bronze Age or later. The epic does, however, remember always that heroic swords were of bronze, not steel; and the epithet ἀργυρόηλον ('with studs of silver'), used of the sword in several of the arming-scenes, takes us back to early Mycenaean times. Sword-hilts throughout the Mycenaean period often had gold-headed rivets (cf. Fig. 13, p. 346); but silver-headed rivets, so far as we know, occur only in L.H. I and II. The phrase ξίφος ἀργυρόηλον is therefore likely to have entered the epic tradition, if it was ever used with historical accuracy, in reference to an earlier generation of heroes, fortes ante Agamemnona. The non-occurrence in Homer of the historically more appropriate χρυσόηλος is doubtless due to its metrical impossibility.

THE SPEAR

In the arming-scenes discussed above it will be noticed that Paris and Achilles each take up one spear (ἔγχος) while Agamemnon and Patroclus each take a pair of spears (δοῦρε), and we are clearly told that Patroclus did not use the ἔγχος of Achilles because it was too heavy for him. It might be conjectured from these facts, taken alone, that the single ἔγχος is a heavy lance for thrusting at close quarters, and the δοῦρε are lighter, for throwing from a distance. But we find that the two words are as interchangeable in the epic as ξίφος and φάσγανον, and that both are normally used for throwing. (There is an exception in the funeral games, Ψ 816 ff., where Ajax and Diomede fight hand-to-hand with spears.)

Hints of an original difference can nevertheless be detected. The ἔγχος unlike δόρυ is described in Homer as ὄβριμον, as βριθύ, μέγα, στιβαρόν. After Homer the word survives only in poetry, though it is found in ordinary prose use in Mycenaean Greek. Its replacement by δόρυ could readily be explained if we knew of an actual change in spear-types during or after the Mycenaean period; but such a change cannot be traced from archaeological evidence. What we do know from representations in art is that in early Mycenaean times a heavy thrusting-spear was common (cf. Pl. 33), and that lighter spears, for throwing, were in use at least in Attica in the Geometric period. How widespread the throwing-spear then was, and when it came into fashion we cannot at present say. It was presumably familiar to the poet of the *Iliad*; but that need not make it an anachronism in scenes of the Trojan War.

THE BOW

In the *Iliad* the bow plays a comparatively small part, and is more a foreign weapon than a Greek one. It is especially characteristic of the Lycians and of their leader Pandaros, though the Carians and Paeonians are also archers (ἀγκυλότοξοι Κ 428). Paris fights with the bow (and the fact seems to be used as a reproach against him by Diomede in Λ 385); so does Helenus (Ν 576 ff.) and so does Dolon (Κ). Among the Greeks, it is matter for comment by the narrator that the Locrians fought primarily with bows (Ν 712 ff.); and only three major heroes are regularly bowmen. Of these Philoctetes takes no part in the action, since he was marooned on Lemnos. The others are Teucer (brother of Ajax, son of Telamon), specifically described (Ν 313 f.) as the best archer among the Achaeans; and Meriones of Crete, the island which in historical times was the chief source of Greek archers. These two were the only entrants in the archery contest in the funeral games for Patroclus (Ψ 850 ff.); Meriones won. On the only occasion in the *Iliad* when we find Odysseus armed with a bow (Κ 260) it is borrowed from Meriones.

Of the bows and arrows themselves the poet says little. But while most arrows have heads of bronze — χαλκήρης and χαλκοβαρής are the common adjectives — we may note that those of Pandaros are pointed with iron (Δ 123). His bow too is unusual, though the description is not easily intelligible (Δ 105 ff.). The distinctive feature is that it was made from the exceptionally long horns of a wild goat, which Pandaros himself had killed; and it was tipped with gold. We should not visualize a

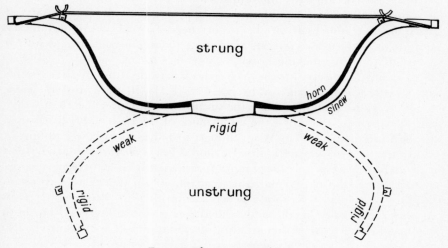

FIG. 58. The composite bow

bow consisting of two curving horns joined by their butt-ends, for such a bow would be of little or no practical use. What is presumably intended is what is usually called a *composite* bow (Fig. 58), made partly of wood, partly of sinews and horn, the latter acting in effect as powerful springs. Such bows, known both in antiquity and in modern times, are readily recognizable when represented in art from the characteristic reverse curvature of the tips. They are more powerful than the ordinary bow: to string them is difficult, and it cannot be accomplished by one pair of hands unless the stringer sits or squats and braces the bow under one thigh and over the other knee (Fig. 59). The type was familiar in classical Greece as the characteristic weapon of the Scythians. From *c.* 600 B.C.

FIG. 59. Stringing the composite bow: from a 5th-century coin of Thebes

onwards both it and the method of stringing it are illustrated in vase-paintings, where it appears in the hands not only of Scythians but of other foreigners (especially the Amazons) and of certain heroes, notably Herakles (as in Fig. 59) and Paris. An early form of the composite bow must have been known to the Mycenaean Greeks also, again as a foreign weapon, in areas like Syria, Cyprus, and probably Asia Minor, where it is known to have been used. It would also have been known in Crete, for it appears occasionally in Minoan art from M.M. III onwards; and in some of the Knossos tablets there appear representations of curved goats' horns [a] which, from the occurrence of other items of military equipment in the same context, Sir Arthur Evans convincingly identified as raw material for making bows.

In mainland Greece in the Mycenaean period, although arrowheads are occasionally found in tombs as late as L.H. III, the composite bow does not appear at all in art, and the simple bow not after the Shaft Grave period. Perhaps, therefore, the importance of the bow had really waned by the time of the Trojan War (though to judge from vase-paintings it was to the fore in Geometric times); and if this is correct it is proper that it plays little part in the *Iliad*, and appears mainly as a foreign weapon. In this connection it is remarkable that one of the few heroes to retain the bow as a major weapon, Teucer, is brother to Ajax, who retains another earlier fashion, the body-shield (see p. 510 f. above). Do both brothers belong to an earlier stratum of epic tradition? Again, when in the *Doloneia* (K 260) Odysseus borrows a bow from Meriones he also borrows a boar's-tusk helmet which is described as an heirloom from an earlier generation. Indeed, as was pointed out many years ago by Martin Nilsson, in Greek legend generally the heroes who use the bow (*e.g.*, Herakles) belong usually to an older generation than that of the Trojan War. It looks as though Homer's historical perspective in regard to the bow was correct.

The rôle of the bow in the *Odyssey* needs no recapitulation. It can, however, only be fully appreciated in the light of what has been said about the composite bow. The suitors could not string Odysseus's bow because it was of this unfamiliar type. They stood up to try, and failed. Odysseus did it sitting down — not because he was stronger, but because he knew the way. The bow episode is so essential to the story that it is reasonable to regard it as one of the earliest elements in it; but our evidence is not such as to prove more absolutely when or where it entered the tradition. Miss Lorimer argues that it was in the post-Mycenaean Greek settlements on the Anatolian coast, where Greeks would meet the composite bow in Asiatic hands. But this is unsound, for, as Miss Lorimer herself pointed out, they could have met it so, as a foreign weapon, far earlier, in Mycenaean times.

---

[a] The animal in question, *Capra aegagrus*, still occurs in a wild state in Crete, where it is called ἀγρίμι.

THE CHARIOT

The Hittites used their chariotry to charge in line and bring the chariot-borne warriors, armed with thrusting spears, quickly within reach of any of the enemy who had not fled at the first onset. The Egyptians improved on this by manning their chariots with archers, who were effective at longer range, whether in attack or pursuit. These tactics cannot have been unknown in the Aegean area at the time of the Trojan War, and it has therefore often been remarked how little trace of them there is in the *Iliad*, where the rôle of the chariot seems to be chiefly as a means of transport to and from the battlefield. Generally the warrior leaps down to fight — his charioteer standing by to carry him out of danger if things go badly. Though he sometimes hurls a spear from his chariot, the *Iliad* knows no chariot-borne archers, and when the great bowman Pandaros fights from Aeneas's chariot he uses a spear (E 278-80). Did the poet fail to understand the proper military functions of chariots? Only once is there clear reference to their concerted use in battle. When Nestor is arraying his forces for the attack (Δ 303-9) he enjoins them to keep in line : no one is to dash ahead or lag behind; they are to use the spear when they get close enough to the opposing chariots. This, he says, is the better way, which was so successful in the past :

> ὧδε καὶ οἱ πρότεροι πόλεας καὶ τείχε' ἐπόρθεον.

These words put in the mouth of ancient Nestor may imply that Homer believed such tactics to be old-fashioned among the Greeks by the time of the Trojan War. Whether they were really so we cannot be sure : there are no representations of chariot-fighting in Mycenaean art later than the period of the Shaft Graves; and though chariots and chariot wheels are freely mentioned among military equipment in the Knossos and Pylos tablets we cannot show how they were used. At any rate Nestor's words are not likely to be an accidental projection into the Trojan War scene from post-Mycenaean times, since they imply the use of thrusting-spears, which are an early Mycenaean weapon, as we have seen above (p. 517 f.). Spears are in fact used by warriors mounted in chariots on the carved *stelai* from the Shaft Graves (Pl. 33), but these carvings portray *individual* chariots only, and provide no evidence for (or against) the massed use of chariots in battle. The *stelai* are designed only to commemorate individual prowess; and we may do well to remember that this purpose was at work in the *Iliad* too.

Of the form and construction of the Homeric chariot little need be said. It seems usually to have been a very light vehicle — even light enough to be carried by one man (K 504-5) — the car (δίφρος) consisting of a wooden frame with sides and floor filled in with interwoven leather thongs, which would give a necessary resilience over rough ground. The wood of the wild fig-tree is mentioned (Φ 37-8) as the material of the ἄντυγες (front and side rails). The leather-work (a feature of classical chariots too) is implied in the adjectives εὔπλεκτος and εὐπλεκέης (Ψ 335, 436). Hera's chariot (E 722 ff.) is, of course, a special one: its eight-spoked (ὀκτάκνημα) wheels and iron axle are doubtless to be regarded as exceptional, no less than its wheel-rims (ἴτυς) of gold, and its hubs (πλῆμναι) and shaft (ῥυμός) of silver; even the thongs of the δίφρος are of gold and silver. Mortal chariots, however, may be ποικίλα χαλκῷ (Δ 226; K 322, 393), and those of Diomede (Ψ 503) and Rhesus (K 438) even have gold and silver or tin about them. Miss Lorimer suggested that such decoration implies a more solidly-built type of chariot than the usual, but that is not necessarily so: ornamentation of shaft, rails, and wheels would be quite enough to merit the descriptions given.

Homer treats these highly-decorated chariots as more like divine than mortal equipment (K 440-1). Probably there was no parallel for them within his own experience; but their presence in the epic may be due not only to poetical imagination but also to traditions of Mycenaean originals. The Pylos tablets show that the late Mycenaean model might have wheels bound with bronze and even silver. At Knossos the tablets record chariots adorned with crimson colouring and with ivory.[a] But what has already been demonstrated in relation to other items of equipment applies here too: in general the poet mentions no features that would not be appropriate to Greek chariots of any age.

NOTE TO CHAPTER 19

The first systematic treatment of this subject was W. Reichel's *Homerische Waffen* (1894), which virtually held the field until the late Miss H. L. Lorimer's *Homer and the Monuments* (1950). Miss Lorimer had originally agreed to write the present chapter, and though she was in the event unable to do so it owes a very great debt to ch. v of her book. This will remain an invaluable survey of the evidence and the earlier literature, even for those who like the present writer do not accept all her conclusions.

Important contributions to the subject since 1950 are: M. S. F. Hood in *BSA*, xlvii. 256 ff. (on the helmet); H. W. Catling in *AIARS*, 4to ser. iii. 21 ff. (for greaves); M. G. F. Ventris and J. Chadwick, *Documents*, ch. xi (evidence of the Linear B tablets); W. E. McLeod in *AJA*, lxii. 397 ff. describes an Egyptian composite bow in the Brooklyn Museum; J. Chadwick in *BSA*, lii. 147 ff. (further discussion of helmet and *thorex* in Knossos tablets).

¶ For the startling discovery at Dendra (since this chapter went to press) of a whole suit of armour—bronze cuirass with neck- and shoulder-pieces (= γύαλα), boar's tusks and bronze cheek-pieces from a helmet, and remains of greaves and (?) shield—of Mycenaean IIIa date see *Archaeological Reports 1960-61*, 9 f. with Figs. 8, 9. The shoulder-pieces strongly suggest that the 'helmet' in Pl. 31, *b* is really another such.

[a] For further discussion of chariots see below, Ch. 22.

CHAPTER 20

FOOD AND AGRICULTURE

by Frank H. Stubbings

FIGHTING is the hero's work; eating and drinking are his proper pleasures, and roast meat and wine his proper food and drink. Epic has its formulae for feasting no less than for arming for battle or running a man through with sword or spear. Any reader of Homer is familiar with the descriptions of slaughtering oxen, sheep, goats, or hogs, of jointing, spitting, roasting, and devouring them; and after the heroes have taken the edge off their appetites in this way they fill the wine bowls and pour every man a bumper while the minstrel strikes up (A 459-74 and elsewhere). Where it all comes from we are not, in the *Iliad* at least, encouraged to inquire; the supply of meat for formal sacrifice and feasting seems endless, and when Achilles receives the embassy from the Greek leaders (I 201 ff.) there are joints of mutton, goat-flesh, and pork at hand in his quarters. Nor are the Trojans behindhand: even after nine years' siege they can still bring out oxen, sheep, wine, and meal from the city when they are to spend the night by their camp-fires in the plain (Θ 545-7). Almost the only reference in all the *Iliad* to the problem of victualling the host is the account (H 467 ff.) of shiploads of wine brought at great expense of bronze, iron, hides, and slaves, from Lemnos. Campaigning in the field, it seems, is no occasion for coarse fare or short commons; every meal is a feast. All seems in strong contrast to what one knows of the comparative rarity of meat in the diet of classical or modern Greece.

But in effect, the first impression is misleading. For, on examination, it will be found that the great feasts of roast meat are normally on ceremonial or religious occasions, or at least when the duties of hospitality demand more than offering pot-luck. Thus the first description of feasting in the *Iliad* is an occasion of sacrifice to Apollo, when Agamemnon has conducted Chryseis back to her father (A 458 ff.); again after the duel of Ajax and Hector the feasting follows a thanksgiving sacrifice (H 313 ff.); the feasting depicted on the shield of Achilles follows a sacrifice in the harvest field (Σ 559 ff.); the funeral feast for Patroclus is obviously ceremonial (Ψ 30 ff.); and so on. Any Greek audience would recognize more readily than the modern reader that this is so; they probably found roast meat as desirable as did the heroes of the epic, but they were used to getting it only on special occasions. The heroes ate *more* of it, but then they were supermen. The poet himself recognizes that the basic human food is bread, as the standard human drink is wine; only the immortals do without these:

οὐ γὰρ σῖτον ἔδουσ᾽, οὐ πίνουσ᾽ αἴθοπα οἶνον,
τοὔνεκ᾽ ἀναίμονές εἰσι καὶ ἀθάνατοι καλέονται;   (E 341-2)

and again, in the *Odyssey*, barley-meal and wheaten flour are characterized as the staff of life, the 'marrow of men', μυελὸν ἀνδρῶν (υ 108). If there are any peoples on earth who are not dependent on wine and bread they are exotics like the Lotus-eaters, or uncivilized savages like the Cyclopes. The latter rely on such crops as grow without the aid of ploughing and sowing (ι 109 ff.), and though they do have wine (or does οἶνον ἐριστά-φυλον in ι 111 and 358 only mean *grapes*?) they are normally content with milk, taken neat (ι 297); Polyphemus is certainly unfamiliar with such supernacular vintages as Odysseus offers.

In the *Odyssey* in general there may at first sight appear to be even more eating than in the *Iliad*. The suitors have little else to do, and do it, for the cattle and sheep and pigs they devour are devoured at Odysseus's expense, and in his absence, and in the hope that he will never return. However, all Ithaca below the suitor class condemns their gluttony, not least Eumaeus, who knows that the produce of his pig-farm was more moderately used in better days before Odysseus went away. (No reader could grudge him his master's porkers to entertain the unknown Odysseus.) But when Telemachus sets out for Pylos it is not with joints of roast pork but with wine and barley-meal that he provisions his ship (β 349 ff.); and that is what Odysseus and his men usually carried, to be supplemented with game when possible. There were wild goats for the shooting on the Cyclops's island (ι 155) and Odysseus bagged a fine stag in Aeaea (κ 158 ff.). It was only when the provisions in the ship gave out, and hunting and fishing failed to supply their needs, that they killed the sacred cattle of the Sun, to their own final undoing (μ 327 ff.); but once they had been persuaded to this by Eurylochus they did their wicked work thoroughly, doubtless on the principle 'as well be hung for a sheep as for a lamb', and slaughtered enough cattle to feast for a week on end.

In both poems, then, it is the roast meat that stands out when there is mention of eating and drinking. The only other type of refreshment actually described is the posset of Pramnian wine mixed with grated cheese, barley meal, and honey, which is offered by Nestor to his visitors (Λ 628 ff.) and by Circe to hers (κ 234 f.). Whether this recipe was descended from Mycenaean times through epic tradition, or was projected into the heroic scene from the poet's own age, is a question of no importance. What is important is that it implies the assumption, the very sensible assumption, by the poet and his audience, that the Greeks of the heroic age would, possessing sheep and goats, have used their milk for cheese, and living among the thyme-scented hills of Greece would have collected and enjoyed wild honey (for reference to bees in similes (as B 87 ff. and M 167 ff.) shows that they were more familiar in the wild state). So, too, no Greek reader or hearer of Homer would ever have supposed (as some modern scholars have, on the strength of the one line in which Odysseus's companions themselves go fishing 'because their bellies ached with hunger') that the Mycenaean Greeks did not normally eat fish as food. They would, rather, have noted with approval the line in which Odysseus speaks of the fish of the sea, like the fruits of the earth, as one of the blessings of nature (τ 113).

In short, the ancient reader would expect and would find in Homeric references to agriculture and food-production nothing unfamiliar. He would assume, as the poet himself would assume, that the resources of the Aegean lands in the heroic age were such as he himself knew. Even nowadays, when Greek agriculture includes such exotics as tobacco, cotton, potatoes, and tomatoes, the basic crops are the same as in Homer: wheat and barley, vines, and olives. Of the fruit trees now grown, ancient Greece knew only figs, pears, apples, and pomegranates. If there is a difference between the Homeric picture and the real Greek world it is simply that of a certain poetic exaggeration.

Though mixed farming would be familiar to any Greek, not every part of Greece is equally adapted to all sides of it. Not many places could be so prodigal of bulls for sacrifice as Nestor's Pylos (γ 6); that part of the Peloponnese had lusher pastures than most. Perhaps the calves frisking in the farmyard as the cows come home from pasture (κ 410), or the herd of cattle by the river (Σ 573), were more familiar in the poet's own Ionia than in Odysseus's Ithaca. But the pictures we find in similes of the baaing ewes at milking time (Δ 433) or the shepherd sorting out the sheep from the goats (B 474) or his dog keeping watch by the fold (K 183) are an essential part of the Greece of all ages. It is no surprise to find that of the livestock listed in the Mycenaean tablets oxen are always considerably less numerous than sheep and goats. Verisimilitude is always preserved. If we ask, for example, how rocky little Ithaca could provide meat for so many ravening suitors, the answer is there (ξ 100 ff.): Odysseus is lord of more than Ithaca, and has twelve herds of cattle, and an equal number of sheep, goats, and pigs, on the mainland. The only flocks and herds in Ithaca itself are goats (which it still supports to-day) and Eumaeus's pigs (ξ ad init.), which would in early times have found adequate feeding on acorns, before deforestation reduced the mountain oaks to mere scrub. Fatted pigs in Homer are referred to as σίαλοι or σύες σίαλοι (Φ 363; β 300; I 208; ξ 41, etc.). This same distinction is found among the swine listed on the Mycenaean tablets: not only is the word σίαλοι attested, but the ideogram for 'pig' is sometimes combined with the syllable-sign for *si*.

We know that in Mycenaean times there were wild boar as well in some parts of Greece — witness the Tiryns fresco of a boar-hunt (Pl. 34, *a*), and the many finds of boar's tusks for helmets.[a]   There is no doubt that the tale of the Calydonian boar, and of the hunt with Autolycus (τ 428 ff.) in which Odysseus got his famous scar, are in strict keeping with the age they portray.   Wild boar and deer could still be hunted in some parts even in classical times ; and some of the frequent similes from the chase — the boar at bay (Λ 414 ; M 146 ; N 471, etc.), the deer or the wild goat pursued or pulled down by the hounds (X 189 ; O 271, 579, etc.) — may have been drawn from life.   But equally they may have been traditional elements in epic.   Huntsmen and deer are both mentioned in Mycenaean texts, and hunting scenes are frequent in Mycenaean art.   One is the more inclined to regard them as traditional, moreover, when they are considered in relation to associated similes.   For the lion at bay (Θ 338 ; M 41) is almost as ready a picture as the wild boar, and there are numerous allusions to lions attacking herds or sheepfolds (E 136, 161 ; K 485 ; Λ 172, 548 ; M 293 ; N 198 ; O 630 ; Π 487, etc.), surprising huntsmen out after stag or wild goat (O 275), or themselves the specific object of the hunt (Υ 164).   Such pictures can hardly have been drawn from the everyday experience of Homer's own archaic period, when the less lively representations of lions in pictorial art suggest the king of beasts was no more familiar in life than he is on the British railways to-day.   In Mycenaean times, however, things may well have been different, and it has been suggested that the tale of Herakles and the lion of Nemea might be a reminiscence of 'the last lion in the Peloponnese'.   We should note also that these similes of beasts of prey — for besides lions we have a leopardess (Φ 573), wolves (Π 156, 352), jackals (Λ 474), and others unspecified (O 323, 586) — are almost entirely confined to the *Iliad*.   This may reflect simply that it is the earlier work, and that the poet was working more closely to tradition ; or it may be due to the subject of the poem, which lends itself to similes from hunting and wild life.

Fishing, as already indicated, was not like hunting an occupation for heroes, and so the references to it are only incidental, in similes.   In one instance (E 487) the fisherman uses nets, elsewhere hook and line (Π 408). Two other passages (Ω 80 ff. and μ 252 ff.) are commonly taken to refer to line-fishing, but may well refer to fish-*spearing*, a method still very common in the translucent coastal waters of Greece.   Finally there is a passage (Π 745-7) in which Patroclus jeeringly compares an opponent who has come a cropper out of his chariot to a man diving into the sea for oysters.   The image may seem far-fetched to us ; but it would not be

[a] *Cf*. Ch. 19.

so to Greeks, familiar with diving for sponges as well as for shellfish. Fishbones and shells of oysters and other molluscs have been found at Mycenae and elsewhere. We know also that sponges were used in Mycenaean times for applying paint to walls and pottery; so there is presumably no anachronism in their Homeric use for washing the blood-stains from Odysseus's furniture or the honest sweat from the brow of Hephaestus (χ 439; Σ 414).

The story of the *Iliad* admits but seldom of reference to the processes of agriculture, except in similes and other incidental ways; but these are such as to give vivid and authentic glimpses of the Greek countryside. Ploughing and harvest and vintage are all depicted on the shield of Achilles. The ploughing is perhaps idealized, with a cup of wine for the ploughmen at every furrow's end, though it has been pointed out that the adjective τρίπολος applied to the field ('thrice ploughed' is the usual translation) may imply that this is in fact a ritual scene, in which the first three furrows were cut with special ceremony. The harvesting is on a king's estate (τέμενος βασιλήϊον); the reapers, of course, work with sickles, and are followed by others who tie the sheaves and boys who gather them up; the king himself is present, with heralds superintending the preparations for the harvest sacrifice and supper. The vintage too is accompanied by ceremonial dance and song.

These are the joyful occasions of farming life. The sheer hard toil is elsewhere just as realistically alluded to in both *Iliad* and *Odyssey*. Plough-ing and reaping are both especially laborious (σ 366 ff.). Though one passage states that mules are preferable (Κ 351 ff.) the plough-team was usually a yoke of oxen. Working oxen (βόες Ϝεργάται) are distinguished from others among those listed in Mycenaean texts. It is striking that the Homeric adjective οἶνοψ, commonly taken to be a colour-word, is applied to oxen only where they are described at work (Ν 703; ν 32), a circumstance which would favour the meaning 'foaming' recently suggested (in *Greece and Rome*, n.s. ii. 86); but whatever its true meaning it is certainly as old as the heroic age, for it occurs with other descriptive names of oxen on a tablet from Knossos.

The Homeric methods of threshing and winnowing are still current in the Aegean and the near east, but a different climate and the industrial revolution have made them remote from the English reader. The grain is threshed from the ears by letting the farm cattle trample it on a circular floor of hard-beaten earth (Υ 495; Φ 346); the winnowing is done by tossing it in the wind with a wooden shovel so that the grain falls in a heap while the chaff is blown aside (Ε 499 ff.) (see Pls. 34, *b*, 35, *a*). There might be folk so far from the sea that they did not know what an oar was; but everyone, it could be taken for granted, would know a win-nowing shovel (ἀθηρηλοιγόν λ 128). Milling too was totally unmechanized in ancient Greece : the corn was ground at home in hand querns. Like spinning and weaving, this was a constant task of the women servants ; in Odysseus's house there were a dozen of them working at it (υ 105 ff.), at the palace of Alcinous more than twice that number (η 103 f.).

The best arable land in Greece being in plains ringed by steep hills (*cf.* Pl. 7), it might be liable to flooding in spring or autumn storms (Π 384 ff.), and the fields must be protected by banks and dykes (E 87 ff.). On the other hand the hot summers make irrigation a necessary feature of husbandry for crops other than corn (Φ 257 ff. ; η 129 f.). Vines can be grown in low-lying land if available (*cf.* ι 131 ff.), but often are planted on hill-slopes, terraced with dry-stone walls (αἱμασίαι ω 224), especially where level ground is scarce, as in Ithaca. In the vineyard on the shield of Achilles the vines are trained on poles (κάμακες), a practice nowadays less common in Greece than in Italy. Orchards or vineyards and other planted ground (ἀλωή, φυταλίη) are in Homer as much a recognized part of agricultural wealth as arable land is, and both are regularly specified in describing a king's *temenos* (*e.g.*, Z 194 f. ; I 578-80 ; Ξ 121-3 ; Τ 112 ff.). It is interesting to find the word φυταλία used with this same connotation in the Mycenaean Greek of the tablets. The most familiar Homeric picture of work in the orchard is the description of Laertes, when Odysseus goes out to find him, at the end of the *Odyssey* (ω 225 ff.). There we have mention, besides vines, of pear, apple, and fig trees (ω 340 f.). Similes too give a glimpse of the husbandman's careful tending of the olive sapling or other young plants (P 53 ; Σ 56). The town-bred modern Englishman used to buying almost any fruit at all seasons may tend to forget how much this depends on importation from other latitudes as well as on modern methods of storage ; the great *desideratum* of horticulture must always be a good *succession* of fruits, and this is the ideal in Homer too, achieved to perfection in the marvellous gardens of Alcinous. These have fruit all the year round, summer and winter — pears, pomegranates, apples, figs, and olives (η 114-19), and some vines are just flowering while others are ripening and yet others already being trodden for wine or dried for raisins.

The gardens of Alcinous also contained vegetable-beds, κοσμηταὶ πρασιαί (η 127), though we are not told what grew in them. Beans and peas are briefly alluded to once in Homer (N 588 ff.), in a way that implies they would be grown in quantity ; and their use in Mycenaean times is borne out by the evidence of archaeology.

Olive oil is frequently mentioned in the epic as used for anointing the skin after washing — ἀλείψασθαι λίπ' ἐλαίῳ and χρῖσαι ἐλαίῳ are regular formulae (K 577 ; Ξ 171 ; Ω 587 ; γ 466, etc.), and ὑγρὸν ἔλαιον is also a standard phrase in similar contexts (Ψ 281 ; ζ 79, 215, etc.) ; moreover the tablets show that it was a very common commodity in Mycenaean Greece. Yet oddly enough there are no Homeric references to the actual cultivation of the olive other than those already quoted; and no references at all to the extraction of the oil or the use of it or the olive itself as food. Nor is there mention of oil for lamps; indeed the one reference to a lamp (τ 34) has often been suspected as an 'interpolation': elsewhere artificial lighting is by torches (δαΐδες Σ 492; σ 354; τ 48,

FIG. 60. Mycenaean lamps
(a) Steatite, from Dendra; (b) Marble, from Mycenae; (c) Pottery, from Mycenae; (d) Pottery, from Athens, Acropolis; (e) Bronze, from Dendra
(Scale about 1 : 6)

etc.). But archaeology shows that lamps *were* used in late Mycenaean times (*cf.* Fig. 60), and olive oil would be the natural fuel for them in Greece. We should perhaps conclude that it was the very ubiquity of olive trees and their products that accounts for the rarity of reference in the poems.

To sum up, it may be said that the epics give over all a true and a complete picture of food and agriculture in early Greece. There is no single crop or food-product mentioned that cannot be attested for Mycenaean times by archaeology, either in the way of actual remains (animal bones, carbonized grain, etc.), or by written reference in the tablets of Pylos, Mycenae, and Knossos.

NOTE TO CHAPTER 20

K. F. Vickery, *Food in early Greece* (1936) (*Illinois Stud. Social Sci.* 20. 3) summarized the then available archaeological evidence. This is now supplemented by the Linear B tablets, see Ventris and Chadwick, *Documents*, chs. vii and viii.

See also above, Ch. 8, *ad fin.*

PLATE 35

(*a*) Winnowing (near Corinth)

(*b*) Spinning (Ithaca)

Plate 36

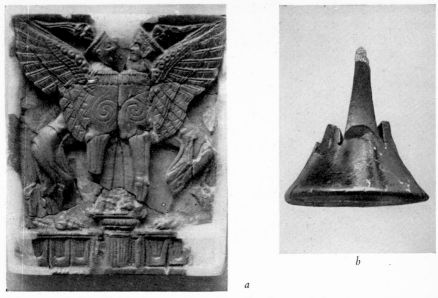

a

b

(*a*) Ivory relief (probably from a piece of wooden furniture) from Mycenae. Width *c*. 3 in. (*b*) Ivory 'foot' (perhaps from a small stool) from Mycenae. Diameter *c*. 2⅜ in.

(*c*) Silver cup, inlaid in gold and *niello*, from Enkomi, Cyprus. Diameter *c*. 6¼ in.

PLATE 37

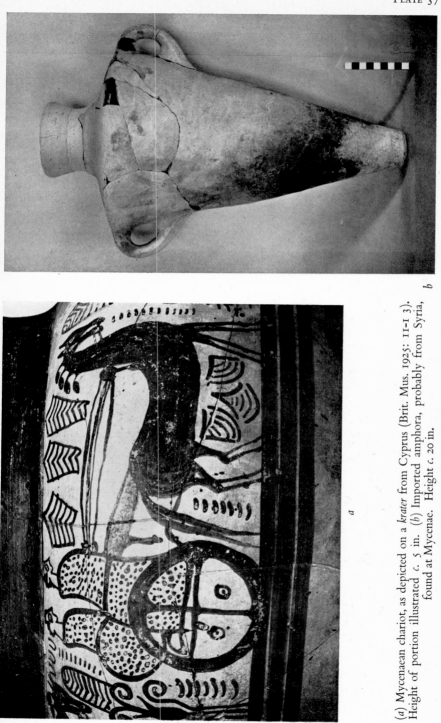

a

b

(*a*) Mycenaean chariot, as depicted on a *krater* from Cyprus (Brit. Mus. 1925: 11-1 3). Height of portion illustrated *c.* 5 in. (*b*) Imported amphora, probably from Syria, found at Mycenae. Height *c.* 20 in.

PLATE 38

(a) Gold patera. Diameter $7\frac{1}{2}$ in.

(b) Ivory lid. Diameter c. $5\frac{1}{2}$ in.

Both from Ugarit (Ras Shamra), fourteenth cent. B.C. In the Louvre

CHAPTER 21

CRAFTS AND INDUSTRIES

by Frank H. Stubbings

REFERENCES to crafts and industries are naturally few in epics primarily concerned with the exploits of a heroic ruling class. Nor, when they do occur, do they need to be very detailed, since to the poet's ancient public the activities of smith and potter, of shipwright and mason, of spinning and weaving, would be everyday sights. These are all special crafts, and even in a simple society not everyone knows *how* they are done; but it is only in modern times, when half the world 'does not know how the other half lives', that *what* is done becomes a mystery. And since the references are rarely detailed the epic picture of crafts, as of farming, for the most part fits any age in the Greek world; only occasionally is there anything which specifically dates the scene.

Spinning and weaving in Homer, as in classical Greece and in many a peasant society to-day, were household crafts, carried on in every home from high to low. As English words and phrases like *spinster* and *the distaff side* still remind us, they were women's tasks; and Telemachus on a famous occasion rudely suggests to his mother that she should stick to them (α 356 ff.). Hand-spinning (Pl. 35, *b*), pulling the raw wool from the mass held on the distaff, and twisting it with right thumb and fore-finger into a continuous thread, kept constantly turning by the aid of the weighted spindle (ἠλακάτη) hanging from its end, is an occupation that can be carried on (like knitting) whenever the hands are free, sitting, standing, even walking, especially talking. It is characteristic in the epic to find the mistress of the house so engaged. Not only the virtuous and housewifely Penelope, or Alcinous's admirable queen Arete (ζ 306), but the witch Circe (κ 222), the nymph Calypso in her grot (ε 62), and even Helen (δ 121 ff.), are all portrayed either spinning or weaving. How far such a picture is true for the historical Mycenaean age we cannot say. Penelope, Helen, or Arete, all had numerous slave-women to spin and weave for them (*cf.* η 105), just as many spinning and weaving women are listed in the Pylos tablets; but it is conceivable that even in a great household the mistress too worked at these tasks, either to superintend the others or because it had become a formal tradition to do so. The description of Helen's golden spindle and her parcel-gilt silver box on wheels to hold the wool, not to mention the *posse* of attendants to bring them in, certainly suggests that *her* spinning is less utilitarian than symbolic — a rather precious and extravagant symbol of her return to domestic virtue. Penelope's weaving (β 93 ff.) is also, of course, a special case ; really necessary weaving would progress at a very different *tempo*, though the suitors seem to have been imperfectly aware of this. In one passage (M 432 ff.) we have a picture, in a simile, of a woman carefully weighing out portions of wool, presumably for spinning, 'so that she may get a scanty living for her children', which though by no means clear suggests she is working for somebody else. But normally spinning and weaving are depicted as essentially home crafts. Though they might in a palace be the specialized occupation of certain slaves (like the γρῆυς εἰροκόμος of Γ 386-7), these were working for the household's own needs, to maintain that extra store of garments and other woven goods, laid up in scented chests (φ 52), which is a regular feature of heroic wealth (*cf.* β 339 ; ε 38 ; Π 221 ff.). Such a store distinguished the kingly household from the commoner's (*cf.* ξ 513 ff.), and could be drawn on for special needs, as when Menelaus and Helen wish to give Telemachus a parting gift (ο 104 ff.). Textiles in Homer are commonly of wool, as would be would be natural in a sheep-raising country ; there are frequent references to χλαῖναι οὖλαι (e.g., δ 50 ; κ 451 ; ρ 89), more rarely to οὖλοι τάπητες (Π 224) and ἐρίοιο τάπητα (δ 124). Whether a precise kind of textile is implied by τάπητες (sometimes purple-dyed, as in I 200) is not clear. They are used for bedcoverings, or to spread over a chair seat. Other materials than wool are less frequently mentioned or implied. The dancing men and maidens pictured on the shield of Achilles were apparently clothed in linen —

τῶν δ' αἱ μὲν λεπτὰς ὀθόνας ἔχον, οἱ δὲ χιτῶνας
εἴατ' ἐϋννήτους ἧκα στίλβοντας ἐλαίῳ.   (Σ 595)

Odysseus's tunic, thin and smooth as an onion-skin (τ 232-4) is perhaps also to be thought of as of superfine linen. How common linen fabrics were in the historical Mycenaean age is not easy to say. The Pylos tablets seem to refer to large quantities of flax or linen produced in the Pylos area ; but in Homer the word λῖτα, specifically meaning 'linen cloths', occurs only rarely (Θ 441 ; α 130) ; and though λίνον is used in two passages (I 661 and ν 73, 118) of linen bed-sheets it is elsewhere used only in reference to thread or nets or fishing-lines (e.g., Υ 128 ; η 198 ; E 487 ; Π 408).

Of industry outside the home we get infrequent but picturesque glimpses. Similes in the *Iliad* several times refer to the felling of timber in the mountains, pine, oak, ash, or poplar, for building ships or waggons (Γ 60 ; Δ 485 ; N 178 ff., 389 ff. ; Π 482). Doubtless, the poet had himself often heard the ring of the axes and the crash of falling branches (Π 633), had seen the woodcutters at their noonday break (Λ 86) and the mules lugging the long timbers down the hillsides (P 742 ff.); and when in Δ 485 he pictures the wainwright with an *iron* axe we may be even more sure that he speaks from his own experience. It was easy for him to envisage the party of men and mules going off up Mount Ida to cut and fetch logs for Patroclus's pyre (Ψ 110 ff.).

Shipbuilding itself must have been an even more familiar sight to Homer than it still is on many a Mediterranean coast; he can talk with confidence of axe and adze and drill and dowels when he describes the building of Odysseus's raft (ε 228-61); and he appeals to a like know-ledge in his public when he tells us the raft was about as broad as the hull

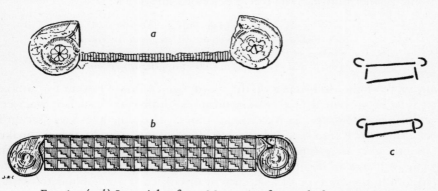

FIG. 61. (*a, b*) Ivory inlay from Mycenaean footstools from Dendra (width 12 in.) and Mycenae (width 16½ in.); (*c*) Linear B ideograms for *ta-ra-nu* (= θρῆνυς)

of a well-found cargo vessel. Apart from this passage and a reference in a simile to drilling ship's timbers (ι 384) there is little occasion for us to see shipwright or carpenter at work.

Furniture of wood is indeed referred to, and phrases like τρητοῖς ἐν λεχέεσσιν (η 345) remind us of the skilful joinery that goes to its making. But generally the emphasis is rather on the decoration applied to bed-steads, chairs, and footstools. This is indicated by adjectives like δαίδαλος and ποικίλος (*e.g.*, α 131 f.), or more specifically by reference to silver studs (θ 65; Σ 389) or inlays of gold, silver, and ivory (τ 55; *cf.* ψ 200). Descriptions of furniture on tablets from Pylos show that in such passages the poet has preserved an authentic tradition from Mycenaean times, and the evidence is corroborated by fragmentary ivory inlays from such furniture found in excavations (*cf.* Fig. 61 and Pls. 27, *b*, 32, *a*, 36, *a, b*). Ivory was, in fact, a favourite decorative material with the Mycenaeans, used not only on furniture but on chariots and horse-trappings (*cf.* ἡνία λεύκ' ἐλέφαντι Ε 583).[1] We may note also in Homer mention of a door key with an ivory handle (φ 6-7). The reference to the staining of ivory, as practised in Maeonia or Caria (Δ 141), is usually taken to reflect an art of Archaic times : we have no evidence that it was practised earlier. But the allusion is in a simile only ; so no question of literary anachronism is involved.

In respect of metalwork, the poet is always aware that his heroes lived in what we call a Bronze Age. Nevertheless, some objects of iron are mentioned — for example, Pandaros's arrowheads (Δ 123), the mace used by Areïthoos (H 141), and the axes used in the archery contest at the end of the *Odyssey*. The precise form of these axes and the nature of the feat required of the archer have been much debated, and deserve some further notice. The feat is described in τ 572 ff. :

> νῦν γὰρ καταθήσω ἄεθλον
> τοὺς πελέκεας, τοὺς κεῖνος ἐνὶ μεγάροισιν ἑοῖσιν
> ἵστασχ᾽ ἑξείης, δρυόχους ὥς, δώδεκα πάντας.
> στὰς δ᾽ ὅ γε πολλὸν ἄνευθε διαρρίπτασκεν ὀϊστόν.

In view of the occurrence of the word ἡμιπέλεκκον (Ψ 851) for an axe, it is to be presumed that πέλεκυς means a 'double axe', such as was very common (in bronze) in Mycenaean times. How the axes were set up is described in φ 120 ff. : Telemachus digs a long straight trench, makes sure the axes are precisely in line, and presses the earth firmly round them. The emphasis on shooting 'through the iron' (τ 587 ; φ 127) has led some to look for some type of axe, current in Greece at a suitable date, with a perforated blade, but without success ; and the solution seems to lie in φ 421-3 :

> πελέκεων δ᾽ οὐκ ἤμβροτε πάντων
> πρώτης στειλειῆς, διὰ δ᾽ ἀμπερὲς ἦλθε θύραζε
> ἰὸς χαλκοβαρής,

where στειλειή must mean the *socket* for the haft (which is called στειλειόν, ε 236). The arrow of Odysseus in no case missed the opening of the socket, but passed right through and out at the other end. The arrangement is illustrated in Fig. 62. The fact that the haftless axe-heads would not stand far above ground-level fits in with the fact that Odysseus shoots from a sitting posture.[2]

Objects of iron in Homer are, however, only such rare exceptions as may actually have occurred in late Mycenaean times. It is, moreover, in keeping with the facts of the Mycenaean age that iron is a number of times mentioned along with bronze and gold as a form of wealth, virtually a precious metal (*e.g.*, Z 48, repeated four times elsewhere ; H 473 ; I 365-6). The lump of iron (σόλον αὐτοχόωνον Ψ 826) offered as a prize in the funeral games might perhaps be grouped with these references, were it not that the subsequent lines imply that such a lump of raw material might be drawn upon for replacing farm implements as required

— surely an Iron Age anachronism in this context. There is only one reference to the actual *manufacture* of iron tools, a description of the tempering process, and that comes in a simile (ι 391-3). That is not to say, however, that allusions to the activities of bronze-smiths are any more frequent. Indeed we only meet the smith at his work in the person of Hephaestus, the divine smith who made the new arms for Achilles. He works not only in bronze, but in precious metals too; Thetis finds him engaged on a set of twenty tripod cauldrons, presumably of bronze, with golden wheels (Σ 373 ff.). Bronze cauldrons with tripod stands were the gifts that Alcinous and his peers presented to Odysseus on his

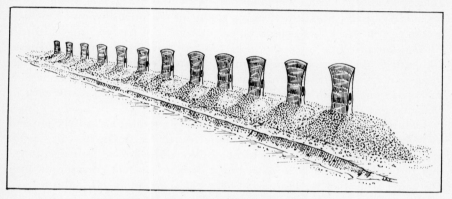

FIG. 62. Arrangement of the axes in *Odyssey* xxi

departure from Phaeacia (ν 13); tripods were also among the treasures that Menelaus brought from Egypt (δ 129); clearly they were objects of great price. Though wheeled tripods with cauldrons attached have not survived from earlier than the Geometric Age (*cf.* Fig. 33, above, p. 420), the existence of wheeled bronze stands from Late Bronze Age Cyprus makes it probable that such articles were in fact used by the Mycenaean Greeks. It is a point of some interest that Hephaestus works in gold and other metals as well as bronze, and had in his time made brooches, necklets, and other ornaments for the Nereids (Σ 400 ff.). To the story it is important, since he is to make for Achilles a shield inlaid with gold, silver, tin, and κύανος (either *niello* or some form of enamel). The shield, like Agamemnon's cuirass,[a] obviously recalls the peculiarly Mycenaean art of applying to bronze objects — daggers and cups especially — pictorial inlays in precious metals (*cf.* Pls. 24, *d*, 36, *c*; Fig. 15) and the craftsmen who made such things must, like Hephaestus, have been bronze-smiths and goldsmiths at once. Of the actual technical methods of such inlay work Homer's account shows no knowledge, and doubtless

[a] See p. 509 f.

he had none. The tools of Hephaestus's trade that are mentioned
(Σ 468-77) are anvil, hammer and tongs, bellows, and crucibles (χόανοι)
for melting bronze, tin, gold, and silver. These, in varying scale and
detail, are necessary gear for any metalworker. Anvil, hammer, and
tongs are similarly the distinctive equipment of the goldsmith (χρυσοχόος,
also called simply χαλκεύς, 'smith') who is summoned by Nestor to gild
the horns of a sacrificial ox (γ 432 ff.) ; and almost as though to forestall
the unsound criticism of some moderns that these are the tools of the
*black*smith, introduced here through ignorance, the poet specifically adds
οἷσίν τε χρυσὸν ἐργάζετο — '[the anvil, etc.] which he used for working
gold'. Even if the epics were contemporary with the action of the story,
we should hardly be justified in expecting of the poet any more explicit
accounts than these of such technical matters. What we might expect
(though an ancient reader would be less sensitive about this) is a general
authenticity of 'period' background. This we do find in Homer in
respect of metalwork inasmuch as the wealth of gold and silver vessels
and ornaments which is characteristic of the epic scene did really exist in
Mycenaean times.

    Admittedly 'Nestor's cup', which was so triumphantly recognized
by Schliemann in a gold cup from the fourth Shaft Grave, can hardly
now be cited as part of the evidence. Not only do we now recognize
that this cup is too early in date, but it does not in fact correspond with
the vessel described by Homer (Λ 632-7) except in so far as both have
figures of doves on the rim by the handles. Nestor's vessel is very large,
suitable for mixing drink in for a party, and too heavy for an ordinary
man to lift from the table when full, while the Shaft Grave cup (Fig. 13, *c*,
p. 346 above) is a goblet only a few inches high. The identification of the
δοιαὶ πυθμένες in the struts below the handles is little more than wishful
thinking. Again, although there is ancient tradition that the Homeric
word δέπας means a drinking cup, we now have some evidence that this
may be no more than a half truth. On an already famous tablet from
Pylos (Pl. 40) we have ideograms for vessels called *di-pa*, showing a
shape which cannot be paralleled among Mycenaean finds by vessels of
drinking-cup type, but can be better compared with a known type of
large bronze vessel of the *krater* or mixing-bowl kind (*cf.* Fig. 14 above,
p. 347). 'Mixing-bowl' will, in fact, be found an appropriate meaning
for δέπας in several other contexts too, though the word may be of wider
application, like 'bowl' in English.

    But though 'Nestor's cup' must be relinquished, the precious objects
that have been recovered by archaeology, and more recently the evidence
of the Knossos and Pylos tablets, do show that the epic rarely if ever
exaggerates the luxury and complex development of Mycenaean civilization, while at times it rather falls short of the truth. For example, we

have now in the tablets evidence for the existence of a specialization of trades and crafts in Mycenaean times such as Homer barely hints at.[3] (It might, of course, be irrelevant for him to do more.)   Only once is the potter mentioned, in a simile (Σ 600), though he must have been very familiar at all times.   There is no reference to working in leather except for the rather special case of Eumaeus making his own sandals from home-grown ox-hide (ξ 23 f.) ; but leather was used for shields and helmets, and in making chariots and harness.[a]   This again could be taken for granted.   We only hear once of a bow-maker, a worker in horn, $\kappa\epsilon\rho\alpha o\xi\acute{o}os$ $\tau\acute{e}\kappa\tau\omega\nu$ (Δ 110), never of the trade of the fuller — though this is attested in the tablets, and was probably familiar in the poet's day too.   Even the craft of the mason, undoubtedly highly developed in Mycenaean times, as the buildings show, is not mentioned by Homer: there is no reason why it should be.

Nor is it right to expect to find in the epic any clear indication of the organization or status of craftsmen, either in Mycenaean or in later times. Any hints there may be are purely incidental, and therefore by no means explicit.   Such are the two references to $\delta\eta\mu\iota o\epsilon\rho\gamma o\acute{\iota}$ (ρ 383 and τ 135). In the first passage it is remarked that men who are $\delta\eta\mu\iota o\epsilon\rho\gamma o\acute{\iota}$, such as the seer, the doctor, the carpenter ($\tau\acute{e}\kappa\tau o\nu\alpha$ $\delta o\acute{u}\rho\omega\nu$ = (?) shipwright), or the bard, are the only kind of strangers one would deliberately send for from outside the community.   The second refers to heralds as among the strangers 'who are $\delta\eta\mu\iota o\epsilon\rho\gamma o\acute{\iota}$'.   In classical Attic $\delta\eta\mu\iota o\upsilon\rho\gamma\acute{o}s$ is used of any creative craftsman, though in some states it was the title of certain magistrates.   In the latter case it would seem to mean originally 'one who does work pertaining to the $\delta\hat{\eta}\mu os$'; and this may perhaps be the real sense in Homer, inasmuch as the $\delta\eta\mu\iota o\epsilon\rho\gamma o\acute{\iota}$ in the Homeric list exercise trades or professions for the service of the whole community — not, like those of farming or spinning and weaving, for their own households.   If this is so, we should perhaps regard craftsmen like smiths and potters too as $\delta\eta\mu\iota o\epsilon\rho\gamma o\acute{\iota}$ in the Homeric sense.   That they are not included in the list in the context could well be because they were to be found in any ordinary community.   Those that do receive mention are those whose crafts are not in sufficiently constant demand for one to be supported in every place.[b]

It is noticeable in the Mycenaean tablets that many persons described by their occupations as, e.g., fuller, potter, etc., are holders of land ; and it has been argued from this that such specialized trades were in that period only part-time occupations, and that the craftsman would normally be a tiller of the soil as well.   This is by no means certain ; the land a man held need not have been worked by him in person.   Again, because the land held by craftsmen is usually of the category tentatively identified as

      [a] See p. 521 f., Ch. 19.   [b] See also Ch. 14, p. 459.

'public' land, it has been suggested that δημιοεργός originally meant 'worker of public land'; but this is equally uncertain; the term in Mycenaean Greek identified as equivalent to 'public' land is not *damios*; nor has the word δημιοεργός yet been found in the tablets. In the epics themselves we should surely not try to make any economic or sociological deductions from the fact that Odysseus himself has considerable skill in boat-building and furniture-making — besides the raft he constructed his own bedstead (ψ c. 200) — or from the fact that the warrior Lycaon goes in person to cut fig-branches for chariot-rails (Φ 37). One Robinson Crusoe is no evidence for a general 'do-it-yourself' trend in society.

NOTES TO CHAPTER 21

1. For furniture inlays see the reports of recent Mycenae excavations in *BSA*, xlviii. 8 with pl. 5; xlix. 235 ff. with pls. 33-6, 38-40; l. 182, 187 f. with pls. 25-7, 30; also Ventris and Chadwick, *Documents*, ch. x. For ivory on chariots, etc., *Documents*, ch. xi, *e.g.*, tablet no. 265.

2. This is substantially the explanation given by W. B. Stanford in his note on τ 572 ff.

3. *Documents*, ch. v. 4 and 7; ch. vi.

CHAPTER 22

COMMUNICATIONS AND TRADE

by Frank H. Stubbings

GREECE is a rugged and mountainous country, and that obvious fact is naturally reflected in the Homeric allusions to means of transport and communication. Even to-day there are many routes that can be traversed only on foot or with pack animals, donkey, or mule. The donkey eluding the donkey boys to browse in the cornfield by the way

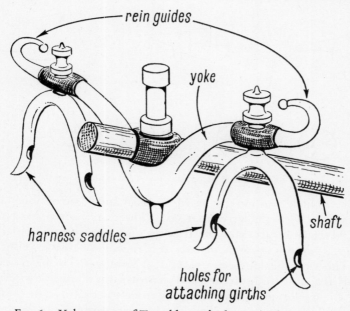

FIG. 63. Yoke-system of Tutankhamen's chariot (14th cent. B.C.)

(Λ 558 ff.) is a vignette that will appeal to everyone who knows the Greek scene. Equally permanent as a beast of burden is the mule, though now that so much of Greece has suffered deforestation, the sight of mules hauling logs and timbers down the mountain paths is not a common one, as it seems to have been for Homer (*cf.* P 742 ff.; Ψ 110 ff.). Wheeled traffic there undoubtedly was, even in Bronze Age times: our earliest evidence, archaeologically, is a little clay model of a four-wheeled cart from Middle Minoan Crete; but the use of carts would inevitably be confined to fairly level ground. Thus Nausicaa and her maids use a mule-cart to take the laundry along the coast to the washing-place (ζ 72 f.) ; and Priam's men use one to carry his gifts across the Trojan plain to Achilles's tent (Ω 265 ff.).

We get a fairly precise picture of Priam's cart: it has a detachable body (πείρινς), four wheels (line 324), and a single shaft (ῥυμός) to which a yoke for two mules is bound on with a long cord or strap (ζυγόδεσμον ἐννεάπηχυ). The yoke has a central knob (ὀμφαλός), and at the outer ends of it are hooks or rings (οἴηκες) to guide the outside reins. Whether

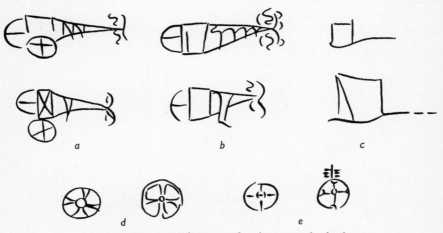

FIG. 64. Linear B ideograms for chariots and wheels

just such a vehicle was current in Mycenaean times, or only in Homer's own world, or in both, we cannot say. There are no representations of carts in Mycenaean art, and the frescoes and vase-paintings of chariots (cf. Pl. 37, a) do not show the details of harness very clearly. But it is at least certain that the Homeric method of lashing the yoke to the shaft (probably the same for both carts and chariots) was in use in the fourteenth century B.C. in Egypt, where we have an actual example from Tutankhamen's tomb. (Fig. 63 shows the yoke in position but without the lashing.) The chariot ideograms of Linear B script seem to imply something similar (see Fig. 64). A distinctive feature of the Mycenaean chariot is the stay running from the top edge of the car to the junction of shaft and yoke. This appears regularly in the vase-paintings, and when in the ideograms the yoke is shown this stay is shown too. This may help to explain the Homeric passage already cited (Ω 265 ff.) : we may understand the κρίκος as a ring or eye at one end of the ζυγόδεσμον, placed over a peg (ἔστωρ) on the front of the chariot frame ; that once in position, the ζυγόδεσμον is carried forward to form a stay as depicted for Mycenaean chariots, and the rest of its otherwise excessive length of nine cubits used to bind the yoke to the shaft.[1]   To judge from vase-paintings the chariots of archaic Greece were not greatly dissimilar in their harnessing arrangements.

Of considerable interest is the Homeric use of chariots not merely in war [a] but for passenger transport.   One would expect the use of chariots, almost as much as carts, to be restricted, not merely by the difficulty or lack of roads, but by the limited amount of country suitable for raising the horses to draw them.   It is a familiar point that such areas, Argos and Elis for example, are unusual enough to be distinguished in Homer by the epithet ἱππόβοτος; and Telemachus comments that the islands (Ithaca especially) are no place for either using or raising horses —

$$οὐ \ γάρ \ τις \ νήσων \ ἱππήλατος, \ οὐδ' \ εὐλείμων— \qquad (δ \ 607)$$

though Ithakesians did own horses on the mainland (δ 635).   We are, therefore, the more surprised that it seems in the poem a matter of course that Telemachus and Peisistratus can go by chariot, in two days' driving, from Pylos to Sparta.   Whatever the route taken, it would involve some steep rough country, and several questions remain unanswered.   Was the poet, and were his audience, unfamiliar with the geography of the Peloponnese ? or did he ignore geography (in a work otherwise careful of verisimilitude) to suit his story ? or was there for him adequate tradition that such journeys really were made in heroic times ?   If they were, there must have been some kind of built roads; and this is not wholly improbable, though our actual evidence of Mycenaean road-works is confined to the remains of bridges over torrent-beds and some traces of paved roads in the vicinity of Mycenae (cf. Fig. 25, and Pl. 18, b).

Of sea communications little need be said : the point needs no labouring that the Greeks have always been seafarers, that the sea is never far off.   There is no reason to doubt that the Homeric descriptions of nautical procedure, both sailing and rowing (e.g., A 475-83, 432-5), are true to their period; and stock lines such as

$$ἐξῆς \ δ' \ ἑζόμενοι \ πολιὴν \ ἅλα \ τύπτον \ ἐρετμοῖς \quad (δ \ 580 \ and \ eight \ other \ places)$$

may well have been traditional in epic for centuries.   Pictures of vessels with many oars have been found at Volo (ancient Iolkos) on a Middle Helladic vase; and though in Mycenaean art representations of ships are excessively rare (one from Cyprus is shown in Fig. 65), yet the archaeological evidence of intercourse with all parts of the eastern Mediterranean and with Sicily and southern Italy leaves us in no doubt that seafaring and sea-borne trade were as essential a feature of the Mycenaean world as they are of the *Odyssey* and the *Iliad*.

[a] *Cf.* Ch. 19.

There are various Homeric references to articles of foreign craftsmanship — usually Phoenician. Helen's silver wool-basket was a gift from
Egypt; from the same source Menelaus had two silver baths and two
tripods, besides ten talents of gold (δ 128 ff.). From the king of the
Sidonioi he had received a silver bowl with a golden rim, which he gives
to Telemachus (δ 615 ff.; ο 115 ff.). A similar Sidonian bowl, brought
across the sea by Phoenician traders, is one of the prizes in the funeral
games (Ψ 741 ff.); and in another passage (Z 289 ff.) we hear of precious
Sidonian textiles brought from Phoenicia to Troy. There are other
passages too where Phoenicians of Sidon are represented as traders and

FIG. 65. Drawing of ship, from a Cypriot Mycenaean vase
(Scale c. 1 : 4)

seafarers whom one might meet in Greek waters. It is on a Phoenician
ship that Odysseus (in one of his fictitious autobiographies) escaped from
Crete (ν 272 ff.); Phoenician seafarers had visited the home of Eumaeus's
childhood, and when after a year's trading they had filled their ship with
merchandise they topped it up with the boy Eumaeus and a Phoenician
slave-woman whom they had 'liberated' from the palace (ο 403-84).
All such allusions to Phoenician ships and merchandise were at one time
supposed to be 'late' elements in the epic, projections of the poet's own
times; for modern knowledge of Greco-Phoenician intercourse began with
the eighth or ninth century B.C. Now, however, it is clear from archaeological evidence that Mycenaean Greece was in frequent contact with
the peoples of the eastern Mediterranean, and there was interchange of
both merchandise and artistic influences. Syrian amphorae (e.g., Pl. 37, b)
have been found at Mycenaean sites. Most probably there were Mycenaean traders permanently resident at Ugarit on the Syrian coast (now
Ras Shamra, a little north of Latakia). There is also the fact that Hittite
records mention Achaean ships going to Syria. We know too that Syria

then as later was a home of craftsmen in gold and ivory (*cf.* Pl. 38) —
textiles too, perhaps, though, of course, they have not survived. Moreover certain Semitic loan-words in Greek — *e.g.*, χρυσός = gold, χιτών =
tunic, σησάμη = sesame — are now known to have been already current
in Mycenaean times; and the names of Sidon and Tyre appear to have
entered Greek in the second millennium B.C., since Greek preserves them
in an ancient form. So there is no anachronism in Homer's Phoenicians;
his picture of the heroic age would indeed be less true without them.[2]

   This eastward trade was doubtless the most important for Mycenaean
Greece, and it is almost the only aspect of trade mentioned in the epic.
The actual exchange of goods is once referred to (H 472 ff.), when the
Greeks at Troy barter bronze, iron, hides, cattle, and slaves, for Lemnian
wine. Barter as the method of exchange is doubtless historically correct;
but cattle are not infrequently a measure of value — witness the adjectives
ἑκατόμβοιος, ἐννεάβοιος (*e.g.*, in the famous exchange of golden for
brazen armour in Z 235 f.). Metals, especially gold, may be measured
in talents (*e.g.*, Ψ 751) and it seems likely that the talent was originally a
weight of metal equivalent to the value of an ox. This is supported by the
currency in Minoan-Mycenaean times of copper ingots of standard weight
shaped to resemble an ox-hide.[3]

   Trade in slaves doubtless existed in Mycenaean times, and in the epic
we have already met it as a sideline of the Phoenician merchants in the
Eumaeus story. In other passages it is the obscure Taphians who appear
as sea-raiders and slave-traders (ξ 452; ο 427; π 426). They too deal
also in kindlier merchandise. Athene on one occasion appears to Telemachus in the guise of the Taphian king Mentes,

πλέων ἐπὶ οἴνοπα πόντον ἐπ' ἀλλοθρόους ἀνθρώπους,
ἐς Τεμέσην μετὰ χαλκόν, ἄγω δ' αἴθωνα σίδηρον.   (α 183-4)

These Taphians are supposed to be a people of north-west Greece,[a] but
unfortunately we do not know where Τεμέση was — Tempsa in Bruttium and Tamassos in Cyprus (a known source of copper) have both
been suggested — or where the cargo of iron is supposed to come from.
There is thus no knowing whether this couplet represents authentic
historical background or not; but the lover of poetry will not be troubled
thereby: the journey to Samarkand is none the less golden for lack of a
map of it.

NOTES TO CHAPTER 22

   1. This account owes much to M. G. F. Ventris and J. Chadwick, *Documents*, 361 ff.,
q.v. for more detail. The explanation of the stay as part of the ζυγόδεσμον is the writer's,
anticipated, however, by M. and C. H. B. Quennell, *Everyday things in Homeric Greece*,
116 f.

                        a See Ch. 9.

2. On Phoenicians in Homer see especially L. A. Stella, 'Importanza degli scavi di Ras Shamra per il problema fenicio dei poemi omerici' in *Archaeologia Classica*, iv. 72 ff.; also her *Il poema di Ulisse* (1955), 38 f.　For the archaeological evidence of Mycenaean intercourse with foreign countries, the following: A. J. B. Wace and C. W. Blegen, 'Pottery as Evidence for Trade and Colonization' in *Klio*, xxxii. 131 ff.; H. Kantor, *The Aegean and the Orient in the Second Millennium B.C.* (=*AJA*, li. 1-103); F. H. Stubbings, *Mycenaean Pottery from the Levant* (1951); Lord William Taylour, *Mycenaean Pottery in Italy and Adjacent Areas* (1958).

3. *Cf.* C. T. Seltman, *Greek Coins* (1933), 4-8 and fig. 1.

CHAPTER 23

WRITING

by Lilian H. Jeffery

1. 'ANCIENT SCRIPTS' IN THE GREEK TRADITION

THE invention of the art of writing was a subject on which the ancient Greeks themselves held a diversity of views. From the fragments of their speculations which survive, mostly in fleeting references or brief quotations only, it seems that at first they followed the usual practice of attributing the invention to a glorious εὑρετής belonging to their own heroic past; but this uncritical viewpoint was inevitably challenged by the travelled logographers, who had seen in other countries inscriptions palpably older than any Greek examples; and these two conflicting lines of thought were fused finally in a series of more or less elaborate accounts compiled by later heurematologists and grammarians, who strove conscientiously but often uncritically to reconcile old traditions with rational inferences.

Our earliest witness, the poet Stesichorus in the first half of the sixth century, ascribed the art to Palamedes, traditionally an inventor of many devices (Bergk, *PLG* iii, fr. 34); and as he had no obvious historical axe to grind here, it may be inferred that he was merely quoting an existing tradition which was attached to the hero. There is no more evidence of sixth-century theories until the end of that century, when the inquiring spirit of Ionian science was already at work. The logographer Hecataeus (*fl. c.* 500 ?), who had visited Egypt and seen the Egyptian hieroglyphic system, maintained that the art of writing was first brought to Greece by Danaus (Jacoby, *FGH* i. 1, F 20); and presumably he had in mind Danaus's connection with Egypt. This theory showed a marked advance beyond the traditional belief, because it admitted that the invention of writing was something distinct from its first appearance in Greece; older systems than the Greek alphabet existed, and the original invention must therefore be sought outside Greece. In the next generation the greatest contribution of any to the problem was put forward by the historian Herodotus, who had once visited Tyre in Phoenicia. Observing that the general term for the Greek alphabet in his own day among Ionic Greeks was 'Phoenician letters' (φοινικήια γράμματα), he concluded that it was the Phoenicians of Cadmus's company who had first brought the art of writing to Greece (v. 58-61). Thenceforward the rival claims of Phoenicia and Egypt appear to have had most weight among the rationalists, although some, notably Epigenes of Byzantium, upheld the great antiquity of Babylonian cuneiform (Pliny, *N.H.* vii. 56), and a certain Dosiadas of Crete made a claim for his island, perhaps from actual observation of inscribed tablets found on deserted sites there (Jacoby, *FGH* iiiB. 458, F 6; see further below, pp. 547 ff.). But there were not lacking other writers who still preferred to assign the invention to a mythical Greek εὑρετής, as Hermes, or Orpheus, or Linus, or Musaeus, or Cecrops; some even derived the φοινικήια from Phoenix, teacher of Achilles, or Phoenice, daughter of Actaeon, or from palm-leaves (φοῖνιξ = a palm), which they held to be the earliest form of writing-material. To reconcile the conflicting arguments of tradition and rationalism, therefore, some authorities suggested that Cadmus introduced the bulk of the alphabet (sixteen or eighteen letters), and the rest were contributed by one of the Greek εὑρεταί (as Palamedes or Linus), or even by the poets Simonides and Epicharmus in the early fifth century. The introduction of such late names may have been due again to rational views, based on a recollection that the Ionic letters *eta*, *xi*, *psi*, and *ōmega*, which were not officially recognized in the Attic alphabet until 403/2 B.C., had first become familiar to the average Athenian through the literary texts of Ionic writers like Simonides. Another compromise suggested was that Cadmus indeed brought the art of writing to Greece, but Linus, or some similar εὑρετής, first adapted this alien script to the sounds of the Greek language.

From the surviving statements it might seem to us that, except possibly for Dosiadas of Crete, the Greeks had no knowledge of the existence of any system of writing in their own country other than their alphabetic 'Phoenician letters' which could be suggested as a rival to the ancient systems of Egypt, Phoenicia, Syria, and Babylonia. But this extreme view would be misleading, a distortion arising from the brevity of our sources, which rarely cite any of the reasons given by the authors whose conclusions they quote. We know from other references that the Greeks did, on occasion, find and puzzle over relics of an unknown script in their own country, which were presumably relics of the old Mycenaean Linear B system. It is true that Herodotus's account (v. 59-61) of dedicatory epigrams by various Greek heroes inscribed in 'Cadmean letters, mostly similar to the Ionic' which he saw on tripods in the Ismenium at Thebes must have been either rank forgeries in pseudo-archaic Greek made by the priests, or genuine archaic Greek dedications on old athletic prizes, barely legible and freely translated; for no inscription written in Linear B characters could possibly be described as 'similar to the Ionic', and an inscription in archaic Phoenician (which might possibly be so described) would hardly be found on a dedicated object so typically

PLATE 39

(*a*) Inscribed stirrup-jar (L.H. IIIb) from Mycenae. Height *c.* 16 in. (*b*) Clay sealing (no. Wt 501) from Mycenae, with Linear B signs inscribed on the reverse. (*c*) Linear B tablet from Mycenae (Au 102). Height 6¾ in.

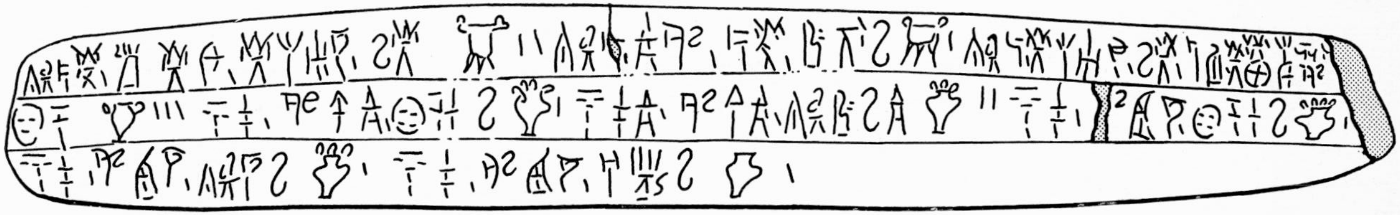

PLATE 40

Line (1) ti-ri-po-de ai-ke-u ke-re-si-jo we-ke TRIPOD 2 ti-ri-po e-me po-de o-wo-we TRIPOD 1 ti-ri-po ke-re-si-jo we-ke a-pu ke-ka-u-me-no ke-re-a₂ no-[pe-re ? TRIPOD 1]

(2) qe-to WINE-JAR ? 3 di-pa me-zo-e qe-to-ro-we POT 1 di-pa-e me-zo-e ti-ri-o-we-e POT 2 di-pa me-wi-jo qe-to-ro-we POT 1

(3) di-pa me-wi-jo ti-ri-jo-we POT 1 di-pa me-wi-jo a-no-we POT 1

Linear B tablet from Pylos (Ta 641), with transliteration. Length 6½ in.

Greek as a bronze tripod. But there are other, more suggestive references. Plutarch records that when a structure known as 'Alcmena's
tomb' at Haliartus in Boeotia was opened in the fourth century there
was found, besides two amphorae and a necklace, a bronze (sic) tablet
inscribed in 'very old, barbaric characters, very like the Egyptian' (De
Gen. Soc. 5). A Roman Liber Memorialis derived from Greek sources
states that in the temple of Apollo at Sicyon were several relics said to
have belonged to Homeric heroes — Agamemnon's shield and sword,
Odysseus's cloak and breastplate, and Palamedes's letters (litterae Pala-
medis; Ampelius, c. 8. 5). By this were probably meant the fatal 'letters
to Priam' by which in the epic Odysseus secured Palamedes's ruin; but
the relics themselves may actually have been clay tablets in Linear B
script like those found elsewhere in the Peloponnese (pp. 548 ff.), just
as some at least of the armour may have been genuine Mycenaean
weapons found in tombs. Again, a confused reference to some system
of writing which was not derived from the Phoenician seems to be preserved in a citation by Diodorus from the works of Dionysius of Mytilene
(Diod. iii. 67). It is said there that Cadmus indeed first brought the
alphabet to Greece, but Linus first adapted it to the language of those then
inhabiting the country, and it was called in general terms 'Phoenician',
but in particular 'Pelasgic', because the Pelasgians first used the adapted
letters. This suggests an uncritical attempt to reconcile two traditions,
one referring to 'Phoenician letters' (i.e., the Greek alphabet), and the
other referring to some other script to which had been given the abori-
ginal-sounding title 'Pelasgic letters'; this would be a natural name to
give any indecipherable Mycenaean tablets found by the Greeks. Lastly,
as was said above, the claim of the Cretan Dosiadas (to which little
attention appears to have been paid by the ancients) that writing was
invented in Crete may have arisen from chance discoveries of tablets in
Linear A or B.

2. WRITING IN THE MYCENAEAN PERIOD

As is now well known, the Cretans had in fact developed the art of
writing during the second millennium B.C. from a hieroglyphic system
to a stylized series of signs generally termed Linear A (Fig. 66), and by the
fifteenth century B.C. there was current at Knossos a kindred system
(Linear B), whose formalized signs retain only faint vestiges of their
pictorial origin (Pls. 39, 40). In 1900, when Sir Arthur Evans made his
first discovery of the vast collection of clay tablets in Linear B stored in
the Palace of Knossos, several Mycenaean sites had been already excavated
on the Greek mainland by Schliemann, Tsountas, and Dörpfeld, and no
vestige of any such tablets had appeared; but at Mycenae had been found

the remains of vases or of storage vessels of the type termed 'stirrup-jar' by archaeologists, on which were incised or painted either single signs or short sign-groups in a script resembling Linear B (*cf*. Pl. 39, *a*); and in later excavations during this century were found the rim of a bowl bearing what may possibly be a line of writing from Asine, a single inscribed stirrup-jar from Orchomenos, another from Eleusis, a series of twenty-eight (some bearing inscriptions of over twelve signs) from the Mycenaean

FIG. 66. Linear A tablet

'Palace of Cadmus' at Thebes, and a number of inscribed fragments from Tiryns. Although these vases (dated provisionally *c*. 1330–1200 B.C.) had every appearance of being local products, the remote possibility remained that they might all be imports from Crete; but in 1939 the final proof appeared in the joint American and Greek excavations at Messenian Pylos, where in a room of the Mycenaean palace Blegen found over five hundred inscribed clay tablets like the Knossian, dated to the Late Helladic IIIb period. Smaller numbers of tablets were further discovered in 1952–5. At Mycenae itself, although all traces of any archive-room within the citadel have been lost, a stray fragment was found on the site in 1950, and in 1952–4 Wace discovered fifty tablets, as well as some inscribed clay sealings (Pl. 39, *b*), in the large building called the House of the Oil Merchant, and the two buildings adjoining it (House of Sphinxes and House of Shields); a few more inscribed stirrup-jars or sherds were also found between 1939 and 1952. All this material is to be assigned to the period Late Helladic IIIa–b (*c*. 1400–1200 B.C.).

The early work of Evans on the Knossian tablets had established that these inscriptions in all probability were written in a syllabary, and were inventories of various objects, written from left to right, the words divided by short vertical strokes (*cf*. Pls. 39, 40). Each entry normally consisted of: name or description of person(s) or object(s); then an ideogram to ensure the identification (a shorthand sketch to represent man, woman, horse, chariot, etc.); and then a numeral or symbol for the relevant number, weight, or measure. The detailed researches of the American scholars, A. Kober and E. L. Bennett, Jr., between 1939 and 1952 had further established the important conclusions that the language of Linear B was inflected on Indo-European lines, that it was not the same language as that of Linear A, and that, though the numeral system was the same for both, the system of weights and measures was not.

Meanwhile the English scholar Michael Ventris had been working for over ten years on the decipherment of Linear B, basing his attack on the unbiased methods used in code-breaking, whereby he succeeded in establishing in a 'grid' (a) the series of those syllables which all began with the same consonant, (b) the series of those which all contained the same vowel, and (c) those which appeared to be pure vowels. Although

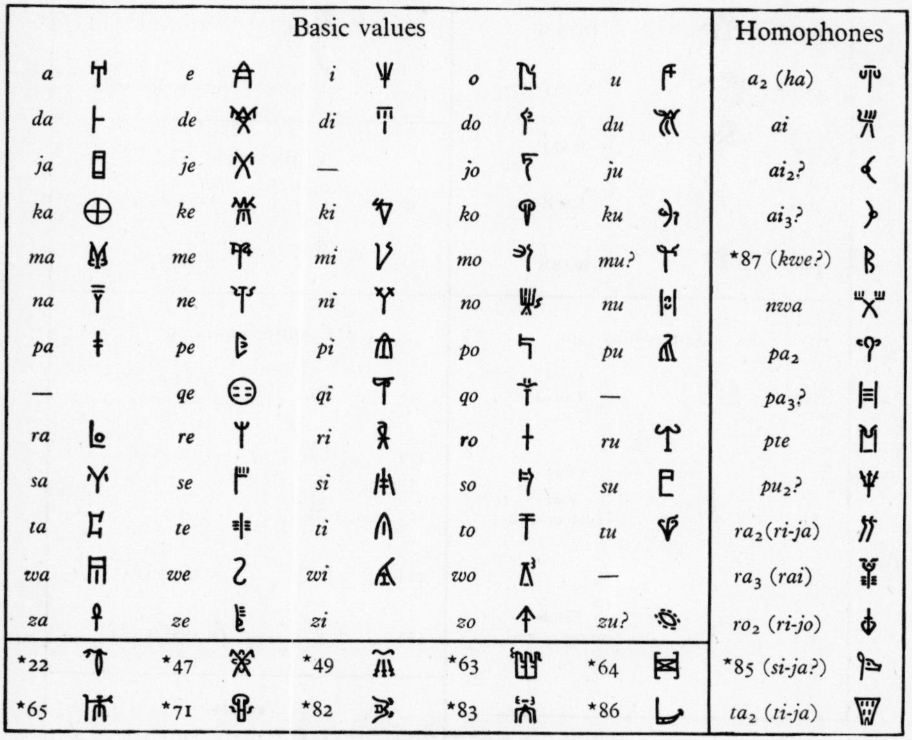

Basic values					Homophones
a	e	i	o	u	a_2 (ha)
da	de	di	do	du	ai
ja	je	—	jo	ju	ai_2?
ka	ke	ki	ko	ku	ai_3?
ma	me	mi	mo	mu?	*87 (kwe?)
na	ne	ni	no	nu	nwa
pa	pe	pi	po	pu	pa_2
—	qe	qi	qo	—	pa_3?
ra	re	ri	ro	ru	pte
sa	se	si	so	su	pu_2?
ta	te	ti	to	tu	ra_2 (ri-ja)
wa	we	wi	wo	—	ra_3 (rai)
za	ze	zi	zo	zu?	ro_2 (ri-jo)
*22	*47	*49	*63	*64	*85 (si-ja?)
*65	*71	*82	*83	*86	ta_2 (ti-ja)

FIG. 67. Values of Linear B signs

at this stage no certain sound-values could be attached to the signs, by June 1952 he had reached the conclusion that the language must be Greek. At this stage began his collaboration with J. Chadwick, and in spring 1953 the suggested sound-values were strikingly confirmed by one of the newly-found tablets at Pylos.[a] The sound-values established by Ventris's grid (Fig. 67) are now generally accepted, and the transliteration and translation of the texts has gone forward rapidly with the collaboration of philologists and archaeologists on both sides of the Atlantic. The language is seen to be an archaic form of Greek, nearest to the Arcado-Cypriot among the classical dialects. Many problems of details remain

[a] See Pl. 40.

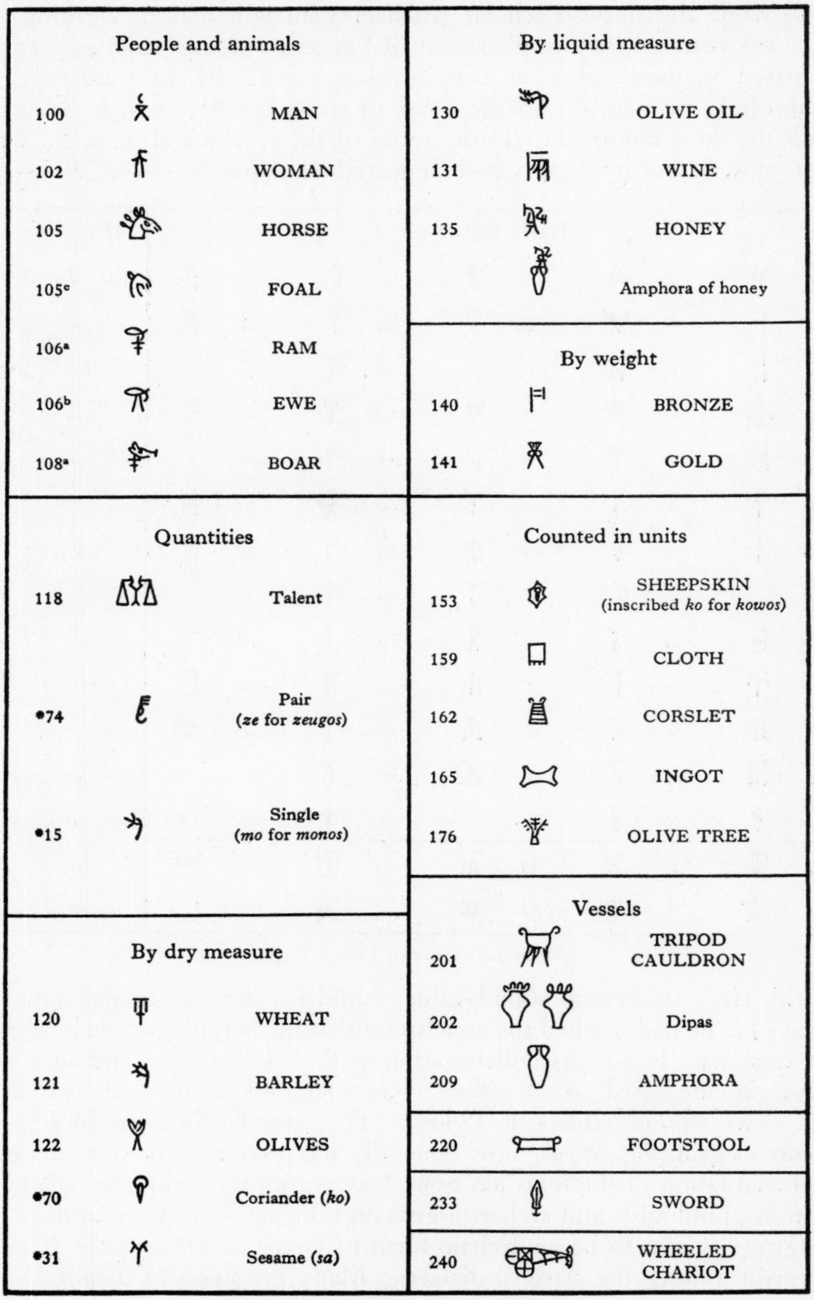

People and animals			By liquid measure		
100		MAN	130		OLIVE OIL
102		WOMAN	131		WINE
105		HORSE	135		HONEY
105ᶜ		FOAL			Amphora of honey
106ᵃ		RAM	**By weight**		
106ᵇ		EWE	140		BRONZE
108ᵃ		BOAR	141		GOLD

Quantities			Counted in units		
118		Talent	153		SHEEPSKIN (inscribed *ko* for *kowos*)
			159		CLOTH
•74		Pair (*ze* for *zeugos*)	162		CORSLET
			165		INGOT
•15		Single (*mo* for *monos*)	176		OLIVE TREE

By dry measure			Vessels		
			201		TRIPOD CAULDRON
120		WHEAT	202		Dipas
121		BARLEY	209		AMPHORA
122		OLIVES	220		FOOTSTOOL
•70		Coriander (*ko*)	233		SWORD
•31		Sesame (*sa*)	240		WHEELED CHARIOT

FIG. 68. Selected Linear B ideograms

to be solved, a fact which may be ascribed to the double difficulty of recovering from a syllabic system whose limited range has necessarily mutilated the words themselves a form of Greek which is at least four centuries earlier than any examples of the language known hitherto. The only slight palliation of this difficulty is the fact that the tablets show throughout a consistency both of script and of dialect which is remarkable in a span of about two centuries.

It is thus established beyond doubt that the Mycenaean age was literate. We should not assume, however, that Homer's heroes could themselves write. Over eighty signs, some highly complex, have been attested in Linear B and there are also many ideograms (Fig. 68) and contractions for signs in combination. Like Egyptian hieroglyphic and Babylonian cuneiform, it was probably confined to a fairly limited class of trained scribes; and this would help to explain its disappearance after the close of the Mycenaean period. A script which was the peculiar property of a trained class might well die out with the downfall of the royal families and wealthy citizens who employed the scribes.

For, as far as we know, the script did disappear from the mainland. There are no traces of it thereafter in the succeeding sub-Mycenaean and Protogeometric periods. Negative evidence at the present stage of archaeological excavation is hardly conclusive; but it is not likely that the Phoenician alphabet would have been adopted by the Greeks had they already possessed an established system of writing in their midst — even a system as cumbersome as the Mycenaean syllabic. It may be objected that in Assyria the alien Aramaic alphabet imposed itself upon the existing native cuneiform and finally drove it out; but the case is not parallel. A large number of North Syrian subjects existed within the Assyrian Empire, who naturally used their own Aramaic script, thus providing the nucleus for its expansion; whereas to bring about the same situation in Greece the Phoenicians would have required an established footing in the country which modern archaeological research utterly denies to them. The case of Cyprus is noteworthy here. The Cypriot Greeks of the classical period used a syllabary composed of an unknown total of signs (between fifty and sixty are identified at present), itself descended from an early system which may possibly have some connection with the Cretan Linear A. The Cypriot syllabary was used for the Greek language — or, to put it more accurately, the joints of the Greek language were wrenched and distorted until it fitted the syllabary; and thus equipped the Greeks of Cyprus ignored the far superior Phoenician system practised by the Phoenician settlers on the same island, and even held out against the Greek alphabet itself as a national script until the Hellenistic period. Convention is a strong force in the history of all writing.

3. THE INTRODUCTION OF THE ALPHABET TO GREECE

It is concluded, therefore, that there was a period of illiteracy again between the disappearance of the mainland syllabic system before it had taken proper root in Greece, and that momentous event in western history when the Greeks adopted the consonantal twenty-two-letter alphabet of the Semitic-speaking Phoenicians, and by their use of it turned it into a flexible instrument for the Indo-European languages (see Fig. 69).

A vestigial trace of this adoption was preserved, as we have seen, in the Ionic Greek name for the alphabet, 'Phoenician letters'. As far as we know, Herodotus was the first to infer this origin from the name. His view is now regarded as clear beyond all doubt, from the similarity in both alphabets (*a*) of the names of the twenty-two letters from *alpha* to *tau* (Phoenician *'ālep*, *bêt*, and so on); (*b*) of their order, both visually in the written *abecedarium* and orally in the recited list, although the Greeks confused the sounds of the sibilants; (*c*) of the basic shapes of the letters, although they underwent some alterations in Greek hands; (*d*) of the retrograde direction of the *abecedarium*; the Phoenicians wrote from right to left continuously, and the general idea that an inscription should begin from right to left was faithfully followed by the Greeks in their early inscriptions; they did not normally, however, continue in a retrograde direction after the first line, but evolved for themselves the system called *boustrophedon*, i.e., turning at the end of a line to return in the reverse direction, as the plough-oxen turned at the end of a furrow.

The process whereby the Greek alphabet of vowels and consonants from *alpha* to *upsilon* arose from the vowel-less Phoenician alphabet is easily traced along its general lines, but certain particulars are still disputed. Of the most important change — that of the Semitic consonants *'ālep*, *hē'*, *wāw*, *yôḏ*, and *'ayin* to the Greek *alpha*, *e(psilon)*, *u(psilon)*, *iota*, and *o(mikron)* — it is perhaps an exaggeration to suggest, as have some authorities, that this was the deliberate work of some brilliant innovator who transformed the Semitic sounds, useless to the Greek language, into the five Greek vowels. It is safer to suggest only that in that first community of Greeks and Phoenicians where Greek learners repeated the alphabet from Phoenician speakers these Phoenician sounds on Greek tongues naturally took on Greek sound-values; for Semitic scholars have pointed out that the Phoenician names *'ālep*, *hē'*, *'ayin* contain in their initial syllables some suggestion of the vowel-sounds *a*, *e*, *o*; so that the Greeks, learning the alphabet on the acrophonic principle ('*ālep* = *a*, *bêt* = *b*, and so on), naturally took those initial sounds to be the Semitic versions of their own vowels. *Wāw* and *yôḏ* had the semi-vocalic values *u* and *i* in Phoenician also, so that here the development to the Greek *u* (both vowel *upsilon* and semivowel *vau* or *digamma*) and *i* was likewise

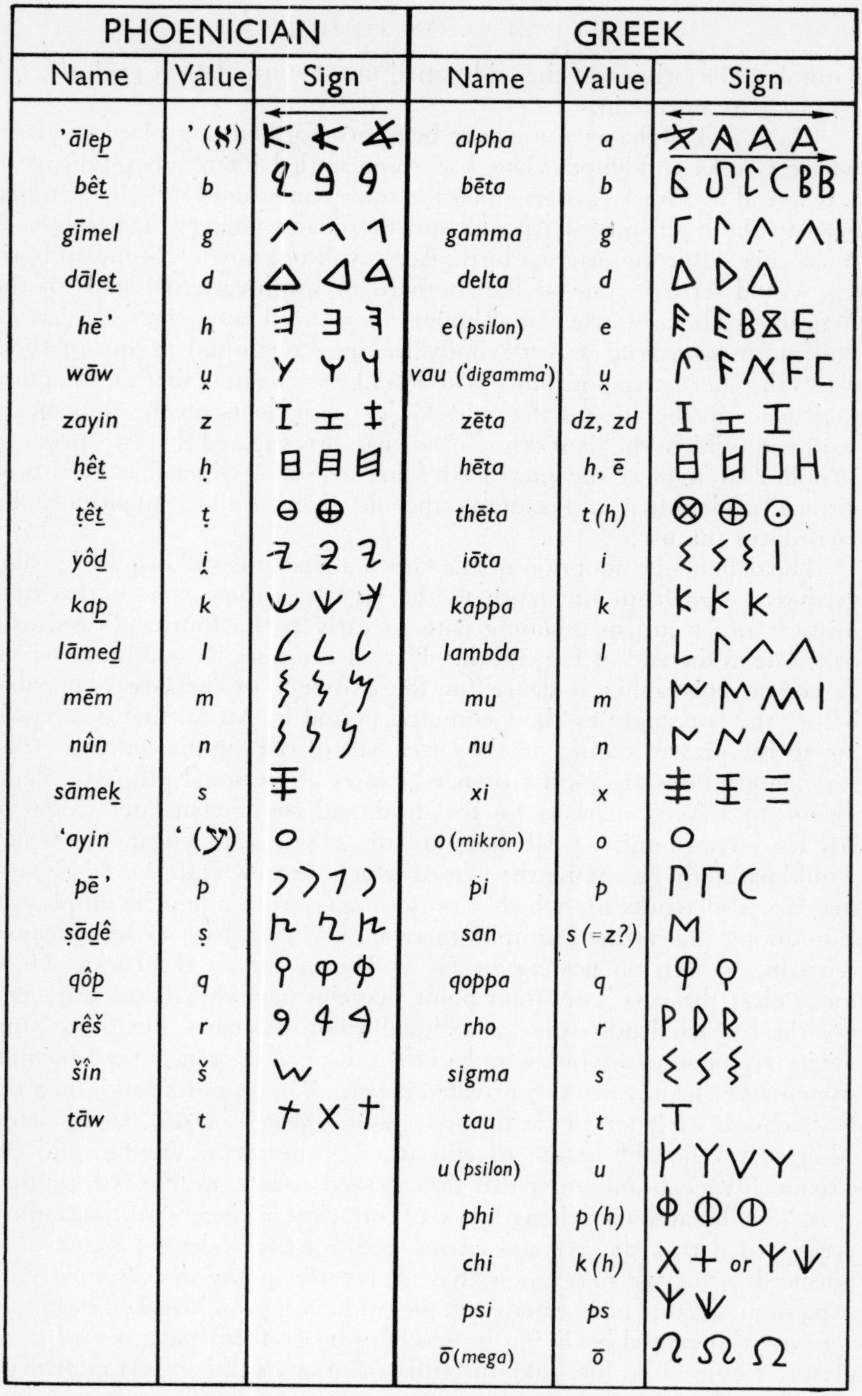

PHOENICIAN			GREEK		
Name	Value	Sign	Name	Value	Sign
'ālep̱	' (א)		alpha	a	
bêṯ	b		bēta	b	
gīmel	g		gamma	g	
dāleṯ	d		delta	d	
hē'	h		e (psilon)	e	
wāw	u̯		vau ('digamma')	u̯	
zayin	z		zēta	dz, zd	
ḥêṯ	ḥ		hēta	h, ē	
ṭêṯ	ṭ		thēta	t (h)	
yôḏ	i̯		iōta	i	
kap̱	k		kappa	k	
lāmeḏ	l		lambda	l	
mēm	m		mu	m	
nûn	n		nu	n	
sāmek̲	s		xi	x	
'ayin	' (ע)		o (mikron)	o	
pē'	p		pi	p	
ṣāḏê	ṣ		san	s (=z?)	
qôp̱	q		qoppa	q	
rêš	r		rho	r	
šîn	š		sigma	s	
tāw	t		tau	t	
			u (psilon)	u	
			phi	p (h)	
			chi	k (h)	or
			psi	ps	
			ō (mega)	ō	

FIG. 69. The Phoenician and archaic Greek alphabets: a selection of typical letter-forms

natural. The origins of the additional, non-Semitic letters (*phi, chi, psi, ō(mega)*) are uncertain.

The Greek alphabet must have been first formed in a place or places where Greeks and Phoenicians had some settled intercourse, whence it was spread by Greek carriers along the trade routes until it had penetrated even to the highlands of Arcadia and the inland villages of Aetolia and Acarnania. But the original birthplace is still unknown. Some authorities would set it in one of the southern or south-eastern islands of the Aegean — Thera, Crete, or Rhodes; but until any traces of actual Phoenician *settlement* (as yet wholly lacking) are found in any of these places the alternative possibility is no less likely : namely that the adoption took place in the area of the early Greek settlements on the Phoenician coast, of which the best known is that investigated by Sir Leonard Woolley in 1938 at the site of Al Mina in Syria, which has been provisionally identified as Posidium, the old Greek colony mentioned by Herodotus (iii. 91).

The date of the adoption of the Greek alphabet is still disputed ; suggestions range from the tenth to the eighth century B.C., with extremists at either end maintaining dates as early as the fourteenth century, or as late as the end of the eighth. Here it can only be said that there is as yet no epigraphic evidence for the existence of the Greek alphabet before the last stages of the Geometric period in Attica, that is, according to the present dating, in the latter half of the eighth century. The early inscriptions are mostly owners' names on personal property, dedications to a deity, markers for the dead, and (somewhat later) codes of law for a community. All these are the obvious, practical uses which would naturally be among the first to which the new craft would be put ; they are also works for which a professional scribe might be employed. But among the earliest examples there are also casual verses and personal remarks, written on pottery or (as at Thera) cut on the rocks, which make clear the very important point that this new alphabetic script was not the restricted possession of a closed guild of scribes, but by its simplicity lay open to anyone who had the means to learn it — vase-painter, stonemason, bronzeworker, private citizen. We do not know when the first schools of letters were opened (γραμματοδιδασκαλεῖα), as the latest addition to the old system of education (gymnastics, singing, and the cithara) ; we can only infer that they existed already in the sixth century at Athens, because Cleisthenes's law of ostracism at the end of the century presupposed that the average citizen could write at least a name on a potsherd. But we may guess that very early in the development and expansion of the new discovery the itinerant γραμματιστής began to appear, who earned his living by teaching his craft for pay, as well as by plying it himself on hire, like the citharist or any other expert craftsman.

4. WRITING IN RELATION TO THE HOMERIC POEMS

There are only two Homeric passages which bear upon the problem of writing, both in the *Iliad*. In one (H 175, 187, 189) the Achaean champions 'make their mark' (σῆμα ἐπιγράφειν) on the pebbles which they cast to decide who shall oppose Hector; and this tells us only that they were illiterate, as warriors might well be, whether in the Mycenaean period or in the Middle Ages, although the art of writing was undoubtedly known at both these times. In the other passage (Z 155 ff.) there is a definite reference to writing, embedded in the tale of Proetus and Bellerophon. Proetus sent Bellerophon from Ephyra to his guest-friend the king of Lycia, and gave him a closed diptych on which he had written many baneful signs:

$$—πόρεν δ' ὅ γε σήματα λυγρά,$$
$$γράψας ἐν πίνακι πτυκτῷ θυμοφθόρα πολλά.$$

This description seems to refer to twin tablets, fastened together with the script inside; which would be equally applicable to two clay tablets like those found at Knossos and Pylos, tied together, or to hinged wooden tablets, wax-coated, of the kind which figures sometimes on Assyrian reliefs. It does not suggest a Phoenician prototype, for the Semitic scribes used mainly papyrus, sherds, or leather. If the verse is regarded as a veiled reference by Homer to a practice of his own time (veiled, because he uses σῆμα for the normal word γράμμα), then the 'folded tablet' was probably wooden, for the post-Mycenaean Greeks, like the Phoenicians, did not use clay tablets. It should be recalled, however, that the saga of Bellerophon, with its weird attendant creatures Pegasus and the Chimaera, is perhaps not Greek but Lycian in origin, and may be very early; the message is an integral part of the story, and therefore any later teller (Lycian or Greek, whenever the Greeks first heard the tale) would continue to repeat the traditional detail of the baneful signs, just as he repeated the account of the Lycian Chimaera, without having necessarily any first-hand knowledge of the thing itself. This theory would mean that the Lycians at an early date knew of a system of writing; which is not impossible, since some non-Greek letters in the classical Lycian alphabet have been held to be survivors of some Anatolian (even Minoan) system. If the story of Bellerophon is as early as the Mycenaean period it may even imply a real possibility of written communication between Greece and Lycia at that time. At least it has to be admitted that the references within the *Iliad* can give no *proof* that the art of writing was practised in Greece when the Homeric poems were composed, and therefore cannot help us in the further problem as to whether the poems themselves were written down at the time of their composition — a

double question which was answered in the negative in the first century
A.D. by Josephus, who was seeking to prove that the Jewish race had
anticipated the Greek in all the latter's alleged inventions (*Contra Apionem*
i. 10-12). Scholars have continued to maintain opposing opinions on the
subject to the present day; but to discuss the evidence afforded by the
study of epic style in general and the Homeric epics in particular is
beyond the scope of this chapter.[a] Have the *Iliad* and *Odyssey* in fact the
distinctive characteristics of works composed for oral recitation ? Or
are major epics of this high quality impossible to achieve without the aid
of a system of writing ? These are literary questions beyond the range
of the epigraphist. But the fact that it is — or was — a perfectly possible
feat for the trained memory to compose and retain for recitation poems
of such length is generally agreed. Can it be established that it would
have been equally possible for a trained writer to write down poems of
such length before the seventh century in Greek lands ?

Obviously, the answer must depend partly at least on the kind of
writing-material available at the time. Apart from those inscriptions
which could suitably be written on existing objects (as law-codes on
temple walls, dedications on the thing dedicated, grave-inscriptions on
the memorials erected above the dead), public texts were usually inscribed
on stone pillars; bronze tablets were also employed, and wood too was
sometimes used, the most famous example of this being the set of wooden
axones on which Solon's law-code was inscribed at Athens. No evidence for the use of clay tablets after the Mycenaean period has been
found as yet in Greece, although a few fragmentary tablets bearing
Carian inscriptions have been found in the post-archaic dumps of the
temple of Zeus at Labranda in Caria (see G. Säflund, *AIARS*, ii (1953),
199 ff.).

Plainly, none of these media would be practicable for a long literary
text. Homer's poems, whenever they were first committed to writing,
could only have been written on some substance like papyrus or leather.
Unfortunately the early history of the papyrus scroll in Greece is still
very obscure. The Greeks must originally have bought their papyrus
not directly from Egypt but *via* Phoenicia, for their usual word for it was
not a derivative from the Egyptian (πάπυρος, which is from the Egyptian,
is late), but βύβλος, the Greek name for the old Phoenician port Gebal
which handled exports from Egypt. It might be argued from this
Phoenician loan-word that Greek knowledge of papyrus as a writing-
material must then antedate the arrival of Greek merchants in Egypt in
the late seventh century and the subsequent establishment of Greek
Naucratis, whence the Egyptian supplies could be imported direct to
Greece; but in fact the use of the loan-word proves only that the Greeks

[a] See Part I.

knew the *material* papyrus at an early date. Was the papyrus brought from Gebal in those early days the specifically-prepared writing-material, or was it merely papyrus in its many other uses, *e.g.*, as the material for ships' cables (φ 390-1)? Papyrus scrolls occur in red-figured vase-paintings of the early fifth century, and are spoken of as the normal medium for writing by Herodotus (v. 58); their use obviously extends back earlier than the fifth century, but how much earlier it is impossible to say with certainty.

The use of leather, on the other hand, is attested as early as the seventh century by ancient authority. It cannot have been a very cheap material — the priests who received the hides of sacrificed victims as their perquisite probably saw to that — but at least it did not have to be imported; moreover it was very durable, and could be re-used simply by being wiped over to remove the ink. The chief testimony to its use is that of Herodotus (v. 58):

καὶ τὰς βύβλους διφθέρας καλέουσι ἀπὸ τοῦ παλαιοῦ οἱ ῎Ιωνες, ὅτι κοτὲ ἐν σπάνι βύβλων ἐχρέωντο διφθέρῃσι αἰγέῃσί τε καὶ οἰέῃσι· ἔτι δὲ καὶ τὸ κατ' ἐμὲ πολλοὶ τῶν βαρβάρων ἐς τοιαύτας διφθέρας γράφουσι, (κτλ.),

i.e., once upon a time, before papyrus was familiar to Greece, the Ionians used to employ leather and the old name διφθέρα was still applied in Ionic to papyrus scrolls. Again, the σκυτάλη (message) consisting of a stick round which was wound an inscribed leather roll, which was used in a special form for secret military dispatches by the Spartans, was known to Archilochus in the first half of the seventh century (fr. 81 Diehl³).

'Archaic' literary texts on both lead and tin are mentioned by Pausanias (ix. 31. 4; iv. 26. 8), but no examples of these metals used as writing material have been found which are earlier than the fifth century (lead) or the fourth (tin); and in both Pausanias's accounts the historical circumstances give grounds for suspicion.

As far as the present meagre evidence goes, therefore, it may be suggested that, if the Homeric poems were written down before the sixth century, they were probably written on leather, the use of which for various documents can be traced as far back as the second quarter of the seventh century, on the evidence of Archilochus. It would be a costly and difficult achievement, but, if the incentive for undertaking it were there, it would be at least technically possible to do so. Evidence for such a proceeding earlier than the seventh century is as yet lacking.

Little can be said, except in general terms, of the other extreme — the establishment of a *terminus ante quem* for the first written copy of the epics, if we subscribe to the theory that they were orally composed. It is not difficult to supply a motive. A rhapsode might no more feel the need to aid his memory by writing down his répertoire than the early

Greek musician felt the need to create a system of notation for perpetuating his music, or the early philosopher the need to write down his theories as well as expounding them orally.   But if the works of contemporary poets were already being committed to writing while the cherished epics of heroic ancestors, though taught to the young, sung at festivals, and even cited as authorities in territorial disputes, were not thus honoured but lay open to any who chose to curtail, expand, or otherwise mutilate them, it could not be long before someone, whether one of the Homeridae or some wealthy patron of the arts, undertook to have a copy made.

The literary evidence offers two names.   One is that of the Spartan lawgiver Lycurgus, who was said to have made a copy of Homer's poems, taking them from the descendants of Creophylus in Samos, and to have first introduced them to the Peloponnese, or, according to another version, to Greece.   While Lycurgus himself remains so nebulous a figure, it is lost labour to probe the accuracy of this claim.   The other name is that of Peisistratus or his son Hipparchus.   This has been already treated in detail elsewhere [a] ; it is enough here to recall briefly the tradition in the Platonic *Hipparchus* 228 B : that Hipparchus (who made a Poets' Circle in Athens, introducing Simonides of Keos and Anacreon of Teos among others) brought Homer's works to Athens and ordained that in the Panathenaic competitions the rhapsodes should take up the recitation one from the other, so that the poems were delivered as a whole, in their proper continuity.   Obviously such a rule could not be enforced without the aid of a definitive version.   Was an existing text then brought to Athens, or was the text first established in Athens, from scattered, orally-transmitted lays ?   Among late authors, and late authors only, a confused tradition persisted that the latter was the case ; some said in fact that Peisistratus himself, not Hipparchus, first collected and edited as a unity the various parts of the epics ; but there is no mention of this in Herodotus's and Thucydides's accounts of Peisistratus's career, although it would be a most important detail.   The Peisistratidae undoubtedly possessed a collection of written oracles, gathered for them by Onomacritus (Hdt. v. 90. 2 and vii. 6. 3-4) ; a tradition of unknown date (in Athenaeus i. 3) says that they had a library of texts.   They and their Poets' Circle may well have established finally the supreme authority of Homer as a poet in Athens ; but that they were the first Greeks to produce a written text of Homer, anticipating any of the Ionians, is hard to believe.   According to the same tradition of Athenaeus, the Samian tyrant Polycrates also possessed a collection of texts.   If there is any truth in this, one would expect such a collection to contain the works of Homer, since Samos was the home of the descendants of Creophylus, the reputed son-in-law of Homer.   It has even been suggested that Hip-

[a] Chs. 6 and 7 above.

parchus might have brought his copy from Samos, as the other tradition said of Lycurgus. In this connection a possible clue should be noted from epigraphy. There are traces of a 'book-hand' in the lettering of Ionic inscriptions of the early sixth century. The lettering is noticeably smaller, hastier, and less regular than that of contemporary work on the mainland. Early inscriptions on stone from Ionia are still too sparse for us to ascertain whether the same is true of their lettering in the seventh century also; but it may at least be suggested that as early as *c.* 600–575 Ionic formal lettering on stone was influenced by some kind of contemporary 'book-hand', which can hardly be other than that of the διφθέραι mentioned by Herodotus.

There may then have been trained scribes in Ionia in the seventh century who could undertake the colossal task of writing out the *Iliad* and *Odyssey* on scrolls. At present, it can only be said that the ability to write was there, and the material; and it seems on the whole safest to regard the last third of the sixth century, the time of Polycrates and the Peisistratidae, as the latest possible, rather than the likeliest, date for the establishment of the poems in writing.

NOTE TO CHAPTER 23

Select bibliography: E. S. Roberts, *An Introduction to Greek Epigraphy*, i (1887); W. Larfeld, *Griechische Epigraphik* ³ (1914); Rhys Carpenter in *AJA*, xxxvii. 8 ff. and xlii. 58 ff.; D. Diringer, *The Alphabet* (1948); G. R. Driver, *Semitic Writing* ² (1954); H. L. Lorimer in *AJA*, lii. 11 ff. and *Homer and the Monuments* (1950), 122 ff.; H. I. Marrou, *Histoire de l'éducation dans l'antiquité* ² (1950); H. T. Wade-Gery, *The Poet of the Iliad* (1952); S. Dow in *AJA*, lviii. 77 ff.; M. Ventris and J. Chadwick, *Documents in Mycenaean Greek* (1956); J. Chadwick, *The Decipherment of Linear B* (1958). D. H. F. Gray in J. N. L. Myres, *Homer and his Critics* (1958).

INDEXES

1. PASSAGES OF HOMER CITED IN THE TEXT

This index should be consulted by readers of Homer who wish to see what the *Companion* may have to say about the form, meaning, grammar, interpretation, etc., of a particular line or passage.

ILIAD

ODYSSEY

2. GENERAL INDEX

Notes: 1. *Greek words* not shown in transliteration in this index should be
sought in the separate *Index of Greek Words*.
   2. Where there are a number of references under one entry, bold
figures indicate the most important.

A

Abdication, 436
Abecedarium, 553
Abioi, 308
Ablaut, 81, 82 f.
Abydos, 302
Acarnania, 272
Achaea :
   agriculture in, 275
   and the kingdom of Mycenae, 290 f.
'Achaean', *see* Dialects, Greek
Achaean empire, 314 f., 316. *See also* Agamemnon, 'empire' of
Achaean wall, 49 f.
Achaeans, 52, 299, 434, 512
   epithets of, 31, 505, 507
   in Hittite records, 315 f., 356
   language, 318
   the name in Homer, 285, 288
Achelous, 271 f., 294
Achilleid, 52, 249 f.
Achilles, 35, 47, 50, 52, 64, 69, 182, 209, 441,
   445, 479, 480, 481, 495, 508
   arming of, 30, 190 f., 505, 517
   arms of, 50, 505, 506, 507, 535
   character of, 67, 206, 451
   conquests in the Troad, 302 f.
   embassy to, 43, 49, 66, 70, 523
   epithets of, 29, 31
   funeral of, 478, 479, 481
   home in Phthia, 99, 296 f.
   kills Hector, 61
   love for Patroclus, 68, 480
   mutilation of Hector, 33, 55, 68
   returns Hector's body, 43, 55
   ritual experience of death, 204
   shield of, *see* Shield
   wrath of, 42, **43**, 52, 56, 61, 64, 247
Addison, 243
Adjectives, 113 f.
Aeaea, 524
'Aegean' linguistic features, *see* Borrowed
   elements
Aegina, 277, 279, 341
Aegisthus, 64, 479
   Tomb of, 393
   traditional burial place, 398

Aelian, on the Peisistratid recession, 241
Aeneas, 71, 301
   aristeia of, 253
Aeolians, arrival in Greece, 89 f., 317
Aeolis, Pelasgians in, 302
Aeolus, 441
Aeschylus, 4
Aetna, Mt., known to Homer, 309
Aetolia, agriculture of, 275
Aetolians, in Homer, 294 f., 299
Aetos, Mt., 414, excavations at, 416 f.,
   419
After-life, in Homer, 447 f., 449
Agamemnon, 48, 51, 64, 69, 320, 357, 434,
   435, 456, 523
   Argos, ruler of, 289, 435
   aristeia, 58, 505
   arming of, 30, 190 f., 505, 517
   breast-plate of, *see* Cuirass
   embassy to Achilles, 49
   'empire' of, 434 f., 453. *See also* Achaean
      empire
   nostos, 292
   offer of 7 towns to Achilles, 291, 435,
      456
   shield of, 513, 547
   traditional burial place, 397
Agora, 432, 433, 437, 438, 446
   meaning in Homer, 454
Agriculture :
   in Homer, 524-30, 531
   in modern Greece, 269-82 *passim*, 525
Aḫḫijawa, 316, 356
Ahrens, 251
Aidôs, 450
Aigialos, in the Catalogue, 290, 293
Ainos, 304
Aithiopes, 307
Ajax, 31, 53 f., 70, 403, 523
   shield of, 511
Ajax, the lesser, 289, 507
Akhenaten, 327
   city of, *see* Tell el Amarna
Akritas, Digenis, 204
Al Mina, 554
Alabastron, 350, 351 ; Fig. 16, *e*
Alamanni, 243
Alcibiades, 218

571

3. GREEK WORDS

ἀγορή, see Agora
αἰδώς, 450
αἴθουσα, 491, 494
ἀντίσιγμα, 223, 224
ἀοιδός, 180, 181, 199, 217, 218. See also Bards
Ἀπορήματα Ὁμηρικά, 239
ἀργυρόηλος, 517
ἀστερισκός, 223, 224
αὐλός, 218
αὐλῶπις, 515

βασιλεύς, 434-7, 455
βουλὴ γερόντων, see Council of Elders

γέρας, 436, 437
γέροντες, see Gerontes
γλῶσσαι, 220, cf. 237
γύαλα, 507 f.

-δε, 26, 107
δέπας, see Depas
δημιοεργοί, 459 f., 537 f.
δημογέρων, 459
δῆμος, 434, 459 f., 537
διαφωνίαι, 241
δίκη, 439, 451
διόρθωσις, 221
διπλῆ, 224
——— περιεστιγμένη, 224
διφθέρα, 557, 559
δμῶες, 433
δοῦλος, 442

ἕδνα, 452
εἴδωλον, 447 f., 481
ἐκδόσεις κατ' ἄνδρα, 221, 237
Ἕλληνες, 285
ἐπάρουρος, 433 f.
ἐπισφύρια, 506
Ἐρεμβοί, 307
ἐριούνιος, 27
ἕστωρ, 540
ἑταῖρος, 437, 441, 457
ἐϋκνήμιδες, 505

ζυγόδεσμον, 540 f.
ζωστήρ, 508

ἦτορ, 447

θέμις, 450, 451, 475
θέμιστες, 436, 439
θεράποντες, 437, 441
θῆτες, 434
θόλος, 493
θυμός, 447
θώρηξ, see Cuirass

ἵππota, 457

κε, 90-2
κεραύνιον, 223
Κήτειοι, 305
κίθαρις, 217
κλέα ἀνδρῶν, 58, 209, 217, 257
κλῆροι, 436, 440
κλῖμαξ, 493
κραδίη, 447
κρήδεμνον, 501 f.
κρίκος, 540
κύανος, 509, 513, 535

λαός, 434, 456 f.
λαύρη, 493 f.
λινοθώρηξ, 507, 508

μεγαλοπρέπεια, 450
μέγαρον, see Megaron
μεσόδμαι, 494 f.
μεταγραμματισμός, 96, 109
μετανάστης, 434, 458
μυχός, 495 f.

Νέκυια, see Odysseus, underworld, visit to
———, second, 46
Νέμεσις, 450
νόος, 447

ξεῖνος, 434, 439

ὄβελος, 222, 223
οἶκος, 433
οἶνοψ, 527
ὀπάων, see Opawon
ὀρσοθύρη, 493, 496
ὄρχαμε λαῶν, 457
οὐδός, 496 f.

Παναχαιοί, 285
Πανέλληνες, 297

THE END

PRINTED BY R. & R. CLARK, LTD., EDINBURGH